OPERATIONAL THEORY AND METHOD IN REGIONAL ECONOMICS

*For Nel*
*keen on sociology*

*and Juliet*
*who teaches chemistry*

# Operational Theory and Method in Regional Economics

JEAN H.P. PAELINCK
*Erasmus University, Rotterdam*

*and*

PETER NIJKAMP
*Free University, Amsterdam*

SAXON HOUSE | LEXINGTON BOOKS

*Published by*

SAXON HOUSE, D.C. Heath Ltd.
Westmead, Farnborough, Hants., England

*Jointly with*

LEXINGTON BOOKS, D.C. Heath & Co.
Lexington, Mass. U.S.A.



ISBN 0 347 01117 9
Library of Congress Catalog Card Number 75–28609
Printed in Great Britain by Butler & Tanner Ltd., Frome and London

# Contents

# Preface

Probably because spatial economics is a relatively new branch of economics, its development has been remarkable. Its roots can be found in the early German literature, starting with Von Thünen. Further important contributions have come from all parts of the world, but particularly from the UK, the USA and a number of European countries. The role of Jean Paelinck in this process is well known, but Peter Nijkamp, too, has produced some noteworthy books and articles on several aspects of spatial economics.

Spatial economics has not only added a new dimension to general economics but also, probably as a result of this, provoked closer integration with related disciplines such as geography and physical planning. The process of integration is now in full progress and gradually a regional science is developing which aims at being both truly inter-disciplinary and truly spatial.

The broadening of the field to be covered by scholars in spatial economics and other disciplines carries no doubt the danger of the study of the separate participating disciplines becoming too superficial, at any rate if each scholar tries to become familiar with all of them. This danger is well-known from the area of physical planning, where efforts to incorporate all aspects in one single approach have not seldom led to vague and unrealistic plans.

It was, therefore, an excellent idea to produce a book that is strictly limited to spatial economics in the narrowest sense of the word. Paelinck and Nijkamp are presenting with this study a valuable textbook, in which not only is classical spatial economic theory well represented but due attention is also paid to newer developments.

The subject has recently gained new importance as a result of the sudden considerable rise in energy prices, the consequences of which are felt particularly in the field of transportation. In recent decades communication costs have played a more and more important role in spatial-economic theory. Recent development in the field of energy will, however, reverse this trend and force us to concentrate, maybe more than ever before, on the role of transportation costs in the narrow sense of the word. For the study of this subject the book has particular relevance.

By the lucid way in which it presents complicated mathematical operations this book will undoubtedly contribute much to the understanding of this new and important branch of economics.

Leo H. Klaassen

# Presentation

Space is a major element of many problems in theoretical and empirical economics.

During recent years an ever-increasing number of economists have realized that the element of space is present in almost every economic problem. Consequently, there has been an increasing demand for new theories and tools in economics which focus on the specific problems of spatial economic analysis.

The present advanced textbook is an attempt to satisfy the need of a synthetic and systematic treatment of regional economic theories and techniques. The authors have tried to pursue systematically three targets in writing this book:

1 A formal presentation of a series of theories, (mainly) developed by several regional economic scholars during the last decades, so that sufficient knowledge of the historical evolution and the present state of regional economics can be obtained.
2 The development of a series of ideas on regional economics along rigorous lines, i.e., stating explicitly the hypotheses from which the argument will be derived, and presenting the results as a series of propositions that should be submitted to empirical tests, in the phase of 'spatial econometrics'*.
3 The introduction of the student or research worker to a series of operational techniques that will lead him – if he really 'works' through the book! – to the mastery of a number of tools that appear to the authors as being indispensable in modern regional analysis.

These considerations explain the curious set-up of some chapters, e.g. the chapter on the history of regional economic analysis; no historian would probably have presented the contributions of Von Thünen, Weber and Lösch in the manner in which they have been exposed there!

Apart from the general introduction, the book is composed of two main ingredients, namely, theory (part I) and method (part II). The theoretical part concentrates primarily on locational problems and related topics, such

* On this topic, a blend of spatial economics and econometrics proper, a later book is planned.

as market-area analysis, since these elements form historically the heart of regional economics. The part devoted to regional economic methods is concerned with data analysis, input–output techniques and mathematical programming methods in regional economics.

The third and last part of the book (synthesis) treats regional problems from a general equilibrium and growth point of view.

The book does certainly not cover *all* the theory and all the techniques of regional analysis; the authors think, however, that they have covered a fair sample, and that the systematic inclusion of numerical exercises will develop a state of mind that will allow student and research worker successfully to master problems in other fields of regional analysis, possibly with other tools.

This, at least, was the result of teaching for six years two-year courses at the Netherlands School of Economics, now Erasmus University Rotterdam, Faculty of Economics. Both authors would like to thank the sympathetic guinea-pigs who willingly submitted themselves to a series of injections and control tests. They seem to be doing quite well in professional life.

This is due also to the *brio* with which our colleague L.H. Klaassen taught a perfectly complementary course on regional research work, based on the permanent regional investigation being carried out at the Netherlands Economic Institute; given the perfect osmosis between the two teachings, he was the right man to write a preface to this book, which we acknowledge very sincerely. We also like to mention that success in obtaining results with the machinery exposed hereafter has been a function of other courses taught in the Regional Economics special course of study at Rotterdam University, of which Economic and Social Geography, as taught by our colleague P.R. Odell, deserves special mention.

The authors hope that they have done justice to all the colleagues in the field from whose work many ideas and techniques have been drawn; they have endeavoured to refer systematically to their original work, and if occasionally some outside contributions to the field were not explicitly mentioned, it was only in order not to overload the text. Complete references have been grouped at the end of each chapter.

L. Hordijk, A.P. Mastenbroek and A. van Delft, assistants at Rotterdam University, made many clarifying remarks; the last-mentioned composed the analytical table. For careful typewriting of parts of a difficult text, we like to thank Mrs C.M. Bakker, Mrs A. Elderson, Miss G. Gebuis and Mrs S. Kleyngeld. Graphs were competently drawn by W. Cristofoletti, while A. de Wit went critically through a last version of the text.

Finally, we thank the North Holland Publishing Company (Amsterdam) for allowing us to reproduce parts of previously published material.

Like so many books, this one too is born 'dal lungo conversare insieme di cantori et sonatori', from a long joint conversing of singers and instrumentalists, as Ercole Bottrigari once put it.

P. Nijkamp
*Free University, Amsterdam*
*Erasmus University, Rotterdam*

J.H.P. Paelinck
*Netherlands Economic Institute*
*and Erasmus University, Rotterdam*

# 1 General Introduction

## 1.1 Outline

The first major subjects to be considered in a textbook concerning operational theories and methods in regional economics are the framework, scope and method of regional (or spatial) economics. Therefore this introductory chapter will deal with a variety of general questions of regional economics, such as fundamentals, methodology, relevance of models, basic principles and spatial concepts. These basic subjects constitute the foundation stones of the spatial economic building, that will be structured in the following chapters.

## 1.2 Regional economics and related disciplines

Regional economics is concerned with an explicit consideration of *spatial elements* in general (theoretical) economics: it studies the spatial dispersion and spatial coherence of activities from an economic point of view. Therefore, regional economics and general economics are closely linked to each other. The rapid development of regional economics in the post-war period is mainly due to the continuing progress in general economic thinking, both in a theoretical/conceptual respect and in an instrumental respect; the two growth paths show similar characteristics. Regional economics should however not be considered as a proper subset of general economics; it also has some unique features with a broader scope.

In the first place, as mentioned already, *spatial factors* are explicitly present in regional economics. The spatial dimension of phenomena can be most easily described by means of a co-ordinate representation in Euclidean space. A *zero*-order spatial dimension may occur in the case of specified point-locations; a *first*-order dimension may be present in transportation and traffic problems produced by distances between paired points (for instance in the case of distance-inputs or transport-inputs; see Ch.6); a *second*-order dimension may be relevant in the case of spatial densities as can be observed in agglomeration phenomena and regional population densities.

A second characteristic of regional economics is *the degree of precision* required in solving regional economic problems at hand. A general statement about 'overall national tendencies' does not, in general, describe adequately the interwoven pattern of regional phenomena. For instance, a clear insight into the effect of a regional economic policy requires more specific judgments concerning the micro-efficiency of regional economic measures based on a refined (inter)regional and sectoral analysis. In addition, the question as to optimal levels for the use of instruments of economic policy (for instance, at a local, regional, national or international level) has to be envisaged, as was considered by Mennes et al. (1969).

A third feature which is present in regional economics is the assumption of a relative *openness* of each region. At the regional–interregional level one observes a higher degree of mobility of goods, services, capital and labour than at the national–international level. This openness of regions results in a complicated interdependent system of regions, which can show considerable fluctuations over time (see Ch.7).

The relevance of considering explicitly spatial factors in economic analysis may be clarified by means of a number of rather arbitrary examples:

1 The element of space is a necessary condition for the existence of a number of spatial price policies. One may discern between policies of spatial price discrimination, of uniform delivered prices, and of uniform mill prices (see Ch.2).
2 The solution of industrial location problems requires a precise knowledge concerning the effect of different spatial locations upon the substitution possibilities between production factors (see Ch.2 and Ch.3).
3 The spatial dispersion and the spatial coherence of relevant economic phenomena gives rise to spatial contiguity effects between adjacent regions (see Ch.4).
4 Interregional migration is not only dependent on the relative payments for labour, but also on the interregional distance, physical, social or psychological (see Ch.7).
5 Migration from region $r_1$ to region $r_2$ may be influenced by the attractive power of a region $r_3$, which is contiguous to $r_2$ (for instance, if $r_3$ is a city and $r_2$ a suburb); such a spatial interaction between different variables is called a *spill-over* effect (see Ch.7).
6 Investments in region $r_1$ may increase owing to a rise in the investments of an adjacent region $r_2$; such a spatial interaction between the same variables is called a *spin-off* effect (see Ch.7).

In addition to regional economics some other disciplines are also concerned with the same field of the spatial dispersion of economic activities. In the first place, *economic geography* should be mentioned. Though the demarcation lines between regional economics and economic geography are hard to trace, one may state from an historical point of view, that economic geography, in general, places more stress on the wide variety of concrete economic landscapes (as is evident from reading a number of applied studies). Therefore, the method of spatial analysis used by economic geography is, generally speaking, rather inductive. Economic geography attempts to explain concrete economic phenomena from a great number of explicative geographical factors. Regional economics, on the contrary, is seeking for more theoretical economic homogeneities. It attempts to find more general possibilities of applying the discovered or assumed regularities. The latter deductive approach requires a higher degree of abstraction, since it reduces spatial economic phenomena to a limited number of essential, explicative economic elements. However, the distinction between economic geography and regional economics is declining more and more, owing to a tendency in both disciplines towards a more formal and quantitative approach (see, for instance, Harvey [1969]). At present, both disciplines possess a considerable area of overlap, and they are complementary to each other rather than competitive; but even then, regional economics starts from typical economic hypotheses on costs, profits, prices, etc. (cf. Berry [1971], Beckmann [1970]).

Furthermore, another discipline which is closely linked to both previous disciplines should be mentioned here. viz, *regional science*. Regional science includes many elements of regional economics and economic geography. In addition, it is more synthetic by considering also the social, demographic, psychologic and political factors. Thus, regional science is a broad discipline, which studies man's activities in relation to his spatial environment; for that reason this discipline also has many elements in common with regional economics (see, for instance, Isard [1960]), though it could be said that a more aggregate view is taken of economic phenomena.

## 1.3 Proposed methodology

The spatial dispersion and coherence of economic activities can be studied and analyzed in different ways. The research field of regional economics can be approached along various paths.

A first path, tred on often in regional economic literature, is a behavioural, verbal and concrete one; good examples of this approach are contained *inter alia* in Courtin and Maillet (1962), Nourse (1968) and Hoover (1971). A second way of attacking spatial economic problems is an analytical, quantitative and abstract approach. The latter method, which dominates in modern regional economic research, is adopted in this book. It should be stressed that both methods are complementary rather than substitutable. The reason why the major focus of this book is on the second method of analysis is the fact that the latter method allows one to present clearly the formal structure and coherence of spatial economic problems. In addition, this approach is completely in line with recent developments in general theoretical economics. This enables one to utilize the modern instruments and methods of economics as developed in the post-war decades.

The theoretical, conceptual and instrumental framework developed in this book intends to provide an *operational* approach to regional economics. Operationality requires a clear exposition of the problem at hand, as well as of the conditions under which a certain phenomenon comes about. In this way a systematic and consistent analysis is possible on the basis of logical, theoretical considerations. Preferably, these considerations are formulated as mathematical expressions, since the latter are more suitable for a coherent way of thinking and for an empirical application. The methodology as set out previously is a crucial element in this book and it constitutes a corner-stone for analyzing and studying the regional economic problems discussed hereafter. For instance, several problems are attacked, in this book, by first stating a set of reasonable hypotheses concerning the problem at hand. On the basis of adequate theoretical considerations and by means of suitable mathematical operations, one may deduce a set of economic propositions (or operational theorems). Ultimately, these propositions should be tested on their empirical validity by carefully checking them against observed facts.[1]

## 1.4 Relevance and use of models

### 1.4.1 *Introduction*

Economic models dominate more and more in modern economic literature. For a clear insight into the recent developments of regional economics a basic knowledge concerning economic models is indispensable. For that reason some elementary aspects of models will now be dealt with.

An economic model is a simplified, abstract representation of a part of the economic reality, and mainly based on quantitative relationships between economic phenomena. By developing theoretical ideas within a model the logical consequences of the *a priori* hypotheses can be investigated more accurately, the analysis becomes more transparent and a more adequate test concerning the empirical validity is possible; to cut a long story short: *a more operational approach of economic problems is possible*.

A model supposes a regularity (or a 'law') in the relationships between economic phenomena. These regularities, which are, in general, formulated by means of mathematical relationships, rest upon a set of reasonable, theoretical hypotheses concerning the problem at hand. The use of such a formal, abstract and mathematical model has many advantages:

1 The assumed regularities are summarized in a *concise and surveyable formulation*. A verbal language may be rather inefficient, particularly in the case of a simultaneous consideration of multiple phenomena. It should be quite clear, that the use of mathematical symbols and of a mathematical language cannot be considered as a replacement of theoretical (regional) economic thinking: mathematics is only an efficient tool for a clear formulation and elaboration of a theory.
2 The application of mathematical techniques forces a scientist to a *precise definition of concepts, hypotheses and variables*, since each mathematical symbol has only one unique meaning. This leads to a more standardized communication between scientists.
3 The continuing tendency towards more *complex theories* requires a more formal approach in order to investigate accurately the effect of various interdependencies, of changes in parameters (sensitivity analysis), of spatial and temporal developments, and of alternative economic decisions.
4 The *consistency* of a theory (as a set of testable consistent regularities) can be checked by means of mathematical tools (for instance, dimensional analysis; cf. De Jong [1967]). In addition, one may study under what conditions the theory will guarantee the attainment of an economic equilibrium (see, for instance, the spatial equilibrium theories in Ch.7).
5 A formal approach has often broader possibilities for *empirical* applications and tests (for instance, by means of mathematical statistics and simulation methods), particularly if one is provided with adequate means for data collection and data storage.

Finally, it should be noted that the validity of the model is completely restricted by the *a priori* hypotheses. If these hypotheses correspond to a certain situation in space or time, the model is valid only for that situation in space or time. In general, a closer connection between theory and practice requires an increase in the number of hypotheses.

A model can be represented in various ways, for instance, in a *figurative* and in a *formal* way. The elementary Keynesian model including investments ($I$), income ($Y$) and consumption ($C$) can be represented as follows:

(a) figuratively: by means of an arrow-scheme often used by Tinbergen (1956):

$$I \longrightarrow Y \rightleftarrows C \tag{1.4.1.1}$$

(b) formally: by means of a system of equations:

$$\left.\begin{aligned} Y &= C + I \\ C &= aY + b \end{aligned}\right\} \tag{1.4.1.2}$$

An intermediate way is a representation by means of a so-called Boolean matrix,[2] in which each row and each column corresponds to a certain variable. If there exists a link between some of the variables, the corresponding elements in a Boolean matrix (if read horizontally) are 1; otherwise the elements are 0 or blank. Then our simple Keynesian example can be written as:

| | $C$ | $Y$ | $I$ |
|---|---|---|---|
| $C$ | | 1 | |
| $Y$ | 1 | | 1 |
| $I$ | | | |

(1.4.1.3)

Obviously, more information is preserved in a formal representation; for this reason models are, in general, constructed in a formal way.

### 1.4.2 *Elements of models*

A model can be considered from different points of view. Each point of view allows one to discern a number of different components within the model. In line with the contents of this book particular attention will be paid to various kinds of economic agents, of variables, of relationships and of time concepts.

If a model is considered from the point of view of the various *economic agents*, one may discern *inter alia* consumers, entrepreneurs, savers, investors and public decision makers. Each category of these agents is supposed to have a characteristic economic behavioural pattern, which determines the structure of the model. Not all agents need to be present in each model: a model is objective-orientated; it depends on the objective concerned, which agents are included in the model. For instance, if one wants to construct a model for (inter)regional economic policy, public agents constitute a necessary component of the model.

Secondly, one may consider *economic variables*. The economic variables, which stand each for a certain economic phenomenon (consumption, income, e.g.), can be classified into *endogenous* and *exogenous* variables. The values of endogenous variables are determined within the model, and they can be solved in terms of exogenous variables; they are the 'unknowns' of the problem. Exogenous variables receive their value from outside the model and they determine the value of the endogenous variables without being affected by these variables; they are 'data' of the problem. For instance, in the previous Keynesian model $C$ and $Y$ are endogenous variables; they can easily be expressed in the exogenous variable $I$. The exogenous variables together with the lagged-endogenous variables are often called *predetermined* variables. It should be noted, however, that it depends completely on the structure of the model (hence on the underlying theoretical conceptions), which variables are considered as endogenous or exogenous. The economic variables may also be distinguished according to their *dimensions* (for instance, volumes and prices), or according to their *level of aggregation* (for instance, micro-economic, semi-aggregate or sectoral, and macro-economic variables).

In the third place, one may inspect the nature of the economic *relationships* between the various variables. Relationships can be distinguished into *equalities* and *functional equations*. Equalities indicate that under certain conditions some phenomena have exactly the same value, while functional relationships indicate how a certain phenomenon is determined or explained by the influence of other phenomena.[3]

The class of equalities contains the following elements:

*definitions* ($\triangleq$); for instance, the balance of trade ($B$) is defined as exports ($E$) minus imports ($M$):

$$B \triangleq E - M \qquad (1.4.2.1)$$

*identities* ($\equiv$); for instance, the simple Keynesian expression for the income formation is:

$$Y \equiv C + I \qquad (1.4.2.2)$$

*equilibrium* conditions ($\overset{\circ}{=}$); for instance, the equilibrium equation imposed on a commodity sector is:

$$D \overset{\circ}{=} S \tag{1.4.2.3}$$

where $D$ represents the demand for a given commodity, and $S$ its supply.

Functional equations can be distinguished into:

*technical* relations; for instance, a production function represents the technical link between a vector of inputs (z) and the resulting output (q):

$$q = f(\mathrm{z}) \tag{1.4.2.4}$$

*behavioural* relations; for instance, the Keynesian consumption equation can be represented as:

$$C = aY + b \tag{1.4.2.5}$$

*institutional* relations; for instance, direct taxes ($T$) are a function of national income:

$$T = f(Y) \tag{1.4.2.6}$$

*empirical* relations; for instance, the number of persons ($n$) receiving an income above a certain level ($x$) is empirically found to satisfy the following relationship (the law of Pareto):

$$n = a\, x^{-\beta} \tag{1.4.2.7}$$

In general, a model contains a set of equalities and functional relationships; the latter represent the essential structure of the economy.

In the fourth place, the element of *time* will be considered. Models may be *static* or *dynamic*. A dynamic model describes an adaptation process of the included variables over a number of time periods: time is an essential internal element in a dynamic model. The endogenous variables of a dynamic model are provided with a specific time index, and their values in a certain time period are a function of the predetermined variables, especially lagged endogenous variables; in a dynamic model, endogenous variables are linked up through time. A static model constitutes only a description of a certain situation with the elimination of time (or without time being considered as an essential element). An intermediate situation is *comparative statics*, where only two equilibrium situations at different points in time are considered, while the adaptation process itself is neglected.

### 1.4.3 *Use of models*

The meaning of a model is dependent on the aim to be attained, in other words: the problem at hand to be solved and the objective to be served by the model determine the contents and the structure of the model. The various objectives aimed at allow one to make a distinction between economic models. In general, a model can be used for one of the following possibilities: economic analysis, economic planning and economic policy.

Economic *analysis* serves to obtain a clear insight into the structure and the interdependency of a part of the economy. A model constructed for economic analysis may serve for illustrative, expository or descriptive purposes (for instance, the Keynesian and Harrod-Domar-type models). In general, such a model can be represented as:

$$\mathbf{f}(\mathbf{y}, \mathbf{x}) = \mathbf{0} \tag{1.4.3.1}$$

or:

$$\left.\begin{array}{l} f_1(y_1, \ldots, y_J; x_1, \ldots, x_K) = 0 \\ \vdots \\ f_J(y_1, \ldots, y_J; x_1, \ldots, x_K) = 0 \end{array}\right\} \tag{1.4.3.2}$$

where $f_j$ ($j = 1, \ldots, J$) is an implicit scalar-valued function including endogenous variables $y_j$ ($j = 1, \ldots, J$) and exogenous variables $x_k$ ($k = 1, \ldots, K$). The functions $f_j$ are derived on the basis of a set of reasonable hypotheses concerning the economic structure, while the various parameters can be estimated by means of econometric methods. The equations as represented in (1.4.3.2) are called *structural* equations. If the various endogenous variables are solved from (1.4.3.2), a *reduced form* system is obtained, in which all endogenous variables are expressed in the exogenous variables and the parameters of the model.[4]

Economic *planning* (or programming) differs from economic analysis, in that it attempts to develop an economic plan (or program) which is derived from certain *a priori* aims, but respects the functioning of the economy. A simple approach to economic planning is to impose upper and lower limits on the development of the endogenous variables, in such a way that the intended aims are realized. A more ambitious approach is to specify an optimality criterion (e.g., a preference or objective function); in the latter way the *optimal* values of the variables of the model can be derived (in principle). An extensive discussion of these problems is contained in Ch.6.

Economic *policy* is a normative approach which prescribes public decision makers what actions to undertake for realizing certain aims. If a model is earmarked for economic policy, it should clearly indicate which variables are instruments of economic policy (for instance, tax rates, regional subsidies). These instruments should be handled in such a way that certain aims of economic policy are realized. One may again discern between a fixed-target-approach (by specifying *a priori* values for the economic targets) and a flexible-target-approach (by specifying an optimality criterion). For more details one should consult Tinbergen (1956) and Theil (1964).

## 1.5 Basic economic principles

### 1.5.1 *Introduction*

Economics (and hence regional economics) is a scientific discipline, which studies alternative possibilities of using activities, taking account of scarce resources. The previous rough description of economics implies three fundamental principles, which are also of particular relevance for regional economics.

First, economics is concerned with the use of certain activities; this gives rise to a so-called *activity-principle* (or $\alpha$-principle). Secondly, activities can be combined in various alternative ways; this leads to the *substitution-principle* (or $\sigma$-principle). Finally, owing to the presence of scarcity each choice should be guided by an optimality criterion in order to assure an efficient allocation of scarce resources; this situation results in the *extremum-principle* (or $\epsilon$-principle).

These basic principles which are (implicitly or explicitly) present in almost each (regional) economic problem are considered more thoroughly in sections 1.5.2 through 1.5.4.

### 1.5.2 *The activity-principle*

An economic activity can be represented in a very simple way by means of a vector containing negative elements (inputs) and positive elements (outputs). For instance, in the productive sector one may represent a production process by means of an *activity vector*, the negative elements of which represent inputs (intermediate products, energy, capital, labour, e.g.) and the positive elements of which represent outputs (e.g. final product, intermediate products, pollution). Then one may obtain the following activity vector:

$$\begin{bmatrix} + \\ - \\ - \\ - \\ + \\ + \\ \cdot \\ \cdot \\ \cdot \\ \cdot \\ \cdot \\ \cdot \end{bmatrix} \qquad (1.5.2.1)$$

where each element of the activity vector represents the volume of input (minus sign) or output (plus sign) of the productive activity concerned, if that activity is operated at a given level. The most simple assumption is a constant input–output-ratio, in which case this linear activity analysis implies fixed technical coefficients.

Different production processes imply different activity vectors. The complete technology of a certain firm or industry can be integrated in an *activity matrix*, which is a set of activity vectors and, therefore, of technical input–output data. Such an activity matrix can be written as:

$$\begin{array}{c} \\ 1 \\ | \\ | \\ I \end{array} \overset{1 - - - - - - - - J}{\begin{bmatrix} & & \\ & a_{ij} & \\ & & \end{bmatrix}} \qquad (1.5.2.2)$$

where the various activities $j$ ($j = 1, \ldots, J$) are listed on top of the matrix, and the various inputs and outputs $i$ ($i = 1, \ldots, I$) on the left of the matrix. In each column of the matrix is recorded the volume of inputs and outputs of the activity listed at the top, if that activity is used at a given level. A good example of activity analysis is contained in Isard et al. (1959), where a detailed activity matrix is used for the planning of an industrial complex at Puerto Rico (an industrial complex is a set of interrelated productive activities settled at the same location; cf. also section 5.19).

In addition to production processes one may deal with other activities also in a similar way. For instance, the economic behaviour of consumers can be described by means of the $\alpha$-principle: goods and services consumed are inputs, utility effects are outputs. Both theories – of production and of consumption – are, in fact, 'isomorphic', i.e. have the same 'formal', theoretical expression. A generalization to the field of economic policy and of social and political activities is straightforward.

### 1.5.3 *The substitution-principle*

Economics is particularly concerned with alternative choices: the major part of economic aims are attainable in various alternative ways. For instance, a certain level of consumer utility can be reached by choosing various alternative combinations of commodities; a certain level of output can be produced by means of various substitutable inputs (for instance, capital and labour); a certain level of regional production can be obtained by using several alternative activities.

In the production sphere the set of all combinations of inputs which can be used for producing a *given* level of output is called an *isoquant*. The isoquant may be a continuous curve (for instance, in the case of a Cobb-Douglas production function) or a number of discrete points (in the case of a limited number of production processes). The situation of discrete substitution corresponds to an activity matrix with a limited number of productive activities.

The $\sigma$-principle was introduced in regional economics by Predöhl (1925; see Ch.2). He stressed the substitution possibilities in the location problems of a firm: an optimal ratio of production factors together with an optimum location is determined by relative factor prices at the mill and by transportation costs from the input sources to the optimum location of the firm; substitution in *factor-space* and in *geographical space* are simultaneous problems.

### 1.5.4 *The extremum-principle*

Economic behaviour can be characterized as optimal decision making (for instance, maximization of individual utility, minimization of costs, maximization of profits, maximization of social welfare). Optimal decision making requires the use of various economic activities (cf. section 1.5.2), which should be combined (cf. section 1.5.3) in such a way that an optimal situation is attained (either in the short run or in the long run). In mathematical terms, this process can be described as the maximization of an objective function (for instance, utility function, profit function) subject to a number of constraints (for instance, budget restriction, production function). It is evident, that the final outcome of an economic problem depends on the optimization criterion chosen beforehand; for instance, the market area of a monopolistic firm can show a considerable difference in the case of cost minimization and of profit maximization (see Ch.3).

## 1.6 The concept of space

### 1.6.1 *Introduction*

As mentioned in section 1.2 a major feature of regional economics is the explicit consideration of space. Space in the sense of a physical extensiveness can be distinguished into *undifferentiated* space and *differentiated* space. Undifferentiated space is an abstract geometric space, in which co-ordinates, distances and densities are dominating concepts.

Differentiated space is provided with (some or all) projections of geographical, social, cultural, economic and physical history; this leads to concepts as transportation networks, industrial concentrations, natural advantages, agglomeration economies, etc.

### 1.6.2 *Undifferentiated space*

Undifferentiated space is, in general, used as the starting-point in theoretical, spatial economic thinking, for instance, in the field of market area analysis, location theory and spatial equilibrium problems (as will be dealt with in the following chapters). Each point of abstract Euclidean space can be uniquely represented by means of *co-ordinates*. In this way each economic phenomenon (for instance, the optimum location of a firm), which is realized at a certain spatial point, can be provided with two-dimensional spatial co-ordinates.

The co-ordinates themselves may be rectangular (Cartesian) co-ordinates (cf. figure 1.6.2.a), polar co-ordinates (cf. figure 1.6.2.b), or any other co-ordinates.

Fig. 1.6.2.a Rectangular co-ordinates

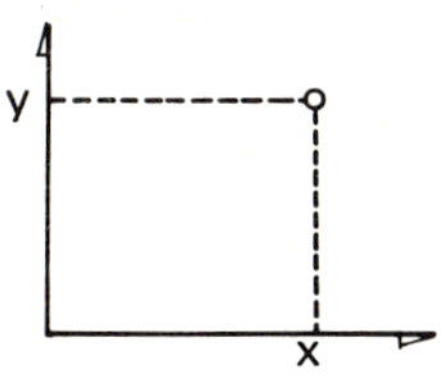


Fig. 1.6.2.b Polar co-ordinates

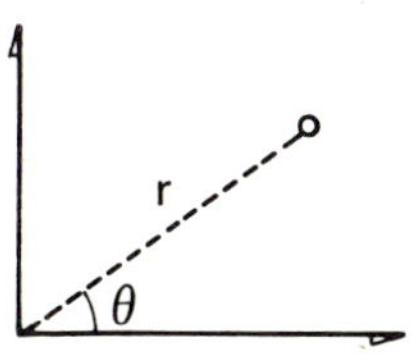

There exists a one-to-one relationship between the rectangular and the polar co-ordinates. This is based upon the following equalities:

$$\left.\begin{aligned} x &= r\cos\theta \\ y &= r\sin\theta \end{aligned}\right\} \qquad (1.6.2.1)$$

and:

$$\left.\begin{aligned} r &= \sqrt{(x^2 + y^2)} \\ \theta &= \operatorname{arctg}\frac{y}{x} \quad \left(\text{note that: } \frac{y}{x} = \frac{r\sin\theta}{r\cos\theta} = tg\,\theta\right) \end{aligned}\right\} \qquad (1.6.2.2)$$

In the case of transportation and traffic problems one meets *distances*. Distance is, in fact, an abstract concept which has to satisfy a set of axiomatic conditions ($d(a, b)$ represents here the distance from point $a$ to point $b$):

$$\left.\begin{aligned} &\text{a.} \quad d(a, b) \geqslant 0 \\ &\text{b.} \quad d(a, a) = 0 \\ &\text{c.} \quad d(a, b) = d(b, a) \\ &\text{d.} \quad d(a, b) \leqslant d(a, c) + d(c, b) \end{aligned}\right\} \qquad (1.6.2.3)$$

[5]

In a two-dimensional case the Euclidean distance $d$ between point $a$ and $b$ (with respective co-ordinates $(x_1, y_1)$ and $(x_2, y_2)$) is equal to (cf. also fig. 1.6.2.c):

$$d = \sqrt{(x_1 - x_2)^2 + (y_1 - y_2)^2} \qquad (1.6.2.4)$$

Fig. 1.6.2.c A representation of distance

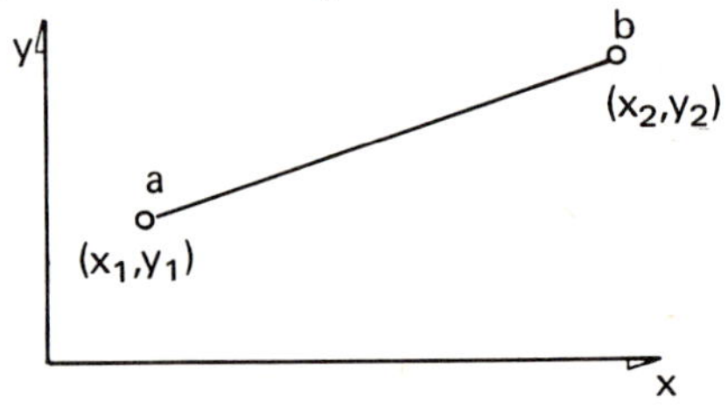


The general concept of spatial distances as developed previously is present in many spatial economic theories; two special cases will be mentioned here.

First, *rectangular networks* (for instance, the traffic network of New York) can be studied by means of the distance concept (see figure 1.6.2.d). For example, in figure 1.6.2.d traffic from point $P_1$ to point $P_2$ must pass point $P_3$. Now the rectangular distance from $P_1$ to $P_2$ (denoted by $d^r(P_1, P_2)$) is equal to the direct physical distance from $P_1$ to $P_3$

Fig. 1.6.2.d A rectangular network

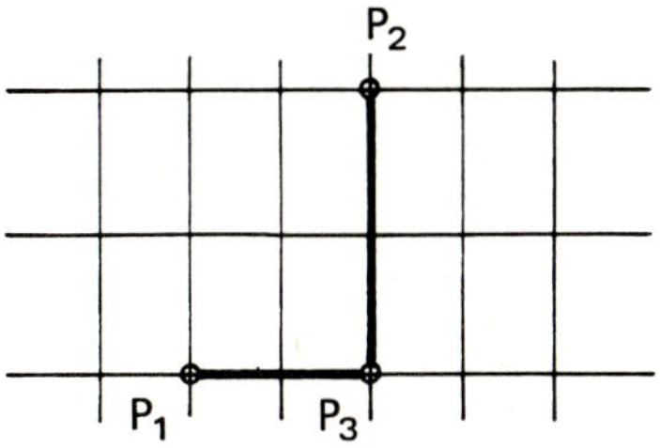


Fig. 1.6.2.e A distance triangle in a rectangular network

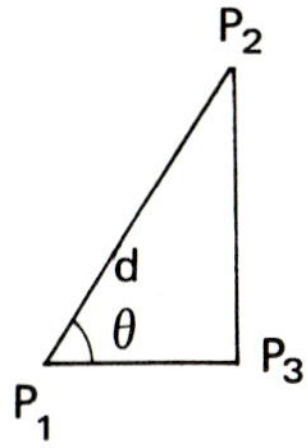


(denoted as $d(P_1, P_3)$) plus the direct physical distance from $P_3$ to $P_2$ (denoted as $d(P_3, P_2)$), so that:

$$d^r(P_1, P_2) = d(P_1, P_3) + d(P_3, P_2) \qquad (1.6.2.5)$$

(see also figure 1.6.2.e).

It can be proved (see Appendix 1A) that a rectangular traffic network (or city block metric) satisfies the axiomatic definitions of abstract distances (see (1.6.2.3)). This implies that the distance concept can also be applied to transportation problems in a city block metric.

Secondly, *structural forms* of growing cities (the so-called 'urban sprawl') can be studied by means of distance concepts (cf. Wingo [1961]). Suppose a city has a network, which is rectangular with respect to two main radials $x$ and $y$ (see figure 1.6.2.f); the origin of the co-ordinate axes is the centre of the city. If the costs of transportation and of traffic from and to the centre are proportional to the rectangular distance with respect to the centre, the evolution of the city will be such that marginal inhabitants living at marginal zones of the city have equal distances with respect to the centre (owing to the $\epsilon$-principle of minimizing transport costs). The set of all points in the first quadrant which have equal

Fig. 1.6.2.f A rectangular structure of a city

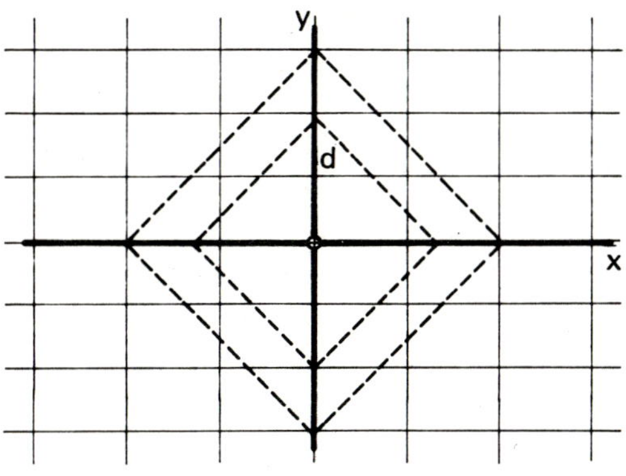

rectangular distances with respect to the centre is represented by the line $y + x = d$, where $d$ is a distance measured along the $y$-axis. In a growing city this line will shift upwards. Since other quadrants will undergo a similar change the structural form of this extending city will be a square (see figure 1.6.2.f). The area $A$ of this square is equal to:

$$A = 2d^2 \tag{1.6.2.6}$$

The effect of enlarging the radials of this city is measured as:

$$\frac{\partial A}{\partial d} = 4d \tag{1.6.2.7}$$

If a city possesses three main radials (represented by the axes $x$, $y$ and $z$) and a network rectangular upon these radials, the result is a star-like structure (see figure 1.6.2.g).

Fig. 1.6.2.g A three-radial structure of a city

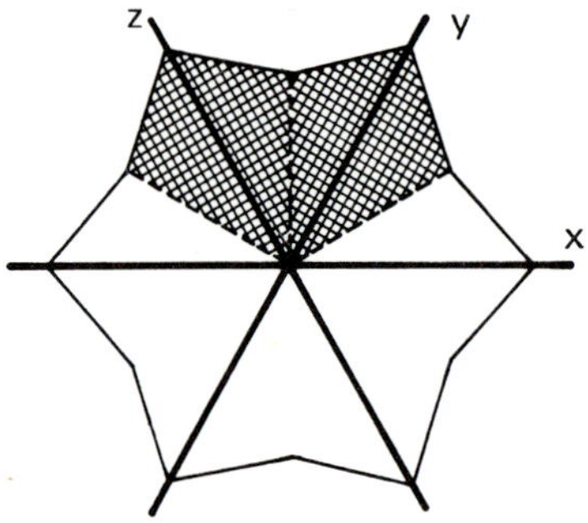


A similar method can be applied to analyze an arbitrary number of radials or alternative patterns of traffic networks. If the number of radials increases, the structural form converges towards a circle. The area $A$ of a circle itself is affected in the following way by an increase of the radius $d$:

$$\begin{aligned} \frac{\partial A}{\partial d} &= \frac{\partial\,(\pi d^2)}{\partial d} \\ &= 2\pi d \end{aligned} \tag{1.6.2.8}$$

Therefore, we may conclude that the effect of an increasing length of the radials upon the area of an arbitrary regular city falls in between $4d$ and $2\pi d$.

Finally, the size of market areas, towns, regions etc. may correspond to densities ($D$), for instance population densities, agricultural production densities. In general, densities can be computed by means of double integrals (denoting two dimensions):

$$D = \int_A \int f(x, y) \, dx \, dy \qquad (1.6.2.9)$$

where $f(x, y)$ is the mathematical representation of the density phenomena studies over domain $A$. Applications of spatial densities are contained in Ch.2.

### 1.6.3 *Differentiated space*

Differentiated space is a (partial) representation of real-world spatial phenomena. Evidently, this differentiated space possesses less regular and ideal structures than the abstract structures of undifferentiated space. In reality one observes irregular spatial concentrations, natural barriers and boundaries, imperfect mobilities of labour, capital and commodities, different levels of regional or national welfare, etc. As a consequence, man's economic activities are dispersed in a rather irregular way. The degree of spatial dispersion (or, inversely, of spatial concentration) is used in table 1.6.3.a for a systematic classification of spatial production and consumption patterns (cf. Beckmann [1968] ).

Table 1.6.3.a A spatial classification of activities

| Spatial classification | | Producers | |
|---|---|---|---|
| | | Concentrated | Dispersed |
| Consumers | Concentrated | I | III |
| | Dispersed | II | IV |

The various cases I–IV of table 1.6.3.a are pure cases. Evidently, reality is less pure than sketched in the previous scheme.

Case I can be considered as a 'point-point' case: both consumers and producers are assumed to be located at certain spatial points. This assumption is implicit in the major part of location theories, for instance those of Weber (1909) and of Predöhl (1925) (see Ch.2).

Case II can be termed a 'market area' case: producers are concentrated, while consumers are supposed to be spread in a regular way all through space. Examples of this case can be found in Christaller (1933) and Lösch (1954) (see Ch.2).

Case III represents a 'supply area' case: a set of dispersed producers have to serve a spatial concentration of consumers. An example of this kind is the circular dispersion of the agriculture around a city, as it is studied by Von Thünen (1842) (see also Ch.2).

Case IV is a 'megalopolis' case: a megalopolis is a diffuse urbanization over an extensive space. An example of this kind is the Philadelphia–Boston region along the north-east coast of the USA, as described by Gottman (1961).

A useful tool in describing and studying problems linked with the dispersion of spatial concentrations is *graph-theory* (cf. Berge [1962], Harary et al. [1966], Lantner [1974] and Ponsard [1966]). All relevant points in a part of the differentiated space can be included in a network, which indicates the way in which the various spatial points are linked up together. These relevant points are called the *nodes* of the network. In the case of a spatial connection between two nodes, one links these nodes by means of an *edge*. In this way one may construct a flow diagram between the various points (see figure 1.6.3.a); if there is no connection between certain points,

Fig. 1.6.3.a A flow-diagram

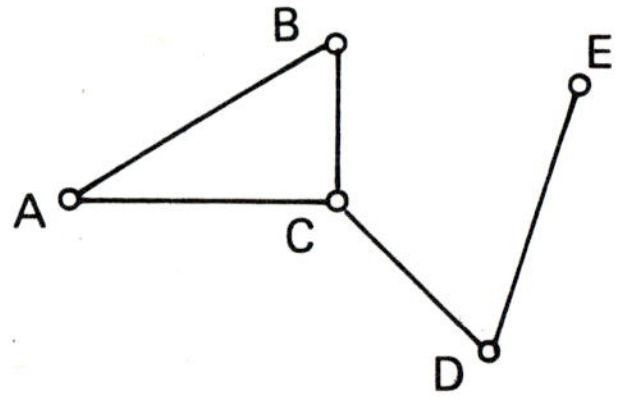


the distance between those points is assumed to be infinite. Figure 1.6.3.a can be extended by indicating the direction of the flows by means of arrows; one then obtains an *orientated flow-diagram* or a *di-graph* (see figure 1.6.3.b). In addition, the oriented flows can be provided with

Fig. 1.6.3.b A di-graph

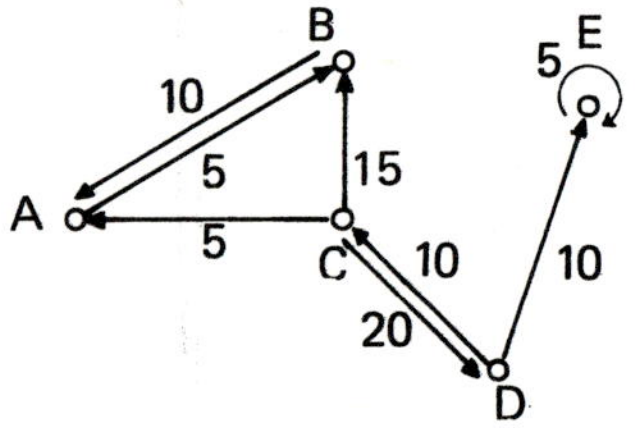


numbers representing the size of the various flows (for instance, in terms of volumes of goods, or of the various distances[6]), as is performed in figure 1.6.3.b. Point *E* appears to have an internal flow.

One can associate with each network a contact-matrix, which is a matrix-representation of a network. For instance, the contact-matrix associated with figure 1.6.3.b is:

| | A | B | C | D | E |
|---|---|---|---|---|---|
| A | | 5 | | | |
| B | 10 | | | | |
| C | 5 | 15 | | 20 | |
| D | | | 10 | | 10 |
| E | | | | | 5 |

(1.6.3.1)

If there exists a flow from one point to another, the size of this flow is represented by means of the corresponding element of the matrix (read horizontally from the left to the right). If there is no flow, the corresponding element is blank. The contact-matrix (1.6.3.1) appears to possess a near block-diagonal structure; this implies that the two blocks are for a major part completely independent with respect to each other. The contact-matrix can also be transformed into a Boolean matrix (cf. (1.4.1.3)):

| | A | B | C | D | E |
|---|---|---|---|---|---|
| A | | 1 | | | |
| B | 1 | | | | |
| C | 1 | 1 | | 1 | |
| D | | | 1 | | 1 |
| E | | | | | 1 |

(1.6.3.2)

Many problems in the field of transportation, traffic and communication can be dealt with by means of network-analysis or contact-matrices. For instance, the evolution of a transportation network or the spatial diffusion of certain economic phenomena over a number of periods can be described by means of the successive corresponding contact-matrices or Boolean matrices. Applications of this type of studies to regional problems are contained *inter alia* in Nystuen and Dacey (1961) and Rouget (1972).

## 1.7 Conclusion

This introductory chapter served to show how a basic knowledge of operational instruments and theories of theoretical economics is a necessary condition for an adequate insight into modern trends in regional economics. In addition to a continuous feed-back from spatial problems towards general theoretical economics, a communication with other disciplines in the same field (for instance, economic geography and regional science) is indispensable. The approach adopted in the first chapter will be elaborated and clarified in the following chapters. So far the field of regional economics has been demarcated in rough lines; the remainder of this book is concerned with more specific topics of regional economics, based on the principles laid down in this first chapter.

## Appendix 1A A rectangular network

In this Appendix the rectangular distance will be proved to satisfy the axiomatic conditions (1.6.2.3).

If one denotes direct distance from $P_1$ to $P_2$ by $d$, one can easily express $d\ (P_1, P_3)$ and $d\ (P_3, P_2)$ in $d$ and the angle $\theta$. Then one obtains (see figure 1.6.2.e):

$$\begin{aligned} d^r\ (P_1, P_2) &= d \cos\theta + d \sin\theta \\ &= d\ (\cos\theta + \sin\theta) \end{aligned} \tag{1A.1}$$

Since the direct distance $d$ satisfies the axiomatic conditions of (1.6.2.3) and since $\cos\theta$ and $\sin\theta$ are positive in the first quadrant, (1A.1) can easily be proved to satisfy conditions a, b and c of (1.6.2.3). Condition d is slightly more complicated, because one has to prove that the rectangular distance (from $P_1$ to $P_2$) via a fourth point $P_4$ is not smaller than the rectangular distance via $P_3$.

If $P_4$ is located within the rectangular area $P_1P_3P_2A$ (see figure 1A.a), one has to prove condition d for the rectangular situation:

$$d^r\ (P_1, P_2) \leqslant d^r\ (P_1, P_4) + d^r\ (P_4, P_2) \tag{1A.2}$$

Fig. 1A.a  A rectangular network

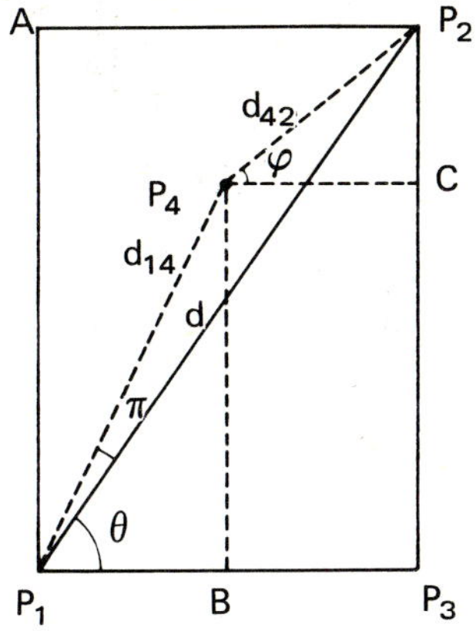


If the direct distances from $P_1$ to $P_4$ and from $P_4$ to $P_2$ are respectively denoted by $d_{14}$ and $d_{42}$, one may apply the results from (1.6.2.5) and (1A.1) to (1A.2) in order to transform the latter condition into:

$$d\,(\cos\theta + \sin\theta) \leqslant d_{14}\ \{\cos(\theta+\pi) + \sin(\theta+\pi)\} + d_{42}\ \{\cos\varphi + \sin\varphi\} \tag{1A.3}$$

Since

$$d\,(P_1, P_3) = d\,(P_1, B) + d\,(P_4, C) \tag{1A.4}$$

and

$$d\,(P_3, P_2) = d\,(B, P_4) + d\,(C, P_2) \tag{1A.5}$$

one can easily prove that

$$d\cos\theta = d_{14}\cos(\theta+\pi) + d_{42}\cos\varphi \tag{1A.6}$$

and

$$d\sin\theta = d_{14}\sin(\theta+\pi) + d_{42}\sin\varphi \tag{1A.7}$$

By adding (1A.6) and (1A.7) condition (1A.3) appears to be satisfied, so that all axiomatic distance conditions are satisfied.

If $P_4$ is located outside the rectangular area $P_1P_3P_2A$ (see figure (1A.b) a similar proof can be found, since condition d of (1.6.2.3) corresponds again to condition (1A.3). Since:

$$d\,(P_1, P_3) = d\,(P_1, B) + d\,(C, P_2) \tag{1A.8}$$

and:

$$d\,(P_3, P_2) \leqslant d\,(B, P_4) + d\,(P_4, C) \tag{1A.9}$$

Fig. 1A.b A rectangular network

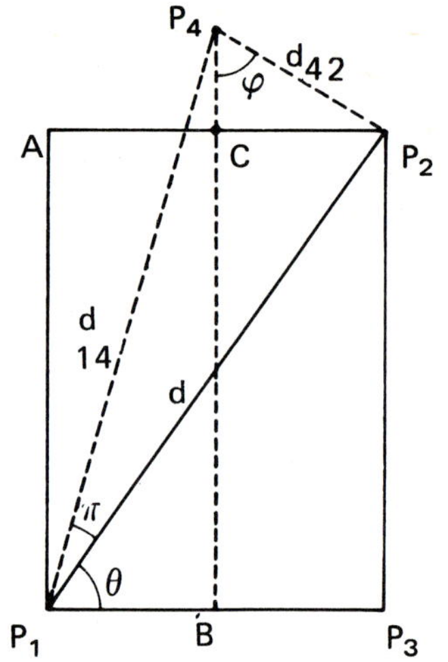


one obtains the following relationships:

$$d \cos \theta = d_{14} \cos (\theta+\pi) + d_{42} \cos \varphi \qquad (1A.10)$$

and:

$$d \sin \theta \leqslant d_{14} \sin (\theta+\pi) + d_{42} \sin \varphi \qquad (1A.11)$$

Addition of (1A.10) and (1A.11) shows that condition (1A.3) is indeed satisfied.[7]

## Notes

[1] This approach, set out among others by Samuelson (1953) and Koopmans (1957), is used here only as a tool of analysis. For further discussion and a critical review, see among others, Goudzwaard (1972) and Nijkamp (1974).

[2] Boolean mathematics is a specific mathematical topic dealing mainly with zero-one variables; see, for instance, Hammer and Rudeanu (1968).

[3] In mathematical terms one may consider a function as a mapping of one space into another space; a function is a prescription which assigns to any element of a given space one and only one image in another given space.

[4] In addition, one may distinguish a normalized structural system. In that case each endogenous variable is expressed exactly once in terms of the other (endogenous and predetermined) variables. Such a system may

be useful in case of numerical solution procedures of systems of equations, such as a Gauss-Seidel method (see, for instance, Saaty and Bram [1964]).

[5] Condition d is called the triangle inequality.

[6] If the distances concerned are *economic* distances, they are not necessarily symmetric in both directions (as in the case of *physical* distances), since e.g. transportation tariffs are not always symmetric in both directions.

[7] It should be noted that there are alternative methods of proving that the rectangular distance or city block metric satisfies condition (1.6.2.3). The distance between two points $P_1$ and $P_2$ (with respective co-ordinates $[x_1, y_1]$ and $[x_2, y_2]$) in a rectangular network is equal to the sum of the absolute difference of their projections on each separate dimension, i.e.,

$$d^r(P_1, P_2) = |x_1 - x_2| + |y_1 - y_2|$$

If this distance relationship is written in the above form, it can also be proved to possess the properties of the abstract concept of distance. This function is, in fact, a special case of a more general distance function, the Minkowski metric, which can be written for a two-dimensional space as:

$$d = \left\{ |x_1 - x_2|^\lambda + |y_1 - y_2|^\lambda \right\}^{1/\lambda}$$

where $\lambda \geqslant 1$ in order to satisfy the triangle inequality. When $\lambda = 1$, one obtains the rectangular distance; when $\lambda = 2$, one obtains the Euclidean distance (1.6.2.4); see Beckenbach and Bellman (1961), Green and Carmone (1970), Huriot and Perreur (1973), and Perreur and Thisse (1973).

## References


Beckenbach, E. and Bellman, R., *An Introduction to Inequalities,* Random House, New York 1961.

Beckmann, M., *Location Theory*, Random House, New York 1968.

Beckmann, M., 'The Analysis of Spatial Diffusion Processes', *Papers and Proceedings of the Regional Science Association*, vol. 25, 1970, pp. 109–117.

Berge, C., *The Theory of Graphs*, Methuen, London 1962.

Berry, B., 'Hierarchical Diffusion; the Basis of Developmental Filtering and Spread in a System of Growth Centers', in: N.M. Hansen (ed.), *Growth Centres in Regional Economic Development*, Free Press, New York 1971, pp. 108–138.

Christaller, W., *Die Zentralen Orte in Süddeutschland*, Fischer, Jena 1933 (English translation by C.W. Baskin: *Central Places in Southern Germany*, Prentice-Hall, Englewood Cliffs 1966).

Courtin, R. and Maillet, P., *Economie Géographique*, Dalloz, Paris 1962.

de Jong, F.J., *Dimensional Analysis for Economists*, North-Holland Publishing Co., Amsterdam 1967.

Gottman, J., *Megalopolis; The Urbanized Northeastern Seaboard of the United States*, The Twentieth Century Fund, New York 1961.

Goudzwaard, B., *Economie en Vooruitgangsidee*, Bohn, Haarlem 1972.

Green, P.E. and Carmone, F.J., *Multidimensional Scaling and Related Techniques in Marketing Analysis,* Allyn and Bacon, Boston, Massachusetts 1970.

Hammer, P.L. and Rudeanu, S., *Boolean Methods in Operations Research and Related Areas*, Springer-Verlag, Berlin 1968.

Harary, F., Norman, R.Z. and Cartright, D., *Structural Models; An Introduction to the Theory of Directed Graphs*, Wiley, New York 1966.

Harvey, D., *Explanation in Geography,* Arnold, London 1969.

Hoover, E.M., *An Introduction to Regional Economics*, Knopf, New York 1971.

Huriot, J.M. and Perreur, J., 'Modèles des Localisations et Distance Rectilinéaire', *Revue d'Economie Politique*, 1973, pp. 640–662.

Isard, W., *Methods of Regional Analysis,* MIT Press, Cambridge 1960.

Isard, W., Schooler, E.W. and Vietorisz, T., *Industrial Complex Analysis and Regional Development: A Case Study of Refinery-Petrochemical-Synthetic-Fiber Complexes and Puerto-Rico*, MIT Press, Cambridge 1959.

Koopmans, T.C., *Three Essays on the State of Economic Science*, McGraw-Hill, New York 1957.

Lantner, R., *Théorie de la Dominance Economique*, Dunod, Paris 1974.

Lösch, A., *The Economics of Location*, Yale University Press, New Haven 1954.

Mennes, L.B.M., Tinbergen, J. and Waardenburg, J.G., *The Element of Space in Development Planning*, North-Holland Publishing Co., Amsterdam 1969.

Nijkamp, P., 'Ekonomie: Norm en Plaats', in: P. Nijkamp et al. (eds.), *Inkomen en Tijd,* Vuurbaak, Groningen 1974, pp. 5–32.

Nourse, H.O., *Regional Economics,* McGraw-Hill, New York 1968.

Nystuen, J.D. and Dacey, M.F., 'A Graph Theory Interpretation of Nodal Regions', *Papers and Proceedings of the Regional Science Association,* vol. 7, 1961, pp. 29–42.

Perreur, J. and Thisse, J.F., 'Central Metrics and Optimal Location',

Credel Research Papers, Liège, Belgium, 1973, 7306 (mimeo).
Ponsard, C., 'Une Application de la Théorie des Graphes à l'Analyse de l'Espace Economique', in: *Techniques Economiques Modernes*, no. 4, Travaux sur l'Espace Economique, Gauthier-Villars, Paris, 1966, pp. 1–21.
Predöhl, A., 'Das Standortsproblem in der Wirtschaftstheorie', *Weltwirtschaftliches Archiv*, vol. XXI, 1925, pp. 294–331.
Rouget, B., 'Graph Theory and Hierarchisation Models, *Regional and Urban Economics*, vol. 2, no. 3, 1972, pp. 263–96.
Saaty, T.L. and Bram, J., *Nonlinear Mathematics*, McGraw-Hill, New York 1964.
Samuelson, P.A., *Foundations of Economic Analysis*, Harvard University Press, Cambridge, Mass. 1953.
Theil, H., *Optimal Decision Rules for Government and Industry*, North-Holland Publishing Co., Amsterdam 1964.
Tinbergen, J., *Economic Policy; Principles and Design*, North-Holland Publishing Co., Amsterdam 1956.
Von Thünen, J.H., *Der Isolierte Staat in Beziehung auf Landwirtschaft und Nationalökonomie,* Léopold, Rostock 1842 (English translation [C.M. Wartenberg] : *Von Thünen's Isolated State*, Pergamon Press, Oxford 1966).
Weber, A., *Über den Standort der Industrien*, Tübingen 1909 (English translation [C.J. Friedrich] : *Alfred Weber's Theory of Location of Industries*, University of Chicago Press, Chicago 1929).
Wingo, L., 'An Economic Model of the Utilization of Urban Land for Residential Purposes', *Papers of the Regional Science Association*, 1961, pp. 191–205.

PART I

# Theories

# 2 Historical Review

## 2.1 Introduction

The explicit consideration and analysis of the spatial dispersion and coherence of economic activities is a rather new element in general theoretical economics. In addition to the element of time one observes, particularly during the post-war years, a stronger emphasis on the element of space in economic thinking, since economic scientists have become more and more aware of the fact that the actions and reactions of the economic agents are not undertaken simultaneously at the same place, but are dispersed over space. The theory of international trade was one of the first topics in economics, which took account of distance factors. The space element implied by these distance factors, however, was only considered with respect to international political boundaries; it was not integrated in local and regional studies.

In this chapter a short review of the history of spatial economics will be presented. It is not the purpose to develop broad historical lines of thought; the purpose is rather to present a limited number of basic historical studies, which are considered to be key-stones in regional economics and which are representative of an operational approach to regional economic problems. A more general and comprehensive survey will not be given here, but can be found *inter alia* in Isard (1956), Ponsard (1958) and Moran (1965).

The major part of the historical review in this chapter is devoted to location theory and market area analysis, since these topics are, from a historical point of view, the heart of regional economics. In the postwar period a number of alternative subjects (for instance, interregional coherence, interregional input–output analysis and mathematical programming of interregional activities) come into the picture. At the moment all these components constitute the basic subjects of regional economics.

The historical development of location theory can be considered from different analytical points of view. In this way one may make the following distinctions[1] :

1 The analysis of *general economic* factors, which guide an entrepreneur in his search for an optimum location ('Standortsbestimmung'), for instance,

the objective of minimization of transportation costs (see Weber, section 2.3).

2 The analysis of *specific regional* factors, with which an entrepreneur is confronted in his decisions for a location ('Standortswirkung'), for instance, the presence of certain inputs or of substitution possibilities between inputs (see Predöhl, section 2.4).

3 The analysis of *regional settlement patterns* ('Standortsgestaltung'), for instance, the way in which market areas are located around a consumption centre (see Von Thünen, section 2.2).

4 The analysis of the *dynamic development of regional location* patterns ('Standortsentwicklung'), for instance, by means of the attraction theory of Klaassen (1967; see also Ch.5).

In accordance with the approach to spatial economic problems, as set out in the introductory chapter, this chapter possesses the following features. The various historical theories are summarized in a set of characteristic hypotheses (denoted by H 1, H 2, etc.); this enables us to apply a more formal or even quantitative analysis. Next, the implications of the various hypotheses are elaborated within a systematic framework, which requires a basic knowledge of theoretical economics and mathematics. Once the analysis has been performed in this way, a set of verifiable conclusions can be drawn on the basis of the final results.

## 2.2 Von Thünen

### 2.2.1 *Introduction*

Von Thünen (1842) studied the different agricultural zones around a city (or consumption centre). He presented an analytical framework for studying the various types of cultivation around a city on the basis of economic relationships between a city and rural areas. Various problems of a spatial exchange economy were considered by Von Thünen, for instance, the influence of a city upon the price formation of agricultural goods, the influence of the distance from the city upon the agriculture and the net income of farmers, and the influence of growing cities upon the cultivated rural area. In the following section Von Thünen's theory of land rent and concentric cultivation will be discussed.

### 2.2.2 *Analysis*

Von Thünen's analysis of land use patterns is based on the following basic hypotheses:

H 1 The existence of non-differentiated agricultural areas with a homogeneous fertility of the soil.
H 2 The existence of a consumer centre, which uses the agricultural products and which has no external relations with respect to other cities or areas ('supply-area'-case; cf. section 1.6).
H 3 Uniform transportation costs as a function of distance, maximum allowable volume of transportation, and value of the products concerned.
H 4 Uniform delivered prices for all products.
H 5 Maximization of rent, i.e. the difference between gross revenues and transportation costs.

Given these hypotheses one can derive a formal relationship between the rent per quantity produced and the distance of a farmer from the consumption centre. Let us define $p$ as the given uniform delivered price of a certain agricultural product, $q$ as the unknown delivered volume of this agricultural product, $\alpha$ as the known quantity of energy required per double unit of distance (this was, in fact, in Von Thünen's time horse-energy, viz. fodder for the horses), $\overline{q}$ as the given maximum allowable gross load per wagon (thus $\overline{q}$ is equal to $q$ plus total requirements of horse-fodder), $d$ as the unknown distance from a farmer to the city, and $T$ as the (unknown) total transportation costs. Von Thünen's approach can be set out in the following equations for the volume of the agricultural product and its transportation costs:

$$q = \overline{q} - \alpha d \tag{2.2.2.1}$$

and:

$$T = (\beta\overline{q} + \gamma p)d \tag{2.2.2.2}$$

where $\beta$ and $\gamma$ can be conceived of as simplified transportation coefficients, which relate $T$ in a rather specific way to volume, price and distance. Now total rent, denoted by $R$, is equal to:

$$R = pq - T \tag{2.2.2.3}$$

which yields after substitution of (2.2.2.1) and (2.2.2.2) into (2.2.2.3):

$$R = p(\overline{q} - \alpha d) - (\beta\overline{q} + \gamma p)d \tag{2.2.2.4}$$

If rent per unit of maximum volume is denoted by $r$, one obtains:

$$\begin{aligned} r &= R/\overline{q} \\ &= p\left\{1 - \left(\frac{\alpha + \gamma}{\overline{q}} + \frac{\beta}{p}\right)d\right\} \end{aligned} \tag{2.2.2.5}$$

This final result shows that the unit rent decreases, as the parameter $a$ is higher (owing to the fact that a rise in $a$ means a rise in the transportation costs). The unit rent appears to decrease, as the distance from the city increases or as the transportation coefficients $\beta$ and $\gamma$ increase (owing to the higher transportation costs). A rise in the price level $p$ affects the unit rent in a positive way, as can be proved by investigating the marginal price effect:

$$\begin{aligned}\frac{\partial r}{\partial p} &= \left\{1-\left(\frac{a+\gamma}{\bar{q}}+\frac{\beta}{p}\right)d\right\}+\frac{\beta d}{p} \\ &= 1-\left(\frac{a+\gamma}{\bar{q}}\right)d > 0\end{aligned} \qquad (2.2.2.6)$$

For each agricultural product a relationship similar to (2.2.2.5) can be derived. If one assumes different prices and different coefficients, one can easily draw a graphical representation of the unit rent for each product as a linear function of distance. This is illustrated in the case of 2 products (1 and 2) in figure 2.2.2.a. Point $P_0$ represents the city, to which all agricultural products have to be transported. Since the objective of the analysis was to find a land use pattern, that maximizes the rent for each product (cf. H 5), the evident solution of the previous land use problem is to choose at the various distances of the city that cultivation pattern, where the respective rents are maximal. Thus, in figure 2.2.2.a the distance $P_0P_1$ represents the area within which the production of good 1 is more profitable; similarly, $P_1P_2$ represents the area with higher rents for good 2.

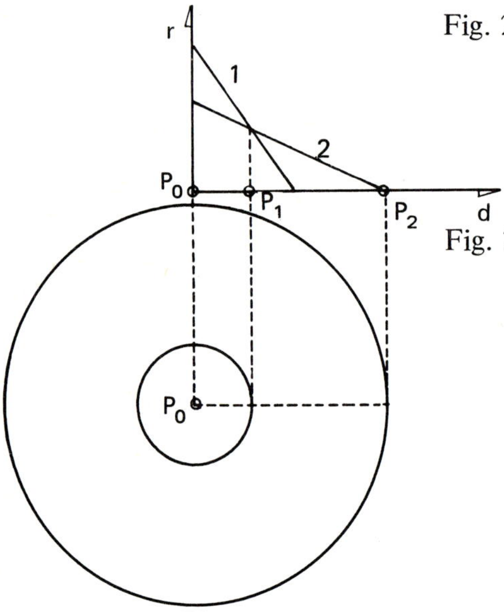


Fig. 2.2.2.a Rent curves of two agricultural products

Fig. 2.2.2.b A concentric cultivation

The demarcation line between both cultivations is determined by the point of intersection of the two rent lines, i.e. point $P_1$. The ultimate result of this maximization procedure is a *concentric* cultivation of the various products around the city. This is represented in figure 2.2.2.b. Once the optimal distances $d_1$ and $d_2$ (and thus the supply areas) have been derived, the remaining unknown variables $q$, $T$, $R$ and $r$ can be calculated in a straightforward way according to (2.2.2.1) – (2.2.2.5).

### 2.2.3 *Conclusion*

Von Thünen has presented an economic explanation of land use patterns based on elementary relationships between city and country. He can be conceived of as a predecessor of the more modern spatial substitution theories (see section 2.4), since he attempted to derive in a simple way an optimal combination of various production factors in terms of cultivated land. The hypothesis of rent maximization (instead of cost minimization) is also a relevant element in Von Thünen's approach. It is easily seen from the previous analysis, that rent maximization leads to an outcome different from cost minimization. Lösch, in particular, has stressed the importance of such a profit maximization instead of cost minimization (cf. section 2.6).

Ultimately, Von Thünen's approach has found a lot of modern applications. His theory is a useful starting-point in modern transportation and city planning, where unit transportation costs and land prices are considered to be a decreasing function of the distance from the city centre. In this framework the degree of accessibility (or inversely the degree of congestion) and the demand for land in the various zones of a city (dependent on the type of activity) are the successive determinants of the unit transportation costs and the land rent. Applications of these theories can be found *inter alia* in Alonso (1964) and Wingo (1961). Population densities and housing markets can be analyzed in a similar way, viz. by assuming that the population density at a certain point is a decreasing exponential function of the distance from that point to the city centre (see, for instance, Clark [1951] and Muth [1961]). Such distance-decay functions are also discussed in Ch.4. Applications in the field of recreation analysis are contained among others in Burton and Fulcher (1968), and in Clawson and Knetsch (1966).

## 2.3 Weber

### 2.3.1 *Introduction*

A new incentive for the development of regional economics, and more in particular of location theory, was given by Weber (1909). He presented a rather abstract and general location theory for the individual firm, while he attempted to analyze the effect of a set of location factors upon the minimum cost decisions of individual entrepreneurs.

His analysis was essentially *partial*: the economic landscape (as, for instance, determined by Von Thünen's approach) was considered as a datum. No general location theory was developed: only the optimal location of firm $N$ is determined, given the known locations of the remaining $N-1$ firms. He obtained a solution by means of an abstract and *mechanical* approach, in which he applied a mechanical experiment with weighted unit transportation costs of final and intermediate products. Other location elements (for example, spatial differences in wage levels and in agglomeration advantages) are stepwise introduced by means of *successive approximations*. This less straightforward way of finding the optimum location was due to the lack of adequate analytical tools at the time Weber worked out his analysis.

### 2.3.2 *Analysis*

The main elements of Weber's location theory can be summarized by means of the following set of basic hypotheses:

H 1 Consideration of only one firm, with a given volume of only one product.
H 2 Known locations of the points of consumption and raw materials.
H 3 Uniform transportation costs per ton-mile.
H 4 Fixed technical production coefficients ('Leontief-approach').
H 5 Minimization of transportation costs.

On the basis of the previous assumptions Weber reduced the location problem to a so-called 'Varignon' problem (cf. Schärlig [1973]). Suppose a known point $P_0$ being a consumption centre (i.e., with given co-ordinates) and two known points $P_1$ and $P_2$ being supply centres for raw materials. Then one may create a location triangle (see figure 2.3.2.a). The optimal location of the firm is found by taking three threads tied together in a knot. The end point of each thread possesses a weight $w_i$ ($i$ = 1, 2, 3), which corresponds to the respective relative unit transportation costs per ton-mile. By letting each thread pass through the corresponding angle of the locational triangle (for instance, by means of a pulley; cf. also figure 2.3.2.a), the knot will move towards an equilibrium position, which is the optimal location of the firm (in terms of minimal transportation costs). This method is also useful, if more points of consumption, or of raw materials, are considered, as long as the location area, i.e. the envelope of the various points, constitutes a *convex* area (for convexity, see Ch. 6).

Fig. 2.3.2.a A location triangle

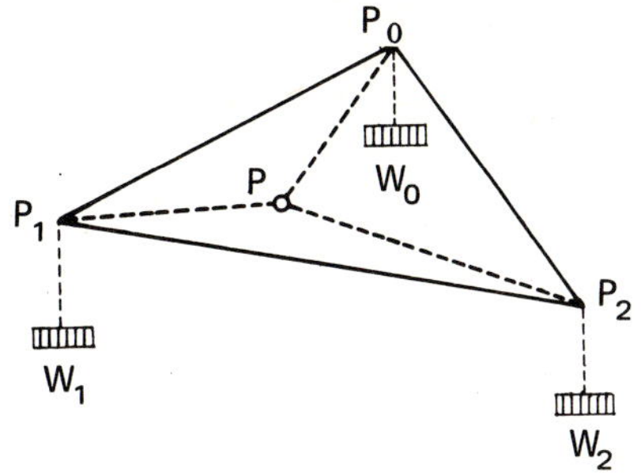


The previous problem can also be formulated in a formal way (though this was not carried out by Weber). If the given volume (i.e., weight) of the product is denoted by $q$, the as yet unknown distance from the firm's location to the consumption centre by $d_0$ and the unit transportation costs per ton-mile by $t_0$, then the unknown transportation costs of the final product, denoted with $T_0$, are:

$$T_0 = t_0 \, d_0 \, q \tag{2.3.2.1}$$

If the fixed technical coefficients of the intermediate products are denoted by $a_i$ $(i = 1, 2)$, where $a_i$ denotes the volume of intermediate product $i$ required to produce one unit of final product, the total requirement for intermediate product $i$ is equal to $a_i q$. If the respective distances and the unit transportation costs of the raw materials are denoted in a similar way by $d_i$ and $t_i$ $(i = 1, 2)$, the total transportation costs of the intermediate product $i$, denoted by $T_i$, are equal to:

$$T_i = t_i \, d_i \, a_i \, q \tag{2.3.2.2}$$

Now the total transportation costs $T$ of the firm are equal to:

$$\begin{aligned} T &= \sum_{i=0}^{2} T_i \\ &= \sum_{i=0}^{2} t_i \, d_i \, a_i \, q \end{aligned} \tag{2.3.2.3}$$

where the parameter $a_0$ is evidently equal to:

$$a_0 = 1 \tag{2.3.2.4}$$

The distance element $d_i$ in (2.3.2.2) is still unknown. According to (1.6.2.4) $d_i$ is written as:

$$d_i = \sqrt{\{(x_i - x)^2 + (y_i - y)^2\}} \quad , \qquad i = 0, 1, 2 \qquad (2.3.2.5)$$

where $x_i$ and $y_i$ are the known co-ordinates, either of the point of consumption or of the points of raw materials; the co-ordinates $x$ and $y$ represent the unknown co-ordinates of the firm's optimal location. These optimal co-ordinates can be found by means of the first-order optimizing condition of (2.3.2.3). By substituting (2.3.2.5) into (2.3.2.3), and differentiating, one finds:

$$\frac{\partial T}{\partial x} = - \sum_{i=0}^{2} t_i a_i q \frac{x_i - x}{\sqrt{\{(x_i - x)^2 + (y_i - y)^2\}}} = 0 \qquad (2.3.2.6)$$

as well as a similar expression for the first-order condition on the $y$-co-ordinate. In this way one obtains two relationships containing two unknown variables. This system of nonlinear equations cannot be solved in an analytical way, however. For that reason one must apply numerical solution procedures as presented in Appendix 2A. In this appendix the general case of multiple products and consumption centres is also formalized.

Once the optimum location of the firm is determined by means of the criterion of minimum transportation costs, one may analyse the effect of *spatial wage differences* within the location area upon the minimum costs of the firm (and thus upon its provisionally optimal location). Weber assumed that the wage costs to be paid by the firm varied from point to point. If the objective of the firm is to minimize total (transportation and labour) costs, the optimum location is co-determined by the spatial differences in wage costs.

Weber solved this additional problem by means of his technique of *isodapanes*. Suppose, one has determined a preliminary, optimal location $P$ on the basis of the minimum transportation cost criterion (2.3.2.3). Then an isodapane is defined as the set of all points, which have an equal rise in transportation costs from the preliminary, optimum location $P$ onwards. If the rise in transportation costs is equal to $\Delta T$ and if the original minimum transportation costs are $T^{\mathrm{O}}$, then the implicit algebraic equation of the corresponding isodapane is:

$$\sum_{i=0}^{2} t_i d_i a_i q = T^{\mathrm{O}} + \Delta T \qquad (2.3.2.7)$$

By substituting (2.3.2.5) into (2.3.2.7) one obtains the mathematical expression of this isodapane in terms of the $x$- and $y$-co-ordinates. By varying $\Delta T$, one may derive an extensive set of isodapanes around the provisionally optimum location $P$ (see figure 2.3.2.b). If the wage rate at point $P$ is higher than at other points within the locational area, this

Fig. 2.3.2.b A set of isodapanes

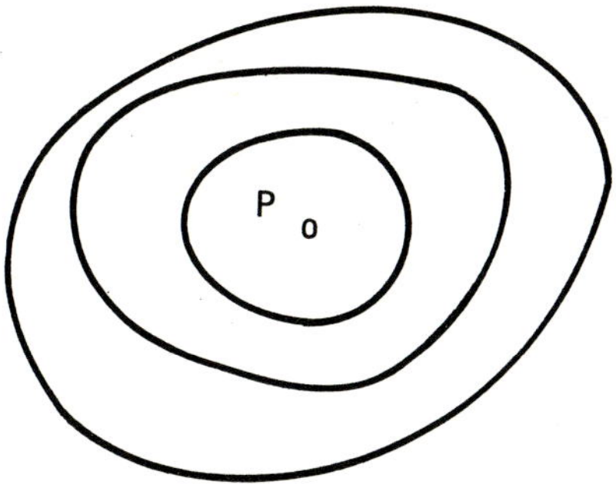


point is perhaps not the location with minimum total (transportation and wage) costs. In order to attack this problem Weber introduced the concept of a *critical isodapane*: a critical isodapane is the set of all points where the rise in transportation costs is exactly equal to the decline in the wage costs. This means that all points on the critical isodapane are indifferent with respect to the original point $P$ for a minimum cost location. This could mean that within Weber's framework multiple solutions can exist.

In order to wipe out the possibility of an indeterminate outcome Weber introduced another location element, viz. the existence of *spatial agglomeration economies,* since the optimum location is co-determined by the effect of agglomeration advantages of the firm concerned with respect to other firms already present in an area. The agglomeration economies arise according to Weber from an additional decline in production and transportation costs consequent upon a spatial clustering of productive activities. These externalities lead to an additional complication in the locational picture, since one has to consider three categories now: transportation costs, wage costs and agglomeration economies.

The latter problem can again be attacked by means of isodapanes. Suppose, one considers two firms, which have a minimum transport location in the respective places $P_1^O$ and $P_2^O$. If they would decide on a joint location somewhere between $P_1^O$ and $P_2^O$ they would get an agglomeration advantage to an amount of $z$ dollars per unit of product. However, at this joint location both firms have an increase in the transportation costs of the inputs. In order to analyse whether a joint location is more profitable, around each point $P_1^0$ and $P_2^0$ a series of isodapanes (net of wage cost differentials) is drawn. The critical isodapane is now the isodapane, where the rise in unit transportation costs (net of wage cost differentials) is exactly equal to the unit agglomeration advantage, i.e. $z$ dollars. If the critical isodapanes intersect (see figure 2.3.2.c), a joint location somewhere within the *agglomeration area* (i.e. the area $A$ of intersection) is more profitable than a separate location, since within the agglomeration area the net rise in transportation costs is compensated (or even overcompensated) by the agglomeration advantage.

Fig. 2.3.2.c Agglomeration and joint location

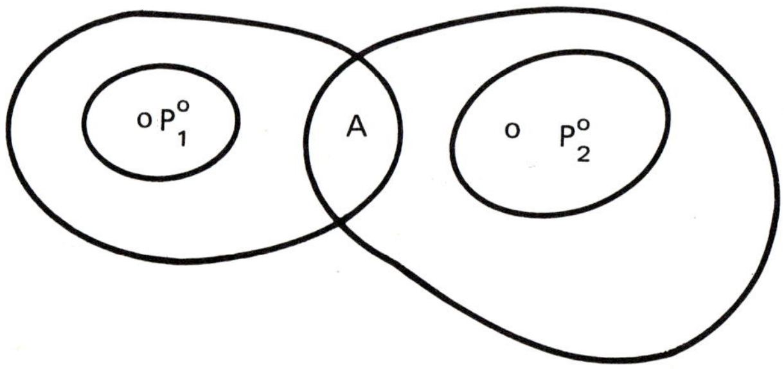


The exact point of joint location in the agglomeration area was not determined by Weber. In fact, the position of this joint production centre is the result of a number of game strategies, carried out by both entrepreneurs. A series of possible strategies for this Weberian problem (for instance, equal-cost-decrement procedures, equal-cost-increment procedures, action-compromise procedures and equidistant-compromise procedures) was proposed by Isard (1969). The relevance of game theory for location problems in the case of restricted competition will be discussed in Ch.3.

It should be noted that the concept of isodapanes and, particularly of a critical isodapane, is not quite clear in Weber's approach. There is no guarantee, that there exists only one unique critical isodapane, since the spatial pattern of wage differences may possess completely arbitrary forms and is not necessarily grouped in a regular way around the minimum-cost point $P$. For that reason the use of the isodapane technique is, in general, not appropriate for an operational approach to the solution of these kinds of location problems, so that a more formal approach must be preferred (cf. Appendix 2A).

Ultimately, Weber has also tried to attack the general location problem. He analyzed the spatial distribution of groups of individual activities and groups of locations within a country, and built up a spatial system consisting of several levels. The first level is the agricultural level (cf. Von Thünen). This first level is used as a starting-point for building a second level, viz. the industrial level. In this way Weber has constructed a hierarchy of activities and locations (cf. Lösch; see section 2.6), though he did not elaborate this system in a formal way.

### 2.3.3 *Conclusion*

In spite of an unsatisfactory formal presentation, Weber has made a far-reaching contribution to regional economics. His approach, based on transport costs, fixed technical coefficients and cost minimization, appeared to be a useful tool, particularly in the field of interregional and sectoral input–output analyses (cf. Ch.5) and of transportation models (cf. Ch.6). Furthermore, his concept of agglomeration forces constitutes the corner stone of modern industrial complex analysis, as developed *inter alia* by Isard et al. (1959), Klaassen (1967) and Nijkamp (1972).

Certain limitations of Weber's theory (in particular, the assumption of fixed technical coefficients and of cost minimization) are reconsidered in Ch.3, where a more general framework is presented.

Finally, Weber's approach of finding an optimal location by minimizing the transportation costs has found a lot of modern applications. It may be useful in the case of a rather homogeneous geographical area, where the transportation network between the various production and consumption points is still being developed. In this way one may also use the Weberian framework for finding a minimum transport cost location for governmental institutions. In addition, the previous approach may be useful for finding an optimal location of a new airport with respect to other airports or of a new power station serving a series of surrounding population centres (cf. also Schärlig [1973] and Serck-Hanssen [1970]).

## 2.4 Predöhl

### 2.4.1 *Introduction*

As mentioned in Ch.1, Predöhl (1925) was the man who introduced the *spatial substitution principle*. This neo-classical approach filled the gaps between general economic theory and location theory. Classical location theory did not take account of substitution possibilities between production factors at various locations (see, for instance, the constant production coefficients in the Weberian framework).

Predöhl can be credited for having developed a neo-classical approach to location problems. He raised the problem of the relation between input substitutions and locational changes of a single firm which produces a given volume of commodities. He integrated shifts along the production isoquant and shifts of the firm's location into one framework. In this way the location problem became a generalization of neo-classical production theory.

### 2.4.2 *Analysis*

Predöhl's neo-classical location theory can be exposed on the basis of the following set of hypotheses:

H 1 Consideration of only one firm with a given volume $q$ of only one product.
H 2 The existence of one consumption centre $P_0$ and of two input sources $P_1$ and $P_2$.
H 3 Uniform transportation costs per ton-mile.
H 4 A given uniform delivered price $p$ of the final product.
H 5 Given f.o.b. prices $p_i^*$ ($i$ = 1, 2) of the inputs.[2]
H 6 A neo-classical production function.
H 7 Minimization of total costs.

Given the previous hypotheses one can study the interrelationship between spatial and input substitutions on the basis of figure 2.4.2.a. The broken line of figure 2.4.2.a represents a circle segment around point $P_0$. Therefore, the points $M_1$ and $M_2$ on this segment have equal distances

Fig. 2.4.2.a. A location area

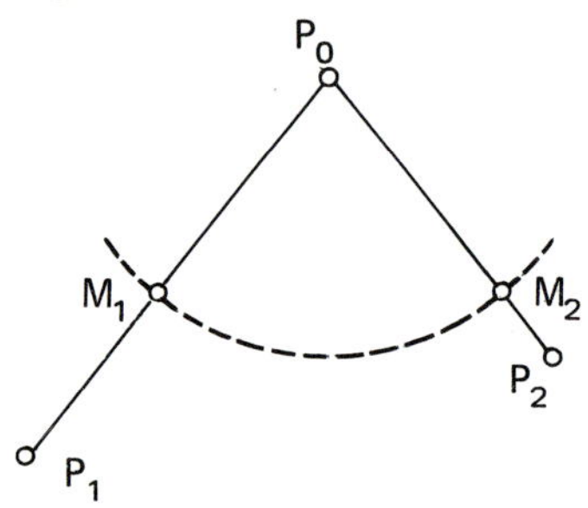


with respect to $P_0$ and, therefore, equal transportation costs of the final product with respect to $P_0$. It is quite evident that $M_1$ and $M_2$ do not possess equal transportation costs with respect to the input sources $P_1$ and $P_2$. If the volume of the raw materials is, respectively, denoted by $z_1$ and $z_2$ (with respective c.i.f. prices $p_1$ and $p_2$), total input costs $C$ are:

$$C = p_1 z_1 + p_2 z_2 \tag{2.4.2.1}$$

The prices $p_1$ and $p_2$ are not constant, but depend on the distances $d_1$ and $d_2$ from the (unknown) optimal location to the input sources $P_1$ and $P_2$. If the unit transportation costs of the inputs are denoted by $t_i$ $(i = 1, 2)$, the c.i.f. input price $p_i$ $(i = 1, 2)$ is:

$$p_i = p_i^* + t_i d_i \qquad (2.4.2.2)$$

By substituting (2.4.2.2) and (2.4.2.1) one obtains:

$$C = (p_1^* + t_1 d_1)\, z_1 + (p_2^* + t_2 d_2)\, z_2 \qquad (2.4.2.3)$$

Thus, the input costs depend on the (unknown) spatial variables $d_1$ and $d_2$, as well as on the (unknown) input variables $z_1$ and $z_2$. Given a certain level of costs $C^*$, the equation for an iso-cost line is:

$$z_1 = \frac{C^*}{p_1^* + t_1 d_1} - \frac{p_2^* + t_2 d_2}{p_1^* + t_1 d_1}\, z_2 \qquad (2.4.2.4)$$

Now each point on the circle segment $M_1 M_2$ of figure 2.4.2.a leads to a certain iso-cost line, since the distances $d_1$ and $d_2$ differ at each point on the segment $M_1 M_2$. For instance, point $M_1$ may give rise to the iso-cost line $A_1 B_1$ of figure 2.4.2.b. In fact, an infinite number of iso-cost lines can be drawn, each of which is related to a certain point on the circle segment $M_1 M_2$. If for the moment only the iso-cost line $A_1 B_1$ is considered, one may draw also the isoquant $QQ$, which is related to the

Fig. 2.4.2.b Iso-cost lines and isoquants

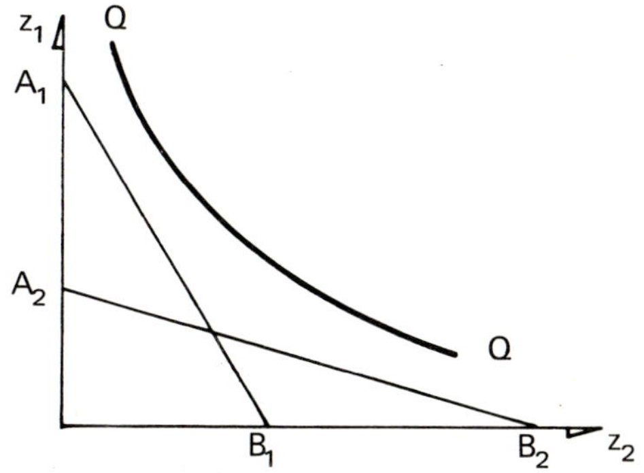


production function of the firm. In non-spatial production theory, the cost-minimizing point is determined as the point of tangency of the isoquant and an iso-cost line. This iso-cost line possesses, in non-spatial production theory, a fixed slope, so that one may attain a point of tangency with the isoquant by a parallel shift (upwards or downwards) (see figure 2.4.2.c). However, adding the space element can significantly

Fig. 2.4.2.c A shift of iso-cost lines

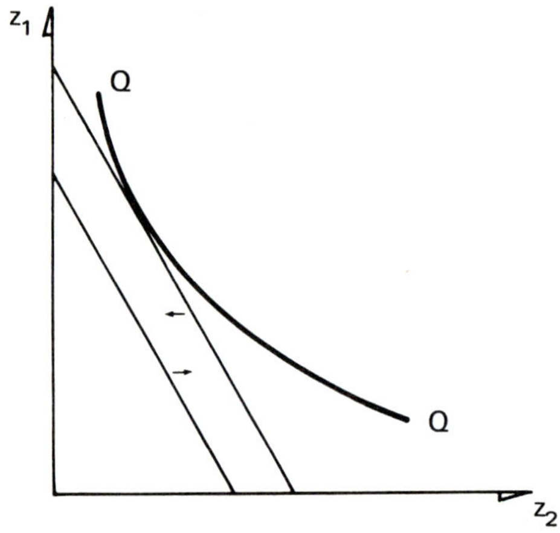


alter the previous analysis, because in the case of distance factors the iso-cost line has a variable direction, dependent on the (as yet unknown) distances $d_1$ and $d_2$ (see [2.4.2.4]). This means that the optimal (i.e. cost minimizing) point cannot be found by a single parallel shift of the iso-cost line (for instance, $A_1B_1$), since there is an infinite number of iso-cost lines with different directions dependent on the distances $d_1$ and $d_2$. The solution of this problem requires a time-consuming procedure in order to select precisely that iso-cost line, which has only one point in common with the isoquant, while it yields minimum total costs. In fact, such a graphical solution procedure requires an inspection of all points of the isoquant: through each point of the isoquant a tangent should be drawn, while, next, the related production costs have to be calculated. In this way one might (in principle) find the cost-minimizing point.

The important fact to be noted is, that there is a one-to-one correspondence between the cost-minimizing factor mix and the optimum location: knowledge of the cost-minimizing factor ratio implies knowledge of the related iso-cost line, while knowledge of this relevant iso-cost line implies according to (2.4.2.4) knowledge of the optimal distances $d_1$ and $d_2$ (and thus of the optimum location). Therefore, the essential element in Predöhl's theory is a simultaneous determination of optimal factor ratios and the optimal location, so that spatial substitution and factor substitution are two sides of the same coin. Input ratios, price ratios and locations are closely linked together according to the generalized $\sigma$-principle (see Ch.1).

Predöhl himself did not solve the previous problem in a satisfactory way. He presented only the essential features of the links between neo-classical production theory and location theory. In addition to the previous figurative way of dealing with Predöhl's problem, one might also use an analytical approach, which is more appropriate for an operational attack of this neo-classical location problem. A generalization of the problem is obtained by taking account of the demand side, viz. by abandoning the assumption of a fixed output and of a fixed output price. In that case the assumption of profit maximization (instead of cost minimization) is more relevant. The result is a completely variable locational problem: inputs, outputs, factor prices, product prices and locations are variables, which are linked to each other by means of substitution relationships. A formal presentation of this generalized neo-classical location theory is contained in Ch.3.

In addition to the partial location theory of a single firm, as described above, Predöhl was also involved in the field of general location theory and of locational patterns. He attempted to reconcile the theories of Von Thünen and Weber with neo-classical substitution theory.

### 2.4.3 *Conclusion*

Predöhl's contribution to regional economics can be summarized in two dominant elements:

1 he introduced the $\sigma$-principle in regional economics; as such he is the founder of modern neo-classical location theories (see Ch.3); and
2 he raised the problem of a general interdependent spatial economic equilibrium on the basis of substitution possibilities between production factors and locations; for the latter reason he can be considered as a predecessor of Palander (see section 2.5), Lösch (see section 2.6) and Isard (see Ch.7).

## 2.5 Palander

### 2.5.1 *Introduction*

The major contribution of Palander (1935) to the development of regional economics was his analysis of a spatial economic equilibrium, particularly in the field of market area analysis. In Palander's opinion, the abstract concept of pure competition is not useful in regional economics, because the spatial dispersion of activities, caused by permanent institutional and climatological factors, obviates the assumption of perfect mobility of products and production factors. For that reason he stressed the importance of situations with restricted competition (for instance, a duopoly). The restricted degree of mobility of activities led Palander to a classification of activities, which linked up better with the real-world dispersion of activities[3] (see table 2.5.a).

Table 2.5.a

A classification of activities

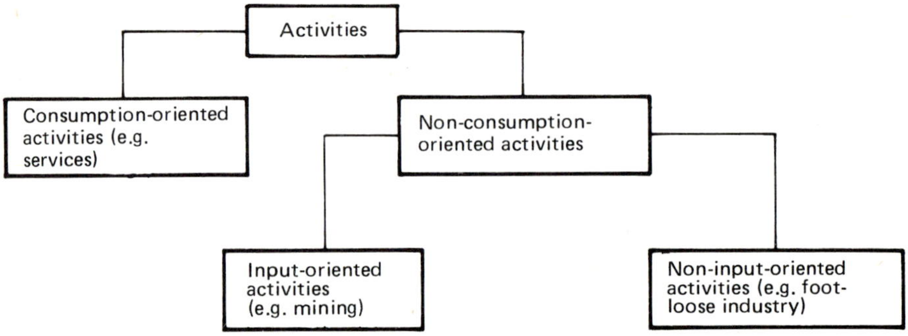


The location problems are dependent on the type of activity used, while the market area is also a direct consequence of the activity concerned. In the following sections attention will be paid to a restricted number of topics, which are selected as relevant elements from Palander's theory. The following subjects will, successively, be dealt with: *market area analysis, the law of refraction,* and *duopolistic pricing and location problems.*

### 2.5.2 *Market area analysis*

Market area analysis is closely linked up with location theory, since it analyses the spatial dispersion and extensiveness of sales areas of entrepreneurs, given their location. In fact, there is a high degree of interdependency between location theory and market area analysis, since the optimality of a certain location is co-determined by the size of the market area (cf. Ch.3). The purpose of market area analysis is to find a set of demarcation lines, by means of which a country or region is divided into a subset of sales areas for each separate entrepreneur. Thus, the whole market area $M$ has to be split up into subsets $M_i$ $(i = 1, \ldots\ldots, I)$, each subset representing the market area of an individual firm $i$. Therefore, the subsets $M_i$ should satisfy the following conditions:

$$\left.\begin{array}{r} \bigcup_{i=1}^{I} M_i = M \\ M_i \cap M_j = \phi \; \forall \, i = j \end{array}\right\} \qquad (2.5.2.1)$$

where the symbols $\cup$, $\cap$ and $\phi$ represent, respectively, the union of sets, their intersection, and the null space. In classical market area analysis it is assumed that each individual firm acts as a monopolist in its own market area. In the latter case, spatial competition only determines the demarcation lines between the sales areas of the firms, but this spatial competition does not affect the sales volume of a certain firm within a given market area. A more modern and realistic approach to market area analysis is the assumption of dominating sales as a criterion for the demarcation of market areas (Beckmann [1971]; see Appendix 2B).

The demarcation lines between sales areas of different entrepreneurs depend *inter alia* on the transportation structure and on the price policy of the entrepreneurs. The transportation structure is determined by various factors, for instance, the means of transport (train, plane, boat, car, etc.), the distance to be bridged, and the weight, value and volume of the product to be shipped. In non-homogeneous space one often observes a less direct relationship between the unit transportation costs and the distance to be bridged.

In order to study the different elements influencing the transportation costs and the related market areas, Palander presented a systematic treatment concerning the concept of *isolines.* Isolines are sets of all points possessing equal spatial properties. The following isolines may be distinguished, assuming non-differentiated space:

| | | |
|---|---|---|
| isodistant | : | the set of all points with equal physical distances to two points; |
| isochrone | : | the set of all points with equal transportation times for a certain good to two points; |
| isotim | : | the set of all points with equal c.i.f. prices for a certain good around a given centre; |
| isovector | : | the set of all points with equal transportation costs for a certain good around a given centre; |
| isostant | : | the set of all points, where the c.i.f. prices of the homogeneous goods of two (or more) competitive sellers are equal, i.e., where the difference in f.o.b. prices of these goods is equal to the difference in transportation costs; and |
| isodapane | : | the set of all points with equal transportation costs (or changes in transportation costs; see section 2.3.2) for several goods (or inputs) around a given centre. |

In fact, the isodapanes can be derived on the basis of a set of known isovectors for the goods concerned. The problems of a *differentiated* space (for instance, natural barriers, national boundaries, transport differentiation and transshipment) can also be considered by means of isolines. In this case an adaptation of the isolines to the specific spatial differentiation at hand is necessary, but, in principle, this distortion can be dealt with in a similar way.

Palander used the concept of isolines for his market area analysis. On the basis of simple hypotheses (*inter alia*, given prices, given unit transportation costs and given locations) he attempted to derive the spatial structure of the market areas of two competing sellers. This analysis is discussed in the present section. A next step, viz. the introduction of various price policies, is more complicated; this duopolistic situation will be dealt with in a following section.

Palander's market area analysis is based on the following set of hypotheses:

H 1 The existence of a non-differentiated market area.
H 2 Two competitive firms (1 and 2) settled at the respective given points $P_1$ and $P_2$.
H 3 A production of only one homogeneous good.
H 4 Uniform transportation costs per ton-mile.
H 5 Given f.o.b. prices $p_i^*$ for each firm $i$ ($i = 1, 2$).
H 6 A price policy of mill pricing.
H 7 An inelastic consumer demand.

The analysis is performed on the basis of figure 2.5.2.a, which is a spatial representation of the locations of both firms. The physical distance between $P_1$ and $P_2$ is assumed to be equal to $l$. In general, $P_1$ and $P_2$ may have any position in Cartesian space. Since the concept of distance, however, is invariant with respect to a translation or rotation of the axes, the points $P_1$ and $P_2$ may be assumed to have respective co-ordinates (0, 0) and ($l$, 0) without lack of generality. The search for the demarcation line

Fig. 2.5.2.a The market area of two firms

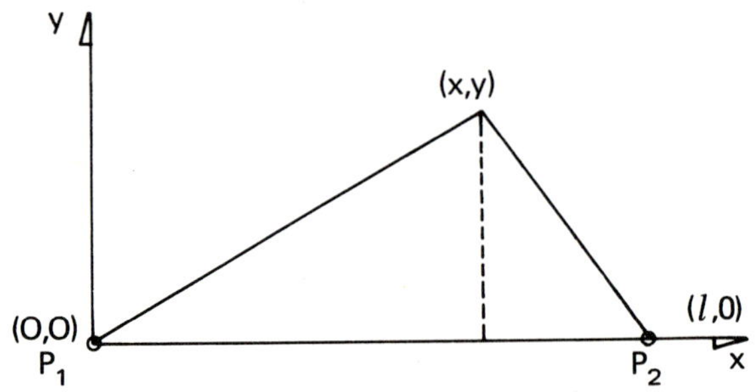


between the market area of firm 1 and 2 means that one should determine the mathematical representation of this demarcation line, i.e. in terms of the moving co-ordinates $x$ and $y$. If the unit transportation costs of the product of firm $i$ ($i = 1, 2$) are again denoted by $t_i$ and the distance from $P_i$ to the market boundary by $d_i$, the demarcation line is characterized by the following condition (supposing the isostant, i.e. the line with equal competitive possibilities, is representative of this demarcation line):

$$p_1^* + t_1 d_1 = p_2^* + t_2 d_2 \qquad (2.5.2.2)$$

After substitution of the distance relationships $d_1$ and $d_2$, calculated on the basis of figure 2.5.2.a, one obtains the characteristic implicit equation for the demarcation line in terms of the $x$- and $y$-co-ordinates:

$$p_1^* + t_1 \sqrt{(x^2 + y^2)} = p_2^* + t_2 \sqrt{(l - x)^2 + y^2} \qquad (2.5.2.3)$$

This general relationship for the demarcation line represents a fourth-degree equation in $x$ and $y$; it has a more easy geometric interpretation, if one assumes some special properties of the parameters $p_1^*$, $p_2^*$, $t_1$, $t_2$ and $l$. These special cases will be successively studied.

The first situation which will be analyzed is:

$$\left.\begin{aligned} p_1^* &= p_2^* \\ t_1 &= t_2 \end{aligned}\right\} \qquad (2.5.2.4)$$

which means equal prices and transportation costs. Substitution of (2.5.2.4) into (2.5.2.3) gives:

$$\sqrt{(x^2 + y^2)} = \sqrt{(l - x)^2 + y^2} \qquad (2.5.2.5)$$

or, after raising (2.5.2.5) to a square:

$$x = \tfrac{1}{2} l \qquad (2.5.2.6)$$

Equation (2.5.2.6) represents a *straight line*, which divides the market area into two equal parts (see also figure 2.5.2.b). This result is reasonable from

Fig. 2.5.2.b A rectilinear market boundary

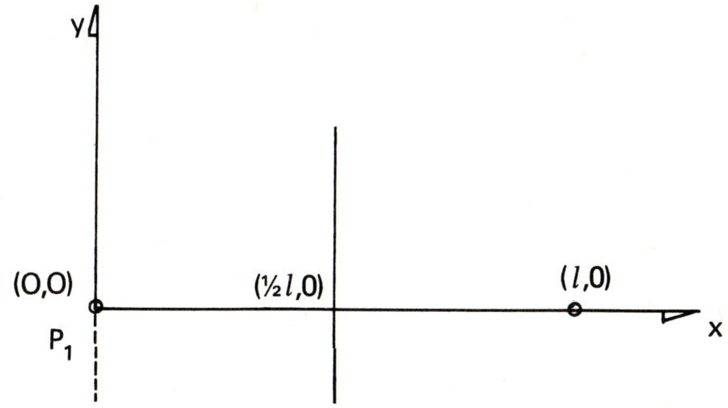

an economic point of view, since an equality both of prices and of transportation costs implies that only the distance element plays a role. The evident solution for the boundary line is an equal division of the market area.

Next, the situation will be analyzed, where:

$$\left.\begin{array}{l} p_1^* = p_2^* \\ t_1 \neq t_2 \end{array}\right\} \qquad (2.5.2.7)$$

i.e., a situation with equal prices, but different transportation costs. Since the unit transportation costs are constant, one may define:

$$t_1/t_2 = a \qquad (2.5.2.8)$$

where the constant parameter $a$ is supposed to satisfy the condition: $a > 1$. Substitution of (2.5.2.7) and (2.5.2.8) into (2.5.2.3) yields:

$$a \sqrt{(x^2 + y^2)} = \sqrt{\{(l - x)^2 + y^2\}} \qquad (2.5.2.9)$$

or, after some operations:

$$\left(x + \frac{l}{a^2 - 1}\right)^2 + y^2 = \frac{a^2 l^2}{(a^2 - 1)^2} \qquad (2.5.2.10)$$

The latter equation is the standard form of a *circle* with centre $(-(l/(a^2-1)), 0)$ and radius $al(a^2-1)$ (see figure 2.5.2.c). This result is also

Fig. 2.5.2.c A circular market boundary

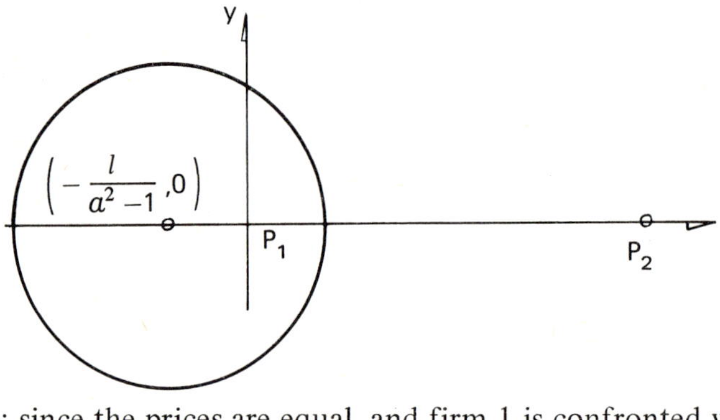


reasonable: since the prices are equal, and firm 1 is confronted with higher transportation costs, the market area of firm 1 will be considerably smaller, even to such a degree that firm 2 conquers the hinterland of firm 1, since in that area the effect of a longer distance is compensated by the lower unit transportation costs. Next, one may calculate the effect of a change in the transport cost ratio $a$ upon the co-ordinates of the centre and on the length of the radius, respectively, as:

$$\frac{\partial\left(\frac{l}{a^2 - 1}\right)}{\partial a} = -\frac{2\,al}{(a^2 - 1)^2} < 0 \qquad (2.5.2.11)$$

and:

$$\frac{\partial\left(\frac{al}{a^2 - 1}\right)}{\partial a} = -\frac{(a^2 + 1)\,l}{(a^2 - 1)^2} < 0 \qquad (2.5.2.12)$$

The maximum distance over which firm 1 can penetrate into the market area of firm 2 is (see figure 2.5.2.c):

$$\frac{al}{a^2 - 1} - \frac{l}{a^2 - 1} = \frac{l}{a + 1} < \tfrac{1}{2}l \qquad (2.5.2.13)$$

which means that this maximum distance is smaller than the market division according to (2.5.2.6).

The next special situation to be studied is:

$$\left.\begin{aligned} p_1^* &\neq p_2^* \\ t_1 &= t_2 \end{aligned}\right\} \qquad (2.5.2.14)$$

which implies equal unit transportation costs, but different prices. An easy way to solve this case is to define:

$$\begin{aligned} \beta &= \frac{p_2^* - p_1^*}{t_1} \\ &= \frac{p_2^* - p_1^*}{t_2} \end{aligned} \qquad (2.5.2.15)$$

where $\beta$ is supposed to satisfy the condition: $\beta > 0$ (i.e. $p_2^* > p_1^*$). Substitution of (2.5.2.14) and (2.5.2.15) into (2.5.2.3) gives:

$$\sqrt{(x^2 + y^2)} - \beta = \sqrt{\{(l - x)^2 + y^2\}} \qquad (2.5.2.16)$$

After some operations, one may obtain:

$$\frac{(x - \tfrac{1}{2}l)^2}{\tfrac{1}{4}\beta^2} - \frac{y^2}{\tfrac{1}{4}(l^2 - \beta^2)} = 1 \qquad (2.5.2.17)$$

Equation (2.5.2.17) is the characteristic equation of a *hyperbola* with centre ($\tfrac{1}{2}l$, 0) (see figure 2.5.2.d). One may draw two branches of the hyperbola, which intersect the $x$-axis, respectively, at the points ($\tfrac{1}{2}(l+\beta)$, 0) and ($\tfrac{1}{2}(l-\beta)$, 0).

Fig. 2.5.2.d A hyperbolic market boundary

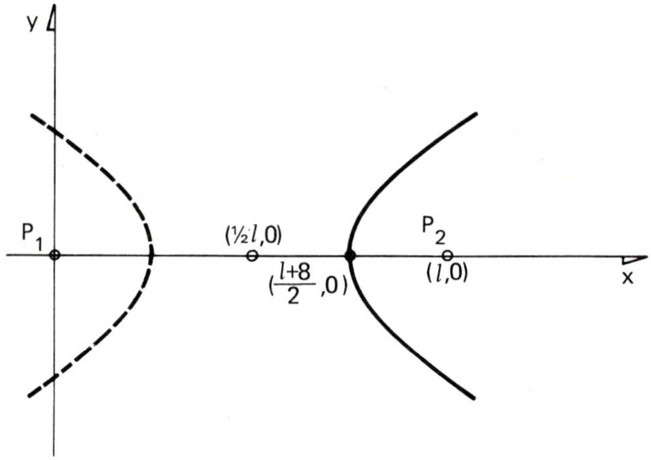


Figure 2.5.2.d shows that this would imply an indeterminate market area owing to the existence of *two* possible market boundaries. However, during the mathematical operations for the derivation of (2.5.2.17), (2.5.2.16) was raised to a square, so that an additional solution has been introduced, which should be cancelled in the ultimate result: one of the two branches is an economically irrelevant solution. It is easily seen that the left-hand branch is not an economically correct solution, since there: $p_1^* < p_2^*$ and $t_1 d_1 < t_2 d_2$ $(= t_1 d_2)$. The latter situation can never be a correct representation of the boundary line, since this situation does not satisfy the characteristic equation of the isostant represented in (2.5.2.2). Thus, only the right-hand hyperbola of figure 2.5.2.d is a relevant representation of the demarcation line. Again, from an economic point of view, since the prices of firm 2 exceed the prices of firm 1, it is obvious that firm 1 will possess a larger market area than firm 2. Only at those points where the smaller distance with respect to firm 2 compensates the lower price of firm 1, one may expect a sales area of firm 2. This sales area appears to have a hyperbolic form.

A border-line case emerges, when $\beta \rightarrow l^4$. Then the intersection point of the hyperbola with the $x$-axis tends to shift towards $P_2$, while the branches of the hyperbola tend to move towards the $x$-axis. If $\beta = l$, the hyperbola is reduced to a straight line coinciding with the $x$-axis from point $P_2$ onwards to the right. In this case the market area of firm 1 covers the entire area including the straight line beyond point $P_2$. This situation can be better understood, if one rewrites (2.5.2.15) as:

$$p_2^* = p_1^* + \beta t_1 \qquad (2.5.2.18)$$

If $\beta = l$, one obtains:

$$p_2^* = p_1^* + l t_1 \qquad (2.5.2.19)$$

which means that the c.i.f. price of firm 1 at the location of firm 2 is exactly equal to the f.o.b. price of firm 2. Since $t_1 = t_2$, it is easily seen that only on the $x$-axis beyond $P_2$ one obtains the characteristic relationship of an isostant.

Finally, if $\beta > l$, relationship (2.5.2.17) would represent an ellipse, but this has no economic meaning. It is easily seen from (2.5.2.19), that in this case the c.i.f. price of firm 2 is everywhere higher than the c.i.f. price of firm 1, so that firm 2 looses its entire market area.

Another special case is the situation where:

$$l = 0 \qquad (2.5.2.20)$$

Then both firms have a joint location. This concentration of the two competitors leads after substitution of (2.5.2.20) into (2.5.2.3) to the following relationship for the isostant (cf. figure 2.5.2.e):

$$p_1^* + t_1 \sqrt{(x^2 + y^2)} = p_2^* + t_2 \sqrt{(x^2 + y^2)} \qquad (2.5.2.21)$$

or:

$$x^2 + y^2 = \left(\frac{p_2^* - p_1^*}{t_1 - t_2}\right)^2 \qquad (2.5.2.22)$$

The latter expression is the standard equation of a *circle* with centre (0, 0) and length of radius $(p_2^* - p_1^*)/(t_1 - t_2)$. This means that the market area of one firm is located within the circular area, while the market area of the

Fig. 2.5.2.e A circular market boundary in the case of a joint location

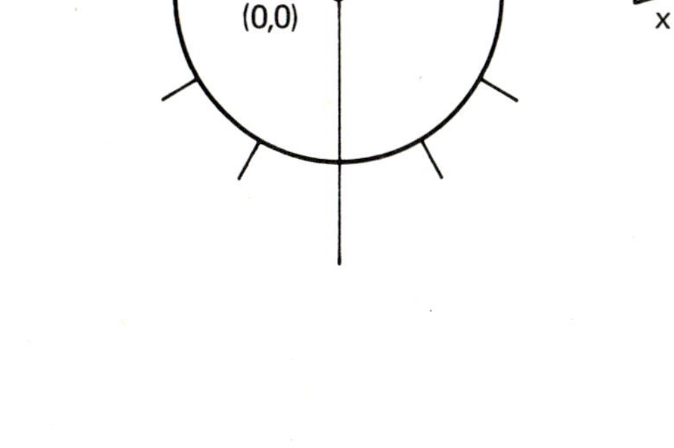

other firm is located outside. The question as to which firm is located inside or outside depends on the values of $p_1^*$, $p_2^*$, $t_1$ and $t_2$. First of all, it is clear that the situations $p_1^* = p_2^*$ or $t_1 = t_2$ are degenerate cases, since in these cases the firm with the highest unit transportation costs, or the highest price, will loose its entire sales area. Therefore, one may assume: $p_1^* \neq p_2^*$ and $t_1 \neq t_2$. When $p_1^* > p_2^*$, firm 2 will only sell its products, if $t_1 < t_2$; otherwise, the c.i.f. price of firm 1 would always be higher than the c.i.f. price of firm 2. A similar reasoning is valid for firm 2. Therefore, the following conditions should be satisfied:

$$\begin{aligned} (p_1^* > p_2^*) \cap (t_1 > t_2) = \phi \\ (p_2^* > p_1^*) \cap (t_2 > t_1) = \phi \end{aligned} \qquad (2.5.2.23)$$

where the symbols $\cap$ and $\phi$ represent again the intersection and the null space. If $p_1^* > p_2^*$, firm 2 will sell within the circle. The reason is, that in the neighbourhood of the centre the c.i.f. price of firm 1 exceeds the c.i.f. price of firm 2. However, from a certain point onwards the lower price of firm 2 will be compensated by the lower transportation costs of firm 1. As soon as the c.i.f. price of firm 1 is smaller than the c.i.f. price of firm 2, firm 1 will start to sell. The set of these boundary points is represented by the radius of the circle. A similar reasoning can be followed for the reverse case.

Ultimately, one may study the degenerate situation:

$$y = 0 \qquad (2.5.2.24)$$

which means a *rectilinear* market area, represented by the $x$-axis. Substitution of (2.5.2.24) into (2.5.2.3) yields the result:

$$p_1^* + t_1 \sqrt{x^2} = p_2^* + t_2\sqrt{(l-x)^2} \qquad (2.5.2.25)$$

or:

$$\boxed{p_1^* + t_1 \mid x \mid = p_2^* + t_2 \mid l - x \mid} \qquad (2.5.2.26)$$

Now the isostant consists of one (or more) *points* on the $x$-axis. The position of this isostant depends on the relative size of $p_1^*$, $p_2^*$, $t_1$ and $t_2$. In fact, one may again distinguish the same number of special cases set out above, viz. (2.5.2.4), (2.5.2.7), (2.5.2.14) and (2.5.2.20).

### 2.5.3 *The law of refraction*

Palander has also studied the effect of *differences in transport tariffs* upon the transportation network. The differences in transportation costs between two or more regions may be caused by natural circumstances or by national boundaries. The different transportation traiffs imply, that the minimum-cost distance between two points does not coincide with the straight line between these points. Palander has derived a mathematical relationship between the different transportation tariffs and an optimal transportation route. This relationship is known as the *law of refraction*. It will be derived on the basis of the following hypotheses:

H 1 The existence of two regions, each of which is homogeneous.
H 2 The existence of different transportation tariffs in each region.
H 3 A rectilinear boundary between the two regions.
H 4 Uniform transportation costs per ton-mile in each region.
H 5 A shipment of only one homogeneous product.
H 6 Minimization of transportation costs.

The analysis will be clarified by means of figure 2.5.3.a, which represents two regions 1 and 2, separated by a boundary line *BB*.

Fig. 2.5.3.a The law of refraction

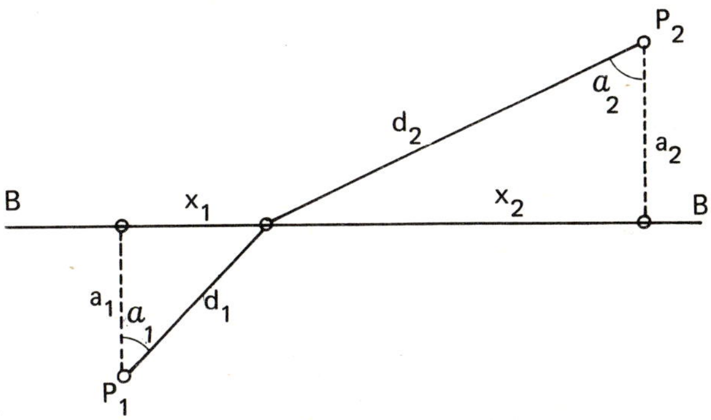


$P_1$ and $P_2$ denote the points between which an optimal transportation route has to be determined. If the unit transportation costs in region 1 and 2 are, respectively, denoted by $t_1$ and $t_2$ (with $t_1 > t_2$), the total transportation costs $T$ between $P_1$ and $P_2$ are equal to:

$$T = t_1 d_1 + t_2 d_2 \tag{2.5.3.1}$$

where $d_1$ and $d_2$ represent the respective unknown distances from $P_1$ and $P_2$ along the transportation route to the boundary line. Therefore, $T$ is rewritten as (see figure 2.5.3.a):

$$T = t_1 \sqrt{(a_1^2 + x_1^2)} + t_2 \sqrt{(a_2^2 + x_2^2)} \tag{2.5.3.2}$$

The known variables are: $t_1, t_2, a_1, a_2$ and $(x_1 + x_2)$. However, $x_1$ and $x_2$ separately are unknown. By defining:

$$x = x_1 + x_2 \qquad (2.5.3.3)$$

one obtains in stead of (2.5.3.2):

$$T = t_1 \sqrt{(a_1^2 + x_1^2)} + t_2 \sqrt{\{a_2^2 + (x - x_1)^2\}} \qquad (2.5.3.4)$$

Minimization of $T$ with respect to the unknown variable $x_1$ gives the following first-order condition:

$$\frac{\partial T}{\partial x_1} = \frac{t_1 x_1}{\sqrt{(a_1^2 + x_1^2)}} - \frac{t_2 (x - x_1)}{\sqrt{\{a_2^2 + (x - x_1)^2\}}} = 0 \qquad (2.5.3.5)$$

or after substitution of (2.5.3.3), and of $d_1$ and $d_2$:

$$\frac{t_1 x_1}{d_1} = \frac{t_2 x_2}{d_2} \qquad (2.5.3.6)$$

By rewriting (2.5.3.6) one finds:

$$\frac{t_1}{t_2} = \frac{x_2}{d_2} \frac{d_1}{x_1} \qquad (2.5.3.7)$$

Since:

$$\sin a_1 = \frac{x_1}{d_1} \qquad (2.5.3.8)$$

and:

$$\sin a_2 = \frac{x_2}{d_2} \qquad (2.5.3.9)$$

the final result is the following condition for the unknown angles $a_i$ $(i = 1, 2)$:

$$\frac{\sin a_2}{\sin a_1} = \frac{t_1}{t_2} \qquad (2.5.3.10)$$

This inverse relationship between the sine of the angles and the unit transportation costs is, owing to its physical analogy, known as the *law of refraction*. This law states in economic terms, that the sine of the angle $a_i$ in a region $i$ $(i = 1, 2)$ will be smaller, as the transportation tariffs in region $i$ are higher, so that a transporter from region 1 to region 2 tends to select a transportation route, along which the transport distance in the region with the highest transportation tariffs will be rather small.

The optimal result (2.5.3.10) satisfies the second-order condition for a minimum, as can easily be checked. A more modern approach to the law of refraction in transportation systems is contained in Werner (1968).

### 2.5.4 *Duopolistic pricing and location problems*

Palander has paid particular attention to spatial price policies under a regime of duopoly. In a duopolistic situation the price policies and their stability conditions appear to depend on the strategies pursued by the participants. Other authors who paid attention to such duopolistic market situations in regional economics were Hotelling (1929), Lösch (1954) and Greenhut (1963).

In this section the effect of mutual price (and quantity) influences will be analyzed, as well as the resulting market areas. The essential difference of this approach, compared to section 2.5.2., is the fact that the assumption of a *given* f.o.b. price is abandoned. The result is an interdependent entrepreneurial behaviour, so that prices, volumes and market areas are unknown variables, which should be determined in such a way that an equilibrium situation is attained.

The following hypotheses are made:

H 1 The existence of a rectilinear market area with length $l$.
H 2 The existence of two competitive sellers 1 and 2, settled at $P_1$ and $P_2$, respectively.
H 3 The production of only one homogeneous commodity.
H 4 A uniform dispersion of consumers along the market line with a unit demand density.
H 5 Uniform transportation costs per ton-mile.
H 6 An inelastic demand for final commodities.
H 7 A mill pricing policy.
H 8 Maximization of individual profits.

The rectilinear market area is represented in figure 2.5.4.a below.

Fig. 2.5.4.a A rectilinear market area

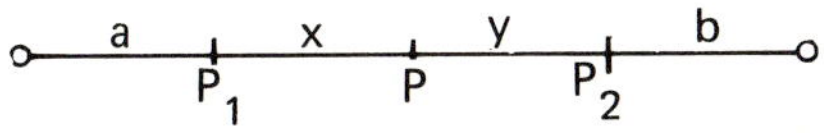


The as yet unknown market boundary between firm 1 and 2 is denoted by $P$. Since $P_1$ and $P_2$ are known locations, $a$ and $b$ are known, while evidently $x$ and $y$ are unknown. The purpose of the analysis is to find the optimal profits and prices of both firms (i.e., the *general* economic variables), as well as their market boundaries (i.e., the *spatial* economic variables). A systematic procedure is a transformation of this problem only into general economic variables. Then, one may first solve the general economic variables and, next, the spatial economic variables after substitution of the general economic variables.

The unknown f.o.b. price of firm $i$ ($i = 1, 2$), denoted by $p_i^*$, is composed of the known production costs per unit of product, denoted by $c_i$, and of unknown profits per unit of product, denoted by $\pi_i$, so that one obtains:

$$p_i^* = c_i + \pi_i \tag{2.5.4.1}$$

Thus, the characteristic equation for the isostant (cf. [2.5.2.2]) is:

$$c_1 + \pi_1 + t_1 x = c_2 + \pi_2 + t_2 y \tag{2.5.4.2}$$

where $t_i$ ($i = 1, 2$) denotes again the unit transportation costs of firm $i$. By solving $x$ from (2.5.4.2), one obtains:

$$x = \frac{c_2 - c_1 + \pi_2 - \pi_1 + t_2 y}{t_1} \tag{2.5.4.3}$$

Furthermore, it is obvious from figure 2.5.4.a, that $y$ is equal to:

$$y = l - a - b - x \tag{2.5.4.4}$$

Substitution of (2.5.4.4) into (2.5.4.3) leads to the result:

$$x = \frac{c_2 - c_1 + \pi_2 - \pi_1 + t_2 (l - a - b)}{t_1 + t_2} \tag{2.5.4.5}$$

Because of the assumption of a unit density of demand, the total sales of firm 1 are equal to the length of the market area of firm 1. Therefore, the total profits of firm 1, denoted by $\Pi_1$, are:

$$\Pi_1 = (a + x)\,\pi_1 \tag{2.5.4.6}$$

After substitution of (2.5.4.5) into (2.5.4.6) one finds:

$$\Pi_1 = \frac{c_2 - c_1 + \pi_2 - \pi_1 + t_2 (l - b) + t_1 a}{t_1 + t_2}\,\pi_1 \tag{2.5.4.7}$$

In a similar way one may calculate the profits of firm 2 as:

$$\Pi_2 = \frac{c_1 - c_2 + \pi_1 - \pi_2 + t_1 (l - a) + t_2 b}{t_1 + t_2}\,\pi_2 \tag{2.5.4.8}$$

It appears from (2.5.4.7) and (2.5.4.8) that the unknown *spatial* economic variables (viz. $x$ and $y$) are eliminated, so that this market area problem is transformed into a problem which encompasses only *general* economic variables. Once the optimal values of these general economic variables are found, they may be substituted into (2.5.4.5) in order to find the unknown spatial economic variables. Furthermore, it appears from (2.5.4.7) and (2.5.4.8), that the profits of each firm depend *inter alia* on the unit profits of its competitor, which is evidently a duopolistic situation. Such duopolistic situations may give rise to various market strategies, for example, a Cournot- and a Von Stackelberg-strategy (see Shubik [1959]).

Since $c_1$, $c_2$, $t_1$ and $t_2$ are fixed constants, for the sake of simplicity the assumption is made, that the production costs per unit of product are equal to zero for both firms (i.e., $c_i = 0$, $i = 1, 2$), and that the unit transportation costs of both firms do not show any difference (i.e., $t_i = t$, $i = 1, 2$). Then (2.5.4.7) and (2.5.4.8) pass into:

$$\Pi_1 = \frac{\pi_2 - \pi_1 + t\,(l + a - b)}{2t}\,\pi_1 \tag{2.5.4.9}$$

and:

$$\Pi_2 = \frac{\pi_1 - \pi_2 + t\,(l - a + b)}{2t}\,\pi_2 \tag{2.5.4.10}$$

In this section attention will be paid only to a strategy set out by Cournot (1897). A Cournot-situation is based on a mutual dependence between duopolistic firms. These firms base their market behaviour on a so-called *reaction function*. Such a reaction function describes the reaction of a firm with respect to actions of its competitor. Formally, a Cournot-equilibrium will be attained, if the simultaneous solution of both reaction equations leads to one unique outcome.

The aforementioned problem of a spatial duopoly can be solved along the same lines. The optimal price decisions of each firm result from the following first-order conditions:

$$\frac{\partial \Pi_1}{\partial \pi_1} = \frac{\pi_2 - 2\,\pi_1 + t\,(l + a - b)}{2t} = 0 \tag{2.5.4.11}$$

and:

$$\frac{\partial \Pi_2}{\partial \pi_2} = \frac{\pi_1 - 2\,\pi_2 + t\,(l - a + b)}{2t} = 0 \tag{2.5.4.12}$$

In fact, (2.5.4.11) and (2.5.4.12) are the implicit relationships for the reaction functions of the duopolistic firms. The equilibrium values of the general economic variables $\pi_1$ and $\pi_2$ can be solved from (2.5.4.11) and (2.5.4.12) as:

$$\pi_1^{\mathrm{O}} = (l + 1/3a - 1/3b)\, t \tag{2.5.4.13}$$

and:

$$\pi_2^{\mathrm{O}} = (l - 1/3a + 1/3b)\, t \tag{2.5.4.14}$$

Substitution of (2.5.4.13) and (2.5.4.14) into (2.5.4.9) and (2.5.4.10) gives:

$$\Pi_1^{\mathrm{O}} = \tfrac{1}{2}t\, (l + 1/3a - 1/3b)^2 \tag{2.5.4.15}$$

and:

$$\Pi_2^{\mathrm{O}} = \tfrac{1}{2}t\, (l - 1/3a + 1/3b)^2 \tag{2.5.4.16}$$

Substitution of $c_i = 0$, $t_i = t$, (2.5.4.13) and (2.5.4.14) into (2.5.4.5) produces the optimal value of the spatial economic variable $x$ and $y$ as:

$$\begin{aligned} x^{\mathrm{O}} &= \tfrac{1}{2}l - 5/6a - 1/6b \\ y^{\mathrm{O}} &= \tfrac{1}{2}l - 1/6a - 5/6b \end{aligned} \tag{2.5.4.17}$$

A situation of Von Stackelberg (1948) can be analysed in a similar way (see also Palander [1935]). A more detailed examination of various adaptations in the process of duopolistic price formation as well as of alternative strategies like basing-point price policies, can also be found in Palander (1935).

### 2.5.5 *Conclusion*

Palander has presented an important contribution to spatial economics, owing to his *formal* approach both to the theory of market areas and to the theory of limited spatial competition. Although his analysis is still a partial and static one, he can be considered as the predecessor of the more modern spatial equilibrium theorists (see Ch.7). A general, interdependent spatial system is not yet present in Palander's theories; the latter problem was first considered by Lösch (see section 2.6). Palander's situation of duopolistic spatial problems will be reconsidered in Ch.3 in relation to game theory.

## 2.6 Lösch

### 2.6.1 *Introduction*

Lösch (1954) has presented a *general theory of interdependent, spatial economic equilibrium*. He was the first economist who presented a comprehensive, systematic analysis of spatial economic phenomena.

He started his study with a *general theory of location*, both for *agricultural* and for *industrial* activities. By considering the *agglomerative* forces between the various activities, he developed a *general equilibrium theory of location patterns*, based on a Walrasian framework of economic interdependences. Next, Lösch analyzed *market areas and networks of markets*, in which field he presented an outstanding contribution to the explanation of the spatial economic landscape. Finally, he paid attention to the theory of *interregional and international trade*, both for products and for production factors.

In line with the objectives adopted in this book the following topics will be dealt with in more detail: Lösch's *location theory, his theory of regions, his general equilibrium system,* the *analysis of regular spatial systems* and the *effect of different price policies.*

### 2.6.2 *Location theory*

In contrast to Weber's partial approach, Lösch's location theory is a *general* theory of location patterns. In addition, this theory integrates the neo-classical elements of the *spatial σ-principle*.

The problem of industrial locations is attacked by Lösch under the assumption of *profit maximization* (rather than cost minimization; cf. Weber). If the demand for industrial products is not a datum, but is assumed to be elastic with respect to prices and income, there may arise a considerable difference in outcomes based on a cost minimization hypothesis or a profit maximization hypothesis.

In the analysis of industrial locations Lösch makes a distinction between an *actual* and an *ideal* location. Actual locations can be studied as the result of historical development tendencies or of various entrepreneurial behavioural patterns. Ideal locations are optimal locations, based on rational assumptions concerning the entrepreneurial behaviour: in a mixed economy-setting, the right location of an individual enterprise is formed by the spatial point, where net profits are at a maximum.

In addition to the previous location theory of the individual firm, Lösch integrates the actions of competitors. The individual firm chooses its ideal location in such a way as to achieve the highest profits as a producer. If one assumes free competition, many competitors will crowd into the market and reduce each other's living space, until the profit advantage disappears. The result of this competitive behaviour is a tendency to maximize the number of individual economic units. In fact, the general location problem is controlled by two counteracting forces: *the maximization of individual profits and the maximization of the number of individual firms.* A spatial equilibrium is the balanced system of these interdependent locational decisions. Lösch has presented an abstract mathematical formulation of this interdependent location problem (see section 2.6.4) without solving this problem empirically.

Lösch's theory of *agricultural* location is more detailed than the earlier theories of Von Thünen. By generalizing Von Thünen's approach one may meet situations, which do not necessarily result in concentric circles. Lösch gives an abstract and general formulation of the location problem of agricultural producers, based on the following elements: unit production costs per square mile, physical revenues per square mile and market prices of the product. The result of Lösch's agricultural location theory may show a considerable difference from Von Thünen's outcomes. One may obtain various different cultivation patterns, for instance a mixed agriculture.

Spatial *agglomerations*, such as towns, are the results of agglomerative forces both in the production and in the consumption sphere. These agglomerative forces may be of a different nature, for instance, economies of scale, external economies and psychological attraction forces. In this way, the general interdependent location problem is closely linked up with the analysis of urban settlement patterns.

### 2.6.3 *Economic regions*

In contrast to Christaller (1933), Lösch gives a non-political and non-administrative description of a 'region'. A region is, in Lösch's opinion, a purely economic concept. The boundary lines between regions rest upon economic considerations. Lösch derives an ideal system of regions on the basis of the following hypotheses:

H 1 The existence of a homogeneous area, which contains regularly dispersed farmers.
H 2 The presence of economies of large scale production.
H 3 The presence of transportation costs.
H 4 The existence of equal individual, elastic demand curves.
H 5 A policy of uniform mill pricing.
H 6 A complete exhaustion of the total area (no 'black corners').
H 7 A uniform and continuous dispersion of population.
H 8 The existence of agglomeration advantages.
H 9 Maximization of profits by the individual firm.
H 10 Minimization of total transportation costs within the entire system.

Lösch's theory of economic regions is based on an agricultural society.

The agricultural production processes are confronted with economies of scale. The latter phenomenon leads to a rise in the profits per unit of product, if the production is enlarged. However, a shipment of this additional production to other population points causes additional transportation costs. Thus, the spatial production pattern rests upon an interplay between economies of scale and transportation costs. Owing to the policy of mill pricing and owing to the elasticity of demand, the total demand for this additional production will be a decreasing function of the distance from the original production centre. The individual demand function itself at each point of the area is represented in figure 2.6.3.a. If the uniform mill price is denoted by $p^*$, and if the transportation

Fig. 2.6.3.a A spatial demand curve

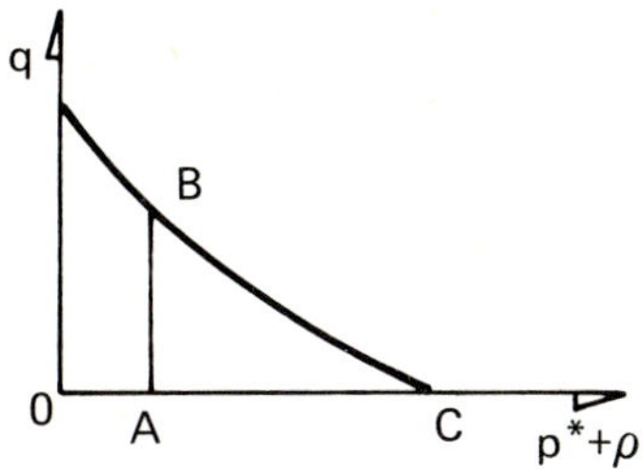


Fig. 2.6.3.b A demand cone

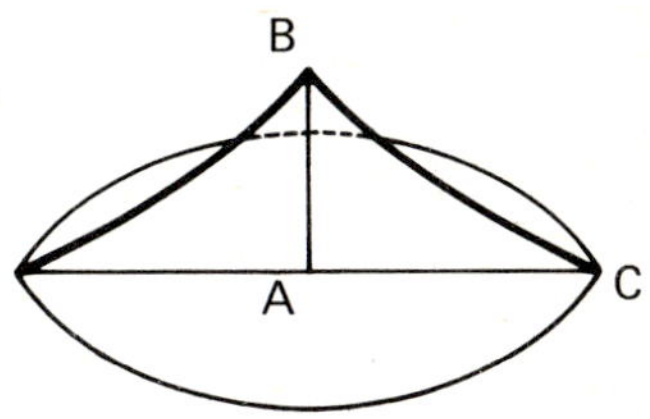


costs per unit of product and per mile are equal to 1, the individual demand function in a point at a certain distance $\rho$ from the production centre is written as:

$$q = f(p^* + \rho) \qquad (2.6.3.1)$$

If the mill price $p^*$ is equal to the length of the line $0A$ in figure 2.6.3.a, $AB$ is the size of individual demand at the production centre itself. The total volume of demand for the additional production of the agricultural production centre concerned is equal to the volume of the cone, which is obtained by rotating the triangle $ABC$ around $AB$ as an axis (see figure 2.6.3.b). If one assumes unit density of demand, this total volume $D$ of demand is calculated as:[5]

$$D = \int_0^r \int_0^{2\pi} \rho f(p^* + \rho)\, da\, d\rho$$

$$= 2\pi \int_0^r \rho f(p^* + \rho)\, d\rho \qquad (2.6.3.2)$$

where the radius $r$ of the circular area is equal to the line $AC$ (see figure 2.6.3.a). However, the circular shape of this so-called demand curve is not consistent with H 6, since a circular market system is incompatible with a complete covering of space. The condition, that all points in space are to be supplied, is only fulfilled by a regular polygonal market system. Therefore, the pattern of market areas can consist of only one of the following types of regular polyhedrons: a triangle, a square or a hexagon.

Of all systems of regular market areas that will cover a plane completely, the *hexagon* appears to possess certain optimal properties, in the sense of minimizing the average transportation costs between supplier and demander, given the volume of demand. These results are derived in section 2.6.5 and presented in table 2.6.5.b. Therefore, the 'optimal' market pattern of every commodity in this sense is a hexagonal trading area.

The reason, why Lösch adopted the assumption of a complete covering of the plane, was his standpoint that *free spatial competition and free market entry* must result in space-filling market areas. This statement was disproved by Mills and Lav (1964), who showed that the spatial picture, resulting from the assumption of profit maximization and free entry, is not necessarily a honeycomb. One may also obtain circles or dodecagons (12-sided regular polygons), albeit that the latter spatial patterns are incompatible with a complete exhaustion of the plane. Therefore, H 6 has only meaning as a *hypothesis* and not as a *theorem* (cf. Hartwick [1973]).

So far, it was assumed that the population was equally and continuously distributed over the plane. In reality, however, the population is spread in a discontinuous way. Therefore, Lösch assumes ultimately, that the population is dispersed in a regular hexagonal way over a large number of settlements. Thus, in addition to a honeycomb scattering of agricultural producers, Lösch assumes also a honeycomb scattering of population settlements.

All the population centres are served by the various farms, in the sense that each centre is provided with products from the nearest farm(s). The twofold dispersion – of farmers and of settlements – may give rise to different spatial pictures. Three possible orientations of the hexagonal system of farms $F_i$ ($i = 1, 2, 3 \ldots$) with respect to the relative positions of the settlements $S_j$ ($j = 1, 2, 3 \ldots$) are represented in figures 2.6.3.c–e. It should be noted that the central production farm is also considered as a settlement. The following comments concerning figures 2.6.3.c–e can be made:

Fig. 2.6.3.c
A settlement pattern at the corners of a hexagon

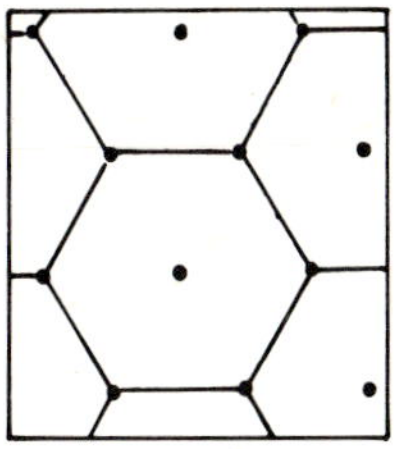

Fig. 2.6.3.d
A settlement pattern on the sides of a hexagon

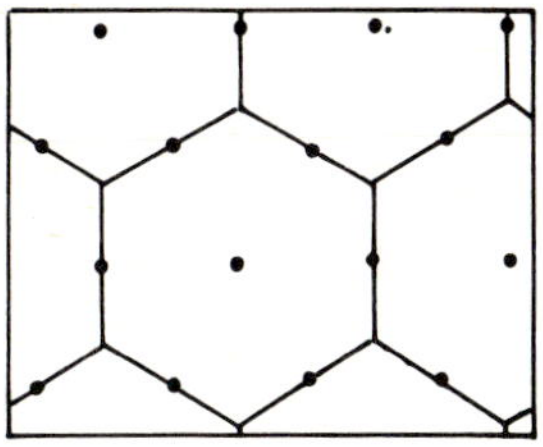

Fig. 2.6.3.e
A settlement pattern throughout the hexagon

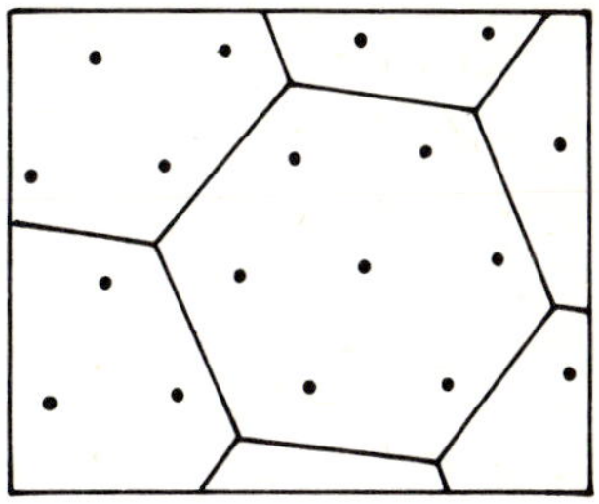

1 figure 2.6.3.c: the settlements are located at the corner points of the hexagons. The total number of settlements to be served with products from one agricultural production unit is (including the central production farm) equal to $1 + (6 \cdot 1/3) = 3$.
2 figure 2.6.3.d: the settlements are located at the midpoints of the sides of the hexagonal market area of the agricultural production unit. Then, the total number of settlements which is oriented towards one central production farm is $1 + (6 \cdot \frac{1}{2}) = 4$.
3 figure 2.6.3.e: the settlements are located in a free, regular way throughout the hexagon. The number of settlements which buy their products from the central production place is $1 + 6 = 7$.

Obviously, one may distinguish more typical spatial pictures than the above mentioned. The general hexagonal pattern allows one to find a simple expression for the distances between the production centres of a hexagonal pattern. The three cases, distinguished in figures 2.6.3.c–e, are presented in table 2.6.3.a.

Table 2.6.3.a Distances between central production units

| Case | Number of settlements completely supplied, including the point of supply | Distance between central production unit and nearest settlement | Distance between two central production units (radius of inscribed circle) |
|---|---|---|---|
| Fig. 2.6.3.c | 3 | $r$ | $r\sqrt{3}$ |
| Fig. 2.6.3.d | 4 | $r$ | $r\sqrt{4}$ |
| Fig. 2.6.3.e | 7 | $r$ | $r\sqrt{7}$ |

By means of complete induction one may derive, that the distance between the production centres of a regular hexogonal pattern is equal to $r\sqrt{n}$, where $n$ is the number of settlements completely supplied.

For each product a honeycomb as described above can be created. The size of the hexagons within this honeycomb will differ from each product. By combining and re-orienting the honeycombs of all products one obtains a superposition of all these honeycombs. All these hexagonal market areas of all different products might form a random spatial mixture, but H 8 and H 10 lead to a more regular pattern. The existence of agglomerative forces leads to a concentration of different production units in one spatial point. This concentration of production is controlled by H 10, which is a general hypothesis, related to the spatial system *as a whole* (and not to *individual* behaviour like H 9). The assumption of agglomeration advantages and of minimization of integral transportation costs, prevents a random mixture of all patterns all over the space from emerging. Rather, it leads to bundles of industrial centres and cities, in which a maximum number of different individual production units will be located at the same place. In this way the economic landscape will show areas with a high and with a low industrial and urban concentration. Thus, a superposition of all hexagonal patterns of all products tends to show a spatial picture, presented arbitrarily in figure 2.6.3.f. The shaded areas of figure 2.6.3.f are characterized by a high, urban and industrial concentration, while the unshaded areas possess little urban and industrial concentrations as well as a diffuse transportation network.

Fig. 2.6.3.f A superposition of hexagonal areas as a regular spatial pattern

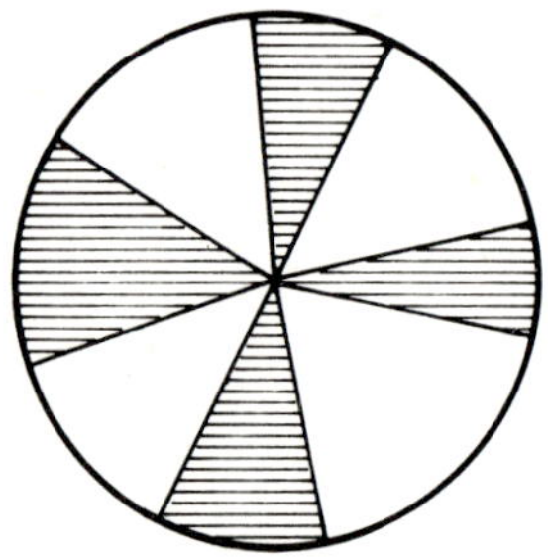

To summarize the previous analysis: one first derives the hexagonal market area surrounding each production centre; second, one creates a net of such areas for every commodity; and third, the so-called ideal economic region is obtained by a systematic spatial re-arrangement of the market areas related to the various commodities.

Ultimately, the previous analysis seems to lead to a certain contradiction between some hypotheses. The hypothesis of an *equal dispersion* of population (H 7) is not compatible with the further course of the analysis, in which urban and industrial *concentrations* arise. This problem is not attacked by Lösch, though it could be solved by eliminating H 7 and by introducing a new hypothesis, for instance, the assumption of external trade equilibrium (see Bos [1964]).

Finally, the previous pure and ideal system of economic regions is based primarily on the following elements: distances, economies of scale and of agglomeration, and competition. Many elements can disturb this abstract system, for example:

1 economic disturbances: differences in price policies (see section 2.6.6), in products or in transportation tariffs;
2 natural disturbances: spatial differences owing to physical or climatological conditions (natural obstacles, differences in fertility, etc.);
3 human disturbances: differences in individual and social behaviour; political disturbances: spatial differences owing to political boundaries.

### 2.6.4 *A general equilibrium system*

The problem of a general economic equilibrium is a very intricate one (see Ch.7). The general objective of an economic equilibrium analysis is to find the conditions under which an interdependent economic system (including consumers and producers) can exist. For this purpose one usually needs a set of behavioural and technical equations describing the internal structure of the economy. For instance, Walras (1954) created an equilibrium system encompassing the following endogenous variables: the volumes of commodities, of services and of production factors, as well as their prices. On the basis of utility functions and production functions one may derive the respective demand and supply functions. The interdependent behaviour of consumers and producers leads to the well-known process of 'tâtonnement' (shuffling), which may result in an equilibrium situation. As long as the monetary sector is not included, all variables have one degree of freedom, since they are expressed as a function of a 'numéraire' (accounting price).

Lösch's contribution to the problem of general economic equilibrium was the introduction of spatial elements. Every economic variable is realized in a certain physical space and bears, therefore, spatial co-ordinates. Lösch gave only an abstract representation of the general spatial economic interdependency without elaborating this system and without proving the existence of an equilibrium situation.

Lösch's equilibrium system is based on the assumption that the spatial economic picture encompasses several production places. There is a continuous economic struggle for space between these production places:

the individual tries to maximize its profits by extending its market, while the economy as a whole tries to maximize the number of independent economic units. This equilibrium will arise in a situation, where countermovements balance; it should satisfy the following conditions:

1 every individual location must be as advantageous as possible;
2 the number of locations is such that the entire space is occupied;
3 abnormal profits may not exist;
4 the areas of supply, production, and sales must have a minimum size; and
5 the boundary lines between economic areas are formed by isolines.

Lösch's equilibrium system will be presented hereafter in a slightly modified notation. Every place of production is a production centre for only one commodity $i$ ($i = 1, \ldots, I$). On the other hand, every commodity $i$ can be produced in one or more production places $j_i$ ($j_i = 1_i, \ldots, J_i$). Thus every place of production is characterized by the commodity concerned and by its rank number. Thus, a production place $P_{j_i}$ means a production centre of good $i$ with rank number $j_i$. This place of production $P_{j_i}$ should be provided with spatial co-ordinates $x_{j_i}$ and $y_{j_i}$ in order to indicate its spatial position. Thus, $P_{j_i}$ $(x_{j_i}, y_{j_i})$ means the $j_i$ th production centre of commodity $i$, located at point $(x_{j_i}, y_{j_i})$. The total number of production centres $P_{j_i}$ for commodity $i$ is equal to $J_i$, while the total number of production centres for all commodities is equal to $J = \Sigma_{i=1}^{I} J_i$. A systematic classification of the various production places, as well as of the commodities, is contained in table 2.6.4.a.

The boundaries of the market areas of every good $i$, produced at production centre $P_{j_i}$, may be represented in the following abstract way:

$$f_{n_{j_i}}(x, y) = 0 \qquad (2.6.4.1)$$

where $n_{j_i}$ ($n_{j_i} = 1_{j_i}, \ldots, N_{j_i}$) is the $n_{j_i}$ th market boundary of commodity $i$, produced at centre $P_{j_i}$. The implicit assumption is, that the market boundaries of a certain product $i$ at production place $P_{j_i}$ can be represented by means of $N_{j_i}$ mathematical expressions (for instance, in the case of a hexagon one has 6 different boundaries). The total number of market boundaries for a certain commodity $i$ is equal to $N_i = \Sigma_{j_i=1_i}^{J_i} N_{j_i}/2$, [6] while the total number of market boundaries for all products is equal to $N = \Sigma_{i=1}^{I} N_i$. Table 2.6.4.a also contains a systematic classification of these market boundaries.

In addition to the previous expressions for the $J$ places of production and the $N$ market boundaries, Lösch's general equilibrium system contains also demand functions, cost functions and profit functions.

If the f.o.b. price of commodity $i$ at production centre $P_{j_i}$ is denoted by $p^*_{j_i}$, the demand function for commodity $i$ is supposed to be:

$$p^*_{j_i} = g(d_{j_i}) \tag{2.6.4.2}$$

where $d_{j_i}$ is the total demand for commodity $i$ at place $P_{j_i}$. Total demand is a function of individual demand, of the location of the production centre, of the market boundaries (i.e. of the market volume), and of the urban and rural population density.

The average costs of producing one unit of commodity $i$ at $P_{j_i}$ are denoted by $c_{j_i}$. These costs are also a function of total demand:

$$c_{j_i} = h(d_{j_i}) \tag{2.6.4.3}$$

Next, the total profits at the production centre $P_{j_i}$ are denoted by $\Pi_{j_i}$; they are equal to:

$$\Pi_{j_i} = (p^*_{j_i} - c_{j_i})\, d_{j_i} \tag{2.6.4.4}$$

Finally, the size of the total market area is fixed and equal to $G$. The individual market areas of a production centre $P_{j_i}$ are supposed to be unknown; their size is denoted by $G_{j_i}$.

The unknown variables of Lösch's spatial system are (their total number is put behind between brackets): $p^*_{j_i}$ ($J$), $G_{j_i}$ ($J$), $J_i$ ($I$), $x_{j_i}$ and $y_{j_i}$ ($2J$), and $f_{n_{j_i}}(x, y)$ ($N$). Thus, the total number of unknown variables is equal to $J + J + I + 2J + N = 4J + I + N$.

Given the previous relationships, Lösch has given a more formal elaboration of the conditions (1)–(5) which are to be satisfied in case of an equilibrium situation (see above). Those equilibrium conditions are, successively, presented below.

$$\frac{\partial \Pi_{j_i}}{\partial x_{j_i}} = 0 \tag{2.6.4.5}$$

Table 2.6.4.a A classification of production places and market boundaries

| Product no. | Place of production: Site | Place of production: Number |
|---|---|---|
| 1 | $P_{1_1}(x_{1_1}, y_{1_1})$ . . . . . . . . . . . . . . . . . . . . . $P_{J_1}(x_{J_1}, y_{J_1})$ | $J_1$ |
| ⋮ | ⋮ . . . . . . . . . . . . . . . . . . . . . ⋮ | ⋮ |
| $I$ | $P_{1_I}(x_{1_I}, y_{1_I})$ . . . . . . . . . . . . . . . . . . . . . $P_{J_I}(x_{J_I}, y_{J_I})$ | $J_I$ |
| | | $J = \sum_{i=1}^{I} J_i$ |

| Product no. | Market boundaries: Formal representation | Market boundaries: Number |
|---|---|---|
| 1 | $f_{1_{1_1}}(x,y)=0, \ldots, f_{N_{1_1}}(x,y)=0, f_{1_{2_1}}(x,y)=0, \ldots, f_{N_{2_1}}(x,y)=0, \ldots$ | $N_1 = \Sigma_{j_1=1_1}^{J_1} N_{j_1}/2$ |
| ⋮ | ⋮ | ⋮ |
| $I$ | $f_{1_{1_I}}(x,y)=0, \ldots, f_{N_{1_I}}(x,y)=0, f_{1_{2_I}}(x,y)=0, \ldots, f_{N_{2_I}}(x,y)=0, \ldots$ | $N_I = \Sigma_{j_I=1_I}^{J_I} N_{j_I}/2$ |
| | | $N = \Sigma_{i=1}^{I} N_i$ |

and:

$$\frac{\partial \Pi_{j_i}}{\partial y_{j_i}} = 0 \qquad (2.6.4.6)$$

Relationships (2.6.4.5) and (2.6.4.6) define the first-order conditions for a maximum profit for each production centre $P_{j_i}$. The total number of these conditions is equal to $2(\Sigma_{i=1}^{I} J_i) = 2J$.

A second condition is concerned with the total covering of the space:

$$\sum_{j_i=1}^{J_i} G_{j_i} = G \qquad (2.6.4.7)$$

The latter condition should be satisifed for each commodity $i$ ($i = 1, \ldots I$). Thus, the total number of these conditions is equal to $I$.

The third condition is related to the absence of abnormal profits, implying that the average production cost per unit are equal to the f.o.b. price:

$$p^*_{j_i} = c_{j_i} \qquad (2.6.4.8)$$

The total number of these relations is equal to $J$, since they relate to each commodity and to each production place.

The fourth condition related to (2.6.4.8) results from a so-called Chamberlin-condition of free entry. The areas of supply, production and sales, will be of a minimum economic size, if an infinitesimal small rise in the market area of a producer leads to an equal change both of the f.o.b. price and of the average costs per unit. In other words:

$$\frac{\partial p^*_{j_i}}{\partial G_{j_i}} = \frac{\partial c_{j_i}}{\partial G_{j_i}} \qquad (2.6.4.9)$$

Evidently, the total number of these conditions is equal to $J$.

Finally, the formal equation of a market boundary is represented by an isostant:

$$p^*_{j_i} + t_{j_i} d_{j_i} = p^*_{j'_i} + t_{j'_i} d_{j'_i} \qquad (2.6.4.10)$$

where $j_i$ and $j'_i$ are supposed to represent two producers with adjacent market areas. The total number of isostants is supposed to be equal to $N$ (see table 2.6.4.a).

The system of equations, described previously in (2.6.4.5)–(2.6.4.10) contains $2J + I + J + J + N = 4J + I + N$ relationships. This means, that the number of equations is exactly equal to the number of unknown variables.

The following comments concerning Lösch's equilibrium system can be made:

1 Lösch's approach is, in a sense, less far-reaching and, from a theoretical point of view, less elegant than the Walrasian approach, since, in Lösch's approach, utility functions and production functions are not present. Lösch starts from demand functions and cost functions. The apparent result is, that there is no degree of freedom in terms of an accounting price (cf. Cassel [1932]): the number of equations is equal to the number of unknown variables (unless a Walras equilibrium condition is satisfied).

2 There is no guarantee, that this system will indeed lead to a (single) equilibrium solution, since only the necessary conditions for a solution are inspected (number of equations equal to number of unknown variables). However, since the system of equations may be highly non-linear, one may obtain multiple solutions or no solution at all. In addition, the second-order (concavity) conditions of the profit-maximizing relationships are not inspected.

3 The isostants, which form the market boundaries, have the general form (2.6.4.1). Their exact specification is contained in (2.6.4.10). However, it is not clear, why the market delimination should not be based on a regular hexagonal pattern. This latter situation, which would be completely in line with Lösch's theory of regions, would reduce the number of unknown market boundaries, since the knowledge concerning the size and site of one hexagonal market of a certain product allows one to find immediately all market boundaries of this regular hexagonal market pattern.

4 The system is over-determined. Once the size and site of $J_i - 1$ market areas $G_{j_i}$ is known (for each product $i$), the last market area can be calculated directly from the additivity condition (2.6.4.7).

5 External economies (for instance, locational and agglomeration advantages) are a basic element in the formation of settlement patterns. However, they do not play a role in Lösch's system.

6 Even the simple equilibrium system, as developed by Lösch, is rather intricate. One does not know beforehand, in how many production centres $P_{j_i}$ a certain commodity $i$ will be produced ($J_i$ is unknown!). However, as long as $J_i$ is unknown, one does not know the total number of profit conditions (2.6.4.5.) and (2.6.4.6.), relating to the commodity $i$ concerned. But, if the number of equations is unknown, Lösch's

equilibrium system can not be solved directly in a *continuous* way (supposed this would be possible). In fact, the ultimate problem of Lösch's equilibrium system is of a combinatorial nature. In addition to the *value* of the unknown variables, one should also determine the *number* of production centres. This means, that Lösch's equilibrium system is a mixed integer-continuous system, which is, from a computational point of view, rather hard to solve (cf. also Ch.3 and Ch.6).

### 2.6.5 *A formal approach to regular market areas*

In this section the idea of 'Lösch regions' will be formalized in a systematic, mathematical way. It should be noted that, although the major part of these formal operations underlies Lösch's theory of regions, it can not be found explicitly in Lösch's contributions.[7]

It will be proved now that the hexagonal pattern is the most efficient space-filling structure, based on a complete covering of the plane. Another hypothesis for the plausibility of a hexagonal structure was suggested by Isard (1956), viz. the stability of a hexagonal pattern with respect to a square market pattern. The latter argument is essentially not an efficiency argument, but a long-term equilibrium argument.

As noted, *the circular market pattern* was not accepted by Lösch, owing to its inability for a complete covering of the space. A strict circular system of market areas implies an unsupplied area between contiguous circles. The relative size of this unsupplied area can be calculated with the aid of figure 2.6.5.a. Suppose three settlements $P_1$, $P_2$ and $P_3$, where

Fig. 2.6.5.a The size of the unsupplied area in the case of a circular market pattern

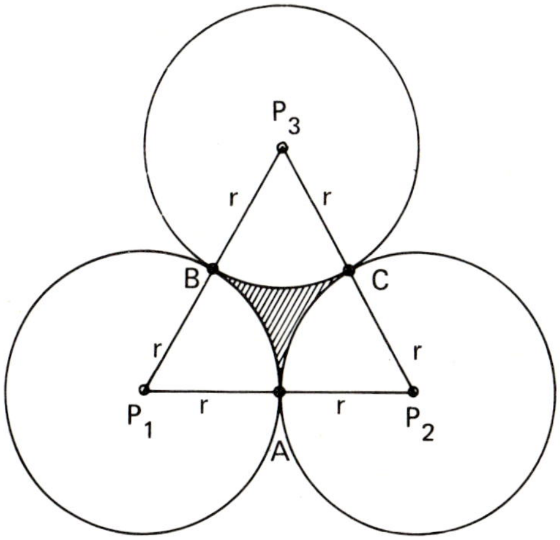

$P_1P_2 = P_1P_3 = P_2P_3 = 2r$. The area of the triangle $P_1P_2P_3$ is equal to $\frac{1}{2} \cdot 2r \cdot r\sqrt{3} = r^2\sqrt{3}$. The areas of the circle segments $P_1AB$, $P_2AC$ and $P_2BC$ are all equal to $1/6\,\pi r^2$. Their aggregate area is equal to $\frac{1}{2}\pi r^2$. Now the relative size of the unsupplied area $ABC$ is easily calculated as:

$$\frac{r^2\sqrt{3} - \frac{1}{2}\pi r^2}{r^2\sqrt{3}} = 1 - \frac{\pi}{2\sqrt{3}} \approx 0{\cdot}092 \qquad (2.6.5.1)$$

The last part of this section will be devoted to *the calculation of average distances in relation to regular market shapes.*[8] It will be proved that from all space-filling regular polygons the hexagon is most efficient.

It will be assumed that unit transportation costs are proportional to distances. Furthermore, the consumers are spread homogeneously over space with a unit demand density, so that the volume of demand in a certain region is equal to the area of that region. The average distance to be bridged between supplier and demanders, is equal to the weighted average of all distances between supplier and demanders, where the weights are formed by the respective volumes of commodities, to be transported. Thus, the general expression for the average distance $\bar{d}$ is equal to:

$$\bar{d} = \frac{\sum_{i=1}^{I} q_i d_i}{\sum_{i=1}^{I} q_i} \qquad (2.6.5.2)$$

where $d_i$ is the distance from the supplier to consumer $i$ (for instance, measured in miles), and $q_i$ the volume of demand of consumer $i$ (for instance, measured in tons). It should be noted that the denominator represents the total volume of consumer demand, while the numerator represents the total transport distance (for instance, measured in ton-miles). On the basis of the previous formula the average distances on a straight line, a circle, a hexagon, a square and a triangle will be calculated. Once the average distances are calculated, the average transportation costs per unit of product can be calculated by multiplying $\bar{d}$ with the freight rate per unit of distance.

The average transport distances will here be calculated under the assumption that each customer is served individually by the production centre. A more realistic assumption might be to calculate average distances in the case where a whole slice of the market is served simultaneously; this generalization, however, is straightforward and will not be dealt with here. Generalizations to average distances when all producers are spread over a line or surface, and exchange of commodities (input-output relations) is possible too. An example of the calculus of average distances to all points in a circle is contained in Van der Rijst (1969).

*A rectilinear market area* with a radius $r$ has an average transport distance, which is equal to $\frac{1}{2}r$. In a formal way, this can be proved by making use of (2.6.5.2). On denoting the numerator of (2.6.5.2) by $N$ and the denominator by $D$, $N$ and $D$ can be calculated for a continuous rectilinear market by means of integrals (being the continuous approximation of a sum of discrete points).

$$N = \int_0^r \rho \, \mathrm{d}\rho = \tfrac{1}{2}r^2 \qquad (2.6.5.3)$$

which results from the fact that, at each point of the continuous line, the volume of demand (i.e., 1) has to be multiplied with its corresponding distance (i.e., $\rho$), followed by a continuous summation (by means of an integral).

$$D = \int_0^r \mathrm{d}\rho = r \qquad (2.6.5.4)$$

which is the continuous expression for the length (or area) of the market (i.e. of the volume of total demand). Therefore, the average distance is:

$$\bar{d} = \frac{N}{D} = \tfrac{1}{2}r \qquad (2.6.5.5.)$$

*A circular market area* has a demand volume, which is again equal to the area of the circle. The calculation of $N$ and $D$ makes again use of integrals.

$$D = \int_0^{2\pi} \int_0^r \rho \, \mathrm{d}\rho \, \mathrm{d}a = \pi r^2 \qquad (2.6.5.6)$$

which is the standard expression for the calculation of a circular area.

At each point at a distance $\rho$ from the centre, the volume of demand (i.e., 1) must again be multiplied with the distance itself in order to find the total transport distance $N$. Therefore:

$$N = \int_0^{2\pi} \int_0^r \rho\rho \, \mathrm{d}\rho \, \mathrm{d}a = 2/3 \, \pi r^3 \qquad (2.6.5.7)$$

so that the average distance is:

$$\bar{d} = \frac{N}{D} = 2/3\ r \qquad (2.6.5.8)$$

It should be noted that the limits of the integrals of $D$ and $N$ should be equal in order to guarantee that the transport volume $N$ and the demand volume $D$ are calculated over the same area.

*The average distances on a hexagon, a square and a triangle* can be calculated by making use of figures 2.6.5.b–d. The regular polyhedrons,

Fig. 2.6.5.b A hexagon

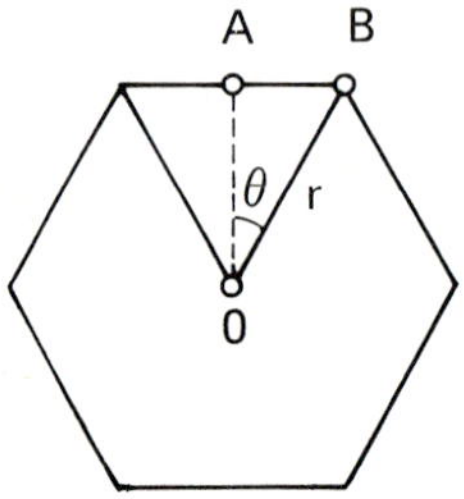


Fig. 2.6.5.c A square

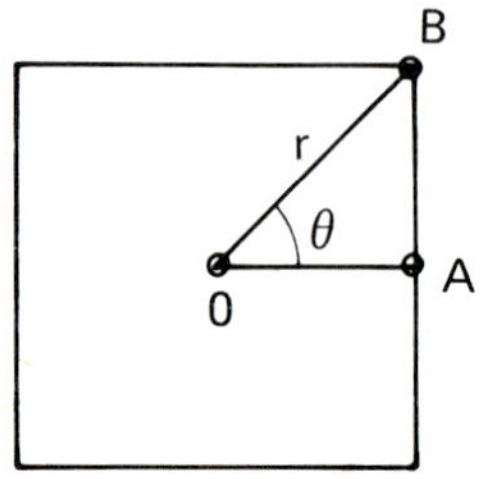


Fig. 2.6.5.d A regular triangle

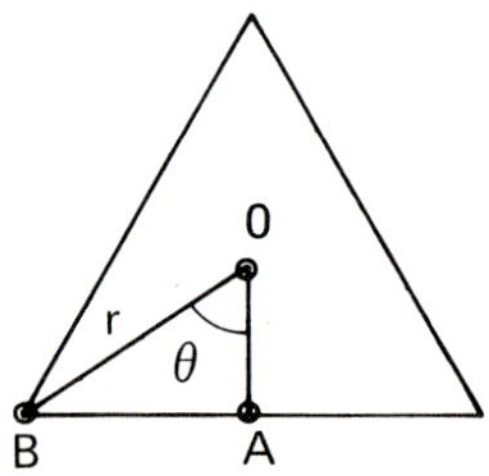


represented in figure 2.6.5.b–d have a circumscribed circle with radius $r$. Each of these regular polyhedrons is composed of a number of elementary rectangular triangles. A regular hexagon, a square and an equilateral triangle contain, respectively, 12, 8 and 6 elementary triangles $OAB$. In order to calculate the average distances over these regular polyhedrons, one needs to calculate only the average distance over the previous elementary rectangular triangles $OAB$. An arbitrary triangle $OAB$ from the figures 2.6.5.b–d is represented in figure 2.6.5.e. A general formula for

Fig. 2.6.5.e An elementary rectangular triangle

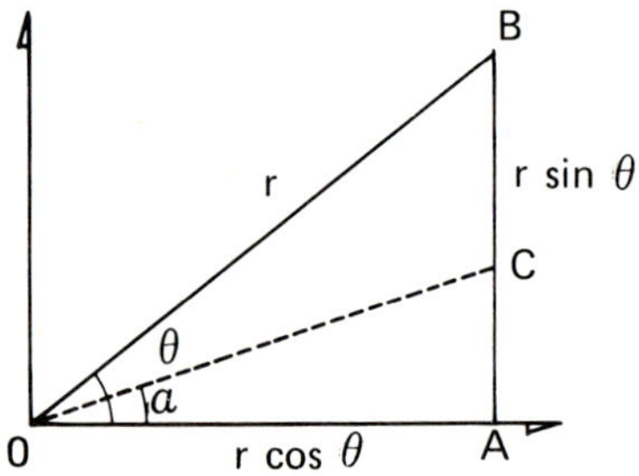


$D$ and $N$, relating to this triangle, will now be derived. The consequence of this general formula is, that the result is not only applicable to the three previous regular polyhedrons, but also to any regular polyhedron, since every regular polyhedron can be built up from a number of elementary rectangular triangles.

It is easily seen that the area of triangle $OAB$ from figure 2.6.5.e is equal to $\frac{1}{2}r^2 \sin\theta \cos\theta$. This result can also be obtained by making use of integrals, similarly to the circular case. The major difference from the circular case is the fact that the circle has a fixed radius $r$, while a rectangular triangle has a radius with a varying length, dependent on the angle $a$, between this radius and the horizontal axis. Therefore, if the angle $a$ varies from 0 to $\theta$, the length of the radius varies from $r \cos\theta$ to $r$ (see figure 2.6.5.e). This means that the calculation of $D$ and $N$ requires a slight adaptation with respect to the circular case. The upper limit of one of the integrals cannot be set equal to $r$, but this upper limit depends on the varying angle $a$. It is easily seen, that the length of the radius varies from 0 to $r$ $(\cos\theta/\cos a)$. If $a = 0$, the length of the radius is $r \cos\theta$, and if $a = \theta$, the length of the radius is $r$. Therefore, after this slight adaptation $D$ and $N$ can be calculated in a way, similar to the circular case, so that:

$$D = \int_0^{\theta} \int_0^{r\frac{\cos\theta}{\cos a}} \rho \, d\rho \, da \qquad (2.6.5.9)$$

and:

$$N = \int_0^{\theta} \int_0^{r\frac{\cos\theta}{\cos a}} \rho\rho \, d\rho \, da \qquad (2.6.5.10)$$

The calculation of $D$ gives:[9]

$$D = \int_0^{\theta} \left(\tfrac{1}{2}r^2 \frac{\cos^2\theta}{\cos^2 a}\right) da \qquad (2.6.5.11)$$

$$= \tfrac{1}{2}r^2 \cos^2\theta \operatorname{tg}\theta$$

$$= \tfrac{1}{2}r^2 \sin\theta \cos\theta$$

The numerator $N$ is calculated as follows:

$$N = \int_0^{\theta} \left(1/3r^3 \frac{\cos^3\theta}{\cos^3 a}\right) da \qquad (2.6.5.12)$$

$$= 1/3r^3 \cos^3\theta \left[\tfrac{1}{2}\frac{\sin\theta}{\cos^2\theta} + \tfrac{1}{2}\left\{\tfrac{1}{2}\ln\left(\frac{1+\sin\theta}{1-\sin\theta}\right)\right\}\right]$$

$$= 1/6r^3 \sin\theta \cos\theta \left[1 + \frac{\cos^2\theta}{\sin\theta}\left\{\tfrac{1}{2}\ln\left(\frac{1+\sin\theta}{1-\sin\theta}\right)\right\}\right]$$

$$= 1/6r^3 \sin\theta \cos\theta \left[1 + \frac{\cos^2\theta}{\sin\theta}\left\{\ln\left(\frac{1+\sin\theta}{\cos\theta}\right)\right\}\right]$$

Therefore, the general expression for an average distance on a rectangular triangle is:

$$\bar{d} = 1/3r \left[1 + \frac{\cos^2 \theta}{\sin \theta} \left\{\ln \left(\frac{1 + \sin \theta}{\cos \theta}\right)\right\}\right] \qquad (2.6.5.13)$$

In the hexagonal, the square and the triangular case, $\theta$ is, respectively, equal to $\pi/6$, $\pi/4$ and $\pi/3$ (see the figures 2.6.5.b–d). By calculating these respective cases, one may construct table 2.6.5.a.

Table 2.6.5.a Average distances in regular market patterns

| Type of market area | $\bar{d}$ | |
|---|---|---|
| Straight line | | $= 0{\cdot}5000\, r$ |
| Circle | | $= 0{\cdot}6666\, r$ |
| Hexagon | $1/3r\,(1 + 3/2 \ln \sqrt{3})$ | $= 0{\cdot}6079\, r$ |
| Square | $1/3r \left\{1 + \tfrac{1}{2}\sqrt{2} \ln (1 + \sqrt{2})\right\}$ | $= 0{\cdot}5407\, r$ |
| Triangle | $1/3r \left\{1 + 1/6\sqrt{3} \ln (2 + \sqrt{3})\right\}$ | $= 0{\cdot}4600\, r$ |

Table 2.6.5.a shows that an equilateral triangle possesses minimum average transport distances, followed respectively by a square, a hexagon and a circle (apart from a straight line). However, it should be noted that this result is based on the assumption of an equal radius $r$ for all four types of market areas; the result is therefore evident, since a triangle with a circumscribed radius $r$ has less consumers, to be supplied at large distances from the centre, than a square etc. For that reason a more appropriate way of comparing the average distances is a comparison, not on the basis of an *equal radius*, but on the basis of an *equal area*. If the spatial efficiency of a certain market pattern is measured by the average transport distances on an equal area, it is evident that the respective radii will differ from each other. If the area of a circle is taken as the standard area, on the basis of which all other areas will be compared, the radii of all these other areas have to be re-scaled with respect to the radius of a circle. If the length of this new radius, is denoted by $r^*$, one may express $r^*$ (of a regular polyhedron) in terms of $r$ (the known radius of a circle with a given area $\pi r^2$). According to (2.6.5.11) the area of a rectangular triangle with radius $r^*$ is equal to $\tfrac{1}{2}r^{*2} \sin \theta \cos \theta$. If the regular polyhedron concerned is composed of $n$ elementary rectangular triangles (for instance, $n$ is 12, 8 or 6), the total area of this regular polyhedron is equal to $\tfrac{1}{2}nr^{*2} \sin \theta \cos \theta$. By setting this result equal to the area of a circle, one can

easily calculate $r^*$ as follows:

$$\tfrac{1}{2} n r^{*2} \sin\theta \cos\theta = \pi r^2 \qquad (2.6.5.14)$$

or:

$$r^* = r \sqrt{\left(\frac{2\pi}{n \sin\theta \cos\theta}\right)} \qquad (2.6.5.15)$$

Thus, the new average distance $\bar{d}^*$ based on equal areas, is calculated on the basis of the old value of $\bar{d}$ as:

$$\bar{d}^* = \bar{d} \sqrt{\left(\frac{2\pi}{n \sin\theta \cos\theta}\right)} \qquad (2.6.5.16)$$

Therefore, table 2.6.5.a is re-calculated on the basis of (2.6.5.16). The new result is presented in table 2.5.6.b.

Table 2.5.6.b
Adjusted average distances in regular market areas

| Type of market area | $\bar{d}^*$ |
|---|---|
| Circle | 0·6666 $r$ |
| Hexagon | 0·6685 $r$ |
| Square | 0·6776 $r$ |
| Triangle | 0·7154 $r$ |

Table 2.6.5.b leads to the conclusion that a circle is the most efficient spatial market area (from the point of view of minimum average distances and minimum average transportation costs). However, from all space-filling regular polygons *the hexagon is the most efficient spatial market pattern.*[10] A more general approach to market areas is contained in Beckmann (1972).

### 2.6.6 *Spatial price policies*

The element of space leads to the existence of different price policies. These spatial price policies were distinguished by Lösch into a policy of *uniform delivered prices*, a policy of *uniform mill prices* and a policy of *price discrimination*. Such policies will be dealt with in more detail now, albeit in a more formal way than Lösch's approach. The approach adopted here shows more resemblance to the presentation of Beckmann (1968). The following hypotheses are presented:

H 1 The existence of a homogeneous area with unit demand density.

H 2 A circular market area with a monopolistic firm at the centre.
H 3 A linear demand function.
H 4 A linear cost function.
H 5 Uniform transportation costs $t$ per ton-mile.
H 6 Maximization of profits.

On the basis of the previous hypotheses various different price policies will be analysed with particular emphasis on a policy of price discrimination.

A policy of *price discrimination* leads to price setting which differs from point to point. Therefore, at each point a price has to be determined in such a way that the profits at that point are at a maximum.

If one assumes the following demand function (with quantity $q$ and c.i.f. price $p$):

$$q = a - bp \tag{2.6.6.1}$$

and the following cost function (with variable costs $c$ and fixed costs $c^*$):

$$C = cq + c^* \tag{2.6.6.2}$$

gross profits $\Pi$ in every point, where the length of the circle radius is equal to $\rho$, are:

$$\begin{aligned} \Pi &= (p - c - t\,\rho)\,q \\ &= (p - c - t\,\rho)\,(a - bp) \end{aligned} \tag{2.6.6.3}$$

If one assumes $t = 1$, the optimal price results from the first-order condition of maximizing $\Pi$:

$$\frac{\partial \Pi}{\partial p} = (a - bp) - b\,(p - c - \rho) = 0 \tag{2.6.6.4}$$

or:

$$p^{\mathrm{O}} = \tfrac{1}{2}\left(\frac{a}{b} + c + \rho\right) \tag{2.6.6.5}$$

It should be noted that the second-order conditions are also satisfied. A graphical representation of the spatial price setting, as described by (2.6.6.5), is contained in figure 2.6.6.a.

Until now the size of the market area was still undetermined. The boundary of the market area is characterized by the fact that there the volume of demand is zero. Thus, the radius $r$ of the market area can be determined by the condition:

$$q = 0 \tag{2.6.6.6}$$

or after substitution of (2.6.6.6.) into (2.6.6.1)

$$p = \frac{a}{b} \qquad (2.6.6.7)$$

Fig. 2.6.6.a A spatial price curve in case of price discrimination

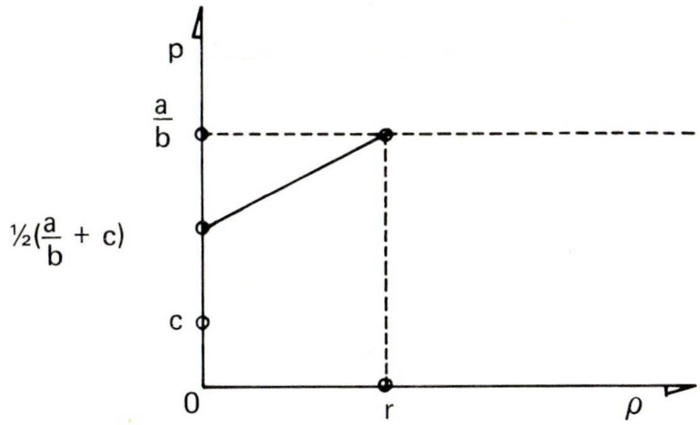


By substituting (2.6.6.7) into (2.6.6.5) one obtains:

$$\frac{a}{b} = ½ \left(\frac{a}{b} + c + \rho\right) \qquad (2.6.6.8)$$

so that the unknown radius $r$ (i.e. the maximum value of $p$) is equal to:

$$r = \frac{a}{b} - c \qquad (2.6.6.9)$$

Thus, the optimal price varies all over the plane. At the centre (where $\rho = 0$), the optimal mill price is:

$$p^{o} = ½ \left(\frac{a}{b} + c\right) \qquad (2.6.6.10)$$

while the optimal price, at a distance $\rho$ from the centre, increases with one half of the transportation costs per unit of product (cf. [2.6.6.5]). This means, that, in case of a price discrimination, nearby customers are charged relatively more with transportation costs than distant customers.

Policies of *uniform delivered prices* and of *mill pricing* can, in principle, be analyzed in a similar way (see Beckmann [1968]). A comparison of these policies shows that a system of mill prices favours nearby consumers, whereas a system of uniform c.i.f. prices favours remote consumers.

### 2.6.7 *Conclusion*

In addition to the topics discussed above, Lösch has dealt with a number of other spatial and regional problems. Among these his theory of international and interregional trade is worth mentioning, since it can be considered as an extension of the earlier theories of Ohlin (1933). In this theory Lösch assumed a complete mobility of goods and services in the short run, and of production factors (labour, e.g.) in the long run. On the contrary, Ohlin assumed an immobility of labour between nations. Lösch's extension of the theory of trade implies that an interregional or international equilibrium can arise from two sides, viz. by transfers of commodities and services in the short run, and by transfers of production factors in the long run. In a more formal way, attention will be paid to these problems in Ch.7 (interregional equilibrium).

Surveying Lösch's theories, one may conclude that he has done path-breaking work in the field of regional economics. He has shaped an integrated framework of regions and economic activities. In this sense Lösch's contributions are a glaring instance of an interplay between economic theory and spatial thinking. He can rightly be considered as the founder of modern regional economics. The way in which Lösch's approach to location theory is linked up with the contributions of Weber, Predöhl and Leontief (cf. Ch.5) is contained in table 2.6.7.a, which synthetizes the main lines of thought of the assumptions concerning the spatial dispersion of economic activities.

Table 2.6.7.a
A classification of hypotheses on location theory

| | Minimization of costs | Maximization of profits |
|---|---|---|
| Fixed technical coefficients (Leontief) | Weber | |
| Substitution between production factors | Predöhl | Lösch |

Ultimately, it should be mentioned that Lösch's work stimulated a lot of discussions in the field of regional economics. Comments on and generalizations of his work are contained *inter alia* in Beckmann (1968), Greenhut (1952), Hyson and Hyson (1950), Isard (1956), Mills and Lav (1964), Ponsard (1954, 1958) and Von Böventer (1963).

## 2.7 Conclusion

The period after Lösch rests for a major part on Lösch's corner-stones.

Many of Lösch's theories were reconsidered and extended. In addition, many new fields of research were and are being explored. A useful survey of the modern developments of regional economics can be found in Meyer (1968). It appears that, in addition to progress in the theoretical field, more and more attention is being paid to operational and empirical studies. This development can be illustrated by the following set of subjects, which are becoming increasingly indispensable instruments to the regional economist:

1 Input–output analysis, applied on the combined regional, interregional and sectoral scale (cf. Ch.5).
2 Mathematical programming of regional and multiregional economic problems, with the allied transportation problems (cf. Ch.6).
3 The general theory of the individual location problem (cf. Alonso [1967] and Ch.3).
4 The relationships between space and limited competition (cf. Smithies [1941] and Ch.3).
5 The general theory of market area analysis (cf. the hypercircles or Descartes ovals, derived by Hyson and Hyson [1950]).
6 The theories of a general spatial economic equilibrium (cf. Isard [1956], Lefeber [1958], von Böventer [1962] and Ch.7).
7 Methods for analyzing regional data (for instance, contiguity and diffusion analysis, distance concepts and factor analysis; see Ch.4).
8 The theory of growth poles and industrial complexes (cf. Ch.5).
9 Integration of regional and urban structures, based on the hypotheses of Christaller [1933] and Lösch [1954]; see Bos [1964] and Ch.3.
10 The theories of regional development (cf. Hirschman [1958], Hartman and Seckler [1970], and Ch.7).

The major part of these topics, as indicated, will be discussed in the next chapters of this book.

## Appendix 2A The Weber problem: a solution algorithm and some generalizations

The derivation of the minimum transport-cost point in a Weberian framework requires the solution of two highly nonlinear equations in terms of the unknown co-ordinates $x$ and $y$ of the firm's location. These nonlinear equations are derived in (2.3.2.6). For the sake of clarity they are presented here for the general case of $I$ sources of input:

$$\sum_{i=0}^{I} t_i a_i q \frac{x_i - x}{d_i} = 0 \tag{2A.1}$$

and

$$\sum_{i=0}^{I} t_i a_i q \frac{y_i - y}{d_i} = 0 \tag{2A.2}$$

where $d_i$ is defined in (2.3.2.5). Since $t_i a_i q$ is known and constant, one may define the so-called 'ideal Weberian weights' $w_i$ as:

$$w_i = t_i a_i q \tag{2A.3}$$

so that (2A.1) and (2A.2) pass into:

$$\sum_{i=0}^{I} w_i \frac{x_i - x}{d_i} = 0 \tag{2A.4}$$

and

$$\sum_{i=0}^{I} w_i \frac{y_i - y}{d_i} = 0 \tag{2A.5}$$

In order to be sure that each (local) extremum of the transportation costs is indeed the global minimum, the transport cost function (2.3.2.3) should be *convex* (convexity is dealt with in Ch.6). Convexity can be proved *inter alia* by inspecting whether the Hessian matrix of second-order derivatives is positive semi-definite. A matrix is positive semi-definite, if and only if its eigenvalues are non-negative. The eigenvalues $\lambda$ of the Hessian matrix $H$ are usually calculated by setting the determinant of the matrix $H - \lambda I$ equal to zero ($I$ is a unit matrix). The Hessian matrix of the distance function $d_i$ is easily calculated as:

$$H = \begin{bmatrix} \frac{\partial^2 d_i}{\partial x^2} & \frac{\partial^2 d_i}{\partial x\, \partial y} \\ \frac{\partial^2 d_i}{\partial x\, \partial y} & \frac{\partial^2 d_i}{\partial y^2} \end{bmatrix} = \begin{bmatrix} d_i^{-1} - (x_i - x)^2 d_i^{-3} & -(x_i - x)(y_i - y) d_i^{-3} \\ -(x_i - x)(y_i - y) d_i^{-3} & d_i^{-1} - (y_i - y)^2 d_i^{-3} \end{bmatrix} \tag{2A.6}$$

If the four elements of $H$ are, respectively, denoted by $h_{11}$, $h_{12}$, $h_{21}$ and $h_{22}$, the determinant $D$ of the matrix $H - \lambda I$ is equal to:

$$D = (h_{11} - \lambda)(h_{22} - \lambda) - h_{12}h_{21}$$
$$= \lambda^2 - (h_{11} + h_{22})\lambda + h_{11}h_{22} - h_{12}h_{21} \quad (2A.7)$$

The roots of this quadratic expression are non-negative, if their sum is positive and their product non-negative. Since the sum and the product are, respectively, equal to $h_{11} + h_{22}$ and $h_{11}h_{22} - h_{12}h_{21}$, and since these expressions can be proved to be, respectively, positive and zero, the Hessian matrix is positive semi-definite, i.e., the distance function is convex. Then the transport cost function (2.3.2.3) is also convex, since it is a positive sum of the convex functions $d_i$. The consequence is that each local extremum of $T$ (and thus each solution of (2A.4) and (2A.5)) is the unique global minimum of this transportation problem.

The *solution algorithm* itself is an iterative (i.e. step-by-step), numerical approximation of the optimum. One starts with a reasonable, initial value of the problem and attempts to find in step-by-step-fashion a new value, which is closer to the optimum. One proceeds in this way, until a converging solution is attained, which shows a negligible difference with respect to the real optimum. A solution algorithm for this location problem was developed by Kuhn and Kuenne (1962). A similar approach is contained in Cooper (1967).

The starting value of the solution procedure is the weighted average of the known co-ordinates $x_i$ and $y_i$ ($i = 0, 1, \ldots, I$), where the weights are equal to the corresponding 'ideal weights' $w_i$ (in fact, this starting value corresponds to the gravity centre of the locational area). If this initial estimate is denoted by $x^1$ and $y^1$, the initial values are:

$$x^1 = \frac{\sum_{i=0}^{I} w_i x_i}{\sum_{i=0}^{I} w_i} \quad (2A.8)$$

and:

$$y^1 = \frac{\sum_{i=0}^{I} w_i y_i}{\sum_{i=0}^{I} w_i} \quad (2A.9)$$

Next, relationships (2A.4) and (2A.5) are rewritten as:

$$x = \frac{\sum_{i=0}^{I} \frac{w_i}{d_i} x_i}{\sum_{i=0}^{I} \frac{w_i}{d_i}} \qquad (2A.10)$$

and:

$$y = \frac{\sum_{i=0}^{I} \frac{w_i}{d_i} y_i}{\sum_{i=0}^{I} \frac{w_i}{d_i}} \qquad (2A.11)$$

In relationships (2A.10) and (2A.11) the unknown co-ordinates $x$ and $y$ are a function of the known variables $w_i$, $x_i$ and $y_i$, and of the unknown variables $d_i$. For this unknown value of $d_i$ one substitutes the known value $d_i^1$, which is defined as the known distance from the initial point $(x^1, y^1)$ to the known point $(x_i, y_i)$:

$$d_i^1 = \sqrt{(x_i - x^1)^2 + (y_i - y^1)^2} \qquad (2A.12)$$

Substitution of (2A.12) into (2A.10) and (2A.11) gives a value of the co-ordinates, which is denoted by $x^2$ and $y^2$. These co-ordinates are used as the second starting point of the solution algorithm. Then the whole procedure is repeated, until ultimately a converging solution is obtained.

The solution algorithm can be clarified by means of the following example concerning one consumption centre and three input sources. The data of this transportation problem are presented in table 2A.a.

Table 2A.a
Data of a location problem

| $i$ | $x_i$ | $y_i$ | $w_i$ |
|---|---|---|---|
| 0 | 0 | 0 | 1 |
| 1 | 1 | 0 | 1 |
| 2 | 0 | 1 | 1 |
| 3 | 5 | 3 | 1 |

The various steps of the solution algorithm are presented in table 2A.b.

Table 2A.b
Successive steps in the solution of a location problem

| 2 | 1 | 2 | 3 | 4 | 5 | 6 | 7 |
|---|---|---|---|---|---|---|---|
| $x^i$ | 1·50 | 0·90 | 0·71 | 0·66 | 0·64 | 0·63 | 0·63 |
| $y^i$ | 1·00 | 0·60 | 0·43 | 0·38 | 0·37 | 0·37 | 0·37 |

The last column of table 2A.b represents the approximate solution of the previous transportation problem. In the previous procedure one should always be aware of corner solutions (where $x^0 = x_i$ and $y^0 = y_i$); in this case $d_i = 0$, so that one of the denominators would become equal to zero.

A generalization of the original Weber problem is obtained by allowing the possibility of multiple consumption centres. If these consumption centres are denoted by an index $j$ ($j = 1, \ldots, J$), one can denote the various commodity flows to these consumption centres by $q_j$ ($j = 1, \ldots, J$). Thus, the total volume of final production is equal to:

$$q = \sum_{j=1}^{I} q_j \tag{2A.13}$$

Owing to the multiple consumption centres the transportation costs of intermediate and final products are:

$$T = \sum_{i=1}^{I} t_i d_i a_i \left( \sum_{j=1}^{J} q_j \right) + \sum_{j=1}^{J} t_0 d_j q_j \tag{2A.14}$$

where $t_0$ represents the unit transportation costs per ton-mile for the final product.

In addition, one may discern between various types of commodities. If a certain commodity class is denoted by the upper index $k$, $q_j^k$ represents the volume of final commodity $k$, earmarked for consumption centre $j$, while $a_i^k$ represents the volume of intermediate product $i$, required for the production of one unit of final commodity $k$. Then the total transportation costs are:

$$T = \sum_{i=1}^{I} t_i d_i \sum_{k=1}^{K} a_i^k \sum_{j=1}^{J} q_j^k + \sum_{j=1}^{J} d_j \sum_{k=1}^{K} t_0^k q_j^k \tag{2A.15}$$

where $t_0^k$ represents the unit transportation costs per ton-mile for the final product of type $k$.

It is easily seen that these generalizations of the Weber problem can be attacked by means of the previous solution algorithm in a similar way as set out above.

Finally, a new generalization can be obtained by assuming a non-proportional relationship between transportation costs and distance (see Cooper [1968]) or by assuming the problem of *multiple* optimal locations. In the latter case, one has to calculate a set of optimal locations (one for each firm), as well as the allocations of the various commodity flows from all sources to all destinations. The latter problem is an integer problem (a 'zero-one' problem), since one should determine whether or not a commodity flow exists between the various spatial points. The solution of the latter problem requires additional heuristic methods (Cooper [1967] and Scott [1971]; see also the transportation problems in Ch.6).

## Appendix 2B Market area analysis: the criterion of dominating sales

In this appendix a more modern version of the market area analysis will be discussed, as developed by Beckmann (1971). The essential idea of this market area analysis is, that not each entrepreneur is a monopolist in his own market area: he has to share the market with other competitors. The market area of a certain entrepreneur is characterized by the fact that his sales in that area dominate the sales of other competitors in that area. Thus, the concept of market areas is linked up with the relative market shares of firms. Below, these ideas are elaborated more formally.

Suppose that two firms (1 and 2), settled at different locations, produce slightly different commodities. If one assumes that the sales ratio of these firms at a certain point is a function $f$ of the difference between the respective distances $d_1$ and $d_2$ from that point to the location of the firms, one may write:

$$\frac{s_1}{s_2} = f(d_2 - d_1) \tag{2B.1}$$

where $s_1$ and $s_2$ represent the sales of the respective firms. The function $f$ is supposed to be a monotonically increasing function. If $d_i$ $(i = 1, 2)$ represents *economic* distance (see also Ch.3) instead of geometric distance, one may postulate that $d_i$ is a monotonically non-decreasing function of geometric distance. Furthermore, one may assume that, in addition to economic distances, the sales ratio is determined by a measure of relative attraction of these firms (for instance, owing to quality differences). If the positive attraction difference of firm 1 with respect to firm 2 is denoted by $a_{12}$, formula (2B.1) passes into:

$$\frac{s_1}{s_2} = f(d_2 - d_1 + a_{12}) \tag{2B.2}$$

In an analogous way one may assume that the sales ratio of firm 2 with respect to firm 1 is equal to:

$$\frac{s_2}{s_1} = f(d_1 - d_2 + a_{21}) \tag{2B.3}$$

The market share of firm 1 (denoted by $m_1$) can now be calculated as:

$$m_1 = \frac{s_1}{s_1 + s_2} = \frac{1}{1 + \frac{s_2}{s_1}} = \frac{1}{1 + f(d_1 - d_2 + a_{21})} \tag{2B.4}$$

The market area of firm 1 is defined as *that* area, where $m_1 > ½$. In this way one may divide the entire region into two sub-areas. The demarcation line between the market areas is the set of all points, where:

$$m_1 = ½ \tag{2B.5}$$

or where:

$$f(d_1 - d_2 + a_{21}) = 1 \tag{2B.6}$$

Furthermore, if one assumes that the relative attraction is symmetric, one may stipulate:

$$a_{12} = -a_{21} \tag{2B.7}$$

so that the boundary line (2B.6) can be written as:

$$f(d_1 - d_2 + a_{21}) = f\{-(d_2 - d_1 + a_{12})\} = 1 \tag{2B.8}$$

In a similar way one may calculate the boundary line with respect to firm 2 as:

$$f(d_2 - d_1 + a_{12}) = 1 \quad \text{(2B.9)}$$

On the basis of (2B.2), (2B.3) and (2B.8) one may conclude:

$$f(d_2 - d_1 + a_{12}) = \frac{1}{f\left\{-(d_2 - d_1 + a_{12})\right\}} \quad \text{(2B.10)}$$

By means of condition (2B.10) one can calculate what value the arguments of the function $f$ should have in order to assure the fulfilment of (2B.8) and (2B.9). Since function $f$ is a positive monotonically increasing function, it is easily seen that the value of the arguments should be:

$$d_2 - d_1 + a_{12} = 0 \quad \text{(2B.11)}$$

Substitution of (2B.11) into (2B.10) gives:

$$f(0) = \frac{1}{f(0)} \quad \text{(2B.12)}$$

so that the evident solution is:

$$f(0) = 1 \quad \text{(2B.13)}$$

which satisfies indeed (2B.8) and (2B.9). It should be noted, that the situation $a_{12} = a_{21} = 0$ corresponds to a Palander situation with homogeneous commodities and equal prices and transportation costs (see [2.5.2.6]).

Ultimately, by making use of (2B.4) one may draw a set of *iso-share lines*. An iso-share line is the set of all points, at which the market share of a firm is a constant. Dependent on the specification of function $f$, one may obtain hyperbolic or elliptic forms for the iso-share lines.

**Notes**

1 The original German names are given in brackets, since this classification stems from the German history of location theory.

2 The abbreviation 'f.o.b.' means free on board; a f.o.b. price means a mill price, i.e. excluding transportation costs, insurance costs, risk costs etc. The abbreviation 'c.i.f.' means cost, insurance, freight; a c.i.f. price has to be paid by the buyer; it includes the costs of transportation, insurance, etc.

3 In fact, Palander's classification bears some resemblance to the more modern theories of Klaassen (1967) concerning demand and supply attraction.

4 The parameter $\beta$ has the dimension of distance, as can be proved by rewriting (2.5.2.15) as: $p_2^* = p_1^* + \beta t_1$.

[5] The mathematics of this derivation can be found in section 2.6.5.

[6] The total number of market boundaries between sales areas should be divided by 2 to avoid double counting.

[7] It should be noted that Lösch's theory of regular market areas can formally be described by means of Dirichlet-regions, as was shown by Dacey (1964). Dirichlet regions rest upon parallelograms, which are conceived of as elementary fundamental regions of a plane lattice. These parallelograms are defined on a six-fold or hexagonal axis. The ultimate Lösch system of regions can be obtained by rotating and translating the fundamental Dirichlet regions.

[8] In allocation-location models these techniques will prove to be useful; see Hordijk and Paelinck (1974).

[9] For the calculation of the integrals one could consult a standard table for integrals (see, for instance, Selby [1968]).

[10] In addition to the fact that section 2.6.5 can be used to prove Lösch's statement, that a hexagonal market pattern is the most efficient space-filling structure, one may also use the general formula (2.6.5.13) to calculate the average travel distances in urban areas to the centre (represented by a single point *P*). For instance, if one assumes a square urban area, in which the centre is not located at the midpoint, one can

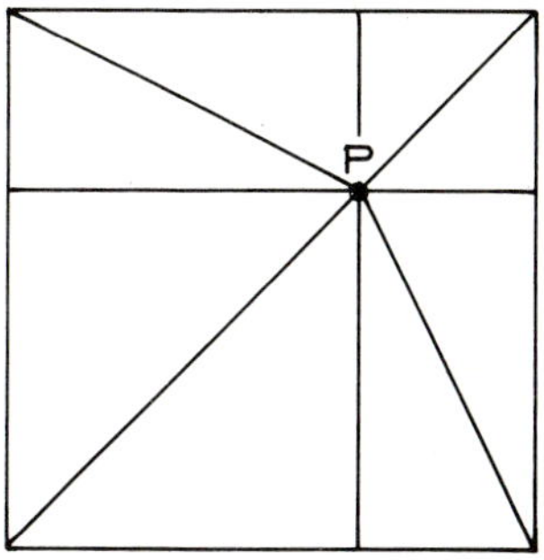


easily calculate the average travel distance to the city as the weighted average distance over all successive rectangular triangles, in which the urban area can be divided (where the weights are formed by the successive areas of the triangles).

## References

Alonso, W., *Location and Land Use, Toward a General Theory of Land Rent*, Harvard University Press, Cambridge 1964.

Alonso, W., 'A Reformulation of Classical Location Theory and its Relation to Rent Theory', *Papers and Proceedings of the Regional Science Association*, vol.19, 1967, pp.23–44.

Beckmann, M., *Location Theory*, Random House, New York 1968.
Beckmann, M., 'Market Share, Distance and Potential', *Regional and Urban Economics*, vol. 1, no. 1, 1971, pp. 1–18.
Beckmann, M., 'Equilibrium versus Optimum; Spacing of Firms, and Patterns of Market Areas', in: R. Funck (ed.), *Recent Developments in Regional Science,* Pion, London 1972.
Bos, H.C., *The Spatial Dispersion of Economic Activity*, Rotterdam University Press, Rotterdam 1964.
Burton, T.L. and Fulcher, M.N., 'Measurement of Recreation Benefits; a Survey', *Journal of Economic Studies*, no. 2, 1968, pp. 35–48.
Cassel, G., *Theoretische Sozialökonomie*, Leipzig 1932.
Christaller, W., *Die Zentralen Orte in Süddeutschland*, Fischer, Jena, 1933 (English translation by C.W. Baskin: *Central Places in Southern Germany*, Prentice-Hall, Englewood Cliffs 1966).
Clark, C., 'Urban Population Densities', *Journal of the Royal Statistical Society*, 1951, Ser. A, no. 114, pp. 490–496.
Clawson, W. and Knetsch, J.L., *The Economics of Outdoor Recreation*, Johns Hopkins, Baltimore 1966.
Cooper, L., 'Solutions of Generalized Locational Equilibrium Models', *Journal of Regional Science*, vol. 7, no. 1, 1967, pp. 1–18.
Cooper, L., 'An Extension of the Generalized Weber Problem', *Journal of Regional Science*, vol. 8, no. 2, 1968, pp. 181–197.
Cournot, A., *Researches into the Mathematical Principles of the Theory of Wealth*, MacMillan, New York 1897.
Dacey, M.F., 'A Note on Some Number Properties of a Hexagonal Hierarchical Plane Lattice', *Journal of Regional Science*, vol. 5, no. 2, 1964, pp. 63–67.
Greenhut, M.L., 'The Size and Shape of the Market Area of a Firm', *Southern Economic Journal*, vol. 19, 1952, pp. 37–50.
Greenhut, M.L., *Micro-economics and the Space Economy*, Scott-Foresman, Chicago 1963.
Hartman, L.M. and Seckler, D., 'Towards the Application of Dynamic Growth Theory to Regions', in: H.W. Richardson (ed.), *Regional Economics*, MacMillan, London 1970, pp. 98-106.
Hartwick, J.M., 'Lösch's Theorem on Hexagonal Market Areas', *Journal of Regional Science*, vol. 13, no. 2, 1973, pp. 213–221.
Hirschman, A.O., *The Strategy of Economic Development*, Yale University Press, New Haven 1958.
Hordijk, L. and Paelinck, J., 'Spatial Econometrics: Some Contributions', in series: *Foundations of Empirical Economic Research*, Netherlands Economic Institute, Rotterdam, (mimeo) 1974.

Hotelling, H., 'Stability in Competition', *Economic Journal*, vol. 39, 1929, pp. 41–57.

Hyson, C.D. and Hyson, W.P., 'The Economic Law of Market Areas', *Quarterly Journal of Economics*, vol. 64, 1950, pp.319–327.

Isard, W., *Location and the Space-Economy*, MIT Press, Cambridge 1956.

Isard, W., *General Theory: Social, Political, Economic and Regional,* MIT. Press, Cambridge 1969.

Isard, W., Schooler, E.W. and Vietorisz, T., *Industrial Complex Analysis and Regional Development: A Case Study of Refinery-Petrochemical-Synthetic-Fiber Complexes and Puerto Rico*, MIT Press, Cambridge 1959.

Klaassen, L.H., *Methods of Selecting Industries for Depressed Areas,* OECD, Paris 1967.

Kuhn, H.W. and Kuenne, R.E., 'An Efficient Algorithm for the Numerical Solution of the Generalized Weber Problem in Spatial Economics', *Journal of Regional Science*, vol. 4, no. 2, 1962, pp. 21–33.

Lefeber, L., *Allocation in Space*, North-Holland Publishing Co., Amsterdam 1958.

Lösch, A., *The Economics of Location*, Yale University Press, New Haven 1954.

Meyer, J.R., 'Regional Economics: A Survey', in: L. Needleman (ed.), *Regional Analysis*, Penguin Books, Baltimore, 1968, pp. 19–60.

Mills, E.S. and Lav, M.R., 'A Model of Market Areas with Free Entry', *The Journal of Political Economy*, vol. 72, 1964, pp. 278–288.

Moran, P., *L'Analyse Spatiale en Science Economique*, Cujas, Paris 1965.

Muth, R.F., 'The Spatial Structure of the Housing Market', *Papers and Proceedings of the Regional Science Association*, vol. 7, 1961, pp. 207–220.

Nijkamp, P., *Planning of Industrial Complexes by means of Geometric Programming*, Rotterdam University Press, Rotterdam 1972.

Ohlin, B., *Interregional and International Trade*, Harvard University Press, Cambridge 1933.

Palander, T., *Beiträge zur Standortstheorie*, Almqvist & Wiksells Boktryckeri A.B., Uppsala 1935.

Ponsard, C., *Economie et Espace*, Sedes, Paris 1954.

Ponsard, C., *Histoire des Théories Economiques Spatiales*, Bodin, Paris 1958.

Predöhl, A., 'Das Standortsproblem in der Weltwirtschaftstheorie', *Weltwirtschaftliches Archiv*, vol. 21, 1925, pp. 294–331.

Schärlig, A., 'About the Confusion between the Center of Gravity and Weber's Optimum', *Regional and Urban Economics,* vol. 3, no. 4, 1973, pp. 371–382.

Scott, A.J., *Combinational Programming, Spatial Analysis and Planning,* Methuen, London 1971.
Selby, S.M., *Standard Mathematical Tables*, Chemical Rubber Co., Cleveland 1968.
Serck-Hanssen, J., *Optimal Patterns of Location*, North-Holland Publishing Co., Amsterdam 1970.
Shubik, M., *Strategy and Market Structure*, Wiley, New York 1959.
Smithies, A., 'Monopolistic Price Policy in a Spatial Market', *Econometrica,* vol. 9, 1941, pp. 63–73.
Van der Rijst, A., *Beschouwingen over de Vestigingsplaats van de Westeuropese Staalindustrie*, Elta, IJmuiden 1969.
Von Böventer, E., *Theorie des Räumlichen Gleichgewichts*, Mohr, Tübingen 1962.
Von Böventer, E., 'Towards a United Theory of Spatial Economic Structure', *Papers of the Regional Science Association*, vol. 10, 1963, pp. 163–187.
Von Stackelberg, H., *Grundlagen der Theoretischen Volkswirtschaftslehre*, Francke Verlag, Bern 1948.
Von Thünen, J.H., *Der Isolierte Staat in Beziehung auf Landwirtschaft und Nationalökonomie,* Léopold, Rostock 1842 (English translation by C.M. Wartenberg: *Von Thünen's Isolated State*, Pergamon Press, Oxford 1966).
Walras, L., *Elements of Pure Economics or the Theory of Social Wealth* (English translation by W. Jaffé, Allen and Unwin, London 1954).
Weber, A., *Über den Standort der Industrien,* Tübingen, 1909 (English translation by C.J. Friedrich: *Alfred Weber's Theory of Location of Industries*, University of Chicago Press, Chicago 1929).
Werner, L., 'The Law of Refraction in Transportation Geography', *Canadian Geographer*, vol. 12, 1968, pp. 28–40.
Wingo, L., *Transportation and Urban Land*, Resources for the Future, New York 1961.

# 3 Location Theory

## 3.1 Introduction

The geographic pattern of economic phenomena shows a spatial dispersion of economic activities. The aim of location theory is to present a systematic exposition and explanation for the spatial organization of these economic activities, in particular of productive activities. General theories on location problems are contained *inter alia* in Beckmann (1968), Bos (1964), Greenhut (1956, 1970), Hoover (1948), Isard (1956), Lösch (1954) and Serck-Hanssen (1970). Furthermore, one may also consult reviews by Lloyd and Dicken (1972), Smith (1966) and Webber (1972). It is obvious that location phenomena are rather complex and hard to disentangle owing to the variety in productive activities and production processes. In addition, the choice in favour of a certain location is co-determined by social, historical, institutional and geographical factors. Therefore, a systematic attack of location problems requires a number of simplifying hypotheses concerning entrepreneurial behaviour, market conditions, degree of competition, etc., in order to derive a set of ultimate propositions. On the other hand, the introduction of simplifying hypotheses implies that the actual situation may deviate considerably from the optimal solution of location problems.

From a spatial economic point of view activities may be classified into *space-consuming* activities (for instance, agriculture, mining), *space-reducing* activities (for instance, transportation and communication services) and *punctiform* (or neutral) activities (for instance, manufacturing industries, services). All these activities take place at certain points in space. This implies that all variables associated with these activities (such as prices, quantities, profits, natural resources, market areas, etc.) are provided with spatial co-ordinates (see section 1.6.2.1). Certain variables are fixed once and for all, for instance the location of natural resources; other ones are variable, either in the *long* run (for instance, the locations for markets and industries), or in the *short* run (for instance, the location of a service apparatus).

Long term and short term location problems give rise to a distinction between *general* and *partial* location problems. *General* location theory attempts at determining the joint spatial distribution of *all* locations and production centres simultaneously, e.g. on the basis of minimum over-all transportation costs (or an equivalent criterion; see section 3.3 and also Ch.7); the only data are the locations of natural resources (see section 3.3). In *partial* location problems, on the contrary, the markets of products and inputs are assumed to be given; here the purpose is to find an (optimal) location of a *single* firm, given the location of the other firms; the optimality criterion itself may be minimization of (transportation) costs or maximization of profits of a single firm. An intermediate problem is an optimal selection of a set of input markets and output markets, together with the selection of a firm's optimal location (see section 3.5).

Three elements of location theory deserve special attention:

a. The existence of *indivisibilities* in many production processes (see, for instance, Manne and Vietorisz [1963]). A non-continuous adaptation of production processes disturbs the global proportionality between inputs and the scale of production. From a certain point onwards indivisibilities lead to increasing returns to scale. These *economies of scale* will lead to a *concentration* in the location of economic activities.
b. The existence of *external economies* (see, for instance, Nijkamp [1972]). External economies are caused by agglomeration advantages (see also sub-section 2.3.2), and they also stimulate spatial *concentration.*
c. The existence of *transportation services.* Availability of a transportation equipment enlarges the mobility of commodities and labour (in fact, a complete immobility implies infinitely high transportation costs). By means of transportation services a dispersion of economic activities is possible. It should be noted that transportation services do not come about automatically, but are a result of a claim upon productive resources (see Ch.7).

The spatial pattern, as it arises from locational decisions, rests upon an interplay between external economies and economies of scale on the one hand, and on space-consuming activities and agglomeration disadvantages on the other hand. The link between both previous phenomena is formed by transportation services. Without space-consuming activities and agglomeration disadvantages production would be concentrated at one point, since in that case transportation costs are zero and external economies and economies of scale are at a maximum. Without indivisibilities and externalities the spatial dispersion of production would be at a maximum, because then transportation costs (with respect to regularly dispersed points) are at a minimum. Without transportation costs production would again be concentrated in order to benefit from externalities and economies of scale.

Ultimately, location problems can also be considered from several formal points of view, viz. from an *analytical,* a *planning* and a *political* point of view (see subsection 1.4.3).

The *analytical* problem deals with the question of the 'how' and the 'why' of a spatial configuration; such problems as locational factors and entrepreneurial behaviour are relevant (cf. Thompson and Mattilla [1959]). The *planning* problem deals with the problem as to the 'what' of an *optimal* spatial structure; here spatial planning and transportation models become relevant (see also Ch.6). The *political* problem tries to find optimal political instruments in order to realize an optimal spatial pattern; in this case the study and the selection of governmental instruments (for instance, subsidies, taxes, and permits) deserves attention.

This chapter deals with *partial* location analysis, *general* location analysis, *game-theoretic* location analysis, and locational problems in *differentiated* space, respectively.

## 3.2 Partial location analysis

### 3.2.1 *Introduction*

The partial location problems, discussed in this section, will be considered from different points of view. First, the *general Lösch-problem* will be presented; next, *market area analysis* and *locational problems* of a single firm will be investigated from a twofold point of view, viz., by assuming *minimum (transportation) costs,* and *maximum profits.* Ultimately, a generalized theory of partial location problems will be presented, followed by the introduction of *elasticities of scale* and *demand elasticities.* The theory of entrepreneurial behaviour, which constitutes a foundation stone of section 3.2, will be presented briefly in a separate Appendix 3A.

### 3.2.2 *The general Lösch-problem*

The general Lösch-problem in partial location theory is rather involved. This general locational problem attempts to find an optimal location of a single firm by including both spatial and temporal factors (i.e., a dynamic locational analysis), as well as a general production function transforming inputs into outputs. In addition, this optimum location of the relevant firm is determined for the rather complicated situation of multi-product activities. For the latter reason, the general Lösch-problem is an intermediate problem, which falls in between the pure partial location problem and the pure general location problem. The optimum locations are determined here on the basis of a *maximization of profits* for all activities of the firm concerned. Beside the *optimum location,* the other economic variables of the Lösch-problem, such as the *optimum market area,* the *optimum production levels,* and the *optimum price level of the outputs,* are determined simultaneously for each period of the time horizon.

By denoting the as yet unknown price and quantity of product $i$ ($i = 1, \ldots, I$) by $p_i$ and $q_i$, it is clear that the unknown gross profits $\Pi$ of the relevant firm depend on $p_i$, $q_i$, $T$ (the time horizon of production and investment), and on the optimum (but unknown) market area. If one assumes a circular market area with (varying) radius $r_i$, for each product $i$, $\Pi$ is equal to the aggregated profits of each individual activity $i$, integrated over all periods within the planning horizon and over all relevant points of the circular market area (see also Ch. 2):

$$\Pi = \sum_{i=1}^{I} \int_0^T \int_{r^*}^{r^*+r_i} \int_{\Theta^*}^{2\pi+\Theta^*} p_i \, q_i \, \gamma(t) \, d\Theta \, d\rho_i \, dt \qquad (3.2.2.1)$$

where the functional relationships of $p_i$ and $q_i$ are, respectively, equal to:

$$p_i = p_i \, (\Theta, r_i - r^*, t) \qquad (3.2.2.2)$$

and:

$$q_i = q_i \, (\Theta, r_i - r^*, t, p_i) \qquad (3.2.2.3)$$

The variables $r^*$ and $\Theta^*$ denote the (as yet unknown) polar co-ordinates of the optimum location of the firm. The variable $q_i$ may represent an amount of *input,* as well as an amount of *output.* If $q_i$ is an output, it is supposed to have a positive sign, and an unknown f.o.b. price $p_i$; if $q_i$ stands for a certain input, it is supposed to have a negative sign and an unknown c.i.f. price $p_i$. Thus, by adding all products, it is easily seen that $\Pi$ represents revenues minus direct costs. The variables $p_i$ and $q_i$ are assumed to be a function of the firm's market area (i.e., of $r_i$ and $\Theta$) during each time period $t$. Therefore, the arguments of $p_i$ and $q_i$ contain the elements $r_i$, $\Theta$, $r^*$ and $t$.[1] In addition, the volume of product $i$ depends on its price $p_i$. The market area not being a circular one, the radius $r_i$ of the market area of commodity $i$ is a function of the angle $\Theta$ and it is written as $r_i(\Theta)$ (see also subsection 2.6.5). Gross profits $\Pi$ are calculated in present value terms by means of a discount function $\gamma(t)$.

The fixed costs of production in each time period are denoted by $c^*$; these fixed costs depend on the relevant time period as well as on the (as yet unknown) optimal location of the firm. Therefore, total fixed costs $C^*$ within the time horizon $T$ are:

$$C^* = \int_0^T c^* \, \gamma(t) \, dt \qquad (3.2.2.4)$$

where the cost function can be written as:

$$c^* = c^* \, (r^*, \Theta^*, t) \qquad (3.2.2.5)$$

Therefore, net profits, $\Pi^*$, are equal to:

$$\Pi^* = \Pi - C^* \qquad (3.2.2.6)$$

The technical process of transforming inputs into outputs is denoted by an implicit production function $f(\mathbf{q})$, where $\mathbf{q}$ is a vector of inputs and outputs. Net profits should be maximized, subject to this production function; this results in the Lagrangean expression:

$$\max L = \Pi^* - \lambda f(\mathbf{q}) \qquad (3.2.2.7)$$

where $\lambda$ is a Lagrange multiplier.

This problem is particularly complicated, since it contains the following endogenous variables: $r^*$, $\Theta^*$, $r_i$, $q_i$ and the prices of the inputs and outputs. A simple solution can not be obtained, although certain analytical properties of the optimal solution can be derived (see below). A more tractable solution can only be attained by a simplification of the problem, for instance, be deleting the time or price problem. This will be assumed in the following sections.

If the constant costs are assumed to play no role, the behaviour of the optimal gross profits $\Pi$ with respect to a change in a location can be studied by differentiating $\Pi$ with respect to $r^*$. The radius $r$ of the corresponding market area is supposed to be the largest one of all radii $r_i$ associated with a certain product $i$. Therefore, the market area concerned may contain points where sales or purchases of certain products of the firm concerned are zero. If this maximum market area is supposed to represent the firm's market area over all its products (inputs and outputs), total gross profits over *all* products can be calculated easily over all time periods and over all points of the market area, given the knowledge of the endogenous variables. If the optimal gross profits in time period $t$ and around a point with spatial co-ordinates $(r, \Theta)$ are denoted by $P$, i.e.,

$$P = P(\Theta, r - r^*, t)\, d\Theta\, d\rho\, dt \tag{3.2.2.8}$$

the optimal total gross profits are:

$$\Pi = \int_0^T \int_{r^*}^{r^*+r} \int_{\Theta^*}^{2\pi+\Theta^*} P\, d\Theta\, d\rho\, dt \tag{3.2.2.9}$$

The effect of a change in the radius $r^*$ (i.e., of a change in the location) is calculated as:[2]

$$\frac{\partial \Pi}{\partial r^*} = \int_0^T \int_{r^*}^{r^*+r} \int_{\Theta^*}^{2\pi+\Theta^*} \frac{\partial P}{\partial r^*}\, d\Theta\, d\rho\, dt \tag{3.2.2.10}$$

$$+ \int_0^T \int_{\Theta^*}^{2\pi+\Theta^*} P\left(1 + \frac{\partial r}{\partial r^*}\right) d\Theta\, dt - \int_0^T \int_{\Theta^*}^{2\pi+\Theta^*} P\, d\Theta\, dt$$

If $r^*$ is a co-ordinate of the optimum location, (3.2.2.10) should satisfy the first-order conditions for a maximum profit. A non-optimal location implies that (3.2.2.10) is positive: in a non-optimal location the profit will always rise. until the optimum itself has been reached.

The first (positive) term of (3.2.2.10) represents the effect of a marginal change in $r^*$ upon gross profits in the *original* market area, except at the limits and at the optimum location. The second (positive) term of (3.2.2.10) is associated with a change of profits at the *limits* of the market area, i.e. at $r^* + r$. Finally, the third (negative) term denotes a change of $\Pi$ near the *original location,* i.e. at $r^*$, caused by a shift of the optimum location. Therefore, the underlying mechanism of a change in the original optimum location of a firm works as follows: *all over* the original market area one observes changes in the firm's policy concerning prices, sales and purchases; at the optimal location these changes are compensated by similar changes at the limits of the market as well as at the centre. Then a stable equilibrium situation has been attained.

In the following sections some simplifying hypotheses concerning the general Lösch-problem will be introduced. First, the problem of an optimum market area itself will be investigated, and, secondly, the problem of an optimum location of a single firm will be analyzed in more detail.

### 3.2.3 *Market area analysis*

Before discussing the partial location problem of a single firm, attention will be paid to the *market area* of a single firm. Therefore, in this section the market area analysis associated with the partial location problem will be studied. A set of simplifying hypotheses will be presented in order to arrive at a simple solution. Next, the optimum market area will be determined, both for a *Weber-situation* (minimization of costs) and for a *Lösch-situation* (maximization of profits); see also Bos (1964).

The following hypotheses are made:

H 1 Existence of a homogeneous area.
H 2 One firm with one single product.
H 3 Absence of external economies.
H 4 A circular market area.
H 5 A stationary situation (i.e., a static analysis).
H 6 Constant marginal costs $c$ and fixed costs $c^*$.
H 7 Constant density of demand $\varphi$.
H 8 A known uniform c.i.f. price $p$.
H 9 Uniform transportation costs $t$ per ton mile.

First, a Weber-solution will be derived on the basis of the previous hypotheses. Weberian analysis is based upon the criterion of cost minimization (either transportation costs, production costs or both); the implications of such a Weber-situation will now be investigated. Total costs $C$ are composed of variable costs, fixed costs and transportation costs. If the production volume is denoted by $q$, and total transportation costs by $T$, one obtains:

$$C = cq + c^* + T \tag{3.2.3.1}$$

or as average costs:

$$\frac{C}{q} = c + \frac{c^*}{q} + \frac{T}{q} \tag{3.2.3.2}$$

Since minimization of *total* costs would lead to a degenerate solution (viz. $q = 0$), the assumption will be made that the *average* costs are to be minimized.

In order to minimize (3.2.3.2) the as yet unknown variables $q$ and $T$ should be expressed in the as yet unknown radius $r$ of the circular market area, so that the cost minimizing problem is specified only in spatial economic variables. Total demand for the commodity concerned is equal to the area of the circular area times the demand density, so that one finds in accordance with (2.6.5.6):

$$q = \varphi \pi r^2 \tag{3.2.3.3}$$

Total transportation costs over the circular area are according to (2.6.5.7) equal to:

$$T = \tfrac{2}{3} \varphi \pi t r^3 \tag{3.2.3.4}$$

Substitution of (3.2.3.3) into (3.2.3.4) results in:

$$T = \tfrac{2}{3} q t r \tag{3.2.3.5}$$

Next, substitution of (3.2.3.3) and (3.2.3.5) into (3.2.3.2) yields the result:

$$\frac{C}{q} = c + \frac{c^*}{\varphi \pi r^2} + \tfrac{2}{3} t r \tag{3.2.3.6}$$

Minimization of (3.2.3.6) with respect to the unknown radius $r$ yields the first-order condition:

$$r = \left\{\frac{3 c^*}{\varphi \pi t}\right\}^{1/3} \tag{3.2.3.7}$$

Formula (3.2.3.7) represents indeed the global minimum of (3.2.3.6), since the second-order conditions are also satisfied at the optimum, as can easily be checked.
Since:

$$\left(\frac{3}{\pi}\right)^{1/3} \approx 1 \tag{3.2.3.8}$$

$r$ is approximately equal to:

$$r \approx \left\{\frac{c^*}{\varphi t}\right\}^{1/3} \tag{3.2.3.9}$$

Formula (3.2.3.9) shows that a rise in the fixed costs will lead to an extension of the market; this implies that a rise in fixed costs will be distributed over a more extensive market area in order to compensate these higher costs. On the contrary, it is obvious that a rise in the transportation rate $t$ will cause a decline in the radius $r$. A rise in $\varphi$ leads to a situation, with a smaller radius of the market area. In this case a less extensive market area is required in order to cover the same costs. The result of the previous simple analysis is laid down in proposition P3.1:

P 3.1 A circular market area of a single firm, which attempts to minimize its average costs, has a size which is positively related to the fixed production costs, and inversely related to the demand density and the freight costs.

It should be noted, that each proposition is only valid within the framework of the *a priori* hypotheses. Given the value of $r$, the other unknown variables ($q$, $T$ and $C$) can be calculated in a straightforward way by substituting (3.2.3.7) into (3.2.3.3), (3.2.3.4) and (3.2.3.6), respectively.

As has already been stated in section 2.6, Lösch preferred the assumption of a profit maximization above a cost minimization as an adequate criterion for entrepreneurial behaviour. By denoting total profits on the product concerned by $\Pi$, one obtains the following profit relationship:

$$\Pi = (p - c)\, q - c^* - T \tag{3.2.3.10}$$

Substitution of (3.2.3.3) and (3.2.3.4) into (3.2.3.10) gives the expression:

$$\Pi = (p - c)\, \varphi\, \pi\, r^2 - c^* - \tfrac{2}{3}\, \varphi\, \pi t\, r^3 \tag{3.2.3.11}$$

The first-order condition for maximization of $\Pi$ with respect to the unknown radius $r$ results in two possible solutions:

$$\begin{cases} r = 0 \\ r = \dfrac{p - c}{t} \end{cases} \tag{3.2.3.12}$$

If $r = 0$, the market area is an empty space, so that the sales will be zero. Then the profits are negative (owing to the existence of the fixed costs $c^*$). The second-order conditions for the maximization of (3.2.3.11) are:

$$\frac{\partial^2 \Pi}{\partial r^2} = 2\,(p - c)\varphi\, \pi - 4\varphi\, \pi t\, r \leq 0 \tag{3.2.3.13}$$

When the solution $r = 0$ is chosen, (3.2.3.13) is non-positive only, if $p \leqslant c$. This, however, would imply even a more negative profit: then production will again be zero, but the fixed costs $c^*$ have still to be paid. Therefore, if $r = 0$, the firm will abandon the market. When $r = \dfrac{p - c}{t}$, the second-order conditions are indeed satisfied, if $p > c$. This result gives rise to a next proposition:

P 3.2 A firm, which attempts to maximize its profits in a circular market area, will abandon the market, if the c.i.f. price of its product is lower than the marginal costs. The firm will maintain its position, if the net price is positive. Then its market area has a radius, which is proportional to the net price and inversely proportional to the freight rate.

Ultimately, one may compare the solutions of the Weber- and Lösch-situations. The solution of the optimal radius $r$ can be proved to be equal both in the Weber- and in the Lösch-situation, if profits $\Pi$ are zero (in the Lösch-situation). If a positive radius is assumed in the Lösch-case (i.e., if $p > c$), substitution of $r = \frac{p - c}{t}$ from (3.2.3.12) into (3.2.3.11) will yield the result:

$$\Pi = (p - c)\varphi\,\pi\left(\frac{p - c}{t}\right)^2 - c^* - \tfrac{2}{3}\,\varphi\,\pi t\left(\frac{p - c}{t}\right)^3 \qquad (3.2.3.14)$$

By putting these profits equal to zero, one obtains the result:

$$\frac{p - c}{t} = \left\{\frac{3\,c^*}{\varphi\,\pi t}\right\}^{1/3} \qquad (3.2.3.15)$$

According to (3.2.3.7) and (3.2.3.12) one may conclude, that a Lösch-solution (the result of profit maximization) is equal to a Weber-solution (the result of cost minimization), if the optimal profits ('rent') are equal to zero. Furthermore, it appears that in case of zero-profits the firm will not abandon the market.

The previous situation can be explained as follows: minimization of average costs leads to a solution, which is the minimum value of the average cost curve (*AC*-curve) of figure 3.2.3.a. Maximization of profits gives rise to an optimal point, where marginal costs (*MC*-curve) are equal to marginal revenues (*MR*-curve), as is sketched in figure 3.2.3.b. The Weber-solution is only equal to the Lösch-solution, if the optimal value of $q$ for the *AC*-curve coincides with the point of intersection of the *MC*- and *MR*-curve (see figure 3.2.3.c). There is, however, one problem concerning figure 3.2.3.c. The usual shape of a *MC*-curve is a convex one (see figure 3.2.3.c). It can be proved, however, that the *MC*-curve resulting from cost function (3.2.3.1) is not convex, but concave. This can easily be shown by solving $r$ from (3.2.3.3), i.e.,

$$r = \left\{\frac{q}{\varphi\,\pi}\right\}^{1/2} \qquad (3.2.3.16)$$

Substitution of (3.2.3.16) into (3.2.3.4) yields:

$$T = \tfrac{2}{3}\, t\, q^{3/2}\, (\varphi\pi)^{-\frac{1}{2}} \qquad (3.2.3.17)$$

while substitution of (3.2.3.17) into (3.2.3.1) gives:

$$C = cq + c^{*} + \tfrac{2}{3}\, t\, q^{3/2}\, (\varphi\pi)^{-\frac{1}{2}} \qquad (3.2.3.18)$$

The formal expression for the *MC*-curve can easily be derived on the basis of the total cost curve (3.2.3.18):

$$\frac{\partial C}{\partial q} = c + tq^{\frac{1}{2}}\, (\varphi\pi)^{-\frac{1}{2}} \qquad (3.2.3.19)$$

Now it has to be proved that (3.2.3.19) is a concave function. Therefore, one has to calculate the second-order derivative of (3.2.3.19).

$$\frac{\partial^3 C}{\partial q^3} = -\tfrac{1}{4}\, tq^{-3/2}\, (\varphi\pi)^{-\frac{1}{2}} < 0 \qquad (3.2.3.20)$$

which proves that the *MC*-curve has the unusual shape of a concave curve (see figure 3.2.3.d). This result, however, has no consequences for the

Fig. 3.2.3.a An average cost curve

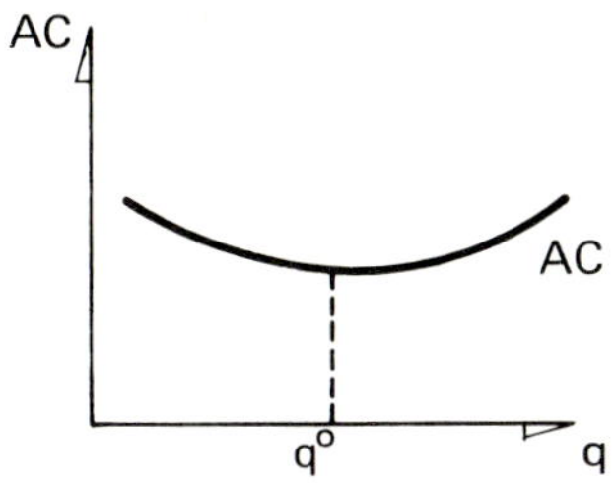


Fig. 3.2.3.b A marginal cost and marginal revenue curve

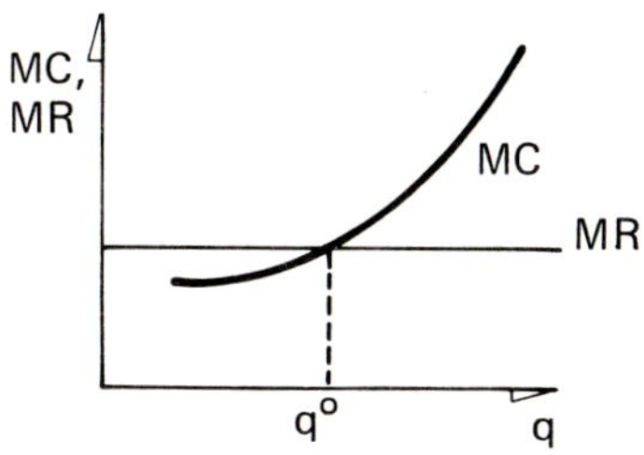


Fig. 3.2.3.c The cost-minimizing point

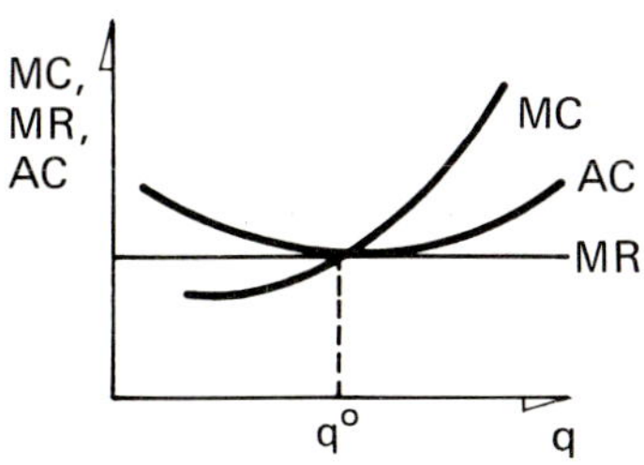


Fig. 3.2.3.d The marginal cost and average cost curve of a Weber-situation

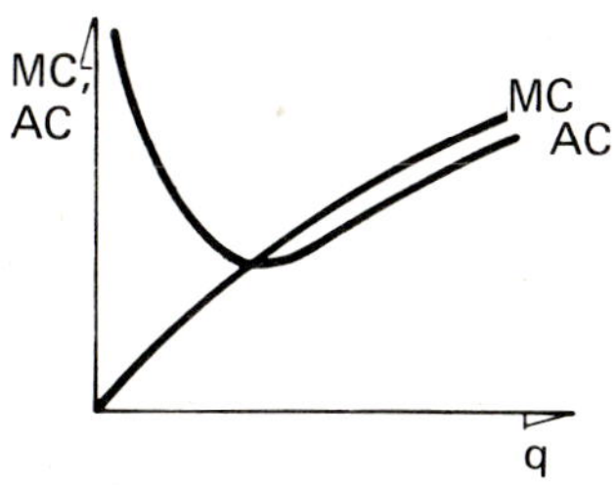


solution, since there is only one point of intersection of the *MC*- and *AC*-curve, viz., exactly the point where *AC* is at a minimum. This can be proved as follows: the $AC$-curve intersects the $MC$-curve at the point(s), where the average costs (calculated from [3.2.3.18]) are equal to the marginal costs (see [3.2.3.19]), i.e.,

$$c + \frac{c^*}{q} + \tfrac{2}{3}\, tq^{1/2}\, (\varphi\pi)^{-1/2} = c + tq^{1/2}\, (\varphi\pi)^{-1/2} \qquad (3.2.3.21)$$

or:

$$q = (\varphi\pi)^{1/3}\, \left(\frac{3\, c^*}{t}\right)^{2/3} \qquad (3.2.3.22)$$

So there is only one point of intersection. This point corresponds to the minimizing value of $q$ for the $AC$-curve, as can easily be checked by substituting (3.2.3.7) into (3.2.3.3).

Ultimately, investigation of relationship (3.2.3.14) and (3.2.3.15) shows, that in case of positive profits the left-hand side of (3.2.3.15) exceeds the right-hand side, i.e., the radius of the market area in a Lösch-situation exceeds the radius of the market area in a Weber-situation. Therefore, the following proposition can be formalized:

P 3.3 A firm seeking to maximize its profits possesses a larger market area than a firm seeking to minimize its average costs.

### 3.2.4 *The partial location problem*

In the previous section the *market area* of a firm was analyzed. The firm's decisions concerning the volume of production were based *inter alia* on a simple cost function, which did not take into account the fact, that a shift in the firm's location might lead to a decline in costs. Therefore, in this section the problem of an *optimum location* of a firm will be investigated (cf. Alonso [1967]).

In order to simplify the analysis the following hypotheses are introduced:

H 1 Existence of a homogeneous area.
H 2 One firm with one single product.
H 3 Absence of external economies.
H 4 A stationary situation (i.e., a static analysis).
H 5 Fixed gross revenues.
H 6 A neo-classical production function.
H 7 Known market points of inputs and outputs.
H 8 Constant freight rates both for inputs and for outputs.
H 9 Given f.o.b. prices of inputs.

H 10 A policy of uniform c.i.f. prices.
H 11 Maximization of profits (Lösch-hypothesis).

H 5 and H 9 imply that the uniform delivered price, $p$, and the volume of production, $q$, are considered to be given. H 6 implies the possibility of input substitution. Therefore, the production function can be written as:

$$q = f(\mathbf{z}) \qquad (3.2.4.1)$$

where the argument $\mathbf{z}$ represents a vector of inputs of order $I$. Each element $z_i$ ($i = 1, \ldots, I$) denotes a volume of input $i$. The fact that those inputs can be substituted for each other means an extension of the Weber-Leontief-approach with fixed technical coefficients (cf. also section 2.3).

The partial location problem, that has to be solved here, requires the determination of an optimum location, i.e., of optimum co-ordinates $x^{\text{O}}$ and $y^{\text{O}}$. The other unknown variables of this problem are the total freight costs, the c.i.f. price $p_i$ and the volume $z_i$ of each input $i$ ($i = 1, \ldots, I$). The f.o.b. price $p_i{}^*$ of each input is assumed to be given, as well as the c.i.f. price $p$ of the known volume of output, $q$. The unknown freight costs, as well as $p_i$ and $z_i$ can only be determined, given the knowledge of $x^{\text{O}}$ and $y^{\text{O}}$. *Therefore, this partial location problem rests on a continuous interplay between theoretical regional economics and general theoretical economics.* An efficient and tractable procedure is to solve this problem first in terms of spatial economic variables (e.g., $x^{\text{O}}$ and $y^{\text{O}}$). Then the unknown general economic variables can easily be solved in terms of $x^{\text{O}}$ and $y^{\text{O}}$.

The criterion for an optimum location is the maximization of profits. Since profits are equal to revenues minus transportation costs on outputs minus input costs (including transportation costs), profits $\Pi$ are equal to:

$$\Pi = (p - td)\, q - \sum_{i=1}^{I} p_i z_i \qquad (3.2.4.2)$$

where $t$ is the constant freight rate on outputs, $d$ the distance from the as yet unknown production centre to the output market ('point-point case'; see section 1.6.3), and $p_i$ the c.i.f. price of the input $i$ ($i = 1, \ldots, I$). The unknown variables in (3.2.4.2) are $d$, $p_i$ and $z_i$. Since $p_i$ is a c.i.f. price, it is equal to:

$$p_i = p_i^* + t_i d_i \qquad (3.2.4.3)$$

where the f.o.b. price $p_i^*$ and the freight rate $t_i$ are known, but where the distance $d_i$ from the production centre to the market of input $i$ is still unknown. It is obvious that both $d$ and $d_i$ ($i = 1, \ldots, I$) depend on the co-ordinates $x^0$ and $y^0$ of the optimum location.

By substituting (3.2.4.3) into (3.2.4.2) one finds:

$$\Pi = (p - td)\, q - \sum_{i=1}^{I} (p_i^* + t_i\, d_i)\, z_i \qquad (3.2.4.4)$$

Relationship (3.2.4.4) has to be maximized subject to the condition (3.2.4.1). It should be noted again that $q$ itself is known; only the input mix required to produce $q$ is unknown. The first-order conditions for a maximum $\Pi$ are (in terms of unknown co-ordinates $x$ and $y$ of the production place):

$$\frac{\partial \Pi}{\partial x} = 0 \qquad (3.2.4.5)$$

and:

$$\frac{\partial \Pi}{\partial y} = 0 \qquad (3.2.4.6)$$

The second-order conditions for a maximum are also supposed to be satisfied (see remarks below).

Since $\partial \Pi / \partial x$ and $\partial \Pi / \partial y$ are symmetric relationships, only $\partial \Pi / \partial x$ will be elaborated. Then one obtains:

$$\frac{\partial \Pi}{\partial x} = -tq\, \frac{\partial d}{\partial x} - \sum_{i=1}^{I} (p_i^* + t_i\, d_i)\, \frac{\partial z_i}{\partial x} - \sum_{i=1}^{I} t_i\, z_i\, \frac{\partial d_i}{\partial x} = 0 \qquad (3.2.4.7)$$

The demand for input $i$, $z_i$, is a function of the unknown distance $d_i$ (and, thus, of $x$ and $y$), since the demand function of input $i$ is a function of all c.i.f. prices $p_{i'}$, ($i' = 1, \ldots, I$), as well as of the production level itself. The validity of this statement rests upon the neo-classical production theory with factor substitution (see Appendix 3A). Since the c.i.f. input prices $p_{i'}$ depend on the unknown distances $d_{i'}$ (see [3.2.4.3]), $z_i$ is a function of $d_{i'}$ ($i' = 1, \ldots, I$), and, therefore, of $x$ and $y$. The expression $\partial z_i / \partial x$ can be elaborated only, if the demand function of input $i$ is known. On the other hand the expressions $\partial d / \partial x$ and $\partial d_i / \partial x$ can easily be elaborated, since the successive unknown distances $d$ and $d_i$ are equal to (see also [2.3.2.5]):

$$d = \sqrt{\{(x - x_M)^2 + (y - y_M)^2\}} \qquad (3.2.4.8)$$

and:

$$d_i = \sqrt{\{(x - x_i)^2 + (y - y_i)^2\}} \qquad (3.2.4.9)$$

where $x$ and $y$ are the (unknown) co-ordinates of the optimum location, $x_M$ and $y_M$ the (known) co-ordinates of the output market, and $x_i$ and $y_i$ the (known) co-ordinates of the market of input $i$. Then expressions (3.2.4.8) and (3.2.4.9) can easily be differentiated with respect to $x$ and $y$ (similarly to [2.3.2.6]). It should be noted that the denominator of (2.3.2.6) should be unequal to zero, which implies that corner solutions (i.e., $x^O = x_M$ and $y^O = y_M$, or $x^O = x_i$ and $y^O = y_i$) are not permitted. Therefore, the conditions (3.2.4.5) and (3.2.4.6) are only relevant in case of interior solutions. In order to simplify the notation of equation (3.2.4.7), the factor $(p_i^* + t_i d_i)$ in the second term of (3.2.4.7) is again replaced by $p_i$ (cf. [3.2.4.3]), so that (3.2.4.7) is equal to:

$$\frac{\partial \Pi}{\partial x} = -tq \frac{\partial d}{\partial x} - \sum_{i=1}^{I} p_i \frac{\partial z_i}{\partial x} - \sum_{i=1}^{I} t_i z_i \frac{\partial d_i}{\partial x} \qquad (3.2.4.10)$$

Now it will be shown that (3.2.4.10) can be considerably simplified, since the second term can be proved to be equal to zero. Since the demand function of input $i$ is a function of all prices, $z_i$ is a function of $p_{i'}$ $(i' = 1, \ldots, I)$, so that one may write $\partial z_i / \partial x$ as:

$$\frac{\partial z_i}{\partial x} = \sum_{i'=1}^{I} \frac{\partial z_i}{\partial p_{i'}} \frac{\partial p_{i'}}{\partial x} \qquad (3.2.4.11)$$

where the c.i.f. price $p_{i'}$ is again defined according to (3.2.4.3). Furthermore, according to formula (3A.7) of Appendix 3A, the cross derivatives of the inputs with respect to the input prices are equal, i.e.,

$$\frac{\partial z_i}{\partial p_{i'}} = \frac{\partial z_{i'}}{\partial p_i} \qquad (3.2.4.12)$$

Substitution of (3.2.4.12) into (3.2.4.11) produces:

$$\frac{\partial z_i}{\partial x} = \sum_{i'=1}^{I} \frac{\partial z_{i'}}{\partial p_i} \frac{\partial p_{i'}}{\partial x} \qquad (3.2.4.13)$$

Therefore, the second term of (3.2.4.10) can be written as:

$$
\begin{aligned}
\sum_{i=1}^{I} p_i \frac{\partial z_i}{\partial x} &= \sum_{i=1}^{I} p_i \sum_{i'=1}^{I} \frac{\partial z_{i'}}{\partial p_i} \frac{\partial p_{i'}}{\partial x} \\
&= \sum_{i=1}^{I} \sum_{i'=1}^{I} p_i \frac{\partial z_{i'}}{\partial p_i} \frac{\partial p_{i'}}{\partial x} \\
&= \sum_{i'=1}^{I} \frac{\partial p_{i'}}{\partial x} \sum_{i=1}^{I} p_i \frac{\partial z_{i'}}{\partial p_i} \\
&= \sum_{i'=1}^{I} \frac{\partial p_{i'}}{\partial x} \frac{z_{i'}}{z_{i'}} \sum_{i=1}^{I} p_i \frac{\partial z_{i'}}{\partial p_i} \qquad (3.2.4.14) \\
&= \sum_{i'=1}^{I} \frac{\partial p_{i'}}{\partial x} z_{i'} \sum_{i=1}^{I} \frac{p_i}{z_{i'}} \frac{\partial z_{i'}}{\partial p_i} \\
&= \sum_{i'=1}^{I} \frac{\partial p_{i'}}{\partial x} z_{i'} \sum_{i=1}^{I} E_{i'i}
\end{aligned}
$$

where $E_{i'i}$ is defined in (3.A.16) as the cross elasticity of input $i'$ with respect to the price of input $i$. Since according to (3.A.19) the sum of the cross elasticities is equal to zero, one finds:

$$
\sum_{i=1}^{I} p_i \frac{\partial z_i}{\partial x} = 0 \qquad (3.2.4.15)
$$

The latter result was overlooked by Alonso (1967) in his location analysis. Substitution of (3.2.4.15) into (3.2.4.10) gives the following ultimate simple result for the first-order conditions:

$$
\frac{\partial \Pi}{\partial x} = -tq \frac{\partial d}{\partial x} - \sum_{i=1}^{I} t_i z_i \frac{\partial d_i}{\partial x} = 0 \qquad (3.2.4.16)
$$

Relationship (3.2.4.16) will contain two unknown variables ($x$ and $y$), if the first-order differentials of $d$ and $d_i$ with respect to $x$ are elaborated (cf. [3.2.4.8] and [3.2.4.9]), and if the demand equation for the inputs (i.e., $z_i$) is written in terms of the c.i.f input prices (cf. [3.A.6]). A similar relationship can be obtained with respect to the $y$-co-ordinate (see [3.2.4.6]), so that ultimately a system of two (non-linear) equations in two unknown variables remains. In principle, such a system can be solved (cf. Ch.2). Once this system has been solved, the optimal co-ordinates $x^{o}$ and $y^{o}$ of the firm's location are known. It is obvious, that then also the unknown distances $d$ and $d_i$ (cf. [3.2.4.8] and [3.2.4.9]) are known, as well as the c.i.f. price and volume of each input $i$.

The first term of (3.2.4.16) represents the *market pull;* it is an indicator for the degree to which (a shift in) the output market affects the profits. The profits are higher, as the market pull is smaller. If the freight costs per unit of output are rising, the profits will decrease. Therefore, the output market exerts a rather strong pull upon the firm's location.

The second term of (3.2.4.16) may be called a *Weberian pull* or *material pull;* it represents the degree to which input sources affect the profits, in particular, if transportation costs are changing (hence, the name Weberian pull; see section 2.3).

The second term of (3.2.4.10), which was deleted ultimately, might be called *Moses-Predöhl pull,* since according to the earlier ideas of Predöhl (see section 2.4) and of Moses (1958) a shift in a location affects the relative input ratio ($\sigma$ -principle !). Therefore, this term reflects the effect of the location on the substitution between the firm's inputs. However, the deletion of this term according to (3.2.4.15) does not imply that the ultimate solution is a pure *Weberian case* (cf. the corresponding formulation [2.3.2.6]), since in the previous problem the variable $z_i$ is *unknown,* whereas in the Weberian case the volume of input is *known,* given the fixed technical coefficients $a_i$ and the volume of output, i.e., $z_i = a_i q$. Therefore, in the previous problem the factor mix is unknown beforehand; this factor mix depends on the as yet unknown optimum location, since $z_i$ is a function of the as yet unknown c.i.f. prices of all inputs (see [3.A.6]). Therefore, *the ultimate solution is not a Weber-solution, but a Predöhl-solution:* both the optimal location and the optimal factor mix are determined simultaneously. This result is summarized in the following proposition:

P 3.4 In case of input substitution the most profitable location is represented by the point, where the market pull and the material pull compensate each other. This point, however, does, in general, not coincide with a minimum transport cost location, since the classical Weberian pull is disturbed by the substitution between the inputs.

One may conclude that the continuous feed-backs between spatial economics and general theoretical economics are very fruitful for solving the firm's location problems. In the next subsection an algorithm will be presented in order to solve the location problem, described above, in a numerical way.

It is obvious, that the assumption of a homogeneous area limits the applicability of the foregoing location analysis. However, for service institutions and governmental institutions, for instance, this analysis may be very useful. Furthermore, as long as the area concerned is still rather homogeneous, the foregoing analysis may also be used to approximate the optimal location. Another application of the previous analysis, which is based on a rather homogeneous space, is the determination of an optimal central station in a network of telecommunications (Schärlig [1973]). Finally, the fundamentals of the location analysis set out above can also be used in combination with network analysis in order to solve location problems in differentiated space (see section 3.5).

### 3.2.5 *A solution method for the partial location problem*

In this section the approach presented in the previous section will be clarified by means of an example. This example will be solved by means of a solution algorithm, based on a grid search procedure (see Nijkamp and Paelinck [1973]).

Suppose two spatial points each of which provides a certain production factor or input. Both production factors or inputs have to be combined in a technical process in order to produce a given amount of a certain commodity. It is assumed that the production process can be described by means of a Cobb-Douglas production function:

$$q = \gamma z_1^{\alpha_1} z_2^{\alpha_2} \tag{3.2.5.1}$$

The optimal location of the firm can be determined on the basis of a maximum profit condition. The profits are according to (3.2.4.4) equal to:

$$\Pi = (p - td)\, q - p_1 z_1 - p_2 z_2 \tag{3.2.5.2}$$

where $p_1$ and $p_2$ are the successive c.i.f. prices of input 1 and 2. The first-order conditions for a maximum profit are according to (3.2.4.16):

$$\frac{\partial \Pi}{\partial x} = -tq \frac{\partial d}{\partial x} - t_1 z_1 \frac{\partial d_1}{\partial x} - t_2 z_2 \frac{\partial d_2}{\partial x} = 0 \tag{3.2.5.3}$$

and:

$$\frac{\partial \Pi}{\partial y} = -tq \frac{\partial d}{\partial y} - t_1 z_1 \frac{\partial d_1}{\partial y} - t_2 z_2 \frac{\partial d_2}{\partial y} = 0 \tag{3.2.5.4}$$

If the (known) co-ordinates of the market, and of both input points are denoted, respectively, by $(x_M, y_M)$, $(x_1, y_1)$ and $(x_2, y_2)$, the successive distances with respect to the firm's location $d$, $d_1$ and $d_2$ can easily be expressed in terms of the unknown co-ordinates $x$ and $y$ by means of (3.2.4.8) and (3.2.4.9). The differentiation of $d$, $d_1$ and $d_2$ with respect to $x$ and $y$ can be performed in a straightforward manner.

In addition to the unknown variables $x$ and $y$, the relationship (3.2.5.3) and (3.2.5.4) contain the unknown variables $z_1$ and $z_2$. The general demand function for production factors can be derived, given the specification of the production function. In case of a Cobb-Douglas function this derivation can be made in the following way. The marginal products of both factors can easily be determined from (3.2.5.1), so that:

$$\frac{\partial q}{\partial z_1} = a_1 \frac{q}{z_1} \qquad (3.2.5.5)$$

and:

$$\frac{\partial q}{\partial z_2} = a_2 \frac{q}{z_2} \qquad (3.2.5.6)$$

According to the well-known marginality principle, the input mix is optimal, if the ratio of the marginal products is equal to the ratio of the input prices, i.e., if:

$$\frac{\partial q/\partial z_1}{\partial q/\partial z_2} = \frac{p_1}{p_2} \qquad (3.2.5.7)$$

or:

$$\frac{a_1 z_2}{a_2 z_1} = \frac{p_1^* + t_1 d_1}{p_2^* + t_2 d_2} \qquad (3.2.5.8)$$

By combining (3.2.5.8) with (3.2.5.1), one can express $z_1$ and $z_2$ in terms of the unknown variables $d_1$ and $d_2$. On the basis of (3.2.5.8) and (3.2.5.1) one can derive, respectively:

$$z_2 = \frac{a_2 \,(p_1^* + t_1 d_1)}{a_1 \,(p_2^* + t_2 d_2)} z_1 \qquad (3.2.5.9)$$

and:

$$z_2 = q^{\frac{1}{a_2}} \gamma^{-\frac{1}{a_2}} z_1^{-\frac{a_1}{a_2}} \qquad (3.2.5.10)$$

Combination of (3.2.5.9) and (3.2.5.10) permits to solve $z_1$ and $z_2$ in terms of $d_1$ and $d_2$. Then one finds the following demand equations for the inputs:

$$z_1 = \left\{ \frac{a_1 \, (p_2^* + t_2 d_2)}{a_2 \, (p_1^* + t_1 d_1)} \right\}^{a_2/(a_1 + a_2)} \left( \frac{q}{\gamma} \right)^{1/(a_1 + a_2)} \qquad (3.2.5.11)$$

and:

$$z_2 = \left\{ \frac{a_2 \, (p_1^* + t_1 d_1)}{a_1 \, (p_2^* + t_2 d_2)} \right\}^{a_1/(a_1 + a_2)} \left( \frac{q}{\gamma} \right)^{1/(a_1 + a_2)} \qquad (3.2.5.12)$$

By substituting (3.2.5.11) and (3.2.5.12) into (3.2.5.3) and (3.2.5.4) one obtains two relationships in two unknown variables $x$ and $y$. These co-ordinates of the spatial location are implicit in $d$, $d_1$ and $d_2$ (see also [3.2.4.8] and [3.2.4.9]). Substitution of (3.2.4.8) and (3.2.4.9), and differentiation of $d_1$ and $d_2$ with respect to $x$ yields the following ultimate first-order condition for the $x$-co-ordinates:

$$\frac{\partial \Pi}{\partial x} = 0 = \frac{-tq(x-x_M)}{\sqrt{\{(x-x_M)^2+(y-y_M)^2\}}} \qquad (3.2.5.13)$$

$$-t_1 \left[ \frac{a_1 \{ p_2^* + t_2 \sqrt{((x-x_2)^2+(y-y_2)^2)} \}}{a_2 \{ p_2^* + t_1 \sqrt{((x-x_1)^2+(y-y_1)^2)} \}} \right]^{a_2/(a_1+a_2)} \left( \frac{q}{\gamma} \right)^{1/(a_1+a_2)} \frac{(x-x_1)}{\sqrt{\{(x-x_1)^2+(y-y_1)^2\}}}$$

$$-t_2 \left[ \frac{a_2 \{ p_1^* + t_1 \sqrt{((x-x_1)^2+(y-y_1)^2)} \}}{a_1 \{ p_2^* + t_2 \sqrt{((x-x_2)^2+(y-y_2)^2)} \}} \right]^{a_1/(a_1+a_2)} \left( \frac{q}{\gamma} \right)^{1/(a_1+a_2)} \frac{(x-x_2)}{\sqrt{(x-x_2)^2+(y-y_2)^2}}$$

A similar (symmetric) expression can be derived with respect to the $y$-co-ordinate of the firm's location. Therefore, the ultimate result consists of a set of 2 highly non-linear equations in two unknown variables $x$ and $y$. The optimal co-ordinates are formed by solving the foregoing non-linear equations. However, the solution of this system of equations represents only an *extreme* point. As long as the second-order conditions are not inspected, there is no guarantee that this extreme point is the *optimal* solution for the firm's location. Furthermore, the solution can only be an interior solution within the location space, i.e., the area of all relevant points (the envelope of all corner-points). The corner points $(x_M, y_M)$, $(x_1, y_1)$ or $(x_2, y_2)$ can not be a solution of this system: it can easily be seen from (3.2.5.13), that in that case the denominator of the corresponding terms in (3.2.5.13) become zero. Finally, the solution of the non-linear system of equations requires an algorithm, which yields in a finite number of steps an (approximated, numerical) solution for the optimum. The algorithm, described in Appendix 2A for the Weberian problem, cannot be applied here owing to the increased complexity of the first-order conditions. Therefore, a new solution method has to be endeavoured (see Nijkamp and Paelinck [1973]).

This solution method has to cope with three problems: (1) are the second-order conditions satisfied? (2) are the corner-solutions not abandoned? (3) can an efficient solution algorithm be found?

The specification of the second-order conditions is rather complicated and will not be given here. It can be proved that the profit relationship (3.2.5.2) is a concave function in the $x$- and $y$-co-ordinates. On the contrary, many examples can be found which show that the objective function is not concave (see the numerical examples below), so that there is no guarantee that the solution of the system of non-linear equations in $x$ and $y$ provides the maximum-profit location of the firm.

Furthermore, the solution algorithm should take account of the fact, that corner points may also be a solution of the location problem. This implies, that the solution algorithm should take into account both interior and corner points.

Therefore, a grid search procedure has been developed, which generates a rectangular grid within the location space (see figure 3.2.5.a). Next, the profits on each intersection point of the lattice are calculated. This can

Fig. 3.2.5.a A rectangular grid

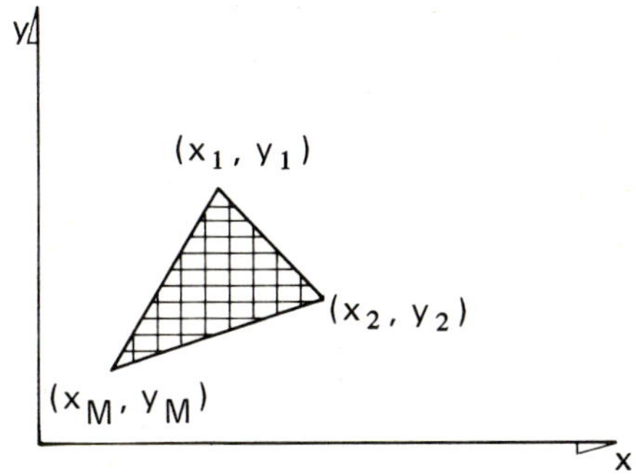


easily be done by substituting (3.2.4.8), (3.2.4.9), (3.2.5.11) and (3.2.5.12) into (3.2.5.2). Next, the profits associated with each lattice point are computed in a straightforward way. It is obvious that the horizontal and vertical lines of the lattice should lay rather closely together, in order to avoid that certain relevant points are overlooked. Although from a theoretical, mathematical point of view there is no guarantee that all extreme points are taken into account, there is a high probability that this situation will not occur in the previous location problem, since the profit surface is rather regular (see also the examples below). Only at the corner-points a more irregular course of the profit surface may be expected. Now the purpose of the first round of the grid procedure is to select those sub-areas from the location space, at which the profits are relatively high. Once a series of near points has been found with relatively higher profits, a new and refined grid search procedure has to be applied in the neighbourhood of these points, in order to find a more accurate approximation of the profits in that area concerned. In this way one may find a rather accurate approximation of the maximum-profit location. If necessary, this grid search procedure may be refined again and again, until the maximum-profit location is approximated with a sufficient accuracy. The foregoing algorithm takes also into account the corner-points $(x_M, y_M)$, $(x_1, y_1)$ and $(x_2, y_2)$, so that these points are also considered as relevant points for the firm's location.

Furthermore, a check on this procedure can be carried out by calculating simultaneously the marginality conditions (3.2.5.13). A necessary condition for a unique optimum is, that an interior point determined in the way described above yields first-order conditions equal to zero. This necessary condition for a maximum-profit location should be inspected simultaneously (except with respect to the corner-points, for which the first-order conditions (3.2.5.13) do not exist).

The solution algorithm, set out above, can also be described in an alternative way as follows: by means of a grid search procedure a point or a series of points is determined which satisfy the first-order conditions for a maximum. Next, the second-order conditions are checked by inspecting the profit surface itself in all points of the lattice. In this way one may select points, which satisfy indeed the first-order conditions, but which do not yield the absolute maximum, but only relative maxima or minima. A series of computer-runs showed, that in spite of a non-concave profit surface, the absolute maximum can be attained in a rather efficient way.

The algorithm described above will be clarified by means of a series of numerical examples. Suppose the following data (see table 3.2.5.a) are available for an individual firm seeking for a maximum profit location:

Table 3.2.5a

Data of the location problem

| $q$ | $\gamma$ | $a_1$ | $a_2$ | $t$ | $t_1$ | $t_2$ | $x_M$ | $y_M$ | $x_1$ | $y_1$ | $x_2$ | $y_2$ | $p$ | $p_1^*$ | $p_2^*$ |
|---|---|---|---|---|---|---|---|---|---|---|---|---|---|---|---|
| 100·0 | 1·0 | 0·1 | 0·9 | 1·0 | 1·0 | 1·0 | 0·0 | 0·0 | 10·0 | 0·0 | 0·0 | 10·0 | 100·0 | 1·0 | 1·0 |

So the location space of the firm can be represented in figure 3.2.5.b in the following way:

Fig. 3.2.5.b The firm's location space

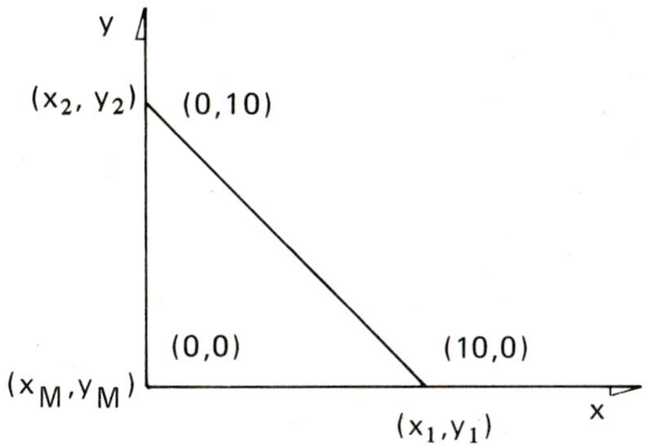


The first and rough grid search procedure puts a rectangular lattice on the location space of figure 3.2.5.b with distances between the lines equal to 1. The resulting values of $\partial\Pi/\partial x$, $\partial\Pi/\partial y$ and $\Pi$ are represented for all lattice points in table 3.2.5.b, 3.2.5.c and 3.2.5.d, respectively. Only the left-upper part of the matrices in table 3.2.5.b–d is represented, since only the points, which satisfy the condition $x + y \leqslant 10$, are relevant points (see the location space in figure 3.2.5.b). The asterisks at some positions denote that the corresponding element does not exist.

Table 3.2.5.b contains mainly negative elements, except in the first column. This means that $\partial\Pi/\partial x$ is only positive, if $x$ possesses a low value, i.e., if $x$ falls in between 0 and 1. Therefore, a positive contribution of $x$ to the firm's profit is attained, only if $x$ is very low: the change in $\Pi$ is inversely related to a change in the value of $x$. Thus, the area $0 < x < 1$ needs further inspection.

Table 3.2.5.c shows that the change in $\Pi$ is mainly positively related to a change in the value of $y$. Furthermore, on the line $x = 0$ the rise in profits is maximal, if $y$ possesses a very high value. Therefore, table 3.2.5.b and 3.2.5.c lead to the conclusion that a maximum profit will be attained, if $x$ is low and $y$ is high.

Finally, inspection of table 3.2.5.d shows that for all relevant points in the table the profits are at a maximum, if $x = 0$ and $y = 10$. This table shows, that the profit surface is declining gradually from the point (0, 10) onwards to the other corner points (0, 0) and (10, 0).

Table 3.2.5.b

The marginality conditions of the $x$-co-ordinate

| $y$ \ $x$ | 0 | 1 | 2 | 3 | 4 | 5 | 6 | 7 | 8 | 9 | 10 |
|---|---|---|---|---|---|---|---|---|---|---|---|
| 0 | * | −97·130 | −107·053 | −115·440 | −121·827 | −125·724 | −126·464 | −122·841 | −112·122 | −86·301 | * |
| 1 | 12·589 | −70·711 | −100·849 | −115·900 | −125·456 | −131·305 | −133·305 | −132·487 | −127·820 | −126·647 | |
| 2 | 11·145 | −48·233 | −87·496 | −111·204 | −126·185 | −135·713 | −141·363 | −144·417 | −147·379 | | |
| 3 | 9·608 | −39·333 | −78·778 | −107·060 | −126·492 | −139·606 | −148·427 | −154·872 | | | |
| 4 | 8·050 | −37·008 | −75·936 | −106·230 | −128·294 | −143·820 | −154·766 | | | | |
| 5 | 6·546 | −38·647 | −78·189 | −109·472 | −132·564 | −149·100 | | | | | |
| 6 | 5·143 | −43·858 | −85·455 | −117·045 | −139·615 | | | | | | |
| 7 | 3·870 | −53·990 | −98·754 | −129·102 | | | | | | | |
| 8 | 2·736 | −73·495 | −119·836 | | | | | | | | |
| 9 | 1·735 | −113·803 | | | | | | | | | |
| 10 | * | | | | | | | | | | |

Table 3.2.5.c

The marginality conditions of the $y$-co-ordinate

| $y$ \ $x$ | 0 | 1 | 2 | 3 | 4 | 5 | 6 | 7 | 8 | 9 | 10 |
|---|---|---|---|---|---|---|---|---|---|---|---|
| 0 | * | 122·723 | 119·514 | 115·127 | 109·806 | 103·805 | 97·342 | 90·564 | 83·504 | 75·978 | * |
| 1 | 24·564 | 51·572 | 73·519 | 81·026 | 81·491 | 78·049 | 71·778 | 62·327 | 46·889 | 16·215 | |
| 2 | 25·095 | 32·968 | 46·786 | 55·205 | 57·581 | 55·438 | 49·711 | 40·311 | 26·111 | | |
| 3 | 26·207 | 28·266 | 34·012 | 38·338 | 39·263 | 36·850 | 31·545 | 23·566 | | | |
| 4 | 27·998 | 27·387 | 27·706 | 27·303 | 25·262 | 21·467 | 16·091 | | | | |
| 5 | 30·140 | 28·001 | 23·922 | 18·850 | 13·319 | 7·588 | | | | | |
| 6 | 33·617 | 29·130 | 20·181 | 10·089 | 0·940 | | | | | | |
| 7 | 37·668 | 29·638 | 13·599 | −2·204 | | | | | | | |
| 8 | 42·929 | 26·235 | −1·432 | | | | | | | | |
| 9 | 50·255 | 3·371 | | | | | | | | | |
| 10 | * | | | | | | | | | | |

Table 3.2.5.d

The profits at the lattice points

| $y$ \ $x$ | 0 | 1 | 2 | 3 | 4 | 5 | 6 | 7 | 8 | 9 | 10 |
|---|---|---|---|---|---|---|---|---|---|---|---|
| 0 | 8477·440 | 8385·730 | 8283·530 | 8172·136 | 8053·317 | 7929·310 | 7862·916 | 7677·822 | 7559·554 | 7458·413 | 7402·833 |
| 1 | 8501·967 | 8466·767 | 8378·758 | 8269·755 | 8148·733 | 8020·065 | 7887·265 | 7753·854 | 7623·480 | 7497·466 | |
| 2 | 8526·748 | 8506·879 | 8437·347 | 8337·043 | 8217·804 | 8086·479 | 7947·667 | 7804·629 | 7658·909 | | |
| 3 | 8552·358 | 8536·982 | 8476·960 | 8383·187 | 8265·788 | 8132·303 | 7988·005 | 7836·247 | | | |
| 4 | 8579·416 | 8564·626 | 8567·483 | 8415·665 | 8297·778 | 8161·258 | 8011·669 | | | | |
| 5 | 8608·577 | 8592·242 | 8533·198 | 8438·649 | 8317·000 | 8175·740 | | | | | |
| 6 | 8640·540 | 8620·800 | 8555·396 | 8453·266 | 8329·273 | | | | | | |
| 7 | 8676·100 | 8650·312 | 8572·640 | 8457·663 | | | | | | | |
| 8 | 8716·275 | 8678·865 | 8579·800 | | | | | | | | |
| 9 | 8762·630 | 8696·867 | | | | | | | | | |
| 10 | 8818·365 | | | | | | | | | | |

It should be noted, however, that until now the precise location, where the profits possess an absolute maximum, has not yet been determined. Only the neighbourhood of the maximum-profit location has been demarcated. Now there are two possibilities: either the corner-point (0, 10) itself is the maximum-profit location (in which case the first-order derivatives do not exist), or a point near the corner-point (0, 10) is the maximum-profit location (in which case the partial derivatives of $\Pi$ with respect to $x$ and $y$ should be zero). Therefore, the neighbourhood of the corner-point (0, 10) should be further inspected. This can be done in a way similar to the grid procedure described above, albeit that now the lattice is restricted to the area $0 \leqslant x \leqslant 1, 9 \leqslant y \leqslant 10$, and $x + y \leqslant 10$, whereas the lattice itself is refined to a 0·1 distance between the lines. This procedure may be repeated again and again. Ultimately, the corner-point (0, 10) itself appears to be the optimal solution. In this particular case even no point, where the partial derivations of $\Pi$ with respect to $x$ only are simultaneously equal to zero, could be found.

The corner-solution, calculated above, appears to be determined by the difference in the production elasticities $a_1$ and $a_2$, since the remaining data (cf. table 3.2.5.a) are symmetric. The production elasticities $a_1$ and $a_2$ can be conceived of as 'geometric' weights, assigned to the corresponding variables $z_1$ and $z_2$. Since $a_1 < a_2$, the first factor receives a lower weight, so that the first factor is relatively less important in the direct input costs. Therefore, the location of the second factor, i.e. (0, 10), becomes more important, reason why the firm's optimal location is mainly determined by the second factor. The fact, that exactly the corner point is attained as the firm's optimal location, depends on the values of the coefficients in table 3.2.5.a. Different data may give rise to *interior* solutions (see below).

In the way described above one may find a solution for each combination of values of coefficients. For instance, if $a_1 = 0{\cdot}3$ and $a_2 = 0{\cdot}7$, while the other data from table 3.2.5.a remain equal, one finds the same solution for the firm's location, viz. the corner point (0, 10). This implies, that the production elasticities play an important role in determining the optimal location of a firm. Next, one may consider the completely symmetric case, where $a_1 = a_2 = 0{\cdot}5$ and where the other data of table 3.2.5.a are still valid. One would expect that in this symmetric case the firm's optimal production place would be located on the bisector through the point (0, 0) (see also figure 3.2.5.a). However, it appears that even in this case a corner solution is obtained, viz. the point (0, 10) or (10, 0). In both points the profits are at a maximum, viz.

8221·742, so that the solution is undetermined. The profit surface itself is not concave in the latter case, as is shown in figure 3.2.5.c, in which a series of intersections of the profit surface corresponding to the location area of figure 3.2.5.b is presented.

The grid search procedure described above has been used to solve a

Fig. 3.2.5.c Cross-sections of the profit-surface

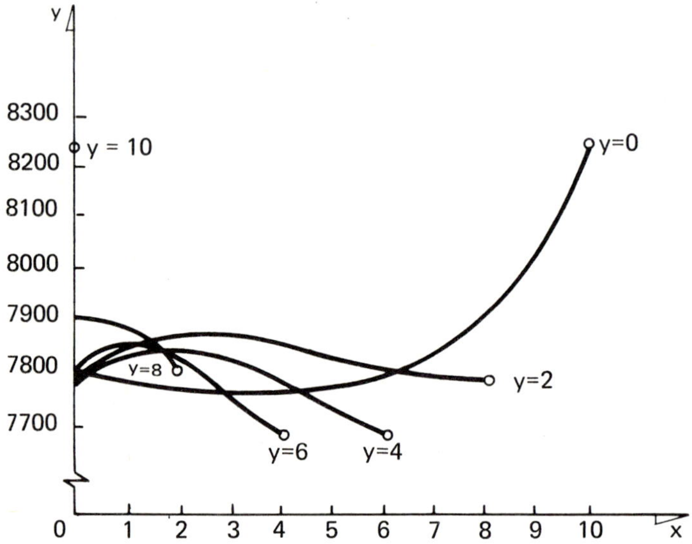


series of partial location problems, each of which is characterized by a different set of parameters. In table 3.2.5.e a series of interesting solutions is presented for given combinations of parameters. Table 3.2.5.e shows many important and interesting features of the partial location problem of a single firm. They will successively be discussed now.

The first three cases show that in these symmetric situations, under varying production elasticities $a_1$ and $a_2$, the optimal solution is always the same corner-point. This corner point is the material point with the highest production elasticity (i.e., $a_2$). This implies, that the input, which possesses the highest elasticity in the production process, exerts a very strong material pull. Furthermore, since there is a high degree of substitution in the Cobb-Douglas production function, the output will mainly be produced with the aid of the production factor with the highest production elasticity. Furthermore, the first three cases of table 3.2.5.e show that the profits are declining, if the production elasticities converge. This phenomenon is also present in the fourth case, which is the entirely symmetric situation discussed already above. The reason why the profits are higher in the case of diverging production elasticities is, that then one production factor (viz. with the highest production elasticity) is the most efficient one in the production process. By locating the firm in this input point, and by making use for the largest part of this input, one produces under very efficient conditions, so that the profits are at a maximum. In case of converging production elasticities the relative advantage of concentrating on one production factor decreases.

Case 5 and 6 are equal to case 3, except the unit freight costs of the first input. A rise of the freight rate from 1 to 2·5 units does not affect the firms optimum location, albeit that the profits are lower. However, a rise of the freight rate to 25 units causes a shift in the optimum location, viz. from (0, 10) to (10, 0). The advantage of location (0, 10), the point with the highest production elasticity, appears to be disturbed by the very high unit transportation costs of the input with the lowest production elasticity. Therefore, the location of the input with the very high freight rate exerts a very strong pull, reason why the optimal location is shifted to the latter point. It is obvious that a rise in transportation costs causes a decline in the profits.

Case 7 and 8 show a reversed situation, viz. with very low transportation costs for the first factor. In that case the total transportation costs of the inputs are so low that the market itself starts to exert a market pull to such a degree, that the market itself becomes the optimal location for the firm. It is clear, that the profits in this situation are much higher than in the third case. The market pull appears to be dominated by the material pull of the most efficient input, when the transportation costs are rising (see case 9). A switch from the market point (0, 0) to the input point (0, 10) occurs, if the freight rate of the first is approximately equal to 0·246.

Next, in case 10 and 11 the effect of a rise in production is presented. It appears, that a reduction of the production to 50 does not influence the firm's optimal location (compared with case 3). It is obvious, that the profits undergo a change. This change appears to be linearly proportional to the change in production: the profits are reduced with a factor ½. If the production rises (see case 11), a similar situation will arise. The reason for this phenomenon is the fact, that the production function specified so far implies constant returns to scale ($a_1 + a_2 = 1$). Substitution of (3.2.5.11) and (3.2.5.12) into (3.2.5.2) shows that $\Pi$ is homogeneous of the first-order in $q$.

A following situation to be studied is the effect of a rise in the f.o.b. prices of the inputs. The cases 12 and 13 indicate that a rise in the f.o.b.

Table 3.2.5.e

Data and solutions of neo-classical location problems

| | $q$ | $\gamma$ | $a_1$ | $a_2$ | $t$ | $t_1$ | $t_2$ | $x_M$ | $y_M$ | $x_1$ | $y_1$ | $x_2$ | $y_2$ | $p$ | $p_1^*$ | $p_2^*$ | solution $x^o$ | solution $y^o$ | solution $\Pi^o$ |
|---|---|---|---|---|---|---|---|---|---|---|---|---|---|---|---|---|---|---|---|
| 1 | 100 | 1 | 0·1 | 0·9 | 1 | 1 | 1 | 0 | 0 | 10 | 0 | 0 | 10 | 100 | 1 | 1 | 0 | 10 | 8818·365 |
| 2 | 100 | 1 | 0·3 | 0·7 | 1 | 1 | 1 | 0 | 0 | 10 | 0 | 0 | 10 | 100 | 1 | 1 | 0 | 10 | 8583·752 |
| 3 | 100 | 1 | 0·4 | 0·6 | 1 | 1 | 1 | 0 | 0 | 10 | 0 | 0 | 10 | 100 | 1 | 1 | { 0<br>10 | 10<br>0 } | 8418·754 |
| 4 | 100 | 1 | 0·5 | 0·5 | 1 | 1 | 1 | 0 | 0 | 10 | 0 | 0 | 10 | 100 | 1 | 1 | 0 | 10 | 8221·742 |
| 5 | 100 | 1 | 0·4 | 0·6 | 1 | 2·5 | 1 | 0 | 0 | 10 | 0 | 0 | 10 | 100 | 1 | 1 | 0 | 10 | 8174·889 |
| 6 | 100 | 1 | 0·4 | 0·6 | 1 | 25 | 1 | 0 | 0 | 10 | 0 | 0 | 10 | 100 | 1 | 1 | 10 | 0 | 7999·084 |
| 7 | 100 | 1 | 0·4 | 0·6 | 1 | 0·05 | 1 | 0 | 0 | 10 | 0 | 0 | 10 | 100 | 1 | 1 | 0 | 0 | 9028·244 |
| 8 | 100 | 1 | 0·4 | 0·6 | 1 | 0·15 | 1 | 0 | 0 | 10 | 0 | 0 | 10 | 100 | 1 | 1 | 0 | 0 | 8807·943 |
| 9 | 100 | 1 | 0·4 | 0·6 | 1 | 0·25 | 1 | 0 | 0 | 10 | 0 | 0 | 10 | 100 | 1 | 1 | 0 | 10 | 8641·130 |
| 10 | 50 | 1 | 0·4 | 0·6 | 1 | 1 | 1 | 0 | 0 | 10 | 0 | 0 | 10 | 100 | 1 | 1 | 0 | 10 | 4209·377 |
| 11 | 250 | 1 | 0·4 | 0·6 | 1 | 1 | 1 | 0 | 0 | 10 | 0 | 0 | 10 | 100 | 1 | 1 | 0 | 10 | 21046·885 |
| 12 | 100 | 1 | 0·4 | 0·6 | 1 | 1 | 1 | 0 | 0 | 10 | 0 | 0 | 10 | 100 | 3 | 3 | 0 | 10 | 7819·719 |
| 13 | 100 | 1 | 0·4 | 0·6 | 1 | 1 | 1 | 0 | 0 | 10 | 0 | 0 | 10 | 100 | 10 | 10 | 0 | 10 | 6211·340 |
| 14 | 100 | 1 | 0·4 | 0·6 | 1 | 1 | 1 | 0 | 0 | 10 | 0 | 0 | 10 | 100 | 20 | 20 | 1·547 | 3·352 | 4199·163 |
| 15 | 100 | 1 | 0·4 | 0·6 | 1 | 1 | 1 | 0 | 0 | 10 | 0 | 0 | 10 | 100 | 20 | 25 | 1·730 | 2·607 | 3617·860 |
| 16 | 100 | 1 | 0·4 | 0·5 | 1 | 1 | 1 | 0 | 0 | 10 | 0 | 0 | 10 | 100 | 1 | 1 | 0 | 10 | 7890·586 |
| 17 | 50 | 1 | 0·4 | 0·5 | 1 | 1 | 1 | 0 | 0 | 10 | 0 | 0 | 10 | 100 | 1 | 1 | 0 | 10 | 3986·411 |
| 18 | 250 | 1 | 0·4 | 0·5 | 1 | 1 | 1 | 0 | 0 | 10 | 0 | 0 | 10 | 100 | 1 | 1 | 0 | 10 | 19429·218 |
| 19 | 50 | 1 | 0·4 | 0·5 | 1 | 2·5 | 1 | 0 | 0 | 10 | 0 | 0 | 10 | 100 | 1 | 1 | 10 | 0 | 3805·379 |
| 20 | 50 | 1 | 0·4 | 0·5 | 1 | 25 | 1 | 0 | 0 | 10 | 0 | 0 | 10 | 100 | 1 | 1 | 10 | 0 | 3805·379 |
| 21 | 100 | 1 | 0·4 | 0·5 | 1 | 25 | 1 | 0 | 0 | 10 | 0 | 0 | 10 | 100 | 1 | 1 | 10 | 0 | 7499·537 |
| 22 | 100 | 1 | 0·3 | 0·6 | 1 | 0·4 | 0·2 | 0 | 0 | 5 | 0 | 0 | 10 | 100 | 20 | 25 | 0 | 0 | 2049·882 |

prices of the inputs lead to a decline in the profits (compared with case 3), whereas preliminary the optimum location remains equal. Only if a formidable rise in the input prices occurs (see case 14 and 15), a shift from the corner solution (0, 10) towards an interior solution will take place. Furthermore, the cases 14 and 15 show that the material pull of an input is stronger, as the freight rate of the input concerned is higher.

If the production function is not linear homogeneous, but if its degree of homogeneity is smaller than one, a decline in the profits (with respect to case 3) will result (case 16), since the production process itself has become less efficient. If the volume of production is decreased to 50 (case 17), or increased to 250 (case 18), the profits are also lower than in the successive corresponding situations 10 and 11. In the cases 17 and 18 the profits are not linearly proportional to the change in $q$ owing to the fact that the production function itself is not linear homogeneous (see the remarks above). The cases 16, 17 and 18 confirm the foregoing remarks, viz. that the input points with the highest production elasticity exert the strongest material pull. On the other hand, if the transportation costs of a certain input are rising, the corresponding input point may exert a material pull, that compensates its less efficient production conditions (see cases 19, 20 and 21).

Finally, case 22 represents a completely asymmetric situation: the production elasticities of the inputs are different, the freight rates are different, the input locations are not symmetric, and the input prices are not equal. In the latter case the optimal location is represented by the market point (the reason for this is that the freight rates of the inputs are rather low).

One may conclude that the grid search procedure described above is capable of solving in a rather efficient way the theoretical location problem of a single firm. The previous solutions show many corner solutions. This implies that one should always be aware of the possibility that the set of first-order conditions for a maximum (cf. [3.2.5.12]) is not sufficient. The fact that corner solutions appear to be a usual phenomenon in location analysis, is co-determined by the assumption of a neo-classical production function. It is precisely the $\sigma$-principle, which allows an easy shift from one corner-point to another.

Finally, the previous locational analysis can be directly generalized by taking account of economies of scale in the firm's production processes and of demand elasticities (see Nijkamp and Paelinck [1973]). In case of economies of scale, the market pull appears to be stronger as the scale elasticity is higher; in case of demand elasticities, the market pull appears to be stronger as the price elasticity of the consumer's decisions is rising.

### 3.2.6 *Conclusion*

Partial location theory, as set out in the previous sections, is indeed rather intricate. Once more one should be aware of a continuous interplay between general theoretical economics and regional economics. Spatial economic variables (for instance, the co-ordinates of the optimum location) are simultaneously determined with general economic variables (for instance, volumes of inputs and outputs, and their prices). A systematic way of attacking these kinds of problems is to transform the location problem either into general economic variables, or into spatial economic variables, and then to solve first this partial problem by means of the grid search procedure. Once the general economic problem or the spatial economic problem has been solved, the remaining variables can be derived in a straightforward way.

Finally, it should be noted that more operational methods of locational analysis are frequently based on a programming approach. This will be discussed in Ch.6.

## 3.3 General location theory

### 3.3.1 *Introduction*

As has already been set out in section 3.1, general location problems concentrate on the spatial division of all economic activities, taking account of interdependencies between these activities. It is obvious, that transportation costs and agglomeration factors play a key role in the spatial distribution of population and production centres. These extremely difficult problems require a set of simplifying hypotheses in order to present a systematic analysis. Based on such simplifying hypotheses, early attempts to attack the general location problem have been undertaken by Christaller (1933) with his central place theory, and by Lösch (1954; see also Ch.2) with his framework of superimposed hexagonal systems. A more modern study by Koopmans and Beckmann (1957) uses location programming models with indivisible plants in order to inspect the possibility of a spatial equilibrium system. In this so-called assignment problem (see Ch.6) a stable equilibrium situation could not always be found. A possible reason for such a disequilibrium (and thus for the absence of a price system on plant location, which sustains an optimal assignment) may be the fact that a spatial concentration of activities was excluded *a priori,* so that agglomeration advantages, which play a crucial role in interdependent location decisions, are abandoned. A systematic survey of general location problems is contained in Scott (1971).

A new impulse to research in the field of general location analysis was given by Tinbergen (1961; 1964), and by Bos (1964). Bos has elaborated Tinbergen's concepts, and the latter approach is the subject of subsection 3.3.2.

### 3.3.2 *The Tinbergen–Bos systems*

The Tinbergen–Bos systems for a general location analysis include many elements: multiple sectors, multiple production centres and multiple market areas. By means of these elements one may study the spatial dispersion of economic activities and its equilibrium conditions, as well as the degree of spatial concentration of certain complementary activities. In addition, one may study alternative combinations of firms and (production and consumption) centres within certain spatial systems by introducing general spatial preference functions for different location and market areas, based on minimization of production and transportation costs.

In order to explain the rather involved spatial picture of the dispersion of production (cf. also section 2.6.4), a set of simplifying assumptions is introduced by Tinbergen and Bos.

A first way of simplifying the spatial picture is a systematic classification of products, production centres and systems of centres. A *production centre* is a spatial point, where one or more products are fabricated. Therefore, a production centre may be characterized either by *one* economic activity (the case of a *separate* location) or by a set of *different* economic activities (the case of a *concentrated* location). A *system* of centres is a spatial set of production centres such that *all* products are fabricated within the spatial system. It is obvious, that production centres may be combined in different ways, so that many systems of centres can be created. Particularly, if one deals with a large number of products, one may find an enormous number of *centres* and *systems of centres.*

For instance, in case of 2 products the maximum number of *types* of centres, where production takes place, is 3, viz., a centre producing only product 1, a centre producing only product 2, and a centre producing product 1 and 2 together. These production centres are denoted by (1), (2) and (1, 2), respectively. On the basis of these three types of production centres one may combine these centres in order to create a *system* of centres, in which both product 1 and product 2 are available.

In a two-product-case 5 systems can be distinguished, as shown in table 3.3.2.a, which shows all possibilities of combining the centres (1), (2) and (1, 2) into a system of centres. Therefore, if only two products are fabricated, a spatial system of centres can be created by combining in 5

Table 3.3.2.a

System of production centres

| system \ type of production centre | (1) | (2) | (3)=(1, 2) |
|---|---|---|---|
| 1 | $x$ | $x$ | $x$ |
| 2 | $x$ | | $x$ |
| 3 | | $x$ | $x$ |
| 4 | $x$ | $x$ | |
| 5 | | | $x$ |

alternative ways the production centres of type (1), (2) and (1, 2). In case of 3 products one may find 7 possible types of centres. In general, $I$ products give rise to $\Sigma_{i=1}^{I} \binom{I}{i} = 2^I - 1$ possible types of production *centres.* One may compute, that the three-product-case leads to 109 possible systems of centres. It is obvious, that in the multiple-product-case an enormous number of possible industrial location systems can be distinguished, and that the problem of finding an optimal location (i.e., the co-ordinates) of each centre, and its market area, is almost unsurmountable.

On the basis of the foregoing classification of *centres* and *systems of centres* a set of simplifying hypotheses is introduced, in order to inspect the possibility of an optimal solution for the general, interdependent location problem, The following hypotheses are made:

H 1 There exist two types of activities, viz., agricultural and industrial activities, within a closed area of a circular shape.
H 2 The agricultural population and the agricultural production are spread continuously and homogeneously over the relevant area of a closed economy.
H 3 The agricultural products may serve as inputs for industries in production centres, and as final products for the population. The income, received from selling agricultural products, is spent on industrial products.

The industries are located in production centres, which are also the place of residence for the industrial workers. The location of these production centres and the settlement of industries is not liable to restrictions, and is based on the criterion of overall minimum transportation costs. All centres are regularly dispersed over the area concerned.

H 4 The industrial products can be used for intermediate and final deliveries.

H 5 The total number of industrial sectors is equal to $I$. Each firm within a certain industrial sector $i$ ($i = 1, \ldots, I$) has an equal minimum production size. At this minimum plant level the unit production costs are at a minimum. The production level of a firm can only be a discrete multiple of the minimum plant size, so that the costs of a production level above the minimum plant size are a multiple of the minimum production costs. The product prices are accounted for at a unit level.

H 6 The transportation costs of a given volume of commodities from one centre to a sufficiently large number of other centres are approximated by the costs of transporting the same volume from this centre over a surrounding continuous circular market with a constant density of demand.[3]

H 7 All people possess the same linear consumption function, in which the marginal rate of consumption is equal to the average rate of consumption. Therefore, the aggregate consumption function for products of sector $i$ is equal to:

$$Y_i = a_i \, Y \tag{3.3.2.1}$$

where $Y_i$, $a_i$ and $Y$ represent the total demand for products of sector $i$, the consumption rate for products of sector $i$, and national income, respectively.

H 8 If the minimum plant size of each firm in sector $i$, is denoted by $\bar{Y}_i$, the total number of firms (or elementary production units) required to produce $Y_i$ (denoted by $n_i$) is easily calculated as:

$$n_i = \frac{Y_i}{\bar{Y}_i} \tag{3.3.2.2}$$

in which $n_i$ is supposed to be an integer. The industrial sectors are ranked according to their number of firms $n_i$ as follows:

$$n_1 > n_2 > \ldots\ldots > n_I (=1) \tag{3.3.2.3}$$

The rank of an industry $i$ relates to a hierarchical ranking of the number of elementary production units $n_i$ in the industrial sector concerned.[4] In (3.3.2.3) industry 1 possesses the lowest rank, viz., 1, whereas industry $I$

possesses the highest rank (viz., $I$). Industry $i$ possesses a higher rank than industry $i'$, if $n_i < n_{i'}$. If $n_I > 1$, the area of the economy concerned is supposed to be subdivided into $n_I$ smaller sub-areas (or regions).

H 9 Each production centre contains only one production-unit (or firm) of the highest-ranking industry. The rank of the latter industry in the production centre concerned is called the *rank of the centre.*

In addition to the previous 9 hypotheses Tinbergen has presented 2 new hypotheses, which allow a more easy computation of the number of centres and their industrial composition. These hypotheses are:

H 10 In a certain centre of rank $i$ only the firm with the highest rank $i$ can export its industrial products (in addition to internal deliveries). These exports are earmarked only for centres of a lower rank and for the rural population. So there is no trade between centres of the same rank. This implies that the exports of a certain product $i$ are delivered only by centres of rank $i$. The remaining products within a centre are earmarked for internal use ('local centre function'). Agricultural products, however, can be imported to centres of any type whatsoever.

H 11 Each centre, characterized by a highest-ranking industry, contains also all industries with a lower rank $i'$ $(i < i')$.
Together with H 9 this hypothesis is called the *hierarchy*-hypothesis.

H 11 implies, that the number of types of centres is equal to the number of industrial sectors. Tinbergen had indicated that under certain conditions the previous simplifying hypotheses (H 1–H 11) may lead to an optimal dispersion of production, based on the criterion of minimum transportation costs. Bos has re-examined Tinbergen's proposition in a more general way, by inspecting the conditions under which a Tinbergen-system is optimal. He omitted H 10 and H 11, so that in Bos' point of view all industries within a certain production centre can export their products to other centres and to agriculture. Only a modified version of H 10 was maintained, viz.,

H 10* Trade between centres of the same rank is excluded.

It is obvious that the number of possible spatial systems of centres will increase if H 10 and H 11 are deleted. On the other hand, a (preliminary) assumption was made, that intermediate deliveries are excluded (the case with input–output relationships will be considered later on). Therefore, instead of H 4 one has to introduce for the moment the simplified hypothesis:

H 4* The industrial production is earmarked for final use.

Finally, a last hypothesis was introduced, viz.,

H 11* There exists a balance of trade (product) equilibrium in all production centres.

On the basis of H 1–H 3, H 4*, H 5–H 9, H 10* and H 11* Bos has created a model which describes the spatial economic structure of the area concerned. In order to clarify the essential ideas of this model, one may construct a table, which represents the possible different types of production centres and their number for a two-product case. If the agricultural sector is denoted by a lower index 0, if the total number of centres of a certain type $k$ within the spatial system is denoted by $n^k$, and if the number of firms within industry $i$ in a centre of type $k$ is denoted by $n_i^k$, one may set up table 3.3.2.b, which shows the relationship between the type of a centre on the one hand, and the number of centres and the number of firms for each industry in a centre on the other hand. It is evident that agriculture does not contain any industrial firm. The second

Table 3.3.2.b

| | Type of centre | | | |
|---|---|---|---|---|
| | (0) | (1) | (2) | (3)=(1, 2) |
| Number of centres | – | $n^1$ | $n^2$ | $n^3$ |
| Number of firms of industry 1 per centre | – | 1 | – | $n_1^3$ |
| Number of firms of industry 2 per centre | – | – | 1 | 1 |

column of table 3.3.2.b shows that there are $n^1$ centres of type 1, each of which contains only one firm (viz., of industrial sector 1; see H 9). The third column can be interpreted in a similar way. The fourth column represents 'mixed' centres, composed of industry 1 and 2. Since industry 2 possesses the highest rank (see also [3.3.2.3]), there is only one firm of the second industrial sector in each centre of type 3 (see H 9). It is obvious that the rank of a centre of type 3 is equal to 2 (the highest-ranking industry). Table 3.3.2.b can be used to combine the various types of production centres (and their numbers) into a set of alternative systems of centres (see table 3.3.2.a).

With the aid of the data of table 3.3.2.b a model for the two-product case can be constructed, which describes the essential relationships within the economy concerned on the basis of the foregoing hypotheses. First the following variables are defined:

$Y$ : total income of the relevant closed system.
$Y_i$ : total production (= income) of industry $i$ ($i = 0, 1, \ldots, I$).
$Y^k$ : total income of all centres of type $k$ ($k = 0, 1, \ldots, K$).
$E_i^k$ : total export of product $i$ by all centres of type $k$ ($i$ is omitted, if a centre of type $k$ includes only one industry).
$E_i^{kk'}$ : total export of product $i$ from all centres of type $k$ to all centres of type $k'$ ($k' = 0, 1, \ldots, K$).

The general system of locations can now be described by means of four types of relationships, viz. trade equations, product equations, income equations, and rank relationships.

The *trade* equations relate to each type of centre (1, 2 and 3). These trade equations impose the condition (see H 11*), that the imports of each type of centre are equal to the exports. For instance, a centre of type 1 imports products from sector 0 and sector 2. The propensities to consume these successive products are equal to $a_0$ and $a_2$. Therefore, the total imports in all centres of type 1, $M^1$, is equal to:

$$M^1 = (a_0 + a_2)\, Y^1 \qquad (3.3.2.4)$$

By abandoning savings the following condition is valid:

$$a_0 + a_1 + a_2 = 1 \qquad (3.3.2.5)$$

or:

$$a_0 + a_2 = 1 - a_1 \qquad (3.3.2.6)$$

By substituting (3.3.2.6) into (3.3.2.4), and by taking account of the condition of trade equilibrium (i.e., $M^1 = E^1$), one finds:

$$E^1 = (1 - a_1)\, Y^1 \qquad (3.3.2.7)$$

In a similar way one finds for centres of type 2:

$$E^2 = (1 - a_2)\, Y^2 \qquad (3.3.2.8)$$

Finally, centres of type 3 need only imports of agricultural products. Therefore, total imports in centres of type 3, $M^3$, are:

$$M^3 = a_0\, Y^3 \qquad (3.3.2.9)$$

Since the total imports should be equal to the total exports of centres of type 3 (i.e., $M^3 = E^3 = E_1^3 + E_2^3$), one obtains:

$$E_1^3 + E_2^3 = a_0 \; Y^3 \qquad (3.3.2.10)$$

The second set of relationships relates to the *product equilibrium* for each sector within the system. For instance, the exports of the agricultural sector are equal to the total demand for agricultural products in all centres of type 1, 2 and 3. Therefore, agricultural exports are equal to:

$$\begin{aligned} E^0 &= a_0 \; (Y^1 + Y^2 + Y^3) \\ &= a_0 \; (Y - Y^0) \end{aligned} \qquad (3.3.2.11)$$

The products of industrial sector 1 can be exported only to centres of type 0 (i.e., the agriculture) and to centres of type 2 (see H 10*). The exports of product 1 can be delivered by centres of type 1 and by centres of type 3. Therefore, total exports of product 1 are:

$$E^1 + E_1^3 = a_1 \; (Y^0 + Y^2) \qquad (3.3.2.12)$$

In a similar way one may prove that exports of product 2 are:

$$E^2 + E_2^3 = a_2 \; (Y^0 + Y^1) \qquad (3.3.2.13)$$

Next, the *income* equations are dealt with. Since savings are abandoned, the production in each sector is equal to the total demand for the products in the sector concerned. For instance, the agricultural production is equal to the demand for agricultural products, i.e.,

$$Y^0 = a_0 \; Y \qquad (3.3.2.14)$$

The industrial sectors yield some complications. The products of sector 1 are fabricated in centres of type 1 and of type 3. The total demand for products of sector 1 is $a_1 Y$. Since the first sector contains $n_1$ firms, the average income per firm in the first sector is equal to $a_1 n_1^{-1} Y$. Since according to table 3.3.2.b a centre of type 1 contains only one firm of the first sector, and since the total number of centres of type 1 is equal to $n^1$, the total number of firms in sector 1, located in centres of type 1, is equal to $n^1$. Therefore, total income of centres of type 1 is equal to:

$$Y^1 = a_1 \frac{n^1}{n_1} \; Y \qquad (3.3.2.15)$$

In a similar way income of centres of type 2 is calculated as:

$$Y^2 = a_2 \frac{n^2}{n_2} \; Y \qquad (3.3.2.16)$$

The income of the 'mixed' centres of type 3 is not calculated separately since it is the residual of the following income indentity:

$$Y \equiv Y^0 + Y^1 + Y^2 + Y^3 \qquad (3.3.2.17)$$

Finally, the *rank* relationships can be derived with the aid of table 3.3.2.b. The number of firms in sector 1 is equal to the total number of firms in all centres of type 1 (i.e., $n^1$) and the number of firms in sector 1, located in centres of type 3. Since the number of firms in sector 1, located in a centre of type 3, is equal to $n_1^3$, and since the total number of centres of type 3 is equal to $n^3$, one can easily calculate the total number of firms in sector 1 as:

$$n_1 = n^1 + n^3 n_1^3 \qquad (3.3.2.18)$$

In a similar way one can derive the number of firms in sector 2 as:

$$n_2 = n^2 + n^3 \qquad (3.3.2.19)$$

The foregoing set of relationships describing the structure of the economy consists of 12 equations, viz. (3.3.2.7), (3.3.2.8), (3.3.2.10)–(3.3.2.19). The variables $Y$, $n_1$ and $n_2$ are supposed to be predetermined, so that 14 unknown variables remain, viz. $Y^0$, $Y^1$, $Y^2$, $Y^3$, $E^0$, $E^1$, $E^2$, $E^3$, $E_1^3$, $E_2^3$, $n^1$, $n^2$, $n^3$, and $n_1^3$. Therefore, the previous system of 12 equations in 14 unknown variables possesses 2 degrees of freedom. A unique solution can not be obtained, unless one introduces an additional criterion to solve these degrees of freedom. This additional criterion is the *minimization of transportation costs within the spatial system.* Two alternative assumptions concerning the transportation costs can be made.

A first simple approach is to assume, that the costs of transporting products between centres are proportional to the volume of the products to be transported. This proportionality factor is denoted by $\Theta_i$ ($i = 0, 1, 2$) for each sector $i$. This is a very simplified version of H 6. Then the total transportation costs $T$ within the spatial system are equal to:

$$T = \Theta_0 E^0 + \Theta_1 (E^1 + E_1^3) + \Theta_2 (E^2 + E_2^3) \qquad (3.3.2.20)$$

To simplify the calculation one may introduce:

$$\mu^1 = \frac{n^1}{n_1} \qquad (3.3.2.21)$$

and:

$$\mu^2 = \frac{n^2}{n_2} \qquad (3.3.2.22)$$

where the new variables $\mu^1$ and $\mu^2$ satisfy the conditions: $0 \leqslant \mu^1 \leqslant 1$ and $0 \leqslant \mu^2 \leqslant 1$. The last two variables are now considered as free variables.

By substituting (3.3.2.21) and (3.3.2.22) into (3.3.2.15) and (3.3.2.16), one finds:

$$Y^1 = a_1 \mu^1 Y \qquad (3.3.2.23)$$

and:

$$Y^2 = a_2 \mu^2 Y \qquad (3.3.2.24)$$

Next, by substituting (3.3.2.14) into (3.3.2.11), and next (3.3.2.14) and (3.3.2.24) into (3.3.2.12), and (3.3.2.14) and (3.3.2.23) into (3.3.2.13), respectively, one finds the successive export equations:

$$E^0 = a_0 (1 - a_0) Y \qquad (3.3.2.25)$$

$$E^1 + E_1^3 = a_1 (a_0 + a_2\mu^2) Y \qquad (3.3.2.26)$$

$$E^2 + E_2^3 = a_2 (a_0 + a_1\mu^1) Y \qquad (3.3.2.27)$$

Substitution of (3.3.2.25)–(3.3.2.27) into the relationship for the transportation costs (3.3.2.20), and division by $Y$ provides the result:

$$\frac{T}{Y} = \Theta_0 a_0 (1 - a_0) + \Theta_1 a_1 (a_0 + a_2\mu^2) + \Theta_2 a_2 (a_0 + a_1\mu^1) \qquad (3.3.2.28)$$

The latter expression contains the unknown (free) variables $\mu^1$ and $\mu^2$. The average transportation costs are at a minimum, if:

$$\mu^1 = \mu^2 = 0 \qquad (3.3.2.29)$$

or, after substitution of (3.3.2.29) into (3.3.2.22) and (3.3.2.21):

$$n^1 = n^2 = 0 \qquad (3.3.2.30)$$

Substitution of (3.3.2.30) into (3.3.2.19) and (3.3.2.18) yields the ultimate result:

$$n^3 = n_2 \qquad (3.3.2.31)$$

and:

$$n_1^3 = \frac{n_1}{n^3} = \frac{n_1}{n_2} \qquad (3.3.2.32)$$

The outcome (3.3.2.30) shows that the second and third column of table 3.3.2.b is empty, so that only the fourth column remains. The number of centres of type 3, and the number of firms of industry 1 in each centre of type 3 are calculated according to (3.3.2.31) and (3.3.2.32).

The previous results permit the derivation of the following proposition:

P 3.5 A system of centres, obtained by minimizing the transportation costs (proportional to the value of the flows of commodities), is composed only of 'mixed' centres.

A similar proposition can be derived, if the transportation costs between two centres are calculated as the maximum costs of transporting the commodities in one of both directions (the case of dominant flows). The previous results can also be shown to be valid, if $I > 2$.

A second way of dealing with the transportation costs is to assume, that the transportation costs depend on the average distance (cf. H 6). The transportation costs over a circular area are specified already in (3.2.3.4). If the transportation costs per ton-mile of the products of industry $i$ are denoted by $t_i$, the total costs of transporting the products of industry $i$ from one centre of type $k$ to all centres of type $k'$ are equal to (see H 6):

$$T_i^{kk'} = \tfrac{2}{3}\, \pi t_i\, \varphi_i^{kk'} (r_i^{kk'})^3 \qquad (3.3.2.33)$$

where $\varphi_i^{kk'}$ is the average density of demand for product $i$, as it results from all centres of type $k'$ with respect to the centre concerned of type $k$, and where $r_i^{kk'}$ is the average distance, over which product $i$ from the centre of type $k$ has to be shipped to all other centres of type $k'$. The transportation costs *within* a centre are supposed to be negligible. It is obvious, that the total transportation costs, caused by all products $i$ exported by *all* centres of type $k$ to all centres of type $k'$, are equal to:

$$\begin{aligned} T_i^{\cdot k'} &= n^k\, T_i^{kk'} \\ &= \tfrac{2}{3}\, n^k\, \pi\, t_i\, \varphi_i^{kk'} (r_i^{kk'})^3 \end{aligned} \qquad (3.3.2.34)$$

where $n^k$ is the total number of centres of type $k$. Next, one may define:

$$R = (n^k)^{1/2}\, r_i^{kk'} \qquad (3.3.2.35)$$

and:

$$E_i^{kk'} = \pi \varphi_i^{kk'} (r_i^{kk'})^2 \qquad (3.3.2.36)$$

where $R$ represents a weighted average distance in the spatial system, and $E_i^{kk'}$ the total export of product $i$ from a certain centre of type $k$ to all centres of type $k'$ (see also [3.2.3.3]). Total exports of product $i$ from all centres of type $k$ to all centres of type $k'$ are denoted by $E_i^{\cdot k'}$, so that (cf. [3.3.2.34]):

$$\begin{aligned} E_i^{\cdot k'} &= n^k\, E_i^{kk'} \\ &= n^k\, \pi \varphi_i^{kk'} (r_i^{kk'})^2 \end{aligned} \qquad (3.3.2.37)$$

Substitution of (3.3.2.35) and (3.3.2.37) into (3.3.2.34) gives as a result for total transportation costs:

$$T_i^{k'} = \tfrac{2}{3}\, t_i\, R\, E_i^{k'} (n^k)^{-\frac{1}{2}} \qquad (3.3.2.38)$$

It is obvious that total transportation cost $T$ within the spatial system is equal to the sum total of transportation cost between all types of centres for all products, i.e.,

$$T = \sum_{i=1}^{I} \sum_{k'=0}^{K} T_i^{k'} \qquad (3.3.2.39)$$

The latter formula can be elaborated for certain special cases, for instance, the case of complete concentration of activities, the case of complete decentralization, and intermediate cases. The tedious derivation of all these cost-minimizing procedures will not be dealt with here, but can be found in Bos (1964). Only the general conclusion, drawn from the previous analysis, will be reported here. It appears that minimization of transportation costs, which depend on distance and volume of transport, leads to a great variety in the dispersion patterns of economic activities. The following proposition can be derived:

P 3.6 The dispersion of economic activities is very sensitive with respect to the value of the freight rate:
(a) a relative high value of the freight rate for agricultural products leads to a decentralization of the industrial production over a large number of small centres.
(b) a relative high value of the freight rate of high-ranking industries (with a small number of production units) leads to a concentration of the production in a small number of larger centres.
(c) a relative high value of the freight rate of a low ranking industry (with a large number of production units) leads to a spatial system, which tends to support H 10 (the Tinbergen-hypothesis, that the exports of product $i$ are only delivered by centres of rank $i$).

The previous proposition is intuitively plausible, since it is obvious that a high value of $t_0$ exerts a heavy burden on $T$ and hence induces dispersion. On the other hand, a high value of $t_i$ (with $i$ a high-ranking industry) induces concentration, while the Tinbergen-system is an intermediate case.

The models described previously can be refined by considering the possibility of intermediate deliveries between industries. Bos (1964) elaborated a situation where certain industries produced *only* intermediate products. These intermediate products had to be shipped to one or a few other industries. In this case an equilibrium situation depends on three factors: the transportation costs of the industrial output, the transportation costs of direct and indirect inputs, and the transportation costs of the consumer goods to be supplied to the industrial workers. Given the assumption of a Tinbergen-system, the spatial structure of centres and industries can be described by means of an extensive set of relationships (see Bos [1964]). It appears that the introduction of input–output relationships leads to a less rigid spatial structure than the original Tinbergen-system with firms producing only final goods.

### 3.3.3 *Evaluation of Tinbergen–Bos systems*

In this subsection the compatibility of a general location system (for instance, the previous Tinbergen–Bos systems) with the theory of entrepreneurial behaviour (for instance, minimization of transportation costs, maximization of profits) will be investigated. On the basis of some simple hypotheses an attempt will be made at evaluating the Tinbergen–Bos systems.

Suppose an economy consisting of two industries, one of which (1) produces only intermediate products, while the other one (2) produces only final goods. Agriculture is spread homogeneously all through space, and the agricultural products are exported to the production centre(s). The purpose of this analysis is to derive the conditions, under which both industries will locate together in one centre, or will locate separately in two centres, if a criterion of minimum transportation costs per unit of product in each centre is introduced. The following hypotheses are made:

H 1 A constant and homogeneous dispersion of agriculture.
H 2 The existence of two industries producing intermediate and final products, respectively.
H 3 Transportation costs per product proportional to distance.
H 4 Minimization of transportation costs.

It is obvious that, in principle, a joint or a separate location for each of the industries is possible. Four possible cases concerning separate or combined location for both industries are investigated below.

The first case is concerned with a *separate location of industry 1* in a certain centre. The total transportation costs in case of separate location for industry 1 consist of two components, viz. transportation costs of agricultural inputs to the centre and transportation costs of final products to be imported from the location of industry 2.

The transportation costs of *agricultural* products, needed as inputs in the centre where industry 1 is located, are denoted by $T_0^1$. If one assumes a circular area, $T_0^1$ is according to (3.3.2.33) equal to:

$$T_0^1 = \tfrac{2}{3}\, \pi\varphi_0\, t_0 r_{01}^3 \tag{3.3.3.1}$$

where $\varphi_0$ represents a constant density of supply of agricultural products (i.e., a unit supply per unit of agricultural area), $t_0$ the freight rate of agricultural products, and $r_{01}$ the radius of the agricultural supply area around city 1. In case of an equilibrium situation total supply $\pi\varphi_0\, r_{01}^2$ (i.e., supply density times circular area) is equal to demand for agricultural products $a_0 Y^1$, where $Y^1$ is income of centre 1:

$$\pi\varphi_0\, r_{01}^2 = a_0 Y^1 \tag{3.3.3.2}$$

By substituting (3.3.3.2) into (3.3.3.1) one obtains:

$$T_0^1 = \tfrac{2}{3}\, t_0 a_0 r_{01} Y^1 \tag{3.3.3.3}$$

which links the transportation costs of agricultural products to the income of the first centre.

Next, the transportation costs of *final* products to be imported from centre 2 to centre 1, are denoted by $T_2^1$. If one assumes a distance $d_{12}$ between the two centres, $T_2^1$ is equal to:

$$T_2^1 = t_2 d_{12} a_2 Y^1 \tag{3.3.3.4}$$

where $t_2$ is the freight rate of the products from industry 2. Then the total transportation costs $T^1$ for centre 1 are:

$$T^1 = T_0^1 + T_2^1 \tag{3.3.3.5}$$

or:

$$T^1 = \tfrac{2}{3}\, t_0 a_0 r_{01} Y^1 + t_2 d_{12} a_2 Y^1 \tag{3.3.3.6}$$

If one denotes the transportation costs per unit of product 1 by $\tau^1$, one obtains:

$$\begin{aligned} \tau^1 &= \frac{T^1}{Y^1} \\ &= \tfrac{2}{3}\, t_0 a_0 r_{01} + t_2 a_2 d_{12} \end{aligned} \tag{3.3.3.7}$$

The second case is concerned with a *joint location of industry 1* and *2* in the same centre. In case industry 1 and 2 are located together in one centre, transportation costs $T^*$ are only determined by agricultural products. The radius of the agricultural supply area ($r_0^*$) exceeds the previous radius $r_0$ (in case of a separate location), because a joint location leads to an increase in demand for agricultural products in the centre concerned. The resulting higher transportation costs have to be spread equally over the production levels $Y^1$ and $Y^2$ of the successive industries. Therefore, the total transportation costs are:

$$T^* = \tfrac{2}{3}\, t_0 a_0 r_0^* Y^* \qquad (3.3.3.8)$$

where $Y^*$ is defined as:

$$Y^* = Y^1 + Y^2 \qquad (3.3.3.9)$$

If one denotes the unit transportation costs by $\tau^*$, one obtains

$$\tau^* = \tfrac{2}{3}\, t_0 a_0 r_0^* \qquad (3.3.3.10)$$

If one abandons external economies between industry 1 and 2, one may assume that industry 1 will choose a location, where the unit transportation costs are at a minimum; in other words, industry 1 will choose the minimum of $\tau^1$ and $\tau^*$. The minimum value of $\tau^1$ or $\tau^*$ determines, whether industry 1 will choose a separate or a joint location, respectively. Since the *optimal* location of industry 1 is determined by the relative ratio of $\tau^1$ and $\tau^*$, one should inspect whether:

$$\frac{\tfrac{2}{3}\, t_0 a_0 r_{01} + t_2 a_2 d_{12}}{\tfrac{2}{3}\, t_0 a_0 r_0^*} \gtrless 1 \qquad (3.3.3.11)$$

or:

$$\frac{r_{01}}{r_0^*} + \frac{3\, t_2 a_2 d_{12}}{2\, t_0 a_0 r_0^*} \gtrless 1 \qquad (3.3.3.12)$$

The latter expression depends obviously on the relative size of the respective ratios of $r_{01}$ and $r_0^*$, $a_2$ and $a_0$, $t_2$ and $t_0$, and $d_{12}$ and $r_0^*$. High values of these respective ratios tend to result in a joint location, because then $\tau_1 > \tau^*$. On the contrary, if $t_0 \rightarrow \infty$, industry 1 will always settle separately, because in this case only the first term of (3.3.3.12) remains. This term is always smaller than 1, since $r_{01} < r_0^*$.

A slight modification in the previous analysis can be made in the following way: instead of determining the average transportation costs over the total income in the joint centre, one may calculate the transportation costs, resulting from spending the income of sector 1 on agricultural products. In this case one determines the transportation costs $T_1^*$ of sector 1, caused by the use of agricultural products, as:

$$T_1^* = \tfrac{2}{3}\, t_0 a_0 r_0^* Y^1 \qquad (3.3.3.13)$$

Next, the average transportation costs $\tau_1^*$, to be paid by sector 1, are obviously equal to (3.3.3.10), i.e.,:

$$\tau_1^* = \frac{T_1^*}{Y^1} = \tfrac{2}{3}\, t_0 a_0 r_0^* \qquad (3.3.3.14)$$

In a way similar to that described above the unit transportation costs for sector 1 can be determined, both for a separate and for a joint location.

In case of a *separate* location the transportation costs to be paid by sector 2 are according to (3.3.3.6) equal to:

$$T^2 = \tfrac{2}{3}\, t_0 a_0 r_{02}\ Y^2 + t_1 d_{12} a_{12}\ Y^2 \qquad (3.3.3.15)$$

where $a_{12} Y^2$ represents the total inputs of intermediate products from industry 1 to industry 2 ($a_{12}$ is a usual input–output coefficient). The average transportation costs for sector 2 in case of a separate location are:

$$\tau^2 = \tfrac{2}{3}\, t_0 a_0 r_{02} + t_1 d_{12} a_{12} \qquad (3.3.3.16)$$

A *joint* location leads to the following average transportation costs for sector 2 (see also [3.3.3.10]):

$$\tau^* = \tfrac{2}{3}\, t_0 a_0 r_0^* \qquad (3.3.3.17)$$

An *optimal* location for industry 2 is again determined by comparing the values of $\tau^2$ and $\tau^*$, i.e., by inspecting whether:

$$\frac{r_{02}}{r_0^*} + \frac{3\, t_1 d_{12} a_{12}}{2\, t_0 a_0 r_0^*} \gtrless 1 \qquad (3.3.3.18)$$

Concerning (3.3.3.18) the same comments can be made as concerning (3.3.3.12).

On the basis of (3.3.3.12) and (3.3.3.18) one may draw some important conclusions concerning concentrated or dispersed patterns of location. In case of a high $t_0$, both expressions are smaller than 1. This implies, that high freight rates for agricultural products give rise to a decentralization of production centres, which corresponds with the conclusions in proposition P 3.6.

In case both expressions give a different outcome ([3.3.3.12] $> 1$ and [3.3.3.18] $< 1$, or reversely), a deviating result is obtained. In this case one industry prefers a joint location, while the other one prefers a separate location. The latter disequilibrium situation may occur, if $a_{12}$ and $a_2$ on the one hand, and $t_1$ and $t_2$ on the other hand, do not move in a symmetric way with respect to $t_0$. The previous analysis gives rise to the following proposition:

P 3.7 Certain market structures (concentration or deconcentration) imply a continuous disequilibrium situation. An equilibrium can only be obtained under special institutional conditions, for instance, with the aid of regional intervention (subsidies, etc.).

The conclusion is that some spatial structures, resulting in a Tinbergen–Bos system from a *general* criterion (for instance, minimization of total transport costs for all firms), do not necessarily agree with the outcomes, resulting from some *individual* preference function (for instance, minimization of individual average transportation costs). The proposition just derived bears some resemblance with the Beckmann–Koopmans case referred to in subsection 3.3.1. The disequilibrium situation is, in a sense, a game-like situation. Such a situation causes locational problems, that cannot be handled with the tools used until now. In the following section some attention will be paid to the use of *game theory* in location analysis.

## 3.4 Location problems and game theory

### 3.4.1 *Introduction*

Frequently, economic phenomena in a spatial context show oligopolistic market structures: spatial factors cause a restricted mobility for production factors, goods, locations and migrations. For that reason regional economics often deals with a limited number of interdependent location decisions, leading to oligopolistic or duopolistic location decisions. One possibility of attacking these kinds of problems is a game-theoretic approach. Some elements of game theory are discussed in Appendix 3B.

In this section some attention will be paid to the usefulness of game theory for location strategies. Other contributions in this field can be found *inter alia* in Isard (1956, 1969), Jacot (1963) and Stevens (1961).

Let us first define a *location game* as a decision game, in which all participants from a group (mostly entrepreneurs) desire to locate some activity somewhere in an area, and in which the optimal location is highly sensitive to the location decisions of the other participants, for instance, because of external (dis)economies. A complete knowledge of the relations, that describe the set of possible outcomes of the location strategies (the 'pay-off matrix'), is assumed. The *location space,* i.e., the set of all relevant locations for a firm, depends on the firm's activity matrix (inputs and outputs). Given this activity matrix, a firm tries to maximize its revenues by choosing an optimal location (taking account of the $\alpha$–, $\sigma$– and $\epsilon$-principle). In this section a location game with a *fixed* and with a *mixed* strategy will successively be dealt with.

### 3.4.2 *The Hotelling problem*

The well-known problem of Hotelling (1929) is concerned with the relationship between prices, market areas and locations of two ice-cream vendors on the beach. This is a duopolistic location problem in a rectilinear market area. Both vendors produce the same homogeneous good, and attempt to determine a location, where the revenues of each individual vendor are at a maximum. The equilibrium location appears to be, under certain conditions, a concentration of both vendors in the centre of the market.

At first, a set of hypotheses is assumed for a game-theoretic approach to the foregoing Hotelling problem. Particular reference is made to the study of Stevens (1961).

H 1 The existence of a rectilinear market area.
H 2 The existence of two competitive sellers *A* and *B*.
H 3 The production of only one homogeneous commodity.
H 4 A uniform dispersion of consumers along the market line with a unit density of demand.
H 5 Uniform transportation costs per ton-mile.
H 6 Inelastic demand.
H 7 A mill price policy.
H 8 Maximization of the revenues by the sellers; minimization of the transportation costs by the consumers.

Since a continuous market line implies an infinite number of locations, it is not possible to allow *continuous* adjustments of locations in a game with a *finite* number of strategies. Therefore, a finite and odd number of relevant locations is assumed, spaced equally along the rectilinear market line. All buyers are assumed to purchase one unit of the commodity concerned, whatever may be the distance. If both sellers choose a joint location, the available market is assumed to be split up equally. In order to obtain a zero-sum game the elements of the pay-off matrix do not indicate absolute revenues, but differences in revenues between the two sellers at their respective locations. Then the sum of both pay-off matrices yields a zero matrix. The sales can be determined by means of figure 3.4.2.a, representing the rectilinear market, along which each seller is competing for a maximum market share. The set of relevant locations is, respectively, denoted by $P_0$, $P_1$, . . . . . . . , $P_I$. Each line sector $P_i P_{i+1}$ is

Fig. 3.4.2.a

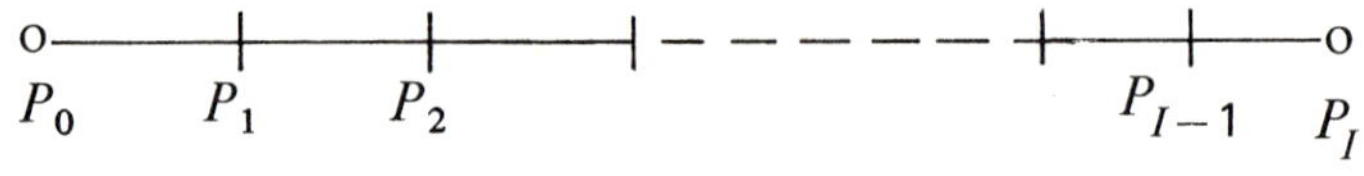


supposed to contain $N$ consumers, so that the total number of consumers is equal to $NI$. If the f.o.b. price is equal to $p^*$, total revenues of both firms are equal to $p^*NI$. If firm $A$ is located in $P_i$, and firm $B$ in $P_{i'}$ (with $i' > i$), their respective revenues $R_A$ and $R_B$ are equal to:

$$R_A = p^*\{N\ \ i + \tfrac{1}{2}(i'-i)\} \qquad (3.4.2.1)$$

and:

$$R_B = p^*\ N\{\ (I-i') + \tfrac{1}{2}(i'-i)\} \qquad (3.4.2.2)$$

If one considers the $I$+1 locations as $I$+1 strategies, a pay-off matrix for seller $A$ can be constructed, the elements of which are the differences in the two respective sales. Thus, the typical element $P^A_{ii'}$ of the pay-off matrix of firm $A$ is:

$$P^A_{ii'} = p^*\ N(i+i'-I)\quad ,\quad i'>i \qquad (3.4.2.3)$$

It is obvious, that the game is symmetric, and that the two sellers are completely interchangeable. The pay-off matrix can be proved to have a saddle-point, if $i=i'=\tfrac{1}{2}I$, in other words: the optimal location, which yields a stable solution, is formed by the centre of the market. This can be illustrated by assuming, that $p^*=1$ and $N=1$, and that there are 5 relevant locations with respective co-ordinates 0, 10, 20, 30 and 40 (cf. Stevens [1961]). By making use of (3.4.2.3) one can easily calculate the pay-off matrix (3.4.2.4). A saddle-point can be found by means of the minimax theorem. A stable equilibrium point is formed by the centre of the market. Therefore, one may conclude that *duopolistic location problems tend to result in a concentrated location at the centre of the market, if demand is completely inelastic.* The foregoing conclusion may be an explanation for the frequent spatial juxtaposition of a number of duopolistic or oligopolistic competitors, for instance, the concentration of air line offices in the main street of a city.

| A \ B | 0 | 10 | 20 | 30 | 40 | Row minima |
|---|---|---|---|---|---|---|
| 0 | 0 | –30 | –20 | –10 | 0 | –30 |
| 10 | 30 | 0 | –10 | 0 | 10 | –10 |
| 20 | 20 | 10 | 0 | 10 | 20 | 0 |
| 30 | 10 | 0 | –10 | 0 | 30 | –10 |
| 40 | 0 | –10 | –20 | –30 | 0 | –30 |
| Column maxima | 30 | 10 | 0 | 10 | 30 | |

(3.4.2.4)

It should be noted, that this minimax solution for a duopoly is not compatible with optimal social welfare. The total revenues of both firms are equal in any location, but the total transportation costs of the consumers would be at a minimum in the case of a location at the points 10 and 30.

A more realistic assumption, considered by Stevens (1961), is a modification of H 6, viz. by assuming that the consumers will buy more goods, if the transportation costs to be paid are low. One may even assume, that the consumers at a large distance from a firm do not buy any goods at all. In this case the two sellers are faced with a moderately *elastic demand.* Their joint sales are not constant (like in the previous case), but depend on their respective locations. The result is that the centre of the market is not necessarily an equilibrium point. A stable equilibrium point is now co-determined by the consumer's demand function and the transport rate. For instance, suppose the transportation costs are \$0·05 per unit good per unit distance. Furthermore, H 6 is modified in the sense, that each consumer buys 2 units of a good, if its c.i.f. price is between \$1 and \$1·25; one unit, if it is between \$1·25 and \$1·50, and no unit, if it exceeds \$1·50. Then the appropriate pay-off matrix can easily be determined for all relevant locations of the firms. Obviously, there are 9 minimax solutions for this problem, viz. 3 strategies for each of the competing sellers. However, the previous problem was formulated in *differences* in revenues and not in *absolute* revenues. It can easily be seen, that the total revenues for each seller are higher in case of a separate location at the points 10 and 30 (viz. 30 units), since at these points there is no need to share the market. Therefore, rational competitors will choose only between 10 and 30, so that the number of rational possibilities is equal to 2. Which of both firms,

| A \ B | 0 | 10 | 20 | 30 | 40 | Row minima |
|---|---|---|---|---|---|---|
| 0 | 0 | −15 | −15 | −15 | 0 | −15 |
| 10 | 15 | 0 | 0 | 0 | 15 | 0 |
| 20 | 15 | 0 | 0 | 0 | 15 | 0 |
| 30 | 15 | 0 | 0 | 0 | 15 | 0 |
| 40 | 0 | −15 | −15 | −15 | 0 | −15 |
| Column maxima | 15 | 0 | 0 | 0 | 15 | |

(3.4.2.5)

however, will settle at 10 and 30, is indeterminate, because both firms are equal in this example. Thus, one may conclude, that *the existence of an elastic demand with respect to c.i.f. prices tends to cause a spatial dispersion of economic activities.*

### 3.4.3 *Mixed location strategies*

The problem of mixed strategies will be elucidated by means of the following location game (cf. Stevens [1961]): suppose a beach owner has available for lease 3 sales points (*a, b* and *c*) for ice-cream with respective expected profitabilities of 3, 4 and 2 units, while there are 2 candidate-sellers *A* and *B*. Each of these sellers is able to serve more than one point simultaneously. Furthermore, both sellers are assumed to possess equal funds in order to pay the amount due to lease. In addition, they are assumed to exhaust their funds entirely, if one or more locations are obtained. In case of more locations the funds of a certain seller are assumed to be equally divided among the respective locations (though a generalization to bids proportional to location profitabilities is possible). Evidently, the beach owner will let on lease his sales points to the highest-bidding seller. The corresponding pay-off matrix in differential profits for *A* is calculated in (3.4.3.1), where *ab, bc* and *abc* denote the corresponding simultaneous locations of a certain seller. The calculation of the elements of this pay-off matrix can be illustrated by means of the entry (*ac, bc*), i.e., a situation where *A* bids on location *a* and *c*, while *B* bids on location *b* and *c*. Evidently, *A* will win location *a*, since *B* did not bid on it; analogously, *B* will obtain location *b*. Since both sellers bid with equal funds on location *c*, neither gains a relative advantage from

| A \ B | a | b | c | ab | bc | ac | abc |
|---|---|---|---|---|---|---|---|
| a | 0 | −1 | 1 | −1 | −3 | 1 | −3 |
| b | 1 | 0 | 2 | 1 | 2 | −1 | −1 |
| c | −1 | −2 | 0 | −5 | −2 | −1 | −5 |
| ab | 1 | −1 | 5 | 0 | 1 | 2 | 5 |
| bc | 3 | −2 | 2 | −1 | 0 | 1 | 3 |
| ac | −1 | 1 | 1 | −2 | −1 | 0 | 1 |
| abc | 3 | 1 | 5 | −5 | −3 | −1 | 0 |

(3.4.3.1)

location *c* (where again the assumption is made that a joint location implies equal profits). Therefore, the advantage of seller *A* with respect to seller *B* is 3 minus 4 units. The value of element (*c, bc*) is calculated in the same way. Evidently, seller *B* will obtain location *b*. On the other hand, seller *A* has now more funds available for location *c* than seller *B*, since *B* has already allocated one half of his funds for obtaining location *b*. Therefore, *A* will obtain point *c*; the differential profit of *A* is 2 minus 4 units. In the same way all elements can be calculated.

The previous pay-off matrix does not have a saddle-point solution, so that the solution should be a mixed strategy. By a generalization of the approach presented in Appendix 3B one finds a mixture of probable locations, viz. a mixture of locations *b, ab* and *ac* with corresponding probabilities: $p_b = 0{\cdot}5$; $p_{ab} = 0{\cdot}25$ and $p_{ac} = 0{\cdot}25$; the other locations receive a zero probability.

### 3.4.4 *Conclusion*

Obviously, the foregoing examples are often far beyond reality, though a number of adaptations can be carried out in a straightforward way, for instance, changes in the entrepreneurial or consumer behaviour. In spite of the simple examples, they can yet provide insight in a number of oligopolistic location strategies, and, more in particular, in the underlying behavioural patterns. In this way one may get a better understanding of the long-term policy problems of a firm, since often the result of a game-theoretic framework is a coalition or a deliberation between the oligopolistic participants. In addition, another reason why some attention has been paid to game theory is its frequent presence in recent urban and regional simulation studies, in which the urban and regional development is simulated on the basis of actions and reactions of the various groups (consumers, planners, entrepreneurs, etc.) in that area.

Other applications of game theory are contained *inter alia* in Gould (1968) (in relation to rural settlement patterns), Isard (1969) (in relation to the Weberian agglomeration problem; see also Ch.2) and in Quirin (1967) (in relation to the location strategies of banks).

The use of game theory for location decisions has some drawbacks. If one uses mixed strategies (with various probabilities for each location), the relevance of game theory is rather small, since the major part of the location decisions leads to one unique (i.e., non-varying) location. In addition, in the field of non-zero sum games with more than two or three participants, one encounters large computational problems, so that, mostly, a game-theoretic approach is only useful in case of a very limited number of participants.

## 3.5 Locational problems in differentiated space

### 3.5.1 *Introduction*

The location problems discussed in section 3.3 were of an abstract, mathematical nature. They did not take into account the differentiated space. Instead, they were based on the assumption of a homogeneous space, each element of which was, in principle, appropriate for the firm's location. On the other hand, the previous approach was extremely useful, since it permitted the derivation of a set of reasonable propositions concerning location problems. In general, such an abstract analysis is not directly applicable to real-world situations. Therefore, practical location problems require some adaptations of the approach set out previously. The main adaptation results from the presence of the *differentiated* space. In subsection 3.5.2 and 3.5.3 two alternative methods for selecting optimum locations in a differentiated space will be dealt with, successively. It is obvious, that a more practical approach to location problems should take account of all relevant location factors (and their financial consequences). Therefore, in figure 3.5.1.a a systematic, figurative scheme is presented, containing a set of relevant factors to be considered by a firm. The arrows, linking the successive location factors, denote the direction of influence of each individual location factor. Figure 3.5.1.a shows once more the close link between regional economics and general economics.

Figure 3.5.1.a is a schematic representation of location factors, but it is

Fig. 3.5.1.a A systematic scheme of location factors

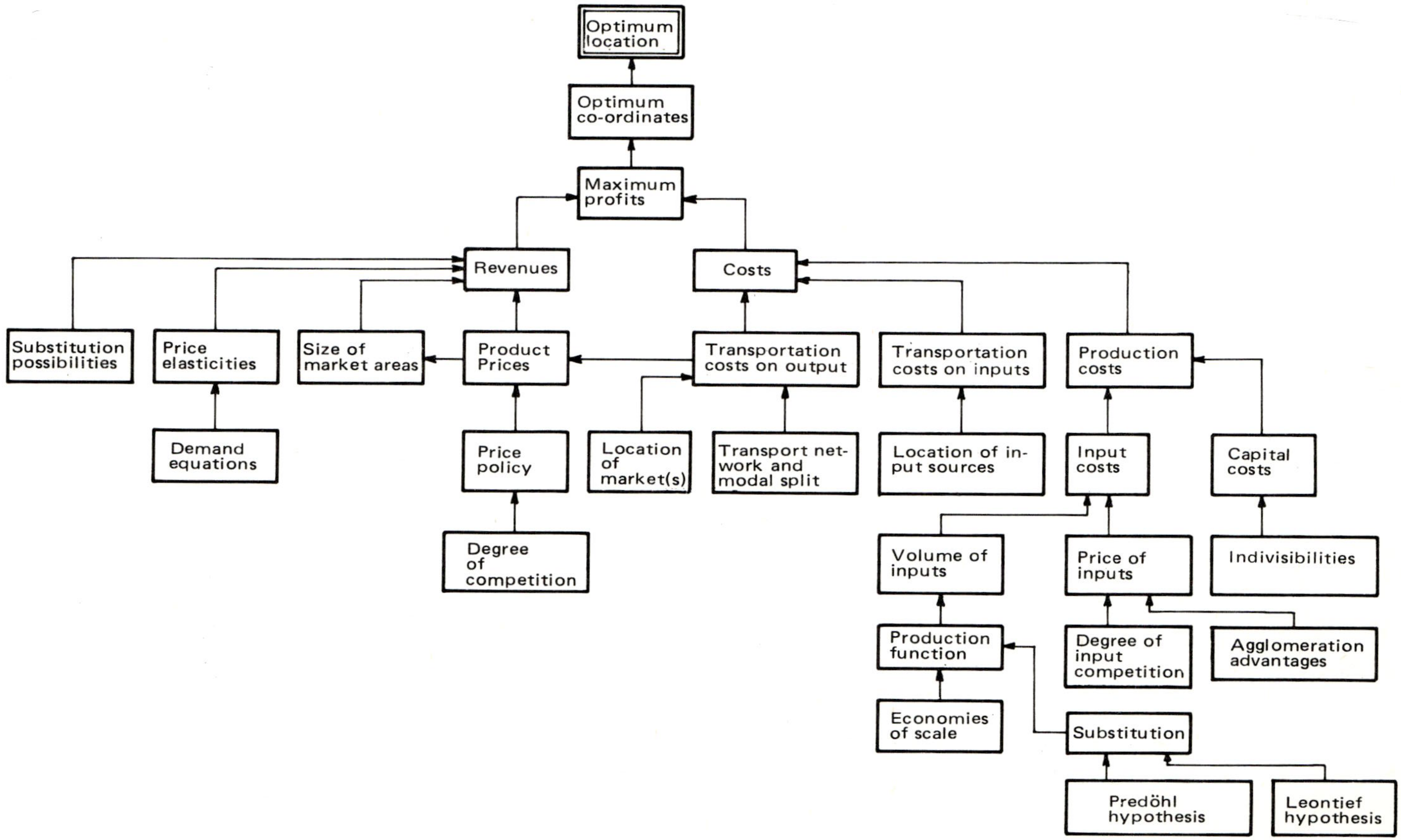

not an operational scheme that explains the relative importance of each successive factor. A more operational contribution in this field is contained in Harris and Hopkins (1972); their approach is based on an interregional, multi-sectoral model that is designed to explain various stimuli to industrial location.

By means of a multivariable regression analysis the relative effects of the successive explanatory variables on industrial location as measured by the change in industrial output are estimated. Explanatory variables are *inter alia* wages, transportation costs, land costs, revenues, agglomeration and infrastructural factors, labour force etc. There are 99 industrial sectors in the regression model, for each of which a regression analysis is performed. The total set of regions used in the regression analysis is formed by 3,112 county-type areas in the United States. For each sector a cross-section analysis over all regions is carried out.

The form of the regression equations used to explain the regional change in sectoral output is:

$$\Delta q_j^r = a_{0_j} + a_{1_j}\tau_j^r + \sum_{j'} \beta_{j'j}\Theta_{j'j} + a_{2_j}w_j^r + a_{3_j}v^r + a_{4_j}q_j^r + a_{5_j}I_j^r + a_{6_j}d^r + \sum_{j''} \gamma_{jj''}b_{jj''}^r$$
$$+ \sum_{j'} \delta_{j'j}s_{j'j}^r + \epsilon_j^r \qquad \begin{array}{l} j = 1, \ldots, J \\ r = 1, \ldots, R \end{array} \qquad (3.5.1.1)$$

The variables used in the previous regression analysis have the following meaning:

$\Delta q_j^r$ : change in output of industry $j$ in region $r$.
$\tau_j^r$ : transport cost of shipping a marginal unit of output from industry $j$ out of region $r$.
$\Theta_{j'j}^r$ : transport cost of obtaining a marginal unit of input from supplying industry $j'$ into region $r$.
$w_j^r$ : annual wage rate in industry $j$ in region $r$.
$v^r$ : value of land in region $r$.
$q_j^r$ : output of sector $j$ in region $r$.
$I_j^r$ : equipment investment by sector $j$ in region $r$.
$d^r$ : population density in region $r$.
$b_{jj''}^r$ : the volume of sector $j''$ in region $r$ buying goods from industry $j$.
$s_{j'j}^r$ : output of supplying sector $j'$ in region $r$ selling goods to industry $j$.
$\epsilon_j^r$ : error term for industry $j$ in region $r$.

The regression coefficients of industry $j$ are $a_{ij}$ ($i$=0,..,6), $\beta_{j'j}$, $\gamma_{jj''}$ and $\delta_{j'j}$, estimated by cross-section analysis.

The results appeared to depend on the specific industry concerned, albeit that transport costs appear to exert a major influence. Further investigations along these lines will be reported on in Ch. 5.

### 3.5.2 *Location problems and network analysis*

In this subsection a first method of considering location problems in a differentiated space will be dealt with. A systematic way in which a practical location analysis can be carried out is provided by the graph theory (see also subsection 1.6.3). This method, proposed among others by Ponsard (1966), Guigou (1971) and Schärlig (1971, 1973), selects an optimal location in a differentiated space on the basis of a set of feasible points, which constitute the nodes of a transport network. Such a discrete method implies a selection among a finite number of points. The advantages of this method are: the elimination *a priori* of impossible or less desirable points (for instance, owing to the physical conditions prevailing in certain points), and the possibility of taking account of spatial differentiations in costs and revenues. Therefore, the application of network analysis requires *a priori* a selection of relevant candidate-locations. The distances between each pair of candidate-locations can be measured on the axes of the network. In principle, the selection of an optimal location is very simple: by inspecting separately each candidate-point and by calculating the revenues and costs in each of these points (for different transport modes, for different input sources, for different output markets, and for different input combinations) the maximum maximorum of the profits over all relevant points can be found. This implies that the choice of the optimal location requires the selection of all relevant candidate-points, the elimination of less appropriate points, and the successive inspection of all remaining points.

It is obvious, however, that the computational work associated with these search procedures is considerable. The main problem in these network procedures is of a combinatorial nature: how to reduce the combinatorial problem of inspecting the enormous set of all relevant locations to a manageable one? An efficient solution procedure for such combinatorial problems requires a systematic comparison of all feasible locations. Before setting out such a systematic solution procedure the location problem at hand will be specified more accurately.

Suppose a firm is seeking for a maximum-profit location. The production process requires a set of inputs $z_i$ $(i = 1, \dots, I)$ in order to produce a set of outputs $q_j$ $(j = 1, \dots, J)$. It is assumed, that each input $z_i$ can be provided by several sources, so that the firm should also make a choice among the various input sources. The same assumption is made for the outputs: the firm can deliver each kind of product to several markets. Therefore, the problem of selecting an optimum location should select simultaneously both an optimal set of input sources and an optimal set of output markets. Therefore, the location problem in a differentiated space requires the construction of three subsets: the subset of relevant, feasible locations, the subset of relevant input sources, and the subset of relevant output markets. The f.o.b. prices of inputs and of outputs are assumed to be given.[5] The f.o.b. prices will, in general, differ at each place. Furthermore, the unit transportation costs of inputs and of outputs between all relevant points of the network are also assumed to be known. These unit transportation costs may also differ for each axis on the network. Therefore, the c.i.f. prices of inputs and outputs in each relevant point can be calculated. Furthermore, the demand markets for the outputs, and the supply markets of the inputs are supposed to have an infinitely elastic capacity. Therefore, the following assumptions are made concerning the location problem:

H 1 A differentiated space, represented by a network.
H 2 A finite, known set of feasible locations.
H 3 Several input sources of each input.
H 4 Several output markets for each output.
H 5 Given f.o.b. prices of inputs and outputs.
H 6 Given unit transportation costs on inputs and outputs.
H 7 A completely elastic demand and supply market.
H 8 Profit maximization.

The selection procedure itself requires a number of successive steps. The first step attempts to select the most advantageous supply market of each input for each feasible location. The second step attempts to find the most advantageous output market for each product for each feasible location. Next, the optimal location is found by confronting the costs and revenues at each feasible location.

The first step to be undertaken is the selection of optimal input markets for each feasible location. The f.o.b. price of each input $z_i$ $(i = 1, \ldots, I)$ at all input sources is known. Because one knows for a given noteworthy location the set of all sources of a certain input, one can easily calculate for that location which source of the input concerned leads to a minimum c.i.f. price. A similar calculation can be made for the c.i.f. prices of each relevant input of the location concerned. Having performed these calculations one knows for the location concerned the set of optimal, i.e. cost-minimizing, sources. Next, one may draw for this location a so-called 'optimal input spider', which indicates an optimal transport network of the inputs for this feasible location. For instance, if a firm requires four inputs, the optimal input spider possesses four 'arms' each of which represents an optimal transportation route for one of the inputs (see figure 3.5.2.a). In a similar way *each* feasible location in figure 3.5.2.a could be provided with an optimal spider for the input sources.

Fig. 3.5.2.a   An optimal input spider in a transport network

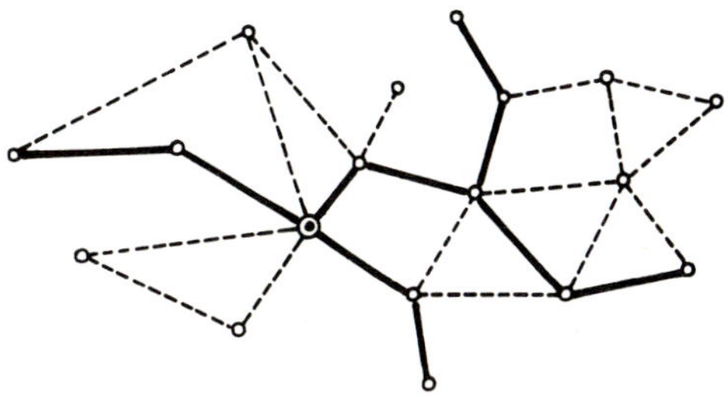

On the basis of the optimal input spider one knows at each feasible location, in principle, the iso-cost lines of the inputs (fixed costs are assumed to be known). Given the total demand for the firm's products, the volume of production can be determined. If one assumes a production process with fixed technical coefficients, the input requirements can be calculated in a straightforward way. If one assumes a neo-classical production function, one should determine the isoquant corresponding to the known production volume. The point of tangency of this isoquant and the iso-cost curve determines an optimal input mix.

The second step is the selection of the output markets. In a similar way as described above one can derive an optimal 'output spider', which indicates for each feasible location the optimal route, along which each product should be shipped from that location to a selected number of output markets. These routes are chosen such that they yield a maximum c.i.f. price for each product. Thus, the optimal output spider of a certain location represents an optimal distribution network of the production at that location.

Until now the determination of optimal volumes of inputs and outputs at each feasible location is dealt with superficially. A first and practical way to find an optimal production volume is to choose the maximum production volume allowed by the firm's capacity or by the total demand at the output markets. In the latter case one has to estimate the demand relationships of each product at each point. A second (more theoretical) method is to assume a technical relationship between inputs and outputs by means of a neo-classical production function (including substitution between inputs). The optimal production level is fixed at the level, where the marginal costs are equal to the marginal revenues. The optimal input mix can be determined in a similar way.

The third and last step is the calculation of the maximal profits for each feasible location on the basis of the optimal product and input mix determined previously by means of the optimal input and output spiders. The location yielding maximum profits of all feasible locations is selected as the optimal location of the firm.

It is obvious, that the previous analysis can be extended in various ways, for instance, by introducing demand relationships, economies of scale and process industries. It should be noted, that the solution method presented above is rather practical, and can be used for location problems of a different nature. If one assumes fixed technical coefficients, one can solve the previous location problems in a formal way by means of linear programming techniques. These solution procedures (for instance, the well-known transportation problems) are dealt with in Ch.6.

### 3.5.3 *Location analysis by comparison of industrial and regional profiles*

Another systematic way in which location problems in a differentiated space can be attacked is a comparison of *industrial* and *regional profiles* (see Paelinck and Jaumotte [1966]). This approach, which might be complementary to the previous network procedure, attempts to confront the locational requirements of a certain industry or firm with relevant factors supplied by certain feasible locations.

One starts with the construction of an *industrial* profile of the activity, for which an optimal location has to be determined. This industrial profile can be represented in a table, which encompasses all aspects of an industrial project, which are relevant for a certain localization (for instance, availability of production factors, and neighbourhood of market). Next, the firm is asked to assign to each of the locational factors a score, which indicates the degree to which the locational factor concerned is preferred. For instance, these scores can be represented on an ordinal scale of increasing priority as: – –, –, 0, +, + +. The element – – represents a strongly negative preference for the factor concerned, whereas the element + + represents a strongly positive preference. In this way an industrial profile is obtained, which indicates a series of weights for the various locational factors, which are relevant for the firm's location decisions (see table 3.5.3.a). In fact, the industrial profile can be considered as the 'demand' side of the location decisions.

In a similar way one can construct a *regional* profile. This table contains the same elements as the industrial profile. A regional profile is, in fact, the 'supply' side of location decisions. By assigning scores to the degree, to which the elements concerned are available or present in the location concerned, one obtains an attraction profile of a certain feasible location (see table 3.5.3.a).

Table 3.5.3.a

Industrial profiles vs. regional profiles

| Locational factors | | Industrial profile | Regional profile |
|---|---|---|---|
| A | *Production factors* | | |
| | Environment | + | ++ |
| | Land | | |
| | – availability | ++ | + |
| | – quality | – | 0 |
| | Raw materials | | |
| | – availability | ++ | ++ |
| | – quality | + | ++ |
| | Etc. | | |
| B | *Economic and technical factors* | | |
| | Markets | – – | 0 |
| | Auxiliary services | + | + |
| | Etc. | | |
| C | *Social factors* | | |
| | Tertiary services | – | – – |
| | Housing | + | 0 |
| | Etc. | | |

By constructing such a regional profile for a number of feasible and relevant locations one may compare the various regional profiles with the industrial profile of the activity concerned. Should there be a close correspondence between the regional profile of a certain location and the industrial profile, the location concerned is very appropriate for attracting that industry. This location analysis is also very useful in case of location problems of non-profit institutions, for instance, governmental services, airports, and so forth.

In general, a unique conclusion in favour of a maximum-profit location is not possible. The use of an ordinal scale obviates a numerical calculation of revenues and costs at the various locations. Furthermore, the technical relationships (for instance, a production function) cannot be represented adequately by means of an industrial profile. This analysis, however, might be complementary to the previous methods, as it takes into account a large series of (sometimes qualitative) factors. In addition, the ultimate number of feasible locations can be considerably reduced by means of a comparison of industrial and regional profiles.

Solution methods for selecting the optimal location by 'vector comparison' are described *inter alia* in Guigou (1974) ('multi-criteria decision rules'). An application of such a multi-criteria analysis to the selection of public projects is contained in Nijkamp (1975); for a purely qualitative solution see Paelinck (1975).

## Appendix 3A Introduction to production theory

In this section some elementary results from neo-classical production theory will be derived, which relate to the location problems of sections 3.2.4 and 3.2.5.

In the first place, the demand function for production factors will be determined. Assume a single firm producing a single product. Each unit of product requires a certain combination of inputs. The way in which the inputs can be combined in a technical production process is reflected by the production function:

$$q = f(\mathbf{z}) \tag{3A.1}$$

where $q$ represents the volume of output and $\mathbf{z}$ a vector of elements $z_i$ ($i = 1, \ldots, I$), each of which represents the volume of a certain input $i$. The firm is assumed to minimize total production costs $C$, defined as:

$$C = \sum_{i=1}^{I} p_i z_i + c^* \tag{3A.2}$$

where $p_i$ represents the known unit costs of input $i$ and $c^*$ the fixed production costs. The unknown factor mix $\mathbf{z}$ can be determined by constructing a Lagrangean function $L$:

$$L = C - \lambda \{ f(\mathbf{z}) - q \} \tag{3A.3}$$

where $\lambda$ is a Lagrange multiplier indicating the marginal costs of a change in the production volume. The first-order conditions for a minimum are:

$$\frac{\partial L}{\partial z_i} = p_i - \lambda \frac{\partial f(\mathbf{z})}{\partial z_i} = 0 \quad , \forall i \tag{3A.4}$$

and:

$$\frac{\partial L}{\partial \lambda} = f(\mathbf{z}) - q = 0 \tag{3A.5}$$

The second-order conditions are also assumed to be satisfied.
Relationship (3A.4) leads to the conclusion that in the case of an optimal factor mix the ratio of the factor prices is equal to the ratio of the marginal products. Relationships (3A.4) and (3A.5) constitute a system of $(I + 1)$ equations in $(I + 1)$ unknown variables $z_i$ $(i = 1, \ldots, I)$, and $\lambda$. In principle, each variable $z_i$ can be determined as a function of the known variables $p_{i'}(i' = 1, \ldots, I)$ and $q$, so that the ultimate general expression for the demand function of factor $i$ is written as:

$$z_i = g_i(\mathbf{p}, q) \tag{3A.6}$$

where $\mathbf{p}$ is a vector with elements $p_i$.

Next, it will be proved that the mutual cross price derivations of two production factors are equal, i.e.,

$$\frac{\partial z_i}{\partial p_{i'}} = \frac{\partial z_{i'}}{\partial p_i} \quad , i, i' = 1, \ldots, I; i \neq i \tag{3A.7}$$

A small change $dp_i$ in $p_i$ has the following effect upon (3A.4):

$$dp_i = \lambda \sum_{i'=1}^{I} \frac{\partial^2 f(\mathbf{z})}{\partial z_i \partial z_{i'}} dz_{i'} + \frac{\partial f(\mathbf{z})}{\partial z_i} d\lambda \tag{3A.8}$$

In a similar way a small change in $q$ allows one to write (3A.5) as a total differential:

$$dq = \sum_{i=1}^{I} \frac{\partial f(\mathbf{z})}{\partial z_i} dz_i \tag{3A.9}$$

By dividing (3A.8) by $\lambda$, there results:

$$\frac{dp_i}{\lambda} = \sum_{i'=1}^{I} \frac{\partial^2 f(\mathbf{z})}{\partial z_i \, \partial z_{i'}} \, dz_{i'} + \frac{\partial f(\mathbf{z})}{\partial z_i} \, \frac{d\lambda}{\lambda} \tag{3A.10}$$

Relationships (3A.9) and (3A.10) can be transformed into matrix notation as a symmetric bordered Hessian:

$$\left[\begin{array}{c|ccc} 0 & \frac{\partial f(\mathbf{z})}{\partial z_1} & \cdots & \frac{\partial f(\mathbf{z})}{\partial z_I} \\ \hline \frac{\partial f(\mathbf{z})}{\partial z_1} & & & \\ \vdots & & \left[\frac{\partial^2 f(\mathbf{z})}{\partial z_i \partial z_{i'}}\right] & \\ \frac{\partial f(\mathbf{z})}{\partial z_I} & & & \end{array}\right] \left[\begin{array}{c} \frac{d\lambda}{\lambda} \\ \hline dz_1 \\ \vdots \\ dz_I \end{array}\right] = \left[\begin{array}{c} dq \\ \hline \frac{dp_1}{\lambda} \\ \vdots \\ \frac{dp_I}{\lambda} \end{array}\right] \tag{3A.11}$$

If the structural matrix of (3A.11) is non-singular, its inverse can easily be calculated. This inverse matrix is also symmetric and is denoted by $F$, so that one obtains:

$$\left[\begin{array}{c} \frac{d\lambda}{\lambda} \\ \hline dz_1 \\ \vdots \\ dz_I \end{array}\right] = \left[ \quad F \quad \right] \left[\begin{array}{c} dq \\ \hline \frac{dp_1}{\lambda} \\ \vdots \\ \frac{dp_I}{\lambda} \end{array}\right] \tag{3A.12}$$

Each element $dz_i$ and $dz_{i'}$ from the first vector of (3A.12) can now be written as a linear combination of $dq$ and $dp_i/\lambda$ ($i = 1, \ldots, I$). If one assumes, that only $dp_{i'} \neq 0$, and that $dq=0$ and $dp_i=0$ ($i = 1, \ldots, I; i \neq i'$), $dz_i$ is a function only of $dp_{i'}/\lambda$. Then $dz_i$ can be written as:

$$dz_i = f_{ii'} \frac{dp_{i'}}{\lambda} \tag{3A.13}$$

where $f_{ii'}$ is the element from the matrix $F$, which is associated with $dz_i$ and $dp_{i'}/\lambda$. In a similar way one may write:

$$dz_{i'} = f_{i'i} \frac{dp_i}{\lambda} \tag{3A.14}$$

It has already been stated that $F$ is a symmetric matrix, so that:

$$f_{ii'} = f_{i'i} \tag{3A.15}$$

Therefore, by combining (3A.13)–(3A.15) one may conclude that relationship (3A.7) is valid. The previous result can also be proved by applying Cramer's rule to (3A.12).

Finally, it can be proved that the sum of the cross elasticities of the inputs with respect to input prices is equal to zero, i.e.:

$$\sum_{i=1}^{I} E_{i'i} = \sum_{i=1}^{I} \frac{\partial z_{i'}}{\partial p_i} \frac{p_i}{z_{i'}} = 0 \tag{3A.16}$$

The proof of this statement is based on (3A.4) and (3A.6). The demand function of inputs (see [3A.6]) is homogeneous of the degree zero in the input prices: an equal percentage change of all input prices does not affect the input mix. This can easily be derived from (3A.4) since:

$$\frac{\partial f(\mathbf{z})\ \partial z_i}{\partial f(\mathbf{z})\ \partial z_{i'}} = \frac{P_i}{P_{i'}} \tag{3A.17}$$

It is obvious, that the production costs themselves undergo a change, if the input prices rise. Furthermore, by making use of Euler's theorem for homogeneous functions the following relationship is valid:

$$\rho z_{i'} = \sum_{i=1}^{I} \frac{\partial z_{i'}}{\partial p_i} P_i \tag{3A.18}$$

where $\rho$ is the homogeneity degree (equal to zero here). Therefore, by dividing (3A.18) by $z_{i'}$ one obtains:

$$0 = \sum_{i=1}^{I} \frac{\partial z_i'}{\partial p_i} \frac{p_i}{z_i'} = \sum_{i=1}^{I} E_i'{}_i \tag{3A.19}$$

## Appendix 3B Elements of game theory

Many economic decision problems can be formulated as the *maximization of an objective function* subject to a number of side-conditions. Examples may be found in the consumption theory, the production theory, the theory of economic policy etc. In other situations, especially in conflict situations with a restricted competition, a pure maximization procedure does not give an adequate description of the decision process (see, for instance, the duopolistic location problems in Ch.2). These conflict situations may occur, when a decision maker does not have a full control of the outcome of his decision, because this outcome depends on the strategies of his competitor(s). These situations can be described in terms of actions and counteractions of a limited number of participants. For instance, a certain maximizing strategy of participant *A* evokes such a counteraction of participant *B*, that the result of both strategies falls below the original maximum aimed at by *A*. The latter result leads *A* to a modification of his original strategy. Whether a stable solution will arise, depends on the joint strategies of *A* and *B*. Problems of this kind may be investigated by means of *game theory*. In this Appendix only a simple introduction will be given. A more extensive treatment of game theory can be found *inter alia* (in decreasing degree of difficulty) in Von Neumann and Morgenstern (1953), Luce and Raiffa (1957), Allen (1960), Baumol (1961), Williams (1954), Theil, Boot and Kloek (1965).

At first, some definitions will be presented:

- strategy : course of action.
- game : set of rules and procedures.
- play : particular realization of the game leading to a definite result.
- choice : decision in favour of a certain alternative.
- payment : revenue or loss at the end of each play.
- finite game : game with a finite number of strategies.
- zero-sum game : game, where the sum of payments is zero.

– pay-off matrix : matrix indicating the amount received or lost by *A* in realizing a certain strategy, given the strategy of *B*. See, for instance, the pay-off matrix **P** in (3B.1).

$$\mathbf{P} = \begin{bmatrix} P_{11} & \cdots & P_{1N} \\ \vdots & & \vdots \\ P_{M1} & \cdots & P_{MN} \end{bmatrix} \tag{3B.1}$$

Every element $p_{mn}$ ($m = 1, \ldots, M$; $n = 1, \ldots, N$) denotes the revenue of a certain strategy $m$ by *A*, given a strategy *n* carried out by *B*. Thus, *A* and *B* have, respectively, *M* and *N* possible strategies. Since for every combination of *m* and *n* the pay-off matrix represents the revenue (or loss) of *A*, the elements of **P** may be positive, zero or negative. In case of a zero-sum game the pay-off matrix of *B* is equal to minus the transposed pay-off matrix of *A*, because the total sum of all payments should be equal to zero.

The use of game theory may be illustrated by means of the following example. Participant *A* is supposed to possess the following (*a priori* known) pay-off matrix, where *A* can choose among 2 actions and *B* among 3 actions:

| A \ B | 1 | 2 | 3 |
|---|---|---|---|
| 1 | 7 | 8 | 4 |
| 2 | 4 | 7 | 2 |

(3B.2)

It appears, that *A* will always make profits, whatever may be the strategy of *B*. For example, if *A* chooses strategy 2 and *B* strategy 1, *A*'s profit is 4 units. *B*, however, will try to minimize his loss by a suitable choice of action. In determining a strategy, *A* will take account of the worst action that *B* can take. Thus, *A* decides on the best (*maximum*) strategy, allowing for the worst (*minimum*) reaction of *B*. At the same time, *B* is making his decisions with an eye on what *A* will do. The action of each participant is then based on *minimax* considerations, a minimum and a maximum being jointly involved in the decisions. Whether the game has a stable outcome or not depends on whether the minimax position aimed at by one player is consistent with that of the other. In the previous example, it is intuitively clear that $A$ will choose the first strategy (i.e., the first row) because in this case his profit is always at a maximum. $B$ will choose strategy 3 (i.e. the third column), yielding the least loss for $B$. Combination of both actions results in a profit for $A$ to an amount of 4.

Mathematically, this two-person zero-sum may be formalized via the *minimax-theorem*: the pay-off matrix **P** yields a stable solution, if the maximum of the row-minima is equal to the minimum of the column-maxima; in other words, if

$$\max_i (\min_j p_{ij}) = \min_j (\max_i p_{ij}) \tag{3B.3}$$

The equilibrium point itself is called a saddle-point, since a minimum and a maximum solution coincide at a saddle-point. In our example the solution can be obtained by means of the following table:

| A \ B | 1 | 2 | 3 | Row minima |
|---|---|---|---|---|
| 1 | 7 | 8 | 4 | ④ |
| 2 | 4 | 7 | 2 | 2 |
| Column maxima | 7 | 8 | ④ | |

(3B.4)

Thus, the result is a fixed strategy 1 by $A$ and a fixed strategy 3 by $B$. This can also be checked by considering $B$'s pay-off matrix. In this case a *pure* or *fixed* strategy can be derived, if both participants play at the same time. Often, however, this simple procedure does not give rise to a saddle-point, as will be illustrated in (3B.5). Suppose the following pay-off matrix:

| A \ B | 1 | 2 | Row minima |
|---|---|---|---|
| 1 | +1 | −1 | −1 |
| 2 | −1 | +1 | −1 |
| Column maxima | +1 | +1 | |

(3B.5)

The latter case shows that $\min_j (\max_i p_{ij})$ and $\max_i (\min_j p_{ij})$ do not always coincide, so that apparently a stable outcome cannot be obtained. Only by a modification in the structure of the problem one can now find a solution, viz. in the following sense: which probabilities have to be attached to the strategies of $A$ and $B$ in order to maximize (minimize) their expected revenues (losses)? In other words, a fixed (pure) strategy has to be replaced by a combination of strategies, while each strategy is weighted with a certain probability. This leads to a so-called *mixed-strategy*. In the foregoing example, it is clear that an equilibrium situation will arise, if both $A$ and $B$ attach a probability of one half to either strategy; this results in an expected revenue (respectively expected loss) of zero for both players (suppose the game is played often enough).

These remarks may be clarified by means of the following example:

| A \ B | 1 | 2 | Row minima |
|---|---|---|---|
| 1 | +2 | −1 | −1 |
| 2 | −1 | +1 | −1 |
| Column maxima | 2 | 1 | |

(3B.6)

The minimax procedure of (3B.3) appears to give no *fixed* solution. Therefore, one has to use *mixed* strategies, the solution of which is derived below. Suppose strategy 1 of $A$ has a probability $p_1$. Since probabilities add to 1, strategy 2 of $A$ has a probability $1-p_1$. $A$'s expected revenue ($E_A$), given strategy 1 of $B$, is equal to:

$$E_A = 2.p_1 - 1\,(1-p_1) = 3p_1 - 1 \tag{3B.7}$$

In the case of strategy 2 of $B$, the expected revenue of $A$ is:

$$E_A = -1.p_1 + 1.\,(1-p_1) = -2p_1 + 1 \tag{3B.8}$$

Combinations of both equations results in figure 3B.a. $A$ tries to find an optimal mixed strategy, viz. a value of $p_1$, for which the expected revenue is still at a maximum in the most unfavourable case. Point $S$, the point of intersection of the two lines, satisfies exactly this condition. Thus, one may conclude that, if $A$ assigns a probability 2/5 to strategy 1, his expected revenue is at a maximum, viz. 1/5.

An analogous method is applicable to $B$. If one compares a *fixed* and a *mixed* strategy, one observes that the essence of the choice problem has been changed. In the first case, only one of the available strategies has to be selected, while in the second case one attempts to specify the probabilities of all actions in a mixed strategy.

Fig. 3B.a The optimum of a mixed strategy

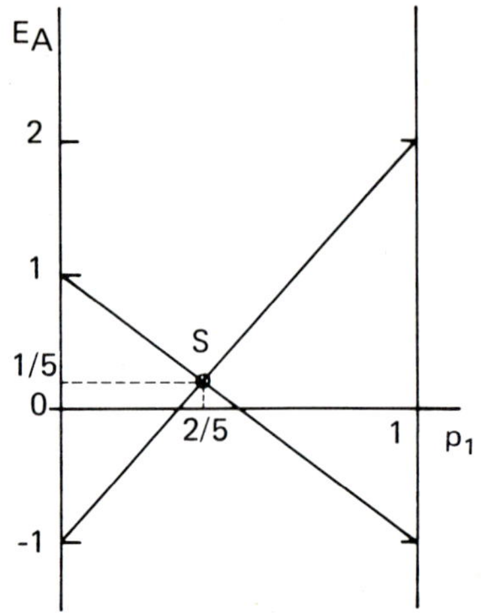


In case of more than two participants, or more than two strategies, a simple geographical solution cannot be obtained. Then linear programming methods may be useful, viz. by maximizing a certain objective function subject to a number of constraints (non-negativity constraints, minimum expected profits, additivity conditions of the probabilities etc.). This, however, is beyond the scope of this appendix.

## Notes

[1] The presence of the argument $r_i - r^*$ in the price and quantity relationships (3.2.2.2) and (3.2.2.3) can be explained with reference to the calculation of a circular area with radius $R$. The area $A$ of a circle is equal to:

$$A = \int_0^{2\pi} \int_0^{R} r \, dr \, d\theta = \pi R^2$$

In the profit relationship (3.2.2.1) use was made of polar co-ordinates, which appeared *inter alia* in the limits of the integrals. It is easily seen that a relationship with a single term $r$ yields the following area $A$ in the case of polar co-ordinates:

$$A = \int_0^{2\pi} \int_{r^*}^{r^*+R} r \, dr \, d\theta = \pi(R^2 + 2r^*R)$$

Since the latter expression is unequal to $\pi R^2$, a correction should be carried out. By replacing the single term $r$ by $r-r^*$ one obtains the correct expression for a circular area in the case of polar co-ordinates:

$$A = \int_0^{2\pi} \int_{r^*}^{r^*+R} (r-r^*)\, dr\, d\theta = \pi R^2$$

[2] Differentiation of an integral-valued function with respect to a parameter $\theta$, which is also present in the limits of the integral, can be carried out according to the following relationship (see, for example, Courant [1967]):

$$\frac{\partial}{\partial\theta} \int_{a(\theta)}^{b(\theta)} f(x,\theta)\mathrm{d}x = \int_{a(\theta)}^{b(\theta)} \frac{\partial f(x,\theta)}{\partial\theta}\, \mathrm{d}x + f\{b(\theta),\theta\}\frac{\partial b(\theta)}{\partial\theta} - f\{a(\theta),\theta\}\frac{\partial a(\theta)}{\partial\theta}$$

[3] The reason for this assumption is that the site of the centres is unknown, so that (in contrast to the partial Weber problem) the point of minimum transportation costs cannot be determined.

[4] If, for instance, in table 3.3.2.a $n_2=1$, system 1 and 3 cannot exist, since system 1 and 3 require that $n_2 > 1$.

[5] The given prices of inputs and outputs may also take account of agglomeration advantages, caused by the presence of complementary activities.

## References


Allen, R.G.D., *Mathematical Economics*, Macmillan, London 1960.

Alonso, W., 'A Reformulation of Classical Location Theory and its Relations to Rent Theory', *Papers and Proceedings of the Regional Science Association*, vol. 19, 1967, pp. 23–44.

Baumol, W.J., *Economic Theory and Operations Analysis*, Prentice-Hall, Englewood Cliffs 1961.

Beckmann, M., *Location Theory*, Random House, New York 1968.

Bos, H.C., *The Spatial Dispersion of Economic Activity*, Rotterdam University Press, Rotterdam 1964.

Christaller, W., *Die Zentralen Orte in Süddeutschland,* Fischer, Jena 1933 (English translation by C.W. Baskin: *Central Places in Southern Germany*, Prentice-Hall, Englewood Cliffs 1966).

Courant, R., *Differential and Integral Calculus*, Blackie, London 1967.

Gould, P.R., 'Man against his Environment', in: L.J. King, R.H.T. Smith and E.J. Taaffe (eds.), *Readings in Economic Geography*, McNally, Chicago 1968, pp. 332–339.

Greenhut, M.L., *Plant Location in Theory and in Practice*, University of North Carolina Press, Chapel Hill 1956.

Greenhut, M.L., *A Theory of the Firm in Economic Space*, Appleton-Century-Crofts, New York 1970.

Guigou, J.L., 'On French Location Models for Production Units', *Regional and Urban Economics*, vol. 1, no. 2, 1971, pp. 107–138.

Guigou, J.L., *Analyse des Données et Choix à Critères multiples*, Dunod, Paris 1974.

Harris, C.C. and Hopkins, F.E., *Locational Analysis*, Heath and Co., Lexington, Massachusetts 1972.

Hoover, E.M., *The Location of Economic Activity*, McGraw-Hill, New York 1948.

Hotelling, H., 'Stability in Competition', *Economic Journal*, vol. 39, 1929, pp. 41–57.

Isard, W., *Location and the Space-Economy*, MIT Press, Cambridge 1956.

Isard, W., *General Theory; Social, Political, Economic and Regional*, MIT Press, Cambridge 1969.

Jacot, S.P., *Stratégie et Concurrence; de l'Application de la Théorie des Jeux à l'Analyse de la Concurrence Spatiale*, SEDES, Paris 1963.

Koopmans, T.C. and Beckmann, M., 'Assignment Problems and the Location of Economic Activities', *Econometrica*, vol. 25, 1957, pp. 53–76.

Lloyd, P.E. and Dicken, P., *Location in Space: A Theoretical Approach to Economic Geography*, Harper and Row, New York 1972.

Lösch, A., *The Economics of Location*, Yale University Press, New Haven 1954.

Luce, R.D. and Raiffa, H., *Games and Decisions,* Wiley, New York 1957.

Manne, A.S. and Vietorisz, T., 'Chemical Processes, Plant Location, and Economies of Scale', in A.S. Manne and H.M. Markowitz (eds.), *Studies in Process Analysis,* Wiley, New York 1963, pp. 136–158.

Moses, L.N., 'Location and the Theory of Production', *Quarterly Journal of Economics*, vol. 72, 1958, pp. 259–272.

Nijkamp, P., *Planning of Industrial Complexes by Means of Geometric Programming*, Rotterdam University Press, Rotterdam 1972.

Nijkamp, P., 'A Multi-criteria Analysis for Project Evaluation', *Papers of the Regional Science Association*, 1975 (forthcoming).

Nijkamp, P. and Paelinck, J.H.P., 'A Solution Method for Neo-classical Location Problems', *Regional and Urban Economics*, vol. 3, nr. 4, 1973, pp. 383–410.

Paelinck, J.H.P., 'Qualitative Multiple-Criteria Analysis, Environmental Protection and Multiregional Development', *Foundations of Empirical Economic Research*, Netherlands Economic Institute, Rotterdam (mimeo), 1975.

Paelinck, J.H.P. and Jaumotte, C., 'Avantages et Inconvénients des Régions Industrielles en Stagnation et des Zones Rurales pour l'Implantation d'Industries Automatisées', in: *Manpower Aspects of Automation and Technical Change*, OECD, Paris, 1966, pp. 331–361.

Ponsard, C., 'Une Application de la Théorie des Graphes à l'Analyse de l'Espace Economique: un Modèle de Localisation Optimale de l'Unité de Production dans une Structure de Concurrence', in: *Travaux sur l'Espace Economique, Techniques Economiques Modernes*, no. 11, Gauthier-Villars, Paris 1966, pp.1–21.

Quirin, G.D., *The Capital Expenditure Decision,* Irwin, Illinois 1967.

Schärlig, A., 'La Localisation Optimale d'une Entreprise', *Revue Suisse d'Economie et de Statistique*, vol. 107, 1971, pp. 599–611.

Schärlig, A., *Où Construire l'Usine*? Dunod, Paris 1973.

Scott, A.J., *Combinatorial Programming, Spatial Analysis and Planning,* Methuen & Co., London 1971.

Serck-Hanssen, J., *Optimal Patterns of Location*, North-Holland Publishing Co., Amsterdam 1970.

Smith, D.M., 'A Theoretical Framework for Geographical Studies of Industrial Location', *Economic Geography*, vol. 42, 1966, pp.95–113.

Stevens, B.H., 'An Application of Game Theory to a Problem in Location Strategy', *Papers and Proceedings of the Regional Science Association*, vol. 7, 1961, pp. 143–157.

Theil, H., Boot, J., and Kloek, T., *Operations Research and Quantitative Economics; an Elementary Introduction*, McGraw-Hill, New York 1965.

Thompson, W.R. and Mattilla, J.M., *An Econometric Model of Postwar State Industrial Development*, Wayne State University Press, Detroit 1959.

Tinbergen, J., 'The Spatial Dispersion of Production: A Hypothesis', *Schweizerische Zeitschrift für Volkswirtschaft und Statistik*, vol. 97, no. 4, 1961, pp. 412–419.

Tinbergen, J., 'Sur un Modèle de la Dispersion Géographique de l'Activité Economique, *Revue d'Economie Politique*, Numéro Spécial, 1964, pp. 30–44.

Von Neumann, J. and Morgenstern, D., *Theory of Games and Economic Behaviour*, Princeton University Press, Princeton 1953.

Webber, M.J., *Impact of Uncertainty on Location*, MIT Press, Cambridge 1972.

Williams, J.D., *The Complete Strategist,* McGraw-Hill, New York 1954.

PART II

# Methods

# 4 Measurement on Regions

## 4.1 Introduction

This chapter is devoted to an introductory exposition of the notion of *regions. Various concepts* of regions will be discussed in detail, while the notion of *interregional distances* will also be introduced. Furthermore, an adequate basis is given to the theory of regions by means of both an *axiomatic* and a *taxonomic* approach. Attention is also paid to a useful tool in regional analysis, viz. *factor analysis*, while the chapter is concluded with two relevant actual problems in multiregional systems, viz. *contiguity* and *diffusion*.

## 4.2 The concept of regions

### 4.2.1 *Introduction*

A *region* is a spatial entity characterized by certain elements. It is evident that various criteria for isolating a region can be distinguished, leading to different types of regions (for instance, districts, areas, provinces, countries). Furthermore, it is clear that a possible demarcation of regions is co-determined by the availability of data; in many research projects the regional classification is highly dependent on the level of available information. Therefore, a necessary condition for progress in regional research is the existence (or development) of regional information systems (for instance, regional data banks).

In the following subsections various concepts of regions will be considered and discussed.

### 4.2.2 *A natural region*

The concept of a *natural* region originates from geography. A natural region is characterized by certain geographical, physical elements; for instance, a classification of natural regions can be based on climatological factors, soil conditions, fertility of land, height above the sea-level, and so forth. Only in as far as certain economic activities (for instance, agriculture, mining, shipbuilding) are linked up with these geographical, physical characteristics, the concept of a natural region is relevant in regional economics; for instance, an investigation into an optimal spatial dispersion of agricultural activities (within the European Economic Community, e.g.), based on transportation costs of agricultural products, should take account of climatological and soil conditions within the countries concerned.

### 4.2.3 *A homogeneous region*

The concept of *homogeneity* is a rather relative one: a region is said to be homogeneous, if it possesses in a certain respect a high degree of *uniformity*. In other words, within a homogeneous region a set of elements can be defined, which show a high degree of correspondence. The characteristics of such a homogeneous region may be the degree of urbanization, the population density, the *per capita* income, and so forth. It is evident, that a homogeneous region depends mainly on the criterion by means of which regional characteristics are distinguished.

The homogeneity concept is relevant in the case of combining elementary regions (for instance, elementary square grid cells, or operational taxonomic units (cf. Johnston [1970]) into a new set of larger regions. Such a regionalization is usually based on the assumption, that each of these new regions should be as homogeneous as possible. For instance, assume an area with elementary grid cells as presented in figure 4.2.3.a. The figures in each grid cell represent the population density.

Fig. 4.2.3.a A system of grid cells

| | | | |
|---|---|---|---|
| 10 | 11 | 19 | 18 |
| 12 | 10 | 21 | 22 |
| 2 | 4 | 5 | 3 |

Fig. 4.2.3.b A grouping within a system

| | | | |
|---|---|---|---|
| 10 | 11 | 19 | 18 |
| 12 | 10 | 21 | 22 |
| 2 | 4 | 5 | 3 |

It is easily seen that the elementary grid cells can be combined into 3 larger regions, which possess a high degree of *internal* uniformity. An indicator for the regional homogeneity may be the standard deviation or the coefficient of variation of the observations in the elementary cells. The standard deviation $\sigma$ is defined as:

$$\sigma = \sqrt{\frac{\sum_{j=1}^{J} (x_j - \bar{x})^2}{J}} \qquad (4.2.3.1)$$

where $x_j$ is the value of the element in the $j^{th}$ cell ($j = 1, \ldots, J$), and where $\bar{x}$ is the average value defined as:

$$\bar{x} = \frac{\sum_{j=1}^{J} x_j}{J} \qquad (4.2.3.2)$$

The coefficient of variation, which is independent of the unit of measurement, is equal to $\sigma/\bar{x}$.

For instance, the standard deviation of the data in all 12 cells of figure 4.2.3.a is equal to 6·861. Owing to the tripartite division into rather homogeneous sub-areas the standard deviation has declined considerably: the standard deviation of the upper left area, of the upper right area and of the lower area is, respectively, equal to 0·829, 1·581 and 1·118. The coefficient of variation for the whole area and for the 3 successive sub-areas is, respectively, equal to 0·601, 0·077, 0·079 and 0·319.

A formal method of forming larger regions is thus to integrate those elementary cells which are connex and which give rise to a relatively low value of $\sigma$ or $\sigma/\bar{x}$. Next, one may decide to add only new elementary cells to an initial set of new regions, if $\sigma$ or $\sigma/\bar{x}$ does not increase. For instance, adding the grid cell with figure 19 to the left region at the top of figure 4.2.3.b would certainly increase the standard deviation of the population density within this region. Therefore, this cell should be added to the right matrix at the top of figure 4.2.3.b. Instead of imposing the condition that $\sigma$ may not rise on adding new cells, one may impose the condition that $\sigma$ should not exceed a certain *a priori* fixed upper limit. It should be noted, that the foregoing variance criterion as such is not sufficient for creating larger regions. One should also impose a restriction on the total number of regions to be formed; otherwise, one would maintain the original grid cells, since the standard deviation is at a minimum (viz. zero) within each cell separately.

If the regionalization rests upon two criteria (instead of one criterion), it will even be more difficult to find homogeneous areas. For instance, if such a criterion is based on the population density and the average *per capita* income, the *intraregional* discrepancy will, in general, increase. In such a multi-criterion situation a maximum degree of internal homogeneity could be attained by minimizing the (weighted) sum of the standard deviations (or the coefficients of variation) of the variables concerned. The previous problem is, in fact, of a combinatorial nature: how to combine elementary grid cells into larger entities on the basis of a variance criterion?

The foregoing problem may be clarified by assuming that the elementary grid cells of figure 4.2.3.a possess another characteristic, viz. the average *per capita* income (see figure 4.2.3.c). If the formation of regions would be based on this second criterion, one would obtain figure 4.2.3.d as a

Fig. 4.2.3.c A system of grid cells

| | | | |
|---|---|---|---|
| 100 | 108 | 200 | 203 |
| 106 | 95 | 205 | 198 |
| 98 | 15 | 12 | 10 |

Fig. 4.2.3.d A grouping within a system

| | | | |
|---|---|---|---|
| 100 | 108 | 200 | 203 |
| 106 | 95 | 205 | 198 |
| 98 | 15 | 12 | 10 |

situation with maximum internal homogeneity. However, if both criteria are combined, the lower cell at the left appears to yield difficulties; according to the criterion of population density this cell should be added to the lower sub-area, while according to the criterion of average *per capita* income it should be added to the left upper sub-area. It depends completely on the weights, attached to the successive standard deviations, to which sub-area this cell should be added. This implies, in fact, that such a procedure of grouping and regionalization depends on the relative importance of each of the relevant variables.

Although a 'multi-criterion' situation leads, in general, to a higher degree of heterogeneity, one may expect that this heterogeneity will be limited, since many regional characteristics are highly correlated. Therefore, rather homogeneous economic regions of a certain size may exist despite the use of multiple criteria. For instance, an industrial area may be characterized by a high degree of industrialization, a high level of income *per capita*, a high degree of urbanization, a high level of infrastructural and social amenities, and so forth.

The concept of a homogeneous region is purely morphologic; it is also closely linked up with geographical analysis. The regionalization described above is, in fact, based on rather simple instruments; more advanced methods in this field are multidimensional scaling techniques, such as factor analysis (cf. also section 4.6). A disadvantage of the previous methods of regionalization is the fact that the internal economic linkages, the intraregional externalities, and the working of a certain regional economic structure are left out of consideration. From this point of view the concept of a polarized region (cf. section 4.2.4) and of a programming region (cf. section 4.2.5) are more adequate tools.

### 4.2.4 *A polarized region*

A *polarized* region (core region, or nodal region) is a connex area, in which the internal economic relationships are more intensive than the relationships with respect to regions outside the area. In other words, a polarized region possesses a high degree of *integration or intradependence*. The polarization criterion depends thus on the number and intensity of internal economic flows (goods, services, traffic, capital, and labour): the internal flows dominate the external relationships. It is clear that a strictly exclusive criterion of polarization is very difficult to indicate. The degree of internal integration of a region is hard to represent by means of one single indicator. The tightness of a certain regional economic structure depends on the relative intensity and the degree of integration of all economic phenomena within that region. Therefore, the study of polarization phenomena should take account of many regional data, such as regional accounts and regional and sectoral input–output tables. Such data are indispensable for a thorough regional analysis, reason why a separate chapter (Ch.5) is devoted to input–output analysis. In spite of the absence of a polarization criterion, in empirical studies often certain conditions for a polarized region are formulated. For instance, Boudeville (1963) states that polarized regions should satisfy *inter alia* the following conditions: (a) a population of more than four million inhabitants; (b) the presence of a basic, integrated industrial complex; (c) a relatively high degree of exports; he considers these conditions to be sufficient for starting a process of accelerated regional growth.

A polarized region integrates both abstract, economic space and concrete, cartographical space. Such a distinction was made by Perroux (1955), who defined economic space not as a concrete, physical space, but as an abstract, topological space characterized by a field of forces between economic sectors or economic activities. It is evident that a polarized region rests on both notions, since both the interwoven pattern of economic activities (or sectors) and the presence of a concrete, physical area are an essential element in the concept of a polarized region: polarization phenomena rest both on economic elements (such as intersectoral commodity flows and externalities), and on spatial elements (such as transportation, traffic, and communication). In general, a polarized region does not rest on a spatial homogeneity, but on a tight, spatial integration of interwoven heterogeneous elements.

As stated, a unique criterion for polarized regions is hard to give. In consequence, there are considerable structural differences among polarized regions, as may be shown by a comparison between the region of Lorraine (France) and Liège (Belgium). After the collection and the analysis of the required regional data, the relative importance of the steel industry (the main industry in both regions) could be calculated, as appears from table 4.2.4.a derived from Davin et al. (1959, p. 321).

Table 4.2.4.a
Economic data concerning Lorraine and Liège

| Region | Internal use of steel products (% of total production) | Net imports of steel products in the region ($) |
|---|---|---|
| Lorraine | 8·5 | $127{\cdot}1 \times 10^6$ |
| Liège | 28·5 | $18{\cdot}1 \times 10^6$ |

Table 4.2.4.a shows that the degree of integration of the steel industry is quite different for both regions. Lorraine appears to possess a rather weak integration of the steel industry, compared to Liège; in addition, the imports of Lorraine are higher than those of Liège.

One may also compare the internal sectors within a polarized region, in particular the effect of a change in certain basic sectors on the regional activity or income level. Such a calculation was performed for the region of Liège by Paelinck (1965), who made a distinction between a *total* regional effect (the percentage increase in total regional value added caused by a unit increase in the activity level of a sector concerned) and an *indirect* regional effect (the percentage increase in production of other branches, as a result of a unit increase in the activity level of a certain sector). These effects, calculated for the steel sector and the chemical sector, are contained in table 4.2.4.b. This table shows that there may be a considerable divergence among the sectors within one region, particularly as far as the total effect on regional value added is concerned. The method of calculating the various effects is based on input–output analysis and input–output multipliers (see Ch.5).

Table 4.2.4.b
Sectoral data concerning Liège

| Sector | Total effect on regional value added (%) | Indirect effect on regional production (%) |
|---|---|---|
| Steel | $\approx 50$ | $\approx 50$ |
| Chemicals | $\approx 8$ | $\approx 35$ |

### 4.2.5 *A programming region*

A *programming region* (planning region, or development region) is considered from the point of view of targets aimed at by a certain region or its inhabitants. A programming region is the spatial basis for certain regional development programs. The regional boundaries are to be fixed in such a way that certain planning objectives are attained in the most efficient way (cf. also the notion of a 'relevant region', developed by Klaassen [1967]). A programming region rests on the idea that economic growth does not come about all through space, but only in certain areas with a high growth potential; these areas are able to transmit economic growth to other regions and to other sectors by means of interregional and intersectoral linkages. Economic growth programs should be based on economic coherence between objectives and instruments; furthermore, they should take account of regional attraction and polarization phenomena, and of the degree of regional openness. Therefore, an optimal policy for a programming region should specify: (a) the objectives aimed at; (b) the constraints to be considered (for instance, the structure of the regional economy represented by input–output linkages). The foregoing exposition shows, that if the boundaries of a programming region depend on the objectives aimed at, the criterion for a programming region can only be given in a concrete situation, because only within the economic structure of a concrete spatial entity the efficiency of certain growth programs can be analyzed. According to Boudeville (1963) a more practical way of delineating programming regions is to select an area with a high degree of economic coherence and growth potentials, or an area with a firm export basis (for instance, a high rate of interregional trade).

A more formal approach to regional growth programs is contained in section 5.19 (a model for a growth centre) and in Ch.6 (multiregional programming), in which the optimality and efficiency of regional growth effects are dealt with in more detail.

### 4.2.6 *An administrative region*

*Administrative* regions form a spatial entity from a political or administrative point of view. The boundaries of an administrative region are often rather arbitrary, particularly as far as the economic structure is concerned. Therefore, from an economic point of view administrative regions do not form an efficient subdivision of an area. If an economic development program is implemented only for a certain administrative region without considering the linkages of the economic structure which may exceed the regional political (or administrative) boundaries, the effect of such a program will not necessarily be an improvement of the existing structure. Therefore, one should always be aware of the fact that a certain homogeneous or integrated economic structure does not necessarily coincide with an administrative region. On the other hand, in practice many regional measures take the administrative region as a starting-point, since administrative regions are frequently the spatial entities for governmental intervention and planning. For that reason a programming region often coincides with an administrative region (or a set of administrative regions). It is clear that the regional basis of economic planning and policy is formed by weighting the regional economic efficiency against the administrative efficiency.

### 4.2.7 *Conclusion*

From an economic point of view regions can be distinguished into homogeneous, polarized and programming regions (see also Boudeville [1961]). Regional economic policy and planning requires a clear distinction between these concepts in order to find suitable analytical methods and tools, and to use efficient instruments of economic policy.

If one considers the three foregoing concepts in relation to the element of time, one may state that a homogeneous region is a static concept, that a polarized region is a dynamic concept, and that a programming region is also a dynamic concept with a particular stress on long-term aims.

The actual determination and distinction of homogeneous, polarized and programming regions is rather complicated, since regional data are frequently stored according to administrative units. In general, a complete correspondence with the objectives of the economic analysis concerned does not exist: the pure cases of homogeneous, polarized and programming regions rarely happen in real-world situations, although one should always be aware of this distinction in regional economic policy and planning.

Efficient regional economic policy and planning requires in the first place the availability of relevant regional data ('data-bank'), in order to obtain an adequate insight in a certain regional economic structure. On the basis of these data one may construct a regional economic model (for instance, an input–output model, or a decision model). The implementation of a regional growth program requires a clear distinction between regional economic objectives and economic instruments. Furthermore, one should specify the relationships between these regional economic objectives (or more concretely the regional economic target variables), and the regional economic instruments which are necessary in order to realize the target variables. A more extensive exposition of these problems was contained in Ch.1.

## 4.3 Interregional economic distances

### 4.3.1 *Introduction*

The concept of Euclidean distances has already been discussed in section 1.6. Such Euclidean distances are relevant in the case of transportation problems between cities or regions, since these transportation problems imply real physical distances. In this section the concept of an economic distance will be dealt with as an analogon of physical distance.

### 4.3.2 *The concept of an economic distance*

The distance concept, developed in vector analysis, can be useful for the calculation of abstract 'economic' distances between regions. Each region $r$ can be characterized by a vector, the elements of which represent a set of regional characteristics, for instance, population, employment, income, degree of urbanization, degree of industrialization, number of service institutions, and so forth. Therefore, an area or a country, composed of $R$ elementary regions $r$ ($r = 1, \ldots, R$), can be characterized in a morphologic way by means of the following data matrix $X$:

$\mathbf{X} =$

| Variable / Region | 1 . . . . . . . . . . . . . . . . . . . . . . . . . . . . . $I$ |
|---|---|
| 1 . . . . . . . . . . $R$ | $[x_{ri}]$ |

(4.3.2.1)

The typical element of this data matrix, $x_{ri}$, represents the value of the $i^{th}$ variable in the $r^{th}$ region. The typical rows of this matrix are denoted by $\mathbf{x}'_{r\cdot}$, which indicates a row vector of order $I$ with the values of all $I$ variables in region $r$. The typical columns of the data matrix are denoted by $\mathbf{x}_{\cdot i}$, which represents a column vector of order $R$ with the values of the $i^{th}$ variable over all $R$ regions. The vectors $\mathbf{x}_{r.}'$ and $\mathbf{x}_{.i}$ arise from a twofold way of analysing a data matrix, viz. in a *horizontal* direction and in a *vertical* direction, respectively. The horizontal direction implies a cross-section within one region over all variables, whereas the vertical direction implies a cross-section of one variable over all regions. Therefore, $\mathbf{x}_{r.}'$ gives a picture of the economic structure of region $r$, while $\mathbf{x}_{.i}$ gives a spatial picture of one variable over all regions. Each vector $\mathbf{x}_{r.}'$ can be represented by means of a point in $I$-dimensional Euclidean space, whereas each vector $\mathbf{x}_{.i}$ can be represented by means of a point in $R$-dimensional space.

The (squared) distance of a point in $I$-dimensional linear vector space with respect to the origin of this $I$-dimensional space is equal to:

$$\begin{aligned} d_{ro}^2 &= \sum_{i=1}^{I} x_{ri}^2 \\ &= \mathbf{x}_{r.}' \, \mathbf{x}_{r.} \end{aligned} \tag{4.3.2.2}$$

or:

$$\begin{aligned} d_{ro} &= \sqrt{(\mathbf{x}_{r.}' \, \mathbf{x}_{r.})} \\ &= || \, \mathbf{x}_{r.} \, || \end{aligned} \tag{4.3.2.3}$$

The foregoing distance concept of a region $r$ with respect to the origin has only a meaning in relation to the distance of all other regions with respect to the origin. By comparing the successive regional distances $d_{ro}$ ($r = 1, \ldots, R$), one obtains an insight concerning the degree to which the successive regional economic structures differ from each other, as far as the relative order of magnitude of the included variables is concerned.

A more meaningful concept is the economic distance between two regions $r$ and $r'$. Such a distance is calculated as (cf. also [1.6.2.4]):

$$\begin{aligned} d_{rr'}^2 &= \sum_{i=1}^{I} (x_{ri} - x_{r'i})^2 \\ &= (\mathbf{x}_{r.} - \mathbf{x}_{r'.})'(\mathbf{x}_{r.} - \mathbf{x}_{r'.}) \end{aligned} \tag{4.3.2.4}$$

or:

$$\begin{aligned} d_{rr'} &= \sqrt{(\mathbf{x}_{r.} - \mathbf{x}_{r'.})'(\mathbf{x}_{r.} - \mathbf{x}_{r'.})} \\ &= || \, \mathbf{x}_{r.} - \mathbf{x}_{r'.} \, || \end{aligned} \tag{4.3.2.5}$$

The interregional economic distance indicates the degree to which regions possess a similar structure. If there is a close correspondence between the economic structure of two regions, the defining variables in both regions will not show considerable differences, so that the economic distance between these regions, measured by adding the squared differences in the various regional characteristics, will be relatively low.

It should be noted that the concept of distance defined above should satisfy the conditions (1.6.2.3). The total number of interregional distances, which have to be calculated in a system of $R$ regions, is equal to $R(R-1)/2$, distances being symmetric in both directions (i.e., $d_{rr'} = d_{r'r}$).

The interregional distances discussed so far are not adequate means for measuring the differences in the economic structure of a set of regions. For several reasons an adaptation of these distances is necessary

In the first place, all regional indicators have to be corrected for the size of the region. An interregional analysis of similarity between economic structures of regions is only meaningful, if the regional indicators are standardized with respect to the size of the region. Examples of such a *standardization* are the population *per square mile* (or population density) instead of total population, the income *per capita* instead of total regional income, and so forth. These standardized variables open a more meaningful possibility for interregional comparisons; they lead to more uniformity in regional characteristics and allow a more adequate computation of interregional distances. Hereafter a standardized variable will be denoted by $x^*_{ri}$ ($r = 1, \ldots, R; i = 1, \ldots, I$), while the modified data table will be denoted by $\mathbf{X}^*$. In a similar way the distances, related to the standardized variables, are denoted by $d^*_{ro}$ and $d^*_{rr'}$.

In the second place, even if a standardized data table is used for the calculation of interregional distances, one may obtain peculiar results, since the variables concerned may possess a high degree of variation owing to a measurement in different dimensions. For instance, if the set of regional indicators contains *inter alia* average regional income (measured in dollars) and the degree of urbanization (measured in percentages), the first variable dominates the second one. The interregional distance would be dominated by (the variation in) the dominant variable. A solution to this problem is to reduce all variables to the same scale, for instance by giving all vectors $\mathbf{x}^*_{\cdot i}$ ($i = 1, \ldots, I$) a unit length. This is called a *normalization* procedure, each vector $\mathbf{x}^*_{\cdot i}$ being divided by its norm $||\mathbf{x}^*_{\cdot i}||$. Such a normalized vector is denoted by $\mathbf{x}^{**}_{\cdot i}$, and it is defined as:

$$\mathbf{x}^{**}_{\cdot i} = \frac{\mathbf{x}^*_{\cdot i}}{||\mathbf{x}^*_{\cdot i}||}$$

$$= \frac{\mathbf{x}^*_{\bullet i}}{\sqrt{((\mathbf{x}^*_{\bullet i})'(\mathbf{x}^*_{\bullet i}))}} \qquad (4.3.2.6)$$

It can easily be checked that $\mathbf{x}^{**}_{\bullet i}$ has unit length. The advantage of this normalization is, that all variables have lost their dimension, whereas all original variables ($x_{ri}$ or $x^*_{ri}$) were expressed in different dimensions (for instance, dollars per head, population per square mile, etc.). In this way a more meaningful interregional comparison is possible. The normalized distances are in a similar way denoted by $d^{**}_{ro}$ and $d^{**}_{rr'}$.

Finally, sometimes an *orthogonalization* procedure is carried out in order to receive only relevant *independent* information from the regional indicators. The regional indicators, as they are present in the regional data vector $\mathbf{x}_{r\bullet}$ are, in general, not independent: they are most of the time highly correlated within each region. For instance, a region with a high degree of industrialization possesses frequently also a high average income. To avoid a strong correlation between these regional indicators, they can be orthogonalized (for instance, by means of a Gram-Schmidt procedure; see, for instance, Murdoch [1957]). Orthogonality of vectors is closely linked up with linear independence of vectors, since each set of mutually orthogonal non-zero vectors is linearly independent. Although an orthogonalization procedure leads indeed to independent variables (hence to independent information concerning a regional economic structure), such a procedure has some drawbacks, since an economic interpretation of the new orthogonal vectors in terms of the original variables is hard to give. An orthogonalization is a mathematical procedure without a clear economic interpretation. Furthermore, an orthogonalization procedure is not necessarily unique. For instance, in the case of two vectors one may choose the first variable as an independent one and put the second variable orthogonal on it, or reversely. Therefore, an orthogonalization procedure should be carefully considered.

A possible way of obtaining orthogonal vectors, proposed by Stone (1960), is the use of a fundamental theorem of factor analysis (factor analysis is dealt with in section 4.6). If the new orthogonal vectors of variables in each region $r$ are denoted by $\mathbf{x}^{***}_{r\bullet}$, the link with the foregoing normalized vectors $\mathbf{x}^{**}_{r\bullet}$ can be represented by means of the following transformation:

$$\mathbf{x}^{**}_{r\bullet} = L\,\mathbf{x}^{***}_{r\bullet} \qquad (4.3.2.7)$$

where $L$ represents a square, nonsingular matrix of order $I$. If the distances with respect to the orthogonal variables are denoted by $d^{***}_{ro}$ and $d^{***}_{rr'}$, they can be calculated, respectively, as:

$$(d_{ro}^{***})^2 = (\mathbf{x}_{r\bullet}^{***})'(\mathbf{x}_{r\bullet}^{***}) \qquad (4.3.2.8)$$

$$= (\mathbf{x}_{r\bullet}^{**})'(\mathbf{LL}')^{-1}(\mathbf{x}_{r\bullet}^{**})$$

and:

$$(d_{rr'}^{***})^2 = (\mathbf{x}_{r\bullet}^{***} - \mathbf{x}_{r'\bullet}^{***})'(\mathbf{x}_{r\bullet}^{***} - \mathbf{x}_{r\bullet}^{***}) \qquad (4.3.2.9)$$

$$= (\mathbf{x}_{r\bullet}^{**} - \mathbf{x}_{r'\bullet}^{**})'(\mathbf{LL}')^{-1}(\mathbf{x}_{r\bullet}^{**} - \mathbf{x}_{r'\bullet}^{**})$$

*Under certain conditions* (cf. section 4.6) the matrix $\mathbf{LL}'$ is equal to the first-order correlation matrix $\mathbf{R}$ between the original standardized (or normalized) variables, i.e.,

$$\mathbf{LL}' = \mathbf{R} \qquad (4.3.2.10)$$

This result can be proved by means of a fundamental theorem from factor analysis (see 4.6.3.3). The orthogonal vectors $\mathbf{x}_{\bullet i}^{***}$ ($i = 1, \ldots, I$) can be conceived of as a set of independent factors (see section 4.6), in terms of which the normalized variables can be expressed. Each vector $\mathbf{x}_{\bullet i}^{**}$ can be written as a linear combination of a set of orthogonal vectors $\mathbf{x}_{\bullet i'}^{***}$ ($i' = 1, \ldots, I$), where the scalars of the linear combination are described by the elements of the $i'^{th}$ row of the matrix $\mathbf{L}$. Therefore, the normalized data matrix can, according to (4.3.2.7), be transformed into:

$$(\mathbf{X}^{**})' = \mathbf{L}(\mathbf{X}^{***})' \qquad (4.3.2.11)$$

where $\mathbf{X}^{**}$, $\mathbf{L}$ and $\mathbf{X}^{***}$ are matrices of order $R \times I$, $I \times I$ and $R \times I$, respectively.

Therefore, one may conclude that relationship (4.3.2.10) permits the calculation of interregional distances for orthogonal regional indicators according to (4.3.2.9). The typical elements of the correlation matrix itself are denoted by $r_{ii'}$; they are defined as:

$$r_{ii'} = \frac{\sum_{r=1}^{R}(x_{ri}^{**} - \bar{x}_i^{**})(x_{ri'}^{**} - \bar{x}_{i'}^{**})}{\sqrt{\sum_{r=1}^{R}(x_{ri}^{**} - \bar{x}_i^{**})^2 \sum_{r=1}^{R}(x_{ri'}^{**} - \bar{x}_{i'}^{**})^2}}$$

$$= \frac{(\mathbf{x}_{\bullet i}^{**} - \bar{\mathbf{x}}_i^{**})'(\mathbf{x}_{\bullet i'}^{**} - \bar{\mathbf{x}}_{i'}^{**})}{\|\mathbf{x}_{\bullet i}^{**} - \bar{\mathbf{x}}_i^{**}\| \cdot \|\mathbf{x}_{\bullet i'}^{**} - \bar{\mathbf{x}}_{i'}^{**}\|} \qquad (4.3.2.12)$$

where $\bar{\mathbf{x}}_i^{**}$ represents the average value of $\mathbf{x}_{ri}^{**}$. Therefore, $\bar{\mathbf{x}}_i^{**}$ is defined as:

$$\overline{x}_i^{**} = \frac{\sum_{r=1}^{R} x_{ri}^{**}}{R} \tag{4.3.2.13}$$

In a similar way the vector $\overline{\mathbf{x}}_i^{**}$ of order $R$ contains the $R$ (equal) elements $\overline{x}_i^{**}$. It should be noted that the correlation matrix can also be calculated on the basis of standardized variables $x_{ri}^{*}$ (instead of normalized variables $x_{ri}^{**}$). The result is the same correlation matrix, since $x_{ri}^{*}$ and $x_{ri}^{*}$ are linear dependent owing to the normalization procedure (4.3.2.6).

Finally, it should be noted that the orthogonalization procedure described above is also not free from criticism. The economic meaning and the theoretical basis of the orthogonalization are not quite clear. On the other hand, the advantage of an orthogonalization is the fact that only independent information is used.

### 4.3.3 *An empirical application*

An empirical application of economic distances was made for the northern part of The Netherlands (see Paelinck [1970]). This area is, in fact, a lagging area with respect to the complementary part of The Netherlands. In order to obtain more insight in the economic structure of this northern part a number of 17 core regions were distinguished. For each of these core regions information concerning 7 variables was available (population density, degree of industrialization, age structure, number of cars, degree of urbanization, average income, active population). On the basis of these 7 (normalized) criteria for each of these 17 core regions the economic distance was calculated with respect to Rotterdam, and with respect to The Netherlands itself. By comparing the differences in economic structure between each of these core regions and Rotterdam (a highly qualified and rapid growing core region) on the basis of economic distances, a quantitative indicator is obtained for the relative difference between a lagging region and a growing region. In a similar way one may compare each of these 17 regions with The Netherlands, in order to investigate how much the economic structure of these core regions deviates from the national average. This analysis was performed for 2 years, viz. 1960 and 1967, in order to inspect whether the differences in economic structure are declining. The results are presented in table 4.3.3.a, which contains the economic distances between the 17 core regions and Rotterdam and The Netherlands (both for 1960 and 1967). These results show that there is a remarkable difference between each of the 17 lagging core regions and the growth pole of Rotterdam. Furthermore, the major part of these core regions possess mutually a rather similar economic structure with respect to Rotterdam. As far as the economic differences with respect to the national economic structure are concerned, they appear to be much lower. The latter phenomenon indicates that the discrepancies of the northern part with respect to the national average are less serious than would be expected. On the other hand, this phenomenon shows that Rotterdam has indeed a tight economic structure with respect to the national average.

Furthermore, table 4.3.3.a shows that the economic discrepancies of the 17 core regions with respect to Rotterdam have decreased during the period 1960–67. There has also been a decrease with respect to the national average. Therefore, one may conclude that the differences in the economic structure between the northern part of The Netherlands and the national economy (and also Rotterdam) have decreased during the period concerned.

Table 4.3.3.a
Economic distances within the Netherlands

| Core region | 1960 | | 1967 | |
|---|---|---|---|---|
| | Rotterdam | The Netherlands | Rotterdam | The Netherlands |
| 1 | 0·91776 | 0·11286 | 0·88546 | 0·10231 |
| 2 | 1·30389 | 0·15641 | 1·03340 | 0·06858 |
| 3 | 1·86003 | 0·09190 | 1·79354 | 0·09003 |
| 4 | 1·83901 | 0·09302 | 1·65929 | 0·02774 |
| 5 | 1·70637 | 0·05172 | 1·59798 | 0·02677 |
| 6 | 1·87204 | 0·09695 | 1·79621 | 0·09052 |
| 7 | 1·39103 | 0·11415 | 0·94195 | 0·10528 |
| 8 | 1·85315 | 0·09698 | 1·78343 | 0·09287 |
| 9 | 1·77321 | 0·04989 | 1·70899 | 0·04503 |
| 10 | 1·71279 | 0·04210 | 1·63505 | 0·03503 |
| 11 | 1·96083 | 0·09543 | 1·78677 | 0·08944 |
| 12 | 1·83321 | 0·09236 | 1·74885 | 0·08548 |
| 13 | 1·74392 | 0·05250 | 1·66834 | 0·04565 |
| 14 | 1·86523 | 0·09206 | 1·79158 | 0·08899 |
| 15 | 1·70075 | 0·01731 | 1·65623 | 0·01462 |
| 16 | 1·83843 | 0·09643 | 1·61565 | 0·01515 |
| 17 | 1·64730 | 0·00633 | 1·60699 | 0·00779 |

## 4.4 Regionalization and classification: axioms

### 4.4.1 *Introduction*

In sections 4.4 and 4.5 concerning regionalization and classification, attention will be paid to grouping procedures for regions. In section 4.4 an axiomatic approach to regionalization procedures will be presented, based on some elements from set theory. A series of applications is also presented; for instance in subsection 4.4.3 a straightforward application of the concept of economic distance for regionalization procedures will be given. In section 4.5 a taxonomic approach to regionalization will be discussed, which is based on a logical, quantitative grouping method. Furthermore, in section 4.6 the use of factor analysis in regional research will be discussed; this multivariate analysis may also be useful in grouping procedures.

### 4.4.2 *Axioms for regionalization*

The *formal axiomatics* of grouping and regionalization procedures can be described by means of *set theory* (see, *inter alia*, Goldberg [1964], Grigg [1965], Rotman and Kneebone [1966], Siebert [1967], Suppes [1965] and Teitz [1962]). In general terms, a set is a collection of objects of any type whatsoever. The objects in a set are called *elements* or *points*. In an abstract way a set $A$ can be represented as follows:

$$A = \{a_i \mid i = 1, \ldots, I\} \tag{4.4.2.1}$$

i.e., $A$ is a set of elements '$a_i$', the index $i$ running from 1 to $I$. An example is a country composed of a number of provinces. Each province is an element of the set, which is formed by the parts of the country. If $a_i$ is an element of $A$, one writes:

$$a_i \in A \tag{4.4.2.2}$$

Otherwise,

$$a_i \notin A$$

The *universal* set is the set of all relevant points in a certain space. In regional analysis the elements of a set have frequently a spatial character (for instance, elementary regions, grid cells, countries, SMSA's, and so forth).

A set $B$ is a *subset* of $A$, if each element of $B$ is an element of $A$. This is written as:

$$B \subset A \tag{4.4.2.3}$$

$B$ is a *proper* subset of $A$, if $B \subset A$ and if $B \neq A$. If $B = A$, both sets will be equal: they contain precisely the same elements. Therefore, $B = A$, if and only if $B \subset A$ and $A \subset B$.

A *union* (the set of all elements in either $A$ or $B$ [or both]) is denoted by:

$$A \cup B \tag{4.4.2.4}$$

whereas the *intersection* of $A$ and $B$ (the set of all elements in both $A$ and $B$) is written as:

$$A \cap B \tag{4.4.2.5}$$

An *empty* set (denoted by $\phi$) does not contain any element. The set of all elements of $A$, which are not elements of $B$, is written as:

$$A - B \tag{4.4.2.6}$$

Therefore, $A - B$ can according to (4.4.2.1) be written as:

$$A - B = \{a_i \,|a_i \in A, a_i \notin B\}$$

A *subset B* can be obtained from a set $A$ on the basis of the *extension-axiom* of set theory, by means of which certain elements of $A$ can be put into a subset $B$ with new characteristics. Such a separation of elements from $A$ requires a certain criterion, which assigns some elements to $B$ owing to certain similar characteristics. If the function $\varphi(a_i)$ represents the criterion, by means of which such an assignment of elements $a_i$ of $A$ is carried out, subset $B$ is characterized by the following condition:

$$a_i \in B \leftrightarrow a_i \in \ A \cap \varphi(a_i) \qquad \forall i \quad {}^{1} \tag{4.4.2.7}$$

which indicates that each element $a_i$ in $A$, which satisfies the criterion $\varphi(a_i)$, is assigned to $B$. The function $\varphi(a_i)$ is a set of certain properties of the elements $a_i$, such that $\varphi(a_i)$ is a mapping of the set of elements of $A$ to subset $B$; in other words: $\varphi(a_i)$ is a rule which assigns to the elements $a_i \in A$ one and only one image $\varphi(a_i) \in B$. If an element $a_i$ satisfies criterion $\varphi(a_i)$, it is called a *linked* element. All elements of $A$, which do not satisfy $\varphi(a_i)$, are supposed to form a subset $C$, which is complementary to $B$. The extension-axiom of set theory, which justifies the above procedure of constructing subsets, is permitted only if the following conditions are satisfied:

$$\exists \ \varphi(a_i) \rightarrow B \cup C = A \qquad \forall i \quad {}^{2} \tag{4.4.2.8}$$

and:

$$\exists \ \varphi(a_i) \rightarrow B \cap C = \phi \qquad \forall i \tag{4.4.2.9}$$

Conditions (4.4.2.8) and (4.4.2.9) require a unique criterion $\varphi(a_i)$, which does not allow any overlap.

If the extension-axiom is used in regional analysis for grouping procedures of regions, still another condition should be satisfied. If one joins elementary regions to larger sub-areas, the newly formed sub-areas should be *connex*, so that each point of a region can be reached from another point in that region without leaving the region. Therefore, a third condition should be imposed in regionalization procedures:

$$\exists \; \varphi(a_i) \rightarrow B \, \rho_c \, C \qquad \forall \, i \tag{4.4.2.10}$$

where the symbol $\rho_c$ represents the connexity condition. Finally, it should be noted that criterion $\varphi(a_i)$ may be of a quantitative or of a qualitative nature: $\varphi(a_i)$ may be a continuous function, as well as a qualitative indicator (for instance, the presence of natural resources). In fact, the σ-criterion in section 4.2.3 can be seen as a simple criterion $\varphi(a_i)$ for regionalization procedures. In the subsections 4.4.3–4.4.5 a number of applications of the axiomatic approach described above will be presented.

### 4.4.3 *Regionalization and distances*

The physical distance between regions can be used as a criterion for grouping procedures. All regions, which possess a low average physical distance with respect to an initial region, are joined into one group, while the other regions with a relatively high physical distance with respect to an initial region are assigned to another group.

For instance, assume a set $A$ of elementary regions $r$ ($r = 1, \ldots, R$). The average distance between each region $r$ and $r'$ ($r, r' = 1, \ldots, R$) is denoted by $d_{rr'}$; $d_{rr'}$ is supposed to be known. Next, one takes the maximum possible distance between each of the regions $r$. The regions which have a maximum distance are denoted by 1 and $R$, so that:

$$d_{1R} = \max_{rr'} d_{rr'} \qquad (r, r' = 1, \ldots, R) \tag{4.4.3.1}$$

The element $d_{1R}$ can easily be found in an interregional distance table. Next, one chooses region 1 and region $R$ as the initial regions for a grouping procedure. Each elementary region $r$, the distance of which with respect to region 1 is lower than its distance with respect to region $R$, is assigned to a subset $B$, and inversely to a subset $C$. Therefore, the grouping procedure considers all elementary regions $r$ ($r = 2, \ldots, R-1$) of set $A$; each of these regions is assigned to $B$ or $C$ according the following respective distance criteria:

$$r \in B \leftrightarrow r \in A \cap (d_{1R} \leqslant d_{rR}) \qquad (4.4.3.2)$$

and:

$$r \in C \leftrightarrow r \in A \cap (d_{1R} > d_{rR}) \qquad (4.4.3.3)$$

Next, the three conditions (4.4.2.8)–(4.4.2.10) must be checked. Condition (4.4.2.8) and (4.4.2.9) are always satisfied because of the $\leqslant$ sign and the $>$ sign. If in both cases equality signs were allowed (thus $\leqslant$ and $\geqslant$), conditions (4.4.2.9) might be invalidated, viz., if a region $r$ could be found such that $d_{1R} = d_{rR}$; then an indeterminate situation would arise, so that $B \cap C = \phi$ is not always guaranteed. The connexity condition is not always satisfied, so that one should always take account of condition (4.4.2.10); if the universal set $A$ is convex and composed of regular elementary regions, condition (4.4.2.10) is satisfied.

As has already been stated, the successive distances can be represented most efficiently in an interregional distance table **D**. The elements $d_{rr'}$ denote the distance between region $r$ and $r'$. In (4.4.3.4) only the right upper part of the distance matrix is represented, since distances are, in general, symmetric in both directions.

$$\mathbf{D} = \begin{array}{c} \\ 1 \\ \vdots \\ R \end{array} \begin{array}{c} 1 \ldots\ldots R \\ \begin{bmatrix} 0 & & d_{rr'} \\ & \ddots & \\ 0 & & 0 \end{bmatrix} \end{array} \qquad (4.4.3.4)$$

In the case of *physical* distances the *intra*regional distances are supposed to be equal to zero, so that the diagonal elements of (4.4.3.4) are zero. The diagonal elements in the distance table of *economic* distances are not equal to zero, since these elements represent the squared distances with respect to the origin.

If the interregional distances are not symmetric, the lower part at the left of the matrix **D** must also be filled in (see 4.4.3.5). Such a situation may arise, if, for instance, distances are measured in time units needed to bridge the interregional physical distances. These time distances are not necessarily symmetric (for instance, upstream and downstream traffic for ships). In such an asymmetric situation the interregional distance can be calculated as a (weighted) average of the distances in either direction.

$$
\mathbf{D} = \begin{array}{c} 1 \\ \vdots \\ \vdots \\ R \end{array}
\overset{1 \;\ldots\ldots\ldots\; R}{\begin{bmatrix} 0 & & d_{rr'} \\ & \ddots & \\ d_{r'r} & & 0 \end{bmatrix}} \qquad (4.4.3.5)
$$

In addition to rectilinear, physical and time distances one may use economic distances as the basis for a regionalization procedure. The economic distances, dealt with in section 4.3, provide a theoretical basis for clustering of regions on the basis of similarity in the successive regional economic structures. Such a clustering procedure requires an extension of the concept of interregional economic distances. Beside a purely economic distance between two regions, one needs a measure for the economic distance between a *subset of regions* contained in one cluster, as well as a measure for the distance between subsets (groups or clusters) of regions. Therefore, these concepts will first be introduced (see also Stone [1960]).

Suppose a set $A$ of elementary regions $r$ ($r = 1, \ldots, R$). By grouping some of these elementary regions one obtains a cluster $c$ ($c = 1, \ldots, C$). A typical region $r$ within a cluster $c$ is denoted by $r_c$ ($r_c = 1_c, \ldots, R_c$). It is clear that the sum of all elementary regions results in the universal set $A$, i.e.,

$$\bigcup_{r=1}^{R} r = A \qquad (4.4.3.6)$$

Furthermore, the sum of all clusters gives also the original set $A$, i.e.,

$$\bigcup_{c=1}^{C} c = A \qquad (4.4.3.7)$$

while the sum of all regions within a cluster gives the cluster itself, i.e.,

$$\bigcup_{r_c=1_c}^{R_c} r_c = c \qquad (4.4.3.8)$$

The first new concept to be introduced is the economic distance between all regions $r_c$ within a cluster $c$, the so-called *compactness*. This compactness can be considered as an average distance between all regions $r_c$ of the cluster $c$. Therefore, the compactness of a cluster $c$ (or the average intracluster distance) is defined as:

$$D_c^2 = \sum_{\substack{r_c = 1_c \\ r_c < r_c'}}^{R_c} \sum_{r_c' = 1_c}^{R_c} d^2_{r_c r_c'} \Bigg/ \frac{R_c (R_c - 1)}{2} \qquad (4.4.3.9)$$

where the squared distances between all regions $r_c$ and $r_c'$ of group $c$ are added only for off-diagonal distances. Because the distance matrix is symmetric, only $r_c < r_c'$ is calculated. For the same reason the aggregated squared distances are divided by $R_c (R_c - 1)/2$, so that $D_c^2$ can be considered as an *average* degree of compactness.

Another new concept is the *intercluster distance*. This concept is defined as the average economic distance between regions $r_c$ ($r_c = 1_c, \ldots, R_c$) and regions $r_{c'}$ ($r_{c'} = 1_{c'}, \ldots, R_{c'}$), belonging to two successive clusters $c$ and $c'$. Therefore, this intercluster distance is defined as:

$$D^2_{cc'} = \sum_{r_c = 1_c}^{R_c} \sum_{r_{c'} = 1_{c'}}^{R_{c'}} d^2_{r_c r_{c'}} \Bigg/ R_c R_{c'} \qquad (4.4.3.10)$$

where the squared distances are divided by the total number of distances between regions of group $c$ and group $c'$, i.e., $R_c R_{c'}$. This can be checked by creating a corresponding distance table $D_{cc'}$ (see [4.4.3.11]).

$D_{cc'} =$ 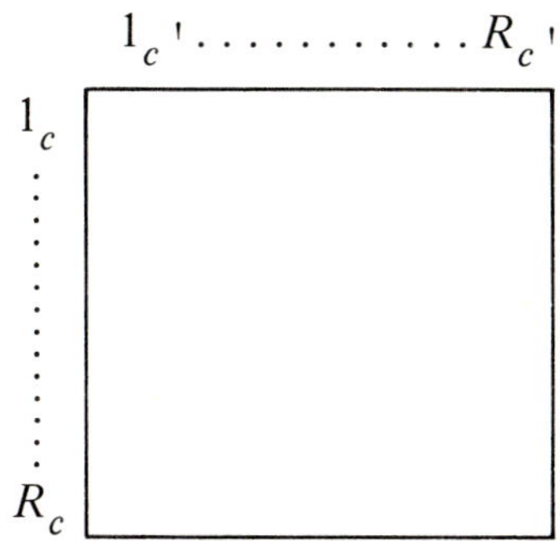

(4.4.3.11)

The total number of elements of $D_{cc'}$ *is equal to* $R_c R_{c'}$. This number corresponds to the $m \times n$ rule of set theory, which states that, if $A$ is a set of $m$ elements, and if $B$ is a set of $n$ elements, and if alternatively from each set one element is drawn, the total number of ordered pairs is equal to $m \times n$.

A systematic grouping procedure for elementary regions will make use of the new distance concepts (4.4.3.9) and (4.4.3.10). Such a procedure starts by assigning the two regions with a minimum distance to a first cluster 1. This minimum distance can easily be read from table (4.4.3.4). Suppose these two regions are denoted by $r_1$ and $r_1'$. The degree of compactness of this first cluster, composed of two regions, can easily be calculated according to (4.4.3.9), but it is clear that this degree of compactness in the case of two regions is exactly equal to the squared economic distance between these regions, i.e. $D_1^2 = d_{rr'}^2$.

Once a first cluster has been created, the region with a minimum distance with respect to this cluster will be included in this cluster. The average distance of this region with respect to the first cluster can easily be calculated by means of (4.4.3.10). Once this region has been included in the original cluster, one may proceed with another region or a set of regions, and so forth. It is clear, that one needs a demarcation criterion for including additional regions; otherwise, one would exhaust in the long run the whole universal set $A$, which would then be transformed in only one new region (built up from the whole original set). Therefore, one should impose the condition that the interregional distance between a new region (or a new set of regions) and the original cluster should not exceed a certain demarcation criterion for distances. For instance, this criterion might be $\alpha D_1^2$ (where $\alpha$ is a constant to be fixed *a priori*). Thus, if the interregional distance between the original cluster and another region (or set of regions), i.e. $D_{12}^2$, exceeds $\alpha D_1^2$, the cluster will not be extended with the region(s) concerned. This region (or set of regions) can then be used as the nucleus of a second group, and so forth, until the universal set $A$ is exhausted. Such a demarcation criterion corresponds to function $\varphi(a_i)$ in (4.4.2.7), and also to the procedure described in (4.4.3.2) and (4.4.3.3).

Instead of criterion $\alpha D_1^2$, which has to be recalculated for each extension of a cluster and for each new cluster, one might choose a more simple criterion, viz. by calculating the average distance $\bar{d}^2$ for all elements in the distance table. Then one may choose criterion $\beta \bar{d}^2$ as a demarcation criterion in the grouping procedure (where $\beta$ is again a constant to be fixed *a priori*).

It should finally be noted, that the regionalization procedure described above does not necessarily yield unique results, since the value of $\alpha$ affects the final results, and more in particular the number of new nuclei. In addition, the value of $\alpha$ (which is fixed *a priori*) should be such that ultimately connex regions are obtained.

The clustering procedure described above can be clarified by means of an example for 3 regions. Suppose one uses the following table of normalized distances as the basis for a grouping procedure:

Table 4.4.3.a

A hypothetical normalized distance table for 3 regions

| | 1 | 2 | 3 |
|---|---|---|---|
| 1 | 0·763 | 0·439 | 0·352 |
| 2 | | 1·578 | 0·243 |
| 3 | | | 0·657 |

The original three regions will be clustered into larger units by means of the foregoing regionalization procedure. The abstract distances between each pair of regions are the starting-point for this procedure. The economic distance between region 2 and 3 appears to be minimal, i.e.,

$$D_1^2 = (d_{23}^{**})^2 \qquad (4.4.3.12)$$

Therefore, region 2 and 3 are clustered into one group $c$. Next, the average distance of region 1 with respect to the cluster $c$ is calculated by means of (4.4.3.10). If region 1 is conceived of as a group $c'$, one finds:

$$\begin{aligned} D_{cc'}^2 &= (0{\cdot}352 + 0{\cdot}439)/2 \\ &= 0{\cdot}396 \end{aligned} \qquad (4.4.3.13)$$

Now it depends on the demarcation criterion, whether or not region 1 will be included in the first cluster. Region 1 will be included, if $D_{cc'}^2 \leqslant aD_1^2$, or: $0{\cdot}396 \leqslant 0{\cdot}243\, a$. Therefore, it depends on the value of $a$, whether the original cluster $c$ will be extended with region 1. The critical value of $a$ is easily calculated as 0·396/0·243 = 1·630. Furthermore, one should check the connexity condition.

Suppose the previous conditions are satisfied. Then the successive steps of this regionalization procedure can be represented in a figurative way by means of a *linkage tree*: such a tree describes at which level each elementary region is included into a larger subset.

Fig. 4.4.3.a A linkage tree

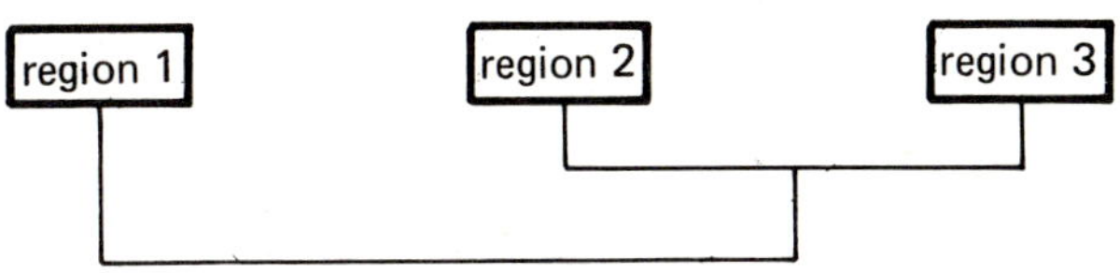


## 4.4.4 *The formation of homogeneous regions*

A homogeneous region contains elementary points which possess, from a given point of view, a high degree of similarity. A homogeneous region can be characterized by geographical, physical properties ('natural' region), by social, political and institutional properties ('administrative' region), or by economic properties.

A simple criterion for constructing homogeneous regions is the following one: the subsets $B$ and $C$ (separated from $A$) are homogeneous, if the elements $a_i$ ($i = 1, \ldots, I$) satisfy the following conditions:

$$a_i \in B \longleftrightarrow a_i \in \quad A \cap (x_i \geqslant \bar{x}) \qquad \forall\ i \tag{4.4.4.1}$$

and:

$$a_i \in C \longleftrightarrow a_i \in \quad A \cap (x_i < \bar{x}) \qquad \forall\ i \tag{4.4.4.2}$$

where $\bar{x}$ denotes a critical level of some variable, and where $x_i$ represents the value of a certain variable in a point $a_i \in A$. For instance, if the homogeneity criterion is the average regional income, $x_i$ represents average income in region $a_i$, and $\bar{x}$ represents average national income. Conditions (4.4.4.1) and (4.4.4.2) satisfy the conditions (4.4.2.8) and (4.4.2.9) from the extension-axiom, albeit that the connexity condition (4.4.2.10) is not always satisfied. If the connexity condition is not satisfied, a larger number of subsets (or subregions) may result: instead of a two-partite division of the universal set, one obtains more and smaller (connex) subsets.

If instead of one criterion two criteria are considered, one can find, in principle, 4 subsets. For instance, assume in addition to $x_i$ another variable $y_i$ with critical level $\bar{y}$. By means of a homogeneous grouping procedure one may obtain 4 subsets, each of which possesses one of the following 4 characteristics: $(x_i \geqslant \bar{x}) \cap (y_i \geqslant \bar{y})$, $(x_i \geqslant \bar{x}) \cap (y_i < \bar{y})$, $(x_i < \bar{x}) \cap (y_i \geqslant \bar{y})$ and $(x_i < \bar{x}) \cap (y_i < \bar{y})$. In general, if $n$ criteria are considered, one may find $2^n$ different homogeneous subsets, although a correlation between the variables may reduce the number of non-empty subsets.

An illustration of the foregoing phenomenon is a regionalization procedure applied to the 9 Belgian provinces. Two variables are considered, viz. the index of the regional income with respect to the average national income, and the regional rate of growth of the average income during the years 1953–1959. The national average values of these variables are considered as the critical values for a regionalization procedure. The data are contained in table 4.4.4.a. A systematic ranking of the Belgian provinces by means of both criteria specified above leads indeed to 4 different subsets. The results are presented in a concise way in table 4.4.4.b, which shows the regional classification based on the question as to whether the two variables exceed their critical values (cf. also Klaassen [1967]).

Table 4.4.4.a Economic data concerning Belgian provinces[3]

| Province \ Variable | Income per head compared to average national income | Rate of growth of income per head (1953–1959) |
|---|---|---|
| Brabant | 128 | 2·2 |
| Liège | 113 | 1·6 |
| Antwerp | 104 | 2·4 |
| National average of Belgium | 100 | 1·9 |
| Hainaut | 96 | 1·5 |
| Namur | 89 | 2·1 |
| East-Flanders | 83 | 2·4 |
| West-Flanders | 79 | 2·3 |
| Limbourg | 73 | 0·3 |
| Luxembourg | 72 | 1·6 |

Table 4.4.4.b A classification of the Belgian provinces

| Rate of growth of income per head \ Income per head | High | Low |
|---|---|---|
| High | Brabant<br>Antwerp | East-Flanders<br>West-Flanders<br>Namur |
| Low | Liège | Hainaut<br>Limbourg<br>Luxembourg |

The notion 'high' and 'low' denotes whether or not a variable in a certain region does exceed its critical value. Table 4.4.4.b is useful for constructing homogeneous regions. One would obtain 4 homogeneous regions, if the provinces in each of the 4 cells would be connex. However, only Brabant and Antwerp, and East-Flanders and West-Flanders are connex regions. Therefore, the ultimate number of remaining (connex) regions is 7, viz. 5 single provinces (Namur, Liège, Hainaut, Limbourg and Luxembourg) and 2 composite provinces (Brabant and Antwerp, and East-Flanders and West-Flanders; see also map 4.4.4.a). It is easily seen that the number of 7 regions can be reduced by decreasing the critical values of both variables.

Map 4.4.4.a Belgium

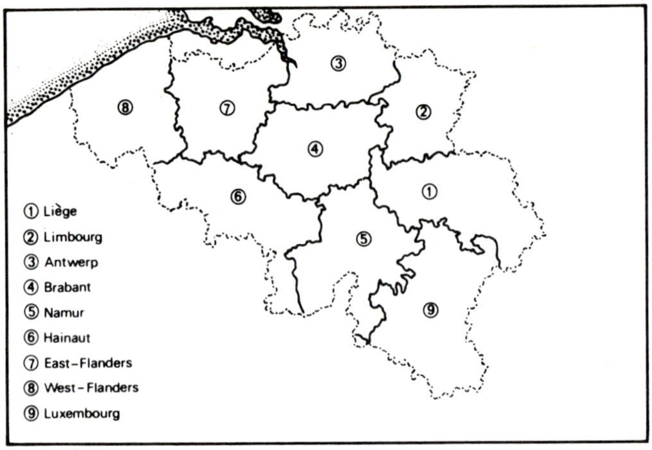


### 4.4.5 *The formation of polarized regions*

It has already been discussed in subsection 4.2.4 that polarized regions contain more intensive *internal* relationships than *external* relationships. Polarized regions are composed of elementary points which have a higher degree of interdependence than other points (cf. also Binswanger [1961, p. 144]). Thus the grouping procedure for polarized regions should be based on a criterion, which describes the degree of interdependence between elementary points or regions. Such an interdependence can be analyzed in various ways.

The flows between elementary points can be represented by means of flow-diagrams, contact-matrices and di-graphs (see subsection 1.6.3; also Boudeville [1966]). For instance, the economic flows between 4 points or elementary regions $r$ ($r = 1, \ldots, 4$) can be represented by means of figure 4.4.5a and 4.4.5b.

Fig. 4.4.5.a A flow-diagram

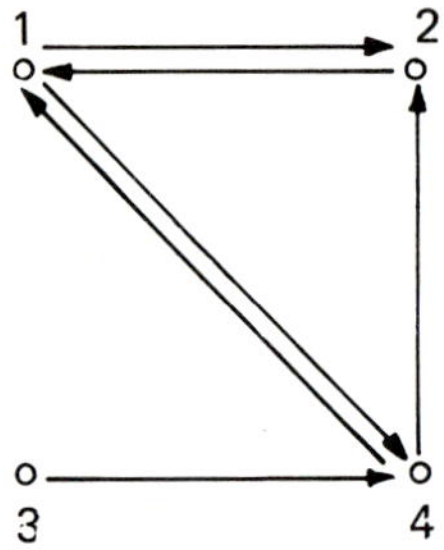


Fig. 4.4.5.b A contact-matrix

| | 1 | 2 | 3 | 4 |
|---|---|---|---|---|
| 1 | . | 1 | . | 1 |
| 2 | 1 | . | . | . |
| 3 | . | . | . | 1 |
| 4 | 1 | 1 | . | . |

The symbol '1' in the Boolean matrix of figure 4.4.5.b denotes the presence of a flow between relevant points in the direction concerned. The size of the flow is left out of consideration. This drawback can be reduced by assigning only a figure '1', if the flow concerned exceeds a certain minimum level. It is evident, that more information is retained, if the value of the flows themselves are represented.

The flow-diagrams and contact-matrices form the starting-point for the determination of connex polarized regions on the basis of flows between elementary regions. If by permutation of rows and columns the contact-matrix can be transformed into a (near-) block-diagonal matrix, the polarized regions can easily be determined: each block represents a polarized region, since it possesses a high degree of intra-dependence. For instance, if a contact-matrix can be transformed into the matrix represented in figure 4.4.5.c, a partition of the universal set *A* into two polarized regions is directly obtained.

Fig. 4.4.5.c A partitioned contact-matrix

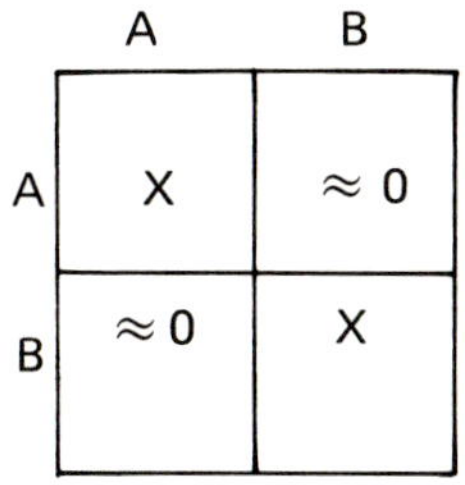


The symbol '*X*' in figure 4.4.5.c means that many elements in that part of the contact-matrix are equal to 1, whereas the symbol '$\approx 0$' means, that the major part of the elements in the block concerned is equal to zero. In this way the two polarized regions *A* and *B* can easily be found.

If a permutation is applied to the contact-matrix of figure 4.4.5.b, the following near-block-diagonal matrix can be obtained:

Fig. 4.4.5.d A permutated contact-matrix

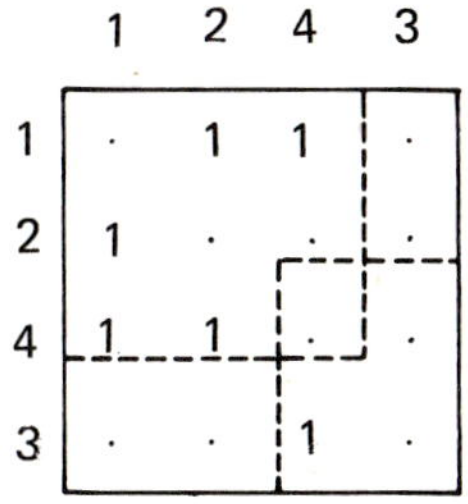

Figure 4.4.5.d shows that the elementary regions 1, 2 and 4 can be considered as a polarized region (supposing they are connex), whereas region 3 can, in a sense, also be considered as a polarized region.

If the contact-matrix can not be partitioned into diagonal blocks, one has to use a systematic algorithm in order to separate polarized regions from the universal set $A = \{ a_i \mid i = 1, \ldots, I \}$. Such a procedure can be started in a systematic way as follows: separate from $A$ a set of connex elementary regions, which have relatively a high degree of interdependence (i.e., the corresponding elements in the incidence-matrix are mainly equal to 1). This first set of elementary regions is denoted by $R_1 = \{ a_i \mid i = 1, \ldots, K; K < I \}$. A new elementary region $a_j$ is added to $R_1$, when the number of flows between $a_j$ and $R_1$, denoted by $N_{a_j R_1}$, exceeds the number of flows between $a_j$ and the remaining set of elementary regions (i.e., $N_{a_j \tilde{R}_1}$), where $\tilde{R}_1$ means the complement of $R_1$ with respect to $A$). By repeating this procedure for each element of $A$, a polarized region $B$ can be created, which satisfies the following formal condition:

$$a_j \in B \longleftrightarrow a_j \in \quad A \cap (N_{a_j R_1} \geqslant N_{a_j \tilde{R}_1}) \qquad (4.4.5.1)$$

The latter condition has some drawbacks, since a unique solution is not guaranteed: the starting-point is arbitrary and influences the outcome. Furthermore, the intensity of the various flows is left out of consideration. Finally, it should be noted, that the connexity condition is not always satisfied. Therefore, a grouping procedure for polarized regions, as described above, should be carefully considered and dealt with.

## 4.5 A numerical taxonomy for regionalization

### 4.5.1 *Introduction*

Section 4.4 was devoted to an axiomatic, operational approach to grouping procedures in regional economics. In this section the use of a systematic taxonomy for grouping procedures will be discussed.

*Quantitative (or numerical) taxonomy* is concerned with the numerical evaluation of affinities or similarities existing between given observation units, and with the subsequent classification of these units on the basis of their affinities. The result is the formation of certain *groups* or *clusters* (or again sets). The grouping of the individual observation units into larger sets should be based on a data analysis, which takes into account all numerical aspects of the original observation units.

The most evident application in regional economics is the formation of macro-regions on the basis of subregions, though many other applications are also possible (classification of towns in categories, of complexes in types, etc.). One should always be aware of the fact that often the *contiguity-condition* works as a constraint (cf. also [4.4.2.10] ). A discussion of a quantitative taxonomy can be found *inter alia* in Benzécri et al. (1973), Chevalier (1971), Guigou (1974), Roux (1968), and Sokal and Sneath (1963).

### 4.5.2 *Operational principles*

Quantitative or numerical taxonomy is a systematic classification procedure, which takes account of a set of *operational principles*. The basis of a numerical taxonomy is formed by ten principles (cf. also Sokal and Sneath [1963] ), although some of them may be debatable. These principles are presented below.

1 The classification is a *function of the objective pursued*. An example of this would be two different, non-overlapping classifications of the same regions, depending on whether one wants to give an accurate, geographical description (for instance, the case of homogeneous regions), or a starting-point for a thorough analysis of the economic structure (for instance, the case of functional or polarized regions).

2 Classification can be based – and is mostly based – on *characteristics of different nature*. It has already been stated in section 3.3, that this heterogeneity raises the problem of units of measurement, and of independence of information (normalization, standardization, orthogonalization).

3 A classification is always *relative*, viz., a function of the available information and the initial hypotheses. This is particularly true in the case of regionalization, in which, in general, only a limited amount of (numerical) characteristics are available.

4 Classification should be based on *objectively apparent characteristics of the entities analyzed at the moment of the analysis*. This exludes, for instance, the possibility that reference is made to historical events, which were responsible for the observed state of affairs. These events, however, could be used later on as a possible *ex post* factor of explanation. An example is that of old coal-and-steel areas, where coal-mines were the historical location factor of the steel industry. A principal component analysis (see section 4.6) revealed a clearly distinguishable factor in these coal-and-steel regions in Europe, for which the explanation was given in a later stage of the analysis (see Paelinck, Molle and Van Holst [1971] ).

5 A classification should be *exhaustive*: there should be no items overlooked in the analysis (see section 4.4).
6 A classification should be *exclusive*: subsets should be non-overlapping (see also section 4.4).
7 For a given target in the analysis, the *same classification principles should be used throughout all stages of the analysis*. This implies that the set of characteristics should be fixed from the start, although, as will be seen later, different levels of decision criteria could generate different groupings.
8 The characteristics, *that separate large groups*, should be considered as *more important* than those referring to *smaller groups*. This might imply an element of arbitrariness, but it is justified by principle 1 (objective-oriented classification), since classification exercises are mostly only an intermediate step to a further analysis.
9 *Qualitative* characteristics should not be excluded, as long as some scale of measurement (for instance, an ordinal scale) can be introduced. Examples of such non-quantitative characteristics in regional and urban economics are the quality of life, the appreciation of the environment, the 'image of the city', etc.
10 Finally, the exercise should lead to a *class-hierarchy*. The way in which such an hierarchy can be achieved will be shown later on.

The previous ten principles constitute the foundation stones for the classification considered in the following subsections.

### 4.5.3 *Similarity between items within a class*

The quantitative starting-point for a numerical taxonomy is the cross-matrix of elementary regions and characteristics, the so-called regional data matrix (see [4.3.2.1]). The most simple way to describe the regional system concerned by means of characteristics, is to assign a value of '0' or '1' to a certain characteristic, according to whether the characteristic concerned is absent or present in the corresponding region (see, for instance, the data matrix [4.5.3.1]).

Such a simple way of dealing with regional data may be caused by lack of precise data. Another reason why the matrix (4.5.3.1) may be relevant is the fact that the 0–1 representation may include qualitative factors. If the characteristics are measured on a certain scale, the 0–1 decision necessarily rests on the acceptance of a threshold-value. Then the mapping can be described as follows:

$$\delta_{ri} = \begin{cases} 1, \text{ if } x_{ri} \geqslant d_i \\ 0, \text{ otherwise} \end{cases} \qquad (4.5.3.2)$$

where $\delta_{ri}$ represents a 0–1 integer for the $i^{th}$ characteristic in region $r$, where $x_{ri}$ represents the value of the $i^{th}$ characteristic in region $r$ (measured on a certain scale), and where $d_i$ represents the relevant threshold-value of the $i^{th}$ characteristic. The choice of $d_i$ will, in general, depend on the interregional distribution of the corresponding characteristic $i$.

| Region \ Characteristic | $1 \ldots\ldots\ldots\ldots I$ |  |
|---|---|---|
| 1 | $1 \ldots\ldots\ldots\ldots 0$ |  |
| . | $1 \ldots\ldots\ldots\ldots 1$ |  |
| . | $\ldots\ldots\ldots\ldots\ldots$ |  |
| . | $\ldots\ldots\ldots\ldots\ldots$ | (4.5.3.1) |
| . | $\ldots\ldots\ldots\ldots\ldots$ |  |
| . | $\ldots\ldots\ldots\ldots\ldots$ |  |
| $R$ | $0 \ldots\ldots\ldots\ldots 1$ |  |

By selecting two row vectors from the matrix in (4.5.3.1), one may compare, on the basis of the presence or absence of the relevant characteristics, the economic structures of both regions concerned. The following table, which shows in an aggregated way the results of table (4.5.3.1), can be used for a further analysis of the similarity between region $r$ and region $r'$.

|  | Region $r'$ |  | Total |
|---|---|---|---|
| Region $r$ | $I^{11}_{rr'}$ | $I^{10}_{rr'}$ | $I^{1}_{r}$ |
|  | $I^{01}_{rr'}$ | $I^{00}_{rr'}$ | $I^{0}_{r}$ |
| Total | $I^{1}_{r'}$ | $I^{0}_{r'}$ | $I$ |

(4.5.3.3)

The element $I^{11}_{rr'}$ represents the total number of times that the characteristics are present both in region $r$ and in region $r'$. In a similar way the element $I^{10}_{rr'}$ represents the total number of times that the characteristics are present in region $r$, but absent in region $r'$, and so forth. The aggregated element $I^1_r$ represents the total number of times that the characteristics are present in region $r$, and so forth (i.e., $I^1_r = I^{11}_{rr'} + I^{10}_{rr'}$). Ultimate, the element $I$ represents the total number of characteristics.

Matrix (4.5.3.3) is a useful tool in order to inspect the similarity between region $r$ and $r'$. A simple way of further analysis is the construction of a so-called *similarity-index* on the basis of the numbers shown in the matrix. Such a similarity matrix indicates the degree to which the regions show a close affinity. The construction of a similarity-index leads to some problems; in particular, should the simultaneous absence of the same characteristic be considered as similarity or dissimilarity? For instance, does the absence of an airport in two regions indicate an affinity between these regions? In case one gives a positive answer, one can construct a similarity index $s_{rr'}$ between region $r$ and $r'$:

$$s_{rr'} \triangleq (I^{11}_{rr'} + I^{00}_{rr'})/I \qquad (4.5.3.4)$$

in which the simultaneous presence or absence of a characteristic in both regions is considered as a similarity. The similarity-indices can be integrated into a so-called similarity-matrix. A *maximum similarity* is obtained, if one observes exclusively a simultaneous presence or absence of all characteristics in both regions. Then $I^{01}_{rr'} = I^{10}_{rr'} = 0$, which implies that $I^{11}_{rr'} + I^{00}_{rr'} = I$, or $s_{rr'} = 1$. In a similar way one can prove that a *maximum dissimilarity* implies $s_{rr'} = 0$. Furthermore, it is evident that $s_{rr'} = s_{r'r}$. A useful feature of $s_{rr'}$ is that a link can be formed with the abstract distance analysis exposed in section 4.3; one can, in fact, define a similarity-index $s^*_{rr'}$ as an inverse function of the distance between region $r$ and $r'$ in the following way:

$$s^*_{rr'} \triangleq (1 + d_{rr'})^{-1} \qquad (4.5.3.5)$$

The latter index bears a close resemblance to (4.5.3.4). It is easily seen, that a minimum distance between region $r$ and $r'$ (i.e., $d_{rr'} = 0$) leads to a maximum similarity, i.e., $s^*_{rr'} = 1$. In a similar way one can prove that a maximum distance (i.e., $d_{rr'} \to \infty$) implies a minimum similarity, i.e., $s^*_{rr'} = 0$. Finally, it is obvious that $s^*_{rr'} = s^*_{r'r}$, since the distance-concept is symmetric. The way in which a similarity-index can be used for regionalization is discussed in the following subsection.

### 4.5.4 *Grouping on the basis of similarity*

In this subsection a simple approach to regionalization will be exposed. A more advanced method is set out in a following subsection.

A simple but intuitive criterion for grouping procedures is that each member of a group should have a smaller distance to the other members of the same group than to members of other groups (see also subsection 4.4.3). The following example may clarify this criterion. Suppose a distance matrix **D** (cf. [4.4.3.4] ), represented in 4.5.4.2). This distance matrix might be calculated on the basis of the abstract economic distances, exposed in section 4.4. Another method of calculating the distance matrix is to make implicitly use of (4.5.3.4) and (4.5.3.5), since one can calculate on the basis of (4.5.3.5);

$$d_{rr'} = (1-s^*_{rr'})/s^*_{rr'} \qquad (4.5.4.1)$$

Next, by assuming that $s^*_{rr}$ corresponds to the similarity index $s_{rr'}$ from (4.5.3.4), one can easily calculate the abstract distance $d_{rr'}$ in (4.5.4.1). An illustration of this approach is the distance matrix, represented in (4.5.4.2).

| Regions | 1 | 2 | 3 | 4 | 5 |
|---|---|---|---|---|---|
| 1 | 0 | 1 | 8 | 10 | 6 |
| 2 | 1 | 0 | 7 | 9 | 5 |
| 3 | 8 | 7 | 0 | 2 | 3 |
| 4 | 10 | 9 | 2 | 0 | 4 |
| 5 | 6 | 5 | 3 | 4 | 0 |

(4.5.4.2)

Next, one can construct a *'nearness' matrix* **N**, showing, row by row, the ranking of the other regions in terms of proximity. For instance, in the first row of (4.5.4.2) the first region receives the rank number 1, the second region the rank number 2, the fifth region the rank number 3, the third region the rank number 4, and the fourth region the rank number 5. In this way all rows of (4.5.4.2) can be dealt with. The resulting nearness matrix is represented in (4.5.4.3):

| Regions | 1 | 2 | 3 | 4 | 5 |
|---|---|---|---|---|---|
| 1 | 1 | 2 | 4 | 5 | 3 |
| 2 | 2 | 1 | 4 | 5 | 3 |
| 3 | 5 | 4 | 1 | 2 | 3 |
| 4 | 5 | 4 | 2 | 1 | 3 |
| 5 | 5 | 4 | 2 | 3 | 1 |

(4.5.4.3)

Matrix (4.5.4.2) is the starting point for a grouping procedure. This grouping procedure again evokes the question as how to attack the combinatorial problem of combining elementary regions into larger units (see also section 4.2–4.4). A useful starting-point for such a cluster procedure is to select first those elementary regions, which possess maximum similarity (or minimum distance). Once an initial cluster of elementary regions has been constructed, one may use this initial cluster for an inclusion of new elementary regions. A first set of regions, which possess a high degree of similarity, is composed of regions 1 and 2. The *partial nearness matrix* $\mathbf{N}_{12}$ between region 1 and 2 is represented in (4.5.4.4):

| | 1 | 2 |
|---|---|---|
| 1 | 1 | 2 |
| 2 | 2 | 1 |

(4.5.4.4)

Next, one may attempt at adding a new region to the previous initial cluster. It appears that region 5 shows the next highest resemblance with respect to the initial cluster. Adding region 5 one finds the extended partial nearness matrix $\mathbf{N}_{125}$

| | 1 | 2 | 5 |
|---|---|---|---|
| 1 | 1 | 2 | 3 |
| 2 | 2 | 1 | 3 |
| 5 | 5 | 4 | 1 |

(4.5.4.5)

Although region 5 is the next nearest to 1 and 2, the reverse case that region 1 and 2 are the next nearest to region 5 is not true. This can be shown in the following way. The partial nearness matrix $\mathbf{N}_{34}$ is exactly equal to $\mathbf{N}_{12}$. Therefore, one may compare the extended partial nearness matrices $\mathbf{N}_{125}$ and $\mathbf{N}_{345}$ in order to inspect which of these possesses a maximum internal homogeneity. Matrix $\mathbf{N}_{345}$ is represented in (4.5.4.6):

| | 3 | 4 | 5 |
|---|---|---|---|
| 3 | 1 | 2 | 3 |
| 4 | 2 | 1 | 3 |
| 5 | 2 | 3 | 1 |

(4.5.4.6)

It appears that $\mathbf{N}_{345}$ possesses a higher degree of internal homogeneity than $\mathbf{N}_{125}$, so that regions 3 and 4 are nearer to region 5 than region 1 and 2. Therefore, one may partition the set of regions into (1, 2) and (3, 4, 5) on the basis of the selected criterion. The previous procedure is, however, *not* necessarily valid in all cases, due to the *lack of symmetry* of **N**. This symmetry is a necessary (though not, as will be set out later on, a sufficient) condition for an unique classification of regions on the basis of a certain technique. If an unique classification of the elementary regions does not succeed, a way out of the difficulty can be found by calculating the average minimal distances between regions or clusters of regions (see subsection 4.4.3). For instance, the average distance between the cluster of regions (1, 2) and region 3 can be calculated as $d_{(1,2)3} = ½\,(d_{13} + d_{23})$. Then $d_{(1,2)3}$ is a possible measure of the distance of region 3 to the regions in cluster (1,2). This is, in fact, the technique used in subsection 4.4.3, so that the grouping procedure from subsection 4.4.3 can be combined with the grouping procedure set out above. The same principle underlies such techniques as quadratic assignment (see Ch.3 and Ch.6; see also Scott [1971]). Another method of grouping elementary regions into larger subsets is discussed in section 4.5.5.

### 4.5.5 *Indexed hierarchies*

In this subsection a new grouping procedure will be set out. It is based on an *indexed hierarchy* (see Roux [1968]), and it gives more insight into the way a regionalization can make use of a relaxation of threshold values of a similarity index.

A *hierarchy* can be considered as a progressive, non-overlapping grouping of all elements of a set in such a way that this grouping has the figurative structure of a tree with branches. Such a linkage tree arises, for instance, during the successive stages of joining elementary regions into larger spatial units (cf. section 4.4.3–4.4.5).

In an axiomatic way a hierarchy can be defined by means of 4 typical properties. A set $H$ with elements $x_i$ ($i = 1, \ldots, I$) is a hierarchy, if:

(1) $H$ is a set of subsets of a universal set $E$ of the observations $x_i$; for instance, if $E = \{ x_1, x_2, x_3 \}$, an example of a hierarchy is: $H = \{ x_1, x_2, x_3, (x_1, x_2), (x_1, x_2, x_3) \}$.
(2) The universal set $E$ as a whole is a subset of the hierarchy, i.e., $E \subset H$.
(3) Each individual element $x_i \in E$ is also an element of $H$.
(4) For all subsets $a \subset H$ and $b \subset H$ the following condition is valid: if $a \cap b \neq \phi$, then $a \subset b$ or $b \subset$ a.

Properties (1)–(3) are obvious; property (4) implies a two-partition of the subsets (or elements) of $H$: the subsets of $H$ are either fully separated (i.e., the subsets are not comparable), or in each pair of subsets one subset is a subset of the other (then the elements of the subsets have some restrictive properties; they can not be obtained by arbitrary combinations of all elementary units from the universal set $E$). For instance, the *power-set* (i.e., the set of all (single and composite) combinations of the elements of $E$) does not satisfy the fourth property. For example, the power-set of the universal set $E = \{x_1, x_2, x_3\}$ is: $\{x_1, x_2, x_3, (x_1, x_2), (x_1, x_3), (x_2, x_3), (x_1, x_2, x_3), \phi\}$. The subsets $\{x_1, x_2\}$ and $\{x_1, x_3\}$ do not satisfy property (4): the fact that $\{x_1, x_2\} \cap \{x_1, x_3\} \neq \phi$ does not imply $\{x_1, x_2\} \subset \{x_1, x_3\}$ nor $\{x_1, x_3\} \subset \{x_1, x_2\}$.

Next, an hierarchy is called *indexed*, if there exists a mapping $s(.)$ from $H$ onto the real interval [0,1], such that, if $a$ and $b$ are subsets of $H$, the two following conditions are satisfied:

(1) If $a$ is a (single) element $x_i$ of $E$, then $s(a) = 1$.
(2) If $a \subset b$, then $s(a) > s(b)$.

The mapping $s(.)$ could, for instance, be derived on the basis of abstract distances between the successive elements of the universal set $E$ (cf. also [4.5.3.5]).

The essential idea of the previous mapping $s(.)$ can be described within this framework as follows: $s(x_i, x_j)$ is the index of the *smallest set* in the hierarchy, that contains $x_i$ and $x_j$. In other words, $s(x_i, x_j)$ is the *highest* value of the indices for those subsets of $H$, which contain $x_i$ and $x_j$. This implies that the index $s(.)$ associated with a group of elements is constructed in such a way that the index of a smaller group of elements exceeds always the index of a larger group of elements which contains the previous smaller group. This may be clarified by means of the following example. Suppose a set of 5 relevant regions, each of which is characterized by means of a certain regional economic indicator $x_i$ ($i = 1, \ldots, 5$). Then the hierarchy, composed of $H = \{x_1, x_2, x_3, x_4, x_5\ (x_1, x_2), (x_3, x_4), (x_1, x_2, x_3, x_4), (x_1, x_2, x_3, x_4, x_5)\}$, can be derived from the universal set $E = \{x_1, x_2, x_3, x_4, x_5\}$. An (arbitrary) example of such an indexing for $H$ is represented in figure 4.5.5.a, which shows a mapping $s$ from $H$ onto the real interval [0,1]. For each subset of the hierarchy a value of $s$ is defined, and, inversely, for each level of $s$, there exists a partition of $E$, $P(s)$, such that:

$$
\left.\begin{array}{lll}
P(1.) & = & \{x_1, x_2, x_3, x_4, x_5\} \\
P(.8) & = & \{(x_1, x_2), x_3, x_4, x_5\} \\
P(.6) & = & \{(x_1, x_2), (x_3, x_4), x_5\} \\
P(.5) & = & \{(x_1, x_2, x_3, x_4), x_5\} \\
P(.2) & = & \{(x_1, x_2, x_3, x_4, x_5)\}
\end{array}\right\} \qquad (4.5.5.1)
$$

Since $s(x_i, x_j)$ is the maximum value of the indices for all subsets of $H$, that contain $x_i$ and $x_j$ (see above), it is obvious that $s(x_1, x_2) = 0{\cdot}8$, $s(x_3, x_4) = 0{\cdot}6$, $s(x_1, x_3) = 0{\cdot}5$, and $s(x_1, x_5) = 0{\cdot}2$. In fact, $s(x_i, x_j)$ can be considered as a similarity index discussed above. Evidently, the mapping $s$ is such that $0 \leqslant s \leqslant 1$. A low value of $s$ implies a low threshold value, in order to assure that the elements concerned can be included in a larger subset. A decline in the threshold value implies that the homogeneity of the subset (i.e., the similarity between the elements) decreases.

Fig. 4.5.5.a An indexed hierarchy

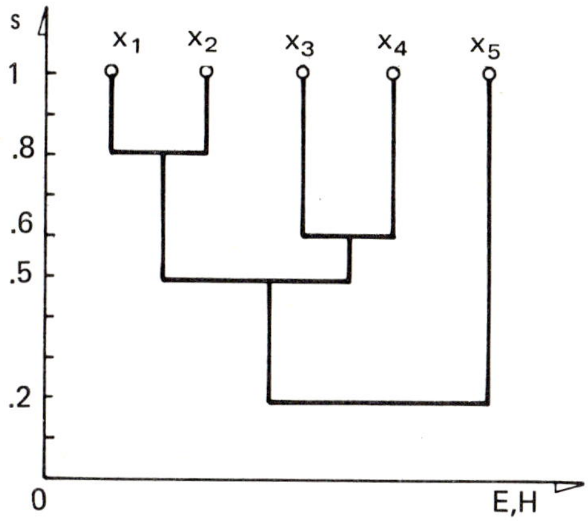


On the basis of figure 4.5.5.a an associated similarity-matrix can be derived in a straightforward way. Such a similarity-matrix is composed of elements the values of which are determined by the mapping $s(.)$, viz. by the highest values of $s(.)$ between the successive paired elements. These elements can be considered as the similarity-indices $s(x_i, x_j)$ derived above; therefore, it is obvious that this matrix is symmetric. The similarity-matrix associated with the previous example is:

| Regions | 1 | 2 | 3 | 4 | 5 |
|---|---|---|---|---|---|
| 1 | 1 | .8 | .5 | .5 | .2 |
| 2 | .8 | 1 | .5 | .5 | .2 |
| 3 | .5 | .5 | 1 | .6 | .2 |
| 4 | .5 | .5 | .6 | 1 | .2 |
| 5 | .2 | .2 | .2 | .2 | 1 |

(4.5.5.2)

The latter similarity-matrix, obtained by means of an indexed hierarchy, can again be used for grouping procedures in the way set out above. For instance, a set of elementary regions can be combined during a series of successive steps into larger units on the basis of a certain regional characteristic. The degree to which this regional characteristic shows a similar pattern among the elementary regions or among sets of elementary regions determines the successive values of $s(.)$. In this way an indexed hierarchy can lead to a systematic regionalization on the basis of similarity. A symmetric similarity matrix, however does *not* in turn necessarily correspond to an indexed hierarchy, as the following matrix shows:

| Regions | 1 | 2 | 3 | 4 | 5 |
|---|---|---|---|---|---|
| 1 | 1 | .5 | .6 | .2 | .8 |
| 2 | .5 | 1 | .8 | .3 | .7 |
| 3 | .6 | .8 | 1 | .4 | .6 |
| 4 | .2 | .3 | .4 | 1 | .5 |
| 5 | .8 | .7 | .6 | .5 | 1 |

(4.5.5.3)

This matrix is not compatible with a hierarchy, as appears from figure 4.5.5.b. For instance, $x_2$ is combined with the element $x_5$ at the level $s = 0{\cdot}7$, whereas $x_1$ (which is included in the cluster $(x_1, x_5)$ at the level $s = 0{\cdot}8$) is combined with $x_2$ at the level $s = 0{\cdot}5$. The matrix (4.5.5.3) contains many of such incompatibilities, so that a symmetric similarity matrix does not necessarily correspond to an indexed hierarchy.

Fig. 4.5.5.b  A false indexed hierarchy

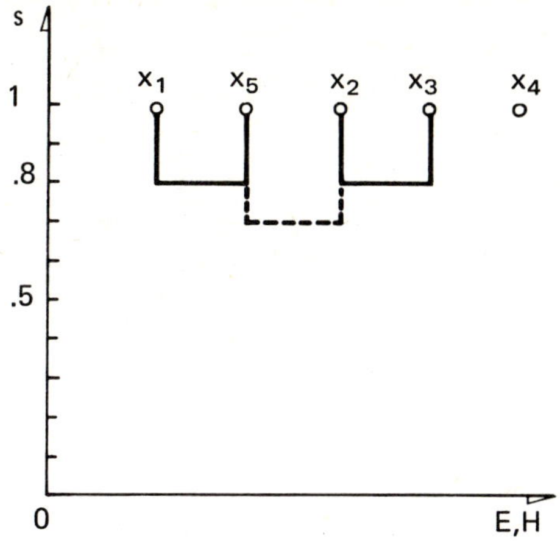


In case of such an incompatible similarity-matrix one way out is to abandon the strict similarity concept and use an approximation to the similarity matrix. For instance, one might again switch to the distance concept by defining a distance $d_{ij}$ as:

$$d_{ij} \triangleq 1 - s(x_i, x_j) \qquad (4.5.5.4)$$

Roux (1968) proposed in such situations the notion of *ultrametric* distances, which are a generalization of the previously defined distance concepts.

Another method, which is more frequently used in grouping procedures, is a *factor analysis*. This method is discussed in section 4.6.

## 4.6 Factor analysis in regional research

### 4.6.1 *Introduction*

*Factor analysis* is a statistical technique by means of which a set of observed values of characteristics (for instance, income, employment, population density, and so forth) can be summarized into a (usually smaller) set of basic categories or *factors*. Such a multidimensional scaling method is particularly useful to select patterns of *association* (or *clusters* of variables) between attributes or phenomena, which form a mutually correlated, complex set of forces. Factor analysis permits a reduction of a large number of variables to a limited number of basic dimensions that yet explain the observations on the original attributes, while all statistically relevant and non-redundant information is maintained.

For instance, average regional income and the degree of industrialization are, in general, correlated. They may, in fact, be reduced to one basic factor, viz., the regional economic structure. The latter factor explains for a major part the levels of the two original variables. If more variables are taken into account, the number of basic explaining variables may also rise, but, in general, a very limited number of factors remains. This limited number of basic factors is often easier to interpret than the original set of variables.

The way in which the factors can be determined will be described below in subsection 4.6.2. The factors themselves are frequently required to be mutually independent. Since orthogonal vectors are independent (see Murdoch [1957]), and thus uncorrelated, the factors are often determined such that they are orthogonal vectors. In this way each factor forms an independent magnitude, that incorporates a part of the fundamental relationships underlying the observations on the structural variables.

The aim of orthogonal factor analysis is to determine a minimum number of independent factors, that represent the variations of the original observations in a multidimensional space. Each of the factors may be associated with one or more of the original variables. On the basis of this linkage one may identify and interpret each factor. A more formal derivation of the way in which factors can be derived is contained in subsection 4.6.2.

Factor analysis is at the moment an instrument which is often used in regional research. An extensive treatment of factor analysis is contained *inter alia* in Harman (1964); other contributions are found *inter alia* in Benzécri et al. (1973), in Broadbent (1968), Cattell (1965), Isard (1960) and King (1969).

### 4.6.2 *A formal exposition*

Factor analysis starts with the construction of a *data matrix*, which encompasses $I$ variables (attributes or characteristics). Furthermore, $J$ observations on each of these $I$ variables are assumed to be available; these observations on each variable may relate to different time periods or to different regions. If the observations relate to different regions, the data matrix that is required, is precisely equal to the regional data matrix (4.3.2.1). The general representation of a data matrix is:

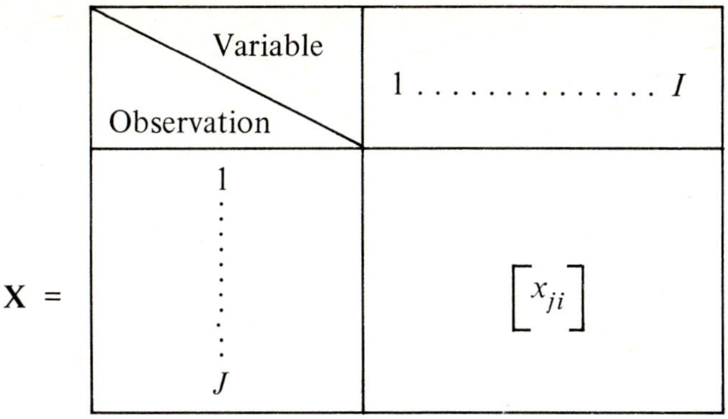


(4.6.2.1)

The typical element $x_{ji}$ ($j = 1, \ldots, J$; $i = 1, \ldots, I$) represents the $j^{th}$ observation on the $i^{th}$ variable. All variables are supposed to be standardized into meaningful units in order to allow comparisons between variables (see subsection 4.3.2).

The elements of the data matrix are used for the calculation of a *correlation matrix*, since a correlation matrix is the basis of a factor-analysis procedure. This correlation matrix is easily determined by transforming the matrix **X** from (4.6.2.1) into a new matrix **Z**, the elements of which are the (statistically) standardized elements of **X**. Therefore, the typical element $z_{ji}$ of the matrix **Z** is:

$$z_{ji} = \frac{x_{ji} - \bar{x}_i}{s_i} \qquad (4.6.2.2)$$

where $\bar{x}_i$ is the mean of $x_{ji}$ ($j = 1, \ldots, J$), i.e.,

$$\bar{x}_i = \frac{\sum_{j=1}^{J} x_{ji}}{J} \qquad (4.6.2.3)$$

and where $s_i$ is the standard deviation of $x_{ji}$, i.e.,

$$s_i = \sqrt{\frac{\sum_{j=1}^{J} (x_{ji} - \bar{x}_i)^2}{J}} \qquad (4.6.2.4)$$

This statistical standardization should be distinguished from the standardization procedure in subsection 4.3.2, which was related to the problem of finding adequate interregional comparison measures. The statistical standardization implies, that $z_{ji}$ has a mean equal to zero and a standard deviation equal to one.

In line with (4.3.2.12) the correlation coefficient $r_{ii'}$ between variable $i$ and $i'$ is equal to:

$$r_{ii'} = \frac{\sum_{j=1}^{J} (x_{ji} - \bar{x}_i)(x_{ji'} - \bar{x}_{i'})}{\sqrt{\sum_{j=1}^{J} (x_{ji} - \bar{x}_i)^2 \sum_{j=1}^{J} (x_{ji'} - \bar{x}_{i'})^2}} = \frac{(\mathbf{x}_{\bullet i} - \bar{\mathbf{x}}_i)'(\mathbf{x}_{\bullet i'} - \bar{\mathbf{x}}_{i'})}{||\mathbf{x}_{\bullet i} - \bar{\mathbf{x}}_i|| \cdot ||\mathbf{x}_{\bullet i'} - \bar{\mathbf{x}}_{i'}||} \qquad (4.6.2.5)$$

where $\mathbf{x}_{\bullet i}$ represents a vector of order $J \times 1$ with elements $x_{ji}$ ($j = 1, \ldots, J$), and where $\bar{\mathbf{x}}_i$ represents a vector of order $J \times 1$ with (equal) elements $\bar{x}_i$. This correlation coefficient is equal to:

$$r_{ii'} = \frac{\sum_{j=1}^{J} z_{ji} z_{ji'}}{\sqrt{\sum_{j=1}^{J} z_{ji}^2 \sum_{j=1}^{J} z_{ji'}^2}} \qquad (4.6.2.6)$$

as is easily seen after substitution of (4.6.2.2) into (4.6.2.5). The correlation coefficient can also be written as:

$$r_{ii'} = \frac{\mathbf{z}'_{\bullet i} \mathbf{z}_{\bullet i'}}{||\mathbf{z}_{\bullet i}|| \cdot ||\mathbf{z}_{\bullet i'}||} \qquad (4.6.2.7)$$

where $\mathbf{z}_{\bullet i}$ is a vector of order $J \times 1$ with typical elements $z_{ji}$ ($j = 1, \ldots, J$). Therefore, the correlation matrix can easily be calculated, if matrix **X** is transformed into **Z**. It should be noted that $r_{ii'}$ is exactly equal to the cosine of the angle between the vectors $\mathbf{z}_{\bullet i}$ and $\mathbf{z}_{\bullet i'}$ (see, for instance, Murdoch [1957]). This justifies the upper and lower limits of $r_{ii'}$, viz.

$$-1 \leqslant r_{ii'} \leqslant +1 \qquad (4.6.2.8)$$

Furthermore, it is easily seen now, that a complete association between two variables $i$ and $i'$ implies that the correlation coefficient is equal to + 1 (positive correlation) or −1 (negative correlation). The case of completely unassociated variables implies a correlation coefficient equal to zero. The correlation matrix itself is a square matrix of order $I$; its elements are symmetric, while the elements on the main diagonal are equal to one. This correlation matrix will be used later on in relation to a factor model.

Factor analysis attempts at reducing a large set of variables to a limited set of basic underlying factors. For that reason the assumption is made that there exists a linear relationship between the original variables $z_{ji}$ and a set of fundamental factors. These factors arise, when the standardized variables ($z_{ji}$) are reduced to certain basic categories. In the case of an orthogonal factor analysis (which will be discussed here), the basic factors are assumed to be *orthogonal* in order to guarantee uncorrelated factors. Each of these factors possesses a weight with respect to each variable. These weights are called loadings; they have to be estimated from the original observation material. The following relationship, the *factor model*, forms the foundation stone of factor analysis:

$$\begin{aligned} \mathbf{z}_{\bullet i} &= l_{i1}\,\mathbf{f}_1 + \ldots . + l_{iK}\,\mathbf{f}_K \\ &= \sum_{k=1}^{K} l_{ik}\,\mathbf{f}_k \end{aligned} \qquad (4.6.2.9)$$

where $l_{iK}$ ($k = 1, \ldots, K$) is the unknown loading, which relates the $i^{\text{th}}$ variable to the $k^{\text{th}}$ factor. The vector $\mathbf{f}_k$ ($k = 1, \ldots, K$) of order $J$ represents the $k^{\text{th}}$ factor in the factor model. The maximum number of factors is equal to $I$, i.e. $K \leqslant I$. The set of factors is unknown, as well as the set of all loadings. This is an essential difference with respect to a normal regression analysis, where only the coefficients have to be estimated. In the previous factor model both the coefficients (i.e., $l_{ik}$) and the 'explaining' variables (i.e., $\mathbf{f}_k$) have to be determined. It is evident, that this situation involves much more degrees of freedom than is the case in regression analysis. Therefore, a unique determination of both $l_{ik}$ and $\mathbf{f}_k$ requires additional hypotheses. These additional hypotheses may be of a different nature: they depend on the problem at hand, and on the aim the factor is used for.

If one assumes that the previous factor model is a *stochastic* model, one may introduce a vector of disturbance terms $\epsilon_{\bullet i}$, i.e.,

$$\mathbf{z}_{\bullet i} = \sum_{k=1}^{K} l_{ik}\,\mathbf{f}_k + \boldsymbol{\epsilon}_{\bullet i} \qquad (4.6.2.10)$$

The following assumptions concerning this stochastic model may be made:[5]

$$\left.\begin{array}{lll} \mathcal{E}(\boldsymbol{\epsilon}_{\bullet i}) = 0 & \mathcal{E}(\mathbf{f}_k' \, \mathbf{f}_k) = 1 & \mathcal{E}(\mathbf{z}_{\bullet i}) = 0 \\ \mathcal{E}(\boldsymbol{\epsilon}_{\bullet i}' \, \epsilon_{\bullet i'}) = 0,\ i \neq i' & \mathcal{E}(\mathbf{f}_k' \, \mathbf{f}_{k'}) = 0,\ k \neq k' & \\ \mathcal{E}(\boldsymbol{\epsilon}_{\bullet i}' \, \epsilon_{\bullet i}) = \sigma_i^2 & \mathcal{E}(\mathbf{f}_k' \, \epsilon_{\bullet i}) = 0 & \end{array}\right\} \qquad (4.6.2.11)$$

The first set of three assumptions states that the disturbances have an expectation equal to zero, a covariance equal to zero, and a variance equal to $\sigma_i^2$, respectively. The second set of three assumptions implies that the factors are normalized (i.e., an expected length equal to 1), that the factors are uncorrelated (i.e., a covariance equal to zero), and that the disturbance terms are uncorrelated with the factors, respectively. The last assumption is the evident assumption that the expectation of $\mathbf{z}_{\bullet i}$ is equal to zero.

The variance of $\mathbf{z}_{\bullet i}$ and the covariances between $\mathbf{z}_{\bullet i}$ and $\mathbf{z}_{\bullet i'}$ $(i \neq i')$ are calculated by making use of (4.6.2.10) and (4.6.2.11):

$$\mathcal{E}(\mathbf{z}_{\bullet i}' \mathbf{z}_{\bullet i'}) = \mathcal{E}\left\{\mathbf{z}_{\bullet i} - \mathcal{E}(\mathbf{z}_{\bullet i})\right\}' \left\{\mathbf{z}_{\bullet i'} - \mathcal{E}(\mathbf{z}_{\bullet i'})\right\}$$

$$= \mathcal{E}\left\{\sum_{k=1}^{K} l_{ik}\,\mathbf{f}_k + \boldsymbol{\epsilon}_{\bullet i}\right\}' \left\{\sum_{k=1}^{K} l_{i'k}\,\mathbf{f}_k + \boldsymbol{\epsilon}_{\bullet i'}\right\}$$

$$= \mathcal{E}\left\{(\sum_{k=1}^{K} l_{ik}\,\mathbf{f}_k)' (\sum_{k=1}^{K} l_{i'k}\,\mathbf{f}_k) + (\sum_{k=1}^{K} l_{ik}\,\mathbf{f}_k)' \boldsymbol{\epsilon}_{\bullet i'} + \boldsymbol{\epsilon}_{\bullet i}' (\sum_{k=1}^{K} l_{i'k}\,\mathbf{f}_k) + \boldsymbol{\epsilon}_{\bullet i}' \boldsymbol{\epsilon}_{\bullet i'}\right\}$$

$$= \sum_{k=1}^{K} l_{ik}\, l_{i'k}\, \mathcal{E}(\mathbf{f}_k' \mathbf{f}_k) + 0 + 0 + \mathcal{E}(\boldsymbol{\epsilon}_{\bullet i}' \boldsymbol{\epsilon}_{\bullet i'})$$

$$= \sum_{k=1}^{K} l_{ik}\, l_{i'k} + \mathcal{E}(\boldsymbol{\epsilon}_{\bullet i}' \boldsymbol{\epsilon}_{\bullet i'}) \qquad (4.6.2.12)$$

Therefore, the variance of $\mathbf{z}_{\bullet i}$, denoted by var $(\mathbf{z}_{\bullet i})$, is equal to:

$$\text{var}\,(\mathbf{z}_{\bullet i}) = \sum_{k=1}^{K} l_{ik}^2 + \sigma_i^2 \qquad (4.6.2.13)$$

while the covariance between $\mathbf{z}_{\bullet i}$ and $\mathbf{z}_{\bullet i'}$ denoted by cov $(\mathbf{z}_{\bullet i}, \mathbf{z}_{\bullet i'})$, is equal to:

$$\text{cov}\,(\mathbf{z}_{\bullet i}, \mathbf{z}_{\bullet i'}) = \sum_{k=1}^{K} l_{ik}\, l_{i'k} \qquad (4.6.2.14)$$

Since according to (4.6.2.2) $\mathbf{z}_{\bullet i}$ is a vector of standardized variables, its variance is equal to 1, so that (4.6.2.13) can be written as:

$$\sum_{k=1}^{K} l_{ik}^2 + \sigma_i^2 = 1 \qquad (4.6.2.15)$$

Next, one may define:

$$h_i^2 = \sum_{k=1}^{K} l_{ik}^2 \qquad (4.6.2.16)$$

in which $h_i^2$ is called the *communality* of variable $i$, i.e., the common part of the variance of variable $i$ with respect to other variables. Next, the term $\sigma_i^2$ is called the *uniqueness* of variable $i$. This part of the variance of variable $i$ is composed of an error variance (owing to the stochastic model) and a specific variance (related to variable $i$).

The factor model, represented in (4.6.2.10), is only related to variable $i$. It is evident that for each vector of observations on a certain variable $i$ a system like (4.6.2.10) can be created. By integrating all these relationships one obtains the following matrix representation of a factor-analytic model:

$$\mathbf{Z}' = \mathbf{L}\mathbf{F}' + \mathbf{E} \qquad (4.6.2.17)$$

where $\mathbf{Z}$ is a matrix of order $J \times I$ with $I$ column vectors representing the successive vectors of observations $\mathbf{z}_{\cdot i}$ ($i = 1, \ldots, I$). The matrix $\mathbf{L}$ is the corresponding (as yet unknown) loading matrix of order $I \times K$ with $K$ column vectors, each of which represents the loading of a variable $i$ ($i = 1, \ldots, I$) on a factor $k$ ($k = 1, \ldots, K$). The (as yet unknown) matrix $\mathbf{F}$ is of order $J \times K$; its columns are the factors $\mathbf{f}_k$ ($k = 1, \ldots, K$). Finally, the matrix $\mathbf{E}$ contains the corresponding disturbance terms.

Next, the variance-covariance matrix $\mathbf{R}$ of $z_{ji}$ (see [4.6.2.13] and [4.6.2.14]) can be written as an $I \times I$ matrix:

$$\mathbf{R} = \mathbf{L}\mathbf{L}' + \hat{\Sigma} \qquad (4.6.2.18)$$

where $\hat{\Sigma}$ is a diagonal matrix of order $I \times I$, in which the elements on the main diagonal are equal to $\sigma_i^2$ ($i = 1, \ldots, I$). The matrix $\mathbf{R}$ can be determined by means of (4.6.2.7): the correlation matrix is equal to the variance-covariance matrix, since the variables $z_{ji}$ are standardized (cf. [4.6.2.2]).

The main problem to be solved in factor analysis is the estimation of the loading matrix $\mathbf{L}$, of the factor matrix $\mathbf{F}$, and of the variance matrix $\hat{\Sigma}$. The only things, which are known *a priori*, are the matrix $\mathbf{Z}$ and, consequently, the matrix $\mathbf{R}$. Without additional criteria this problem does not possess a unique solution. It can easily be proved, that, if $\mathbf{L}^*$ is a solution of (4.6.2.18), i.e.,

$$\mathbf{R} = \mathbf{L}^*\mathbf{L}^{*\prime} + \hat{\Sigma} \qquad (4.6.2.19)$$

there exists a broad class of solutions. The reason is that any matrix product $\mathbf{L}^*\mathbf{T}$, where $\mathbf{T}$ is an orthogonal matrix (i.e., $\mathbf{T}'\mathbf{T} = \mathbf{I}$), is also a solution of (4.6.2.18). By substituting $\mathbf{L}^*\mathbf{T}$ as a solution for $\mathbf{L}$ into (4.6.2.18), one finds:

$$
\begin{aligned}
\mathbf{R} &= (\mathbf{L}^*\mathbf{T})(\mathbf{L}^*\mathbf{T})' + \hat{\Sigma} \\
&= \mathbf{L}^*\mathbf{T}\mathbf{T}'\mathbf{L}^{*\prime} + \hat{\Sigma} \qquad (4.6.2.20) \\
&= \mathbf{L}^*\mathbf{L}^{*\prime} + \hat{\Sigma}
\end{aligned}
$$

which is again equal to (4.6.2.19). Therefore, there is an infinite number of possible solutions.[6] Only by introducing additional requirements a unique solution is obtained. These additional requirements depend entirely on the aim of the factor analysis concerned: a factor analysis is *objective-oriented*. The ultimate objective determines the direction in which the model will be further developed, and the way in which the unknown matrices **L**, **F** and $\hat{\Sigma}$ are estimated. Two broad categories, within which the basic factor model can be further developed, may be discerned, viz. *principal component analysis* and *common factor analysis*. They will be discussed in the following subsection with a particular stress on principal component analysis, since this is a frequently used instrument in regional analysis.

### 4.6.3 *Principal component methods in regional analysis*

*Principal component analysis* is a transformation from a set of originally mutually correlated variables to a new set of independent variables. Principal component analysis is an orthogonal data transformation, in which the original variables are replaced by independent factors. Furthermore, since a principal component analysis is only concerned with the common variances between variables (or communalities), and not with the uniqueness of variables, the terms $\sigma_i^2$ are eliminated from (4.6.2.13); a principal component analysis is a non-stochastic approach. In consequence, the variance of each original variable $i$ is equal to the sum of the squared loadings with respect to the factors. In principle, the number of factors obtained from a principal component analysis is exactly equal to the number of original variables, since a principal component analysis is only an orthogonal data transformation. Therefore, the total variance of all the original variables is equal to the total variance of the new variables. Since a principal component analysis is a frequently used instrument in regional analyses, the major part of this subsection will be devoted to this topic and only a short exposition of common factor analysis will be given.

*Common factor analysis* differs from a methodological point of view from principal component analysis; a common factor analysis aims at representing the variations in a certain set of variables by a small number of underlying factors, which may reproduce the correlations among the original variables. The correlations between a number of variables are assumed to result from some common underlying factors. The number and nature of these factors may be determined *a priori* on theoretical grounds, so that the results of a common factor analysis are testable with respect to the *a priori* hypotheses. The proportion of the variance in each variable $i$, accounted for by the common factor, is equal to the communality $h_i^2$, while the remainder of its variance is the uniqueness $\sigma_i^2$ (see [4.6.2.13]). Common factor analysis may be useful for a systematic classification of regional data into a number of distinguishing features determined *a priori*.

As has already been stated, a *principal component analysis* attempts at extracting a set of uncorrelated factors from a set of mutually correlated observations. The number of independent dimensions is exactly equal to the number of original variables, i.e. $K = I$. Principal component analysis only deals with the common variance of the original variables; the total variance is supposed to remain equal after this orthogonal transformation. The uniqueness is left out of consideration, so that, in fact, the basic factor model is equal to (4.6.2.9), and so that (4.6.2.13) and (4.6.2.14) are transformed into:

$$\text{var}\,(\mathbf{z}_{\bullet i}) = \sum_{k=1}^{I} l_{ik}^2 \tag{4.6.3.1}$$

and:

$$\text{cov}\,(\mathbf{z}_{\bullet i}, \mathbf{z}_{\bullet i'}) = \sum_{k=1}^{I} l_{ik}\, l_{i'k} \tag{4.6.3.2}$$

Therefore, relationship (4.6.2.18) passes into:

$$\mathbf{R} = \mathbf{L}\mathbf{L}' \tag{4.6.3.3}$$

which is a fundamental theorem in factor analysis already used in (4.3.2.7).[7] Since the total variance has to remain equal, a principal component analysis implies a redistribution of the total variance: the variance of each of the $I$ original variables $\mathbf{z}_{\bullet i}$ (cf. [4.6.3.1]) is distributed over the $I$ new independent variables $\mathbf{f}_k$ ($k = 1, \ldots, I$), such that the total variance remains equal. Since $\mathbf{z}_{\bullet i}$ is a standardized variable, its variance is, according to (4.6.2.15), equal to 1, so that the total variance over all variables is equal to $I$.

Next, the problem arises as to how to estimate or to determine both the matrix of factor loadings (i.e., **L**) and the matrix of factors themselves (i.e., **F**). It has already been set out in the previous subsection, that the determination of **L** and **F** requires an additional criterion in order to overcome the large number of degrees of freedom. This criterion for a principal component analysis is a variance criterion. The first factor or first principal component is supposed to account for the greatest part of the common variance (or communalities), i.e., the contribution of the loadings of the first factor to the common variance should be at a maximum. The second factor is supposed to claim the maximum part of the remaining part of the common variance, etc. The mathematical derivations and the formal implications of the previous assumptions are contained in Appendix 4A, in which the extraction of factors in principal component analysis is described.

The results of this derivation are rather striking. It can be proved that the *largest eigenvalue of the correlation matrix* **R** (cf. [4.6.3.3]) is associated with the first factor or principal component. Furthermore, the eigenvector corresponding with the greatest eigenvalue of the correlation matrix is equal to the vector of factor loadings of all original variables with respect to the first factor. By repeating this procedure for the second and all other factors, the complete matrix of factor loadings, **L**, can easily be determined. This implies, that if the model for principal component analysis is written as (cf. [4.6.2.17]):

$$\mathbf{Z}' = \mathbf{L}\,\mathbf{F}' \qquad (4.6.3.4)$$

the matrices $\mathbf{Z}'$ and $\mathbf{L}$ are known. Since the matrix $\mathbf{L}$ is square, the factors (or principal components) can easily be calculated as:

$$\mathbf{F}' = \mathbf{L}^{-1}\,\mathbf{Z}' \qquad (4.6.3.5)$$

supposed the matrix $\mathbf{L}$ is non-singular. In this way all factors $\mathbf{f}_k$ ($k = 1, \ldots, K$) can be determined. Each vector $\mathbf{f}_k$ represents the component scores (or factor scores) of the original observations on the factors. The scores on each factor $k$ can be represented in a graphical way, viz. over all $J$ observations. For instance, if the observations relate to regions, one may construct a multiregional picture of the factor scores of each factor separately.

As has already been stated, the original variables are frequently correlated, so that not each variable is equally important for explaining the differences in a certain economic structure. In consequence, the number of relevant factors will, in general, be smaller than the number of variables, i.e., $K < I$. The problem as to how to select a reduced number of independent factors is not necessarily solvable in a unique way. A frequently used method is to fix a critical lower limit or threshold-value for the eigenvalues, associated with the successive factors (the eigenvalues represent the variance explained by the corresponding factors; see Appendix 4A). Each factor with a corresponding eigenvalue below this critical level (for instance, $\leqslant 1$) is eliminated. A second method is to eliminate those factors, the corresponding eigenvalues of which show a significant, rapid decline (or break-down) with respect to the eigenvalues of the previous factors.

Anyhow, the result of such an elimination procedure is that the matrix **F**, determined according to (4.6.3.5), is no longer a square matrix, but a matrix of $J \times K$, where $K < I$. In general, $K$ will be relatively small, for instance 3 or 4. The loading matrix **L** can be reduced in a similar way, so that **L** is no longer a square matrix either. Then formula (4.6.3.5) can not be applied directly in order to calculate **F**'. In a way similar to regression analysis one may determine **F**' as follows:

$$\mathbf{F}' = (\mathbf{L}'\mathbf{L})^{-1}\ \mathbf{L}'\mathbf{Z}' \tag{4.6.3.6}$$

supposed **L**'**L** is non-singular.

An additional reason, why the number of factors should be reduced, is the fact that a low number of factors facilitates the identification and interpretation of the factors. Such an interpretation is easier, if certain loadings which are hardly significant are dropped out (according to the eigenvalue criterion set out above). The identification and interpretation of the factors is based on the loadings, which link the factors to the variables. In fact, each factor can be identified and named on the basis of and with the aid of the variables, which possess a high loading coefficient with respect to the factor concerned.

The identification of the factors can be facilitated by determining the factors such that only one variable possesses a high loading on a certain factor. This procedure requires a rotation of the factors, and is called a Varimax-criterion. According to this criterion the variance of a certain variable with respect to one component is maximized, while the variance with respect to other components is minimized. In this way one may obtain higher loadings of certain variables on some factors, so that a more accurate identification of the factors concerned is possible. Such a rotation of the co-ordinate axes does affect only the relative positions of the factors, and hence the loading matrix.

Finally, some attention should be paid to common factor analysis. Common factor analysis is a stochastic approach, which takes account of disturbances in the factor model (see [4.6.2.10] and [4.6.2.17]). The procedure of a common factor analysis bears some resemblance to the principal component method. The main difference is of a methodological nature. In common factor analysis the number of underlying orthogonal factors is fixed *a priori* (and not *ex posteriori* by means of an eigenvalue criterion like in principal component analysis).

The components themselves are determined in the following way. First the matrix of single correlation coefficients, **R**, has to be determined. This matrix is represented in (4.6.2.18). As has already been set out above, the disturbances are not dropped out like in principal component analysis. Therefore, the correlation matrix **R**, used in common factor analysis, differs from the correlation matrix in principal component analysis owing to the presence of the diagonal matrix $\hat{\Sigma}$. This implies that only the diagonal elements of the correlation matrix in common factor analysis differ from the correlation matrix in principal component analysis. These diagonal elements of the correlation matrix **R** from (4.6.2.18) are frequently estimated with the aid of the multiple correlation coefficient of the corresponding variable with respect to all other variables (see Harman [1964] and King [1969]). Once these diagonal elements have been estimated, the principal component procedure is applied to this correlation matrix. Then one can determine in a way, similar to the principal component analysis, the factor matrix **F**. This matrix contains exactly as many factors as there are variables, i.e. $I$. Next, this number of $I$ factors is reduced to the number of factors which was fixed *a priori*. If this number is equal to $K$, one selects the first $K$ factors $\mathbf{f}_1, \ldots, \mathbf{f}_K$. These known factors $\mathbf{f}_k$ $(k = 1, \ldots, K)$ are now used as 'explaining' variables in the factor model (4.6.2.9). By applying a least squares procedure to this model the as yet unknown loading coefficients $l_{ik}$ $(i = 1, \ldots, I; k = 1, \ldots, K)$ can be estimated in this regression model.

The previous factor-analytic methods may be tractable instruments for regional scientists in order to disentangle rather involved and complicated regional and interregional relationships, particularly in the case of a large number of variables. By reducing a large set of data to a restricted number of factors, one may find more systematic facts and trends in regional phenomena. The identification of the factors requires some experience, particularly since the factors themselves are frequently named on rather subjective grounds.

It is obvious that factor-analytic methods are not free from criticism, since they bear all drawbacks of orthogonalization procedures (see also subsection 4.3.2). From a theoretical *economic* point of view these methods are rather heuristic. Furthermore, *theoretical* linkages between the original, relevant regional economic variables are abandoned. Instead, the *numerical* issue of the transformed observations shows some underlying relationships, without explaining the 'how' and 'why'. The only links between observations and factors are the loadings. The mutual influence between regional phenomena is not analyzed in a theoretical, deductive way, but only in a heuristic way.

In spite of these drawbacks factor analysis may be useful. In the first place, factor analysis may be an important instrument for a systematic classification of a huge amount of regional information, particularly in a first stage of research (see subsection 4.6.4). Such a classification of regional data may be helpful for constructing a regional or interregional model. Secondly, factor analysis may be useful to test certain hypotheses concerning dominating factors underlying regional phenomena (particularly, in the case of a common factor analysis). In the third place, a factor analysis may be helpful in grouping and regionalization procedures. If the original observations relate to regions (i.e., $x_{ji}$ is the value of the $i^{\text{th}}$ variable in the $j^{\text{th}}$ region), the factor scores $f_{jk}$ (the typical element from the matrix $F$) will also relate to regions. Therefore, each element $f_{jk}$ ($k = 1, \ldots, K$) can be considered as an indicator for the economic structure of region $j$. By considering all elements $f_{jk}$ as regional characteristics, one may calculate the interregional distances, based on the factor scores $f_{jk}$ (see section 4.3). By means of certain cluster methods (see subsection 4.4.3) these interregional distances can be used for grouping and regionalization procedures (see also Berry [1967]). More advanced concepts ($Q$- and $R$-mode analysis, correspondence analysis) can be found, among others, in Benzécri et al. (1973) and King (1969).

### 4.6.4 *An empirical application*

In this section the use of factor analysis for regional research will be illustrated on the basis of an empirical application, performed by Jaumotte and Paelinck (1971). The purpose of this factor analysis was to determine the principal components defining implicitly the economic structure of the Belgian provinces, as well as their evolution, and to give them an operational interpretation. The Belgian provinces themselves have already been presented in map 4.4.4.a. For each province a series of data were collected during 7 years (1959–1965). The data were assumed to be indicators for demography, employment, investment, productivity, production, private consumption and standards of living in each province. The total number of variables was equal to 29. These data can for each year be represented in a regional data matrix (see also 4.3.2.1). The aim of the study was to find for each year the underlying explaining factors that are common to all 9 regions for the explanation of the regional phenomena. Next, the evolution of the structural characteristics of the regions can be studied during the observation period 1959–1965. The method used is a principal component analysis. For a comment on this approach, see Dawson and Mather (1971).

After a standardization of the observation material the correlation matrix **R** with typical elements $r_{ii'}$ (cf. [4.6.2.7]) can easily be constructed. By inspecting this matrix of single correlation coefficients one may obtain more insight into the correlations among the original variables.

Next, the correlation matrix **R** is used in a principal component analysis in order to determine the eigenvalues and eigenvectors. In this way the loading matrix **L** can easily be calculated (see Appendix 4A). By making use of (4.6.3.5) the matrix of component scores is also easy to compute. For each period such a procedure has been carried out.

Only 2 factors or components were selected. Inspection of (4A.13) showed that these 2 factors accounted for a large proportion of the total variance. Therefore, only the first and second factor were further inspected. An analysis of the loading matrix showed that the following variables had a high loading on the first factor: residential population, total employment, industrial employment, employment in services, value added of the sectors commerce, insurance, banking and services, value added of the sector dwellings, and the relative importance of the value added of the agricultural sector. From the point of view of the provincial economic system the first factor is closely associated with regional state and structural variables. Therefore, the first factor could be identified as a structural factor.

The second factor appeared to be characterized by high loadings with respect to the following original variables: rate of unemployment, industrial productivity, rate of gross domestic product per capita, and the number of cars per 10,000 inhabitants. Therefore, the second factor is named a potential or dynamic component, since it includes many elements which can be associated with regional growth.

Furthermore, the structural factor and the potential factor have both relatively high loadings with respect to the following variables: rate of birth, percentage of salary earners in total employment, productivity in services, industrial liabilities, total liabilities, number of building licenses, and numbers of doctors per 10,000 inhabitants. Therefore, the first and second factor share also the explanation of the variances of these foregoing 7 variables. The factor scores, both of the first and the second factor, are presented for each year in table 4.6.4.a (derived from Jaumotte and Paelinck [1971]).

Obviously, the number of independent factors cannot exceed the rank of **R** (i.e., g).

Table 4.6.4.a can be analysed in a threefold way. In the first place one may compare for each period the separate elements of each individual

Table 4.6.4.a
Scores of the Belgian provinces on factor 1 and 2

| | Province \ Year | 1959 | 1960 | 1961 | 1962 | 1963 | 1964 | 1965 |
|---|---|---|---|---|---|---|---|---|
| Scores on factor 1 | Antwerp | 0·88 | 0·86 | 0·60 | 0·69 | 0·53 | 0·76 | 0·59 |
| | Brabant | 2·13 | 2·12 | 2·18 | 2·27 | 2·28 | 2·25 | 2·32 |
| | West-Flanders | −0·11 | 0·11 | 0·16 | 0·03 | 0·03 | −0·15 | −0·18 |
| | East-Flanders | 0·18 | 0·19 | 0·17 | 0·04 | 0·13 | 0·15 | 0·09 |
| | Hainaut | −0·03 | −0·38 | −0·19 | −0·18 | −0·06 | −0·10 | −0·11 |
| | Liège | 0·16 | 0·28 | 0·36 | 0·22 | 0·20 | 0·16 | 0·28 |
| | Limbourg | −1·07 | −0·98 | −1·09 | −1·05 | −0·94 | −0·97 | −0·87 |
| | Luxembourg | −1·36 | −1·33 | −1·30 | −1·29 | −1·42 | −1·29 | −1·30 |
| | Namur | −0·78 | −0·88 | −0·89 | −0·71 | −0·74 | −0·80 | −0·83 |
| Scores on factor 2 | Antwerp | 0·52 | 0·50 | 0·62 | 0·48 | 0·83 | 0·83 | 0·30 |
| | Brabant | −0·59 | −0·61 | −0·43 | −0·58 | −0·94 | −0·79 | −0·61 |
| | West-Flanders | 0·50 | 0·65 | 0·71 | 1·04 | 1·05 | 0·50 | 0·51 |
| | East-Flanders | 1·10 | 1·24 | 1·17 | 1·52 | 1·03 | 1·00 | 1·02 |
| | Hainaut | 0·21 | −0·13 | −0·22 | −0·26 | −0·08 | 0·02 | −0·24 |
| | Liège | −0·94 | −1·12 | −1·18 | −1·02 | −0·61 | −0·58 | 0·04 |
| | Limbourg | 1·71 | 1·65 | 1·57 | 1·13 | 1·27 | 1·63 | 1·72 |
| | Luxembourg | −1·22 | −1·14 | −0·87 | −1·06 | −1·41 | −1·37 | −0·88 |
| | Namur | −1·28 | −1·04 | −1·37 | −1·25 | −1·14 | −1·24 | −1·86 |

factor. Thus, one may compare in each year the elements $f_{11}, \ldots, f_{91}$ of the first factor $\mathbf{f}_1$, and next of the second factor. Table 4.6.4.a shows a high degree of variation for the scores on factor 1 in each province. The province Brabant appears to yield relatively very high scores on factor 1, whereas Luxembourg provides rather low values of the factor scores. This may be an indication that Brabant has a very tight economic structure, and Luxembourg a very weak economic structure. This hypothesis could be tested by analyzing and comparing the average regional values added (see below). In a similar way one may compare the elements of the second factor. Table 4.6.4.a shows that East-Flanders and Limbourg possess rather high scores on factor 2, whereas Namur possesses a very low score on factor 2. This might imply that East-Flanders and Limbourg possess a high rate of growth potential, and that Namur possesses a rather bad growth potential. This hypothesis might be tested by comparing the growth rates of the regional values added (see below).

Next, one may compare factor 1 and factor 2 mutually. It appears that factor 1 and 2 show a tendency to a reversed pattern for each province:

frequently, a province with a good economic structure appears to possess a rather bad growth potential, and *vice versa*. It will be shown below, that the average value added and the growth rate of value added shows a similar pattern for each province.

In the third place, one may study the evolution of the factors over time. They appear to possess rather little variation during the period 1959–1965. This relative stability implies the provincial economic systems are dominated by constant permanent influences during the observation periods.

As had been remarked above, the previous global results of the foregoing factor analysis might be checked by inspecting the average regional value added and the growth rate of regional value added. In this, use is made of a shift and share analysis (cf. Perloff et al. [1960]), by means of which the difference between the regional rate of growth and the national rate of growth are separated into two parts, the first of which corresponds to the structural elements, and the second to the growth element. If the average rate of growth of value added is denoted by $\rho$, and if the value added itself is denoted by $v$, one may write:

$$\rho = \Delta v / v \qquad (4.6.4.1)$$

where $\Delta v$ represents the change in $v$. Since $\Delta v$ is composed of the changes in values added of all sectors $i$ ($i = 1, \ldots, I$), $\Delta v$ can be written as:

$$\Delta v = \sum_{i=1}^{I} \Delta v_i \qquad (4.6.4.2)$$

By substituting (4.6.4.2) into (4.6.4.1) one finds:

$$\rho = \frac{\sum_{i=1}^{I} \Delta v_i}{v} \qquad (4.6.4.3)$$

$$= \sum_{i=1}^{I} \frac{\Delta v_i}{v_i} \frac{v_i}{v}$$

$$= \sum_{i=1}^{I} \rho_i s_i$$

where $\rho_i$ is the rate of growth of value added in sector $i$, and $s_i$ the share of value added of sector $i$ in the total value added. Next, one may write the average rate of growth of regional value added as:

$$\rho_r = \sum_{i=1}^{I} \rho_i^r \, s_i^r \qquad (4.6.4.4)$$

where the index $r$ refers to a certain region $r$ ($r = 1, \ldots, R$). The difference between the average rate of growth of region $r$ and the national rate of growth of region $r$ and the national rate of growth can be written as:

$$\rho_r - \rho = \sum_{i=1}^{I} \rho_i^r s_i^r - \sum_{i=1}^{I} \rho_i s_i \qquad (4.6.4.5)$$

$$= \sum_{i=1}^{I} (s_i^r - s_i)\, \rho_i + \sum_{i=1}^{I} (\rho_i^r - \rho_i)\, s_i^r$$

The first term on the right hand side of (4.6.4.5) represents a *structural* effect, since it explains the difference between $\rho_r$ and $\rho$ by differences in the initial economic structures, viz. the relative shares in the sectoral values added. The second term on the right hand side of (4.6.4.5) describes a *dynamic* effect, since this term explains the difference between $\rho_r$ and $\rho$ by differences in the sectoral rates of growth. By applying the previous method to the Belgian provinces one may construct table 4.6.4.b (derived from Jaumotte and Paelinck [1971]). There are some discrepancies between the third, fourth and fifth column due to the fact that each column is calculated separately, so that the additivity condition (4.6.4.5) is not exactly satisfied. The percentages in the last two columns may have either sign, since they may be composed of negative and positive terms in the right hand side of (4.6.4.5). For the same reason these percentages may exceed the value of 100.

Table 4.6.4.b can be used as a check on the results of the factor analysis. Both table 4.6.4.a and 4.6.4.b show a structural effect and a dynamic effect. By comparing these tables one may conclude that both tables show a corresponding pattern (except some small discrepancies). Therefore, the factor analysis used in the foregoing analysis has been proved to be reliable *a posteriori.*

## 4.7 Contiguity analysis

### 4.7.1 *The concept of a spatial correlation coefficient*

In section 4.3 attention has been paid to the fact that regional indicators within a certain regional economic structure may be mutually correlated. By means of an orthogonalization procedure an attempt was made at obtaining relevant, independent information from a set of observations.

Table 4.6.4.b

Structural and dynamic effects of value added in the Belgian provinces

| Province | $\rho_r$ (%) | $\rho$ (%) | $\rho_r - \rho$ | $\sum_{i=1}^{I} (s_i^r - s_i)\rho_i$ | $\sum_{i=1}^{I} (\rho_i^r - \rho_i)s_i^r$ | Structural effect (%) | Dynamic effect (%) |
|---|---|---|---|---|---|---|---|
| Antwerp | 44·55 | 34·37 | 10·18 | 3·23 | 6·95 | 31·7 | 68·3 |
| Brabant | 35·57 | 34·47 | 1·20 | 1·86 | −0·60 | 137·3 | (−)37·3 |
| West-Flanders | 35·00 | 34·37 | 0·63 | −3·05 | 3·77 | (−)462·3 | 562·3 |
| East-Flanders | 32·71 | 34·37 | −1·66 | −1·17 | −0·34 | 77·4 | 22·6 |
| Hainaut | 27·78 | 34·37 | −6·59 | −0·47 | −6·27 | 7·0 | 93·0 |
| Liège | 25·39 | 34·37 | 8·98 | 3·64 | −12·52 | (−)41·0 | 141·0 |
| Limbourg | 45·75 | 34·37 | 11·38 | −12·02 | 23·40 | (−)105·6 | 205·6 |
| Luxembourg | 20·98 | 34·37 | −13·39 | −9·52 | −4·09 | 69·9 | 30·1 |
| Namur | 31·71 | 34·37 | −2·66 | −3·76 | 1·04 | 138·0 | (−)38·0 |

In section 4.6 a similar problem came up in relation to a regional classification and in relation to a structure analysis of regions. Factor analysis appeared to be a tool for dealing with a large set of observations on highly correlated variables. In this section another kind of correlation will be considered: not a correlation between *different* variables within a spatial entity, but a correlation between the observations on *one single* variable, dispersed over several regions. Such a correlation arises owing to the fact that a regional classification almost never leads to autonomous and autarchic regions: a region is an open spatial system and it has many (often intricate) relationships with other regions. Therefore, an observation on a certain phenomenon (for instance, average regional income) is frequently also dependent on the levels of that phenomenon in contiguous regions. In this section an attempt will be made at presenting a test and a measure for spatial contiguity effects between observations on one phenomenon within a spatial system of regions.

A *spatial correlation analysis* or *contiguity analysis* is based on the assumption that between adjacent regions the probability of spatial correlation is very high. Such a situation with first ring of adjacent regions around a given central region is called a *first-order contiguity*. The second ring of regions (second-order contiguity) is supposed to possess less influence on the central region: the area of influence is restricted by the physical distance between regions; third-order contiguity has even less influence on the central region, and so forth.

The aforementioned situation bears a close resemblance to auto-correlation in time series analysis, where the observation on a certain variable is co-determined by its realization in previous periods. A test on the presence of auto-correlation is *inter alia* the well-known Von Neumann ratio (see, for instance, Malinvaud [1970]). There is, however, an essential difference between auto-correlation and spatial correlation: auto-correlation implies only *one* (chronological) direction of influence (a certain variable at time $t$ is determined *inter alia* by the same variable at time $t-1$), whereas a spatial correlation implies different (spatial) directions (a certain regional phenomenon is determined *inter alia* by the same phenomenon in many surrounding regions, while this phenomenon in each of the surrounding regions is also determined by the same phenomenon in the central region). There is a higher degree of interdependence in spatial correlation analysis, reason why the Von Neumann ratio for auto-correlation can not be applied directly as a reasonable test for spatial correlation.

Geary (1954), however, has proposed a generalization of the Von Neumann ratio as an adequate test for spatial contiguity effects. Geary's correlation coefficient for contiguity effects is defined as the ratio of the sum of the squared differences between contiguous realizations of a certain variable, and the general spatial variance. An extension of this correlation coefficient was given by Lebart (1966) by taking account of the distance between the regions. Another approach to the generalization of Geary's correlation coefficient was proposed by Fisher (1971). Further applications of and contributions to spatial correlation tests are contained *inter alia* in Cliff and Ord (1969, 1970, 1973), Dacey (1968), Hordijk (1974) and Moran (1950).

If $k$ is the order of contiguity (i.e., $k = 1, 2, \ldots$), the general *spatial correlation coefficient* of contiguity order $k$, denoted by $c_k$, is defined as:

$$c_k = \frac{\sum_{r=1}^{R} \sum_{i_{kr}=1_{kr}}^{I_{kr}} (x_r - x_{i_{kr}})^2}{2 I_k} \cdot \frac{R-1}{\sum_{r=1}^{R} (x_r - \bar{x})^2} \tag{4.7.1.1}$$

where $x$ is a known value of a certain indicator in region $r$ $(r = 1, \ldots, R)$, for instance, average regional income or population density. The subscript $i_{kr}$ $(i_{kr} = 1_{kr}, \ldots, I_{kr})$ pertains to each region $i_{kr}$, which possesses a $k^{\text{th}}$ order contiguity with respect to region $r$. Therefore, the total number of $k^{\text{th}}$ connections for region $r$ is equal to $I_{kr}$, while $I_k$ is defined as the total number of connections of order $k$ within the whole system, i.e.,

$$I_k = \sum_{r=1}^{R} I_{kr} \tag{4.7.1.2}$$

Finally, $\bar{x}$ is defined as the national average of the indicator concerned, i.e.,

$$\bar{x} = \sum_{r=1}^{R} x_r / R \tag{4.7.1.3}$$

The first factor of (4.7.1.1) can be conceived of as the statistical contiguity variance: it represents the aggregated squared differences of the variable concerned between a central region and surrounding regions, measured over all regions of the spatial system. These squared differences are divided by the total number of connections of the corresponding order $k$, i.e. $I_k$. Furthermore, these squared differences are divided by a factor 2, in order to guarantee that the absence of spatial correlation of order $k$ implies $c_k = 1$ (see Appendix 4B). Both the numerator and the denominator of the first factor of (4.7.1.1) involve double countings: the contiguity of region $r$ with respect to region $r'$ is considered, as well as the contiguity of region $r'$ with respect to region $r$.[8]

The second factor of (4.7.1.1) represents the inverse of the statistical variance of the variable concerned within the whole spatial system: this expression contains the aggregated squared differences between the observations in the variable concerned in each region, and the national average. This expression is divided by $R-1$ (and not by $R$) in order to obtain an unbiased estimate of the variance. Therefore, $c_k$ is the ratio of the contiguity variance of order $k$, and the general spatial variance.

The value of $c_k$ is an indicator for the presence of spatial correlation of order $k$. This value can be used as a test on the presence of spatial contiguity effects. It can be proved (see Appendix 4B) that there is no spatial correlation (or order $k$) between the regional observations on a certain variable if $c_k = 1$. Furthermore, if $c_k < 1$, there is a positive contiguity effect; this means that within the spatial system a high value of a certain variable in a given region tends to be accompanied by a high value in surrounding regions (of order $k$). In a similar way one may state that $c_k > 1$ implies a negative spatial correlation.

Instead of $c_k$ one may use a complementary coefficient $\gamma_k$, defined as:

$$\gamma_k = 1 - c_k \qquad (4.7.1.4)$$

where $\gamma_k$ is called the *coefficient of spatial influence*. If $\gamma_k = 0$, there is no spatial dependency between regions, if $\gamma_k > 0$ and $\gamma_k < 0$, there is a positive and a negative contiguity effect, respectively. This coefficient of spatial influence bears, in fact, a close resemblance to the well-known correlation coefficient.

The spatial correlation coefficient (or the complementary concept of the coefficient of spatial influence) varies according to the order of contiguity. If $k = 1$, then $c_k$ measures the direct spatial correlation, caused by the first ring of contiguous regions. If $k = 2$, $c_k$ measures the indirect spatial influence of a second ring of surrounding regions. It is clear, that the various spatial effects depend mainly on the order of contiguity.

The significance of the influence of each order $k$ can be represented in a so-called spatio-correlogram, which indicates the relationship between $c_k$ and $k$: each contiguity order $k$ gives rise to a value of $c_k$ (see figure 4.7.1.a). The figurative example of a spatio-correlogram, represented in figure 4.7.1.a, denotes a positive spatial influence within a first order contiguity system, a negative spatial influence within a second-order contiguity system, etc. In general, $c_k$ tends to increase for higher-order systems.

If one assumes a large set of observations on the spatial correlation coefficient $c_k$, the spatial correlation coefficient $c_k$ can be conceived of as a stochastic variable, which possesses a certain probability distribution. For a set of French departments it was shown by Lebart (1966) that $c_k$ had a normal distribution with a mean equal to 1 and a standard deviation equal to 0·08. Then one may conclude, that *if* $c_k = 1$, nearly at least 95% of the observations on $c_k$ will fall within the $2\sigma$ limits, i.e. will fall between 0·84 and 1·16. In general, the standard deviations of the spatial correlation coefficients depend on the number of contiguous regions (see Geary [1954] and Cliff and Ord [1969]).

Fig. 4.7.1.a A spatio-correlogram

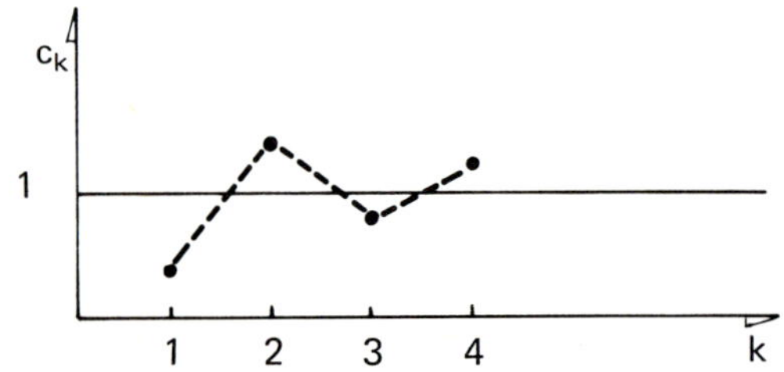


The foregoing spatial analysis deals with a single variable, observed within a set of regions. A similar analysis may be carried out for each arbitrary variable separately. Then one obtains for each variable a set of spatial correlation coefficients $c_k$ ($k = 1, \ldots, K$). By comparing the spatial correlation coefficients of each variable separately, in relation to a certain contiguity order, one may evaluate the spatial spheres of influence: if there is a similarity in the spatial correlation coefficients of each variable, one may identify the underlying pattern of spatial influence and spatial interdependence. For instance, if one observes that for a set of variables the corresponding first-order spatial correlation coefficients are $\ll 1$, one may conclude that there is a strong positive interdependence between strictly contiguous regions. Another way of dealing with these multivariate situations has already been discussed in section 4.6.

### 4.7.2 *An empirical application*

The foregoing analysis of and test on contiguity effects have been applied on the eleven Dutch provinces, in order to investigate whether there are evident contiguity effects between these provinces. This analysis of spatial autocorrelation has been applied not for a single provincial property, but for 5 different properties, viz. regional population density, regional population growth, regional employment, per capita regional gross value added (at market prices), and per capita regional disposable income. Furthermore, this analysis was performed for two different years, viz. 1960 and 1965, in order to investigate a possible shift in the spatial contiguity effects.

The data of this analysis are contained in table 4.7.2.a, which presents the observations on the 5 variables, both for 1960 and 1965. In addition, the average national values of these variables are represented at the bottom of the table.

Table 4.7.2.a

Data table of the Dutch provinces

| Variables / Provinces | | Number of inhabitants per square kilometer (1) | | Rate of growth of population (2) | | Employment per square kilometer (3) | | Per capita gross value added in factor prices (Dfl.) (4) | | Per capita available income (Dfl.) (5) | |
|---|---|---|---|---|---|---|---|---|---|---|---|
| | | 1960 | 1965 | 1960 | 1965 | 1960 | 1965 | 1960 | 1965 | 1960 | 1965 |
| 1 | Groningen | 205 | 216 | 0·64 | 1·02 | 70 | 75 | 3520 | 5150 | 2241 | 3609 |
| 2 | Friesland | 141 | 148 | 0·35 | 0·86 | 45 | 47 | 2960 | 4610 | 2023 | 3225 |
| 3 | Drente | 119 | 129 | 1·04 | 1·71 | 40 | 42 | 2950 | 4280 | 1920 | 3251 |
| 4 | Overijssel | 205 | 229 | 1·62 | 2·23 | 77 | 83 | 3350 | 4950 | 2183 | 3493 |
| 5 | Gelderland | 231 | 253 | 1·39 | 1·83 | 77 | 84 | 3130 | 4790 | 2165 | 3540 |
| 6 | Utrecht | 518 | 562 | 1·93 | 1·67 | 171 | 192 | 3270 | 5080 | 2530 | 4120 |
| 7 | North-Holland | 771 | 811 | 0·91 | 1·02 | 274 | 300 | 4050 | 6150 | 2795 | 4404 |
| 8 | South-Holland | 950 | 995 | 1·05 | 1·07 | 325 | 356 | 4030 | 6250 | 2670 | 4290 |
| 9 | Zeeland | 160 | 165 | 0·07 | 0·64 | 53 | 55 | 3370 | 5050 | 2255 | 3756 |
| 10 | North-Brabant | 305 | 336 | 1·89 | 2·00 | 104 | 114 | 3400 | 5180 | 2092 | 3445 |
| 11 | Limburg | 403 | 436 | 1·35 | 1·61 | 137 | 148 | 3300 | 4840 | 2133 | 3427 |
| The Netherlands | | 364 | 389 | 1·11 | 1·42 | 125 | 136 | 3394 | 5121 | 2237 | 3687 |

The number of connections of the various orders can be calculated for each province on the basis of a map of the Netherlands (map 4.7.2.a). The provinces in this map are enumerated according to table (4.7.2.a). The provinces North-Holland and Friesland are considered as adjacent regions (first-order contiguity) owing to the Closing Dike, which connects North-Holland and Friesland. The map can be used to construct a contiguity table, which represents the connections of each order *k* between the Dutch provinces. This contiguity table can be constructed up to the fourth order contiguity; the connections of the various orders are contained in a condensed way in table 4.7.2.b. The provinces are enumerated according to table 4.7.2.a.

The symbol ‘x’ means a first-order contiguity, the symbol ‘o’ means a second-order contiguity, the symbol ‘+’ means a third-order contiguity, and the symbol ‘*’ means a fourth-order contiguity.

Map 4.7.2.a The Netherlands

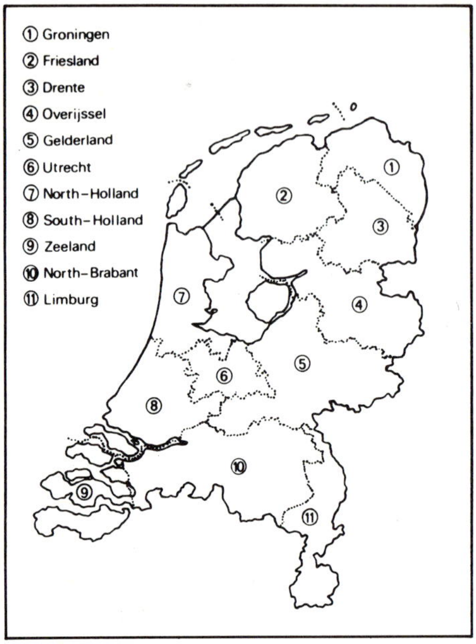


By making use of table 4.7.2.a and 4.7.2.b one can easily calculate for each of the five variables the contiguity correlation coefficients $c_k$ of each order $k$, both for the year 1960 and for 1965. The results are presented in table 4.7.2.c, where the variables are enumerated according to table 4.7.2.a. Table 4.7.2.c can be inspected in a threefold way, each of which analyses a certain aspect of table 4.7.2.c.

At first, one may consider the value of $c_k$ ($k = 1, \ldots, 4$) for each variable separately. By comparing the successive values of $c_k$ for a given variable one obtains insight into the degree of spatial correlation for various contiguity orders of this variable. This idea underlies a spatio-correlogram (see figure 4.7.1.a). Table 4.7.2.c shows a tendency towards a (slightly) positive spatial correlation for the first contiguity order (except the 4$^{th}$ variable), a negative spatial correlation for the second and third contiguity order (except the 4$^{th}$ and 5$^{th}$ variable of order 3), followed by a positive spatial correlation for the fourth contiguity order (except the 2$^{nd}$ variable). Therefore, it appears that there is, in general, a significant difference between the $c_k$-values of most variables in the successive $k^{th}$-order contiguity systems ($k = 1, \ldots, 4$). This is also indicated by a superficial inspection of table 4.7.2.a.

Table 4.7.2.b

A complete contiguity table for the Netherlands

| Provinces | Presence of $k^{th}$-order connections ($k = 1, 2, 3, 4$) | | | | | | | | | | | Number of first-order connections ('x') | Number of second-order connections ('o') | Number of third-order connections ('+') | Number of fourth-order connections ('*') |
|---|---|---|---|---|---|---|---|---|---|---|---|---|---|---|---|
| | 1 | 2 | 3 | 4 | 5 | 6 | 7 | 8 | 9 | 10 | 11 | | | | |
| 1 | | x | x | o | + | + | o | + | * | * | * | 2 | 2 | 3 | 3 |
| 2 | x | | x | x | o | o | x | o | + | + | + | 4 | 3 | 3 | – |
| 3 | x | x | | x | o | + | o | + | * | + | + | 3 | 2 | 4 | 1 |
| 4 | o | x | x | | x | o | o | o | + | o | o | 3 | 6 | 1 | – |
| 5 | + | o | o | x | | x | o | x | o | x | x | 5 | 4 | 1 | – |
| 6 | + | o | + | o | x | | x | x | o | o | o | 3 | 5 | 2 | – |
| 7 | o | x | o | o | o | x | | x | o | o | + | 3 | 6 | 1 | – |
| 8 | + | o | + | o | x | x | x | | x | x | o | 5 | 3 | 2 | – |
| 9 | * | + | * | + | o | o | o | x | | x | o | 2 | 4 | 2 | 2 |
| 10 | * | + | + | o | x | o | o | x | x | | x | 4 | 3 | 2 | 1 |
| 11 | * | + | + | o | x | o | + | o | o | x | | 2 | 4 | 3 | 1 |
| | | | | | | | | | | | | $I_1 = 36$ | $I_2 = 42$ | $I_3 = 24$ | $I_4 = 8$ |

Table 4.7.2.c
Spatial correlation coefficients for the Dutch provinces

| Variable | Contiguity order | | | | | | | |
|---|---|---|---|---|---|---|---|---|
| | 1 | | 2 | | 3 | | 4 | |
| | 1960 | 1965 | 1960 | 1965 | 1960 | 1965 | 1960 | 1965 |
| 1 | 0·88 | 0·87 | 1·26 | 1·26 | 1·02 | 1·04 | 0·09 | 0·10 |
| 2 | 0·83 | 0·83 | 1·02 | 1·13 | 1·16 | 0·98 | 1·16 | 1·21 |
| 3 | 0·90 | 0·88 | 1·27 | 1·27 | 1·00 | 1·00 | 0·08 | 0·08 |
| 4 | 1·07 | 0·92 | 1·10 | 1·15 | 0·97 | 1·10 | 0·25 | 0·25 |
| 5 | 0·69 | 0·66 | 1·43 | 1·43 | 0·99 | 1·01 | 0·24 | 0·25 |

In the second place, one may compare the value of the spatial correlation coefficient of a certain order *k* between the five variables. These $c_k$'s do not show a considerable difference for any one of the five variables. They show a similar pattern over each order *k* ($k = 1, \ldots, 4$). Only the second variable in the fourth contiguity order shows a deviating outcome. The reason is that there is a considerable difference in population growth between fourth-order contiguous provinces (Groningen with respect to Zeeland, North-Brabant, and Limburg, as well as Drente with respect to Zeeland).

Finally, one may study the intertemporal pattern of the $c_k$'s. This pattern appears to be rather stable: only slight variations occur in the period 1960–1965.

The foregoing three remarks can be illustrated by constructing the spatio-correlograms for each variable separately, both for the year 1960 and 1965. In figure 4.7.2.a and 4.7.2.b the spatio-correlograms associated with variables 1 and 2 are presented. The pattern of the spatio-correlograms of variables 3, 4 and 5 is almost similar to that of variable 1.

Fig. 4.7.2.a Two spatio-correlograms for 1960

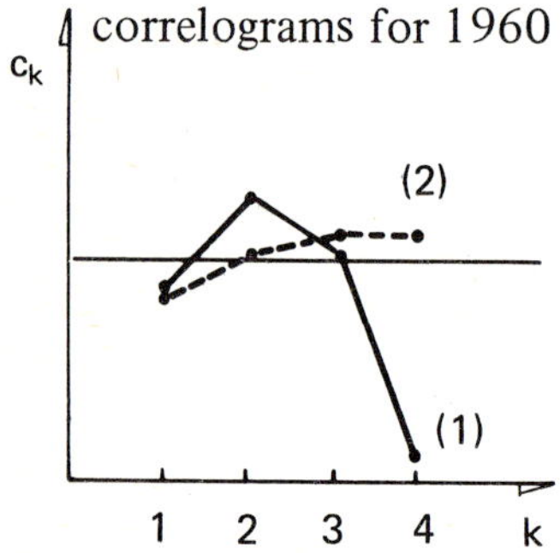


Fig. 4.7.2.b Two spatio-correlograms for 1965

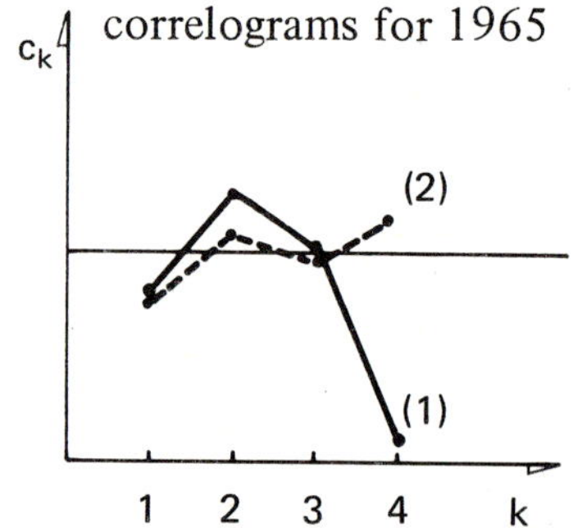

Figure 4.7.2.a and 4.7.2.b show that all variables (except the second one) possess a similar pattern with a maximum spatial correlation coefficient at the order 2. This situation can be explained as follows. The population density, for instance, appears to have a positive spatial correlation in the first-order adjacent ring of provinces, and a negative spatial correlation in the second-order ring of regions. The reason is that in the first-order ring provinces with corresponding population densities are correlated (Overijssel and Gelderland, North-Holland and South-Holland, North-Brabant and Limburg), whereas, in the second-order contiguity system the regions with a high population density (Utrecht, South-Holland and North-Holland) are correlated with regions with a low population density (Groningen, Drente, Overijssel and Zeeland). The fourth-order spatial correlation coefficient is smaller than one, i.c. the fourth-order contiguity system involves a positive spatial correlation. This can be explained by realizing that the fourth-order connexity links regions with a low population density (for instance, Groningen and North-Brabant, Drente and Zeeland, Groningen and Zeeland). The value of $c_k$ for the third, fourth and fifth variable can be explained in a similar way. The growth rate of population possesses a different pattern. In contrast with the other variables the highest values of the growth-rate of population are found in the more central regions (Utrecht, Gelderland, and Overijssel) and the southern regions (North-Brabant and Limburg). Since the lowest values of the growth rate of population occur in the northern regions and in Zeeland, the correlation coefficients of order 3 and 4 are at a maximum for this variable.

A comparison of the $c_k$'s for all variables over the years 1960 and 1965 leads to the conclusion that the interregional contiguity have undergone only slight changes, except the effect of the growth of population. Inspection of table 4.7.2.a shows that indeed the growth rate of population shows significant differences over the period 1960–1965. The growth rates of the northern provinces and Zeeland show in 1965 less differences with respect to the growth rates of the more central regions. Therefore, the third-order spatial correlation coefficient has undergone a decline.

One may conclude that the results presented above show a slight tendency to negative spin-off effects between the Dutch provinces (except for adjacent regions). A reason might be that there are certain provinces (North-Holland, South-Holland, for instance) with favourable economic conditions (employment, income, etc.), which act as attraction forces with respect to surrounding provinces.

Finally, the spatial correlation coefficients can be used in grouping procedures. It was already pointed out in section 4.3, that economic distances between regions can be used as a tool for deriving regional indicators. These regional indicators receive normally an equal weight. By assigning to each indicator, used for the calculation of the economic distance between two regions, a weight that corresponds to the inverse[9] of the spatial correlation coefficient of corresponding order, the clustering of regions is based more adequately on the economic interregional structure of the spatial system concerned.

## 4.8 Spatial diffusion analysis

### 4.8.1 *Introduction*

The explicit introduction of the element of space in regional economics (for instance, in the case of regional classification) implies, that a certain economic phenomenon is not realized in an equal, uniform way all through space. Instead one observes a spatial spread of economic phenomena. Such a diffusion in space does, in general, not occur at random, but it shows certain patterns (see also the contiguity analysis in the preceding section). In this way one may study the spatial spread of income, of cities, of population, and so forth. In this section the *spatial diffusion* of economic phenomena will be considered, while particular attention will be paid to the problem as to whether regular spatial spread patterns càn be found. At first, trend-surfaces will be considered, and, next, the spatial-temporal aspects of diffusion phenomena will be discussed.

### 4.8.2 *Spatial trend-surfaces*

It has already been pointed out in section 4.7, that certain regions (or spatial points) may act as attraction centres, which generate high income levels in the region itself, while surrounding regions show a slowly declining level of income. The problem as to whether there exist spatial influences between regions can be tested by means of a spatial correlation coefficient. In this subsection attention is paid to the spatial diffusion itself of a certain phenomenon. A useful tool for such a diffusion is a *trend-surface* (see, for instance, Chorley and Haggett [1965], Haggett [1968], Robinson [1970] and Robinson and Salih [1971]). A trend-surface is an isoline, the points of which are characterized by the fact that a certain phenomenon (for instance, income) has equal values on that line. Such a trend-surface can be used to analyse the effect of growth centres or polarized regions upon surrounding areas as a result of growth in the centre or region itself; a trend-surface can also be used to derive the spatial spread of consumption of a certain commodity (for instance, televisions), so that it also allows the determination of market areas between firms.

The concentric development of a certain phenomenon around a centre can be distorted by physical conditions (for instance, mountains or rivers). This implies that a trend-surface is, in general, not a regular line; it will show many disturbances. Furthermore, there are often in addition to a dominating spatial centre several secondary centres, which also exert a considerable influence on the spatial diffusion of a phenomenon. In spite of these variations in the spatial spread of an economic variable, the actual pattern often shows a certain degree of regularity. Such a rather regular spatial distribution of a phenomenon permits one to consider the area concerned as a continuous space, in which the points at which the phenomenon is observed are conceived of as sample points. In this way one may attempt at approximating the regular spatial patterns by means of certain higher order polynomials, expressed in the spatial co-ordinates of the area concerned. Such an approximation can use a regression analysis, in which the observations on a phenomenon are considered as dependent variables and in which the co-ordinates of the sample points are considered as independent variables. In this way trend-surface analysis can be used to test hypotheses concerning the spatial dispersion of certain economic phenomena.

The statistical technique itself of trend-surfaces is based on a least-squares curve-fitting procedure. The regression equation may have the form of a polynomial equation of any order, but, in general, the highest order used is a third order. If one considers the geographical co-ordinates as the two independent variables to describe the spatial diffusion of a dependent variable, one may estimate the parameters of this regression procedure in the normal way. Therefore, the regression equation of a trend-surface has the following shape:

$$z = f(x, y) + \epsilon \tag{4.8.2.1}$$

where $z$ is the value of a phenomenon at the sample point with co-ordinates $x$ and $y$, and where $\epsilon$ represents the disturbance term. The function $f(x, y)$ is a polynomial of the first, second or third order, represented in (4.8.2.2)–(4.8.2.4), respectively.

$$z = c + a_1 x + b_1 y + \epsilon \tag{4.8.2.2}$$

$$z = c + a_1 x + a_2 x^2 + b_1 y + b_2 y^2 + d_1 xy + \epsilon \tag{4.8.2.3}$$

$$z = c + a_1 x + a_2 x^2 + a_3 x^3 + b_1 y + b_2 y^2 + b_3 y^3 + d_1 xy + d_2 xy^2 + d_3 x^2 y + \epsilon \tag{4.8.2.4}$$

The coefficient $c$ represents a constant term in the regression equation, while the other coefficients $a_i$, $b_i$ and $d_i$ are the normal regression coefficients.

By mapping the estimated equations of the trend-surfaces for a number of successive levels of the variable $z$, one may draw a set of isolines, so that one obtains more insight in the (approximated) dispersion of the phenomenon concerned. An example of such a set of isolines is presented in figure 4.8.2.a for the case of a quadratic trend-surface (cf. [4.8.2.3]). The points, presented in figure 4.8.2.a, are the sample points, the successive co-ordinates of which are used in the regression equation (4.8.2.3) to estimate the unknown parameters $c$, $a_1$, $a_2$, $b_1$, $b_2$ and $d_1$. In this example the variable $z$ may represent any arbitrary phenomenon, for instance population density, average income, and so forth.

Fig. 4.8.2.a A set of trend-surfaces

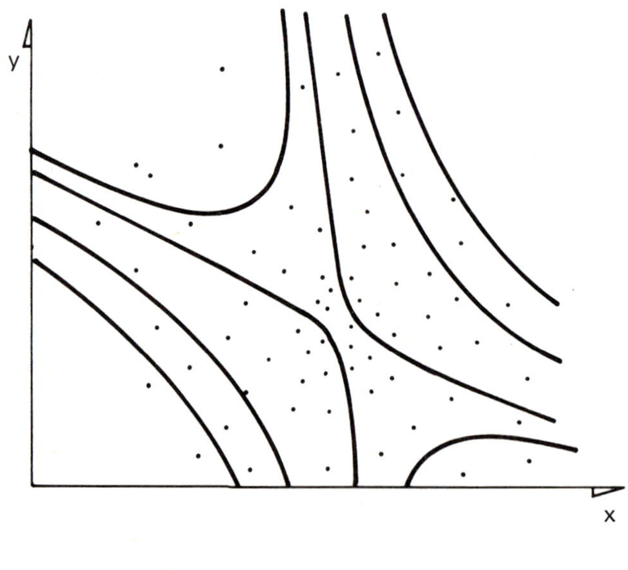


Finally, by analyzing the spatial diffusion of economic variables during more periods, a more reliable picture concerning interregional (or interurban) dynamics is obtained. A more dynamic approach to the spatial dispersion of phenomena is presented in the following section, where innovation diffusion in spatial systems will be discussed.

### 4.8.3 *Spatial-temporal diffusion*

In the foregoing section the concept of a trend-surface has been dealt with as a tool for analyzing the spatial diffusion of economic phenomena. However, the spatial diffusion of a phenomenon is not a static fact, but it often undergoes a dynamic evolution (for instance, the spread of television sets (see Berry [1972]), regional average incomes, or the growth rates of population (cf. table 4.7.3.a)). This implies that frequently a diffusion process is a simultaneous space-time process. Therefore, both time and distance play an essential role in diffusion analysis. This, however, does not imply that time and space are equivalent concepts (see subsection 4.7.1), but a series of studies in this field have shown that a simultaneous consideration of a spatial-temporal process is often capable of explaining the changes in geographical spread of certain phenomena. Contributions to diffusion analysis are contained *inter alia* in Casetti (1969), Hägerstrand (1967a, 1967b), Hudson (1969), Monin et al. (1973), Morrill and Pitts (1967), Morrill (1968), Morrill (1970), Nijkamp and Paelinck (1974) and Pedersen (1970).

The essential idea that underlies a diffusion analysis is that there is a high degree of interdependence in a spatial system (for instance, by means of communication flows, by means of attraction and repulsion forces, and so forth). This interdependence causes the spatial diffusion of phenomena, but this diffusion is limited through time and distance constraints. For instance, the spatial consequence of an innovation is, that this innovation is at first clustered around a centre, and that next the diffusion of this innovation occurs as a wave outwards from this centre according to a distance decay function. The evolution of the phenomenon over time may be represented by means of a S-shaped logistic curve (see figure 4.8.3.a). The variable $x$ on the vertical axis of figure 4.8.3.a represents the value of the phenomenon concerned during each time period. If the phenomenon concerned relates to a new commodity (for instance, television sets), $x$ represents the proportion of acceptance of this commodity, and the dashed line represents the ultimate saturation level.

Fig. 4.8.3.a A logistic curve

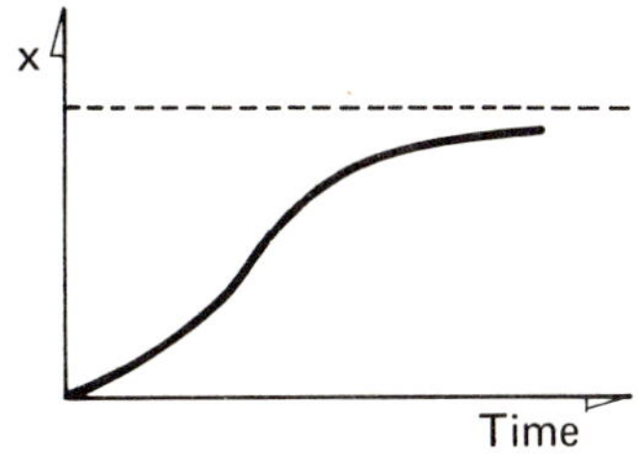


Fig. 4.8.3.b A distance decay function

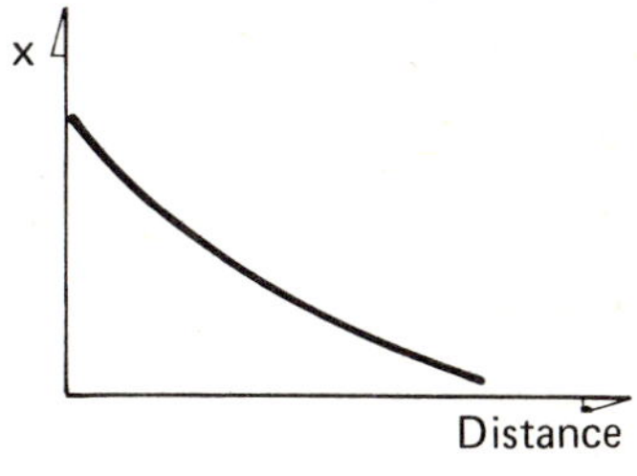

If the phenomenon concerned relates to an economic variable (for instance, the income level), $x$ represents the average value of this variable during each time period, and the dashed line is the long-run equilibrium level. Next, one may represent the *spatial* spread of the phenomenon concerned with respect to a centre. If a distance decay function is assumed, one obtains figure 4.8.3.b, in which the vertical axis measures the level of the phenomenon concerned at a certain distance from the origin. It should be noted that this distance decay function undergoes a shift in each time period. The mathematical representations of the logistic curve (figure 4.8.3.a) and the distance decay function are contained in (4.8.3.1) and (4.8.3.2); they are, respectively, equal to:

$$x = \frac{c}{1 + ae^{-bt}} \qquad (4.8.3.1)$$

where $t$ is a time index, $c$ the saturation (or equilibrium) level, and $a$ and $b$ certain constants, and:

$$x = ae^{-\beta d} \qquad (4.8.3.2)$$

where $d$ represents the distance, $\beta$ a friction coefficient of distance, and $a$ a constant. It should be noted that in addition to an exponential distance decay function alternative mathematical specifications can be used, for instance, a Pareto function, i.e.,

$$x = ad^{-\beta} \qquad (4.8.3.3)$$

or a Pareto exponential function, i.e.,

$$x = a\, d^{-\beta}\, e^{-\gamma d} \qquad (4.8.3.4)$$

The coefficients $a$ and $\beta$ are not equal in the various specifications (4.8.3.2)–(4.8.3.4).

Finally, one may combine figure 4.8.3.a and 4.8.3.b in a three-dimensional figure, which represents the value of $x$ at different time periods and at different distances from the origin. This figure may show spatial-temporal waves of the dispersion of a certain phenomenon (see figure 4.8.3.c). Such a wave-like phenomenon may have various shapes. A usual shape in the case of innovation diffusion is a Poisson-like function:

$$x = \frac{a\, e^{-\beta d}\, d^{t}}{t!} \qquad (4.8.3.5)$$

Fig. 4.8.3.c Spatial-temporal waves of dispersion

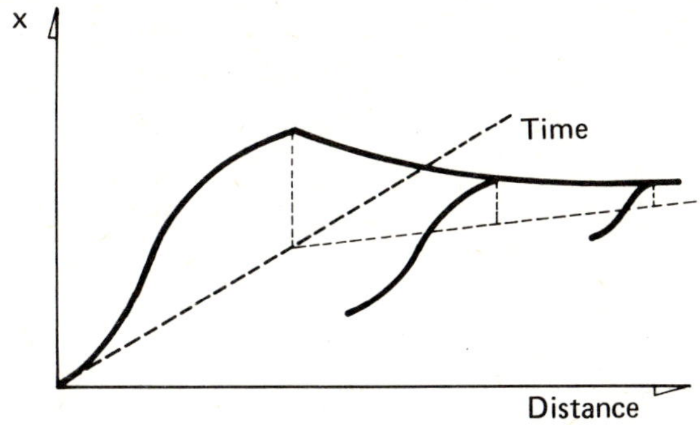


The previous problem with simultaneous spatial-temporal elements is not only relevant for the diffusion of one single phenomenon; it arises also in the case of dynamic urban or (inter) regional models, in which the spatial and temporal evolutions of many variables are integrated (see also Ch.7). The evolution of such a dynamic model might also be represented in the figurative way set out above.

Finally, it should be noted that in many simulation studies in diffusion analysis use is made of *diffusion operators*. A diffusion operator is a spatial representation of expected or estimated regularities in the flows or contacts between spatial points (for instance, between elementary grid cells). These operators are estimated on the basis of past observations on spatial diffusion phenomena. Once these operators have been estimated, they can be used to generate simulated patterns of flows or contacts between points in a spatial system. There is a wide variety of diffusion operators in simulation studies, for instance the *mean information fields* (cf. Hägerstrand [1967b], Marble and Nystuen [1963], and Morrill and Pitts [1967]) or the *linear diffusion operators* (cf. Tinline [1970]). A disadvantage of these diffusion operators is the fact that they rest, in general, mainly on statistical regularities in spatial systems, but that behavioural relationships (apart from a distance decay function) are frequently left out of consideration. In general, the use of regional and urban models including behavioural assumptions is preferred. These behavioural assumptions in spatial systems are elaborated in various ways in the following chapters. A specific application of a diffusion process in a spatial and dynamic context is contained in Ch.7.

## Appendix 4A The use of principal component methods in factor analysis

It has already been set out in section 4.6, that a principal component method is a non-stochastic approach to an orthogonal transformation of mutually correlated variables into a set of independent characteristics. Therefore, the assumption is made that the common variance of the original variables can be explained by a new set of an equal number of orthogonal factors (see, for instance, Harman [1964] and Tintner [1952]). Therefore, the basic principal component model is equal to (4.6.2.9). Since a principal component method abandons the uniqueness, the variance and the covariance of the original variables $\mathbf{z}_{\bullet i}$ is equal to (4.6.3.1) and (4.6.3.2), respectively.

As has already been stated in section 4.6, an additional criterion is necessary in order to derive unique estimations of the loading matrix $\mathbf{L}$ with typical elements $l_{ik}$ $(i = 1, \ldots, I; k = 1, \ldots, I)$. This criterion states, that the first factor accounts for the greatest amount of the communalities, so that the contribution of its corresponding loadings to the common variance is maximal. Furthermore, the condition is imposed that the original covariances between the variables $\mathbf{z}_{\bullet i}$ and $\mathbf{z}_{\bullet i'}$ should remain equal, i.e., (4.6.3.2) should be satisfied. The contribution of the first factor or first principal component, $\mathbf{f}_1$, to the total variance of all variables $\mathbf{z}_{\bullet i}$ $(i = 1, \ldots, I)$ is equal to:

$$S_1 = \sum_{i=1}^{I} l_{i1}^2 \qquad (4A.1)$$

Therefore, $l_{ik}$ $(i = 1, \ldots, I; k = 1, \ldots, I)$ should be determined such that the following program is solved:

$$\left.\begin{aligned} &\max S_1 = \sum_{i=1}^{I} l_{i1}^2 \\ &\text{s.t.}^{10} \\ &r_{ii'} = \sum_{k=1}^{I} l_{ik}\, l_{i'k} \end{aligned}\right\} \qquad (4A.2)$$

where $r_{ii'}$ represents the correlation coefficient between $\mathbf{z}_{\bullet i}$ and $\mathbf{z}_{\bullet i'}$ (it should be noted that $r_{ii'} = \text{cov}\,(\mathbf{z}_{\bullet i}, \mathbf{z}_{\bullet i'})$, because $\mathbf{z}_{\bullet i}$ and $\mathbf{z}_{\bullet i'}$ are standardized variables).

Solution of the previous program gives the following result (cf. Harman [1964]):

$$l_{i1} \sum_{i=1}^{I} l_{i1}^2 - \sum_{i'=1}^{I} r_{ii'}\, l_{i'1} = 0 \qquad (4A.3)$$

Since system (4A.3) is valid for any value of $i$, the complete system can be written as:

$$\begin{bmatrix} 1 & r_{12} & \cdots & r_{1I} \\ r_{21} & \ddots & & \vdots \\ \vdots & & \ddots & \vdots \\ r_{I1} & \cdots & \cdots & 1 \end{bmatrix} \begin{bmatrix} l_{11} \\ \vdots \\ \vdots \\ l_{I1} \end{bmatrix} = \sum_{i=1}^{I} l_{i1}^{2} \begin{bmatrix} l_{11} \\ \vdots \\ \vdots \\ l_{I1} \end{bmatrix} \tag{4A.4}$$

or:

$$\mathbf{R}\mathbf{l}_{\bullet 1} = \lambda_1 \mathbf{l}_{\bullet 1} \tag{4A.5}$$

where $\mathbf{R}$ is the known matrix of correlation coefficients, $\mathbf{l}_{\bullet 1}$ the, as yet unknown, first column vector from the loading matrix $\mathbf{L}$ (with typical elements $l_{i1}$ ), and $\lambda_1$ an unknown scalar defined as:

$$\lambda_1 = \sum_{i=1}^{I} l_{i1}^{2} \tag{4A.6}$$

System (4A.5) is the standard expression for the calculation of eigenvalues and eigenvectors of the matrix $\mathbf{R}$, where $\lambda_I$ stands for an eigenvalue and $\mathbf{l}_{\bullet 1}$ for an eigenvector (see Hadley [1961]). The eigenvalue $\lambda_1$ appears to be equal to the squared length of the eigenvector $\mathbf{l}_{\bullet 1}$. System (4A.5) has a non-trivial solution, if the determinant of the matrix of coefficients is equal to zero; in other words, if:

$$|\mathbf{R} - \lambda_1 \mathbf{I}| = 0 \tag{4A.7}$$

Relationship (4A.7) is called the characteristic equation for the calculation of eigenvalues and eigenvectors. This equation is a polynomial of the $I^{\text{th}}$ degree in the unknown eigenvalue $\lambda_1$. This implies, that in principle $I$ different eigenvalues can be calculated (owing to the symmetry of $\mathbf{R}$ the eigenvalues are real numbers; see Murdoch [1957]. The problem as to how to find only one unqiue solution can easily be solved by realizing that $\lambda_1$ (cf. [4A.6]) is equal to the variance criterion $S_1$ (cf. [4A.1]). Since $S_1$ should be maximized, one has to select from the range of $I$ eigenvalues the maximum value of $\lambda_1$ as the solution of system

(4A.5): the greatest eigenvalue is associated with the first principal component. Once the eigenvalue $\lambda_1$ has been determined, the corresponding eigenvector $\mathbf{l}_{\bullet 1}$ can be determined by substituting $\lambda_1$ into system (4A.5). This eigenvector as such is not unique, since each scalar multiple of $\mathbf{l}_{\bullet 1}$ is also a solution of (4A.5). In order to guarantee a unique solution for the eigenvector $\mathbf{l}_{\bullet 1}$ an additional condition is imposed, viz. a *normalization* condition (cf. [4.3.2.6]). This implies that the ultimate solution of $\mathbf{l}_{\bullet 1}$, denoted by $\mathbf{l}^*_{\bullet 1}$, should be equal to:

$$\mathbf{l}^*_{\bullet 1} = \frac{\mathbf{l}_{\bullet 1}}{||\mathbf{l}_{\bullet 1}||} \tag{4A.8}$$

Once this normalized eigenvector has been calculated, the first column of the loading matrix is known. Therefore, the elegant result is attained, that the determination of the loadings according to a principal component method implies the calculation of the eigenvectors of the original, known correlation matrix.

Next, the loadings in the second column of **L** are calculated in an analogous way. Then the new criterion is, that the contribution of the second factor to the total variance should be maximized.

By repeating this procedure, all loadings $l_{ik}$ $(i = 1, \ldots, I; k = 1, \ldots, I)$ can be determined. Evidently, the condition holds:

$$S_1 > S_2 > \ldots . > S_I \tag{4A.9}$$

Each factor $\mathbf{f}_k$ accounts for a certain part of the contribution to the total variance. This part is for each factor $\mathbf{f}_k$ equal to $\lambda_k$ (cf. [4A.1] and [4A.6]). The total variance is equal to $I$ (as has already been set out in subsection [4.6.3]. This can be checked by realizing that the total variance, $S$, is according to (4.6.3.1) equal to:

$$S = \sum_{i=1}^{I} \sum_{k=1}^{I} l_{ik}^2 \tag{4A.10}$$

According to (4A.6) $S$ is equal to:

$$S = \sum_{k=1}^{I} \lambda_k \tag{4A.11}$$

Since the *trace* of the (symmetric) correlation matrix is equal to the sum of the eigenvalues (cf. Murdoch [1957]), one may derive:

$$\sum_{k=1}^{I} \lambda_k = I \tag{4A.12}$$

Therefore, the relative contribution of a factor $\mathbf{f}_k$ to the total variance, $s_k$, is equal to:

$$s_k = \frac{\lambda_k}{I} \tag{4A.13}$$

Ultimately, one may conclude that the determination of loadings and factor scores is extremely simple. This determination requires only the calculation of the eigenvalues and eigenvectors of the (known) correlation matrix of the original variables.

## Appendix 4B Some properties of the spatial correlation coefficient

Section 4.7 was devoted to contiguity analysis, and more in particular to spatial correlation coefficients. This coefficient was defined in (4.7.1.1).

The first factor of (4.7.1.1) was identified as the contiguity variance. If this first factor is denoted by $F_1$, one may write:

$$\begin{aligned}
F_1 &= \frac{\sum_{r=1}^{R} \sum_{i_{kr}=1_{kr}}^{I_{kr}} (x_r - x_{i_{kr}})^2}{2I_k} \\
&= \frac{\sum_{r=1}^{R} \sum_{i_{kr}=1_{kr}}^{I_{kr}} (x_r^2 - 2x_r x_{i_{kr}} + x_{i_{kr}}^2)}{2I_k} \qquad (4B.1)\\
&= \frac{\sum_{r=1}^{R} I_{kr} x_r^2 - 2 \sum_{r=1}^{R} \sum_{i_{kr}=1_{kr}}^{I_{kr}} x_r x_{i_{kr}} + \sum_{r=1}^{R} \sum_{i_{kr}=1_{kr}}^{I_{kr}} x_{i_{kr}}^2}{2I_k} \\
&= \frac{\sum_{r=1}^{R} I_{kr} x_r^2}{2I_k} - \frac{\sum_{r=1}^{R} \sum_{i_{kr}=1_{kr}}^{I_{kr}} x_r x_{i_{kr}}}{I_k} + \frac{\sum_{r=1}^{R} \sum_{i_{kr}=1_{kr}}^{I_{kr}} x_{i_{kr}}^2}{2I_k}
\end{aligned}$$

Next, the simplifying hypothesis may be made, that all regions $r$ ($r = 1, \ldots, R$) have an equal number of connections of a certain order (for instance, in the case of a regular regional pattern). This implies, that $I_{kr}$ is constant for each region $r$, i.e.,

$$I_{kr} = I_k^* \tag{4B.2}$$

It should be noted, that this simplifying hypothesis is not necessary (cf. Hordijk [1974]), but it serves to reduce the computational work. Then the system is said to be homogeneous of order $k$. It should be noted, that (4B.2) does not imply that the number of connections of region $r$ over all contiguity orders $k$ is constant. Since each region $r$ possesses $I_k^*$ connections of order $k$, the total number of connections of order $k$ within the spatial system is $RI_k^*$, i.e.,

$$I_k = RI_k^* \tag{4B.3}$$

Substitution of (4B.2) and (4B.3) into the first term of (4B.1) yields:

$$\frac{\sum_{r=1}^{R} I_{kr} x_r^2}{2I_k} = \frac{\sum_{r=1}^{R} I_k^* x_r^2}{2RI_k^*} = \frac{\sum_{r=1}^{R} x_r^2}{2R} \tag{4B.4}$$

In a similar way one may substitute (4B.2) and (4B.3) into the third term of (4B.1). Then one obtains:

$$\frac{\sum_{r=1}^{R} \sum_{i_{kr}=1}^{I_{kr}} x_{i_{kr}}^2}{2I_k} = \frac{\sum_{r=1}^{R} I_k^* x_r^2}{2RI_k^*} = \frac{\sum_{r=1}^{R} x_r^2}{2R} \tag{4B.5}$$

The operation in (4B.5), in which the terms $x_{i_{kr}}^2$ are transformed into $x_r^2$, is justified, because each term $x_{i_{kr}}^2$ in the summation is added $I_k^*$ times. The implication is, that the first and third term of (4B.1) are exactly equal.

Finally, the second term can be rewritten as:

$$\frac{\sum_{r=1}^{R}\sum_{i_{kr}=1_{kr}}^{I_{kr}} x_r x_{i_{kr}}}{I_k} = \frac{\sum_{r=1}^{R}\sum_{i_{kr}=1_{kr}}^{I_k^*} x_r x_{i_{kr}}}{RI_k^*} \tag{4B.6}$$

$$= \frac{\sum_{r=1}^{R}\sum_{i_{kr}=1_{kr}}^{I_k^*} (x_r - \overline{x})(x_{i_{kr}} - \overline{x}) + RI_k^*\overline{x}^2}{RI_k^*}$$

where $\overline{x}$ is defined in (4.7.1.3). The latter operation is permitted, since

$$\sum_{r=1}^{R}\sum_{i_{kr}=1_{kr}}^{I_k^*} (x_r - \overline{x})(x_{i_{kr}} - \overline{x}) = \sum_{r=1}^{R}\sum_{i_{kr}=1_{kr}}^{I_k^*} (x_r x_{i_{kr}} - \overline{x}x_r - \overline{x}x_{i_{kr}} + \overline{x})^2$$

$$= \sum_{r=1}^{R}\sum_{i_{kr}=1_{kr}}^{I_k^*} x_r x_{i_{kr}} - \overline{x}I_k^* \sum_{r=1}^{R} x_r - \overline{x} \sum_{r=1}^{R}\sum_{i_{kr}=1_{kr}}^{I_k^*} x_{i_{kr}} + RI_k^* \overline{x}^2$$

$$= \sum_{r=1}^{R}\sum_{i_{kr}=1_{kr}}^{I_k^*} x_r x_{i_{kr}} - \overline{x}I_k^*(R\overline{x}) - \overline{x}(RI_k^*\overline{x}) + RI_k^*\overline{x}^2$$

$$= \sum_{r=1}^{R}\sum_{i_{kr}=1_{kr}}^{I_k^*} x_r x_{i_{kr}} - RI_k^*\overline{x}^2 \tag{4B.7}$$

Substitution of (4B.4), (4B.5) and (4B.6) into (4B.1) gives the result:

$$F_1 = \frac{\sum_{r=1}^{R} x_r^2}{R} - \frac{\sum_{r=1}^{R}\sum_{i_{kr}=1_{kr}}^{I_k^*} (x_r - \overline{x})(x_{i_{kr}} - \overline{x})}{RI_k^*} - \overline{x}^2 \tag{4B.8}$$

The second term of (4B.8) represents the correlation coefficient of a regional variable with respect to the same variable in contiguous regions of order $k$ (see also [4.3.2.12]). If there is no spatial correlation (and thus no sphere of influence of the regions), this correlation coefficient will be equal to zero. Then $F_1$ is equal to:

$$F_1 = \frac{\sum_{r=1}^{R} x_r^2 - R\overline{x}^2}{R} = \frac{\sum_{r=1}^{R} (x_r - \overline{x})^2}{R} \tag{4B.9}$$

By substituting (4B.9) into (4.7.1.1) one finds the expression for the contiguity correlation coefficient $c_k$ in the case of no spatial correlation:

$$c_k = \frac{\sum_{r=1}^{R} (x_r - \overline{x})^2}{R} \cdot \frac{R-1}{\sum_{r=1}^{R} (x_r - \overline{x})^2} \tag{4B.10}$$

$$= \frac{R-1}{R} \approx 1$$

supposed $R$ is sufficiently large. One may prove (see Lebart [1966]), that the mathematical expectation of $c_k$ is exactly equal to 1, if there is no spatial correlation. Therefore, one may conclude that $c_k = 1$, if there is no contiguity effect of order $k$. Furthermore, in the case of a positive spatial correlation $F_1$ is smaller than (4B.9), so that a positive spatial correlation implies $c_k < 1$. In the reverse case of a negative spatial correlation one may prove that $c_k > 1$.

## Notes

1 The symbol '$\forall$' means 'for each value of'.

2 The symbol '$\exists$' means 'there exists'.

3 Source: National Institute of Statistics, Belgium, 1959.

4 An unbiased estimation of the variance obtained, if the aggregated squared differences are divided by $J-1$ instead of by $J$.

5 The symbol '$\mathcal{E}$' means 'the mathematical expectation of'.

6 This undetermined solution can be interpreted in a geometric way as follows:

(a) each vector $\mathbf{z}_{\bullet i}$ can be transformed into a $K$-dimensional vector space by means of (4.6.2.9), in which $\mathbf{f}_1, \ldots, \mathbf{f}_K$ are orthogonal axes.

(b) the coefficients $l_{ik}$ ($k = 1, \ldots, K$) are the components of $\mathbf{z}_{\bullet i}$ with respect to the new system of orthogonal axes. A rotation of this system of axes does not influence the length of the vector $\mathbf{z}_{\bullet i}$ and their mutual angles, i.e., the variances and covariances remain equal. Therefore, a rotation does only affect **L**. but not $h_i^2$ and $\sigma_i^2$.

[7] In fact, the orthogonalized variables $\mathbf{x}_{r\bullet}^{***}$ from (4.3.2.7) are the orthogonal factors or components of a factor-analytic model, while the transition matrix **L** is the matrix with factor loadings.

[8] The connection between the various regions can also be described by means of a Boolean matrix, which represents for each order $k$ the corresponding connections between regions (see also subsection 1.6.3).

[9] The inverse spatial correlation coefficient is used, since a low value of a spatial correlation coefficient implies a high degree of spatial correlation (see also Appendix 4B).

[10] The abbreviation 's.t.' means 'subject to the condition'.

## References


Benzécri, J.P. et al., *L'Analyse des Données; I, La Taxinomie; II, L'Analyse des Correspondances*, Dunod, Paris 1973.

Berry, B.J.L., 'Grouping and Regionalization; An Approach to the Problem Using Multivariate Analysis', in: W.L. Garrison and D.F. Marble (eds.), *Quantitative Geography*, Part I, *Economic and Cultural Topics*, Studies in Geography, North-western University, Illinois 1967, pp. 219–251.

Berry, B.J.L., 'Hierarchical Diffusion: The Basis of Developmental Filtering and Spread in a System of Growth Centers', in: N.M. Hansen (ed.), *Growth Centers in Regional Economic Development*, Free Press, New York 1972, pp. 108–138.

Binswanger, H.C., 'Das Intro-Regionale Gleichgewicht (zur Integration von Standorttheorie und Theorie des Internationalen Handels)', *Schweizerische Zeitschrift für Volkswirtschaft und Statistik*, 1961, pp. 129–164.

Boudeville, J.R., *Les Espaces Economiques*, 'Que sais-je,', no. 950, Presses Universitaires de France, Paris 1961.

Boudeville, J.R., *Les Programmes Economiques*, 'Que sais-je.', no. 1073, Presses Universitaires de France, Paris 1963.

Boudeville, J.R., *Problems of Regional Economic Planning*, Edinburgh University Press, Edinburgh 1966.

Broadbent, T.A., *An Introduction to Factor Analysis and its Application in Regional Science*, Working Paper no. 13, Centre for Environmental Studies, London 1968.

Casetti, E., 'Why Do Diffusion Processes Conform to Logistic Trends?', *Geographical Analysis*, vol. 1, 1969, pp. 101–105.

Cattell, R.B., 'Factor Analysis: An Introduction to Essentials I and II', *Biometrics*, vol. 21, 1965, pp. 190–215, 405–435.

Chevalier, J.C., *Classification et Régionalisation; Analyse des Méthodes Quantitatives*, Mémoire, Dijon 1971.

Chorley, R.J. and Haggett, P., 'Trend-Surface Mapping in Geographical Research', *Transactions of the Institute of British Geographers*, vol. 37, 1965, pp. 47–67.

Cliff, A.D. and Ord, J.K., 'The Problem of Spatial Autocorrelation', in: A.J. Scott (ed.), *Studies in Regional Science*, Pion Press, London 1969, pp. 25–55.

Cliff, A.D. and Ord, J.K., 'Spatial Autocorrelation: A Review of Existing and New Measures with Applications', *Economic Geography*, vol. 46, no. 2, 1970, pp. 269–292.

Cliff, A.D. and Ord, J.K., *Spatial Autocorrelation*, Pion Press, London 1973.

Dacey, M.F., 'A Review on Measures of Contiguity for Two and *k*-Color Maps', in: B.J.L. Berry and D.F. Marble (eds.), *Spatial Analysis: A Reader in Statistical Geography*, Prentice-Hall, Englewood Cliffs 1968, pp. 479–490.

Davin, L.E., Degeer, L. and Paelinck, J.H.P., *Dynamique Economique de la Région Liégeoise*, Presses Universitaires de France, Paris 1959.

Dawson, J.A. and Mather, P.M., 'The Differential Economic Structures of the Belgian Provinces – A Comment', *Regional and Urban Economics*, vol. 1, no. 3, 1971, pp. 317–322.

Fisher, W.A., 'Econometric Estimation with Spatial Dependence', *Regional and Urban Economics*, vol. 1, no. 1, 1971, pp. 19–40.

Geary, R.C., 'The Contiguity Ratio and Statistical Mapping', *The Incorporated Statistician*, vol. 5, 1954, pp. 115–145.

Goldberg, R.R., *Methods of Real Analysis*, Blaisdell Publishing Co., Waltham 1964.

Grigg, D.B., 'The Logic of Regional Systems', *Annals of the Association of American Geographers*, vol. 55, 1965, pp. 465–491.

Guigou, J.L., *Analyse des Données et Choix à Critères Multiples*, Dunod, Paris 1974.

Hadley, G., *Linear Algebra*, Addison-Wesley Publishing Co., Reading, Massachusetts 1961.

Hägerstrand, T., *Innovation Diffusion as a Spatial Process* (Translated by A. Pred), University of Chicago Press, Chicago 1967a.

Hägerstrand, T., 'On Monte Carlo Simulation of Diffusion', in: W.L. Garrison and D.F. Marble (eds.), *Quantitative Geography*, Part I, *Economic and Cultural Topics*, Studies in Geography, North-western University, Illinois, 1967b, pp. 1–32.

Haggett, P., 'Trend-Surface Mapping in the Interregional Comparison of Intra-Regional Structures', *Papers and Proceedings of the Regional Science Association,* vol. 20, 1968, pp. 19–28.

Harman, H.H., *Modern Factor Analysis*, Chicago University Press, Chicago 1964.

Hordijk, L., 'Spatial Correlation in the Disturbances of a Linear Interregional Model', *Regional and Urban Economics*, vol. 4, nr. 2, 1974, pp. 117–140.

Hudson, J.C., 'Diffusion in a Central Place System', *Geographical Analysis*, vol. 1, 1969, pp. 45–58.

Isard, W., *Methods of Regional Analysis: An Introduction to Regional Science,* MIT Press, Cambridge 1960.

Jaumotte, Ch. and Paelinck, J.H.P., 'The Differential Economic Structures of the Belgian Provinces', *Regional and Urban Economics*, vol. 1, no. 1, 1971, pp. 41–75.

Johnston, R.J., 'Grouping and Regionalizing: Some Methodological and Technical Observations', *Economic Geography*, vol. 46, no. 2, 1970, pp. 293–305.

King, L.J., *Statistical Analysis in Geography*, Prentice-Hall, Englewood Cliffs 1969.

Klaassen, L.H., *Methods of Selecting Industries for Depressed Areas*, OECD, Paris 1967.

Lebart, L., 'Les Variables Socio-Economiques Départementales ou Régionales', I, *Méthodes Statistiques d'Etude,* IEDES, Paris 1966.

Malinvaud, E., *Statistical Methods of Econometrics,* North-Holland Publishing Co., Amsterdam 1970.

Marble, D.F. and Nystuen, J.D., 'An Approach to the Direct Measurement of Community Mean Information Fields', *Papers and Proceedings of the Regional Science Association*, vol. 11, 1963, pp. 99–109.

Monin, J.P., Bénayoun, R. and Sert, B., *Initiation des Mathêmatiques des Processus de Diffusion*, Gauthiers-Villars & Mouton, Paris, The Hague, 1973.

Moran, P.A.P., 'A Test for Serial Independence of Residuals', *Biometrika,* vol. 37, 1950, pp. 178–181.

Morrill, R.L., 'Waves of Spatial Diffusion', *Journal of Regional Science*, vol. 8, no. 1, 1968, pp. 1–18.

Morrill, R.L., 'The Shape of Diffusion in Space and Time, *Economic*

*Geography*, vol. 46, no. 2, 1970, pp. 259–268.
Morrill, R.L. and Pitts, F.R., 'Marriage, Migration, and the Mean Information Field: A Study in Uniqueness and Generality', *Annals of the Association of American Geographers*, vol. 57, 1967, pp. 401–422.
Murdoch, D.C., *Linear Algebra for Undergraduates*, Wiley, New York 1957.
Nijkamp, P. and Paelinck, J.H.P., 'Diffusion of Development Processes in Regional and Urban Systems', *Foundations of Empirical Economic Research*, Netherlands Economic Institute, Rotterdam (mimeo) 1974.
Paelinck, J.H.P., 'Analyse Quantitative de Certains Phénomènes du Développement Régional Polarisé, in: *Problèmes de Conversion Economique*, Actes du IVe Colloque de l'ASRDLF, Génin, Paris 1965, pp. 341–387.
Paelinck, J.H.P., 'Het Noorden van Nederland Gezien in het Licht van de Algemene Theorie der Regionaal-Economische Ontwikkeling', in: *Akademiedagen 21*, North-Holland Publishing Co., Amsterdam 1970, pp. 7–22.
Paelinck, J.H.P., Molle, W.T.M. and Van Holst, B., 'Complejos Siderometalúrgicos en Europa', in: *La Industria Siderometalúrgica en Asturias*, Sociedad Asturiana de Estudios Económicos e Industriales (SADEI) and Netherlands Economic Institute (NEI), Asturias 1971.
Pedersen, P.O., 'Innovation Diffusion within and between National Urban Systems', *Geographical Analysis*, vol. 2, 1970, pp. 203–254.
Perloff, H., Dunn, E.S., Lampard, P. and Muth, R., *Regions, Resources and Economic Growth*, The Johns Hopkins Press, Baltimore 1960.
Perroux, F., 'Note sur la Notion de Pôle de Croissance', *Economie Appliquée*, no. 1 and 2, 1955.
Robinson, G., 'Some Comments on Trend-Surface Analysis', *Area*, no. 3, 1970, pp. 31–36.
Robinson, G. and Salih, K.B., 'The Spread of Development around Kuala Lumpur: A Methodology for an Exploratory Test of Some Assumptions of the Growth-Pole Model', *Regional Studies*, vol. 5, 1971, pp. 303–314.
Rotman, B. and Kneebone, G.T., *The Theory of Sets and Transfinite Numbers,* Oldbourne, London 1966.
Roux, M., *Un Algorithme pour Construire une Hiérarchie Particulière*, Thèse Sciences, Paris 1968.
Scott, A.J., *Combinatorial Programming, Spatial Analysis and Planning,* Methuen, London 1971.
Siebert, H., 'Die Anwendung der Mengentheorie für die Abgrenzung von Regionen', *Jahrbuch für Sozialwissenschaft*, vol. 18, 1967, pp. 215–222.
Sokal, R.R. and Sneath, P.H.A., *Principles of Numerical Taxonomy*, Freeman, San Francisco 1963.

Stone, J.R.N., 'A Comparison of the Economic Structures of Regions Based on the Concept of Distance', *Journal of Regional Science*, vol. 2, no. 2, 1960.
Suppes, P., *Axiomatic Set Theory*, Van Nostrand Co., Princeton 1965.
Teitz, M.B., 'Regional Theory and Regional Models', *Papers of the Regional Science Association*, 1962, pp. 35–52.
Tinline, R., 'Linear Operators in Diffusion Research', in: M. Chisholm, A.E. Frey and P. Haggett (eds.), *Regional Forecasting*, Butterworths, London 1970, pp. 71–91.
Tintner, G., *Econometrics*, Wiley, New York 1952.

# 5 Regional and Interregional Input-Output Analysis

## 5.1 Introduction

The purpose of regional economics is to analyse, to explain and to predict the material aspects and operations of a region or a system of regions. The field of study concentrates on economic activities both at a micro scale (for instance, the individual location decisions) and at a medium and macro scale (for instance, the problem of regional classification). In general, regional economics requires much information at a disaggregated level. This disaggregation relates to the *space* (viz., a division according to regions, areas, districts, etc.), as well as to the *economic activities* (viz., a division according to sectors, industries, etc.). A powerful instrument for analyzing intersectoral and interregional relationships is the *input–output analysis* (I–O analysis). I–O analysis is a study of inter-industry relationships, which takes into consideration the product flows, which emerge, if a national economy is distinguished by industry or by region.

I–O analysis is an empirical approach to sectoral and regional phenomena. It consists of a set of technical and definitional relationships between economic phenomena. The reason why the use of I–O analysis has undergone a rapid growth is the fact that this applied economic analysis is based on production statistics, that can actually be collected. Furthermore, the various classifications made and the degree of disaggregation is rather flexible, since they can easily be adapted to the problem at hand and to the available information. Ultimately, I–O analysis provides a useful framework of a spatially dispersed production system; it is capable of a quantitative analysis and of a theoretical approach to optimization techniques (cf. Ch.6).

The division of production statistics by sectors and regions allows one to connect final demand for the output of the various sectors with the sectoral demand for primary inputs, so that the entire system of intermediate industrial requirements can be analyzed both for each sector and for each region. Spatial and economic linkages in the cost structure of each industry can be analyzed as well by means of I–O tabulation. In fact, I–O analysis is a method which is based on a relatively stable pattern of commodity flows between the spatial areas of an economy; it provides a detailed statistical framework of an economy, which is suitable for a manipulation by economic theory. This method becomes more important, as the possibilities for a large data storage increase (for instance, by means of data banks and computers).

This chapter is devoted to a set of regional and multiregional I–O models. The first sections of this chapter deal with the formal background and the essential elements of I–O analysis. Not all problems are discussed in detail, but appropriate introductions into and applications of I–O analysis can be found *inter alia* in Bródy and Carter (1970a), 1970b, 1972), Chenery and Clark (1959), Czamanski (1972, 1973), Isard (1960), Leontief (1951, 1953, 1966), Miernyk (1966), Rasmussen (1956), Richardson (1972), Stone (1961) and Tilanus (1965). After the formal introduction, presented in sections 5.2–5.4, a number of regional and interregional I–O studies and methods will be treated.

## 5.2 Taxonomic problems

As mentioned in the foregoing section, one may disaggregate an economy in various ways. The flows within an economy may be distinguished by different aspects. In the most general way, a certain flow $x$ (for instance, goods or services) can be provided with a seven-fold index:

$$({}_{i,\,j}^{\;k}x_{i'\,j'}^{k'})_t \tag{5.2.1}$$

which represents a flow of commodity $j$, produced in a certain production process $i$ at location $k$, to production process $i'$ at location $k'$, which uses commodity $j$ as an intermediate product for commodity $j'$, while the index $t$ stands for the time period concerned.

The flows described above are the most elementary flows, containing all information of economic streams. On the other hand, they are rather difficult to deal with and they require much detailed information. For that reason most economic flows are represented in a less detailed form. This less detailed structure of economic flows can be obtained by an aggregation over the various indices. For instance, if $t$ is a time index representing days, one may aggregate over all days in order to get years, in which case the flows relate to annual magnitudes (as is usually done). One may also aggregate over all production processes $i$ and $i'$, in which case the flows are only distinguished by product and not by production process. Obviously, this means a loss of information, since a certain commodity can be produced by different productive activities, while a given productive activity can give rise to several different products (cf. the activity matrix (1.5.2.2.); see also section 5.9). Furthermore, one may aggregate over $k$ and $k'$. For instance, if one applies a *complete* aggregation, one obtains the *national* flows of the various products; if one applies a *partial* aggregation, one obtains regional flows. The size of these regions is determined by the degree of partial aggregation. In this way one may obtain provinces, states, districts, cities, Standard Metropolitan Statistical Areas (SMSA), Economic Geographical Areas, etc., dependent on the problem at hand and on the degree of accuracy required. Finally, one may also aggregate over the product indices $j$ and $j'$. A complete aggregation would imply the creation of only one commodity category. Usually, one applies a partial aggregation in order to obtain a set of homogeneous commodity categories (or sectors).

The previous methods of aggregating the commodity flows in various ways is known as the *principle of multiple aggregation,* by means of which a bulk of detailed information can be reduced through combination of origin and destination. The degree of aggregation is closely allied with the *principle of multiple classification,* by means of which semi-aggregated entities are combined into *homogeneous* groups. For instance, products are aggregated in such a way, that a classification is obtained, the items of which are characterized by a maximal technological homogeneity. This sectoral analysis leads to homogeneous activity groups, for instance, mining, building, manufacturing, and public utilities. Such a homogeneity of commodity categories within the industrial branches is useful for I–O analysis, because any simple, fixed linear relationship between inputs and outputs is difficult to justify, if there is much variability of the constituent outputs within a branch. Apart from the condition of *exhaustiveness* the multiple classification should satisfy the condition of *exclusiveness,* since otherwise it will be hard to decide to which category a certain product should be assigned. Finally, it should be noted that the number of items of the classification (for instance, the number of sectors) is dependent on the problems at hand and on the degree of accuracy required.

A basic assumption of I–O analysis is a two-fold division of commodities: commodities can be absorbed either by *intermediate* use or by *final* use. If no further distinction is made within these two categories, it is said that the product flows are represented in *consolidated* form. In general, however, one makes a further classification. The *intermediate* products can be classified by sector, so that one obtains insight in the origins and destinations of the intermediate deliveries of each sector during a given period. The *final* products can also be subdivided between some constituents, for instance, final consumption and capital accumulation (or investments). Once the foregoing classification has been made, the sources of the costs associated with the intermediate and final outputs can also be analyzed by subdividing the gross value added in all forms of production between incomes accruing from the productive activities and provisions for depreciation.

The picture of the various commodity flows in a closed economy, and its cost components, is represented in table 5.2.a, where three industrial sectors 1, 2 and 3 are assumed, and where $C$, $I$, $Y$ and $D$ represent, respectively, consumption (private and public), investments (private and public), income accruing (net value added) and depreciations[1]. By inspecting table 5.2.a the essential principles of I–O methods can easily be comprehended. This table can be read in two ways, viz. in *horizontal* and *vertical* direction. The first three (horizontal) rows of table 5.2.a show how the production of each sector is distributed among the other productive sectors (intermediate deliveries) and the final components ($C$ and $I$). The last two rows represent the net value added and depreciation resulting from each sector. The first three (vertical) columns of the previous table show how each sector obtains from the other sectors its needed inputs of commodities (intermediate deliveries), as well as its needed labour inputs and its needed provisions for depreciation. The last two columns represent the composition of final demand and asset formation, as it is delivered by the different productive sectors. In this way one obtains a detailed double-entry bookkeeping of an economy, which is the basis of I–O analysis (see section 5.3).

Table 5.2.a

A pattern of commodity flows

| | 1 | 2 | 3 | $C$ | $I$ |
|---|---|---|---|---|---|
| 1 | | | | | |
| 2 | | | | | |
| 3 | | | | | |
| $Y$ | | | | | |
| $D$ | | | | | |

Frequently, all flows are measured in *monetary units,* since this basis of measurement has many computational advantages. The valuation of these commodity flows is usually based on *market prices.* A valuation at *factor costs* might be more appropriate, if the indirect taxes on a given product vary greatly between the different users (for instance, intermediate and final users).

## 5.3 Elements of I–O analysis

On the basis of the taxonomic approach presented in the foregoing section some essential principles of I–O analysis will now be dealt with. I–O analysis can be regarded as a systematic and comprehensive data storage about an economic system, composed of several different sectors. More particularly, I–O tabulation permits the determination of the interdependent effects in the production sector consequent upon the change in an exogenous variable.

If one introduces foreign trade, one may represent table 5.2.a in a more formal and general way as follows:

Table 5.3.a

A pattern of commodity flows in an open economy

| | | c | i | e |
|---|---|---|---|---|
| | $Q$ | | | |
| y' | | | | $x$ |
| d' | | $s$ | | $z$ |
| m' | | | | |

**Q**, **c**, **i**, **e**, **y**, **d** and **m** represent, respectively, intermediate deliveries, consumption, investments, exports, net value added, depreciation and imports. The typical elements of the flow matrix **Q** are represented by $q_{ii'}$, i.e., the intermediate deliveries from sector $i$ to sector $i'$ $(i, i' = 1, \ldots, I)$. In a similar way the typical elements $c_i$, $i_i$ and $e_i$ (respectively, from the column vectors **c**, **i** and **e**) represent the amount of products of sector $i$, which are used, respectively, for consumption, asset formation and exports. Correspondingly, the typical elements $y_i$, $d_i$ and $m_i$ of the successive row vectors, $\mathbf{y}'$, $\mathbf{d}'$ and $\mathbf{m}'$ are the net value added in, the depreciation provisions made by, and the imports absorbed into sector $i$, respectively. Frequently, the matrix right at the bottom contains many zero elements: some elements, which are non-zero, are, for instance, the elements $s$, $x$ and $z$: the total savings of the economy, the total net income payments from abroad and the net amount borrowed from abroad, respectively. The components **e** and $\mathbf{m}'$ are often replaced by one column vector of net exports.

If the elements consumption, investments and net exports are consolidated in one column vector **f** of final demand, and if the elements net value added and depreciation are consolidated in one row vector $\mathbf{v}'$, one obtains the following matrix of national accounts:

Table 5.3.b

A classical I–O tabulation

| | |
|---|---|
| **Q** | **f** |
| $\mathbf{v}'$ | **0** |

If table 5.3.b is read in a *horizontal* direction, one may write for each sector the balance equation between the value of total supply (denoted by means of the product vector **q**) and total demand (intermediate and final demand) as:

$$\mathbf{q} \equiv \mathbf{Q}\mathbf{i} + \mathbf{f} \qquad (5.3.1)$$

where **i** is a summation vector containing only unit elements. Relationship (5.3.1) is a formalization of the idea, that the production can be absorbed either by intermediate use or by final use.

Next, a basic assumption in I–O analysis is made, viz. by stipulating a linear relationship between the inputs and the output of each sector. This leads to constant *technical or input coefficients* (the 'Leontief-hypothesis'). If the intermediate deliveries from sector $i$ to sector $i'$ are denoted by $q_{ii'}$ and if the total production volume of sector $i'$ is denoted by $q_{i'}$, one obtains the following relationship:

$$q_{ii'} = a_{ii'} q_{i'} \tag{5.3.2}$$

where the input coefficient $a_{ii'}$ represents the quantity of the output of sector $i$ absorbed by sector $i'$ per unit of its total output $q_{i'}$. It should be noted that the element of space (and hence problems of an open economy) are abandoned for the moment. Next, one may write (5.3.2) as:

$$a_{ii'} = \frac{q_{ii'}}{q_{i'}} \tag{5.3.3}$$

Relationship (5.3.3) can be written in matrix notation as:

$$\mathbf{A} = \mathbf{Q}\,\hat{\mathbf{q}}^{-1} \tag{5.3.4}$$

where **A** is the matrix of I–O coefficients (also called the *structural* matrix), and where $\hat{\mathbf{q}}$ is a diagonal matrix in which the main diagonal is formed by **q**. Correspondingly, (5.3.2) can be written in matrix notation as:

$$\mathbf{Q} = \mathbf{A}\,\hat{\mathbf{q}} \tag{5.3.5}$$

Substitution of (5.3.5) into (5.3.1) gives:

$$\begin{aligned} \mathbf{q} &= \mathbf{A}\,\hat{\mathbf{q}}\,\mathbf{i} + \mathbf{f} \\ &= \mathbf{A}\,\mathbf{q} + \mathbf{f} \end{aligned} \tag{5.3.6}$$

which is the usual matrix representation of an I–O tabulation, if read horizontally.

In addition to a horizontal balance equation one may distinguish a vertical balance equation, which relates the values of the outputs to the direct factor costs in each of the industries. This balance equation is based on the fact that the value of the total production on the one hand and the value of input requirements and value added on the other hand are balanced. Therefore:

$$\mathbf{q} \equiv \mathbf{Q}'\mathbf{i} + \mathbf{v} \tag{5.3.7}$$

Substitution of (5.3.5) into (5.3.7) yields as a result for the cost side:

$$\mathbf{q} = \hat{\mathbf{q}}\,\mathbf{A}'\mathbf{i} + \mathbf{v} \qquad (5.3.8)$$

where each element $q_i$ of **q** can be regarded as $q_i$ 'dollars worth'.

The two fundamental I–O relationships (5.3.6) and (5.3.8) permit the calculation of the effects of a rise in final demand or in gross value added upon all sectors throughout the economic system. An essential concept for analyzing the interdependent production effects is the *matrix multiplier*. A matrix multiplier bears a close resemblance to the well-known classical Keynesian multiplier, representing the total (direct and indirect) effect on endogenous variables after an exogenous impulse. A similar concept arises in I–O analysis. Assume an economy consisting of 3 industries and a final demand sector, where:

$$\mathbf{A} = \begin{bmatrix} 0 & 0 & 0 \\ 0{\cdot}25 & 0 & 0 \\ 0{\cdot}20 & 0{\cdot}40 & 0 \end{bmatrix} \text{ and } \mathbf{f} = \begin{bmatrix} f_1 \\ f_2 \\ f_3 \end{bmatrix} \qquad (5.3.9)$$

Given a certain level of final demand $f_i$ $(i = 1, 2, 3)$ the production levels $q_i$ $(i = 1, 2, 3)$, required for intermediate and final use, can be calculated as (cf. [5.3.6]):

$$\begin{aligned} q_1 &= f_1 \\ q_2 &= 0{\cdot}25\, q_1 + f_2 = 0{\cdot}25\, f_1 + f_2 \\ q_3 &= 0{\cdot}20\, q_1 + 0{\cdot}40\, q_2 + f_3 = 0{\cdot}30\, f_1 + 0{\cdot}40\, f_2 + f_3 \end{aligned} \qquad (5.3.10)$$

Now suppose that the final demand for commodities of industry 1 rises with one unit. In the first place, it is necessary to produce one additional unit of output in industry 1. But in the second place, this additional unit of output of industry 1 requires 0·25 of a unit of intermediate output from industry 2 and 0·20 of a unit of intermediate output from industry 3 (see [5.3.9]). Next, the production of 0·25 unit of output in industry 2 requires an additional intermediate output from industry 3 to an amount of $0{\cdot}40 \times 0{\cdot}25 = 0{\cdot}10$ units. These successive steps can be extended, if the structural matrix contains less zero-elements. The relationships (5.3.10) show that, given the information embodied in (5.3.9), a rise in the final demand of the first sector leads to a series of interdependent production effects owing to the existence of intermediate deliveries. The foregoing effects can also be written in matrix form, respectively, as:

$$\begin{bmatrix} q_1 \\ q_2 \\ q_3 \end{bmatrix} = \begin{bmatrix} 0 & 0 & 0 \\ 0{\cdot}25 & 0 & 0 \\ 0{\cdot}20 & 0{\cdot}40 & 0 \end{bmatrix} \begin{bmatrix} q_1 \\ q_2 \\ q_3 \end{bmatrix} + \begin{bmatrix} f_1 \\ f_2 \\ f_3 \end{bmatrix} \qquad (5.3.11)$$

or:

$$\begin{bmatrix} 1 & 0 & 0 \\ -0{\cdot}25 & 1 & 0 \\ -0{\cdot}20 & -0{\cdot}40 & 1 \end{bmatrix} \begin{bmatrix} q_1 \\ q_2 \\ q_3 \end{bmatrix} = \begin{bmatrix} f_1 \\ f_2 \\ f_3 \end{bmatrix} \qquad (5.3.12)$$

or:

$$\begin{bmatrix} q_1 \\ q_2 \\ q_3 \end{bmatrix} = \begin{bmatrix} 1 & 0 & 0 \\ 0{\cdot}25 & 1 & 0 \\ 0{\cdot}30 & 0{\cdot}40 & 1 \end{bmatrix} \begin{bmatrix} f_1 \\ f_2 \\ f_3 \end{bmatrix} \qquad (5.3.13)$$

where (5.3.13) corresponds to (5.3.10). The series of steps, which are the result of a rise in an exogenous variable, appear to show a close correspondence to the classical multiplier effect. This gives rise to the notion of a *matrix multiplier,* which indicates the total (direct and indirect) product requirements in each sector as a consequence of a unit increase in the final demand sector.

The value added of all these production effects can be determined by multiplying each additional production level by the value added per unit of output and adding the amounts so obtained together. Owing to the condition of additivity the value added per unit of output of the respective industries is easily calculated on the basis of (5.3.9) as (1–0·25–0·20), (1–0·40) and 1. The respective additions to the output as a consequence of a rise of one unit in final demand in sector 1 are according to (5.3.10) equal to 1, 0·25 and 0·30. Thus, the rise in value added is equal to $1 \times 0{\cdot}55 + 0{\cdot}25 \times 0{\cdot}60 + 0{\cdot}30 \times 1 = 1$, which is the value of the rise in final demand in sector 1.

In a more formal way, the notion of a matrix multiplier can be derived on the basis of (5.3.6) as:

$$\mathbf{q} = (\mathbf{I} - \mathbf{A})^{-1}\,\mathbf{f} \qquad (5.3.14)$$

where the matrix multiplier $(\mathbf{I} - \mathbf{A})^{-1}$, often called the inverse Leontief matrix, is supposed to be non-singular. The successive steps related to this multiplier can be better understood by expanding $(\mathbf{I} - \mathbf{A})^{-1}$ in a Neumann-series:[2]

$$(\mathbf{I} - \mathbf{A})^{-1} = \mathbf{I} + \mathbf{A} + \mathbf{A}^2 + \mathbf{A}^3 + \ldots\ldots \qquad (5.3.15)$$

where $\mathbf{I}$ is a unit matrix representing the direct production needed to satisfy a rise in final demand, $\mathbf{A}$ a matrix representing the intermediate production needed as an input into the direct production requirements, etc. The expansion of $(\mathbf{I} - \mathbf{A})^{-1}$ in a geometric series is permitted, because:

$$\lambda_i (\mathbf{A}) < 1, \quad \forall i \tag{5.3.16}$$

where $\lambda_i$ (**A**) is the $i^{\text{th}}$ eigenvalue of the structural matrix **A**. The proof of this statement can be found *inter alia* in Gilbert (1970, p. 259) and Nikaido (1970, p. 118).

In addition to this *horizontal* matrix multiplier, which is related to the production effects, one may distinguish a *vertical* matrix multiplier, which is related to the various cost components of the output. Correspondingly, this vertical matrix multiplier shows the total (direct and indirect) rise in the unit prices of each sector, if one of the cost components of the production (for instance, wages, salaries, profits, depreciation and indirect taxes) undergo a change. In a more formal way, one may derive these cost effects by premultiplying (5.3.8) by $\hat{\mathbf{q}}^{-1}$. This results in:

$$\mathbf{i} = \mathbf{A}'\,\mathbf{i} + \hat{\mathbf{q}}^{-1}\,\mathbf{v} \tag{5.3.17}$$

where **i** is again a vector containing only unit elements. Relationship (5.3.17) means that a unit value of output in each sector (i.e., one 'dollar worth' in each sector) is composed of the value of the unit intermediate requirements ($\mathbf{A}'\mathbf{i}$) and of gross value added per unit of output ($\hat{\mathbf{q}}^{-1}\,\mathbf{v}$).The cost effect of a rise in one or more components of **v** can be calculated by rewriting (5.3.17) as:

$$\mathbf{i} = (\mathbf{I} - \mathbf{A}')^{-1}\,\hat{\mathbf{q}}^{-1}\,\mathbf{v} \tag{5.3.18}$$

which allows one to calculate the percentage price effect (measured in indices with a basis equal to 1) as a consequence of changes in the cost structure of production. The previous relationship for the vertical multiplier $(\mathbf{I} - \mathbf{A}')^{-1}$ is only valid for a closed economy. In an open economy some adaptations should be made (see section 5.5).

## 5.4 Evaluation

Before introducing the more regional aspects of I–O analysis it may be worthwhile to give a brief evaluation of the I–O analysis discussed so far. An I–O tabulation has the advantage of presenting a surveyable and consistent table of relations between the various sectors of an economy, both in relation to the productive structure as well as in relation to the cost structure. I–O analysis is an efficient tool for the compilation and presentation of sectoral and spatial production relationships.

The usefulness of I–O analysis is mainly based on a set of simple relationships between inputs and outputs remaining approximately constant during the period of analysis. The rigorous assumptions concerning the regularity in the flows imply that the input–output coefficients remain equal. This assumption of constant production coefficients may be questionable from different points of view, which will successively be discussed.

First of all, the coefficients are assumed to be the same over an *entire country*, which is furthermore assumed to be closed. However, because each country shows regional variations in the production structure, it is reasonable to make a regional division of the country and, next, to construct regional and interregional I–O tables. Problems of a spatial division and, hence, of an open economy (either between countries or between regions) are dealt with in section 5.5.

In the second place, the estimation of I–O coefficients is based on the assumption of the *absence of technological change.* The estimation problems of the I–O coefficients, as well as of its variations, are discussed in section 5.6.

*Changes in the price structure* of an economy lead to structural changes in I–O tables, if the commodity flows are measured in value terms. The effect of price changes is set out in section 5.7.

In the fourth place, *economies of scale* are not included in the normal I–O analysis, since there exists a fixed relationship between inputs and outputs. Structural changes in the I–O tabulation owing to scale advantages can be attacked in a similar way as technological progress (see section 5.6). If one assumes also linear relationships between the required capital and labour inputs on the one hand and the output on the other hand, one obtains, respectively, *fixed capital and labour coefficients.* The scale problems related to capital and labour inputs can be introduced by means of so-called *technological* or *engineering functions* (see section 5.8). Problems of indivisibilities in the investment sector are more difficult to deal with, but they are discussed later on in relation to programming problems (see Ch.6).

Next, the static I–O analysis does not allow any substitution between the inputs: each output is the result of a fixed combination of inputs. A more flexible approach is obtained by the use of *activity analysis,* where several alternative production processes are allowed (see section 1.5.2). The elaboration of I–O analysis within the framework of activity analysis is contained in section 5.9.

In the sixth place, the final demand is assumed to be exogenous. By introducing *behavioural* assumptions both for the investment and for the consumption sector the rather rigid I–O analyis (based only on technical and definitional relationships) can be extended in a more flexible way. This is carried out in section 5.10.

The I–O production structure for capital and, particularly, labour permits the calculation of the capital and labour requirements. However, the broader economic consequences for changes in population and service institutions are abandoned. This problem can be attacked by means of *spatial (or urban) interaction models* (and corresponding multipliers). Such an extension can be found in section 5.11.

Finally, the classical I–O analysis does not take account of *agglomerative forces* between complementary activities. Some methods for considering agglomeration economies in relation to I–O analysis are presented in section 5.12 and 5.19.

In the coming sections it will be shown that many of the objections, mentioned above in the use of I–O analysis, can be met. For the moment the conclusion is justified, that I–O analysis is an indispensable instrument for regional analysis and planning, provided this analysis is used in a flexible way and complemented with a set of additional methods and assumptions.

## 5.5. The element of space in I–O analysis

As has already been stated, problems of spatial division of economic activities were for a major part abandoned in section 5.3. The element of space was only (implicitly) present in table 5.3.a, where imports and exports were included. A more advanced method of including a spatial division of economic activities is constructing an *interregional* I–O table (either between regions or between countries), where commodity flows between the sectors of the regions concerned are considered.

Obviously, such an interregional I–O table requires a lot of detailed information. As far as the quantity of information is concerned, one may distinguish between a *full information* (F.I.) and a *limited information* (L.I.) flow table. An *F.I. flow table* is based on a completely detailed knowledge concerning the intersectoral flows, both within and between the regions. Such an F.I. flow table may be illustrated by assuming two economic sectors 1 and 2, and two regions $A$ and $B$. The elements of such a table are $q_{ij}^{ab}$, $f_i^{ab}$, $q_i^a$ and $v_i^a$ ($i = 1, 2; j = 1, 2; a = A, B; b = A, B$); they represent the commodity flow from sector $i$ in region $a$ to sector $j$ in region $b$, the commodity flow from sector $i$ in region $a$ to the final demand sector in region $b$, the production volume of sector $i$ in region $a$, and the value added of sector $i$ in region $a$, respectively (see table 5.5.a). It is obvious from table 5.5.a, that an F.I. table involves the knowledge of the origins and destinations of all flows, both between sectors and between regions. The *intra*sectoral flows are assumed to be zero.

Table 5.5.a

An F.I. I–O table

| | | *A* 1 | *A* 2 | *B* 1 | *B* 2 | | $\mathbf{f}^A$ | | $\mathbf{f}^B$ | | $\mathbf{q}$ |
|---|---|---|---|---|---|---|---|---|---|---|---|
| *A* | 1 | – | $q_{12}^{AA}$ | – | $q_{12}^{AB}$ | | $f_1^{AA}$ | | $f_1^{AB}$ | | $q_1^A$ |
| | 2 | $q_{21}^{AA}$ | – | $q_{21}^{AB}$ | – | | $f_2^{AA}$ | | $f_2^{AB}$ | | $q_2^A$ |
| *B* | 1 | – | $q_{12}^{BA}$ | – | $q_{12}^{BB}$ | + | $f_1^{BA}$ | + | $f_1^{BB}$ | = | $q_1^B$ |
| | 2 | $q_{21}^{BA}$ | – | $q_{21}^{BB}$ | – | | $f_2^{BA}$ | | $f_2^{BB}$ | | $q_2^B$ |

+

| | | | | |
|---|---|---|---|---|
| $\mathbf{v}'$ | $v_1^A$ | $v_2^A$ | $v_1^B$ | $v_2^B$ |

=

| | | | | |
|---|---|---|---|---|
| $\mathbf{q}'$ | $q_1^A$ | $q_2^A$ | $q_1^B$ | $q_2^B$ |

An *L.I. table* is based on a less detailed information: the regions of origin of the intermediate flows, and the allocations of the exports over intermediate and final commodities are unknown. Obviously, this leads to a slightly condensed table (see table 5.5.b). The elements of this L.I. table are $q_{ij}^a$, $q_i^{ab}$, $f_i^a$, $r_i^a$ and $v_i^a$ ($i = 1, 2; j = 1, 2; a = A, B; b = A, B$); they represent the commodity flow from sector *i* to sector *j* in region *a*, the commodity flow from sector *i* in region *a* to region *b*, the final demand in region *a* for commodity *i*, the total requirements of sector *i* in region *a*, and the value added of sector *i* in region *a*, respectively.

Table 5.5.b

An L.I. I–O table

| | | *A* 1 | *A* 2 | *B* 1 | *B* 2 | | **f** | | **r** |
|---|---|---|---|---|---|---|---|---|---|
| *A* | 1 | – | $q_{12}^{\cdot A}$ | $q_{1}^{\cdot AB}$ | – | | $f_{1}^{\cdot A}$ | | $r_{1}^{\cdot A}$ |
| | 2 | $q_{21}^{\cdot A}$ | – | – | $q_{2}^{\cdot AB}$ | + | $f_{2}^{\cdot A}$ | = | $r_{2}^{\cdot A}$ |
| *B* | 1 | $q_{1}^{\cdot BA}$ | – | – | $q_{12}^{\cdot B}$ | | $f_{1}^{\cdot B}$ | | $r_{1}^{\cdot B}$ |
| | 2 | – | $q_{2}^{\cdot BA}$ | $q_{21}^{\cdot B}$ | – | | $f_{2}^{\cdot B}$ | | $r_{2}^{\cdot B}$ |
| | | | + | | | | | | |
| **v**' | | $v_{1}^{A}$ | $v_{2}^{A}$ | $v_{1}^{B}$ | $v_{2}^{B}$ | | | | |
| | | | = | | | | | | |
| **r**' | | $r_{1}^{\cdot A}$ | $r_{2}^{\cdot A}$ | $r_{1}^{\cdot B}$ | $r_{2}^{\cdot B}$ | | | | |

The reason for redefining the various commodity flows in an L.I. table is the fact, that, owing to the limited information, the imports should be redistributed over the various original commodity flows. Therefore, the element $q_{12}^{\cdot A}$ is composed of the *intra*regional deliveries from sector 1 in region *A* to sector 2 in region *A* (i.e., $q_{12}^{AA}$) and the *inter*regional deliveries from sector 1 in region *B* to sector 2 in region *A* (i.e. $q_{12}^{BA}$); this shows that the regions of origin for intermediate deliveries are supposed to be unknown in an L.I. table. In a similar way, the element $q_{1}^{\cdot AB}$ represents the export from sector 1 in region *A* to region *B*, so that $q_{1}^{\cdot AB}$ is composed of $q_{12}^{AB}$ (the exports for intermediate use) and $f_{1}^{AB}$ (the exports for final use). Correspondingly, the element $f_{1}^{\cdot A}$ is composed of $f_{1}^{AA}$ and $f_{1}^{BA}$. In this way, all elements of the intermediate and final deliveries in an L.I. table can be redefined and easily calculated on the basis of an F.I. table. It is obvious that the reverse procedure (viz. from a situation with limited information to a situation with full information) is impossible. The value added in each sector remains equal in both situations, because the value added of each sector does not depend on the way in which the computational framework is constructed. The total requirements **r** differ from the total production **q** owing to the presence of imports: the requirements represent the total available amount of a certain product (production plus imports). Therefore, if the intermediate requirements and the imports are denoted by **y** and **m**, respectively, the following identity relates **r** to **q**:

$$\begin{aligned} \mathbf{r} &\equiv \mathbf{q} + \mathbf{m} \\ &\equiv \mathbf{y} + \mathbf{v} + \mathbf{m} \end{aligned} \tag{5.5.1}$$

The method of transforming an F.I. flow table into an L.I. flow table may be illustrated by means of the following example, where table 5.5.c represents an F.I. table.

Table 5.5.c.

An illustrative example of an F.I. I–O table

| | | | | | | | | | |
|---|---|---|---|---|---|---|---|---|---|
| — | 2 | — | 4 | | 10 | | 2 | | 18 |
| 3 | — | 1 | — | | 5 | | 3 | | 12 |
| | | | | + | | + | | = | |
| — | 5 | — | 6 | | 2 | | 5 | | 18 |
| 7 | — | 8 | — | | 1 | | 10 | | 26 |
| | + | | | | | | | | |
| 8 | 5 | 9 | 16 | | | | | | |
| | = | | | | | | | | |
| 18 | 12 | 18 | 26 | | | | | | |

The corresponding L.I. table, which can be constructed by means of the aforementioned rules, is represented in table 5.5.d.

Table 5.5.d

An illustrative example of an L.I. I–O table

| | | | | | | | |
|---|---|---|---|---|---|---|---|
| — | 2 + 5 = 7 | 4 + 2 = 6 | — | | 10 + 2 = 12 | | 25 |
| 3 + 7 = 10 | — | — | 1 + 3 = 4 | | 5 + 1 = 6 | | 20 |
| | | | | + | | = | |
| 5 + 2 = 7 | — | — | 6 + 4 = 10 | | 2 + 5 = 7 | | 24 |
| — | 7 + 1 = 8 | 8 + 1 = 9 | — | | 10 + 3 = 13 | | 30 |
| | + | | | | | | |
| 8 | 5 | 9 | 16 | | | | |
| | = | | | | | | |
| 25 | 20 | 24 | 30 | | | | |

Obviously, the latter table is easier to construct than the foregoing F.I. table, since the L.I. table requires less information. Therefore, one often uses L.I. I–O tables. The imports are implicitly present in an L.I. table, but they cannot be calculated in a direct way from such a table. The way in which the imports affect the I–O tabulation in the case of an L.I. situation can not be analyzed, unless one makes additional assumptions concerning the import rates. Similar assumptions are usually made in the Keynesian type of models for an open economy. A usual assumption is a linear relationship between the imports for each sector and the national requirements:

$$\mathbf{m} = \hat{\mu}\,(\mathbf{Aq} + \mathbf{f}^i) \qquad (5.5.2)$$

where $\hat{\mu}$ is a diagonal matrix the diagonal elements of which represent the fixed linear import rates, and where $\mathbf{f}^i$ is a vector the elements of which represent the *internal* final demand (final demand net of exports). The balance equation (5.3.6) for national production is corrected for imports and exports as follows:

$$\mathbf{q} + \mathbf{m} = \mathbf{Aq} + \mathbf{f}^i + \mathbf{e} \qquad (5.5.3)$$

Substitution of (5.5.2) into (5.5.3) yields:

$$\mathbf{q} = \mathbf{Aq} + \mathbf{f}^i + \mathbf{e} - \hat{\mu}\,(\mathbf{Aq} + \mathbf{f}^i) \qquad (5.5.4)$$

or:

$$\mathbf{q} = \{ \mathbf{I} - (\mathbf{I} - \hat{\boldsymbol{\mu}})\mathbf{A} \}^{-1} \{ (\mathbf{I} - \hat{\boldsymbol{\mu}}) \mathbf{f}^i + \mathbf{e} \} \tag{5.5.5}$$

provided the matrix $\mathbf{I} - (\mathbf{I} - \hat{\boldsymbol{\mu}})\mathbf{A}$ is non-singular. The latter result bears a close resemblance to the Keynesian analysis, where imports are supposed to be a fraction of national income.

A refinement can be introduced by assuming different import rates for intermediate and for final products. Then one obtains:

$$\mathbf{m} = \hat{\boldsymbol{\mu}}_a \mathbf{A}\mathbf{q} + \hat{\boldsymbol{\mu}}_f \mathbf{f}^i \tag{5.5.6}$$

Substitution of (5.5.6) into (5.5.3) gives:

$$\begin{aligned} \mathbf{q} &= \mathbf{A}\mathbf{q} + \mathbf{f}^i + \mathbf{e} - \hat{\boldsymbol{\mu}}_a \mathbf{A}\mathbf{q} - \hat{\boldsymbol{\mu}}_f \mathbf{f}^i = \\ &= (\mathbf{I} - \hat{\boldsymbol{\mu}}_a)\, \mathbf{A}\mathbf{q} + (\mathbf{I} - \hat{\boldsymbol{\mu}}_f)\, \mathbf{f}^i + \mathbf{e} \end{aligned} \tag{5.5.7}$$

or:

$$\mathbf{q} = \{ \mathbf{I} - (\mathbf{I} - \hat{\boldsymbol{\mu}}_a)\, \mathbf{A} \}^{-1} \{ (\mathbf{I} - \hat{\boldsymbol{\mu}}_f)\, \mathbf{f}^i + \mathbf{e} \} \tag{5.5.8}$$

supposed $\mathbf{I} - (\mathbf{I} - \hat{\boldsymbol{\mu}}_a)\mathbf{A}$ is non-singular.

The national price level, as represented by (5.3.18), undergoes a similar change in consequence of the introduction of imports and exports. Relationship (5.5.7) shows that the original I–O matrix $\mathbf{A}$ undergoes a change owing to the presence of imports and exports; the corrected I–O matrix becomes $(\mathbf{I} - \hat{\boldsymbol{\mu}}_a)\mathbf{A}$. The latter implies that the way in which primary inputs affect the price level undergoes a similar change. Therefore, the original relationship (5.3.18) should be adapted in the following way:

$$\mathbf{i} = \{ \mathbf{I} - \mathbf{A}'(\mathbf{I} - \hat{\boldsymbol{\mu}}_a) \}^{-1}\, \hat{\mathbf{q}}^{-1}\, \mathbf{v} \tag{5.5.9}$$

The latter relationship permits the calculation of the effect of price changes in primary inputs on the national price level.

## 5.6 Technical coefficients in I–O analysis

The estimation of the I–O coefficients is a rather simple matter, if a single input–output table for only one period is available. Then there is only one observation for each interindustrial flow, so that the I–O coefficient $a_{ii'}$ can easily be determined as (cf. [5.3.3]):

$$a_{ii'} = \frac{q_{ii'}}{q_{i'}} \tag{5.6.1}$$

However, if one possesses observations on the interindustrial flows during more periods, the estimation of the I–O coefficients presents a more intricate problem.

Then, a first method of estimating the I–O coefficients is taking the average value of the I–O coefficients over all time periods $t$ ($t = 1, \ldots, T$), so that:

$$a_{ii'} = \frac{\sum_{t=1}^{T} a_{ii'}(t)}{T} \qquad (5.6.2)$$

Instead, one may determine $a_{ii'}$ as the ratio of the sum total of the interindustrial flows during all time periods with respect to the sum total of the production values during these periods, i.e.:

$$a_{ii'} = \frac{\sum_{t=1}^{T} q_{ii'}(t)}{\sum_{t=1}^{T} q_{i'}(t)} \qquad (5.6.3)$$

The previous methods, however, are rather rigid, and do not include error terms. Therefore, from a statistical point of view it is more appropriate to estimate the I–O coefficients by means of regression analysis. Then, the matrix **A** of unknown parameters can be estimated by introducing a matrix **E** of error terms into relationship (5.3.5). Then one obtains the following relationship, which can be estimated by means of least squares:

$$\mathbf{Q} = \mathbf{A}\hat{\mathbf{q}} + \mathbf{E} \qquad (5.6.4)$$

However, if the estimation of I–O coefficients is based on observations during a certain time period, they are assumed to be constant during this time period. This means, that changes in the production structure (for instance, technological changes) are left out of consideration. The latter objection is particularly important, if a certain I–O table, which is estimated on the basis of past data, is used for projection. Then one should take account of structural changes in the production structure ('updating').

A well-known method of taking account of technical changes in I–O matrices is the RAS-method (see Stone [1963]). This method of updating I–O tables uses new row and column totals for a later year and alters the coefficients of an old I–O table according to a mathematical rule, so that one obtains an updated, consistent I–O matrix. The

RAS-method attempts at gauging simultaneously two effects, viz. the effect of relative shifts in the input proportions of a certain activity (i.e., *substitution*), as well as the effect of changes in the *productivity* (i.e., less inputs per unit of output). The assumption is that both effects exert a systematic uniform influence upon the rows and columns of an (already known) I–O matrix. A systematic relative shift in the input proportions requires a systematic adaptation of the successive *rows* of this I–O matrix, while a systematic change in the productivity of each sector requires a systematic adaptation of the successive *columns* of this I–O matrix. An adaptation of the rows of a matrix can be obtained by premultiplying the matrix with a diagonal matrix $\hat{\mathbf{r}}$, while an adaptation of the columns can be obtained by postmultiplying the matrix with a diagonal matrix $\hat{\mathbf{s}}$. Therefore, the new I–O matrix $\mathbf{A}^*$ is related to the former I–O matrix $\mathbf{A}$ in the following way:

$$\mathbf{A}^* = \hat{\mathbf{r}}\,\mathbf{A}\,\hat{\mathbf{s}} \tag{5.6.5}$$

The foregoing adaptation can only be carried out, if $\hat{\mathbf{r}}$ and $\hat{\mathbf{s}}$ are known. The estimation of $\hat{\mathbf{r}}$ and $\hat{\mathbf{s}}$ for a certain year should be based on a set of production data for this year concerned. One needs the following data: the vector of total production ($\mathbf{q}$), the vector of primary inputs ($\mathbf{v}$) and the vector of final demand ($\mathbf{f}$). These three vectors permit the calculation of the vector of total intermediate output of commodities ($\mathbf{u}$) and the vector of total intermediate input into commodities ($\mathbf{y}$), since the following relationships are valid:

$$\mathbf{u} \equiv \mathbf{q} - \mathbf{f} \tag{5.6.6}$$

and

$$\mathbf{y} \equiv \mathbf{q} - \mathbf{v} \tag{5.6.7}$$

It is obvious from (5.3.6) and (5.3.8), that the known vectors $\mathbf{u}$ and $\mathbf{y}$ are, respectively, equal to:

$$\mathbf{u} = \mathbf{A}^*\mathbf{q} \tag{5.6.8}$$

and

$$\mathbf{y} = \hat{\mathbf{q}}(\mathbf{A}^*)'\mathbf{i} \tag{5.6.9}$$

Substitution of (5.6.5) into (5.6.8) and (5.6.9) yields:

$$\hat{\mathbf{r}}\,\mathbf{A}\,\hat{\mathbf{s}}\mathbf{q} = \mathbf{u} \tag{5.6.10}$$

and:

$$\hat{\mathbf{q}}\,\hat{\mathbf{s}}\,\mathbf{A}'\mathbf{r} = \mathbf{y} \tag{5.6.11}$$

The relationships (5.6.10) and (5.6.11) represent two systems of equations connecting the unknown vectors **r** and **s**; they are usually called the RAS-equations. Since the other elements (**A**, **q**, **u** and **y**) are known, and since the number of equations is exactly equal to the number of unknown variables (**r** and **s**), one can solve system (5.6.10) and (5.6.11) in principle. A method of solving this non-linear system of equations is presented in Appendix 5A. Once the unknown elements **r** and **s** have been determined, the corrected I–O matrix (5.6.5.) can easily be calculated.

The RAS-method described above is a rather simple instrument to take account of intertemporal variations in the structural matrix of an I–O framework. A more rigorous method of taking account of intertemporal variations in I–O analysis is the use of dynamic I–O analysis. In this, the structural matrix may undergo a change in each time period. It is obvious that the dynamic I–O analysis requires a lot of information, so that its use in practice is rather limited.

Finally, it should be mentioned that in addition to the RAS-method other methods of updating I–O tables may be used, viz. the linear programming method (see Matuszewski, Pitts and Sawyer [1964]), a statistical correction method (see Tilanus [1965]), and a quadratic programming method (see Nijkamp and Paelinck [1974]).

Finally, the estimation of technical coefficients in an *interregional* I–O framework deserves some attention, because one should distinguish between an L.I. I–O framework and an F.I. I–O framework.

In accordance with table 5.5.b from section 5.5 an L.I. technical coefficient of intermediate deliveries from sector $i$ to sector $i'$ within region $A$ is defined as:

$$a_{ii'}^{\cdot A} = \frac{q_{ii'}^{\cdot A}}{q_{i'}^{A}} = \frac{q_{ii'}^{\cdot A}}{r_{i'}^{\cdot A} - q_{i'}^{\cdot BA}} \qquad (5.6.12)$$

This coefficient is a pure, technical coefficient; it is supposed to be constant in the Leontief I–O analysis.

In a similar way one may define an F.I. technical coefficient as:

$$a_{ii'}^{A} = \frac{q_{ii'}^{AA}}{q_{i'}^{A}} \qquad (5.6.13)$$

It is obvious, that the following relationship exists between both technical coefficients (cf. section 5.5):

$$
\begin{aligned}
a^{A}_{ii'} &= \frac{q^{\cdot A}_{ii'}}{q^{A}_{i\cdot}} \; \frac{q^{AA}_{ii'}}{q^{\cdot A}_{ii'}} \\
&= \frac{a^{\cdot A}_{ii'} \, (q^{\cdot A}_{ii'} - q^{BA}_{ii'})}{q^{\cdot A}_{ii'}} \\
&= a^{\cdot A}_{ii'} \left(1 - \frac{q^{BA}_{ii'}}{q^{\cdot A}_{ii'}}\right) \\
&= a^{\cdot A}_{ii'} \, (1 - t^{AB}_{ii'})
\end{aligned}
\qquad (5.6.14)
$$

where the trade coefficient $t^{AB}_{ii'}$ represents the ratio of the import of intermediate deliveries with respect to the total input requirements, i.e., the proportion of regional input, which is imported. This ratio is not necessarily constant over time, since trade flows show often much variation. Therefore, the F.I. technical coefficient $a^{A}_{ii'}$ is built up by a constant L.I. technical coefficient $a^{\cdot A}_{ii'}$ and by a variable trade coefficient $t^{AB}_{ii'}$. For the latter reason, the use of L.I. technical coefficients in an interregional I–O framework is often preferred, even if F.I. statistics are available.

## 5.7 The effect of price changes

Until now the I–O data were expressed at constant prices. For instance, the technical coefficient $a_{ii'}$, defined in (5.3.3), is calculated on the basis of fixed prices for all intermediate deliveries. However, if one allows the possibility of varying prices, the value of the intermediate deliveries will have to be split into a price component and a volume component. Therefore, one obtains:

$$
a_{ii'} = \frac{p_i \, x_{ii'}}{p_{i'} \, x_{i'}} \qquad (5.7.1)
$$

where $p_i$ and $p_{i'}$ represent the price of good $i$ and good $i'$, respectively, and where $x_{ii'}$ and $x_{i'}$ represent the quantity of intermediate deliveries from sector $i$ to $i'$, and the production volume of sector $i'$, respectively. The prices are relative prices, i.e. price index-numbers with respect to a certain basis year. The value of $a_{ii'}$ in that basis year is supposed to be known.

If after some time periods the prices of intermediate deliveries have undergone a change, one should recalculate $a_{ii'}$. This new value of $a_{ii'}$ is denoted by $a^*_{ii'}$. The new element $a^*_{ii'}$ is calculated by correcting $a_{ii'}$ by means of price indices, which correspond to the relative changes in the prices with respect to the basis year. Therefore, $a^*_{ii'}$ is equal to:

$$a^*_{ii'} = \frac{p^*_i}{p^*_{i'}} a_{ii'} \tag{5.7.2}$$

where $p^*_i$ and $p^*_{i'}$ are the new price indices of commodity $i$ and $i'$.

In matrix notation, one finds instead of (5.7.2):

$$\mathbf{A}^* = \hat{\mathbf{p}}\, \mathbf{A}\, \hat{\mathbf{p}}^{-1} \tag{5.7.3}$$

where $\hat{\mathbf{p}}$ is a diagonal matrix with the new price indices on the main diagonal. The matrix multiplier will also change as a result of varying prices. The new matrix multiplier $(\mathbf{I} - \mathbf{A}^*)^{-1}$ is calculated as (cf. [5.3.14]):

$$\begin{aligned} (\mathbf{I} - \mathbf{A}^*)^{-1} &= (\mathbf{I} - \hat{\mathbf{p}}\, \mathbf{A}\, \hat{\mathbf{p}}^{-1})^{-1} \\ &= (\hat{\mathbf{p}}\, \hat{\mathbf{p}}^{-1} - \hat{\mathbf{p}}\, \mathbf{A}\, \hat{\mathbf{p}}^{-1})^{-1} \\ &= \left\{\hat{\mathbf{p}}\, (\mathbf{I} - \mathbf{A})\, \hat{\mathbf{p}}^{-1}\right\}^{-1} \\ &= \hat{\mathbf{p}}\, (\mathbf{I} - \mathbf{A})^{-1}\, \hat{\mathbf{p}}^{-1} \end{aligned} \tag{5.7.4}$$

The latter method of introducing price changes is a second way of updating I–O matrices.

## 5.8 Economies of scale

As mentioned in section 5.4 a usual assumption in I–O analysis is the assumption of fixed capital and labour coefficients. This assumption implies that the required capital and labour inputs of each industry are a fixed proportion of its output. Economies of scale, which are frequently present in capital and labour requirements, are abandoned in this way.

Scale advantages of capital and labour can be introduced by means of *technological* or *engineering functions*. They are usually represented by means of power functions, which reflect the technical relationships between the activitiy scale ($q$) and the input scale of labour ($L$) or of capital investments ($I$). Therefore, these generalized I–O relationships can be written as:

$$\frac{I}{I_o} = \left(\frac{q}{q_o}\right)^{\alpha} \tag{5.8.1}$$

and

$$\frac{L}{L_o} = \left(\frac{q}{q_o}\right)^{\beta} \tag{5.8.2}$$

where the lower index o denotes technical minimum levels of the variables concerned. The constant elasticities $\alpha$ and $\beta$ are usually called plant factor and labour factor, respectively. In figure 5.8.a and 5.8.b these functions are represented in a graphical way. It is obvious, that a necessary condition for the occurrence of scale advantages is: $0<\alpha<1$ and $0<\beta<1$.

Fig. 5.8.a A technological function for investments

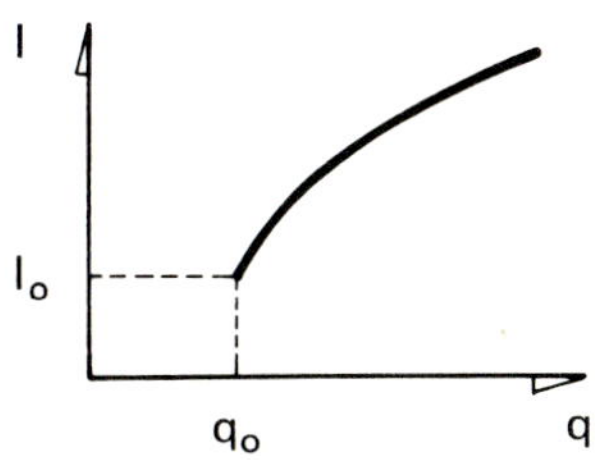


Fig. 5.8.b A technological function for labour

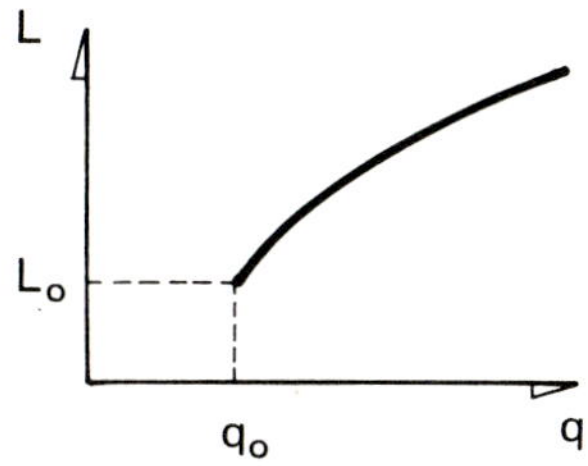


These technological functions are present in several regional and national planning frameworks. They were used *inter alia* by Chenery (1952), Isard et al. (1959), Kornai et al. (1967), Manne and Vietorisz (1963) and Nijkamp (1972). A more fundamental treatment of these functions is contained in De Meester (1970).

Empirical estimations of $\alpha$ and $\beta$ showed that their values were dependent on the kind of activity studied. In general, $\alpha$ and $\beta$ appeared to fall within the following range: $0{\cdot}40 \leqslant \alpha \leqslant 0{\cdot}85$ and $0{\cdot}15 \leqslant \beta \leqslant 0{\cdot}60$.

A combination of technological functions with the more rigid I–O analysis permits a greater flexibility in the empirical research concerning industrial processes (see, for instance, Isard et al. [1959] and also section 5.19).

## 5.9 Multi-product activities

The classical I–O analysis described above does not take into consideration the possibility of alternative production processes for the production of the same commodity. Each activity was assumed to produce exactly one product, which is typical for this activity. It is obvious that multi-product activities are difficult to integrate in a single commodity category (cf. the classification- and aggregation-principle in section 5.2).

A more adequate integration of multi-product activities is obtained by using *activity matrices,* where each column represents the inputs and outputs per unit of a certain productive activity (see section 1.5.2). An activity matrix indicates that a certain product can be produced in more than one production process.

In this section a method of integrating multi-product activities into the usual I–O framework will be discussed. It is evident that a simultaneous consideration of *commodities* and of *activities* implies a considerable extension of the I–O analysis. In this so-called commodity-by-industry approach it is assumed that each industry is able to produce multiple commodities and that any commodity may be produced by multiple industries (cf. also Victor [1972]).

Suppose an activity matrix **A**, the elements of which denote the input requirements per unit activity of a certain industry. Given the scale of the various activities (denoted by $\boldsymbol{\lambda}$), the vector of input requirements (denoted by **q**) can easily be determined as:

$$\mathbf{q} = \mathbf{A}\boldsymbol{\lambda} \tag{5.9.1}$$

Relationship (5.9.1) permits the calculation of the required input levels, given a known activity matrix and a known activity scale of an economy.

It is evident that the realization of a certain production level exerts a claim on other productive activities. Since, however, a certain product can be produced by *multiple* activities, one should know the composition of the product structure, i.e. the allocation of products among activities. This requires a distribution matrix **R** that indicates which industry produces and sells a commodity or a set of commodities. Therefore, one obtains:

$$\boldsymbol{\lambda} = \mathbf{R}\,\mathbf{q} \tag{5.9.2}$$

where $\boldsymbol{\lambda}$ represents again the vector of activity scales required to generate the production vector **q**. The columns of the matrix **R** satisfy the additivity condition that total production should indeed be realized, i.e.,

$$\mathbf{i}'\mathbf{R} = \mathbf{i}' \tag{5.9.3}$$

where **i** is a vector of unit elements. Therefore, a typical element $r_{ij}$ of **R** indicates that a proportion $r_{ij}$ of commodity $j$ is produced by activity $i$. It is obvious that the columns and rows of **R** are associated with products and with activities, respectively.

In general, **A** is a non-square matrix, so that the number of elements of **q** and **λ** is unequal. Therefore, the matrix **R** may possess various shapes.

If **R** is equal to **I** (the identity matrix), there is a one-to-one relationship between each commodity and each activity. This is, in fact, the classical I–O situation, where each sector produces only one typical product.

If there are more products than activities, the matrix **A** possesses more rows than columns. Then the matrix **R** is also rectangular and it contains more columns than rows: the specification of **R** in (5.9.2) shows that the columns of **R** represent products and the rows activities. The matrix **R** may have any arbitrary shape, provided all elements are non-negative and all columns add up to 1. For instance, one may assume the particular case:

$$\mathbf{R} = \begin{bmatrix} 1 \ldots\ldots 1 & & & 0 \\ & 1 \ldots\ldots 1 & & \\ & & \ddots & \\ 0 & & & 1 \ldots\ldots 1 \end{bmatrix} \qquad (5.9.4)$$

The matrix **R**, specified in (5.9.4), implies that each activity can produce several products, while each product can be the output of only one activity. An example of a completely filled distribution matrix is:

$$\mathbf{R} = \begin{bmatrix} 0{\cdot}2 & 0{\cdot}3 & 0{\cdot}6 \\ 0{\cdot}8 & 0{\cdot}7 & 0{\cdot}4 \end{bmatrix} \qquad (5.9.5)$$

The latter distribution matrix shows, that, for instance, commodity 1 is produced for 20 per cent by activity 1, and for 80 per cent by activity 2. For the moment **R** is assumed to represent *fixed* proportions between activities and commodities. The problem of finding *optimal* combinations of activities for producing commodities is analyzed in Ch.6.

The working mechanism of a distribution matrix **R** in relation to an activity matrix **A** bears a close resemblance to the classical I–O multiplier. If one assumes an exogenous change in production (for instance, a new level **f*** of final demand), one can easily calculate the direct effect on the required level of relevant activities by means of a distribution matrix $\mathbf{R}_0$, which indicates the degree to which this final production induces activities (cf. [2.9.2]):

$$\boldsymbol{\lambda}_0 = \mathbf{R}_0 \mathbf{f}^* \qquad (5.9.6)$$

The implementation of the activities up to the level $\boldsymbol{\lambda}_0$ requires a set of inputs. The level of the input vector results from the activity matrix, which relates activities to production volumes. If one assumes, that this activity matrix during the first step is equal to $\mathbf{A}_1$, one may use (5.9.1) in order to calculate the input requirement for the first step:

$$\mathbf{q}_1 = \mathbf{A}_1 \boldsymbol{\lambda}_0 \tag{5.9.7}$$

Next, the deliveries of the first inputs, $\mathbf{q}_1$, require the implementation of new activities. The sectoral distribution of these activities is represented by means of the distribution matrix $\mathbf{R}_1$, so that one obtains:

$$\boldsymbol{\lambda}_1 = \mathbf{R}_1 \mathbf{q}_1 \tag{5.9.8}$$

In the version of rectangular matrices presented here the distribution matrix of the final commodities is supposed to differ from the distribution matrix of the input requirements for the first step. If the market distribution is the same for both commodity categories, one may use the same distribution matrix during each stage of the process.

The new level of activities for inputs, $\boldsymbol{\lambda}_1$, requires, on its turn, new inputs, which can be calculated by means of a new activity matrix $\mathbf{A}_2$ for the second step. Then one obtains:

$$\mathbf{q}_2 = \mathbf{A}_2 \boldsymbol{\lambda}_1 \tag{5.9.9}$$

It should be mentioned that in the version presented here the first-step activity matrix, $\mathbf{A}_1$, differs from the second-step activity matrix, $\mathbf{A}_2$, since each stage of the production chain is supposed to be subject to different technologies. Should such a difference be negligible, one may use the same activity matrix during all stages.

It is obvious, that the procedure described above can be repeated infinitely. By substituting (5.9.6) into (5.9.7), and by substituting this result into (5.9.8), one obtains:

$$\boldsymbol{\lambda}_1 = \mathbf{R}_1 \mathbf{A}_1 \mathbf{R}_0 \mathbf{f}^* \tag{5.9.10}$$

It is easily seen that by aggregating the successive activity levels $\boldsymbol{\lambda}_0$, $\boldsymbol{\lambda}_1$, $\boldsymbol{\lambda}_2$, . . . . , one obtains the following series:

$$\sum_{i=0}^{\infty} \boldsymbol{\lambda}_i = (\mathbf{I} + \mathbf{R}_1 \mathbf{A}_1 + \mathbf{R}_2 \mathbf{A}_2 \mathbf{R}_1 \mathbf{A}_1 + \ldots\ldots) \, \mathbf{R}_0 \mathbf{f}^* \tag{5.9.11}$$

The latter series represents the aggregated activities to be implemented as a consequence of a new level of final demand. The total level of production is then equal to:

$$\begin{aligned} \mathbf{f}^* + \sum_{i=1}^{\infty} \mathbf{q}_i &= \mathbf{f}^* + \sum_{i=1}^{\infty} \mathbf{A}_i \boldsymbol{\lambda}_{i-1} \\ &= \mathbf{f}^* + (\mathbf{A}_1 + \mathbf{A}_2 \mathbf{R}_1 \mathbf{A}_1 + \mathbf{A}_3 \mathbf{R}_2 \mathbf{A}_2 \mathbf{R}_1 \mathbf{A}_1 + \ldots\ldots) \, \mathbf{R}_0 \mathbf{f}^* \end{aligned} \tag{5.9.12}$$

The two series represented in (5.9.11) and (5.9.12) form a converging series, if the absolute value of the eigenvalues of each matrix product $\mathbf{R}_i\mathbf{A}_i$ is smaller than 1 (cf. [5.3.16]). If one assumes that during each stage of the process $\mathbf{R}_i$ and $\mathbf{A}_i$ are constant and equal to **R** and **A**, respectively, the series (5.9.11) and (5.9.12) are equal to:

$$\sum_{i=0}^{\infty} \boldsymbol{\lambda}_i = \left\{ \mathbf{I} + \mathbf{RA} + (\mathbf{RA})^2 + \ldots\ldots \right\} \mathbf{Rf}^* \\ = (\mathbf{I} - \mathbf{RA})^{-1} \mathbf{Rf}^* \tag{5.9.13}$$

and:

$$\mathbf{f}^* + \sum_{i=1}^{\infty} \mathbf{q}_i = \mathbf{f}^* + \mathbf{A}\,(\mathbf{I} - \mathbf{RA})^{-1}\,\mathbf{R}\,\mathbf{f}^* \\ = \left\{ \mathbf{I} + \mathbf{A}\,(\mathbf{I} - \mathbf{RA})^{-1}\,\mathbf{R} \right\} \mathbf{f}^* \tag{5.9.14}$$

provided **I–RA** is nonsingular and the absolute value of the eigenvalues of **RA** is smaller than 1. The series (5.9.13) and (5.9.14) bear a close resemblance to the Leontief series (5.3.14) and (5.3.15). The main differences of the rectangular approach with respect to the Leontief approach are the assumptions of a different technology during each stage of the process, and the absence of a unique link between each product and each activity. Finally, it should be remarked that the advantage of a higher degree of realism in the rectangular approach is counterbalanced by the enormous quantity of required technical information. This is the main reason why rectangular I–O matrices have found, until now, little application in regional economics. An example of an application of this technique can be found in a study concerning the Quebec region, carried out by the Bureau de la Statistique du Québec (1967), and also in Aidenoff (1970) and Gigantes (1970).

## 5.10 Integration of final demand

The I–O analysis discussed so far was mainly based on technical, definitional and balance equations. Apart from the import sector (see section 5.5) no behavioural relationships were included. A higher degree of flexibility of the rather rigid I–O relationships is obtained by assuming that the final sector is not a datum. By introducing *consumption* and *investment* functions the final demand components can be conceived of as endogenous variables. The result is, that the sectoral production levels are no longer determined by the final demand sector, but that now both the sectoral production levels and the final demand components are determined simultaneously (see Paelinck [1970]).

By assuming 2 economic sectors the following basic I–O system may be created:

$$\begin{bmatrix} q_1 \\ q_2 \end{bmatrix} = \begin{bmatrix} 0 & a_{12} \\ a_{21} & 0 \end{bmatrix} \begin{bmatrix} q_1 \\ q_2 \end{bmatrix} + \begin{bmatrix} c_1 \\ c_2 \end{bmatrix} + \begin{bmatrix} i_1 \\ i_2 \end{bmatrix} + \begin{bmatrix} x_1 \\ x_2 \end{bmatrix} \quad (5.10.1)$$

where $c_i$, $i_i$ and $x_i$ represent the consumption, the investments and the net exports delivered by sector $i$ ($i = 1, 2$). If necessary, one may split the net exports into imports and exports, and make assumptions concerning the imports similar to section 5.5.

A first behavioural assumption relates to the consumption. In line with the classical consumption theory, consumption is supposed to depend on income (wages, salaries and profits) and, all things being equal, the prices. The aggregated gross value added, $v$, is composed of 2 elements, viz. net value added (wages, salaries and profits), and depreciations and retained profits. If these 2 elements are denoted by $v^*$ and $v^{**}$, respectively, one may write:

$$v \equiv v^* + v^{**} \quad (5.10.2)$$

If one assumes that consumption is a linear function of income, the following demand function is valid:

$$c_i = \alpha_i \, v^* + \beta_i \quad i = 1, 2 \quad (5.10.3)$$

where $\alpha_i$ and $\beta_i$ are the marginal propensity to consume and a constant term, respectively ($i = 1, 2$). The previous specification of the demand function implies that the final products from both industrial sectors are sold to the consumption sector, the marginal consumption rates of which differ for each industrial sector.

It is clear that now circular relationships arise, since the production volume is determined by the final demand, and the final demand by net value added, whereas net value added on its turn is determined by the production volume. Total net value added is formed by both industrial sectors in different proportions. One may assume the following relationship for this income formation:

$$v^* = \gamma_1 \, q_1 + \gamma_2 \, q_2 \quad (5.10.4)$$

where $\gamma_1$ ($i = 1, 2$) represents a coefficient that denotes which proportion of the disposable income is generated in either sector. In this way the production volume, the consumption and income are determined simultaneously.

A second behavioural assumption is concerned with industrial investments. In this section two important theories concerning investment behaviour will be dealt with, viz. the *acceleration theory* (see Koyck [1954]) and the *disposable funds theory* or *liquidity theory* (see Meyer and Kuh [1957]).

The *acceleration theory* explains the firm's investment behaviour by assuming that the investments, implemented in each sector, are a fixed proportion $\kappa$ of the change in output from one year to another. Then one obtains the following investment equation:

$$I_i = \kappa_i \, (\triangle q_i) \quad i = 1, 2, \tag{5.10.5}$$

where $I_i$ are the investment requirements of sector $i$, and $(\triangle q)_i$ the change in the output of sector $i$. The coefficient $\kappa_i$ is a marginal capital coefficient.[3] The element $\triangle q_i$ is a dynamic element in this static model, since it is equal to $q_{i,t} - q_{i,\,t-1}$ (where the lower index $t$ stands for the time period concerned). This additional difficulty can be overcome by assuming that $q_i$ is rising linearly during a number of years, so that the average change in $q_i$ for each year is equal to:

$$\triangle q_i = \frac{q_{i,t} - q_{i,o}}{t} \tag{5.10.6}$$

where $q_{i,o}$ is the production level of industry $i$ in a certain basis year. Substitution of (5.10.6) into (5.10.5) yields

$$\begin{aligned} I_i &= \kappa_i \, \left(\frac{q_{i,t} - q_{i,o}}{t}\right) \\ &= \kappa_i^* \, q_{i,t} + \kappa_i^{**} \end{aligned} \tag{5.10.7}$$

where $\kappa_i^*$ and $\kappa_i^{**}$ are defined, respectively, as:

$$\kappa_i^* = \kappa_i / t \tag{5.10.8}$$

and:

$$\kappa_i^{**} = -\frac{\kappa_i q_{i,o}}{t} \tag{5.10.9}$$

In each time period a relationship between $I_i$ and $q_i$ can be found on the basis of (5.10.7).

It should be remarked now, that the element $I_i$, introduced in (5.10.5), is unequal to the element $i_i$, introduced in (5.10.1). The reason is that $i_i$ represents the investments, *delivered and produced* by sector $i$. Therefore, before integrating $I_i$ in the I–O framework, a relationship has to be found between $I_i$ and $i_i$. This relationship can be justified by assuming that the production of investment goods in sector $i$ is used for implementing investments in sector $i$ itself, as well as in other sectors. The relative proportions of these sectoral investments can be calculated by means of transition coefficients $t_{ii'}$ $(i,i' = 1,2)$, which denote the required deliveries of investments from sector $i$ to sector $i'$, if the investments implemented by sector $i'$ are at a unit level. Such a system can be extracted from a BIG SAM of a national economy. Therefore one obtains:

$$\begin{bmatrix} i_1 \\ i_2 \end{bmatrix} = \begin{bmatrix} t_{11} & t_{12} \\ t_{21} & t_{22} \end{bmatrix} \begin{bmatrix} I_1 \\ I_2 \end{bmatrix} \tag{5.10.10}$$

or, after substitution of (5.10.5):

$$\begin{bmatrix} i_1 \\ i_2 \end{bmatrix} = \begin{bmatrix} t_{11}\kappa_1 & t_{12}\kappa_2 \\ t_{21}\kappa_1 & t_{22}\kappa_2 \end{bmatrix} \begin{bmatrix} \Delta q_1 \\ \Delta q_2 \end{bmatrix} \tag{5.10.11}$$

The coefficients $t_{ii'}, \kappa_{i'}$ $(i, i' = 1, 2)$ in the matrix of (5.10.11) are called *sectoral capital coefficients.* These coefficients denote the additional volume of investments, delivered by sector $i$ to sector $i'$, if the production in sector $i'$ undergoes a unit increase. They are very usual in growth models; see, for instance, Tinbergen and Bos (1962). Next, substitution of (5.10.7) into (5.10.10) yields:

$$\begin{aligned} \begin{bmatrix} i_1 \\ i_2 \end{bmatrix} &= \begin{bmatrix} t_{11}\kappa_1^* & t_{12}\kappa_2^* \\ t_{21}\kappa_1^* & t_{22}\kappa_2^* \end{bmatrix} \begin{bmatrix} q_1 \\ q_2 \end{bmatrix} + \begin{bmatrix} t_{11}\kappa_1^{**} + t_{12}\kappa_2^{**} \\ t_{21}\kappa_1^{**} + t_{22}\kappa_2^{**} \end{bmatrix} \\ &= \begin{bmatrix} \tau_{11} & \tau_{12} \\ \tau_{21} & \tau_{22} \end{bmatrix} \begin{bmatrix} q_1 \\ q_2 \end{bmatrix} + \begin{bmatrix} \tau_1^* \\ \tau_2^* \end{bmatrix} \end{aligned} \tag{5.10.12}$$

where $\tau_{ii'}$ and $\tau_i^*$ $(i, i' = 1, 2)$ are defined as $t_{ii'}\kappa_{i'}^*$ and $\sum_{i'=1}^{2} t_{ii'}\kappa_{i'}^{**}$, respectively. By substituting (5.10.12) into (5.10.1) the investments in this I–O framework have also become endogenous variables.

The *theory of disposable funds* assumes that investments are dependent on the disposable funds of a firm. Therefore, one may assume a linear relationship between investments on the one hand, and depreciations and retained profits on the other hand. Furthermore, the depreciations and retained profits in each sector $i$, $\nu_i^{**}$, are assumed to be a fixed proportion $\varphi_i$ of the output in sector $i$, so that one may assume:

$$\nu_i^{**} \equiv \varphi_i\, q_i \quad i = 1, 2 \tag{5.10.13}$$

It is obvious, that the following additivity condition should be satisfied:

$$\begin{aligned} \nu^{**} &\equiv \nu_1^{**} + \nu_2^{**} \\ &= \varphi_1\, q_1 + \varphi_2\, q_2 \end{aligned} \tag{5.10.14}$$

The linear relationship, assumed between $I_i$ and $v_i^{**}$, gives rise to the following expression:

$$\begin{aligned} I_i &= \delta_i\, v_i^{**} + \epsilon_i \\ &= \delta_i\, \varphi_i\, q_i + \epsilon_i \end{aligned} \qquad (5.10.15)$$

By substituting (5.10.15) into (5.10.10) one obtains the following system of equations:

$$\begin{bmatrix} i_1 \\ i_2 \end{bmatrix} = \begin{bmatrix} t_{11} & t_{12} \\ t_{21} & t_{22} \end{bmatrix} \begin{bmatrix} \delta_1\varphi_1 q_1 + \epsilon_1 \\ \delta_2\varphi_2 q_2 + \epsilon_2 \end{bmatrix}$$

$$= \begin{bmatrix} t_{11}\delta_1\varphi_1 & t_{12}\delta_2\varphi_2 \\ t_{21}\delta_1\varphi_1 & t_{22}\delta_2\varphi_2 \end{bmatrix} \begin{bmatrix} q_1 \\ q_2 \end{bmatrix} + \begin{bmatrix} t_{11}\epsilon_1 + t_{12}\epsilon_2 \\ t_{21}\epsilon_1 + t_{22}\epsilon_2 \end{bmatrix}$$

$$= \begin{bmatrix} \lambda_{11} & \lambda_{12} \\ \lambda_{21} & \lambda_{22} \end{bmatrix} \begin{bmatrix} q_1 \\ q_2 \end{bmatrix} + \begin{bmatrix} \mu_1 \\ \mu_2 \end{bmatrix} \qquad (5.10.16)$$

where the elements $\lambda_{ii'}$ and $\mu_i$ $(i, i' = 1, 2)$ are defined as $t_{ii'}\delta_{i'}\varphi_{i'}$ and $\sum_{i'=1}^{2} t_{ii'}\epsilon_{i'}$, respectively. In this way the investment deliveries are again a function of the production levels in both sectors. System (5.10.16) possesses a structure similar to (5.10.12). Should the parameters of both systems be estimated directly by means of the respective relationships (5.10.16) and (5.10.12) (and not indirectly by means of the foregoing composing elements), both systems would possess even the same coefficients.

A synthesis between the acceleration theory and the disposable funds theory is obtained by assuming that the investment decisions in each sector $i$ are determined by both theories, so that the actual investment decision is a weighted average of 'acceleration investments' ($I_i^A$) and 'disposable funds investments' ($I_i^D$). Then $I_i$ can be written as:

$$I_i = \omega_i I_i^A + (1 - \omega_i)\, I_i^D \qquad (5.10.17)$$

where $\omega_i$ is a weighting coefficient ($0 \leqslant \omega_i \leqslant 1$). $I_i^A$ and $I_i^D$ can be related to the output by means of (5.10.7) and (5.10.5), respectively. Therefore, $I_i$ is equal to:

$$\begin{aligned} I_i &= \omega_i\kappa_i^* q_i + \omega_i\kappa_i^{**} + (1 - \omega_i)\,\delta_i\varphi_i q_i + (1 - \omega_i)\,\epsilon_i \\ &= \left\{ \omega_i\kappa_i^* + (1 - \omega_i)\,\delta_i\varphi_i \right\} q_i + \omega_i\kappa_i^{**} + (1 - \omega_i)\epsilon_i \end{aligned} \qquad (5.10.18)$$

Substitution of (5.10.18) into (5.10.10) yields the result:

$$\begin{bmatrix} i_1 \\ i_2 \end{bmatrix} = \begin{bmatrix} t_{11} & t_{12} \\ t_{21} & t_{22} \end{bmatrix} \left[ \begin{bmatrix} \{\omega_1 \kappa_1{}^* + (1-\omega_1)\,\delta_1 \varphi_1\}\, q_1 \\ \{\omega_2 \kappa_2{}^* + (1-\omega_2)\,\delta_2 \varphi_2\}\, q_2 \end{bmatrix} + \begin{bmatrix} \omega_1 \kappa_1{}^{**} + (1-\omega_1)\,\epsilon_1 \\ \omega_2 \kappa_2{}^{**} + (1-\omega_2)\,\epsilon_2 \end{bmatrix} \right]$$

$$= \begin{bmatrix} t_{11}\{\omega_1\kappa_1{}^* + (1-\omega_1)\,\delta_1\varphi_1\} & t_{12}\{\omega_2\kappa_2{}^* + (1-\omega_2)\,\delta_2\varphi_2\} \\ t_{21}\{\omega_1\kappa_1{}^* + (1-\omega_1)\,\delta_1\varphi_1\} & t_{22}\{\omega_2\kappa_2{}^* + (1-\omega_2)\,\delta_2\varphi_2\} \end{bmatrix} \begin{bmatrix} q_1 \\ q_2 \end{bmatrix} +$$

$$+ \begin{bmatrix} t_{11}\{\omega_1\kappa_1{}^{**} + (1-\omega_1)\,\epsilon_1\} + t_{12}\{\omega_2\kappa_2{}^{**} + (1-\omega_2)\,\epsilon_2\} \\ t_{21}\{\omega_1\kappa_1{}^{**} + (1-\omega_1)\,\epsilon_1\} + t_{22}\{\omega_2\kappa_2{}^{**} + (1-\omega_2)\,\epsilon_2\} \end{bmatrix}$$

$$= \begin{bmatrix} \nu_{11} & \nu_{12} \\ \nu_{21} & \nu_{22} \end{bmatrix} \begin{bmatrix} q_1 \\ q_2 \end{bmatrix} + \begin{bmatrix} \xi_1 \\ \xi_2 \end{bmatrix} \tag{5.10.19}$$

where $\nu_{ii'}$ and $\xi_i$ ($i, i' = 1, 2$) are defined as $t_{ii'}\ \{\omega_{i'}\kappa_{i'}^{*} + (1-\omega_{i'})\delta_{i'}\varphi_{i'}\}$ and $\sum_{i'=1}^{2} t_{ii'}\ \{\omega_{i'}\kappa_{i'}^{**} + (1-\omega_{i'})\,\xi_{i'}\}$, respectively. The structure of (5.10.19) is again equal to (5.10.16) or (5.10.12).

If one supposes that (5.10.19) represents the ultimate investment equation, one may integrate (5.10.19) together with (5.10.1) and (5.10.3) into one framework. This framework represents the structure of an economy, in which production, consumption, investments and value added are endogenous elements. By combining (5.10.1), (5.10.2), (5.10.3), (5.10.4), (5.10.14) and (5.10.19) into a normalized system of equations (i.e., a system where all endogenous variables are placed on one side of the = sign), one obtains:

$$\left[\begin{array}{cc|ccccc|cc} 1 & -a_{12} & -1 & 0 & -1 & 0 & 0 & 0 & 0 \\ -a_{21} & 1 & 0 & -1 & 0 & -1 & 0 & 0 & 0 \\ \hline 0 & 0 & 1 & 0 & 0 & 0 & -a_1 & 0 & 0 \\ 0 & 0 & 0 & 1 & 0 & 0 & -a_2 & 0 & 0 \\ -\nu_{11} & -\nu_{12} & 0 & 0 & 1 & 0 & 0 & 0 & 0 \\ -\nu_{21} & -\nu_{22} & 0 & 0 & 0 & 1 & 0 & 0 & 0 \\ -\gamma_1 & -\gamma_2 & 0 & 0 & 0 & 0 & 1 & 0 & 0 \\ \hline -\varphi_1 & -\varphi_2 & 0 & 0 & 0 & 0 & 0 & 1 & 0 \\ 0 & 0 & 0 & 0 & 0 & 0 & -1 & -1 & 1 \end{array}\right] \left[\begin{array}{c} q_1 \\ q_2 \\ c_1 \\ c_2 \\ i_1 \\ i_2 \\ \nu^* \\ \hline \nu^{**} \\ \nu \end{array}\right] = \left[\begin{array}{c} x_1 \\ x_2 \\ \beta_1 \\ \beta_2 \\ \xi_1 \\ \xi_2 \\ 0 \\ \hline 0 \\ 0 \end{array}\right] \tag{5.10.20}$$

By denoting the matrix of coefficients, the vector of endogenous variables and the vector of constant terms and exogenous variables by **B**, **y** and **z**, respectively, system (5.10.20) can be written as:

$$\mathbf{B}\ \mathbf{y} = \mathbf{z} \tag{5.10.21}$$

or:

$$y = B^{-1} z \qquad (5.10.22)$$

provided **B** is non-singular.

The matrix $\mathbf{B}^{-1}$ bears a resemblance to the Leontief matrix multiplier $(\mathbf{I} - \mathbf{A})^{-1}$, because **B** is composed of a unit matrix **I** (see the main diagonal) and a remaining matrix (denoted by **B***). Therefore, **B*** is comparable to the I–O matrix **A**. **B*** only differs from **A** in the order of magnitude of the elements. The column sums of an I–O matrix may not exceed 1, i.e., $\mathbf{i}'\mathbf{A} \leqslant \mathbf{i}'$ (where **i** is a unit vector), whereas the column sums of **B*** are not subject to this restriction. Therefore, the I–O matrix multiplier is always convergent (cf [5.3.16]), but $\mathbf{B}^{-1}$ does not necessarily converge, so that an exogenous disturbance does not always result in a convergent equilibrium process.

The structure of **B** is worth further inspection. One may split **B** into 3 parts, separated by means of dotted lines. The first matrix, left at the top, represents the purely technical part of the system (the I–O relationships). The second part represents the behavioural relationships, while the last part represents definitional equations. The last two elements, $\nu^{**}$ and $\nu$, can be separated from the structural system; these elements can be calculated, once the foregoing 7 elements have been determined. The reason for this phenomenon is the fact that the matrix **B** is *block-triangular* with respect to the last two elements (block-triangularity of a matrix is discussed in Appendix 5B.)This separation of elements of the matrix **B** and this solution in terms of the foregoing 7 variables is *only* possible for the last two elements $\nu^{**}$ and $\nu$. The remaining 7 variables can only be solved simultaneously and not separately, since the corresponding upper left-hand part of the matrix **B** (i.e., the square matrix of order 7) is indecomposable ([in] decomposable matrices are also discussed in Appendix 5B). Therefore, these 7 elements cannot be solved in a separate or recursive way, and a triangularization or diagonalization of the corresponding matrix of coefficients is not possible. Each of these 7 elements is linked up with the remaining 6 variables. This indecomposability of the matrix can also be illustrated by means of the flow diagram represented in figure 5.10.a. The arrows denote the forces exerted by the variables on each other. The figures between brackets denote the rank of the successive equations $n$ ($n = 1, \ldots, 7$), as it results from system (5.10.20). The flow diagram shows the direct and indirect linkages between the variables.

One may conclude that the introduction of consumption and investment functions implies an extension of the *technical* I–O analysis to a larger system with *behavioural* relationships. In this way the broader

Fig. 5.10.a    A flow-diagram of an I–O model

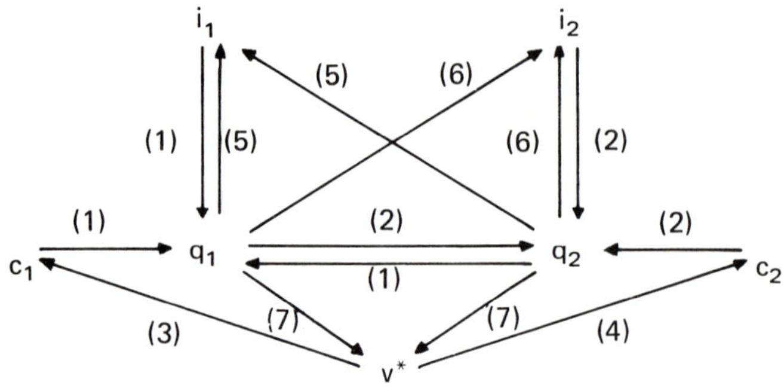


consequences of a change in the exogenous variables can be analyzed more profoundly (see [5.10.22]). The model itself is a comparative static model: it permits the calculation of a new equilibrium situation. The adaptation process itself, however, cannot be studied by means of static models.

A dynamic model can be created by introducing time-lags in the relationships, for instance, in the consumption and investment equations. If a time-lag is introduced in the acceleration theory for investments, even a double time-lag is obtained. Therefore, one might find instead of (5.10.3) and (5.10.5) the following relationships:

$$c_{i,t} = a_i \, v^*_{t-1} + \beta_i \qquad (5.10.23)$$

and

$$\begin{aligned} I_{i,t} &= \kappa_i \, (\Delta q_{i,t-1}) \\ &= \kappa_i \, (q_{i,t-1} - q_{i,\,t-2}) \end{aligned} \qquad (5.10.24)$$

The inclusion of these dynamic equations results in a non-homogeneous dynamic system of the second order with constant coefficients. The adaptation process of a certain variable, in consequence of an exogenous push, can have various forms, for instance, figure 5.10.b and 5.10.c. The first situation is an explosive one; since the variable concerned, $y_i$, remains rising (without external intervention). The second situation represents a growth towards a new equilibrium situation.[4] A more detailed analysis of regional growth models will be presented in Ch.7.

## 5.11    I–O analysis and spatial interaction models

The I–O framework discussed so far concentrated mainly on economic

Fig. 5.10.b A diverging growth path

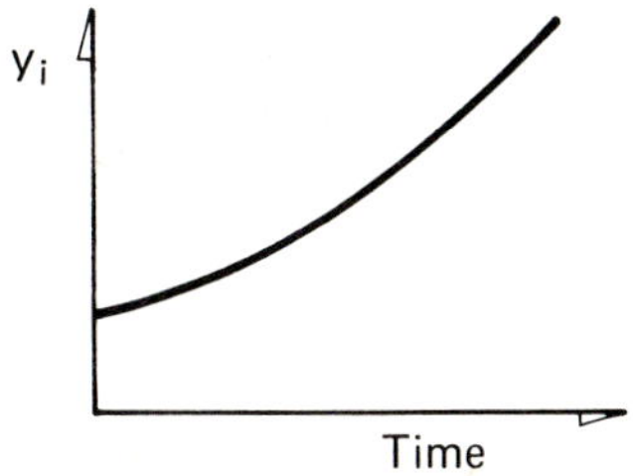


Fig. 5.10.c A converging growth path

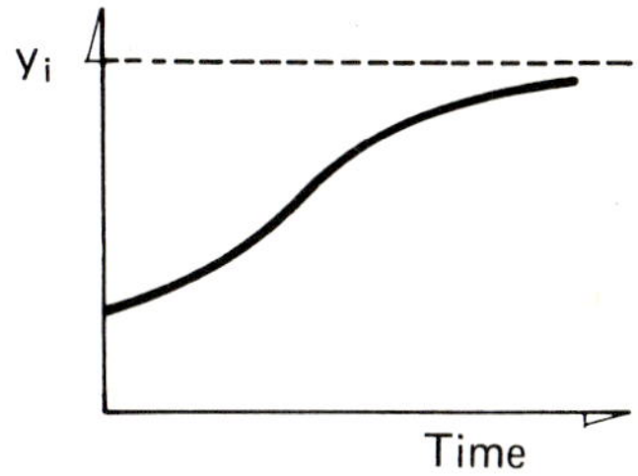


variables, such as production, intermediate deliveries, value added etc. Demographic phenomena were not taken into account. Furthermore, this framework was supposed to be rather rigid: the introduction of new basic activities into the existing structure was abandoned. In this section a link is created between changes in an original (regional) structure and demographic changes.

Suppose a region or city meets an exogenous change in final demand of all sectors. If this change is denoted by $\Delta\mathbf{f}$, the resulting change in the regional or urban activity is:

$$\Delta\mathbf{q} = (\mathbf{I} - \mathbf{A})^{-1}\Delta\mathbf{f} \tag{5.11.1}$$

By assuming a vector of constant labour coefficients, $\mathbf{l}$, the additional demand for labour in consequence of a rise in the output is equal to:

$$\Delta L_1 = \mathbf{l}'\Delta\mathbf{q} \tag{5.11.2}$$

where $\Delta L_1$ represents the initial change in total labour requirements. A similar result is obtained, if a new propulsive activity is included in the existing regional or urban structure.[5] Then the initial push to the employment can also be denoted by $\Delta L_1$.

If one assumes a situation of full employment, an employment push will lead to a rise in regional or urban population. This rise in population is only possible by migration from other regions or cities. The ratio of the economically active population with respect to total population is called the *activity rate.* The activity rate $r$ may also be distinguished by sector, and by age and sex groups; for instance, see Bowers (1970). In a formal way, one obtains:

$$r = L/P \tag{5.11.3}$$

where $P$ represents the total regional or urban population. On the basis of (5.11.3) one may write:

$$\triangle P_1 = \pi(\triangle L_1) \qquad (5.11.4)$$

where $\pi$ is the inverted marginal activity rate, and where $\triangle P_1$ is the initial rise in regional or urban population.

The rise in population, $\triangle P_1$, leads to an increase in the demand for *private* services in that area (shopping, education, e.g.). If this initial rise in demand for services is denoted by $\triangle S_1^P$, one may assume the following relationship:

$$\triangle S_1^P = \kappa(\triangle P_1) \qquad (5.11.5)$$

where $\kappa$ is a proportionality factor between the rise in population and in services. Substitution of (5.11.4) into (5.11.5) gives:

$$\triangle S_1^P = \kappa\pi(\triangle L_1) \qquad (5.11.6)$$

Furthermore, the increase in industrial activity is assumed to exert also an effect on the demand for *industrial* services (repair services, e.g.). If the initial rise in demand for industrial services is denoted by $\triangle S_1^i$, one may assume the following proportional relationship between $\triangle S_1^i$ and the initial change in the industrial employment ($\triangle L_1$):

$$\triangle S_1^i = \sigma(\triangle L_1) \qquad (5.11.7)$$

where $\sigma$ is again a proportionality factor.

Now the total secondary push to employment as a consequence of a rise $\triangle L_1$ in the basic employment is equal to:

$$\begin{aligned}\triangle L_2 &= \triangle S_1^p + \triangle S_1^i \\ &= \kappa\pi(\triangle L_1) + \sigma(\triangle L_1) \qquad (5.11.8) \\ &= (\kappa\pi + \sigma)(\triangle L_1)\end{aligned}$$

Once the secondary change in employment has been calculated, the previous steps (5.11.4)–(5.11.8) can be repeated with respect to $\triangle L_2$. By applying (5.11.4) one may find the rise in population in consequence of the rise in employment in the service sector. Therefore, one obtains:

$$\triangle P_2 = \pi^*(\triangle L_2) \qquad (5.11.9)$$

in which the inverted activity rate of the service sector, $\pi^*$, is not necessarily equal to the original inverted activity rate of the industrial sector, $\pi$ (see Bowers [1970]).

Furthermore, the new rise in population causes an additional demand for private services, which is according to (5.11.6) equal to:

$$\triangle S_2^p = \kappa\pi^*(\triangle L_2) \qquad (5.11.10)$$

If necessary, $\kappa$ may be replaced by a new value, $\kappa^*$, during the second stage. Beside the *private* services the *industrial* services may also undergo a secondary rise, viz. as a result of the attraction forces of the industrial services already established in the previous period. If the fraction of industrial services, which are generated as a result of the initial rise of the employment in the service sector, is denoted by $\sigma^*$, the following result is found according to (5.11.7):

$$\Delta S_2^i = \sigma^* (\Delta L_2) \qquad (5.11.11)$$

Therefore, the total effect on the employment is equal to:

$$\begin{aligned} \Delta L_3 &= \Delta S_2^P + \Delta S_2^i \\ &= \kappa\pi^* (\Delta L_2) + \sigma^* (\Delta L_2) \\ &= (\kappa\pi^* + \sigma^*) (\Delta L_2) \end{aligned} \qquad (5.11.12)$$

Substitution of (5.11.8) into (5.11.12) yields the result:

$$\Delta L_3 = (\kappa\pi^* + \sigma^*) (\kappa\pi + \sigma) (\Delta L_1) \qquad (5.11.13)$$

The last series of steps (5.11.9) – (5.11.13) can be repeated *ad infinitum.* It is evident that during each stage of the repetition the successive changes in employment and population will decrease. The ultimate total effect on the employment and population sector can be calculated by means of the following series, respectively:

$$\begin{aligned} \sum_{i=1}^{\infty} (\Delta L)_i &= \left[1 + (\kappa\pi + \sigma) \left\{ 1 + (\kappa\pi^* + \sigma^*) + (\kappa\pi^* + \sigma^*)^2 + \ldots \right\}\right] (\Delta L_1) \\ &= \left\{1 + \frac{\kappa\pi + \sigma}{1 - (\kappa\pi^* + \sigma^*)}\right\} (\Delta L_1) \end{aligned} \qquad (5.11.14)$$

and:

$$\begin{aligned} \sum_{i=1}^{\infty} (\Delta P)_i &= \left[\pi + \pi^* (\kappa\pi + \sigma) \left\{ 1 + (\kappa\pi^* + \sigma^*) + (\kappa\pi^* + \sigma^*)^2 + \ldots \right\}\right] (\Delta L_1) \\ &= \left\{\pi + \frac{\pi^* (\kappa\pi + \sigma)}{1 - (\kappa\pi^* + \sigma^*)}\right\} (\Delta L_1) \end{aligned} \qquad (5.11.15)$$

provided $\kappa\pi^* + \sigma^* < 1$. Now the *employment multiplier* ($m_E$), which is defined as the aggregate effect on the employment given an exogenous rise in regional or urban activity, is equal to:

$$m_E = 1 + \frac{\kappa\pi + \sigma}{1 - (\kappa\pi^* + \sigma^*)} \qquad (5.11.16)$$

In a similar way the *population multiplier* ($m_p$) is equal to:

$$m_p = \pi + \frac{\pi^* (\kappa\pi + \sigma)}{1 - (\kappa\pi^* + \sigma^*)} \qquad (5.11.17)$$

For instance, if one assumes the following values for the parameters: $\pi = 3$, $\kappa = 0{\cdot}1$, $\sigma = 0{\cdot}05$, $\pi^* = 3$, and $\sigma^* = 0{\cdot}1$, the employment and population multiplier are, respectively, $m_E = 1{\cdot}58$; $m_p = 4{\cdot}75$. The working mechanism of employment and population multipliers is entirely similar to the classical Keynesian multiplier in which each step towards a new equilibrium situation takes place by means of step-wise declining impulses. The interactions between the various sectors can be represented in a figurative way as follows:

Fig. 5.11.a

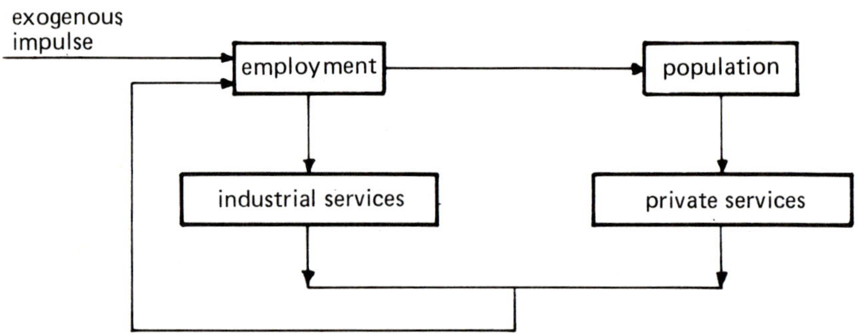


If one starts in the foregoing analysis with a situation of unemployment in the industrial sector, the introduction of a new basic activity will enhance employment without attracting additional population. This situation may occur in a stagnating region, where a development program is implemented by introducing propulsive activities. In this case one meets a situation where $\pi = 0$. It is obvious that this leads to a decline in the multiplier effect (see [5.11.16] and [5.11.17]). Similar situations arise, if $\pi^* = 0$, $\sigma = 0$, $\sigma^* = 0$, or $\kappa = 0$.

It is evident that the previous situation is a partial one, because the migration flows from other regions or cities lead also to structural changes in these areas. By linking up all these elements one obtains a complex spatial system with spatial interactions, controlled by attraction or gravity forces of the various areas. A formalization of this approach can be found *inter alia* in Cahen and Ponsard (1963), Cordey-Hayes and Wilson (1971), Crowther and Echenique (1972), Lowry (1964), and Wilson (1974).

Such an approach is also useful for analyzing trip distribution and shopping behaviour.

## 5.12 Attraction theory

Classical I–O analysis describes the technical linkages between economic activities, and is essentially demand-oriented. The nature of these linkages, however, may be such that various activities seek for a spatial concentration. Such a spatial concentration arises owing to the existence of *agglomeration advantages* (for instance, see the Weber analysis in section 2.3). These agglomeration advantages are composed *inter alia* of a decline in transportation and communication costs. Communication costs are a broader concept than transportation costs. Communication costs involve all costs caused by the need for contact with input and output markets (for instance, face-to-face contact). One of the first operational approaches to these external linkages between economic activities was developed by Klaassen (1967). Other contributions can be found *inter alia* in Klaassen and Van Wickeren (1969), and Klaassen (1972). In essence, Klaassen's approach is a neo-Weberian analysis concentrating on transportation and communication costs. Klaassen's so-called *attraction theory* assumes that the attraction forces between activities are formed by the existence of transportation and communication costs. The resultant of the attraction forces between the activities determines the ultimate location of a firm. Relatively high transportation costs for intermediate products between complementary economic activities tend to cause an industrial concentration of these activities, whereas relatively high transportation costs for final commodities tend to result in a location near the consumer market.

The static version of the attraction theory can be developed on the basis of the following assumptions. The total transportation and communication costs of a certain activity, located in a certain region, are composed of input and output costs. Given the presence of input and output markets in a certain region, and given the levels of intermediate products for a certain activity as well as the level of final products in that region, one can calculate, on the basis of the actual location pattern, the implicit weights of the transportation and communication costs both for inputs and outputs. For instance, if a certain industry, settled in a given region, is exporting the major part of its final products, and if it is using as intermediate products only products originating from the region itself, this industry is said to be *input-oriented,* since the transportation and communication costs of the output possess a relatively low weight, whereas the transportation and communication costs of the intermediate deliveries possess a relatively high weight. In the reverse case the industry would be *output-oriented.* An industry which does not show an orientation either to the input market or to the output market is called a *footloose* industry. The assumption is made that within the region concerned (the so-called '*relevant region*') the transportation and communication costs are negligible. Therefore, the total transportation and communication costs are caused by exports of final products and imports of intermediate products.

In a formal way the attraction theory can be represented in the following way. If the total production of activity $i$ in region $r$ is denoted by $q_i^r$, the following identity is valid:

$$q_i^r \equiv d_i^r + e_i^r \tag{5.12.1}$$

where $d_i^r$ represents the deliveries of sector $i$ within region $r$ (these deliveries are according to [5.5.3] composed of intermediate and final products), and where $e_i^r$ represents the total exports of commodity $i$ from region $r$ to all other regions $r'$ ($r' = 1, \ldots, R; r' \neq r$).

Furthermore, the imports of intermediate products to sector $i$ in region $r$ are calculated as the net total of all input requirements of sector $i$ in region $r$ minus the regional production of these inputs. If $q_{i'i}$ represents the total (intraregional and interregional) flow of input $i'$ earmarked for production process $i$ in region $r$ ($i, i' = 1, \ldots I; i \neq i'$), if $m_{i'i}^r$ represents the imports (i.e. the interregional flow) of input $i'$ to production process $i$ in region $r$, and if $q_{i'i}^r$ represents the intraregional intermediate deliveries of sector $i'$ to sector $i$ (both within region $r$), one may write the following identity:

$$m_{i'i}^r \equiv q_{i'i} - q_{i'i}^r \tag{5.12.2}$$

Next, $q_{i'i}$ and $q_{i'i}^r$ can be rewritten by means of I–O coefficients. Then one obtains:

$$q_{i'i} = a_{i'i}^r q_i^r \tag{5.12.3}$$

where $a_{i'i}^r$ is a well-known I–O coefficient which indicates the total volume of input $i'$ required for the production of one unit of product $i$ in region $r$. Furthermore, one may write:

$$q_{i'i}^r = b_{i'i}^r q_{i'}^r \tag{5.12.4}$$

where the allocation coefficient $b^r_{i'i}$ represents which fraction of the regional production of sector $i'$ is earmarked for intermediate deliveries to sector $i$. This allocation coefficient can be calculated from a normal regional I–O table. If the transport rate for the exports $e^r_i$ is denoted by $t^r_i$, and the transport rate for the imports $m^r_{i'i}$ by $t^r_{i'i}$, the total transportation and communication costs of sector $i$ in region $r$, $T^r_i$, are equal to:

$$T^r_i = t^r_i \, e^r_i + \sum_{\substack{i'=1 \\ i' \neq i}}^{I} t^r_{i'i} \, m^r_{i'i} \tag{5.12.5}$$

Substitution of (5.12.1) and (5.12.2) into (5.12.5) gives:

$$T^r_i = t^r_i \, (q^r_i - d^r_i) + \sum_{\substack{i'=1 \\ i' \neq i}}^{I} t^r_{i'i} \, (q_{i'i} - q^r_{i'i}) \tag{5.12.6}$$

while substitution of (5.12.3) and (5.12.4) into (5.12.6) yields the result:

$$\begin{aligned} T^r_i &= t^r_i \, (q^r_i - d^r_i) + \sum_{\substack{i'=1 \\ i' \neq i}}^{I} t^r_{i'i} \, (a^r_{i'i} \, q^r_i - b^r_{i'i} \, q^r_{i'}) \\ &= (t^r_i + \sum_{\substack{i'=1 \\ i' \neq i}}^{I} t^r_{i'i} \, a^r_{i'i}) \, q^r_i - t^r_i d^r_i - \sum_{\substack{i'=1 \\ i' \neq i}}^{I} t^r_{i'i} \, b^r_{i'i} \, q^r_{i'} \end{aligned} \tag{5.12.7}$$

Next, one may make an assumption concerning the transportation costs. A first assumption is to relate $T^r_i$ by means of I–O coefficients to the total output of the transportation sector. A second assumption, which will be made here, is to relate $T^r_i$ to the output of sector $i$, so that the following relationship is valid (apart from stochastic elements; see also Paelinck [1973] and Klaassen [1974]).

$$T^r_i = a^r_{ti} \, q^r_i \tag{5.12.8}$$

where $a^r_{ti}$ represents the transportation and communication costs per unit of output in sector $i$ in region $r$. Substituting (5.12.8) into (5.12.7) yields:

$$a^r_{ti} \, q^r_i = (t^r_i + \sum_{\substack{i'=1 \\ i' \neq i}}^{I} t^r_{i'i} a^r_{i'i}) q^r_i - t^r_i d^r_i - \sum_{\substack{i'=1 \\ i' \neq i}}^{I} t^r_{i'i} \, b^r_{i'i} \, q^r_{i'} \tag{5.12.9}$$

or:

$$q_i^r = \frac{t_i^r d_i^r + \sum_{\substack{i'=1 \\ i' \neq i}}^{I} t_{i'i}^r b_{i'i}^r q_{i'}^r}{t_i^r + \sum_{\substack{i'=1 \\ i' \neq i}}^{I} t_{i'i}^r a_{i'i}^r - a_{ti}^r} \tag{5.12.10}$$

By defining:

$$\lambda_i^r = \frac{t_i^r}{t_i^r + \sum_{\substack{i'=1 \\ i' \neq i}}^{I} t_{i'i}^r a_{i'i}^r - a_{ti}^r} \tag{5.12.11}$$

and:

$$\lambda_{i'i}^r = \frac{t_{i'i}^r}{t_i^r + \sum_{\substack{i'=1 \\ i' \neq i}}^{I} t_{i'i}^r a_{i'i}^r - a_{ti}^r} \tag{5.12.12}$$

relationship (5.12.10) is written as:

$$q_i^r = \lambda_i^r d_i^r + \sum_{\substack{i'=1 \\ i' \neq i}}^{I} \lambda_{i'i}^r b_{i'i}^r q_{i'}^r \tag{5.12.13}$$

If $q_i^r$, $d_i^r$, $b_{i'i}^r$ and $q_{i'}^r$ are known in a certain period (or during more periods), the unknown regression coefficients $\lambda_i^r$ and $\lambda_{i'i}^r$ can be estimated for each sector by means of least squares. This estimation can be based on a time series of observations (if available), or on a cross-section (over regions). The latter procedure implies that the transportation and communication structure of a certain sector is assumed to be equal in all regions. This is, of course, a rigorous assumption, but frequently the lack of observation materials leads to such an assumption. The relative values of $\lambda_i^r$ and $\lambda_{i'i}^r$ indicate for each sector the degree to which a certain sector is demand- or supply-oriented. Therefore, they are called *attraction coefficients.* For instance, if $\lambda_{i'i}^r = 0$ ($i, i' = 1, \ldots, I$), the activity concerned is entirely demand- or market-oriented. On the other hand, if $\lambda_i^r = 0$, the activity concerned is entirely supply-oriented. In general, one does not meet such extreme situations; most estimations of $\lambda_i^r$ and $\lambda_{i'i}^r$ show intermediate cases. If the regional production $q_i^r$ and $q_{i'}^r$ of the activities $i$ and $i'$ $(i, i' = 1, \ldots, I)$ is unknown, one can also use regional employment data per sector, provided the gross output per worker in each sector is known.

Once the attraction coefficients have been estimated for each sector, one has some evidence concerning the attraction forces exerted by the sectors upon each other. Therefore, this attraction theory can be considered as an operational and manageable approach to agglomeration phenomena. In a series of studies very promising results were obtained, with rather reasonable correlation coefficients. The knowledge of the attraction coefficients is very important in regional development and planning efforts, since these attraction coefficients provide a reliable basis for the selection of complementary activities (see also section 5.19).

It should be mentioned that the theoretical concept of a 'relevant' region discussed above meets many difficulties in practice, since this concept would imply a different 'relevant' region for each activity. The size of such a 'relevant' region is determined by the level of transportation and communication costs, because within a 'relevant' region transportation and communication costs are supposed to be negligible. However, transportation and communication costs are frequently not exactly measurable, so that then the size of the 'relevant' region is unknown. Therefore, in practice most attraction studies are based on the existing regional division of a country, for which production data are available. Furthermore, if the attraction coefficients are estimated by means of a cross-section over all regions, one should be aware of the assumption of an equal transportation and communication structure in all 'relevant' regions.

The attraction theory described above does not contain behavioural relationships; it is based only on balance and technical equations. This may be the reason for the relatively high correlation coefficients. There is only one implicit behavioural assumption, viz. that a firm's location is determined by transportation and communication costs. However, this assumption is not tested in a direct way (for instance, by seeking for a minimum cost location), but only in an indirect way (viz. by assuming that the actual location is optimal, in the sense that the attraction coefficients are a reliable representation of the agglomeration forces, which determine the firm's location). Furthermore, the previous assumption does not include the element of time. An elaboration of the original theory including behavioural assumptions and dynamic elements will be given below.

The attraction theory is a theory of interindustry relations; as such it bears a certain resemblance to the classical I–O analysis. The relationship between the attraction theory and the I–O theory will now be dealt with. First, relationship (5.12.13) will be written in matrix notation. Then one obtains for each region $r$:

$$\mathbf{q}^r = \hat{\boldsymbol{\lambda}}\, \mathbf{d}^r + \Lambda\, \mathbf{q}^r \qquad (5.12.14)$$

where $\mathbf{q}^r$ is a vector of order $I$ encompassing the sectoral production levels in region $r$, $\hat{\boldsymbol{\lambda}}$ a diagonal matrix with market attraction coefficients for each sector, $\mathbf{d}^r$ a vector of intraregional demand, and $\Lambda$ a matrix of order $I \times I$ with typical elements $\lambda^r_{i'i}\, b^r_{i'i}$ $(i, i' = 1, \ldots, I)$. Since the total demand in region $r$ is composed of intermediate demand and internal final demand, the vector $\mathbf{d}^r$ is written as:

$$\mathbf{d}^r = \mathbf{A}^r \mathbf{q}^r + \mathbf{f}^r \qquad (5.12.15)$$

where $\mathbf{A}^r$ is the usual I–O matrix and $\mathbf{f}^r$ the regionalised final demand.

Substitution of (5.12.15) into (5.12.14) gives:

$$\begin{aligned} \mathbf{q}^r &= \hat{\boldsymbol{\lambda}}(\mathbf{A}^r \mathbf{q}^r + \mathbf{f}^r) + \Lambda\, \mathbf{q}^r \\ &= (\hat{\boldsymbol{\lambda}}\mathbf{A}^r + \Lambda)\, \mathbf{q}^r + \hat{\boldsymbol{\lambda}}\mathbf{f}^r \end{aligned} \qquad (5.12.16)$$

or, provided $\mathbf{I} - \hat{\boldsymbol{\lambda}}\,\mathbf{A}^r - \Lambda$ is non-singular:

$$\mathbf{q}^r = (\mathbf{I} - \hat{\boldsymbol{\lambda}}\mathbf{A}^r - \Lambda)^{-1}\, \hat{\boldsymbol{\lambda}}\, \mathbf{f}^r \qquad (5.12.17)$$

where the matrix $\mathbf{I} - \hat{\boldsymbol{\lambda}}\ \mathbf{A}^r - \Lambda$ is called the *attraction matrix*. Relationship (5.12.17) bears a resemblance to the Leontief expression (5.3.14). There are two differences: (a) The I–O matrix $\mathbf{A}$ is replaced in the attraction theory, by the more general matrix $\hat{\boldsymbol{\lambda}}\,\mathbf{A}^r + \Lambda$, which shows that the attraction forces are an essential element in the interindustry relations of the attraction theory.[6] (b) The Leontief final demand $\mathbf{f}$ is equal to $\mathbf{f}^r + \mathbf{e} - \mathbf{m}$, whereas the final demand in the attraction theory is equal to the internal final deliveries $\mathbf{f}^r$. Therefore, we may conclude that the classical I–O analysis is demand-oriented, whereas the attraction analysis is both demand-oriented (via $\hat{\boldsymbol{\lambda}}\ \mathbf{A}^r$) and supply-oriented (via $\Lambda$).

So far the attraction theory does not encompass behavioural relationships and dynamic elements. In this final part concerning the attraction theory both elements will be introduced. A first step into this direction was made by Van Wickeren (1971).

Instead of the attraction model (5.12.16) one may assume the following dynamic model for each region:

$$\mathbf{q}_t = \mathbf{B}\, \mathbf{q}_{t-1} + \hat{\mathbf{b}}\, \mathbf{f}^i_{t-1} + \hat{\mathbf{d}}\, (\Delta\mathbf{e})_t + \mathbf{c}_{t-1} \qquad (5.12.18)$$

where $\mathbf{B}$ is supposed to be a matrix of supply and demand attraction coefficients, $\hat{\mathbf{b}}$ a diagonal matrix of attraction coefficients for the final demand $\mathbf{f}^i$, $\hat{\mathbf{d}}$ a matrix representing the influence of export changes, and $\mathbf{c}_{t-1}$ a vector of exogenous impulses; $\mathbf{q}_t$ represents the regional production in period $t$.

Furthermore, one may assume the following consumption function:

$$\mathbf{f}^i_{t-1} = \boldsymbol{\alpha}\, \nu_{t-1} + \boldsymbol{\beta} \tag{5.12.19}$$

where $\nu$ represents the net regional value added. This relationship bears a close resemblance to (5.10.3). In accordance with (5.10.4) $\nu$ is generated as follows:

$$\nu_{t-1} = \boldsymbol{\gamma}'\, \mathbf{q}_{t-1} \tag{5.12.20}$$

where $\boldsymbol{\gamma}$ is a vector of regional value added per sector. Substitution of (5.12.20) into (5.12.19) gives:

$$\mathbf{f}^i_{t-1} = \boldsymbol{\alpha}\,(\boldsymbol{\gamma}'\, \mathbf{q}_{t-1}) + \boldsymbol{\beta} \tag{5.12.21}$$

Next, in accordance with (5.5.6) one may assume the following relationship for the imports:

$$\mathbf{m}_t = \hat{\boldsymbol{\mu}}_a\, \mathbf{A}\, \mathbf{q}_t + \hat{\boldsymbol{\mu}}_f\, \mathbf{f}^i_t \tag{5.12.22}$$

where $\mathbf{A}$ is again the well-known I–O matrix satisfying the regional product equilibrium (5.5.3):

$$\mathbf{q}_t = \mathbf{A}\, \mathbf{q}_t + \mathbf{f}^i_t + \mathbf{e}_t - \mathbf{m}_t \tag{5.12.23}$$

or in absolute changes:

$$(\Delta\mathbf{q})_t = \mathbf{A}\,(\Delta\mathbf{q})_t + (\Delta\mathbf{f}^i)_t + (\Delta\mathbf{e})_t - (\Delta\mathbf{m})_t \tag{5.12.24}$$

or:

$$(\Delta\mathbf{e})_t = (\mathbf{I} - \mathbf{A})\, \mathbf{q}_t - (\mathbf{I} - \mathbf{A})\, \mathbf{q}_{t-1} - \mathbf{f}^i_t + \mathbf{f}^i_{t-1} + \mathbf{m}_t - \mathbf{m}_{t-1} \tag{5.12.25}$$

Substituting (5.12.21) and (5.12.22) into (5.12.25) yields the result:

$$(\Delta\mathbf{e})_t = (\mathbf{I} - \mathbf{A})\mathbf{q}_{t-1} - (\mathbf{I} - \mathbf{A})\mathbf{q}_{t-1} - \boldsymbol{\alpha}(\boldsymbol{\gamma}'\mathbf{q}_t) + \boldsymbol{\alpha}(\boldsymbol{\gamma}'\mathbf{q}_{t-1}) + \hat{\ }_a\mathbf{A}\mathbf{q}_t + \hat{\boldsymbol{\mu}}_f\, \mathbf{f}^i_t - \boldsymbol{\mu}_a\, \mathbf{A}\mathbf{q}_{t-1} - \acute{\boldsymbol{\mu}}_f\mathbf{f}^i_{t-1} \tag{5.12.26}$$

Substitution of (5.12.21) and (5.12.26) into (5.12.18) gives:

$$\begin{aligned} q_t = {} & Bq_{t-1} + \hat{b}\, a(\gamma' q_{t-1}) + \hat{b}\,\beta + \hat{d}\,(I - A)q_t - \hat{d}(I - A)q_{t-1} - \hat{d}\, a(\gamma' q_t) + \\ & + \hat{d}\, a(\gamma' q_{t-1}) + \hat{d}\,\hat{\mu}_a A q_t + \hat{d}\,\hat{\mu}_f\, a\,(\gamma' q_t) + \hat{d}\,\hat{\mu}_f \beta - \hat{d}\,\hat{\mu}_a A q_{t-1} \\ & - \hat{d}\,\hat{\mu}_f\, a(\gamma' q_{t-1}) - \hat{d}\,\hat{\mu}_f\, \beta + c_{t-1} \end{aligned} \quad (5.12.27)$$

or:

$$(I - C)q_t = (B + \hat{b}\, a\, \gamma' - C)q_{t-1} + \hat{b}\,\beta + c_{t-1} \quad (5.12.28)$$

where **C** is defined as:

$$C = \hat{d}\,\left\{ (I - A) - a\,\gamma' + \hat{\mu}_a A + \hat{\mu}_f\, a\,\gamma' \right\} \quad (5.12.29)$$

Therefore, the final result is:

$$q_t = (I - C)^{-1} \left\{ (B + \hat{b}\, a\,\gamma' - C)q_{t-1} + \hat{b}\,\beta + c_{t-1} \right\} \quad (5.12.30)$$

provided the matrix **I – C** is non-singular. This result is a system of first-order difference equations, the solution of which describes the motion of this dynamic system. Regional growth models are dealt with more thoroughly in Ch.7.

Finally, the previous attraction analysis can be generalized by taking account of several regions simultaneously. Such a multiregional attraction analysis is able to give a more adequate description of the ex-post results of locational choices as a function of the locations of demand and supply (see Paelinck [1973]).

## 5.13 The dispersion coefficient

Before considering a set of *interregional* I–O models a last important characteristic of an I–O matrix will be introduced. If one assumes the basic relationship (5.3.14), one can easily calculate the effect of a change in the final demand for one or more sectors. Then relationship (5.3.14) can be written as:

$$\Delta q = B\,\Delta f \quad (5.13.1)$$

where **B** is defined as:

$$B = (I - A)^{-1} \quad (5.13.2)$$

If only the final demand for sector *i* undergoes a rise, viz., one unit, (5.13.1) becomes:

$$\begin{bmatrix} \Delta q_1 \\ \vdots \\ \Delta q_I \end{bmatrix} = \begin{bmatrix} b_{11} & \cdots & b_{1I} \\ \vdots & & \vdots \\ b_{I1} & \cdots & b_{II} \end{bmatrix} \begin{bmatrix} 0 \\ \vdots \\ 1 \\ \vdots \\ 0 \end{bmatrix} \tag{5.13.3}$$

or:

$$\mathbf{\Delta q} = \mathbf{b}_i \tag{5.13.4}$$

where $\mathbf{b}_i$ is the $i^{th}$ column of the matrix **B**. Therefore, the total (direct and indirect) production effect of a unit increase in the final demand for sector $i$ is equal to:

$$D_i = \mathbf{i}' \mathbf{\Delta q} = \mathbf{i}' \mathbf{b}_i \tag{5.13.5}$$

where **i** is a vector with unit elements. An equivalent formulation of (5.13.5) is:

$$D_i = \sum_{i'=1}^{I} \Delta q_{i'} = \sum_{i'=1}^{I} b_{i'i} \tag{5.13.6}$$

The coefficient $D_i$ is called a *sectoral dispersion coefficient:* it represents the aggregate change in production in consequence of a rise in final demand for sector *i.*

Next, one may assume that all elements of **f** undergo a unit of increase. Then the effect on the total production level is:

$$\sum_{i=1}^{I} D_i = \mathbf{i}' \mathbf{\Delta q} = \mathbf{i}' \mathbf{B}\, \mathbf{i} \tag{5.13.7}$$

The average effect over all sectors is called the *dispersion coefficient,* and this is equal to:

$$D = \frac{\sum_{i=1}^{I} D_i}{I} = \frac{\mathbf{i}'\mathbf{\Delta q}}{I} = \frac{\mathbf{i}'\,\mathbf{B i}}{I} \tag{5.13.8}$$

An equivalent specification is again:

$$D = \frac{\sum_{i'=1}^{I} \sum_{i=1}^{I} b_{i'i}}{I} \tag{5.13.9}$$

Such a dispersion coefficient measures the average dispersion throughout the economy in consequence of exogenous impulses (see also Rasmussen [1956]).

Finally, it is obvious that the influence on each production sector $i'$ in consequence of a unit increase of final demand for *all* sectors is measured by the row total of the matrix **B**, i.e. $\sum_{i=1}^{I} b_{i'i}$.

The previous remarks may be clarified by calculating the dispersion coefficients of the I–O matrix (5A.11). The Leontief inverse of this matrix is equal to:

$$(\mathbf{I} - \mathbf{A})^{-1} = \begin{bmatrix} 1{\cdot}2264 & 0{\cdot}2493 & 0{\cdot}2623 \\ 0{\cdot}6570 & 1{\cdot}5298 & 0{\cdot}5677 \\ 0{\cdot}4003 & 0{\cdot}3412 & 1{\cdot}5465 \end{bmatrix} \tag{5.13.10}$$

The sectoral dispersion coefficients are equal to: $D_1 = 2{\cdot}2837$, $D_2 = 2{\cdot}1203$ and $D_3 = 2{\cdot}3765$, whereas the average dispersion coefficient is equal to: $D = 2{\cdot}2602$. So a change in the final demand for products of sector 3 induces the highest change in total production. It is clear that a dispersion coefficient is particularly valuable in comparing the structure of different (regional or national) economies.

Finally, it should be mentioned that in case of interregional I–O linkages (see section 5.5) the computation of $D$ should take account of L.I. and F.I. situations. The way in which an exogenous impulse works out through the I–O structure of an economy depends on the assumptions or knowledge concerning the imports. Such a computation of $D$ is discussed in section 5.14 after a formal introduction of interregional I–O linkages. For a generalisation re $a_{ij}$ changes, see Klaassen and Paelinck (1975).

## 5.14 A formalization of multiregional I–O analysis

So far multiregional I–O models were discussed very superficially. Only section 5.5 contained a two-region situation with I–O linkages, which will be dealt with now in a more formal way. By introducing I–O coefficients table 5.5.a can be rewritten in the following way (cf. also [5.3.6]).

$$\begin{bmatrix} \mathbf{q}^A \\ \hline \mathbf{q}^B \end{bmatrix} = \left[\begin{array}{c|c} \mathbf{A}^{AA} & \mathbf{A}^{AB} \\ \hline \mathbf{A}^{BA} & \mathbf{A}^{BB} \end{array}\right] \begin{bmatrix} \mathbf{q}^A \\ \hline \mathbf{q}^B \end{bmatrix} + \begin{bmatrix} \mathbf{f}^A \\ \hline \mathbf{f}^B \end{bmatrix} \tag{5.14.1}$$

where $\mathbf{q}^A$ and $\mathbf{q}^B$ are the respective production vectors in region $A$ and $B$, and $\mathbf{f}^A$ and $\mathbf{f}^B$ the respective vectors of final demand for products from region $A$ and $B$.[7] The matrices $\mathbf{A}^{AA}$ and $\mathbf{A}^{BB}$ describe the *intraregional* I–O linkages, whereas the matrices $\mathbf{A}^{AB}$ and $\mathbf{A}^{BA}$ describe the *interregional* I–O linkages (i.e., the import coefficients).

System (5.14.1) can be split into the following 2 subsystems:

$$\mathbf{q}^A = \mathbf{A}^{AA}\mathbf{q}^A + \mathbf{A}^{AB}\mathbf{q}^B + \mathbf{f}^A \qquad (5.14.2)$$

and:

$$\mathbf{q}^B = \mathbf{A}^{BA}\mathbf{q}^A + \mathbf{A}^{BB}\mathbf{q}^B + \mathbf{f}^B \qquad (5.14.3)$$

Relationship (5.14.3) can be written as:

$$\mathbf{q}^B = (\mathbf{I} - \mathbf{A}^{BB})^{-1}(\mathbf{f}^B + \mathbf{A}^{BA}\mathbf{q}^A) \qquad (5.14.4)$$

while substitution of (5.14.4) into (5.14.2) yields the result:

$$\mathbf{q}^A = \mathbf{A}^{AA}\mathbf{q}^A + \mathbf{A}^{AB}(\mathbf{I} - \mathbf{A}^{BB})^{-1}(\mathbf{f}^B + \mathbf{A}^{BA}\mathbf{q}^A) + \mathbf{f}^A \qquad (5.14.5)$$

or:

$$\mathbf{q}^A = \{\mathbf{I} - \mathbf{A}^{AA} - \mathbf{A}^{AB}(\mathbf{I} - \mathbf{A}^{BB})^{-1}\mathbf{A}^{BA}\}^{-1}\{\mathbf{f}^A + \mathbf{A}^{AB}(\mathbf{I} - \mathbf{A}^{BB})^{-1}\mathbf{f}^B\} \qquad (5.14.6)$$

In a similar way the production level of region **B** can be calculated. The matrix $\{\mathbf{I} - \mathbf{A}^{AA} - \mathbf{A}^{AB}(\mathbf{I} - \mathbf{A}^{BB})^{-1}\mathbf{A}^{BA}\}^{-1}$ is again called a multiplier. This interregional multiplier can be considered as an extension of the classical multiplier $(\mathbf{I}-\mathbf{A})^{-1}$, viz. with interregional production effects. The first part of the interregional multiplier, $\mathbf{I}-\mathbf{A}^{AA}$, represents the total *intraregional* effect of an exogenous impulse. The remaining part, $\mathbf{A}^{AB}(\mathbf{I}-\mathbf{A}^{BB})^{-1}\mathbf{A}^{BA}$, represents the feed-back effect of the imports from region **A** to **B** (viz. $\mathbf{A}^{AB}$), which are required as inputs by region **B** in order to produce the export commodities earmarked for region **A** (viz. $(\mathbf{I}-\mathbf{A}^{BB})^{-1}\mathbf{A}^{BA}$). The exogenous part of (5.14.6) is composed of a purely *intraregional* exogenous impulse (viz. $\mathbf{f}^A$), and an impulse induced by the final demand in region **B**, since the production of these final products requires imports from region $A$ to region $B$ (cf. the multiplier effect $\mathbf{A}^{AB}(\mathbf{I}-\mathbf{A}^{BB})^{-1}$).

It is obvious that the interregional framework described above can be applied for any arbitrary number of regions. Such an interregional framework presents a detailed picture of the working of a spatially divided economy.

The regional division itself is a complicated matter (see also Ch.4). Such a division depends on the problem at hand, the degree of homogeneity of the area concerned, and last but not least on the availability of data. Therefore, the scale of regions may vary from urban districts to states or counties. In general, the regional classification and the industrial classification are closely linked together, since the fund of available data on industrial linkages determines the regional classification.

Finally, as mentioned in the previous section, the calculation of dispersion coefficients depends on an F.I. or L.I. hypothesis.

If one assumes that region $A$ is entirely open and that the import sector has a feed-back effect with region $B$, the dispersion coefficient of region $A$ is calculated by aggregating the elements of the matrix $\{\mathbf{I}-\mathbf{A}^{AA}-\mathbf{A}^{AB}(\mathbf{I}-\mathbf{A}^{BB})^{-1}\mathbf{A}^{BA}\}^{-1}$.

The previous F.I. case can also be used in a slightly modified way, viz. by assuming that region $A$ is again entirely open and that products not available are imported, however, without a feed-back effect. Then the dispersion coefficient of region $A$ is calculated on the basis of the matrix $(\mathbf{I}-\mathbf{A}^{AA})^{-1}$.

In the third place, one may assume that no information is available, in the sense that region $A$ is supposed to be autarchic, i.e., region $A$ can meet all its input requirements. The dispersion coefficients of such an L.I. situation are calculated by adding up the matrices $\mathbf{A}^{AA}$ and $\mathbf{A}^{BA}$ (see table 5.5a and 5.5b in section 5.5), and, next, by calculating the dispersion coefficient on the basis of this new L.I. I–O matrix.

The previous threefold computation of dispersion coefficients was applied to Belgium by Van Straelen (1965). In this case Belgium was split into a region Antwerp (an inportant core region) and the remaining part of Belgium.

The first F.I. situation resulted in: $D$ = 1·18, the second one into $D$ = 1·15, while the L.I. situation resulted in $D$ = 1·31. These outcomes are very reasonable. The L.I. structure implies that all additional inputs are delivered by the region itself, so that in this situation an exogenous impulse induces a maximum production effect. The second F.I. case is based on the assumption of an openness of the region, in the sense that imports are allowed, but no feed-back effects. This situation implies that a considerable part of an exogenous impulse flows to other regions, so that the dispersion coefficient will be rather low. Next, the first F.I. case with imports and feed-back effects implies that a part of the import effect returns in the region itself by means of the feed-back effect. Obviously, the dispersion coefficient is higher in this case.

The previous procedure for partitioning an economy into regions can also be applied in a straightforward way for a partition of an economy into basic and non-basic sectors. For instance, if the basic sectors of a certain region are formed by the activities included in an industrial complex (see section 5.19) settled in the region concerned, the I–O matrix related to these interrelated activities is almost entirely filled. The relationships with respect to the non-basic activities are rather weak. This leads to a more or less block-diagonal structure of the total regional I–O matrix. If the basic and the non-basic sectors are denoted by $B$ and $N$, respectively, one obtains an I–O framework similar to (5.14.1):

$$\begin{bmatrix} \mathbf{q}^B \\ \hline \mathbf{q}^N \end{bmatrix} = \left[\begin{array}{c|c} \mathbf{A}^{BB} & \mathbf{A}^{BN} \\ \hline \mathbf{A}^{NB} & \mathbf{A}^{NN} \end{array}\right] \begin{bmatrix} \mathbf{q}^B \\ \hline \mathbf{q}^N \end{bmatrix} + \begin{bmatrix} \mathbf{f}^B \\ \hline \mathbf{f}^N \end{bmatrix} \tag{5.14.7}$$

Although the upper indices $B$ and $N$ have a meaning different from the upper indices $A$ and $B$ from (5.14.1), the formal analysis is completely analogous. In a way similar to (5.14.2)–(5.14.6) one may derive:

$$\mathbf{q}^B = \left\{ \mathbf{I}-\mathbf{A}^{BB} - \mathbf{A}^{BN} (\mathbf{I}-\mathbf{A}^{NN})^{-1} \mathbf{A}^{NB} \right\}^{-1} \left\{ \mathbf{f}^B + \mathbf{A}^{BN} (\mathbf{I}-\mathbf{A}^{NN})^{-1} \mathbf{f}^N \right\} \tag{5.14.8}$$

The multiplier working of (5.14.8) is also entirely identical to the multiplier mechanism of (5.14.6), albeit that one has to speak now in terms of intra- and intersectoral impulses instead of intra- and interregional impulses. Therefore, the 4 components of (5.14.8) have the following meaning: (a) $\mathbf{I} - \mathbf{A}^{BB}$ represents the direct multiplier working of the basic activities (without linkages with non-basic activities); (b) $\mathbf{A}^{BN} (\mathbf{I}-\mathbf{A}^{NN})^{-1} \mathbf{A}^{NB}$ represents a correction on the previous direct multiplier, caused by linkages with non-basic activities (this feed-back effect indicates the indirect influence of an exogenous impulse on the basic activities, viz. via the multiplier effect of related non-basic activities); (c) $\mathbf{f}^B$ represents the internal final demand plus net exports of final products of sector $B$; (d) $\mathbf{A}^{BN} (\mathbf{I}-\mathbf{A}^{NN})^{-1} \mathbf{f}^N$ represents the indirect effect on the basic sector, caused by a rise in the final demand of the non-basic sector (this effect results again from the multiplier of intermediate deliveries from sector $B$ to sector $N$).

The aforementioned 4 components were calculated for the region Basse-Sambre (Belgium) by Paelinck (1970), where the basic activities were formed by the glass and metal industry. The relative degree of influence of each of these 4 components was also calculated, which implied the calculation of the percentage distribution of the total production of all basic activities over the four components: intermediate deliveries within the basic sector (a), intermediate feed-back deliveries to the non-basic sector (b), final deliveries (local demand plus net exports) (c) and intermediate deliveries to the non-basic sector for final production (d). The following outcomes were obtained for the cases (a)–(d): (a) 9·0%; (b) 4·1%; (c) 1·3% (local final demand) and 82·6% (net exports from the region); (d) 3·0%.

The previous outcomes lead to the conclusion that the region concerned is *export-oriented*. This is a consequence of the openness of the region, which was rather small and which had a rather specialized production structure. Furthermore, the internal direct multiplier working of the basic activities is rather small, which indicates weak I–O relationships between the basic industries: the basic production processes are not entirely integrated. Finally, the I–O relationships with the non-basic sector (banking, services, other small industries) are also relatively small. Therefore, one may conclude that the region in question has a rather weak production structure: a situation of rapid economic growth will be attained only by creating a new economic structure.

## 5.15 Interregional product flows

In the foregoing section attention was paid to the elementary structure of interregional I–O models. Before dealing with more complicated multiregional I–O systems in more detail, interregional product flows will be considered more thoroughly.

Suppose one economic sector and a set of regions $r$ ($r = 1, \ldots, R$). The products of this sector are entirely mobile, so that a pattern of multiregional product flows exists. This multiregional pattern is represented in the matrix **Q** in (5.15.1):

$$\mathbf{Q} = \begin{bmatrix} q_{11} & \cdots & q_{1R} \\ \vdots & & \vdots \\ q_{R1} & \cdots & q_{RR} \end{bmatrix} \qquad (5.15.1)$$

where $q_{rr'}$ $(r, r' = 1, \ldots, R; r \neq r')$ represents a commodity flow from region $r$ to region $r'$. It should be noted that $q_{rr'}$ represents an *interregional* flow rather than an intersectoral flow. For all sectors of the economy a system like (5.15.1) can be created.

If one assumes an L.I. situation, in which only the row and the column totals are known, the diagonal elements of **Q** can easily be calculated as residual elements, when the off-diagonal elements are known. However, these off-diagonal elements are supposed to be unknown for the moment.

The number of unknown elements can be reduced, if there is prior information available concerning certain flows. This prior information may result from interregional accounts and statistics, or from other mathematical and analytical methods. If such *a priori* information is not available, additional hypotheses concerning interregional flows may be helpful to estimate these flows.

A reasonable hypothesis is to assume a relationship between the volume of interregional trade and the average economic distance between regions (the notion of economic distance is discussed in Ch.1 and Ch.4). If the distance between region $r$ and $r'$ is denoted by $d_{rr'}$ one may write:

$$q_{rr'} = (a_r - b_r d_{rr'})\, q_{r.} \quad r,r' = 1, \ldots, R;\ r \neq r' \tag{5.15.2}$$

where $a_r$ and $b_r$ are typical (as yet unknown) distance coefficients of region $r$, and where $q_{r.}$ is defined as:

$$q_{r.} = \sum_{\substack{r'=1 \\ r' \neq r}}^{R} q_{rr'} \tag{5.15.3}$$

If the foregoing hypothesis is valid, the number of degrees of freedom is reduced to $2R$ (the total number of unknown coefficients $a_r$ and $b_r$; $r = 1, \ldots, R$).

Next, one may aggregate all interregional product flows over the regions of destination, so that one obtains:

$$\begin{aligned} \sum_{\substack{r'=1 \\ r' \neq r}}^{R} q_{rr'} = q_{r.} &= \sum_{\substack{r'=1 \\ r' \neq r}}^{R} (a_r - b_r\, d_{rr'})\, q_{r.} \\ &= \left\{ (R-1)a_r - b_r \sum_{\substack{r'=1 \\ r' \neq r}}^{R} d_{rr'} \right\} q_{r.} \end{aligned} \tag{5.15.4}$$

or:

$$1 = \left\{ (R-1)\, a_r - b_r \sum_{\substack{r'=1 \\ r' \neq r}}^{R} d_{rr'} \right\} \tag{5.15.5}$$

The final result is:

$$a_r - b_r \sum_{\substack{r'=1 \\ r' \neq r}}^{R} d_{rr'} \,/(R-1) = 1/(R-1) \quad , r=1, \ldots, R \tag{5.15.6}$$

Relationship (5.15.6) can be written as a system of $R$ equations in $2R$ unknown variables $a_r$ and $b_r$. The expression $\sum_{\substack{r'=1 \\ r' \neq r}}^{R} d_{rr'}/(R-1)$ is the average distance from region $r$ to all other regions $r'$.

Furthermore, relationship (5.15.2) can be aggregated over all regions of origin, in which case one obtains:

$$\sum_{\substack{r=1 \\ r \neq r'}}^{R} q_{rr'} = q_{.r'} = \sum_{\substack{r=1 \\ r \neq r'}}^{R} (a_r - b_r d_{rr'}) q_{r.} \tag{5.15.7}$$

$$= \sum_{\substack{r=1 \\ r \neq r'}}^{R} a_r \, q_{r.} - \sum_{r=1}^{R} b_r \, d_{rr'} \, q_{r.}$$

It is obvious that (5.15.7) is also a system of $R$ equations in $2R$ unknown coefficients $a_r$ and $b_r$. Therefore, (5.15.6) and (5.15.7) represent a system of $2R$ equations in $2R$ unknown variables. It should be noted, however, that these $2R$ equations are not entirely independent. There is one dependent relationship, since the sum of the row totals ( $\sum_{r=1}^{R} q_{r.}$ ) is equal to the sum of the column totals ( $\sum_{r'=1}^{R} q_{.r'}$). Therefore, knowledge of $2R - 1$ balance equations implies the knowledge of the remaining balance equation. Consequently, the ultimate result is a system of $2R - 1$ independent equations in $2R$ unknown variables so that $a_r$ and $b_r$ can be estimated up to a multiplicative constant. Therefore, in addition to information concerning $d_{rr'}$, $q_{r.}$ and $q_{.r'}$ one needs statistical or other prior information concerning one flow in order to obtain an exact estimation of $a_r$ and $b_r$. Furthermore, one should be aware of the condition that $a_r$ and $b_r$ should be such that $q_{rr'} \geqslant 0$ $(r,r' = 1, \ldots, R)$. The latter condition could also be introduced by solving $a_r$ and $b_r$ by means of linear programming methods (see Ch.6). Therefore, one may conclude that the previous hypotheses permit the estimation of all $R(R-1)$ interregional product flows on the basis of $2R$ observed relationships, which implies an empirical observation of $\dfrac{2R}{R(R-1)} \cdot 100 = \dfrac{2}{R-1} \cdot 100$ per cent.

## 5.16 Pooling models in interregional I–O analysis

An interregional *pooling model* attempts to construct an equilibrium model for interregional shipments. In such a model the assumption is made that interregional commodity movements can be considered as shipments from regional supply pools to regional demand pools of that commodity. The interregional commodity distribution is supposed to be determined by distance factors, transportation costs and so forth.

A first, simple pooling model for I – O analysis was developed by Leontief (1953). Leontief's model is an I – O framework containing 2 types of sectors, viz. local sectors ($L$) and national sectors ($N$). Local commodities are produced and delivered within a delimitated region. National commodities are supposed to exceed the boundaries of the region concerned; in fact, they possess a high degree of mobility. It is obvious that this two-fold commodity classification is very sensitive with respect to the regional classification (for instance, town, SMSA, district, county and state). The local sector will decline, as the region is smaller. Such a model can be used to calculate the differential local impact in consequence of an exogenous impulse from the national sector.

The starting point is a set of I–O relations which bears a close resemblance to (5.14.7):

$$\begin{bmatrix} \mathbf{q}_r^N \\ \hline \mathbf{q}_r^L \end{bmatrix} = \left[\begin{array}{c|c} \mathbf{A}^{NN} & \mathbf{A}^{NL} \\ \hline \mathbf{A}^{LN} & \mathbf{A}^{LL} \end{array}\right] \begin{bmatrix} \mathbf{q}_r^N \\ \hline \mathbf{q}_r^L \end{bmatrix} + \begin{bmatrix} \mathbf{f}_r^N \\ \hline \mathbf{f}_r^L \end{bmatrix} \tag{5.16.1}$$

where $\mathbf{q}_r^N$, $\mathbf{q}_r^L$, $\mathbf{f}_r^N$ and $\mathbf{f}_r^L$ represent the production vector of national sectors in region $r$, the production vector of local sectors in region $r$, the net final demand vector for national goods in region $r$, and the net final demand vector for local goods in region $r$, respectively. The I – O matrix is partitioned in a similar subdivision and is assumed to be equal for each region.

The assumption of the previous model is that the *national* products are pooled over all regions, without considering the interregional flows themselves. Next, the production volume of *national* goods in region $r$ is supposed to be known (for instance, on the basis of an interregional model for national products), so that $\mathbf{q}_r^N$ is known. The as yet unknown production volume of *regional* (or *local*) goods in region $r$ can be solved, if the final demand for regional goods in region $r$ is known (for instance, on the basis of budget and demand studies). The latter statement can be proved by writing the second subsystem of (5.16.2) as:

$$\mathbf{q}_r^L = \mathbf{A}^{LN} \mathbf{q}_r^N + \mathbf{A}^{LL} \mathbf{q}_r^L + \mathbf{f}_r^L \tag{5.16.2}$$

or:

$$\mathbf{q}_r^L = (\mathbf{I} - \mathbf{A}^{LL})^{-1} (\mathbf{A}^{LN} \mathbf{q}_r^N + \mathbf{f}_r^L) \tag{5.16.3}$$

However, Leontief's approach seems to have some peculiar implications.

If $\mathbf{q}_r^N$ and $\mathbf{f}_r^L$ are given, and if $\mathbf{q}_r^L$ is known, the net final demand for national products is necessarily endogenous, as can easily be seen by writing the first subsystem of (5.16.1) as:

$$\mathbf{q}_r^N = \mathbf{A}^{NN}\,\mathbf{q}_r^N + \mathbf{A}^{NL}\,\mathbf{q}_r^L + \mathbf{f}_r^N \tag{5.16.4}$$

In system (5.16.4) $\mathbf{f}_r^N$ is necessarily the only vector of variables, which can be unknown. A coherence in this model can only be obtained by splitting the net final demand for national products in region $r$ into internal final demand, imports and exports:

$$\mathbf{f}_r^N = \mathbf{f}_r^{N*} + \mathbf{e}_r^N - \mathbf{m}_r^N \tag{5.16.5}$$

where $\mathbf{f}_r^{N*}$, $\mathbf{e}_r^N$ and $\mathbf{m}_r^N$ represent the internal final demand for national products in region $r$, the exports of national products and the imports of national products, respectively. It should be noted that the final demand for local goods can not be split in this way, since local goods are not exported nor imported. In general, $\mathbf{f}_r^{N*}$ is known (for instance, on the basis of demand relations and income data). Then the necessary consequence is that net exports $\mathbf{e}_r^N - \mathbf{m}_r^N$ are unknown, so that a solution of Leontief's pooling model leads to an implicit estimation of the net exports of national products in each region $r$.

A specific application and generalization of interregional I–O models is the multiregional gravity trade model constructed by Leontief and Strout (1966). This model is an intersectoral model combined with a gravity transportation model, and it allows the computation and projection of regional outputs and interregional commodity shipments. It is evident that the implementation of such a model requires a set of reliable interregional I–O tables.

The theoretical gravity trade model contains 4 basic sets of relationships ([5.16.6]–[5.16.9]).

The first relationship is the well-known balance equation:

$$q_i^{or} = \sum_{i'=1}^{I} a_{ii'}^r q_{i'}^{ro} + f_i^r \tag{5.16.6}$$

where $q_i^{or}$ represents the total amount of commodity $i$ (i.e., production + imports – exports) demanded by all intermediate and final sectors in region $r$, where $a_{ii'}^r$ represents the amount of commodity $i$ required by sector $i'$ in region $r$ to produce one unit of output of sector $i'$, where $q_{i'}^{ro}$ represents the total output of sector $i'$ in region $r$, and where $f_i^r$ represents the total amount of commodity $i$ demanded by final users in region $r$.

The second relationship is an additivity condition for the production in region $r$:

$$q_i^{ro} = \sum_{r'=1}^{R} q_i^{rr'} \qquad (5.16.7)$$

where $q_i^{rr'}$ represents the amount of commodity $i$ produced in region $r$ and shipped to region $r'$.

The third relationship is an additivity condition for the regional demand:

$$q_i^{or} = \sum_{r'=1}^{R} q_i^{r'r} \qquad (5.16.8)$$

Finally, the fourth relationship satisfies a gravity specification; it states that the amount of commodity $i$ shipped from region $r$ to region $r'$ is proportional to the total production of commodity $i$ in region $r$, and also proportional to the total consumption of commodity $i$ in region $r'$, while it is inversely proportional to the total output of commodity $i$ in all regions (represented by $q_i$):

$$q_i^{rr'} = \tau_i^{rr'} \frac{q_i^{ro} q_i^{or'}}{q_i} \qquad (5.16.9)$$

where the proportionality factor $\tau_i^{rr'}$ represents a trade coefficient which is a function of the cost of shipping commodity $i$ from region $r$ to region $r'$ ($\tau_i^{rr'} = 0$, if $r = r'$). It should be noted that this relationship allows cross-hauling (simultaneous shipments of the same sector in both directions between two regions). This situation is, in general, not allowed in the transportation models discussed in Ch.6.

Substitution of (5.16.9) into (5.16.7) gives:

$$q_i^{ro} = \sum_{\substack{r'=1 \\ r' \neq r}}^{R} \tau_i^{rr'} \frac{q_i^{ro} q_i^{or'}}{q_i} + q_i^{rr} \qquad (5.16.10)$$

$$= \frac{q_i^{ro}}{q_i} \sum_{\substack{r'=1 \\ r' \neq r}}^{R} \tau_i^{rr'} q_i^{or'} + q_i^{rr}$$

where $q_i^{rr}$ represents the amount of commodity $i$ produced and sold in region $r$. In a similar way, substitution of (5.16.9) into (5.16.8) gives:

$$q_i^{or} = \sum_{\substack{r'=1 \\ r' \neq r}}^{R} \tau_i^{r'r} \frac{q_i^{r'o} q_i^{or}}{q_i} + q_i^{rr}$$

$$= \frac{q_i^{or}}{q_i} \sum_{\substack{r'=1 \\ r' \neq r}}^{R} \tau_i^{r'r} q_i^{r'o} + q_i^{rr} \qquad (5.16.11)$$

By combining (5.16.10) and (5.16.11), one finds:

$$q_i q_i^{ro} - q_i^{ro} \sum_{\substack{r'=1 \\ r' \neq r}}^{R} \tau_i^{rr'} q_i^{or'} = q_i q_i^{or} - q_i^{or} \sum_{\substack{r'=1 \\ r' \neq r}}^{R} \tau_i^{r'r} q_i^{r'o} \qquad (5.16.12)$$

where the intraregional flows are eliminated.
The previous relationships can also be written as:

$$q_i^{ro} (q_i - \sum_{\substack{r'=1 \\ r' \neq r}}^{R} \tau_i^{rr'} q_i^{or'}) = q_i^{or} (q_i - \sum_{\substack{r'=1 \\ r' \neq r}}^{R} \tau_i^{r'r} q_i^{r'o}) \qquad (5.16.13)$$

Since:

$$q_i = \sum_{r'=1}^{R} q_i^{or'} = \sum_{r'=1}^{R} q_i^{r'o} \qquad (5.16.14)$$

one may write (5.16.13) as:

$$q_i^{ro} (\sum_{r'=1}^{R} q_i^{or'} - \sum_{\substack{r'=1 \\ r' \neq r}}^{R} \tau_i^{rr'} q_i^{or'}) = q_i^{or} (\sum_{r'=1}^{R} q_i^{r'o} - \sum_{\substack{r'=1 \\ r' \neq r}}^{R} \tau_i^{r'r} q_i^{r'o}) \qquad (5.16.15)$$

or:

$$q_i^{ro} \left\{ \sum_{\substack{r'=1 \\ r' \neq r}}^{R} (1 - \tau_i^{rr'}) q_i^{or'} + q_i^{or} \right\} = q_i^{or} \left\{ \sum_{\substack{r'=1 \\ r' \neq r}}^{R} (1 - \tau_i^{r'r}) q_i^{r'o} + q_i^{ro} \right\} \qquad (5.16.16)$$

By defining:

$$\lambda_i^{rr'} = 1 - \tau_i^{rr'}, i = 1, \ldots, I; r, r' = 1, \ldots, R, r \neq r' \qquad (5.16.17)$$

and by eliminating the term $q_i^{ro}\ q_i^{or}$ on both sides of (5.16.16), one obtains instead of (5.16.16):

$$q_i^{ro} \left\{ \sum_{\substack{r'=1 \\ r' \neq r}}^{R} \lambda_i^{rr'} q_i^{or'} \right\} = q_i^{or} \left\{ \sum_{\substack{r'=1 \\ r' \neq r}}^{R} \lambda_i^{r'r} q_i^{r'o} \right\} \qquad (5.16.18)$$

The latter system is not an independent set of relationships; for each sector one equation is redundant. This can be proved by summing the latter system over all regions $r$, which results in an identity (the superscripts $r$ and $r'$ may be freely interchanged). Consequently, any one of the $R$ equations (5.16.18) for a given sector can be derived from the other $R-1$ equations, so that for each sector one equation can be omitted. On the other hand, one should now impose the condition that total supply in each other sector is equal to total demand in each sector (see relationship [5.16.14]).

Therefore, the ultimate model compasses $2IR$ independent equations ([5.16.6], [5.16.14] and [5.16.18]), and also $2IR$ unknown variables.

The solution of the previous model is facilitated, if the nonlinear relationships (5.16.18) are linearized. Such a linearization can be accomplished by writing all variables as deviations from their base-year values. If the known value of a variable in a base-year is denoted by a bar, and a deviation from this value is denoted by the increment sign $\triangle$, one may write instead of (5.16.18):

$$(\bar{q}_i^{ro} + \triangle q_i^{ro}) \left\{ \sum_{\substack{r'=1 \\ r' \neq r}}^{R} \lambda_i^{rr'} (\bar{q}_i^{or'} + \triangle q_i^{or'}) \right\} = (\bar{q}_i^{or} + \triangle q_i^{or}) \left\{ \sum_{\substack{r'=1 \\ r' \neq r}}^{R} \lambda_i^{r'r} (\bar{q}_i^{r'o} + \triangle q_i^{r'o}) \right\} \tag{5.16.19}$$

A linear expression in the absolute changes of the variables is obtained by dropping out the products of two deviations of variables (i.e., the multiplicative terms are eliminated). Furthermore, one should be aware of the fact that relationship (5.16.18) is also valid in the base year (i.e., all variables replaced by barred variables). If this latter condition is also introduced into (5.16.19), one finds ultimately:

$$\triangle q_i^{ro} \Big( \sum_{\substack{r'=1 \\ r' \neq r}}^{R} \lambda_i^{rr'} \bar{q}_i^{or'} \Big) + \bar{q}_i^{ro} \Big( \sum_{\substack{r'=1 \\ r' \neq r}}^{R} \lambda_i^{rr'} \triangle q_i^{or'} \Big) = \triangle q_i^{or} \Big( \sum_{\substack{r'=1 \\ r' \neq r}}^{R} \lambda_i^{r'r} \bar{q}_i^{r'o} \Big) + \bar{q}_i^{or} \Big( \sum_{\substack{r'=1 \\ r' \neq r}}^{R} \lambda_i^{r'r} \triangle q_i^{r'o} \Big) \tag{5.16.20}$$

or:

$$\bar{q}_i^{ro} \sum_{\substack{r'=1 \\ r' \neq r}}^{R} \lambda_i^{rr'} \triangle q_i^{or'} - \Big( \sum_{\substack{r'=1 \\ r' \neq r}}^{R} \lambda_i^{r'r} \bar{q}_i^{r'o} \Big) \triangle q_i^{or}$$

$$= \bar{q}_i^{or} \sum_{\substack{r'=1 \\ r' \neq r}}^{R} \lambda_i^{r'r} \Delta q_i^{r'o} - \Big( \sum_{\substack{r'=1 \\ r' \neq r}}^{R} \lambda_i^{rr'} \bar{q}_i^{or'} \Big) \Delta q_i^{ro} \tag{5.16.21}$$

By substituting the regional index $r''$ for $r'$ in the second and fourth term of (5.16.21), one finds:

$$\bar{q}_i^{ro} \sum_{\substack{r'=1 \\ r' \neq r}}^{R} \lambda_i^{rr'} \Delta q_i^{or'} - \Big( \sum_{\substack{r''=1 \\ r'' \neq r}}^{R} \lambda_i^{r''r} \bar{q}_i^{r''o} \Big) \Delta q_i^{or} \tag{5.16.22}$$

$$= \bar{q}_i^{or} \sum_{\substack{r'=1 \\ r' \neq r}}^{R} \lambda_i^{r'r} \Delta q_i^{r'o} - \Big( \sum_{\substack{r''=1 \\ r'' \neq r}}^{R} \lambda_i^{rr''} \bar{q}_i^{or''} \Big) \Delta q_i^{ro}$$

Next, one defines:

$$\mu_i^{rr'} = \begin{cases} \bar{q}_i^{ro} \lambda_i^{rr'} & r' \neq r \\ - \sum_{\substack{r''=1 \\ r'' \neq r}}^{R} \lambda_i^{r''r} \bar{q}_i^{r''o} & r' = r \end{cases} \tag{5.16.23}$$

and:

$$\nu_i^{rr'} = \begin{cases} \bar{q}_i^{or} \lambda_i^{r'r} & r' \neq r \\ - \sum_{\substack{r''=1 \\ r'' \neq r}}^{R} \lambda_i^{rr''} \bar{q}_i^{or''} & r' = r \end{cases} \tag{5.16.24}$$

By substituting (5.16.23) and (5.16.24) into (5.16.22), one finds the linear expression for the interregional product equilibrium:

$$\sum_{r'=1}^{R} \mu_i^{rr'} \Delta q_i^{or'} = \sum_{r'=1}^{R} \nu_i^{r'r} \Delta q_i^{r'o}, \quad r = 1, \ldots, R; \; i = 1, \ldots, I \tag{5.16.25}$$

where the coefficients $\mu_i^{rr'}$ and $\nu_i^{r'r}$ can easily be determined from (5.16.23) and (5.16.24)

In addition to the latter system, relationships (5.16.6) and (5.16.14) should also be written in deviations. Then one obtains, respectively:

$$\Delta q_i^{or} = \sum_{i'=1}^{I} a_{ii'}^{r} \Delta q_{i'}^{ro} + \Delta f_i^{r} \tag{5.16.26}$$

and:

$$\sum_{r'=1}^{R} \Delta q_i^{or'} = \sum_{r'=1}^{R} \Delta q_i^{r'o} \qquad (5.16.27)$$

The last three systems should be used now to estimate the unknown variables $\Delta q_i^{or}$ and $\Delta q_i^{ro}$ ($r = 1, \ldots, R$; $i = 1, \ldots, I$). An efficient way of solving these variables is to replace $\Delta q_i^{or'}$ in relationship (5.16.25) by its balance identity (see [5.16.26]). Then one obtains:

$$\sum_{r'=1}^{R} \nu_i^{r'r} \Delta q_i^{r'o} = \sum_{r'=1}^{R} \sum_{i'=1}^{I} \mu_i^{rr'} a_{ii'}^{r'} \Delta q_{i'}^{r'o} + \sum_{r'=1}^{R} \mu_i^{rr'} \Delta f_i^{r'} \qquad (5.16.28)$$

System (5.16.28) can be considered as a system of $IR$ equations. It has already been stated that this system is redundant: it contains $I\,(R-1)$ independent equations.

In a similar way one may substitute the balance identity (5.16.26) into (5.16.27):

$$\sum_{r'=1}^{R} \Delta q_i^{r'o} = \sum_{r'=1}^{R} \sum_{i'=1}^{I} a_{ii'}^{r'} \Delta q_{i'}^{r'o} + \sum_{r'=1}^{R} \Delta f_i^{r'} \qquad (5.16.29)$$

which is a system of $I$ independent equations. Therefore, (5.16.28) and (5.16.29) form a system of $IR$ independent equations in $IR$ unknown variables $\Delta q_i^{r'o}$ ($r' = 1, \ldots, R$; $i = 1, \ldots, I$). These variables can be determined by solving the previous system by means of matrix algebra.

Such a matrix representation, as well as an application and empirical implementation of the foregoing gravity trade model is contained in Polenske (1970). On the basis of data for the nine Japanese provinces (interregional I–O coefficients, interregional trade coefficients, data of base year variables, and data on changes in final demand), the development of intraregional and interregional commodity flows could be estimated, and tested against the real interregional development in the past. In addition, the previous model (with changes in variables) permits also a projection of interregional developments.

The complete matrix specification of the previous model will take too much space here. In the following section a more simple matrix representation of an interregional trade model (without a gravity approach) will be given.

## 5.17 Interregional trade and I–O analysis

In contrast with Leontief's pooling model the interregional trade model of Moses (1955) does not possess a gravity approach for interregional flows.

Moses' model assumes a closed economy divided into $R$ regions each of which possesses interregional trade flows with the other regions. Furthermore, the number of productive sectors is supposed to be equal to $I$. Such a system can be considered again as a detailed framework of interregional I–O relations. The solution of such a system requires a lot of information, because both the regional production levels and the interregional product flows should be determined. Therefore, additional assumptions concerning the production structure and the commodity flows are necessary in order to estimate the entire set of unknown variables.

A first assumption concentrates on the regional production structure, viz. by assuming that the volume of each product absorbed by every industry within region $r (r = 1, \ldots, R)$ is strictly proportional to the output of that industry. Therefore, one may assume:

$$q^{r}_{ii'} = a^{r}_{ii'} \, q^{ro}_{i'} \qquad i, i' = 1, \ldots, I \tag{5.17.1}$$

where $q^{r}_{ii'}$ is the amount expended on sector $i$ by sector $i'$ in region $r$, $q^{ro}_{i'}$ the output of sector $i'$ in region $r$, and $a^{r}_{ii'}$ the corresponding I–O coefficient. Therefore, one may construct for each region a regional I–O matrix $\mathbf{A}^{r}$ of order $I \times I$, the coefficients of which describe the technical structure of all sectors in region $r$. The total demand in region $r$ for commodity $i$ is designated by $q^{or}_{i}$; it is composed of the total intermediate demand and final demand, so that one obtains:

$$q^{or}_{i} = \sum_{i'=1}^{I} q^{r}_{ii'} + f^{r}_{i} \tag{5.17.2}$$

where $f^{r}_{i}$ represents the final demand for commodity $i$ in region $r$. Substituting (5.17.1) into (5.17.2) gives:

$$q^{or}_{i} = \sum_{i'=1}^{I} a^{r}_{ii'} \, q^{ro}_{i'} + f^{r}_{i} \tag{5.17.3}$$

or, in matrix notation for each region:

$$\mathbf{q}^{or} = \mathbf{A}^{r} \, \mathbf{q}^{ro} + \mathbf{f}^{r} \tag{5.17.4}$$

By integrating system (5.17.4) to a multiregional pattern one obtains:

$$\begin{bmatrix} \mathbf{q}^{o1} \\ \vdots \\ \mathbf{q}^{oR} \end{bmatrix} = \begin{bmatrix} \mathbf{A}^{1} & & \mathbf{O} \\ & \ddots & \\ \mathbf{O} & & \mathbf{A}^{R} \end{bmatrix} \begin{bmatrix} \mathbf{q}^{1o} \\ \vdots \\ \mathbf{q}^{Ro} \end{bmatrix} + \begin{bmatrix} \mathbf{f}^{1} \\ \vdots \\ \mathbf{f}^{R} \end{bmatrix} \tag{5.17.5}$$

or, in compact matrix notation:

$$\mathbf{q}^o = \mathbf{A}\,\mathbf{q} + \mathbf{f} \qquad (5.17.6)$$

where **A** is a block diagonal matrix with successive diagonal blocks $\mathbf{A}^r$ ($r = 1, \ldots, R$), and $\mathbf{q}^o$ and $\mathbf{q}$ the respective vectors of demand and output.

A second assumption is concerned with the interregional flows, viz. by assuming that each region purchases its requirements of every good according to a constant regional supply pattern. Such a stable supply pattern can be represented by means of a set of trade coefficients for each sector. A trade coefficient $t_i^{rr'}$ represents the amount of product $i$ from region $r$, which is bought by all (intermediate and final) sectors in region $r'$, as a proportion of the total demand for product $i$ in region $r'$. Therefore, one may write:

$$q_i^{rr'} = t_i^{rr'}\, q_i^{or'} \qquad (5.17.7)$$

where $q_i^{rr'}$ represents a flow of commodity $i$ from region $r$ to region $r'$. Since $t_i^{rr'}$ is a proportion, the trade coefficients add up to 1, if they are aggregated over all regions of origin (including region $r'$ itself). In this way one can create for each sector $i$ a matrix $T_i$ of trade coefficients (of order $R \times R$). Such a matrix describes the per unit trading patterns of all regions for this sector. It should be noted that this assumption is much simpler than the gravity specification (5.16.9). Therefore, (5.17.7) is written in matrix notation as:

$$\begin{bmatrix} q_i^{11} & \cdots & q_i^{1R} \\ \vdots & & \vdots \\ q_i^{R1} & \cdots & q_i^{RR} \end{bmatrix} = \begin{bmatrix} t_i^{11} & \cdots & t_i^{1R} \\ \vdots & & \vdots \\ t_i^{R1} & \cdots & t_i^{RR} \end{bmatrix} \begin{bmatrix} q_i^{o1} & & \mathbf{O} \\ & \ddots & \\ \mathbf{O} & & q_i^{oR} \end{bmatrix} \qquad (5.17.8)$$

If one defines the output of region $r$ as:

$$q_i^{ro} = \sum_{r'=1}^{R} q_i^{rr'} \qquad (5.17.9)$$

system (5.17.8) can be written as:

$$\begin{bmatrix} q_i^{1o} \\ \vdots \\ q_i^{Ro} \end{bmatrix} = \begin{bmatrix} t_i^{11} & \cdots & t_i^{1R} \\ \vdots & & \vdots \\ t_i^{R1} & \cdots & t_i^{RR} \end{bmatrix} \begin{bmatrix} q_i^{o1} \\ \vdots \\ q_i^{oR} \end{bmatrix} \qquad (5.17.10)$$

or, in compact matrix notation:

$$\mathbf{q}_i = \mathbf{T}_i \, \mathbf{q}_i^o \tag{5.17.11}$$

where $\mathbf{q}_i$ and $\mathbf{q}_i^o$ are the respective vectors of output and demand in sector $i$. Combining (5.17.11) for each sector $i$ gives:

$$\begin{bmatrix} \mathbf{q}_1 \\ \hline \vdots \\ \hline \mathbf{q}_I \end{bmatrix} = \begin{bmatrix} \mathbf{T}_1 & & \mathbf{O} \\ & \ddots & \\ \mathbf{O} & & \mathbf{T}_I \end{bmatrix} \begin{bmatrix} \mathbf{q}_1^o \\ \hline \vdots \\ \hline \mathbf{q}_I^o \end{bmatrix} \tag{5.17.12}$$

The main ordering of (5.17.12) is according to sectors $i(i = 1, \ldots, I)$, while the main ordering of (5.17.6) is according to regions $r(r = 1, \ldots, R)$. System (5.17.12) can be reordered according to regions by means of a permutation matrix. Such a permutation matrix reorders the output vector of (5.17.12) in such a way, that the first element of this vector is equal to $q_1^{1o}$, the second one to $q_2^{1o}$ (instead of $q_1^{2o}$), the third to $q_3^{1o}$ (instead of $q_1^{3o}$), etc. In this way the output vector of (5.17.12) obtains a structure similar to the output vector in (5.17.6). When this permutation has been carried out, system (5.17.12) is written in compact matrix notation as:

$$\mathbf{q} = \mathbf{T} \, \mathbf{q}^o \tag{5.17.13}$$

Substitution of (5.17.6) into (5.17.13) gives:

$$\mathbf{q} = \mathbf{T} \, \mathbf{A} \, \mathbf{q} + \mathbf{T} \, \mathbf{f} \tag{5.17.14}$$

or:

$$\mathbf{q} = (\mathbf{I} - \mathbf{TA})^{-1} \, \mathbf{T} \, \mathbf{f} \tag{5.17.15}$$

provided $\mathbf{I} - \mathbf{TA}$ is nonsingular. Therefore, once the coefficient matrices $\mathbf{T}$ and $\mathbf{A}$ have been estimated in a certain base year, they can be used to estimate the entire interregional production pattern in other periods. An empirical application of the foregoing analysis is contained in Moses (1955).

Finally, if one should possess more observations, one could make a distinction in the trade pattern between intermediate and final commodities for instance, by means of a successive matrix of trade coefficients $\mathbf{T}_1$ and $\mathbf{T}_2$. Then one would obtain instead of (5.17.14):

$$q = T_1 \, Aq + T_2 \, f \tag{5.17.16}$$

or:

$$q = (I - T_1 A)^{-1} \, T_2 \, f \tag{5.17.17}$$

It is obvious that the implementation of the latter model requires a lot of information. Moreover, like the previous models, it is essentially demand-oriented, whereas multiregional attraction (or generalized: profile) analysis introduces also supply elements and other locational factors (cf. Paelinck [1973]).

## 5.18 Pollution and I–O analysis

Environmental deterioration in the form of air pollution, water pollution and soil pollution appears to become an ever-increasing problem for industrialized and urbanized areas. The control of this environmental pollution deserves the full-scale attention of scientists and planners. In order to maintain a desired level of environmental and ecological conditions and to reduce the emission of pollutants into men's physical environment, a more detailed knowledge concerning the pollution phenomena is indispensable. In this section an attempt is made at constructing an interregional model, which embodies the various kinds of pollution. This model may be helpful to obtain a full understanding as to what pollutant discharges are to be expected in the various regions of a country, since it provides an operational framework for waste management and environmental pollution control. A more detailed presentation of such a model and its possibilities for application are contained in Nijkamp and Paelinck (1973).

The approach adopted here concentrates on a country consisting of a set of regions. The regional distinction is assumed to be based on a set of relevant characteristics (for instance, population density, production structure). The regions of such a spatial system are interlinked in various ways (for instance, interregional product flows, transportation networks, interregional migration flows and interregional dispersion of pollution). In the model presented here major attention is paid to interregional pollution effects.

These interregional pollution effects can be analyzed in a way which bears a close resemblance to the regional and interregional production effects set out in the previous sections. The discharges into the atmosphere of an industry in a certain region are not limited to the region itself, but will often exceed the regional boundaries. Therefore, surrounding regions will endure the external diseconomies of a polluting industry settled in a certain region. The degree to which surrounding regions suffer from the pollution effects of such a region depends on the size of the region, the direction of wind and its average speed, and other physical and climatological conditions. In general, the pollution is at a maximum near the source and declines with the distance from this source. In principle, however, one may construct a *dispersion matrix* for each region, which indicates for each pollutant what percentage of its emission remains on the average within the region and what percentage of its emission is on the average dispersed to all other regions. The pollutants themselves can be distinguished, for instance, into carbon monoxide, nitrogen oxide, etc. The typical element of such a dispersion matrix for region $r$ is designated by $h_k^{rr'}$; it represents the proportion of pollutant $k$ ($k = 1, \ldots, K$) originating from region $r$ and ending up in region $r'$ ($r, r' = 1, \ldots, R$). The dispersion matrix of region $r$ is represented by:

$\mathbf{H}^r =$

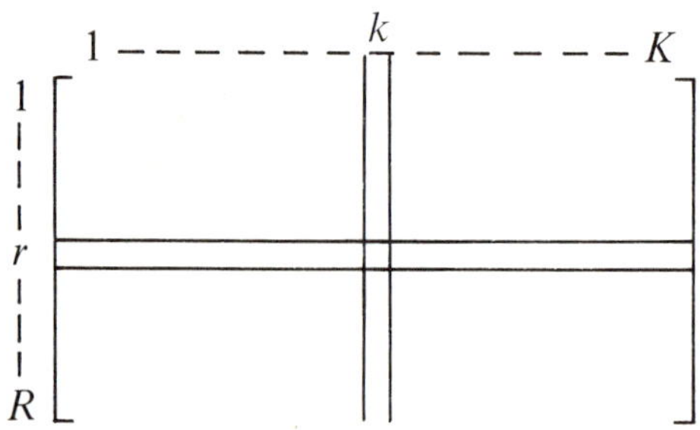


(5.18.1)

Column $k$ of $\mathbf{H}^r$ represents a spatial picture of pollutant $k$, originating in region $r$ and divided over all other regions. Row $r$ of $\mathbf{H}^r$ represents the 'internal' pollution of region $r$, while row $r'$ ($r' \neq r$) represents the 'external' pollution of region $r$, viz. in region $r'$. It is obvious, that row $r$ of $\mathbf{H}^r$ will possess, in general, elements with high percentages, since most pollution remains within the region itself. For each region $r$ one may create such a spatial dispersion matrix of environmental pollution. The construction of these dispersion matrices and the estimation of the dispersion coefficients require an adequate knowledge concerning technological production processes and of physical environmental conditions.

Next, the dispersion coefficients can be related to the levels of the various pollutants. The element $t_k^r$ is defined as the amount of pollutant $k$, which originates from productive activities in region $r$. In this way one may construct a regional pollution vector $\mathbf{t}^r$ of order $K \times 1$. Now one may write the following relationship:

$$d_k^{rr'} = h_k^{rr'} \cdot t_k^r \qquad (5.18.2)$$

where $d_k^{rr'}$ represents the average amount of pollutant $k$ present in region $r'$ in consequence of productive activities in region $r$. In matrix notation, (5.18.2) can be written as:

$$\mathbf{D}^r = \mathbf{H}^r \, \hat{\mathbf{t}}^r \qquad (5.18.3)$$

where $\hat{\mathbf{t}}^r$ is a diagonal matrix with diagonal elements $t_k^r$. Furthermore, it is easily seen that $\sum_{r=1}^{R} d_k^{rr'}$ represents the total ('internal' and 'external') pollution in region $r'$ resulting from pollutant $k$ from all regions (including region $r'$). In a similar way one may add up all matrices $\mathbf{D}^r$. If one defines:

$$\mathbf{D} = \sum_{r=1}^{R} \mathbf{H}^r \, \hat{\mathbf{t}}^r = \sum_{r=1}^{R} \mathbf{D}^r \qquad (5.18.4)$$

**D** represents a pollution picture of a country, observed in the regions where the pollutants end up.

Next, the various pollutants can be related to the regional production levels of each sector. This requires an extension of the classical I–O analysis by assuming a linear relationship between the level of production per sector and the various levels of resulting pollutants. This idea was first proposed by Leontief (1970). In this way production and pollution can be linked up with 'pollution I–O' coefficients. The 'pollution I–O' matrix of region $r$ is denoted by $\mathbf{B}^r$ with typical elements $b_{ki}^r$ $(k = 1, \ldots, K; i = 1, \ldots, I)$. This element $b_{ki}^r$ represents the volume of emission of pollutant $k$, if activity $i$ in region $r$ works at a unit level. If one defines a vector $\mathbf{q}^r$ of order $I \times 1$ as a vector of regional production levels, one can relate the pollution in region $r$ to the production in region $r$ as follows (see also section 6.7.2).

$$\mathbf{t}^r = \mathbf{B}^r \, \mathbf{q}^r \qquad (5.18.5)$$

System (5.18.5) permits the calculation of the total volume of emission of pollutants in region $r$, if the production takes place at a given level. Such a system can again be created for each region. By writing (5.18.5) as a diagonal matrix, i.e.

$$\hat{\mathbf{t}}^r = (\widehat{\mathbf{B}^r \, \mathbf{q}^r}) \,, \qquad (5.18.6)$$

one may substitute (5.18.6) into (5.18.4):

$$\mathbf{D} = \sum_{r=1}^{R} \mathbf{H}^r \, (\widehat{\mathbf{B}^r \, \mathbf{q}^r})$$

The latter system permits the calculation of the dispersion of pollutants over all regions, given the production levels in the regional system. Such a detailed knowledge is a necessary condition for pollution control. Finally, it should be noted that in a similar way as described above the pollution of final demand and transportation can be analyzed.

## 5.19 A planning model for activities in an industrial complex

### 5.19.1 *Introduction*

This section can be conceived of as a linkage between the I–O analysis of Ch.5 and the programming approach in Ch.6. It presents a formal framework for interrelated activities within an industrial complex, as well as a planning strategy for building up such a complex.

As has already been mentioned, the classical I–O analysis does not consider explicitly the external economies between interlinked activities, which are located at the same place. A first attempt at taking account of demand and supply influences has been undertaken in the attraction theory (section 5.12). In this section the external economies resulting from agglomeration advantages will be considered as a pivot element in the activities of an industrial complex. These agglomeration effects are responsible for the spatial juxtaposition of economic activities (or the so-called *polarization phenomena*). The notion of a polarization has led to the well-known *growth pole* idea in regional economics. A growth pole is a set of activities which are able to transmit growth impulses to all sectors of an economy. Such a transmission may occur by means of I–O relations with other sectors. Contribution to growth pole analysis can be found *inter alia* in Darwent (1969), Hansen (1972) and Kuklinski and Petrella (1972). The growth pole idea is now a current concept in regional economics and regional planning. Particularly in struggling or developing areas the concept of a growth pole is a useful tool in order to set in motion a process of accelerated regional development. If such a regional development is aimed at by means of industrialization programmes, an industrial complex is the obvious means for a rapid regional growth.

An *industrial complex* is a set of industrial activities located at a certain place, while these activities possess a high degree of mutual economic and technological linkages. Examples of industrial complex programmes can be found, *inter alia*, in the region of Mezzogiorno (Italy), Konin (Poland) and Puerto Rico.

More particularly, each industrial complex has the following characteristic features:

(a) The existence of *interindustrial relations* owing to mutual deliveries. These relations can be most adequately described in terms of input–output analysis. If $q_i$ is the production volume of activity $i$ ($i = 1, \ldots, I$) and $q_{i'i}$ the volume of intermediate deliveries from activity $i'$ ($i' = 1, \ldots, I$; $i' \neq i$) to activity $i$, the following relationship will exist between activity $i$ and $i'$:

$$q_{i'i} = a_{i'i} q_i \qquad (5.19.1.1)$$

where $a_{i'i}$ is the input–output coefficient between activity $i$ and $i'$;
(b) The existence of *internal scale advantages* for each separate activity. These can be described in a simple way by means of the technological (or engineering) functions discussed in section 5.8; and
(c) The existence of *agglomeration advantages* between the various members of the industrial complex. It will be assumed here, that the decline in transportation and communication costs (in a broad sense) between the members of the complex leads to a decline in the unit costs of intermediate deliveries. This decline in intermediate costs is assumed to be more important, as the production level of the supplier of the intermediaries rises (see Paelinck [1972]). Therefore, if the original price of intermediate deliveries from activity $i'$ to $i$ is denoted by $p_{i'}$, and if the new (varying) price of intermediate deliveries is denoted by $p_{i'}^*$, one may represent the situation with agglomeration advantages between activity $i$ and $i'$ in the following figure:

Fig. 5.19.1.a

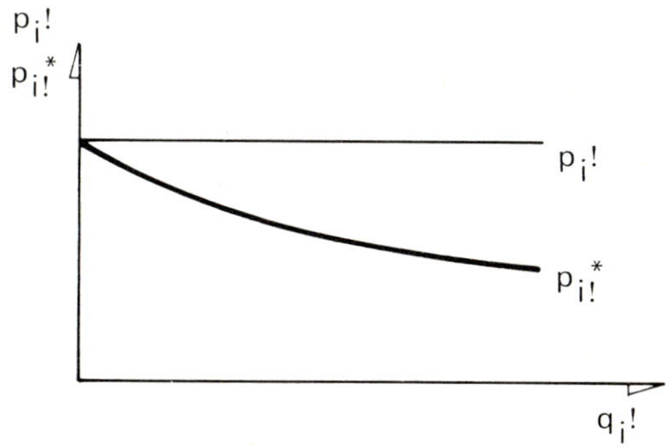


Figure 5.19.1.a corresponds to decreasing marginal costs in the transportation and communication sector. In mathematical terms, one may represent the situation sketched in figure 5.19.1.a by means of the following relationship:

$$p^*_{i'} = p_{i'} q_{i'}^{-a_{i'i}} \qquad (5.19.1.2)$$

where $a_{i'i}$ indicates the degree of agglomeration advantages between member $i'$ and $i$. The parameter $a_{i'i}$ is assumed to be zero, if there are no interindustrial linkages or external economies between activity $i$ and $i'$.

The elements discussed previously should be present (implicitly or explicitly) in industrial complex analysis. This section uses the previous ideas in order to find an optimal strategy of planning the various activities of a certain industrial complex. It will be assumed that a decision maker (for instance, policy maker or planning board) has taken a decision in favour of a certain given industrial complex (for example, a chemical complex). Then the question arises as to how to include the various activities in this complex in an optimal sequential manner within the planning horizon. This question consists of two parts: in the first place, one should determine which activities should be included during the various periods of the planning horizon (i.e. the *discrete* or *integer* problem); in the second place, one should determine an optimal production level of the activities, once they are included in the complex (i.e. the *continuous* problem). These questions are rather intricate, since they are closely linked together. The optimal production level of a given activity depends on the presence or absence of complementary activities, owing to the externalities between the members of the complex (see [5.19.1.2]). On the other hand, the optimal successive building up of the complex depends on the production volume of the individual activities. The purpose of this section is to disentangle this rather complicated problem. In the following sections a simplified approach is presented for an optimal industrial complex policy. This planning model concentrates on an optimal time schedule for the activities of the complex. In addition to this planning strategy a method is proposed for solving extensive non-linear models.

### 5.19.2 *The planning model*

The notion of optimal planning (related to time, production volume, or sequential strategies) needs a criterion by means of which decisions or solutions can be evaluated. In this section a very simple criterion will be assumed, viz. minimization of the investment costs during each stage of the planning process. Alternative strategies (for instance, minimization of total production costs, maximization of total production value and maximization of total income resulting from the activities of the complex) will not be dealt with here, but are contained in Nijkamp (1972). Therefore, the objective to be handled is:

$$\min \phi = \sum_{i=1}^{I} p_i^c \, I_i \tag{5.19.2.1}$$

where $p_i^c$ represents the price index of investments $I_i$ of activity *i*.

In addition to this objective function a set of constraints has to be specified. Based on the assumption of a mixed economy-setting, it is supposed that each member of the complex must fix its production volume at such a level, that at least a desired level of profitability on investments is attained. If the wage rate, the rate of depreciation and profit rate of activity *i* is denoted by $w_i$, $\rho_i$ and $\pi_i$, respectively, the profitability condition of activity *i* will be represented as:

$$p_i q_i - \sum_{\substack{i'=1 \\ i' \neq i}}^{I} p_{i'}^* q_{i'i} - w_i L_i - \rho_i p_i^c I_i \geqslant \pi_i p_i^c I_i \quad \forall_i \tag{5.19.2.2}$$

Substitution of (5.19.1.1), (5.19.1.2), (5.8.1) and (5.8.2) into (5.19.2.2) produces the following result:

$$p_i q_i - \sum_{\substack{i'=1 \\ i' \neq i}}^{I} p_{i'} q_{i'}^{-a_{i'i}} a_{i'i} q_i - w_i L_{io} q_{io}^{-\beta_i} q_i^{\beta_i} - (\rho_i + \pi_i) p_i^c I_{io} q_{io}^{-a_i} q_i^{a_i} \geqslant 0 \tag{5.19.2.3}$$

This profitability condition should be satisfied for each activity, once it is set in operation. It can be seen from (5.19.2.3), that owing to the internal scale advantages a higher production level has a better change of satisfying the profitability condition. Furthermore, owing to the agglomeration advantages a firm with high interindustrial linkages has a better chance of satisfying the profitability requirements.

The previous remarks imply that the production level which satisfies the profitability conditions depends both on *internalities* (i.e. internal scale advantages) and on *externalities* (i.e. mutual agglomeration advantages). A systematic comparison of internalities and externalities is facilitated by creating an *internality–externality matrix* (I–E matrix) **M**. The typical elements of **M** are denoted by $m_{i'i}$. If $i' = i$, the (diagonal) element $m_{ii}$ will represent the internal scale advantage of activity *i*. In other words, $m_{ii}$ is defined as:

$$m_{ii} = p_i q_i - \sum_{\substack{i'=1 \\ i' \neq i}}^{I} p_{i'} a_{i'i} q_i - w_i L_{io} q_{io}^{-\beta_i} q_i^{\beta_i} - \rho_i p_i^c I_{io} q_{io}^{-a_i} q_i^{a_i} \tag{5.19.2.4}$$

If $i' \neq i$, the (off-diagonal) element $m_{i'i}$ will represent the rise in profits of activity $i$ owing to the agglomeration advantages with respect to activity $i'$. Therefore, $m_{i'i}$ is defined as:

$$m_{i'i} = p_{i'} a_{i'i} q_i \left(1 - q_{i'}^{-a_{i'i}}\right) \qquad (5.19.2.5)$$

In this way one may construct a complete I–E matrix for the industrial complex concerned. The $i^{\text{th}}$ column of this matrix represents the various components of the profit of activity $i$, viz. internal scale profits (if $i' = i$) and external agglomeration profits ($i' \neq i$). The I–E matrix is represented in (5.19.2.6).

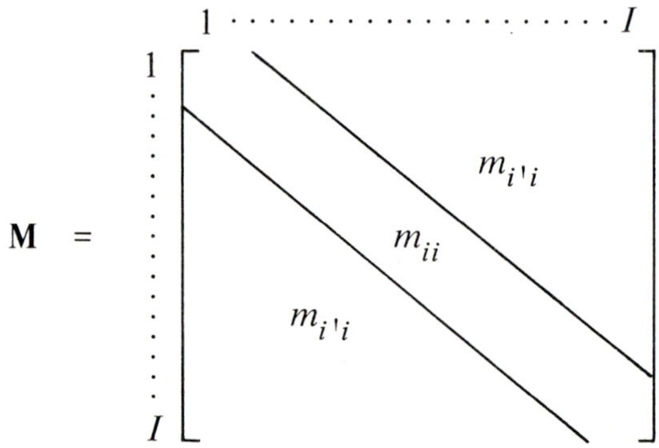


(5.19.2.6)

However, the elements of the I–E matrix discussed so far were still undetermined, since the optimal scale of production had not yet been determined. In addition to this continuous problem the integer problem (i.e. the intertemporal selection of candidate-activities) has still to be solved. The solution procedure of the integer problem is given in section 5.19.3, while section 5.19.4 is devoted to the solution of the continuous problem.

### 5.19.3 *The integer problem*

The problem as to which activities should be included in each stage of the planning process gives rise to enormous combinatorial possibilities. For instance, one might start with activity 1 or activity 2 or both activities, etc. If the number of activities is equal to $I$, the total number of combinatorial possibilities will be:

$$\sum_{i=1}^{I} \binom{I}{i} = 2^I - 1 \qquad (5.19.3.1)$$

For each combination of activities one should calculate the continuous programme and determine the minimum value of the objective function. Then the minimum minimorum of all these $2^I - 1$ combinations of activities is the first-period solution of the investment program. It is evident that a normal-sized industrial complex (20 to 50 activities) gives rise to insuperable computational problems. For that reason some heuristic methods have to be applied (for instance, based on the branch-and-bound principle) in order to truncate the combinatorial problem to a manageable one. Before indicating how the original master problem can be decomposed into a manageable subset of individual continuous problems, the continuous investment planning model is represented for the sake of clarity (where the objective function results from [5.19.2.1] and [5.8.1]).

$$\left.\begin{array}{ll}\min \phi = \sum_{i=1}^{I} \gamma_i q_i^{a_i} & \\ \text{s.t.} & \\ p_i q_i - \sum_{\substack{i'=1 \\ i' \neq i}}^{I} \bar{a}_{i'i} q_{i'}^{-a_{i'i}} q_i - \delta_i q_i^{\beta_i} - \epsilon_i q_i^{a_i} \geqslant 0 & \forall_i \\ q_i \geqslant q_{io} & \forall_i \end{array}\right\} \quad (5.19.3.2)$$

where the parameters $\gamma_i$, $\bar{a}_{i'i}$, $\delta_i$ and $\epsilon_i$ are defined as:

$$\left.\begin{array}{l}\gamma_i = p_i^c I_{io} q_{io}^{-a_i} \\ \bar{a}_{i'i} = p_{i'} a_{i'i} \\ \delta_i = w_i L_{io} q_{io}^{-\beta_i} \\ \epsilon_i = (\rho_i + \pi_i)\, p_i^c I_{io} q_{io}^{-a_i}\end{array}\right\} \quad (5.19.3.3)$$

The program as formulated in (5.19.3.2) is not an intertemporal planning program, since the specification of (5.19.3.2) implies that all activities are simultaneously selected. Therefore, one should impose the condition that not all activities should be included in the first period (i.e. for some activities $i : q_i = 0$), but that at least one activity should be selected.

The way in which this selection procedure can be attacked is based on a systematic comparison of an optimal first-order program (i.e., the minimum investment program of all activities separately) with a set of relevant higher-order programs (i.e., programs including more firms).

Therefore, one starts with the determination of an optimal first-order program. This minimum investment program is, in fact, the solution of (5.19.3.2) for each individual activity (i.e., without external linkages). The most simple method of solving all $I$ individual programs is to start by checking whether $q_{io}$ satisfies the profitability conditions of each separate activity. The reason is that $q_{io}$ is the minimum technical production volume of activity $i$; the production level cannot decline below $q_{io}$. Therefore, if there were no profitability conditions for activity $i$, the investment level $I_{io}$ would yield minimum investment costs. Hence, if $q_{io}$ satisfies the profitability condition, the minimum investment costs of activity $i$ will be $p_i^c I_{io}$. However, if $q_{io}$ does not satisfy the profitability requirements, the production level should be increased in order to guarantee the minimum profit desired. This means that one should determine which production level $q_i$ ($q_i > q_{io}$) satisfies the profit conditions exactly. This could be done by solving the geometric program (see section 5.19.4) associated with activity $i$, but a more straightforward manner in this individual case is to calculate $q_i$ on the basis of a Newton-Raphson procedure[9] for solving nonlinear relationships. If the latter solution is denoted by $q_i^o$, the minimum investment costs of activity $i$ are $\gamma_i(q_i^o)^{a_i}$. Therefore, the minimum investment costs of activity $i$ in a first-order program are either $p_i^c I_{io}$ or $\gamma_i(q_i^o)^{a_i}$. A similar procedure can be followed for each individual activity $i$. The minimum value of all these $I$ minimum investment costs is the optimal solution of a first-order program for the first period. It will be denoted by $\phi(1)$.

However, there is no guarantee that a second-order program (including two firms simultaneously) will yield higher investment costs, since the externalities between firms lead to a decrease in investment costs. For that reason second- and higher-order firms must also be considered. However, the optimal first-order solution can now be used to truncate the combinatorial possibilities, since no single higher-order program may yield higher investment costs than the optimal first-order program.

Consequently, one can again use a systematic inspection of second- and higher-order programs. For instance, if one considers firm 1 and 2 with respective minimum technical production levels $q_{1o}$ and $q_{2o}$, one inspects whether $p_i^c I_{1o} + p_2^c I_{2o}$ exceeds the optimal first-order investment costs $\phi(1)$. If $p_1^c I_{1o} + p_2^c I_{2o} \geqslant \phi(1)$, the activities 1 and 2 will produce higher investment costs than the minimum first-order program, as a result of which activity 1 and 2 (as well as higher-order combinations of activity 1 and 2) can be excluded from further inspection. If $p_1^c I_{1o} + p_2^c I_{2o} \leqslant \phi(1)$, activity 1 and 2 may be considered for a further inspection. Then one has to solve the mathematical program including activity 1 and 2 (see section 5.19.4). Only if this solution gives lower investment costs than $\phi(1)$, activity 1 and

2 may be relevant activities for a first-period program. In a similar way all other second-order programs can be dealt with. Once the optimal second-order solution has been obtained, one may use the minimum value of the first- and second-order program as a similar truncation criterion for $k^{\text{th}}$-order programs ($k > 2$). In this way the original master problem can be truncated to a subset of manageable programs.

If an optimal first-period set of activities is selected, the remaining activities can be dealt with in a similar way during the second period by assuming that the first-period solution has already been realized. Higher-period solutions can be obtained in a similar sequential way, until the set of candidate-investors is completely exhausted. In this way an optimal intertemporal building up of industrial complexes can be attained (see figure 5.19.3.a).

Fig. 5.19.3.a

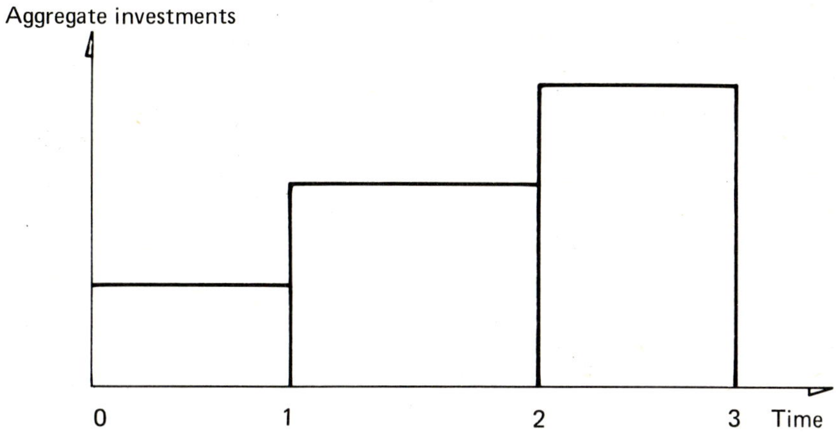


It should be noted that according to (5.19.2.5) the individual profits rise, according as more activities are included in the industrial complex. The program presented so far is of an elementary nature, but it can easily be extended by including market conditions, labour conditions or capital conditions. Examples of alternative constraints, and of alternative objective functions are contained in Nijkamp (1972).

### 5.19.4 *The continuous problem*

Each series of steps of the integer problem described in section 5.19.3 requires the solution of the continuous program (5.19.3.2). It will be shown that this program can be formulated as a geometric program, for which an efficient solution algorithm has recently been developed. The details of this solution algorithm can be found in Nijkamp (1972). The continuous program (5.19.3.2) can be reformulated as:

$$\left.\begin{aligned} &\min \phi = \sum_{i=1}^{I} \gamma_i \, q_i^{a_i} \\ &\text{s.t.} \\ &\sum_{\substack{i'=1 \\ i' \neq i}}^{I} a^*_{i'i} \, q_{i'}^{-a_{i'i}} + \delta^*_{i} q_i^{\beta_i - 1} + \epsilon^*_i q_i^{a_i - 1} \leqslant 1 \quad \forall i \\ &q_{io} q_i^{-1} \leqslant 1 \qquad\qquad \forall i \end{aligned}\right\} \qquad (5.19.4.1)$$

where the coefficients $a^*_{i'i}$, $\delta^*_i$ and $\epsilon^*_i$ are defined as $\bar{a}_{i'i}\bar{p}_i^{-1}$, $\delta_i p_i^{-1}$ and $\epsilon_i p_i^{-1}$, respectively. This program satisfies the standard formulation of a geometric program, as presented in (5C.1) of Appendix 5C. Once the previous program concerning industrial complexes has been formulated as a geometric program, it can be solved by means of a constrained gradient algorithm. Therefore, we may conclude that geometric programming allows one to deal with an extensive class of nonlinear programming problems. It can be considered as an appropriate instrument in modern regional planning and policy making.

It appears from the foregoing planning model that programming is an indispensable instrument in modern regional economics. Therefore, the next chapter is devoted to a more thorough analysis of programming methods in regional economics.

## Appendix 5A The solution of the RAS equations

As set out in section 5.6, the solution of the RAS equations requires the solution of system (5.6.10) and (5.6.11), viz.,

$$\hat{\mathbf{r}}\,\mathbf{A}\,\hat{\mathbf{s}}\,\mathbf{q} = \mathbf{u} \qquad (5A.1)$$

and:

$$\hat{\mathbf{q}}\,\hat{\mathbf{s}}\,\mathbf{A}'\mathbf{r} = \mathbf{y} \qquad (5A.2)$$

A tractable method of solving the previous system is an iterative method.

This implies that one attempts to approximate the solution in a series of successive steps.

The first step to be undertaken is to concentrate on **r** and to delete **s**, so that one obtains instead of (5A.1):

$$\hat{\mathbf{r}}\,\mathbf{A}\,\mathbf{q} = \mathbf{u} \tag{5A.3}$$

from which one can easily solve the vector from the first step, $\mathbf{r}_1$, as:

$$\mathbf{r}_1 = (\widehat{\mathbf{A}\,\mathbf{q}})^{-1}\,\mathbf{u} \tag{5A.4}$$

However, the previous operation implies, that the vertical balance is disturbed. Therefore, an adaptation is required by means of the matrix $\hat{\mathbf{s}}$. Then one obtains (cf. [5A.2]):

$$\hat{\mathbf{q}}\,\hat{\mathbf{s}}\,\mathbf{A}'\mathbf{r}_1 = \mathbf{y} \tag{5A.5}$$

Relationship (5A.5) permits the calculation of the vector from the first step in vertical direction, $\mathbf{s}_1$, in terms of the known elements $\hat{\mathbf{q}}$, **A** and $\mathbf{r}_1$. This results in:

$$\mathbf{s}_1 = (\widehat{\mathbf{A}'\mathbf{r}_1})^{-1}\,\hat{\mathbf{q}}^{-1}\,\mathbf{y} \tag{5A.6}$$

It is obvious, however, that now the horizontal balance is disturbed. Therefore, the first step, $\mathbf{r}_1$, should again be adapted, so that one obtains a second step, $\mathbf{r}_2$, on the basis of the following relationship (cf. [5A.1] and [5A.3]):

$$\hat{\mathbf{r}}_2\,\hat{\mathbf{r}}_1\,\mathbf{A}\,\hat{\mathbf{s}}_1\,\mathbf{q} = \mathbf{u} \tag{5A.7}$$

from which $\mathbf{r}_2$ can easily be calculated.

The vertical balance requires also an adaptation by means of a second step, $\mathbf{s}_2$, so that one obtains (cf. [5A.2] and [5A.5]):

$$\hat{\mathbf{q}}\,\hat{\mathbf{s}}_2\,\hat{\mathbf{s}}_1\,\mathbf{A}'\hat{\mathbf{r}}_1\,\mathbf{r}_2 = \mathbf{y} \tag{5A.8}$$

By repeating this procedure, one may obtain under certain conditions a converging solution of $\hat{\mathbf{r}}$ and $\hat{\mathbf{s}}$, where $\hat{\mathbf{r}}$ and $\hat{\mathbf{s}}$ are defined, respectively, as:

$$\begin{aligned}\hat{\mathbf{r}} &= \hat{\mathbf{r}}_N\,\hat{\mathbf{r}}_{N-1}\,\ldots\ldots\ldots\,\hat{\mathbf{r}}_2\,\hat{\mathbf{r}}_1\\ &= \prod_{n=1}^{N}\hat{\mathbf{r}}_n\end{aligned} \tag{5A.9}$$

and:

$$\hat{\mathbf{s}} = \prod_{n=1}^{N}\hat{\mathbf{s}}_n \tag{5A.10}$$

and where $N$ is the total number of iterations. The final steps of $\hat{\mathbf{r}}_n$ and $\hat{\mathbf{s}}_n$

should converge towards the unit matrix. Some properties of this RAS-procedure (particularly, the convergence and uniqueness) are discussed by Bacharach (1965).

A numerical example of the RAS-method is worked out here on the basis of an I–O matrix derived from Isard (1960). This matrix is in the basis year equal to:

$$\mathbf{A} = \begin{bmatrix} 0{\cdot}083 & 0{\cdot}125 & 0{\cdot}111 \\ 0{\cdot}333 & 0{\cdot}250 & 0{\cdot}222 \\ 0{\cdot}167 & 0{\cdot}125 & 0{\cdot}278 \end{bmatrix} \tag{5A.11}$$

Suppose the following data are available in the basis year:

$$\mathbf{q} = \begin{bmatrix} 12 \\ 24 \\ 18 \end{bmatrix} ; \mathbf{v} = \begin{bmatrix} 5 \\ 12 \\ 7 \end{bmatrix} ; \mathbf{f} = \begin{bmatrix} 6 \\ 10 \\ 8 \end{bmatrix} \tag{5A.12}$$

It should be noted that the sum of the value added components (**v**) should be equal to the sum of the final demand components (**f**). Next, some periods later the following observations are assumed to be available:

$$\mathbf{q} = \begin{bmatrix} 13{\cdot}2 \\ 26{\cdot}1 \\ 20{\cdot}0 \end{bmatrix} ; \mathbf{v} = \begin{bmatrix} 7{\cdot}0 \\ 16{\cdot}4 \\ 11{\cdot}9 \end{bmatrix} ; \mathbf{f} = \begin{bmatrix} 7{\cdot}7 \\ 14{\cdot}2 \\ 13{\cdot}4 \end{bmatrix} \tag{5A.13}$$

By means of (5.6.6) and (5.6.7) one can easily calculate the vectors **u** and **y**:

$$\mathbf{u} = \begin{bmatrix} 5{\cdot}5 \\ 11{\cdot}9 \\ 6{\cdot}6 \end{bmatrix} ; \mathbf{y} = \begin{bmatrix} 6{\cdot}2 \\ 9{\cdot}7 \\ 8{\cdot}1 \end{bmatrix} \tag{5A.14}$$

By means of the procedure set out above the following successive steps of the RAS iteration procedure were obtained:

$$\hat{\mathbf{r}}_1 \ \mathbf{A} \ \hat{\mathbf{s}}_1 = \begin{bmatrix} 0{\cdot}076 & 0{\cdot}104 & 0{\cdot}087 \\ 0{\cdot}284 & 0{\cdot}193 & 0{\cdot}162 \\ 0{\cdot}110 & 0{\cdot}075 & 0{\cdot}156 \end{bmatrix} \tag{5A.15}$$

$$\hat{\mathbf{r}}_2 \ \hat{\mathbf{r}}_1 \ \mathbf{A} \ \hat{\mathbf{s}}_1 \ \hat{\mathbf{s}}_2 = \begin{bmatrix} 0{\cdot}077 & 0{\cdot}105 & 0{\cdot}087 \\ 0{\cdot}281 & 0{\cdot}191 & 0{\cdot}160 \\ 0{\cdot}111 & 0{\cdot}075 & 0{\cdot}158 \end{bmatrix} \tag{5A.16}$$

while further steps gave a more accurate approximation, which was beyond the degree of precision required here. Since $\hat{\mathbf{r}}_2$ and $\hat{\mathbf{s}}_2$ converge towards the unit matrix, a converging solution for the new I–O matrix is obtained, so that the new I–O matrix **A*** may be approximated by means of:

$$\mathbf{A}^* = \hat{\mathbf{r}}_2 \, \hat{\mathbf{r}}_1 \, \mathbf{A} \, \hat{\mathbf{s}}_1 \, \hat{\mathbf{s}}_2 \qquad (5A.17)$$

## Appendix 5B The structure of matrices

The elements of a matrix may have any arbitrary value. Frequently, one or more elements of a matrix are equal to zero. If it is possible to rank the zero-elements of a matrix in a special pattern, the matrix may possess certain important properties. For instance, if all elements of a matrix are equal to zero except the elements on the main diagonal, one obtains a diagonal matrix. If the coefficient matrix **B** in (5.10.20) would be diagonal, all endogenous variables could be solved separately, since then each endogenous variable is only determined by the exogenous terms. In a similar way a triangular matrix gives rise to certain specific properties.

The occurrence of *(block-)diagonality* and *(block-)triangularity* can be analyzed by means of the concept of *(in)decomposability.* A solution matrix **B** (see [5.10.20]) is said to be decomposable, if one may obtain a *triangular* or *diagonal* matrix by means of a permutation of its rows and columns. A *weak decomposability* gives rise to a *triangular* matrix, whereas a *strong decomposability* gives rise to a *diagonal* matrix. The decomposability may be related both to elements and blocks of a matrix. Therefore, one may obtain the following systematic scheme:

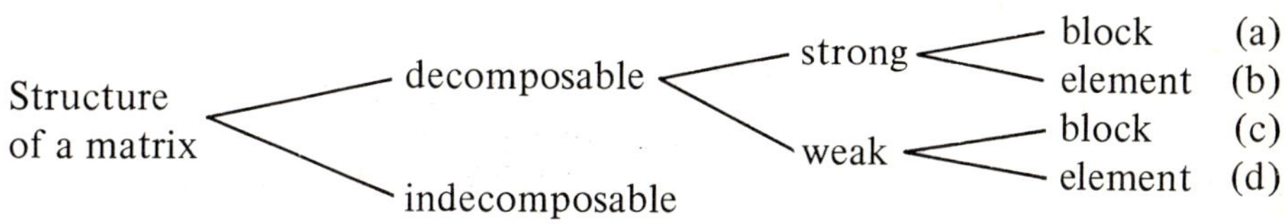


The various situations of decomposability are represented in figure 5B.a–d, respectively. The non-shaded parts of these matrices represent zero-elements.

Fig. 5B.a A block-diagonal matrix

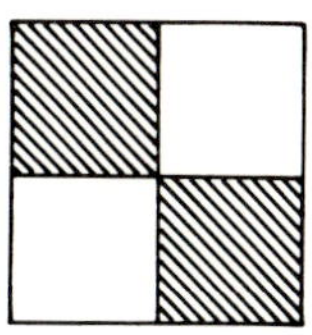

Fig. 5B.b A diagonal matrix

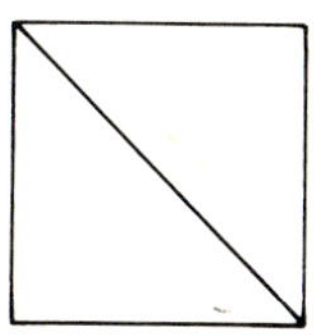

Fig. 5B.c A block-triangular matrix

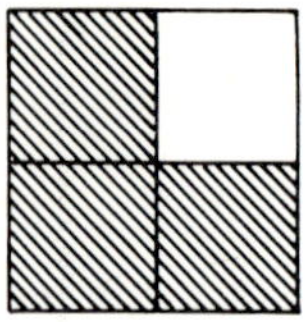

Fig. 5B.d A triangular matrix

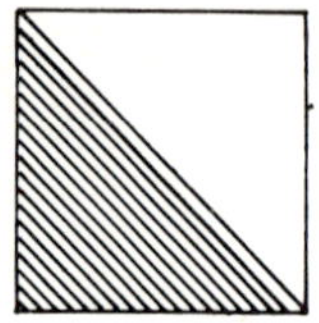

Figure 5B.a shows that this solution matrix can be divided into 2 separate blocks each of which can be handled independently. Each block itself represents an interdependent system. For instance, in a block-diagonal I–O matrix each block might represent a certain interwoven industrial complex of allied activities.

Figure 5B.b is a diagonal matrix, each element of which can be dealt with in a separate way.

Figure 5B.c shows a block-triangular structure. Such a system can be solved in a *block-recursive* way, i.e. once the system related to the first block has been solved, the next systems can be solved on the basis of the solution of this first block. A model is said to be *recursive*, if there exists an ordering of the endogenous variables and an ordering of the equations such that the $i^{th}$ equation can be considered to describe the determination of the value of the $i^{th}$ endogenous variable during period $t$ as a function of the predetermined variables and of the endogenous variables of index less than $i$. A model is *interdependent*, if it is not recursive; see Malinvaud (1968) and Wold (1954). A *block-recursive* system of equations can be solved by means of a recursive causal chain of blocks.

Figure 5B.d is a triangular matrix. Once the first variable has been determined, the second one can be determined on the basis of the first variable, and so forth according to a recursive chain.

A matrix is *indecomposable,* if it is not decomposable. A check on the (in)decomposability of matrices can be carried out by means of the following theorem (see Kuenne [1963]):

A necessary and sufficient condition for indecomposability of a normalized matrix is that a *chain* of non-zero coefficients from that matrix can be formed such that *all* column and row indices of the matrix occur at least once (diagonal elements being excluded), and that the order of the chain (i.e., the number of elements) is equal to or larger than the order of the matrix. This chain of elements $b_{ij}$ from a matrix $B$ consists of elements which are linked together as follows:

$$b_{ij} \rightarrow b_{jk} \rightarrow b_{kl} \rightarrow \dots \qquad (5B.1)$$

In general, there is no systematic method of finding such a chain, so that this method is mostly based on a trial-and-error-procedure. The indecomposability can be illustrated by means of the square left upper matrix of order 7 in (5.10.19), since on the basis of this matrix the following chain can be created:

$$b_{26} \rightarrow b_{61} \rightarrow b_{13} \rightarrow b_{37} \rightarrow b_{72} \rightarrow b_{24} \rightarrow b_{47} \rightarrow b_{71} \rightarrow b_{15} \rightarrow b_{52} \tag{5B.2}$$

The latter result proves that the matrix concerned is indecomposable, so that this matrix cannot be simplified by means of triangularization or diagonalization.

## Appendix 5C Geometric programming

Geometric programming is a recently developed method of handling a broad class of nonlinear programming problems (see Duffin et al. [1967]). It is useful for programming problems written as posynomials, i.e. positive sums of multiplicative power functions. The standard format is:

$$\left.\begin{array}{l}
\min \phi = c_{01}\, x_1^{a_{11}^{o}}\, x_2^{a_{12}^{o}} \ldots . x_I^{a_{1I}^{o}} + c_{02}\, x_1^{a_{21}^{o}}\, x_2^{a_{22}^{o}} \ldots . x_I^{a_{2I}^{o}} + \ldots . \\
\text{s.t.} \\
c_{11} x_1^{a_{11}^{1}}\, x_2^{a_{12}^{1}} \ldots . x_I^{a_{1I}^{1}} + c_{12}\, x_1^{a_{21}^{1}}\, x_2^{a_{22}^{1}} \ldots . + \ldots .. \leqslant 1 \\
\cdot \\
\cdot \\
\cdot \\
c_{K1}\, x_1^{a_{11}^{K}}\, x_2^{a_{12}^{K}} \ldots . x_I^{a_{1I}^{K}} + c_{K2}\, x_1^{a_{21}^{K}}\, x_2^{a_{22}^{K}} \ldots .. + \ldots . \leqslant 1 \\
x_i \geqslant 0 \quad (i = 1, \ldots, I)
\end{array}\right\} \tag{5C.1}$$

The coefficients of this program are denoted by $c_{kj}(k = 0, 1, \ldots K;$ $j = 1, \ldots, J)$, i.e. the coefficient in the $j^{\text{th}}$ term of the $k^{\text{th}}$ side-condition ($K = 0$, means the objective function itself). These coefficients are assumed to be positive (hence the name 'posynomials'). The exponent $a_{ji}^{k}$ denotes the exponent in the $j^{\text{th}}$ term of the $k^{\text{th}}$ side-condition related to the $i^{\text{th}}$ variable $(i = 1, \ldots, I)$.

The previous (primal) geometric program is difficult to solve, but it has a dual formulation which is more manageable. On denoting the dual variables by $y_{kj}$ the dual program reads as:

$$
\left.\begin{array}{l}
\max \tau = \left(\dfrac{c_{01}}{y_{01}}\right)^{y_{01}} \left(\dfrac{c_{02}}{y_{02}}\right)^{y_{02}} \ldots \times \left(\dfrac{c_{11}}{y_{11}}\right)^{y_{11}} \left(\dfrac{c_{12}}{y_{12}}\right)^{y_{12}} \ldots \times \left(\dfrac{c_{K1}}{y_{K1}}\right)^{y_{K1}} \left(\dfrac{c_{K2}}{y_{K2}}\right)^{y_{K2}} \\
\quad \times (y_{11} + y_{12} + \ldots)^{y_{11} + y_{12} + \ldots} \ldots \times (y_{K1} + y_{K2} + \ldots)^{y_{K1} + y_{K2} \ldots} \\
\text{s.t.} \\
y_{01} + y_{02} + \ldots y_{0J} = 1 \\
a_{11}^{0} y_{01} + a_{21}^{0} y_{02} + \ldots + a_{11}^{1} y_{11} + a_{21}^{1} y_{12} + \ldots + a_{11}^{K} y_{K1} + a_{21}^{K} y_{K2} + \ldots = 0 \\
\cdot \\
\cdot \\
\cdot \\
a_{1I}^{0} y_{01} + a_{2I}^{0} y_{02} + \ldots + a_{1I}^{1} y_{11} + a_{2I}^{1} y_{12} + \ldots + a_{1I}^{K} y_{K1} + a_{2I}^{K} y_{K2} + \ldots = 0 \\
y_{kj} \geqslant 0
\end{array}\right\} \tag{5C.2}
$$

The dual program is more tractable owing to the linear equality restrictions. Since the primal and dual programs are related to each other by means of primal-dual relationships, one needs to solve only the dual program in order to find the primal solution. The solution of the dual geometric program and the identification of active or inactive primal constraints make use of a constrained gradient method, which is a particular kind of a so-called hill-climbing method (see Nijkamp [1972]). It should be mentioned that the dual formulation (in a logarithmic form) bears a close resemblance to a generalized entropy expression (see section 6.4.5; see also Nijkamp and Paelinck [1974a, 1974b]).

**Notes**

1 Table 5.2.a is sometimes called a BIG SAM (Social Accounting Matrix), since it comprises a big table with all interindustrial deliveries. If table 5.2.a is consolidated such, that the table with intermediate deliveries is reduced to single elements, it is called a BABY SAM; see Stone (1962).

2 The expansion can be verified by premultiplying (5.3.15) by the matrix **I**–**A**.

3 If one assumes a fixed relationship between the *stock* of capital and the *level* of output, one will have a constant *average* capital-output ratio (or capital coefficient).

4 The latter S-shaped curve is often called a Lorenz-curve. It is a very

usual representation of regional growth phenomena (for instance, the growth of cities).

[5] Structural changes in an I–O matrix in consequence of the entrance of new industrial sectors are frequently denoted by *polarization* effects (see section 5.19).

[6] The matrix multiplier $(\mathbf{I} - \hat{\boldsymbol{\lambda}}\mathbf{A}^r - \Lambda)^{-1}$ has the same working as the Leontief multiplier $(\mathbf{I} - \mathbf{A})^{-1}$, albeit that in attraction theory convergence is not guaranteed *a priori* (the eigenvalues of $\hat{\boldsymbol{\lambda}}\mathbf{A}^r + \Lambda$ are not necessarily smaller than 1).

[7] The vectors $\mathbf{f}^A$ and $\mathbf{f}^B$ are composed of *intraregional* final demand plus exports of final products.

[8] One might also assume a negative exponential relationship for the distance relationship, in which case (5.15.2) would pass into $q_{rr'} = a_r e^{-\beta_r d_{rr'}} q_{r.}$ (where $\beta_r$ is a friction coefficient of distance).

[9] A Newton-Raphson procedure is a mathematical method of solving non-linear equations; see, for instance, Saaty and Bram (1964).

## References


Aidenoff, A., 'Input–Output Data in the United Nations System of National Accounts', in: A. Bródy and A.P. Carter (eds.), *Applications of Input–Output Analysis*, North-Holland Publishing Co., Amsterdam 1970 pp. 349–368.

Bacharach, M., 'Estimating Nonnegative Matrices from Marginal Data', *International Economic Review*, vol. 6, no. 3, 1965, pp. 294–310.

Bowers, J., *The Anatomy of Regional Activity Rates*, Cambridge University Press, London 1970.

Bródy, A. and Carter, A.P. (eds.), *Applications of Input–Output Analysis*, North-Holland Publishing Co., Amsterdam 1970a.

Bródy, A. and Carter, A.P. (eds.), *Contributions to Input–Output Analysis*, North-Holland Publishing Co., Amsterdam 1970b.

Bródy, A. and Carter, A.P. (eds.), *Input–Output Techniques*, North-Holland Publishing Co., Amsterdam 1972.

Bureau de la Statistique du Québec, *Le Système de Comptabilité Economique du Québec*, Université Laval (Laboratoire d'Econométrie), 1967.

Cahen, L. and Ponsard, C., *La Répartition Fonctionnelle de la Population des Villes et son Utilisation pour la Détermination des Multiplicateurs d'Emploi*, Ministère de la Construction, Paris 1973 (2 vol.)

Chenery, H.B., 'Overcapacity and the Acceleration Principle', *Econometrica,* vol. 20, 1952, pp. 1–28.
Chenery, H.B. and Clark, M.G., *Interindustry Economics,* Wiley, New York 1959.
Cordey-Hayes, M. and Wilson, A.G., 'Spatial Interaction', *Socio-Economic Planning Sciences,* vol. 5, 1971, pp. 73–95.
Crowther, D. and Echenique, M., 'Development of a Model of Urban Spatial Structure', in: L. Martin and L. March (eds.), *Urban Space and Structures,* Cambridge University Press, Cambridge 1972, pp. 175–218.
Czamanski, S., *Regional Science Techniques in Practice; The Case of Nova Scotia*, Heath, Lexington 1972.
Czamanski, S., *Regional and Interregional Social Accounting,* Heath, Lexington, 1973.
Darwent, D.F., 'Growth Poles and Growth Centers in Regional Planning; a Review', *Environment and Planning,* vol. 1, no. 1, 1969, pp. 5–31.
De Meester de Ravestein, J.C., *Une Fonction de Production Technique Néoclassique,* Ceruna, University of Namur, Namur 1970.
Duffin, R.J., Peterson, E.L. and Zener, C.J., *Geometric Programming,* Wiley, New York 1967.
Gigantes, T., 'The Representation of Technology in Input–Output Systems', in: A Bródy and A.P. Carter (eds.), *Contributions to Input–Output Analysis,* North-Holland Publishing Co., Amsterdam 1970, p. 270–290.
Gilbert, J.D., *Elements of Linear Algebra,* International Textbook Company Scranton, Pennsylvania 1970.
Hansen, N.M. (ed.), *Growth Centers in Regional Development Policy*, Free Press, Glencoe, Illinois, 1972.
Isard, W., *Methods of Regional Analysis: An introduction to Regional Science,* MIT Press, Cambridge 1960.
Isard, W., Schooler, E.W. and Vietorisz, T., *Industrial Complex Analysis and Regional Development: A Case Study of Refinery–Petrochemical–Synthetic Fiber Complexes and Puerto Rico,* MIT Press, Cambridge 1959.
Klaassen, L.H., *Methods of Selecting Industries for Depressed Areas,* OECD, Paris, 1967.
Klaassen, L.H., 'Growth Poles in Economic Theory and Policy', in: A. Kuklinski and R. Petrella (eds.), *Growth Poles and Regional Policies,* Mouton, The Hague, 1972.
Klaassen, L.H., 'Some Further Considerations on Attraction Analysis', *Foundations of Empirical Economic Research,* Netherlands Economic Institute, Rotterdam (mimeo) 1974.

Klaassen, L.H. and Paelinck, J.H.P., 'Uncovering Regional Growth Potentials from an Input–Output Table', *Foundations of Empirical Economic Research*, Netherlands Economic Institute, Rotterdam (mimeo) 1974.

Klaassen, L.H. and Van Wickeren, A.C., 'Interindustry Relations: An Attraction Model', in H.C. Bos (ed.), *Towards Balanced International Growth* (essays presented to J. Tinbergen), North-Holland Publishing Co., Amsterdam 1969.

Kornai, J. (with T. Liptak and P. Wellish), *Mathematical Planning of Structural Decisions,* North-Holland Publishing Co., Amsterdam 1967.

Koyck, L.M., *Distributed Lags and Investment Analysis,* North-Holland Publishing Co., Amsterdam 1954.

Kuenne, R.E., *The Theory of General Economic Equilibrium,* Princeton University Press 1963.

Kuklinski, A. and Petrella, R. (eds.), *Growth Poles and Regional Policies,* Mouton, The Hague, 1972.

Leontief, W., *The Structure of American Economy,* 1919–1939, Oxford University Press, New York 1951.

Leontief, W., *Studies in the Structure of the American Economy,* Oxford University Press, New York 1953.

Leontief, W., *Input–Output Economics,* Oxford University Press, New York 1966.

Leontief, W., 'Environmental Repercussions and the Economic Structure: An Input–Output Approach', *Review of Economics and Statistics,* vol. 52, 1970, pp. 262–271.

Leontief, W. and Strout, A., 'Multiregional Input–Output Analysis', in: W. Leontief (ed.), *Input–Output Economics,* Oxford University Press, New York, 1966, pp. 223–257.

Lowry, I., *Model of Metropolis,* Report No. RM-4125-RC, Rand Corporation, Santa Monica 1964.

Malinvaud, E., *Statistical Methods of Econometrics,* North-Holland Publishing Co., Amsterdam 1968.

Manne, A.S. and Vietorisz, T., 'Chemical Processes, Plant Location and Economies of Scale', in: A.S. Manne and H.M. Markowitz (eds.), *Studies in Process Analysis,* Wiley, New York 1963, pp. 136–158.

Matuszewski, T.I., Pitts, R.R., and Sawyer, J.R., 'Linear Programming Estimates of Changes in Input Coefficients', *The Canadian Journal of Economics and Political Science,* vol. 30, no. 2, 1964, pp. 203–210.

Meyer, J. and Kuh, E., *The Investment Decision,* Harvard University Press, Cambridge 1957.

Miernyk, W.H., *Elements of Input–Output Analysis,* Random House, New York 1966.

Moses, L.N., 'The Stability of Interregional Trading Patterns and Input–Output Analysis', *The American Economic Review,* vol. 45, no. 5, 1955, pp. 803–832.

Nijkamp P., *Planning of Industrial Complexes by Means of Geometric Programming,* Rotterdam University Press, Rotterdam 1972.

Nijkamp P. and Paelinck, J.H.P., 'An Interregional Model of Environmental Choice', *Papers of the Regional Science Association,* vol. 31, 1973, pp. 51–72.

Nijkamp P., and Paelinck, J.H.P., 'Some Methods for Updating Input–Output Tables', *Foundations of Empirical Economic Research,* Netherlands Economic Institute Rotterdam (mimeographed) 1974.

Nijkamp, P., and Paelinck, J.H.P., 'Geometric Programming and Entropy Maximizing Models', *Bulletin de Statistique, Recherche Opérationnelle et Informatique,* nr. 2, 1974a.

Nijkamp, P., and Paelinck, J.H.P., 'A Dual Interpretation and Generalization of Entropy Models in Regional Science', *Papers of the Regional Science Association,* vol. 33, 1974b, pp. 13–31.

Nikaido, H., *Introduction to Sets and Mappings in Modern Economics,* North-Holland Publishing Co., Amsterdam, 1970.

Paelinck, J.H.P., 'De Quelques Aspects Opératoires dans l'Usage de Techniques d'Entrée et de Sortie au Niveau Régional et Interrégional', *Revue Juridique et Economique du Sud-Ouest,* Série Economique, no. 1, 1970, pp. 1–11.

Paelinck, J.H.P., 'Programming a Viable Minimal Investment Industrial Complex for a Growth Center', in: N.M. Hansen (ed.), *Growth Centers in Regional Development Policy,* Free Press, Glencoe, Illinois, 1972, pp. 139–159.

Paelinck, J.H.P., 'Models for Multiregional Economic Policy Based on Attraction Analysis', *Foundations of Empirical Economic Research,* Netherlands Economic Institute, Rotterdam, (mimeo) 1973.

Polenske, K.R., 'Empirical Implementation of a Multiregional Input–Output Gravity Trade Model', in: A. Bródy and A.P. Carter (eds.), *Contributions to Input–Output Analysis.* North-Holland Publishing Co., Amsterdam 1970, pp. 143–163.

Rasmussen, P.N.,*Studies in Inter-sectoral Relations,* North-Holland Publishing Co. Amsterdam 1956.

Richardson, H.W., *Input–Output and Regional Economics,* Weidenfeld & Nicolson, London 1972.

Saaty, T.L. and Bram, J., *Nonlinear Mathematics,* McGraw–Hill, New York 1964.

Stone, J.R.S., *Input–Output and National Accounts,* OECD, Paris 1961.
Stone, J.R.S. (ed.), *A Social Accounting Matrix for 1960* (Series: A Programme for Growth), Chapman and Hall, London 1962.
Stone, J.R.S. (ed.), *Input–Output Relationships, 1954–1966* (Series: A Programme for Growth), Chapman and Hall, London 1963.
Tilanus, C.B., *Input–Output Experiments: The Netherlands 1948–1961,* Rotterdam University Press, Rotterdam 1965.
Tinbergen, J. and Bos, H.C., *Mathematical Models of Economic Growth,* North-Holland Publishing Co., Amsterdam 1962.
Van Straelen, R.A., 'Polarisatiestructuren en de Groei van een Grootstad', *Economisch en Sociaal Tijdschrift,* nr. 1 en 2, 1965, pp. 3–20.
Van Wickeren, A.C., *Interindustry Relations; Some Attraction Models,* Ph.D., Netherlands School of Economics, Rotterdam 1971.
Victor, P.A., *Economics of Pollution,* MacMillan, London 1972.
Wilson, A.G., *Urban and Regional Models in Geography and Planning,* Wiley, New York 1974.
Wold, H., 'Causality and Econometrics', *Econometrica,* vol. 22, 1954, pp. 162–177.

# 6 Regional and Multiregional Programming

## 6.1 Introduction

This chapter is devoted to theoretical foundations and regional applications of mathematical programming techniques. After a short treatment of general mathematical programming the theory of linear programming will be dealt with more thoroughly. Then some illustrative examples and ultimately an extensive set of spatial economic applications will be presented. The purpose of this chapter is to stress the importance of efficiency criteria (for instance, cost minimization) in problems concerning the spatial dispersion of economic activities.

## 6.2 Theory of mathematical programming

### 6.2.1 *Introduction*

Generally speaking, economic problems can be conceived of as *optimization problems:* in mathematical terms this statement can be translated as determining an optimum (maximum, minimum, minimax) of a certain objective function (for instance, utility function, cost function, social welfare function, etc.). In general, however, pure optimization is seldom relevant, since in most economic problems a number of constraints (equalities and/or inequalities) have to be taken into account. This is frequently due to the fact that economics deals with scarce resources, which act as a constraint in an optimization procedure.

Once an economic problem has been formulated as a constrained optimization problem, the question arises as to how to solve such an optimization problem. Therefore, the following successive stages must be considered: the specification of an *objective function,* the formulation of *all relevant constraints,* and the determination of a *solution procedure.*

*Mathematical programming* (for instance, linear programming, quadratic programming, stochastic programming, geometric programming) is a general optimization method, which can be used both in constrained and unconstrained optimization problems. Mathematical programming can be described in the following general and formal way:

$$\min_{x \in K} \omega = f(\mathbf{x}) \qquad (6.2.1.1)$$

where $K = \{\mathbf{x} | \mathbf{x} \in R^J, g_i(\mathbf{x}) \leqslant 0, i = 1, ..., I\}$. Function $f(\mathbf{x})$ is a scalar-valued *objective function* (with a vector of arguments $\mathbf{x}$), which has to be minimized with respect to the vector $\mathbf{x}$ over a feasible region $K$. If $f(\mathbf{x})$ would have to be maximized, one should invert the sign of $f(\mathbf{x})$. $K$ can be conceived of as the set of all relevant constraints $g_i(\mathbf{x})$ on $\mathbf{x}$. The condition $\mathbf{x} \epsilon R^J$ means that $\mathbf{x}$ is a vector of order $J$ in $J$–dimensional Euclidean space. In a sufficiently large neighbourhood around the optimal point $\mathbf{x}^O$, the function $f(\mathbf{x})$ is assumed to be *continuous* and *single-valued.* If $f(\mathbf{x}^O) < f(\mathbf{x})$, $\mathbf{x}^O$ is called a *strong* minimum; otherwise, if $f(\mathbf{x}^O) \leqslant f(\mathbf{x})$, $\mathbf{x}^O$ is called a *weak* minimum. A minimization problem can, therefore, also be formulated as: determine $\mathbf{x}^O \epsilon K$, such that $f(\mathbf{x}^O) \leqslant f(\mathbf{x})$ for any $\mathbf{x} \epsilon (K \cap E)$, where $E$ is a neighbourhood of $\mathbf{x}^O$.

The constraints $g_i(\mathbf{x})$ of an optimization problem should be *consistent,* i.e. the intersection of all constraints should not produce the null space; in other words: $\bigcap_{i=1}^{I} g_i(\mathbf{x}) \neq \phi$. A constraint $i$ is *binding* (*effective,* or *active*) with respect to $\mathbf{x}^O$, if $\mathbf{x}^O$ lies on the boundary line of the constraint; in other words, if $g_i(\mathbf{x}^O) = 0$. In general, one requires that the feasible set $K$ is *convex*. This means in a two-dimensional case, that any straight line between two points of $K$ should also belong to $K$. A more *formal* definition of a convex *set* is: A set $K$ is convex over a number of relevant points, if for any pair of $J$–dimensional points $(P_1, P_2)$ belonging to $K$, the following condition is satisfied:

$$\lambda P_1 + (1 - \lambda) P_2 \epsilon K, \qquad 0 \leqslant \lambda \leqslant 1 \qquad (6.2.1.2)$$

Convexity of *sets* can be distinguished from convexity of *functions.* A function in a two-dimensional space is convex, if any straight line between two points of that function lies entirely above the function (or coincides with it). Convexity of *functions* is in a more formal way defined as follows: A function $f(\mathbf{x})$ is convex over a relevant range of $\mathbf{x}$, if for any pair of points $(\mathbf{x}_1, \mathbf{x}_2)$ the following condition is satisfied:

$$f\{\lambda \mathbf{x}_1 + (1 - \lambda)\mathbf{x}_2\} \leqslant \lambda f(\mathbf{x}_1) + (1 - \lambda) f(\mathbf{x}_2), \quad 0 \leqslant \lambda \leqslant 1 \qquad (6.2.1.3)$$

Concavity is defined as the inverse case. If $f(\mathbf{x})$ is a convex function defined on a convex set $K$, then any *local* minimum can be proved to be an *absolute* minimum. This can be demonstrated in the following way. Suppose $f(\mathbf{x})$ possesses an absolute minimum in the feasible point $\mathbf{x}^*$ and a local minimum in the feasible point $\mathbf{x}^O$. If $f(\mathbf{x})$ is a convex function, the following condition is valid according to (6.2.1.3):

$$f\left(\lambda x^* + (1-\lambda)x^o\right) \leqslant \lambda f(x^*) + (1-\lambda) f(x^o), 0 \leqslant \lambda \leqslant 1 \quad (6.2.1.4)$$

Since $f(x^*)$ is an absolute minimum and $f(x^o)$ a local minimum, it is evident that:

$$f(x^*) < f(x^o) \quad (6.2.1.5)$$

Relationship (6.2.1.5) can be rewritten as:

$$\lambda f(x^*) + (1-\lambda) f(x^o) < f(x^o) \quad (6.2.1.6)$$

By combining (6.2.1.4) and (6.2.1.6) one finds:

$$f\left(\lambda x^* + (1-\lambda)\, x^o\right) < f(x^o) \quad (6.2.1.7)$$

or:

$$f(x) < f(x^o) \quad (6.2.1.8)$$

in which x represents an arbitrary point between $x^*$ and $x^o$, viz. the following linear combination of $x^*$ and $x^o$:

$$x = \lambda x^* + (1-\lambda)\, x^o \quad (6.2.1.9)$$

Since $f(x)$ is defined on a convex set $K$, one may locate x at an infinitely small distance from $x^o$. If this is the case, (6.2.1.8) states that a point very near the local minimum $x^o$ leads to a lower value of the function. This contradiction can be solved only if $x^o$ is not a local minimum unless $x^o$ coincides with $x^*$. This implies that under the given conditions any local minimum is an absolute minimum.

In a similar way one can show that any *local maximum* of $f(x)$ is an absolute maximum, if $f(x)$ is a *concave* function defined on a convex set.

The previous notions are extremely important in the theory of mathematical programming. For instance, linear programming is a method of finding an optimum of a linear objective function defined on a set of linear (in)equalities. A certain extreme point once selected is always an absolute minimum (maximum), since linear programming implies the minimization (maximization) of a convex (concave) function defined on a convex set. This can be proved by showing that a linear function is always convex, and that a set of linear inequalities is a convex set.

Suppose the following function:

$$f(x) = a' x \quad (6.2.1.10)$$

where a is a vector of known coefficients. By selecting two arbitrary points $x_1$ and $x_2$ and by applying condition (6.2.1.3) one finds:

$$\mathbf{a}'\left(\lambda \mathbf{x}_1 + (1 - \lambda)\, \mathbf{x}_2\right) = \lambda \mathbf{a}'\, \mathbf{x}_1 + (1 - \lambda)\, \mathbf{a}'\, \mathbf{x}_2 \qquad (6.2.1.11)$$

which demonstrates the convexity of a linear function. Suppose this function is minimized subject to the following set of linear inequalities:

$$\mathbf{A}\, \mathbf{x} \geqslant \mathbf{b} \qquad (6.2.1.12)$$

where **A** and **b** are a matrix and a vector of coefficients, respectively. If one selects again two arbitrary points $\mathbf{x}_1$ and $\mathbf{x}_2$, one obtains

$$\mathbf{A}\, \mathbf{x}_1 \geqslant \mathbf{b} \qquad (6.2.1.13)$$

and:

$$\mathbf{A}\, \mathbf{x}_2 \geqslant \mathbf{b} \qquad (6.2.1.14)$$

Next, by choosing an intermediate point $\mathbf{x}^*$ between $\mathbf{x}_1$ and $\mathbf{x}_2$, it is evident that $\mathbf{x}^*$ can be written as linear combination of $\mathbf{x}_1$ and $\mathbf{x}_2$, i.e.,

$$\mathbf{x}^* = \lambda \mathbf{x}_1 + (1 - \lambda)\, \mathbf{x}_2, \quad 0 \leqslant \lambda \leqslant 1 \qquad (6.2.1.15)$$

Premultiplication of (6.2.1.15) with the matrix **A**, and substitution of (6.2.1.13) and (6.2.1.14) yields:

$$\begin{aligned} \mathbf{A}\, \mathbf{x}^* &= \lambda\, \mathbf{A}\, \mathbf{x}_1 + (1 - \lambda)\, \mathbf{A}\, \mathbf{x}_2 \\ &\geqslant \lambda\, \mathbf{b} + (1 - \lambda)\, \mathbf{b} = \mathbf{b} \end{aligned} \qquad (6.2.1.16)$$

This implies that condition (6.2.1.2) is satisfied; any convex combination of two feasible points results again in a feasible point, which means that the entire feasible set is convex. In consequence, a local minimum of a linear programming problem is always an absolute minimum. It is easily seen that a linear objective function is also a *concave* function, so that a local maximum of a linear programming problem is always an absolute maximum.

A more detailed exposition of mathematical and, in particular, of linear programming is contained *inter alia* in Allen (1960), Baumol (1961), Dorfman et al. (1958), Gale (1960), Lancaster (1968), and Miller (1972). A condensed survey of programming problems is contained in a following section.

### 6.2.2 *A typology of programming problems*

Programming problems are concerned with the determination of optimal decisions. They can be of a different nature. In this section a typology of programming problems will be presented, which is based on the characteristics of constraints on programming models. The following classes will be dealt with, respectively: an *unconstrained* (or free) optimization, an optimization with *equality* constraints, an optimization with *non-negativity* constraints, and an optimization with *inequality* constraints.

A An unconstrained optimization

An unconstrained (or free) optimization implies the absence of constraints, so that the only problem to be solved is (in terms of a maximizing program):

$$\max \omega = f(\mathbf{x}) \tag{6.2.2.1}$$

where $\mathbf{x}$ is a vector of order $J$ with typical elements $\mathbf{x}_j$ ($j = 1, \ldots, J$).

This classical problem can, in general, be solved by equating to zero the first partial derivatives of $f(\mathbf{x})$ with respect to $\mathbf{x}_j$ (the so-called gradient). This yields the following set of first-order conditions:

$$\left.\begin{array}{l} \dfrac{\partial f(\mathbf{x})}{\partial x_1} = 0 \\ \vdots \\ \dfrac{\partial f(\mathbf{x})}{\partial x_J} = 0 \end{array}\right\} \tag{6.2.2.2}$$

The latter system of $J$ equations encompasses $J$ unknown variables $x_j$, and can in principle be solved, for instance, by means of Newton-Raphson methods (see Saaty and Bram [1964]). The optimum conditions (6.2.2.2) are necessary conditions. The solution should also satisfy the second-order conditions, i.e. concavity of the objective function $f(\mathbf{x})$.

B Optimization problems with equality constraints (Lagrange problems)

Many 'neoclassical' optimization problems (for instance, utility maximization subject to budget constraints) give rise to the following program:

$$\left.\begin{array}{l} \max \omega = f(\mathbf{x}) \\ \text{s.t.} \\ g_i(\mathbf{x}) = 0, \; i = 1, \ldots, I \end{array}\right\} \tag{6.2.2.3}$$

The condition has to be imposed that $I \leqslant J$, since otherwise the equality constraints $g_i(\mathbf{x}) = 0$ would lead to incompatibilities or redundancies ($I$ equations with $J$ variables).

The solution of this program requires the construction of the following Lagrangean function $L(\mathbf{x}, \boldsymbol{\lambda})$, where $\boldsymbol{\lambda}$ represents a vector of $I$ Lagrange multipliers $\lambda_i$ $(i = 1, \ldots, I)$:

$$L(\mathbf{x}, \boldsymbol{\lambda}) = f(\mathbf{x}) - \boldsymbol{\lambda}' g(\mathbf{x}) \qquad (6.2.2.4)$$

in which $g(\mathbf{x})$ represents a vector of $I$ elements $g_i(\mathbf{x})$. By putting the gradient of $L(\mathbf{x}, \boldsymbol{\lambda})$ with respect to $\mathbf{x}$ and $\boldsymbol{\lambda}$ equal to zero, a system of $J + I$ equations containing $J + I$ unknown variables ($\mathbf{x}$ and $\boldsymbol{\lambda}$) is obtained, from which the optimal value of the variables can be derived, supposed the second-order conditions are satisfied. The Lagrange multipliers have an extremely important interpretation, which can be demonstrated in the following way. Construct the total differential of $f(\mathbf{x})$:

$$\mathrm{d}f(\mathbf{x}) = \sum_{j=1}^{J} \frac{\partial f(\mathbf{x})}{\partial x_j} \mathrm{d}x_j \qquad (6.2.2.5)$$

The first-order condition of the Lagrangean function (6.2.2.4) is:

$$\frac{\partial L(\mathbf{x}, \boldsymbol{\lambda})}{\partial x_j} = \frac{\partial f(\mathbf{x})}{\partial x_j} - \sum_{i=1}^{I} \lambda_i \frac{\partial g_i(\mathbf{x})}{\partial x_j} = 0, \ \forall j \qquad (6.2.2.6)$$

or:

$$\frac{\partial f(\mathbf{x})}{\partial x_j} = \sum_{i=1}^{I} \lambda_i \frac{\partial g_i(\mathbf{x})}{\partial x_j} \qquad (6.2.2.7)$$

Substitution of (6.2.2.7) into (6.2.2.5) gives:

$$\mathrm{d}f(\mathbf{x}) = \sum_{j=1}^{J} \sum_{i=1}^{I} \lambda_i \frac{\partial g_i(\mathbf{x})}{\partial x_j} \mathrm{d}x_j \qquad (6.2.2.8)$$

Furthermore,

$$\mathrm{d}g_i(\mathbf{x}) = \sum_{j=1}^{J} \frac{\partial g_i(\mathbf{x})}{\partial x_j} \mathrm{d}x_j \qquad (6.2.2.9)$$

so that substitution of (6.2.2.9) into (6.2.2.8) gives:

$$\mathrm{d}f(\mathbf{x}) = \sum_{i=1}^{I} \lambda_i \mathrm{d}g_i(\mathbf{x}) \qquad (6.2.2.10)$$

If only *one* constraint $g_i(\mathbf{x})$ is supposed to undergo a small shift $\mathrm{d}g_i(\mathbf{x})$, there results:

$$df(\mathbf{x}) = \lambda_i dg_i(\mathbf{x}) \tag{6.2.2.11}$$

or, since this implies essentially a partial derivative:

$$\boxed{\frac{\partial f(\mathbf{x})}{\partial g_i(\mathbf{x})} = \lambda_i} \tag{6.2.2.12}$$

The importance of Lagrange multipliers leans on the fact that they indicate the *marginal shift in the value of the objective function on relaxing a corresponding constraint.* This marginality condition will turn out to be extremely important for the interpretation of dual ('shadow') variables and dual programs.

C Optimization problems with non-negativity constraints (Kuhn-Tucker problems)

If the feasible area of the decision variables $x_j$ ($j = 1, \ldots, J$) is limited to positive values of $x_j$, the following program (an extension of the previous one) has to be considered:

$$\left.\begin{array}{l} \max \omega = f(\mathbf{x}) \\ \text{s.t.} \\ g_i(\mathbf{x}) = 0, \; i = 1, \ldots, I \\ x_j \geqslant 0, \quad j = 1, \ldots, J \end{array}\right\} \tag{6.2.2.13}$$

In case of such a program the following (so-called Kuhn-Tucker) conditions for an optimal solution have to be satisfied (see, for instance, Lancaster [1968] and Miller [1972]):

$$\frac{\partial L(\mathbf{x}, \boldsymbol{\lambda})}{\partial x_j} = \frac{\partial f(\mathbf{x})}{\partial x_j} - \sum_{i=1}^{I} \lambda_i \frac{\partial g_i(\mathbf{x})}{\partial x_j} \leqslant 0, \; \forall j \tag{6.2.2.14}$$

and

$$\frac{\partial L(\mathbf{x}, \boldsymbol{\lambda})}{\partial x_j} x_j = 0, \; \forall j \tag{6.2.2.15}$$

The first condition is the classical Lagrangean condition, which is now not necessarily equal to zero. This expression may possess a negative value, depending on the fact whether one of the optimal values of $x_j$ ($j = 1, \ldots, J$) is equal to zero (in other words, whether the condition $x_j \geqslant 0$ is binding). The reason for this phenomenon is, that owing to the condition $x_j \geqslant 0$ a certain value of $x_j$, which is equal to zero, can only undergo a shift in a positive direction. If then the condition $\partial L(\mathbf{x},\boldsymbol{\lambda}) / \partial x_j > 0$ would be satisfied, the original zero-value of $x_j$ could not represent an optimum, because in this case it appeared to be possible to increase $L(\mathbf{x}, \boldsymbol{\lambda})$. On the other hand, small variations of $x_j$ in the negative direction are not permitted, so the condition $\partial L(\mathbf{x}, \boldsymbol{\lambda}) / \partial x_j < 0$ cannot be ruled out as non-optimal. If $x_j^o > 0$, then according to (6.2.2.15) the following condition is valid:

$$\frac{\partial L(\mathbf{x}, \boldsymbol{\lambda})}{\partial x_j} = 0 \qquad (6.2.2.16)$$

If $x_j^o = 0$, then $\partial L(\mathbf{x}, \boldsymbol{\lambda}) / \partial x_j$ is (analytically) negative, which implies:

$$\frac{\partial f(\mathbf{x})}{\partial x_j} - \sum_{i=1}^{I} \lambda_i \frac{\partial g_i(\mathbf{x})}{\partial x_j} < 0 \qquad (6.2.2.17)$$

D Optimization problems with inequality constraints

Many modern optimization problems do not only include equality and non-negativity constraints, but also inequality constraints. This gives rise to the following program:

$$\left.\begin{array}{l} \max \omega = f(\mathbf{x}) \\ \text{s.t.} \\ g_i(\mathbf{x}) \leqslant 0, i = 1, \ldots, I \\ x_j \geqslant 0, j = 1, \ldots, J \end{array}\right\} \qquad (6.2.2.18)$$

The solution of such a constrained optimization problem should satisfy the first-order conditions (6.2.2.14) and (6.2.2.15). However, owing to the inequality constraint $g_i(\mathbf{x})$, the following condition should be satisfied in addition to (6.2.2.14) and (6.2.2.15):

$$g_i(\mathbf{x})\lambda_i = 0, \quad \forall i \qquad (6.2.2.19)$$

This condition states that a positive Lagrange multiplier $\lambda_i$ implies an active constraint $g_i(\mathbf{x})$, while a negative value of the constraint $g_i(\mathbf{x})$ at the optimum requires that the corresponding Lagrange multiplier $\lambda_i$ is zero. It is evident, that the solution of this constrained optimization problem should satisfy the second-order conditions.

The optimal value of the objective function will be affected in the following way, if a certain constraint $g_i(\mathbf{x})$ undergoes a slight change (cf. Lancaster [1968]):

$$\frac{\partial f(\mathbf{x})}{\partial g_i(\mathbf{x})} = \lambda_i + \sum_{j=1}^{J} \left\{ \frac{\partial f(\mathbf{x})}{\partial x_j} - \sum_{i'=1}^{I} \lambda_{i'} \frac{\partial g_{i'}(\mathbf{x})}{\partial x_j} \right\} \frac{\partial x_j}{\partial g_i(\mathbf{x})} \qquad (6.2.2.20)$$

It is easily seen that the second term of (6.2.2.20), which contains the first-order Lagrangean expression (6.2.2.6) will be deleted, if all constraints $g_{i'}(\mathbf{x})$ are binding. In this case $\lambda_i$ has again the marginality interpretation, derived in (6.2.2.12).

In fact, the problems dealt with sub A, B and C, are particular types of the general mathematical program, specified in (6.2.2.18). This general mathematical programming problem can also be analyzed within the framework of the Lagrangean theory. On the basis of program (6.2.2.18) one can again construct a Lagrangean function, viz.

$$L(\mathbf{x}, \boldsymbol{\lambda}) = f(\mathbf{x}) - \boldsymbol{\lambda}'\mathbf{g}(\mathbf{x}) - \boldsymbol{\mu}'\mathbf{x} \qquad (6.2.2.21)$$

where $\boldsymbol{\mu}$ is a vector of $J$ Lagrange multipliers $\mu_j$, associated with the constraint $x_j \geqslant 0$. Then the following so-called 'Kuhn-Tucker-Lagrange' conditions should be satisfied at the optimum:

$$\frac{\partial L(\mathbf{x}, \boldsymbol{\lambda})}{\partial x_j} = \frac{\partial f(\mathbf{x})}{\partial x_j} - \sum_{i=1}^{I} \lambda_i \frac{\partial g_i(\mathbf{x})}{\partial x_j} - \mu_j \leqslant 0 \qquad (6.2.2.22)$$

The latter condition provided $J$ relationships in $2J + I$ unknown variables ($J$ $x_j$'s, $I$ $\lambda_i$'s and $J$ $\mu_j$'s). In order to arrive at a complete system of equations, the following so-called *slack-duality* conditions should be added:

$$g_i(\mathbf{x})\,\lambda_i = 0, \quad \forall\, i \qquad (6.2.2.23)$$

and:

$$x_j \mu_j = 0, \quad \forall\, j \qquad (6.2.2.24)$$

These slack-duality conditions state that a non-binding constraint $g_i(\mathbf{x})$ implies a zero-Lagrange multiplier $\lambda_i$. Analogously, a positive $x_j$ leads to a zero-Lagrange multiplier $\mu_j$.

A difficulty in all programming problems is to determine *which* constraints $g_i(\mathbf{x})$ are binding and *which* variables $x_j$ are zero at the optimum. There is, in general, no prior knowledge concerning the relative stringency of the constraints. The latter problem can be solved in various ways, for instance by using an iterative procedure (for example, a Simplex-technique) in order to determine in a systematic stepwise manner, which feasible solutions optimize the objective function; in other words, which solutions satisfy the Kuhn-Tucker (-Lagrange) optimality conditions. These Kuhn-Tucker (-Lagrange) conditions are valid for each programming problem, since the Kuhn-Tucker-Lagrange theory is an entirely general theory. Therefore, each solution should satisfy these conditions, whatever may be the way in which the solution is attained. In fact, looking for a solution is a *combinatorial* problem, where one has to find out which constraints are binding. Once this is known, the solution can be found by solving the corresponding system of first-order Lagrange equations.

The solution procedures for mathematical programming problems may be of a different nature. They will not be discussed here any further, since this would be beyond the scope of this book. A large number of solution algorithms is available at the moment (for instance, methods of feasible directions, gradient methods, cutting plane methods, Newton-Raphson methods, etc.). For certain classes of problems standard algorithms are available (for instance, for linear programming, quadratic programming, and geometric programming). The derivation of efficient algorithms is a rather time-consuming and technical activity. A survey of certain methods can be found *inter alia* in Miller (1972), Wilde and Beightler (1967), and Zangwill (1969). In a following sub-section only a few simple numerical examples will be presented in order to illustrate the necessity and usefulness of the Kuhn-Tucker (-Lagrange) theory.

### 6.2.3 *Some examples*

In this section two numerical examples will be dealt with in order to clarify the theory of mathematical programming.

Suppose a regional planning committee has disposable funds to an amount of 0·2 monetary units. This amount can be used for 2 items, viz. economic overhead capital (for instance, productive investments) and social overhead capital (for instance, schools and hospitals). The respective prices of economic overhead capital and social overhead capital are supposed to be 1 and 0·5. The planning committee is supposed to possess a quadratic preference function, which serves as a decision criterion for allocating the disposable funds over both items. The formal frame-work of such a decision problem could be represented as follows:

$$\left.\begin{array}{l} \max f(\mathbf{x}) = x_1 - \tfrac{1}{2}x_1^2 + x_2 - \tfrac{1}{2}x_2^2 \\ \text{s.t.} \\ x_1 + \tfrac{1}{2}x_2 = 0{\cdot}2 \\ x_1, x_2 \geqslant 0 \end{array}\right\} \qquad (6.2.3.1)$$

where $x_1$ and $x_2$ represent the volume of economic overhead capital and of social overhead capital, respectively. The most simple approach to this type of problems is a *relaxation* of the problem, viz. by solving the problem by means of the classical Lagrangean method without considering the non-negativity conditions. Once an optimal solution has been obtained, one can easily check whether the non-negativity conditions are satisfied.

The latter procedure is frequently applied in the classical theory of consumer behaviour. The neo-classical production theory and the theory of economic policy (cf. Theil [1964]) are, in general, attacked in a similar way. The relaxation of problem (6.2.3.1) yields the following Lagrangean function:

$$L = x_1 - \tfrac{1}{2}x_1^2 + x_2 - \tfrac{1}{2}x_2^2 - \lambda\,(x_1 + \tfrac{1}{2}x_2 - 0{\cdot}2) \qquad (6.2.3.2)$$

The first-order conditions for this maximization procedure are:

$$\left.\begin{aligned} \frac{\partial L}{\partial x_1} &= 1 - x_1 - \lambda = 0 \\ \frac{\partial L}{\partial x_2} &= 1 - x_2 - \tfrac{1}{2}\lambda = 0 \end{aligned}\right\} \qquad (6.2.3.3)$$

The solution of this system gives:

$$\left.\begin{aligned} x_1 &= -0{\cdot}04 \\ x_2 &= \phantom{-}0{\cdot}48 \end{aligned}\right\} \qquad (6.2.3.4)$$

These values imply that the non-negativity conditions are not satisfied. Therefore, (6.2.3.4) is *not* the optimal solution of program (6.2.3.1). This can also be demonstrated by means of figure 6.2.3.a.

Fig. 6.2.3.a A graphical representation of the optimization problem

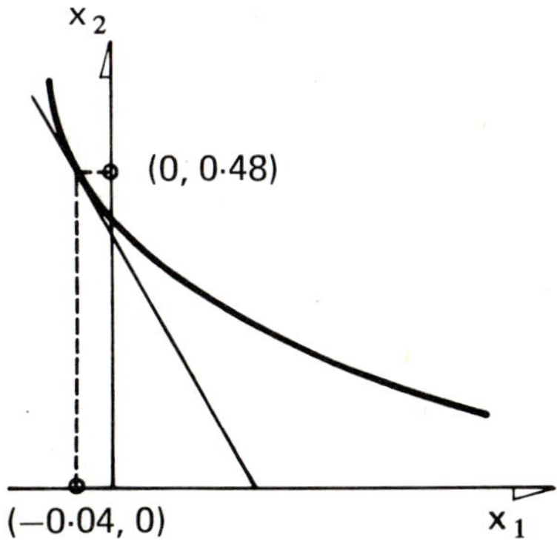


It is evident from figure 6.2.3.a, that the value of $x_1$ should be put equal to zero in order to satisfy simultaneously the non-negativity constraints. At this point one can easily check the Kuhn-Tucker-Lagrange conditions (6.2.2.22), (6.2.2.23) and (6.2.2.24). If $x_1 = 0$, then $\mu_1$ should be (analytically) non-zero; a positive value of $x_2$ implies that $\mu_2 = 0$. Therefore, one obtains:

$$\left.\begin{aligned} &\frac{\partial L}{\partial x_1} = 1 - \lambda - \mu_1 = 0 \\ &\frac{\partial L}{\partial x_2} = 1 - x_2 - ½\lambda = 0 \\ &½x_2 = 0{\cdot}2 \end{aligned}\right\} \qquad (6.2.3.5)$$

The solution of the latter system gives:

$$\left.\begin{aligned} x_2^0 &= 0{\cdot}4 \\ x_1^0 &= 0 \\ \lambda &= 1{\cdot}2 \\ \mu_1 &= -0{\cdot}2 \end{aligned}\right\} \qquad (6.2.3.6)$$

These results show that the Kuhn-Tucker-Lagrange conditions are satisfied, which means that an optimum solution has been attained. Apart from a relaxation of the problem, alternative tools for solving programs with linear equality constraints can be used, for instance a constrained gradient method (see Nijkamp [1972]).

## 6.3 Linear programming

### 6.3.1 *Introduction*

The use of L.P. models will first be illustrated by means of an example. Suppose a regional planning committee wants to implement two projects each of which has different unit costs. These projects are to be combined such that the total costs of these projects are minimized. Each of these projects requires two types of labour inputs (for instance, skilled and unskilled labour). In addition, the requirement is imposed that for each of these two categories of labour at least a certain predetermined level of employment has to be attained. Given these side-conditions the planning committee wants to determine an optimal mix of the expenditures spent on the first and second project.

The following data are available: one unit of the first project requires 1 unit of labour category 1 and 4 units of labour category 2, while one unit of the second project requires 2 units of labour category 1 and 3 units of labour category 2. The unit costs of project 1 and 2 are equal to 4 and 6, respectively. The minimum standards of labour category 1 and 2 are 4 and 10, respectively. Minimization of the joint costs of both projects results in the following objective function:

$$\min \omega = 4\,x_1 + 6\,x_2 \qquad (6.3.1.1)$$

in which $x_1$ and $x_2$ represent the volume of project 1 and 2, respectively. The constraints concerning the employment conditions can be specified as:

$$\left.\begin{aligned} x_1 + 2\,x_2 &\geqslant 4 \\ 4x_1 + 3\,x_2 &\geqslant 10 \end{aligned}\right\} \qquad (6.3.1.2)$$

Finally, the non-negativity conditions of $x_1$ and $x_2$ should also be imposed:

$$\left.\begin{aligned} x_1 &\geqslant 0 \\ x_2 &\geqslant 0 \end{aligned}\right\} \qquad (6.3.1.3)$$

The problem formulated above is a L.P. problem: the purpose is to find values of $x_1$ and $x_2$ resulting in a minimum value of $\omega$ subject to the constraints. This problem can easily be solved in a graphical way, as is shown in figure 6.3.1.a.

Fig. 6.3.1.a The solution space of a L.P. model

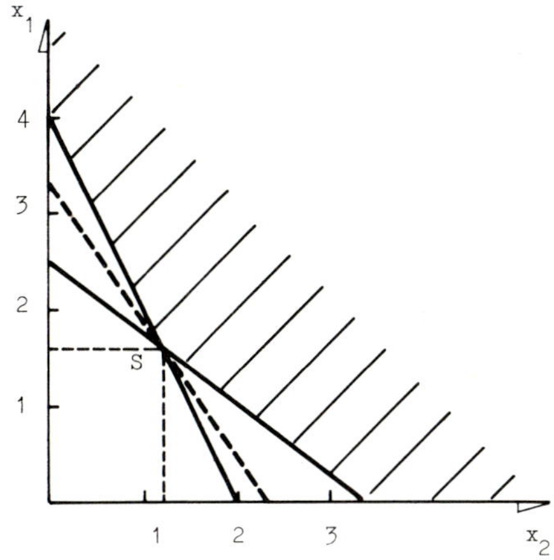


The shaded area represents the set of all points in which all constraints are satisfied simultaneously. The objective function is written as $x_1 = -3/2\,x_2 + \frac{1}{4}\omega$, and shifted through the solution space, until $\omega$ becomes minimal taking account of the side-conditions. The points $S$ (6/5, 8/5) appears to be the point at which all constraints are satisfied and at which $\omega$ is at a minimum. In this case the optimal point $S$ is the point of intersection of both side-conditions. Therefore, the optimal decision is: $x_1^0 = 8/5; x_2^0 = 6/5$ with minimal costs equal to 13 3/5.

If the slope of the objective function would have been equal to one of the slopes of the constraints, an infinite number of optimal solutions would have been obtained.

### 6.3.2 *Formal specification of a L.P. problem*

In general, a L.P. problem can be formulated in matrix notation as:

$$\left.\begin{array}{l} \min \omega = \mathbf{c}'\,\mathbf{x} \\ \text{s.t.,} \\ \mathbf{A}\mathbf{x} \geqslant \mathbf{b} \\ \mathbf{x} \geqslant \mathbf{0} \end{array}\right\} \qquad (6.3.2.1)$$

where the vector $\mathbf{x}$ of order $J$ x 1 represents decision variables, and where the matrix $\mathbf{A}$ $(I \times J)$, and the vectors $\mathbf{b}$ $(I \times 1)$ and $\mathbf{c}$ $(J \times 1)$ represent known coefficients. The constraints can also be written as:

$$\begin{bmatrix} \mathbf{A} \\ \mathbf{I} \end{bmatrix} \mathbf{x} \geqslant \begin{bmatrix} \mathbf{b} \\ 0 \end{bmatrix} \qquad (6.3.2.2)$$

where $\mathbf{I}$ is the identity matrix,
or as:

$$\mathbf{A}^*\,\mathbf{x} \geqslant \mathbf{b}^* \qquad (6.3.2.3)$$

Sometimes the inequality constraints are replaced by equalities by introducing so-called slack-variables $t_i$ $(i = 1, \ldots, I)$. The number of slack-variables is equal to the number of side-conditions. Then instead of (6.3.2.1) the following canonical form of a L.P. model is obtained:

$$\left.\begin{array}{l} \min \omega = \mathbf{c}'\,\mathbf{x} \\ \text{s.t.} \\ \mathbf{A}\mathbf{x} - \mathbf{t} = \mathbf{b} \\ \mathbf{x} \geqslant \mathbf{0} \end{array}\right\} \qquad (6.3.2.4)$$

In case of a reversed inequality-sign the vector of slack-variables must be added instead of subtracted. Apart from the non-negativity conditions the side-conditions represent a system of $I$ equations in $I + J$ unknown variables $\mathbf{x}$ and $\mathbf{t}$. The alternative constraints (6.3.2.3) can be written in terms of slack-variables as:

$$\mathbf{A}^*\mathbf{x} - \mathbf{t}^* = \mathbf{b}^* \quad (6.3.2.5)$$

All solutions satisfying simultaneously the constraints are called *feasible* solutions. All solutions of (6.3.2.4), for which the number of non-zero-valued variables (ordinary and slack-variables) is equal to the total number of constraints, are called *basic* solutions. The set of basic solutions of a linear program is formed by the corner points of the feasible area satisfying all constraints. The objective function possesses always an *optimum* solution at one of the basic points, so that the number of optimal non-zero-variables $x_j$ $(j = 1, \ldots, J)$ en $t_i$ $(i = 1, \ldots, I)$ will never exceed the total number of constraints. In consequence, only a restricted number of points, viz. all basic solutions, need to be inspected in order to find the optimum.

It is evident that the general L.P. problem cannot be solved in a graphical way. However, by means of a successive inspection of all basic solutions the constrained optimum can, in principle, be determined. Such a computational work for rather extensive programs can be reduced by applying standard iterative solutions procedures, for instance a Simplex-technique. This technique requires the construction of a Simplex-tableau, which contains in a systematic way all coefficients of the L.P. problem. By selecting successively efficient pivotal elements, a set of solutions converging towards the optimum can be obtained in an iterative way. This technique will not be discussed here any further. Instead, more attention will be paid to duality relationships in L.P. models and to other formal properties of L.P. models.

### 6.3.3 *The dual L.P. problem*

Each L.P. problem possesses a dual problem: a minimum problem is always linked up with a maximum problem and *vice versa.* The economic interpretation of this phenomenon is that allocation of scarce resources and pricing are two sides of the same coin. Therefore, consideration of a dual problem may be very useful to obtain more insight into the structure of an optimization problem and into its relationships with prices.

The duality concept can be clarified with reference to the minimization problem discussed in section 6.3.1. Let $y_1$ and $y_2$ be the unknown unit value of labour category 1 and 2, respectively. The total imputed (or accounting) value of the amount of labour is equal to:

$$\varphi = 4y_1 + 10y_2 \quad (6.3.3.1)$$

in which 4 and 10 represent the known minimum amount of each labour category imposed *a priori*. It is a very reasonable assumption to maximize the intrinsic value of these labour inputs given the fact that the unit costs of each project may not exceed their predetermined levels. Therefore, the intrinsic value of labour associated with project 1 and 2 should be determined such that the unit costs of project 1 and 2 are lower than (or equal to) 4 and 6, respectively. For instance, it is known from section 6.3.1 that one unit of project 1 requires 1 unit of labour category 1 (with accounting price $y_1$) and 4 units of labour category 2 (with accounting price $y_2$). It is evident that the total intrinsic value of the labour components, required for one unit of project 1, cannot exceed the unit costs of project 1, so that there results:

$$y_1 + 4y_2 \leqslant 4 \tag{6.3.3.2}$$

In an analogous way one finds for the second project:

$$2y_1 + 3y_2 \leqslant 6 \tag{6.3.3.3}$$

The dual problem can now be formulated as:

$$\left.\begin{array}{l} \max \varphi = 4y_1 + 10y_2 \\ \text{s.t.} \\ y_1 + 4y_2 \leqslant 4 \\ 2y_1 + 3y_2 \leqslant 6 \\ y_1, y_2 \quad \leqslant 0 \end{array}\right\} \tag{6.3.3.4}$$

This dual L.P. problem can also be solved in a graphical way (see figure 6.3.3.a).

Fig. 6.3.3.a  The solution space of a dual L.P. model

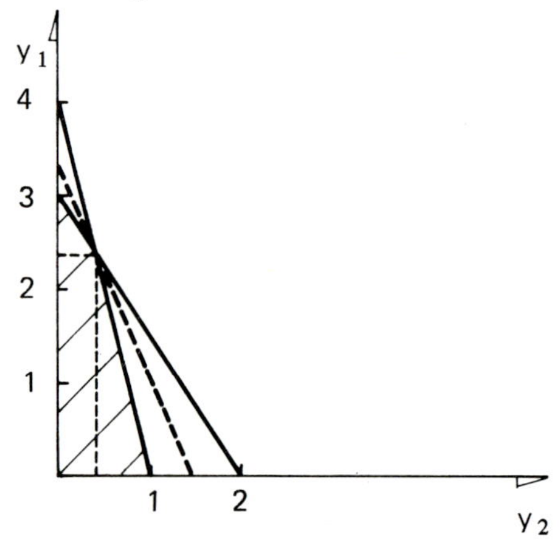

The values of $y_1$ and $y_2$ can be determined in the same way as $x_1$ and $x_2$. They appear to be: $y_1^0 = 2\ 2/5$ and $y_2^0 = 2/5$, while the maximum value of $\varphi = 13\ 3/5$.

The dual model appears to result in the same optimum for $\varphi$ as the primal for $\omega$. This implies that the minimum costs of both projects (given the minimum labour requirements) are equal to the total maximum accounting value of the labour components (given the unit costs of the projects). In other words, the optimal expenditure (to an amount of 13 3/5) can be used either to buy 8/5 units of project 1 and 6/5 units of project 2, or 4 units of labour component 1 (with implicit value 2 2/5) and 10 units of labour component 2 (with implicit value 2/5). In fact, in the dual model both labour categories receive non-negative values such that the total material value of each project does not exceed its market price. These intrinsic values of the labour components are determined such that the total material value, implicit in both projects at minimum costs, is at a maximum.

Therefore, one may conclude that allocation of resources and pricing problems are dual aspects of the same problem. In case of absence of market prices for the resources, imputed (fictitious, accounting, dual or shadow) prices have to be computed (see the previous example).

### 6.3.4. *Formal specification of a dual L.P. model*

In a formal way a dual L.P. problem can be written as:

$$\left.\begin{array}{r} \max \varphi = \mathbf{b}'\mathbf{y} \\ \mathbf{A}'\mathbf{y} \leqslant \mathbf{c} \\ \mathbf{y} \geqslant \mathbf{0} \end{array}\right\} \qquad (6.3.4.1)$$

The constraints of the latter system can be written in a way similar to (6.3.2.2) and (6.3.2.3):

$$\begin{bmatrix} \mathbf{A}' \\ -\mathbf{I} \end{bmatrix} \mathbf{y} \leqslant \begin{bmatrix} \mathbf{c} \\ \mathbf{0} \end{bmatrix} \qquad (6.3.4.2)$$

or:

$$(\mathbf{A}')^* \quad \mathbf{y} \leqslant \mathbf{c}^* \qquad (6.3.4.3)$$

The dual problem appears to contain exactly as many variables as there are constraints ($I$) in the original problem, and as many constraints ($J$) as there are variables in the original problem. It is easily seen that the dual of the dual yields again the primal problem.

The following fundamental theorem, the so-called *duality theorem*, can be proved to be valid (see, for instance, Lancaster [1968]). The primal and the dual problem of the same L.P. problem have either the same solution for the objective function, i.e.

$$\mathbf{c}'\mathbf{x}^{\mathrm{o}} = \mathbf{b}'\mathbf{y}^{\mathrm{o}} \tag{6.3.4.4}$$

(with $\mathbf{x}^{\mathrm{o}}$ and $\mathbf{y}^{\mathrm{o}}$ optimal values of the variables concerned), or no solution at all.

It is evident that there are close links between primal and dual programs. The relationships between primal and dual L.P. problems can be summarized as follows:

1 If the primal variables constitute a vector of order $J$, the dual variables form a vector of order $I$.
2 The elements of the constraint vector of the primal program are the coefficients of the dual objective function, and the coefficients of the primal objective function are the constraint vector of the dual program.
3 The sign of the inequalities in the dual model is reversed with respect to the sign of the inequalities in the primal model.
4 The dual of a minimizing primal program is a maximizing program and *vice versa.*
5 Each column of coefficients in the constraint matrix of the original problem becomes a row of coefficients in the constraint matrix of the dual program.
6 The non-negativity conditions on the variables are not reversed.

### 6.3.5 *Further properties of primal-dual systems*

In this section a set of properties will be discussed which add substantially to our understanding of L.P. models. It was already pointed out that the optimum of an L.P. problem is located at a corner-point of the feasible area; this optimum represents an absolute (global) and not a local optimum. Inspection of the dual system associated with a primal system may shed new light on this absolute optimum, the corresponding price system, and other properties of L.P. models. Four aspects of L.P. models will be considered and discussed successively.

At first, inspection of the dual system may result in a *more rapid computation* of the optimum value of the primal objective function, particularly if the primal program has one or two constraints and if it contains $J$ variables ($J > 2$). This primal problem cannot be solved in a graphical way. However, in this case the dual system has one or two variables with $J$ constraints. Such a dual problem with one or two variables can be solved directly in a graphical way, from which the optimum value of the objective function results. In addition, *the consistency of a primal program can be checked* by inspecting the dual program, since both a primal and a dual model have to be defined within a *feasible* area. For instance, the following L.P. problem does not have an optimal solution (apart from the infinity-solution)

$$\left.\begin{array}{l} \max \omega = \tfrac{1}{2} x_1 + 1\tfrac{1}{2} x_2 + 3x_3 \\ \text{s.t.} \\ -x_1 - 3x_2 - x_3 \leqslant 4 \\ -x_1 - x_2 - 2x_3 \leqslant 2 \\ -x_1, x_2, x_3 \leqslant 0 \end{array}\right\} \qquad (6.3.5.1)$$

It is easily seen that the dual program associated with (6.3.5.1). shows incompatible constraints:

$$\left.\begin{array}{l} \min \omega = 4y_1 + 2y_2 \\ \text{s.t.} \\ -y_1 - y_2 \geqslant \tfrac{1}{2} \\ -3y_1 - y_2 \geqslant 1\tfrac{1}{2} \\ -y_1 - 2y_2 \geqslant 3 \\ y_1, y_2 \geqslant 0 \end{array}\right\} \qquad (6.3.5.2)$$

The non-negativity constraints on $y_1$ and $y_2$ are not compatible with the other constraints.

In the second place, the dual system contains computed (accounting or shadow) prices, when the primal problem contains quantity variables. It has already been pointed out that this phenomenon results from an *optimal allocation* of *scarce resources.* For instance, in the previous example, the shadow prices represent the maximum values that can be imputed to the various labour categories. The sum total of these value amounts adds up exactly to the same level as total minimum project costs. In addition, the dual variables have an extremely important significance in relation to the marginality conditions which will be discussed below.

Next, the problem of bindingness of constraints will be considered, viz. the problem whether in the optimizing point $\mathbf{x}^0$ the constraints are equalities or inequalities. This problem can be solved by means of the *equilibrium theorem* of L.P., which relates primal programs to dual programs. This theorem states that at the optimum point the $i^{\text{th}}$ variable of a dual program is zero whenever the $i^{\text{th}}$ constraint of the corresponding primal program is not binding (or ineffective, or inactive). In a more formal way this theorem states that *any feasible program of primal and dual problems is optimal, if and only if:* $y_i = 0$, *whenever* $\mathbf{a}_i' \mathbf{x} > b_i$; $\mathbf{a}_i'$ represents the $i^{\text{th}}$ row vector of the matrix $\mathbf{A}$, and corresponds to the $i^{\text{th}}$ constraint of the primal program, while $b_i$ represents the $i^{\text{th}}$ element of $\mathbf{b}$. The previous theorem is also valid in the reverse way, viz. whenever the $j^{th}$ constraint of a dual program is inactive, the corresponding $j^{th}$ primal variable is equal to zero. First, both the *necessary* and the *sufficient* condition of the equilibrium theorem will be proved successively.

The *necessary* condition of this theorem can be proved as follows. The following conditions are satisfied at the optimum (according to the primal and dual L.P. constraints):

$$\mathbf{A}\mathbf{x}^{o} \geqslant \mathbf{b} \tag{6.3.5.3}$$

and:

$$\mathbf{A}'\mathbf{y}^{o} \leqslant \mathbf{c} \tag{6.3.5.4}$$

Premultiplication of (6.3.5.3) and (6.3.5.4) with $\mathbf{y}^{o\prime}$ and $\mathbf{x}^{o\prime}$ gives:

$$\mathbf{y}^{o\prime}\mathbf{A}\mathbf{x}^{o} \geqslant \mathbf{y}^{o\prime}\mathbf{b} \tag{6.3.5.5}$$

and:

$$\mathbf{x}^{o\prime}\mathbf{A}'\mathbf{y}^{o} \leqslant \mathbf{x}^{o\prime}\mathbf{c} \tag{6.3.5.6}$$

Because:

$$\mathbf{x}^{o\prime}\mathbf{A}'\mathbf{y}^{o} = \mathbf{y}^{o\prime}\mathbf{A}\mathbf{x}^{o} \tag{6.3.5.7}$$

one may derive the following results

$$\mathbf{b}'\mathbf{y}^{o} \leqslant \mathbf{x}^{o\prime}\mathbf{A}'\mathbf{y}^{o} \leqslant \mathbf{c}'\mathbf{x}^{o} \tag{6.3.5.8}$$

By making use of (6.3.4.4) one may conclude that the following result (the 'saddle-point' theorem) is valid in the optimal point:

$$\mathbf{c}'\mathbf{x}^{o} = \mathbf{x}^{o\prime}\mathbf{A}'\mathbf{y}^{o} = \mathbf{b}'\mathbf{y}^{o} \tag{6.3.5.9}$$

The second part of the latter equality yields:

$$\mathbf{x}^{o\prime}\mathbf{A}'\mathbf{y}^{o} = \mathbf{b}'\mathbf{y}^{o} \tag{6.3.5.10}$$

or:

$$(\mathbf{A}\mathbf{x}^{o} - \mathbf{b})'\mathbf{y}^{o} = 0 \tag{6.3.5.11}$$

where $(\mathbf{A}\mathbf{x}^{o} - \mathbf{b})'$ represents a row vector of order $I$, and $\mathbf{y}^{o}$ a column vector of order $I$. The product of these vectors must be equal to zero (according to [6.3.5.11] ). The respective elements of both vectors are non-negative (since $\mathbf{A}\mathbf{x}^{o} \geqslant \mathbf{b}$ and $\mathbf{y}^{o} \geqslant \mathbf{0}$). Then the only way in which condition (6.3.5.11) can be satisfied is that any term of the vector sum $(\mathbf{A}\mathbf{x}^{o} - \mathbf{b})'\mathbf{y}^{o}$ is equal to zero; in other words, any element $i$ should satisfy the following condition:

$$\mathbf{a}_i'\mathbf{x}^o - b_i = 0 \text{ or } y_i^o = 0 \qquad (6.3.5.12)$$

The latter result leads to the following conclusion: in the optimal point of an L.P. problem, $y_i^o = 0$ whenever $\mathbf{a}_i'\mathbf{x}^o - b_i > 0$.

The *sufficient* part of the equilibrium theorem states that the feasible vectors **x** and **y** are the optimal solutions of the L.P. program, if each element $y_i$ of **y** is equal to zero, whenever $\mathbf{a}_i'\mathbf{x} - b_i > 0$. The proof of the optimality of **x** and **y** can be directly provided. Each term of the series $(\mathbf{Ax} - \mathbf{b})'\mathbf{y}$ is equal to zero since: a) $\mathbf{a}_i'\mathbf{x} - b_i > 0$ implies $y_i = 0$, i.e. $(\mathbf{a}_i'\mathbf{x} - b_i)y_i = 0$; b) $\mathbf{a}_i'\mathbf{x} - b_i = 0$ implies $(\mathbf{a}_i'\mathbf{x} - b_i)y_i = 0$.
Therefore:

$$(\mathbf{Ax} - \mathbf{b})'\mathbf{y} = 0 \qquad (6.3.5.13)$$

or:

$$\mathbf{x}'\mathbf{A}'\mathbf{y} = \mathbf{b}'\mathbf{y} \qquad (6.3.5.14)$$

Analogously:

$$\mathbf{x}'\mathbf{A}'\mathbf{y} = \mathbf{c}'\mathbf{x} \qquad (6.3.5.15)$$

Combination of (6.3.5.14) and (6.3.5.15) yields:

$$\mathbf{b}'\mathbf{y} = \mathbf{c}'\mathbf{x} \qquad (6.3.5.16)$$

The latter situation is according to (6.3.4.4) only valid at the optimum.

This theorem explains directly, why in an optimum point the number of non-zero variables in each (primal or dual) program will never exceed the number of constraints in that program. Furthermore, it appears that a certain active constraint implies a positive corresponding dual variable and a zero-value of the corresponding slack variable. On the other hand, inactiveness of constraints results in zero-values of corresponding *dual* variables and in non-zero values of corresponding *slack* variables.

The procedure of selecting active constraints can be described in terms of vector analysis as follows: at the optimum a set of independent row vectors (viz. a basis of a vector space) is selected from the coefficient matrix of the constraints such that a set of equalities is obtained. These row vectors are selected such that the corresponding objective function is minimized. The remaining constraints represent a feasible area within which the optimum point is an interior point (and no corner-solution). Therefore, the ultimate result of these L.P. models is only the minimization of an objective function subject to a number of *selected* equalities.

In the fourth place, dual variables considered from the previous point of view have an extremely important interpretation. This can be clarified as follows: consider the primal L.P. problem specified in (6.3.2.1) and its corresponding dual specified in (6.3.4.1). Denote the respective optimum values by $\mathbf{x}^o$ and $\mathbf{y}^o$. Assume a change in the level of the constraints, viz. a change in $\mathbf{b}$ to an amount of $\Delta\, \mathbf{b}$. Assume furthermore, that the original effective constraints remain effective, so that $\mathbf{x}^o$ shifts to $\bar{\mathbf{x}}$, but $\mathbf{y}^o$ remains equal. The resulting change in the primal objective function $\omega$, can be determined by making use of the duality theorem (6.3.4.4). In the initial situation the following condition is valid:

$$\mathbf{c}'\mathbf{x}^o = \mathbf{b}'\mathbf{y}^o \tag{6.3.5.17}$$

After the change in $\mathbf{b}$ the duality theorem can be formalized as:

$$\mathbf{c}'\bar{\mathbf{x}} = (\mathbf{b} + \Delta\mathbf{b})'\mathbf{y}^o \tag{6.3.5.18}$$

so that:

$$\begin{aligned} \Delta\omega &= \mathbf{c}'\bar{\mathbf{x}} - \mathbf{c}'\mathbf{x}^o \\ &= (\mathbf{b} + \Delta\mathbf{b})'\mathbf{y}^o - \mathbf{b}'\mathbf{y}^o \\ &= (\Delta\mathbf{b})'\mathbf{y}^o \end{aligned} \tag{6.3.5.19}$$

If only one element $i$ of $b$ has been changed, one may write:

$$\frac{\partial\omega}{\partial b_i} = y_i^o \tag{6.3.5.20}$$

The latter result permits the following interpretation of dual variables (see also [6.2.2.12]): a dual variable indicates the degree to which the primal target function is affected if the corresponding elements of the level of constraints ($\mathbf{b}$) are slightly changed; in other words, a dual variable indicates the marginal value to the optimal program on relaxing the $i^{th}$ constraint. For instance, in the example of section 6.3.1 and 6.3.3 the dual variables (i.e., the shadow prices) reflected marginal costs, viz. the least costs of an additional unit of the required minimum levels of the labour inputs. In other problems dual variables may represent marginal revenues, marginal productivities, etc. If a dual variable $y_i$ is zero, a slight change in $b_i$ will not have any effect on the optimum level of the objective function, since in the latter case the $i^{th}$ constraint is not binding. The marginality relationships are only relevant for binding constraints, i.e. constraints satisfying exactly the equality. The latter situation is entirely comparable to the classical case of optimizing an objective function subject to a number of equality conditions (see section 6.2.2). The Lagrange multipliers in these kinds of problems represented also shadow prices, and denoted the marginal rates of change of the optimal value of the objective function with respect to a small relaxation of a certain equality. These marginality interpretations of Lagrange multipliers correspond to the interpretation of dual variables in L.P. problems.

In the following sections of this chapter a set of applications of linear and non-linear programming models in regional economics will be presented (for instance, transportation models, assignment models, investment allocation models etc.). These models are based on the programming problems discussed so far.

## 6.4 Transportation models

### 6.4.1 *A simple transportation problem*

Transportation models are one of the most well-known programming models in regional economics. A description of these types of models can be found among others in Dantzig (1951), Dorfman et al. (1958), Ghosh (1965), Miller (1972), Rogers (1971), and Quandt (1960).

In general terms a transportation problem is characterized as the minimization of a cost function for the allocation of commodities. In addition, a set of constraints is imposed on both the supply points of these commodities (i.e. the points of origin) and the demand points (i.e. the points of destination). Therefore, a transportation problem is concerned with the optimal spatial distribution of products from a set of sources to a number of destinations, given the unit transportation costs between each origin and destination. The purpose is to find an optimal transportation pattern, that minimizes total transportation costs within the system, subject to side-conditions on capacity levels of plants at the origin and on consumption requirements at the destination.

For instance, assume a certain branch of industry is composed of $J$ plants $j$ ($j = 1, \ldots, J$). The total production of this industry has to be shipped to $I$ consumption points $i$ ($i = 1, \ldots, I$). The costs of shipping a unit of the commodity from $j$ ($j = 1, \ldots, J$) to $i$ ($i = 1, \ldots, I$) are a constant proportion of the total amount shipped from $j$ to $i$; these known unit transportation costs are denoted by $\tau_{ji}$. Each plant $j$ has a known capacity $c_j$ which cannot be surpassed, while each locality $i$ has a level of demand $r_i$ which should at least be satisfied. The decision variables in this problem are the quantities of the product to be shipped from each point $j$ to each point $i$, and they are denoted by $x_{ji}$. It is obvious that there is an enormous number of feasible routings. A transportation model serves to select a flow pattern with minimum transportation costs.

The foregoing problem can be formulated in L.P. terms as:

$$\left.\begin{aligned}
&\min \omega = \sum_{j=1}^{J} \sum_{i=1}^{I} \tau_{ji} x_{ji} \\
&\text{s.t.} \\
&\sum_{i=1}^{I} x_{ji} \leqslant c_j \qquad \forall j \\
&\sum_{j=1}^{J} x_{ji} \geqslant r_i \qquad \forall i \\
&x_{ji} \geqslant 0 \qquad \forall i \text{ and } j
\end{aligned}\right\} \tag{6.4.1.1}$$

Commonly still another constraint is introduced, viz. the condition that total quantity supplied (i.e., the capacity) is equal to total quantity demanded (i.e. the consumption), so that:

$$\sum_{j=1}^{J} c_j = \sum_{i=1}^{I} r_i \tag{6.4.1.2}$$

It is obvious, that the foregoing problem is not only applicable to one single industry with one type of commodity, but also to problems concerning the spatial distribution of multiple commodities. The L.P. problem specified above has an extremely simple structure, because all decision variables $x_{ji}$ in the constraints possess a unit coefficient. If the previous types of problems are rather small, they can frequently be solved without the use of a computer (see, for instance, Dorfman et al. [1958]), viz. by distributing initially in a feasible way all $x_{ji}$'s. Next, by means of an iterative procedure the first results may be improved, until the constrained maximum has been attained. For more complicated problems one may use standard solution algorithms for transportation problems such as the Simplex-technique, the reduced-matrix-method or network algorithms (see, for instance, Dortman et al. [1958], Hadley [1964], Houthakker [1955], Rogers [1971] and Von Böventer [1961]).

The standard structure associated with the primal problem specified in (6.4.1.1) is constructed as follows:

$$\left.\begin{aligned}
&\min \omega = \sum_{j=1}^{J} \sum_{i=1}^{I} \tau_{ji} x_{ji} \\
&\text{s.t.} \\
&\sum_{i=1}^{I} x_{ji} \geqslant - c_j \qquad \forall j \\
&\sum_{j=1}^{J} x_{ji} \geqslant r_i \qquad \forall i \\
&x_{ji} \geqslant 0 \qquad \forall i, j
\end{aligned}\right\} \tag{6.4.1.3}$$

The construction of the dual program is facilitated by writing the constraints of the standard primal program in matrix notation:

$$\left[\begin{array}{ccc|c|ccc} 1 & & 0 & & 1 & & 0\\ & \ddots & & \cdots & & \ddots & \\ 0 & & 1 & & 0 & & 1 \\ \hline -1 & \cdots & -1 & & & 0 & \\ & & & \cdots & & & \\ & 0 & & & -1 & \cdots & -1 \end{array}\right] \begin{bmatrix} x_{11}\\ \vdots \\ x_{1I} \\ \vdots \\ x_{j1} \\ \vdots \\ x_{JI}\end{bmatrix} \geqslant \begin{bmatrix} r_1 \\ \vdots \\ r_I \\ -c_1 \\ \vdots \\ -c_J\end{bmatrix} \qquad (6.4.1.4)$$

### 6.4.2 *The dual transportation model*

The dual L.P. model associated with the primal transportation model can be determined by transposing the matrix of system (6.4.1.4) according to the primal-dual relationships set out in section 6.3. Application of the primal-dual rules for a standard L.P. problem gives the following dual transportation model:

$$\left.\begin{array}{ll} \max \varphi = \sum_{i=1}^{I} r_i y_i^r - \sum_{j=1}^{J} c_j y_j^c & \\ \text{s.t.} & \\ y_i^r - y_j^c \leqslant \tau_{ji} & \forall i, j \\ y_i^r \ , \ y_j^c \geqslant 0 & \forall i, j \end{array}\right\} \qquad (6.4.2.1)$$

The dual variables $y_i^r$ and $y_j^c$ correspond to the primal $r_i$- and $c_i$- constraints, respectively. They are the respective shadow prices of demand and of capacity. The particular form of the dual constraints results from transposition of the coefficient matrix of the primal constraints. The dual variables $y_i^r$ represent the marginal transportation costs if the level of $r_i$ *rises,* while the dual variables $y_j^c$ represents the marginal costs if $c_j$ *declines.*

The *dual objective function* to be maximized is the surplus of total imputed value of products delivered at all consumption points $i$ over total imputed value of products produced at all plants $j$. The dual *constraints* state that the imputed value differential between origin and destination cannot exceed the transportation costs necessary to make the shipments from plant $j$ to locality $i$; in other words, the marginal value of the produce delivered may not exceed its marginal mill price plus its transportation costs. In a similar way Stevens (1961) presented a dual interpretation in terms of location rents. A positive delivery from $j$ to $i$ and $i'$ (i.e. $x_{ji} > 0$ and $x_{ji'} > 0$) implies that the corresponding dual constraints are active, so that

$$y_i^r - y_j^c = \tau_{ji} \tag{6.4.2.2}$$

and:

$$y_{i'}^r - y_j^c = \tau_{ji'} \tag{6.4.2.3}$$

or:

$$y_i^r - y_{i'}^r = \tau_{ji} - \tau_{ji'} \tag{6.4.2.4}$$

Relationship (6.4.2.4) states that the difference in two imputed c.i.f. prices is equal to the difference in the corresponding transportation rates.

### 6.4.3 *An empirical application of a transportation model*

The transportation model discussed in section 6.4.1 has been applied to solid fuel flows between 43 Dutch regions. The following data were available for this problem: the transportation rates $\tau_{ji}$ between each successive region $j$ and $i$, the total volume of commodities to be shipped *from* region $j$ (i.e. the *origin* constraint $c_j$), and the total volume of commodities to be shipped *to* region $i$ (i.e. the *destination* constraint $r_i$). The transportation rates (in Dutch guilders) are presented in the body of table 6.4.3.a, while the commodity constraints on the origins and on the destinations are presented in the last column and the last row (in 100 tons), respectively. By minimizing total transportation costs an optimal interregional flow pattern of commodities is obtained. The results of this L.P. model are contained in table 6.4.3.b. The value of minimum overall transportation costs associated with these results is equal to 27 million Dutch guilders.

The *actual* total interregional transportation costs were calculated by means of transportation statistics; they appeared to be equal to 33 million Dutch guilders.

The L.P. results show that a considerable reduction in transportation costs could have been obtained, if the optimal flow patterns could be realized. (For computations see Specker and Kok [1973].)

It should be noted that the results show also a very specific property

# Table 6.4.3.a

## Data of a transportation model for solid fuel

| | 1 | 2 | 3 | 4 | 5 | 6 | 7 | 8 | 9 | 10 | 11 | 12 | 13 | 14 | 15 | 16 | 17 | 18 | 19 | 20 | 21 | 22 | 23 | 24 | 25 | 26 | 27 | 28 | 29 | 30 | 31 | 32 | 33 | 34 | 35 | 36 | 37 | 38 | 39 | 40 | 41 | 42 | 43 | $c_j$ |
|---|---|---|---|---|---|---|---|---|---|---|---|---|---|---|---|---|---|---|---|---|---|---|---|---|---|---|---|---|---|---|---|---|---|---|---|---|---|---|---|---|---|---|---|---|
| 1 | 4·7 | 8·2 | 4·7 | 8·2 | 12·2 | 12·2 | 9·0 | 8·2 | 12·2 | 13·8 | 14·9 | 15·3 | 20·0 | 22·0 | 22·5 | 24·9 | 20·0 | 26·6 | 25·3 | 23·2 | 26·0 | 21·6 | 23·2 | 28·0 | 24·9 | 26·6 | 30·9 | 34·3 | 31·4 | 32·1 | 36·7 | 29·3 | 42·8 | 43·8 | 38·4 | 31·0 | 32·6 | 29·7 | 32·6 | 29·7 | 35·0 | 39·3 | 40·0 | 513 |
| 2 | | 4·7 | 8·2 | 9·0 | 15·6 | 15·6 | 12·8 | 11·7 | 13·8 | 16·8 | 17·8 | 20·0 | 20·2 | 25·3 | 26·0 | 28·0 | 22·5 | 29·3 | 28·0 | 26·0 | 20·3 | 24·9 | 26·6 | 30·9 | 27·6 | 29·7 | 34·3 | 37·1 | 35·0 | 35·4 | 40·0 | 33·0 | 46·2 | 47·2 | 41·7 | 36·0 | 35·4 | 33·0 | 35·4 | 33·0 | 37·7 | 42·8 | 43·4 | 14 |
| 3 | | | 4·7 | 8·2 | 12·2 | 12·2 | 9·0 | 8·2 | 12·2 | 13·8 | 14·9 | 15·3 | 20·0 | 22·0 | 22·5 | 24·9 | 20·0 | 26·6 | 25·3 | 23·2 | 26·0 | 21·6 | 23·2 | 28·0 | 24·9 | 26·6 | 30·9 | 34·3 | 31·4 | 32·1 | 36·7 | 29·3 | 42·8 | 43·8 | 38·4 | 31·0 | 32·6 | 29·7 | 32·6 | 29·7 | 35·0 | 39·3 | 40·0 | 47 |
| 4 | | | | 4·7 | 14·9 | 14·9 | 12·8 | 8·2 | 10·2 | 13·8 | 15·8 | 15·3 | 18·7 | 22·0 | 22·5 | 24·9 | 19·7 | 26·0 | 25·3 | 23·2 | 26·0 | 24·4 | 26·0 | 27·6 | 24·9 | 26·9 | 32·1 | 33·7 | 31·4 | 32·1 | 36·7 | 29·3 | 42·8 | 43·8 | 38·4 | 32·6 | 32·6 | 29·7 | 32·1 | 29·7 | 34·3 | 39·3 | 40·0 | 193 |
| 5 | | | | | 4·7 | 4·7 | 8·2 | 13·6 | 16·8 | 13·6 | 13·8 | 15·3 | 21·0 | 22·5 | 22·0 | 24·4 | 19·1 | 24·9 | 23·7 | 21·6 | 22·5 | 15·8 | 17·3 | 22·0 | 23·2 | 20·6 | 24·9 | 29·7 | 26·9 | 28·7 | 32·6 | 26·0 | 40·5 | 40·0 | 34·3 | 31·4 | 30·9 | 28·7 | 31·4 | 29·3 | 33·7 | 38·4 | 39·3 | 10 |
| 6 | | | | | | 4·7 | 8·2 | 13·6 | 16·8 | 13·6 | 13·8 | 15·3 | 21·0 | 22·5 | 22·0 | 24·4 | 19·1 | 24·9 | 23·7 | 21·6 | 22·5 | 15·8 | 17·3 | 22·0 | 23·2 | 20·6 | 24·9 | 29·7 | 26·9 | 28·7 | 32·6 | 26·0 | 40·5 | 40·0 | 34·3 | 31·4 | 30·9 | 28·7 | 31·4 | 29·3 | 33·7 | 38·4 | 39·3 | 662 |
| 7 | | | | | | | 4·7 | 10·2 | 13·8 | 12·2 | 12·8 | 16·5 | 19·7 | 21·0 | 21·0 | 23·2 | 18·4 | 24·4 | 23·2 | 21·0 | 24·4 | 18·7 | 20·0 | 25·3 | 22·5 | 23·7 | 27·6 | 32·1 | 29·7 | 30·4 | 35·0 | 26·9 | 41·2 | 42·1 | 36·7 | 30·9 | 30·4 | 28·0 | 30·0 | 28·0 | 32·6 | 37·7 | 38·4 | 340 |
| 8 | | | | | | | | 4·7 | 9·4 | 11·0 | 12·8 | 14·9 | 15·3 | 19·7 | 20·0 | 22·0 | 15·3 | 23·2 | 22·0 | 20·0 | 23·2 | 21·6 | 23·2 | 24·9 | 21·6 | 24·4 | 29·3 | 30·9 | 28·7 | 29·3 | 33·7 | 26·0 | 40·0 | 41·2 | 35·4 | 29·7 | 29·3 | 26·9 | 29·3 | 26·9 | 31·4 | 36·7 | 37·1 | 1111 |
| 9 | | | | | | | | | 4·7 | 12·2 | 15·5 | 15·5 | 14·9 | 18·4 | 19·1 | 21·0 | 16·5 | 22·5 | 22·5 | 20·6 | 23·2 | 24·9 | 26·6 | 25·3 | 22·0 | 24·4 | 29·3 | 30·9 | 28·7 | 29·3 | 33·7 | 26·6 | 40·0 | 41·2 | 35·4 | 29·7 | 28·7 | 26·0 | 28·0 | 26·0 | 30·4 | 35·4 | 36·0 | 2250 |
| 10 | | | | | | | | | | 4·7 | 6·6 | 10·2 | 14·9 | 15·8 | 15·6 | 17·3 | 12·8 | 18·7 | 17·8 | 15·8 | 18·4 | 20·6 | 22·0 | 20·0 | 15·3 | 19·7 | 24·4 | 26·0 | 23·2 | 23·7 | 28·7 | 21·0 | 34·3 | 36·0 | 30·4 | 24·9 | 24·4 | 21·6 | 24·4 | 22·0 | 26·6 | 31·4 | 32·1 | 441 |
| 11 | | | | | | | | | | | 4·7 | 10·2 | 16·5 | 16·5 | 15·8 | 17·8 | 13·6 | 18·7 | 15·3 | 15·6 | 18·4 | 19·1 | 20·6 | 17·7 | 15·3 | 19·1 | 23·7 | 25·3 | 23·2 | 23·7 | 28·0 | 20·6 | 34·3 | 35·4 | 29·7 | 24·4 | 24·4 | 21·6 | 24·9 | 22·0 | 26·9 | 31·4 | 32·1 | 440 |
| 12 | | | | | | | | | | | | 4·7 | 12·8 | 11·7 | 11·7 | 13·8 | 8·2 | 15·6 | 14·9 | 12·8 | 15·8 | 21·0 | 21·0 | 17·3 | 14·9 | 16·8 | 20·6 | 22·5 | 20·0 | 20·6 | 25·3 | 18·4 | 30·9 | 32·1 | 26·9 | 21·6 | 20·6 | 18·4 | 20·6 | 18·7 | 22·5 | 26·9 | 28·0 | 533 |
| 13 | | | | | | | | | | | | | 4·7 | 12·2 | 14·9 | 16·8 | 13·6 | 18·7 | 19·1 | 15·3 | 20·6 | 26·9 | 26·6 | 22·0 | 19·1 | 21·6 | 26·0 | 26·9 | 25·3 | 24·9 | 29·7 | 22·5 | 35·4 | 37·1 | 31·4 | 26·0 | 23·7 | 21·0 | 23·2 | 21·0 | 25·3 | 30·4 | 30·9 | 1383 |
| 14 | | | | | | | | | | | | | | 4·7 | 8·2 | 11·0 | 9·4 | 13·6 | 15·6 | 14·5 | 17·3 | 23·7 | 22·5 | 19·1 | 16·5 | 18·4 | 21·0 | 21·6 | 20·6 | 19·7 | 24·4 | 18·7 | 29·7 | 30·9 | 26·0 | 20·0 | 18·7 | 16·5 | 18·4 | 16·5 | 20·0 | 24·9 | 25·3 | 1232 |
| 15 | | | | | | | | | | | | | | | 4·7 | 6·6 | 8·2 | 9·4 | 12·2 | 11·0 | 14·5 | 20·6 | 18·7 | 16·5 | 13·6 | 15·6 | 18·4 | 18·7 | 17·8 | 16·8 | 21·0 | 15·8 | 26·6 | 27·6 | 22·5 | 17·3 | 15·8 | 13·6 | 15·6 | 13·6 | 17·3 | 21·6 | 22·0 | 712 |
| 16 | | | | | | | | | | | | | | | | 4·7 | 11·0 | 9·4 | 12·8 | 12·2 | 14·9 | 21·6 | 21·0 | 16·8 | 14·9 | 16·8 | 18·7 | 18·4 | 17·8 | 16·8 | 20·6 | 16·5 | 25·3 | 27·6 | 22·0 | 15·8 | 13·8 | 11·0 | 13·6 | 11·0 | 15·6 | 19·7 | 20·0 | 97 |
| 17 | | | | | | | | | | | | | | | | | 4·7 | 12·8 | 12·8 | 10·2 | 13·8 | 20·0 | 19·1 | 15·6 | 12·8 | 14·9 | 18·7 | 20·0 | 18·4 | 18·7 | 22·5 | 16·5 | 28·7 | 29·7 | 24·4 | 19·1 | 18·4 | 15·8 | 17·8 | 15·8 | 19·7 | 23·7 | 24·9 | 933 |
| 18 | | | | | | | | | | | | | | | | | | 4·7 | 9·0 | 10·2 | 12·8 | 19·7 | 18·7 | 14·5 | 12·2 | 14·5 | 16·5 | 14·9 | 13·8 | 12·8 | 17·3 | 13·6 | 22·0 | 23·7 | 18·7 | 13·8 | 12·2 | 9·0 | 13·6 | 13·8 | 17·8 | 21·0 | 21·6 | 662 |
| 19 | | | | | | | | | | | | | | | | | | | 4·7 | 6·6 | 6·6 | 15·6 | 14·9 | 9·4 | 7·4 | 9·4 | 12·8 | 14·5 | 11·7 | 12·8 | 16·8 | 9·0 | 22·0 | 23·2 | 18·4 | 13·6 | 14·5 | 11·7 | 15·6 | 17·3 | 19·7 | 23·2 | 23·7 | 911 |
| 20 | | | | | | | | | | | | | | | | | | | | 4·7 | 9·0 | 16·5 | 15·8 | 11·7 | 7·4 | 11·0 | 14·9 | 16·5 | 14·5 | 14·9 | 18·7 | 11·7 | 24·4 | 25·3 | 20·0 | 15·6 | 14·9 | 12·2 | 15·8 | 16·8 | 21·0 | 23·7 | 24·4 | 381 |
| 21 | | | | | | | | | | | | | | | | | | | | | 4·7 | 13·6 | 12·8 | 6·6 | 6·6 | 6·6 | 12·8 | 15·6 | 12·8 | 13·8 | 17·3 | 10·2 | 23·7 | 23·7 | 18·7 | 14·9 | 15·8 | 13·6 | 16·8 | 18·7 | 21·0 | 24·9 | 25·3 | 224 |
| 22 | | | | | | | | | | | | | | | | | | | | | | 4·7 | 4·7 | 12·2 | 13·8 | 11·3 | 14·9 | 19·1 | 16·8 | 18·4 | 21·6 | 15·8 | 29·3 | 28·7 | 23·2 | 21·6 | 22·5 | 20·0 | 23·7 | 26·0 | 28·7 | 32·6 | 33·0 | 627 |
| 23 | | | | | | | | | | | | | | | | | | | | | | | 4·7 | 11·0 | 13·6 | 10·2 | 13·8 | 18·4 | 15·8 | 17·3 | 20·6 | 14·9 | 28·0 | 27·6 | 22·0 | 20·6 | 21·6 | 19·7 | 22·5 | 25·3 | 28·0 | 32·1 | 32·6 | 24 |
| 24 | | | | | | | | | | | | | | | | | | | | | | | | 4·7 | 9·0 | 6·6 | 10·2 | 14·5 | 11·3 | 13·6 | 16·8 | 9·0 | 23·7 | 23·2 | 18·4 | 16·5 | 17·3 | 15·6 | 18·4 | 20·6 | 23·2 | 26·9 | 27·6 | 329 |
| 25 | | | | | | | | | | | | | | | | | | | | | | | | | 4·7 | 7·4 | 14·5 | 16·8 | 14·5 | 14·9 | 19·1 | 12·2 | 24·4 | 25·3 | 20·6 | 15·8 | 16·5 | 14·5 | 17·3 | 19·1 | 22·0 | 26·0 | 26·6 | 878 |
| 26 | | | | | | | | | | | | | | | | | | | | | | | | | | 4·7 | 11·3 | 15·8 | 13·6 | 14·5 | 17·8 | 11·0 | 24·9 | 24·4 | 19·1 | 16·8 | 17·3 | 15·6 | 18·4 | 20·6 | 23·2 | 26·9 | 26·6 | 2380 |
| 27 | | | | | | | | | | | | | | | | | | | | | | | | | | | 4·7 | 11·3 | 7·4 | 10·2 | 13·8 | 9·0 | 21·0 | 20·0 | 15·6 | 14·5 | 16·5 | 16·8 | 19·7 | 22·0 | 24·9 | 28·0 | 29·3 | 3159 |
| 28 | | | | | | | | | | | | | | | | | | | | | | | | | | | | 4·7 | 8·2 | 8·2 | 10·2 | 11·0 | 18·4 | 16·8 | 12·2 | 12·8 | 14·9 | 15·6 | 18·4 | 21·0 | 23·2 | 26·6 | 26·9 | 173 |
| 29 | | | | | | | | | | | | | | | | | | | | | | | | | | | | | 4·7 | 7·4 | 11·3 | 7·4 | 19·1 | 18·4 | 13·6 | 11·3 | 14·5 | 14·5 | 17·3 | 20·0 | 22·0 | 26·0 | 26·6 | 1336 |
| 30 | | | | | | | | | | | | | | | | | | | | | | | | | | | | | | 4·7 | 11·3 | 9·0 | 16·8 | 18·4 | 13·6 | 9·0 | 11·3 | 13·6 | 15·6 | 19·1 | 20·0 | 23·2 | 24·4 | 984 |
| 31 | | | | | | | | | | | | | | | | | | | | | | | | | | | | | | | 4·7 | 13·6 | 15·8 | 14·5 | 9·0 | 12·2 | 14·5 | 16·5 | 17·8 | 21·0 | 22·5 | 26·0 | 26·9 | 329 |
| 32 | | | | | | | | | | | | | | | | | | | | | | | | | | | | | | | | 4·7 | 20·0 | 19·7 | 14·9 | 13·6 | 13·8 | 13·8 | 16·8 | 19·1 | 21·6 | 25·3 | 26·0 | 307 |
| 33 | | | | | | | | | | | | | | | | | | | | | | | | | | | | | | | | | 4·7 | 8·2 | 12·8 | 15·8 | 18·4 | 20·0 | 21·0 | 25·3 | 26·6 | 30·4 | 30·9 | 931 |
| 34 | | | | | | | | | | | | | | | | | | | | | | | | | | | | | | | | | | 4·7 | 11·0 | 17·8 | 19·7 | 22·0 | 23·2 | 26·9 | 28·7 | 32·1 | 32·6 | 439 |
| 35 | | | | | | | | | | | | | | | | | | | | | | | | | | | | | | | | | | | 4·7 | 13·6 | 15·6 | 17·3 | 18·2 | 22·0 | 23·7 | 26·9 | 27·6 | 79 |
| 36 | | | | | | | | | | | | | | | | | | | | | | | | | | | | | | | | | | | | 4·7 | 7·4 | 11·0 | 11·3 | 15·8 | 16·8 | 20·0 | 20·6 | 988 |
| 37 | | | | | | | | | | | | | | | | | | | | | | | | | | | | | | | | | | | | | 4·7 | 7·4 | 9·0 | 13·6 | 14·9 | 17·8 | 18·7 | 507 |
| 38 | | | | | | | | | | | | | | | | | | | | | | | | | | | | | | | | | | | | | | 4·7 | 9·0 | 12·2 | 14·9 | 17·8 | 18·7 | 379 |
| 39 | | | | | | | | | | | | | | | | | | | | | | | | | | | | | | | | | | | | | | | 4·7 | 10·2 | 11·0 | 14·9 | 15·6 | 1289 |
| 40 | | | | | | | | | | | | | | | | | | | | | | | | | | | | | | | | | | | | | | | | 4·7 | 11·0 | 15·6 | 15·8 | 594 |
| 41 | | | | | | | | | | | | | | | | | | | | | | | | | | | | | | | | | | | | | | | | | 4·7 | 10·2 | 11·0 | 653 |
| 42 | | | | | | | | | | | | | | | | | | | | | | | | | | | | | | | | | | | | | | | | | | 4·7 | 7·4 | 13702 |
| 43 | | | | | | | | | | | | | | | | | | | | | | | | | | | | | | | | | | | | | | | | | | | 4·7 | 268 |
| $r_i$ | 510 | 9 | 120 | 248 | 20 | 654 | 251 | 1212 | 1614 | 331 | 591 | 717 | 1189 | 1453 | 638 | 264 | 1478 | 733 | 951 | 454 | 293 | 718 | 476 | 442 | 464 | 2422 | 3429 | 564 | 1268 | 656 | 333 | 387 | 1092 | 156 | 249 | 1227 | 888 | 699 | 1895 | 760 | 1077 | 7827 | 2685 | 43444 |

# Table 6.4.3.b

## Results of an L.P. model for solid fuel shipments

| | 1 | 2 | 3 | 4 | 5 | 6 | 7 | 8 | 9 | 10 | 11 | 12 | 13 | 14 | 15 | 16 | 17 | 18 | 19 | 20 | 21 | 22 | 23 | 24 | 25 | 26 | 27 | 28 | 29 | 30 | 31 | 32 | 33 | 34 | 35 | 36 | 37 | 38 | 39 | 40 | 41 | 42 | 43 | $c_j$ |
|---|---|---|---|---|---|---|---|---|---|---|---|---|---|---|---|---|---|---|---|---|---|---|---|---|---|---|---|---|---|---|---|---|---|---|---|---|---|---|---|---|---|---|---|---|
| 1 | 445 | | 68 | | | | | | | | | | | | | | | | | | | | | | | | | | | | | | | | | | | | | | | | | 513 |
| 2 | | 9 | 5 | | | | | | | | | | | | | | | | | | | | | | | | | | | | | | | | | | | | | | | | | 14 |
| 3 | | | 47 | | | | | | | | | | | | | | | | | | | | | | | | | | | | | | | | | | | | | | | | | 47 |
| 4 | | | | 193 | | | | | | | | | | | | | | | | | | | | | | | | | | | | | | | | | | | | | | | | 193 |
| 5 | | | | | 10 | | | | | | | | | | | | | | | | | | | | | | | | | | | | | | | | | | | | | | | 10 |
| 6 | | | | | 10 | 652 | | | | | | | | | | | | | | | | | | | | | | | | | | | | | | | | | | | | | | 662 |
| 7 | | | | | | 2 | 251 | | | | | | | | | | | | | | | 87 | | | | | | | | | | | | | | | | | | | | | | 340 |
| 8 | | | | | | | | 1111 | | | | | | | | | | | | | | | | | | | | | | | | | | | | | | | | | | | | 1111 |
| 9 | 65 | | | 55 | | | | 101 | 1614 | 41 | | 184 | | | | | 190 | | | | | | | | | | | | | | | | | | | | | | | | | | | 2250 |
| 10 | | | | | | | | | | 290 | 151 | | | | | | | | | | | | | | | | | | | | | | | | | | | | | | | | | 441 |
| 11 | | | | | | | | | | | 440 | | | | | | | | | | | | | | | | | | | | | | | | | | | | | | | | | 440 |
| 12 | | | | | | | | | | | | 533 | | | | | | | | | | | | | | | | | | | | | | | | | | | | | | | | 533 |
| 13 | | | | | | | | | | | | | 1189 | 194 | | | | | | | | | | | | | | | | | | | | | | | | | | | | | | 1383 |
| 14 | | | | | | | | | | | | | | 1232 | | | | | | | | | | | | | | | | | | | | | | | | | | | | | | 1232 |
| 15 | | | | | | | | | | | | | | 27 | 638 | | 47 | | | | | | | | | | | | | | | | | | | | | | | | | | | 712 |
| 16 | | | | | | | | | | | | | | | | 97 | | | | | | | | | | | | | | | | | | | | | | | | | | | | 97 |
| 17 | | | | | | | | | | | | | | | | | 933 | | | | | | | | | | | | | | | | | | | | | | | | | | | 933 |
| 18 | | | | | | | | | | | | | | | | | | 662 | | | | | | | | | | | | | | | | | | | | | | | | | | 661 |
| 19 | | | | | | | | | | | | | | | | | | | 911 | | | | | | | | | | | | | | | | | | | | | | | | | 911 |
| 20 | | | | | | | | | | | | | | | | | | | | 381 | | | | | | | | | | | | | | | | | | | | | | | | 381 |
| 21 | | | | | | | | | | | | | | | | | | | | | 111 | | | 113 | | | | | | | | | | | | | | | | | | | | 224 |
| 22 | | | | | | | | | | | | | | | | | | | | | | 607 | 20 | | | | | | | | | | | | | | | | | | | | | 627 |
| 23 | | | | | | | | | | | | | | | | | | | | | | 24 | | | | | | | | | | | | | | | | | | | | | | 24 |
| 24 | | | | | | | | | | | | | | | | | | | | | | | | 329 | | | | | | | | | | | | | | | | | | | | 329 |
| 25 | | | | | | | | | | | | | | | | | | | | | | | | | 464 | 416 | | | | | | | | | | | | | | | | | | 878 |
| 26 | | | | | | | | | | | | | | | | | | | | | | | 372 | | | 2008 | | | | | | | | | | | | | | | | | | 2380 |
| 27 | | | | | | | | | | | | | | | | | | | | | | | | | | | 3159 | | | | | | | | | | | | | | | | | 3159 |
| 28 | | | | | | | | | | | | | | | | | | | | | | | | | | | | 173 | | | | | | | | | | | | | | | | 173 |
| 29 | | | | | | | | | | | | | | | | | | | | | | | | | | | 68 | | 1268 | | | | | | | | | | | | | | | 1336 |
| 30 | | | | | | | | | | | | | | | | | | | | | | | | | | | | 328 | | 656 | | | | | | | | | | | | | | 984 |
| 31 | | | | | | | | | | | | | | | | | | | | | | | | | | | | | | | 329 | | | | | | | | | | | | | 329 |
| 32 | | | | | | | | | | | | | | | | | | | | | | | | | | | | | | | | 307 | | | | | | | | | | | | 307 |
| 33 | | | | | | | | | | | | | | | | | | | | | | | | | | | | | | | | | 931 | | | | | | | | | | | 931 |
| 34 | | | | | | | | | | | | | | | | | | | | | | | | | | | | | | | | | 161 | 156 | 122 | | | | | | | | | 439 |
| 35 | | | | | | | | | | | | | | | | | | | | | | | | | | | | | | | | | | | 79 | | | | | | | | | 79 |
| 36 | | | | | | | | | | | | | | | | | | | | | | | | | | | | | | | | | | | | 988 | | | | | | | | 988 |
| 37 | | | | | | | | | | | | | | | | | | | | | | | | | | | | | | | | | | | | | 507 | | | | | | | 507 |
| 38 | | | | | | | | | | | | | | | | | | | | | | | | | | | | | | | | | | | | | | 379 | | | | | | 379 |
| 39 | | | | | | | | | | | | | | | | | | | | | | | | | | | | | | | | | | | | | | | 1289 | | | | | 1289 |
| 40 | | | | | | | | | | | | | | | | | | | | | | | | | | | | | | | | | | | | | | | | 594 | | | | 594 |
| 41 | | | | | | | | | | | | | | | | | | | | | | | | | | | | | | | | | | | | | | | | | 653 | | | 653 |
| 42 | | | | | | | | | | | | | | | | 167 | 308 | 71 | 40 | 73 | 182 | | 84 | | | | 202 | 63 | | | 4 | 80 | | | 48 | 239 | 381 | 320 | 606 | 166 | 424 | 7827 | 2417 | 13702 |
| 43 | | | | | | | | | | | | | | | | | | | | | | | | | | | | | | | | | | | | | | | | | | | 268 | 268 |
| $r_i$ | 510 | 9 | 120 | 248 | 20 | 654 | 251 | 1212 | 1614 | 331 | 591 | 717 | 1189 | 1453 | 638 | 264 | 1478 | 733 | 951 | 454 | 293 | 718 | 476 | 442 | 464 | 2422 | 3429 | 564 | 1268 | 656 | 33 | 387 | 1092 | 156 | 249 | 1227 | 888 | 699 | 1895 | 760 | 1077 | 7827 | 2685 | 43444 |

of L.P. models, viz. that the number of non-zero variables cannot exceed the number of independent constraints. In consequence, the total number of non-zero variables for our commodity allocation problem is equal to 85. An extension of this number can be obtained only if the number of constraints increases, or if an alternative approach is chosen (for instance, an entropy maximizing model [see section 6.4.5]).

### 6.4.4 *A generalized transportation model*

In this section an extension of the original transportation model will be presented (cf. also Beckmann and Marschak [1955]). In the first place, the Weberian assumption of minimal transportation costs will be replaced by the assumption of a profit maximization. Secondly, the pattern of product flows and of transportation costs will be complicated by considering multiple products, in particular intermediate products. In the third place, the intermediate products are related to final production by means of linear activity coefficients. By means of a L.P. model one can determine the optimal spatial pattern for the allocation of products between supply sources, plants and output markets, given the product prices and the transportation rates.

One assumes again an industry made up of $J$ firms at $J$ different production places denoted by $1, \ldots, J$. The markets supplied by the firms are indicated by $1, \ldots, I$. Each firm requires $L$ different inputs $l(l = 1, \ldots, L)$ for the production of the (homogeneous) commodities. These inputs originate from $K$ supply points $k(k = 1, \ldots, K)$. The volume of commodities shipped from $j$ to $i$ is denoted by $x_{ji}$ (with corresponding unit transportation costs $\tau_{ji}$). The c.i.f. price of the commodity concerned differs from market to market, and is denoted by $p_i$. The volume of input $l(l = 1, \ldots, L)$, shipped from $k$ to $j$, is denoted by $m^l_{kj}$ (with corresponding price $p^l_{kj}$ and unit transportation costs $\tau^l_{kj}$). All prices and unit transportation costs are supposed to be known, while the decision variables $x_{ji}$ and $m^l_{kj}$ have to be derived from a L.P. model, that describes the spatial allocation problem for a profit-maximizing industry.

The objective function becomes:

$$\max \omega = \sum_{i=1}^{I} \sum_{j=1}^{J} p_i x_{ji} - \sum_{k=1}^{K} \sum_{l=1}^{L} \sum_{j=1}^{J} p^l_{kj} m^l_{kj} - \sum_{i=1}^{I} \sum_{j=1}^{J} \tau_{ji} x_{ji} - \sum_{k=1}^{K} \sum_{l=1}^{L} \sum_{j=1}^{J} \tau^l_{kj} m^l_{kj} \tag{6.4.4.1}$$

where total gross profits $\omega$ are composed of the following four terms, respectively: total revenues, f.o.b. costs of inputs, transportation costs on outputs and transportation costs on inputs. The objective function can be written as:

$$\max \omega = \sum_{i=1}^{I} \sum_{j=1}^{J} (p_i - \tau_{ji}) x_{ji} - \sum_{k=1}^{K} \sum_{l=1}^{L} \sum_{j=1}^{J} (p^l_{kj} + \tau^l_{kj}) m^l_{kj} \qquad (6.4.4.2)$$

in which the first term represents net revenues of output after subtraction of transportation costs, and the second term gross procurement costs of all inputs.

In addition to an objective function a number of constraints have to be specified. The first constraint leans on the assumption that production activities can be described by means of constant technical coefficients based on linear activity analysis; in other words, one assumes a constant ratio between inputs and outputs. The amount of input $l$ required per unit of output is denoted by $a^l$. If $a^l$ would not be independent on the location $j$, it should be provided with a subscript $j$. Therefore, the total amount of input $l$ required for the total production of firm $j$ ($\sum_{i=1}^{I} x_{ji}$) is equal to $a^l \sum_{i=1}^{I} x_{ji}$. These total input requirements cannot exceed the total flows of inputs $l$ from all supply points $k$ to firm $j$:

$$a^l \sum_{i=1}^{I} x_{ji} \leqslant \sum_{k=1}^{K} m^l_{kj} \qquad \forall\, l, j \qquad (6.4.4.3)$$

Moreover, one may impose the condition that the shipments from a supply point $k$ to all firms cannot exceed the productive capacity of that point:

$$\sum_{j=1}^{J} m^l_{kj} \leqslant b^l_k \qquad \forall\, l, k \qquad (6.4.4.4)$$

where $b^l_k$ denotes the maximum amount of input $l$ available at point $k$ per unit of time. Furthermore, one may impose the constraint discussed in section 6.4.1:

$$\sum_{i=1}^{I} x_{ji} \leqslant c_j \qquad \forall j \qquad (6.4.4.5)$$

$$-\sum_{j=1}^{J} x_{ji} \leqslant -r_i \qquad \forall\, i \qquad (6.4.4.6)$$

and:

$$x_{ji} \geq 0 \quad \forall i, j \tag{6.4.4.7}$$

$$m^{l}_{kj} \geq 0 \quad \forall k, j, l \tag{6.4.4.8}$$

It is obvious that the resulting model is a L.P. model, that possesses the standard form of the L.P. models discussed in par. 6.3. The solution of this L.P. problem gives the firm's 'location decisions' in terms of amounts of inputs from resource deposits and outputs to all market areas for each production program at each location.

### 6.4.5 *Entropy maximizing models*

Entropy maximizing models are a very specific type of optimizing models that bear a close resemblance to transportation models. The concept of entropy stems originally from thermodynamics. It is a well-known fact that closed physical systems can adopt numerous states. In general, however, the elements of such a system tend towards an arrangement which can be organized in as many ways as possible (a maximum 'disorder'). Such a tendency is called the maximization of the entropy of a system: for a closed physical system 'disorder' is much more probable than 'order'.

In addition to the *physical* concept of entropy, this concept plays also an important role in *information* theory. In this field entropy represents expected information: it indicates the degree of uncertainty about the realizations of events in information systems, represented by a discrete probability distribution. The mathematical specification of entropy in information systems bears a close resemblance to that used in physics, because both concepts are based on a common statistical background, for instance by making use of Bayesian statistics and maximum likelihood functions.

Recently the concept of entropy has also found applications in regional systems (for instance, trip distribution, freight flows, migration flows, and activity allocations). The entropy concept attempts at determining the most probable spatial configurations of a system, which can adopt numerous uncertain spatial states. In this sense entropy maximizing models can be used to assess the most probable spatial flows of trips, commodities, migrations, and so forth. A systematic survey of these models is contained in Wilson (1970).

Furthermore, entropy can be used as a measure for the degree of organization in a spatial system. In this way the concept of entropy is a tool for studying spatial differentiation, for instance, by inspecting whether certain point patterns are completely arbitrary and disordered, or whether these spatial configurations show a certain degree of spatial organization or regularity. Attempts in this field have been made among others by Berry (1964), Medvedkov (1967), and Gurevitch (1969).

The entropy concept in regional research is related to the *state* of a spatial system; it is a characteristic concerning the assignment of elements to a spatial structure. In this section attention will be paid to commodity flows from an origin $j$ to a destination $i$. It is obvious, however, that a similar reasoning can be applied to all other problems concerning the (spatial) distribution of flows.

There are numerous possibilities to assign the interregional commodity flows of an origin-destination table, given the column and row totals, and given the total costs within the system. Each particular spatial configuration can be obtained in many different ways, dependent on the number of possible states associated with a certain configuration. Anyhow, each distribution of flows within an origin-destination table should satisfy a set of *additivity* conditions. Therefore, the following relationships can be specified:

$$\sum_{i=1}^{I} x_{ji} = c_j \qquad \forall j \tag{6.4.5.1}$$

$$\sum_{j=1}^{J} x_{ji} = r_i \qquad \forall i \tag{6.4.5.2}$$

$$\sum_{j=1}^{J} \sum_{i=1}^{I} \tau_{ji} x_{ji} = C \tag{6.4.5.3}$$

where $x_{ji}$ represents again a flow from origin $j$ to destination $i$, and where $c_j$ and $r_i$ represent the row and column totals, respectively. The parameter $\tau_{ji}$ represents the unit transportation costs, while $C$ represents the total (known) transportation costs. Instead of assuming an upper constraint on the total transportation costs one may assume a total travel time budget of the spatial system concerned.

Next, the problem arises as to which spatial distribution of the trips is the most probable arrangement within the system defined by (6.4.5.1)–(6.4.5.3). According to the entropy assumption the most probable arrangement is formed by the spatial configuration which possesses the greatest number of states associated with it. If one denotes the total volume of commodities within the system by $x$, i.e.,

$$x = \sum_{j=1}^{J} \sum_{i=1}^{I} x_{ji} \tag{6.4.5.4}$$

the number of ways the individual commodities can be assigned to a particular origin-destination table with elements $x_{ji}$ is equal to:

$$\omega(x_{ji}) = \frac{x!}{x_{11}!(x-x_{11})!} \cdot \frac{(x-x_{11})!}{x_{12}!(x-x_{11}-x_{12})!} \cdot \ldots = \frac{x!}{\prod_{j=1}^{J} \prod_{i=1}^{I} x_{ji}!} \qquad (6.4.5.5)$$

The maximum value of $\omega(x_{ji})$ represents the maximum number of assignments of commodities to an origin-destination matrix. The maximum number of states of a spatial configuration dominates the number of states of alternative arrangements to such a degree, that the spatial allocation of the commodity flows associated with this maximum is the most likely one. This implies that the entropy approach is a probability approach: the 'optimal' spatial arrangement of a system is formed by the most probable arrangement, which is characterized by the fact that $\omega(x_{ji})$ of this arrangement is at a maximum.

Since $\omega(x_{ji})$ is invariant against a monotonically increasing transformation, the objective function of the spatial system can be written in a logarithmic form as:

$$\ln\omega(x_{ji}) = \ln x! - \sum_{j=1}^{J} \sum_{i=1}^{I} \ln x_{ji}! \qquad (6.4.5.6)$$

or after Stirling's approximation for $x_{ji}!$:

$$\ln\omega(x_{ji}) \approx \ln x! - \sum_{j=1}^{J} \sum_{i=1}^{I} (x_{ji} \ln x_{ji} - x_{ji}) \qquad (6.4.5.7)$$

Since $\ln x!$ is a constant, it can be left out of consideration in the maximization procedure, so that the ultimate program to be solved is:

$$\left.\begin{array}{ll} \max \ln \omega(x_{ji}) = - \sum_{j=1}^{J} \sum_{i=1}^{I} (x_{ji} \ln x_{ji} - x_{ji}) & \\ \text{s.t.} & \\ \sum_{i=1}^{I} x_{ji} = c_j & \forall j \\ \sum_{j=1}^{J} x_{ji} = r_i & \forall i \\ \sum_{j=1}^{J} \sum_{i=1}^{I} \tau_{ji} x_{ji} = C & \end{array}\right\} \qquad (6.4.5.8)$$

The outcome of program (6.4.5.8) is easily obtained by constructing a Lagrangean function $L$ for this constrained maximization problem, i.e.,

$$L = \ln \omega(x_{ji}) + \sum_{j=1}^{J} \lambda_j (c_j - \sum_{i=1}^{I} x_{ji}) + \sum_{i=1}^{I} \mu_i (r_i - \sum_{j=1}^{J} x_{ji})$$
$$+\beta(C - \sum_{j=1}^{J} \sum_{i=1}^{I} \tau_{ji} x_{ji}) \tag{6.4.5.9}$$

where $\lambda_j$, $\mu_i$ and $\beta$ are the Lagrange multipliers associated with (6.4.5.1), (6.4.5.2) and (6.4.5.3), respectively.

The necessary conditions for a maximum are:

$$\frac{\partial L}{\partial x_{ji}} = -\ln x_{ji} - \lambda_j - \mu_i - \beta\tau_{ji} = 0 \tag{6.4.5.10}$$

or:

$$x_{ji} = e^{-\lambda_j - \mu_i - \beta\tau_{ji}} \tag{6.4.5.11}$$

Next, writing

$$A_j = \frac{e^{-\lambda_j}}{c_j} \tag{6.4.5.12}$$

and

$$B_i = \frac{e^{-\mu_i}}{r_i} \tag{6.4.5.13}$$

one obtains:

$$x_{ji} = A_j B_i c_j r_i e^{-\beta\tau_{ji}} \tag{6.4.5.14}$$

By making use of (6.4.5.1) and (6.4.5.2) it is easily seen that:

$$A_j = \left\{ \sum_{i=1}^{I} B_i r_i e^{-\beta\tau_{ji}} \right\}^{-1} \tag{6.4.5.15}$$

and

$$B_i = \left\{ \sum_{j=1}^{J} A_j c_j e^{-\beta\tau_{ji}} \right\}^{-1} \tag{6.4.5.16}$$

It can be proved that the second-order conditions for a maximum are also satisfied ($\ln \omega(x_{ji})$ is a concave function), so that there is only one (absolute) maximum.

The final result (6.4.5.14) represents the most probable flow between each origin $j$ and each destination $i$. This spatial distribution function of the flows within the system concerned appears to possess a *gravity* specification. Such a gravity model is frequently used in regional research in order to analyze or estimate the flows between two spatial masses (cf. Isard [1960]). The spatial distribution of trips, represented by (6.4.5.14), can be used for several purposes.

In the first place, the result can be used to derive an 'optimal' (i.e. most likely) trip distribution in a spatial system, given $c_j$, $r_i$ and $C$. This implies that the *most probable state* of the system will be determined on the basis of the known totals $c_j$, $r_i$ and $C$. Then one has to determine first the parameters $A_j$, $B_i$ and $\beta$. Such a (numerical) estimation can be carried out in an iterative way, for instance by starting with initial values of all $B_i$'s and of $\beta$, by calculating the resulting values of all $A_j$'s by means of (6.4.5.15), by calculating on its turn a new series of $B_i$ by means of (6.4.5.16), and so forth, until the procedure converges to an equilibrium point. By substituting the resulting values of $A_j$ and $B_i$ into (6.4.5.14), and, next, by substituting $x_{ji}$ into (6.4.5.3), one can try to calibrate $\beta$, given the value $C$. Once $A_j$, $B_i$ and $\beta$ have been assessed, the 'optimal' (i.e., most likely) flows $x_{ji}$ can be determined. Such a most probable equilibrium state can be used as a planning objective in a spatial system. Next, if $C$ is unknown (which is frequently the case), $A_j$ and $B_i$ can be estimated up to a multiplicative constant (viz., the exponential cost function). By varying the parameter $\beta$, different states of the system are found. In this way one might also approximate the *actual* state of the system for a particular value of $\beta$.

As a further step formula (6.4.5.15) can be used for projecting spatial flows. Then the *actual* observation on $x_{ji}$ from the past are used to estimate the unknown parameters $A_j$, $B_i$ and $\beta$. In this case, the parameters $A_j$, $B_i$ and $\beta$ are determined by means of regression methods, for instance, by taking the natural logarithm from both sides of (6.4.5.14), Then, by assuming that $x_{ji}$ can be explained from $c_j$, $r_i$ and $\tau_{ji}$, one can estimate the corresponding parameters. Once the parameters $A_j$, $B_i$ and $\beta$ are known, (6.4.5.15) can be used as a relationship projecting the most likely future development of the spatial system concerned, given the knowledge of $c_j$ and $r_i$. In this case, one should keep in mind, however, the specific assumption about the invariance of $\lambda_j$, $\mu_i$ and $\beta$, whereas it is obvious that a change in the future structure of the system

# Table 6.4.5.a

## Results of an entropy model for solid fuel

| | 1 | 2 | 3 | 4 | 5 | 6 | 7 | 8 | 9 | 10 | 11 | 12 | 13 | 14 | 15 | 16 | 17 | 18 | 19 | 20 | 21 | 22 | 23 | 24 | 25 | 26 | 27 | 28 | 29 | 30 | 31 | 32 | 33 | 34 | 35 | 36 | 37 | 38 | 39 | 40 | 41 | 42 | 43 | $c_i$ |
|---|---|---|---|---|---|---|---|---|---|---|---|---|---|---|---|---|---|---|---|---|---|---|---|---|---|---|---|---|---|---|---|---|---|---|---|---|---|---|---|---|---|---|---|---|
| 1 | 235 | 3 | 56 | 32 | 1 | 20 | 26 | 94 | 14 | 6 | 8 | 10 | 1 | 1 | 0 | | 3 | | | | | 2 | 1 | | | | | | | | | | | | | | | | | | | | | 513 |
| 2 | 6 | 1 | 1 | 2 | | | 1 | 2 | 1 | | | | | | | | | | | | | | | | | | | | | | | | | | | | | | | | | | | 14 |
| 3 | 22 | | 5 | 3 | | 2 | 2 | 9 | 1 | 1 | 1 | 1 | | | | | | | | | | | | | | | | | | | | | | | | | | | | | | | | 47 |
| 4 | 30 | 1 | 7 | 69 | | 3 | 3 | 49 | 16 | 3 | 3 | 5 | 1 | 1 | | | 2 | | | | | | | | | | | | | | | | | | | | | | | | | | | 193 |
| 5 | | | | | | 8 | 0 | | | | | | | | | | | | | | | 1 | | | | | | | | | | | | | | | | | | | | | | 10 |
| 6 | 14 | | 3 | 3 | 15 | 484 | 43 | 13 | 3 | 7 | 16 | 12 | 1 | 1 | 1 | | 5 | | | 1 | | 31 | 10 | | | 3 | 1 | | | | | | | | | | | | | | | | | 662 |
| 7 | 35 | | 8 | 4 | 3 | 83 | 120 | 35 | 6 | 9 | 16 | 5 | 1 | 1 | 1 | | 4 | | | | | 6 | 2 | | | 1 | | | | | | | | | | | | | | | | | | 340 |
| 8 | 100 | 1 | 25 | 56 | 1 | 19 | 27 | 666 | 74 | 30 | 34 | 20 | 13 | 5 | 2 | | 30 | 1 | 1 | 1 | | 4 | 1 | | 1 | 1 | | | | | | | | | | | | | | | | | | 1111 |
| 9 | 60 | 3 | 14 | 74 | 1 | 16 | 19 | 300 | 1474 | 56 | 34 | 45 | 46 | 23 | 8 | 2 | 56 | 2 | 3 | 3 | 1 | 3 | 1 | 1 | 2 | 3 | 1 | | | | | | | | | | | | | | | | | 2250 |
| 10 | 4 | | 1 | 2 | | 7 | 4 | 18 | 9 | 134 | 147 | 48 | 6 | 9 | 4 | 1 | 29 | 1 | 2 | 2 | 1 | 2 | 1 | 1 | 3 | 3 | 1 | | | | | | | | | | | | | | | | | 441 |
| 11 | 2 | | | 1 | | 6 | 3 | 8 | 2 | 55 | 273 | 41 | 3 | 6 | 3 | 1 | 19 | 1 | 5 | 3 | | 4 | 1 | 1 | 3 | 3 | 1 | | | | | | | | | | | | | | | | | 440 |
| 12 | 1 | | | 1 | | 2 | 1 | 3 | 1 | 10 | 23 | 288 | 9 | 30 | 12 | 2 | 124 | 3 | 5 | 6 | 1 | 1 | 1 | 1 | 2 | 5 | 2 | | 1 | | | 1 | | | | | | 1 | | | | | | 533 |
| 13 | 1 | | | 1 | | 1 | 1 | 10 | 9 | 7 | 9 | 53 | 1066 | 116 | 16 | 4 | 67 | 4 | 4 | 11 | 0 | 1 | | 1 | 2 | 4 | 1 | | | | | 1 | | | | | | 1 | 1 | 1 | | | | 1383 |
| 14 | | | | | | | | 1 | 1 | 2 | 3 | 31 | 20 | 895 | 88 | 14 | 138 | 12 | 6 | 6 | 1 | 1 | 1 | 1 | 2 | 5 | 2 | 1 | 1 | 1 | | 1 | | | | 1 | 1 | 2 | 1 | 1 | | | | 1232 |
| 15 | | | | | | | | | | 1 | 3 | 20 | 4 | 139 | 231 | 51 | 141 | 42 | 16 | 15 | 2 | 2 | 2 | 2 | 5 | 10 | 5 | 2 | 2 | 2 | | 2 | | | | 2 | 3 | 5 | 3 | 3 | | | | 712 |
| 16 | | | | | | | | | | | | 2 | | 10 | 23 | 24 | 10 | 9 | 3 | 2 | | | | | 1 | 0 | 1 | | | | | | | | | 1 | 0 | 3 | 1 | 2 | | | | 97 |
| 17 | | | | | | 1 | 0 | 3 | 1 | 4 | 8 | 82 | 7 | 87 | 57 | 9 | 592 | 11 | 12 | 21 | 3 | 2 | 2 | 3 | 7 | 15 | 4 | 1 | 2 | 1 | | 2 | | | | 1 | 1 | 2 | 1 | 1 | | | | 923 |
| 18 | | | | | | | | | | | 1 | 5 | 1 | 18 | 39 | 19 | 25 | 310 | 64 | 23 | 5 | 3 | 2 | 4 | 9 | 18 | 11 | 8 | 13 | 10 | 2 | 5 | | | 0 | 11 | 12 | 35 | 7 | 3 | | | | 662 |
| 19 | | | | | | | | | | 1 | 3 | 5 | 1 | 7 | 11 | 4 | 22 | 48 | 312 | 86 | 48 | 13 | 10 | 30 | 55 | 119 | 42 | 8 | 26 | 9 | 2 | 32 | | | 1 | 10 | 4 | 12 | 3 | 1 | | | | 911 |
| 20 | | | | | | | | | | 1 | 3 | 7 | 2 | 6 | 10 | 3 | 34 | 16 | 79 | 101 | 10 | 5 | 4 | 6 | 30 | 34 | 10 | 2 | 5 | 2 | 1 | 6 | | | | 3 | 2 | 5 | 1 | | | | | 381 |
| 21 | | | | | | | | | | | | 1 | | 1 | 1 | | 3 | 2 | 33 | 7 | 24 | 6 | 5 | 21 | 17 | 82 | 9 | 1 | 4 | 0 | | 4 | | | | 0 | 0 | 0 | | | | | | 224 |
| 22 | | | | | | 1 | | | | | | | | | | | | | 1 | 1 | 1 | 376 | 219 | 4 | 2 | 21 | 7 | | 1 | | | 1 | | | | | | | | | | | | 627 |
| 23 | | | | | | | | | | | | | | | | | | | | | | 15 | 8 | | | 1 | | | | | | | | | | | | | | | | | | 24 |
| 24 | | | | | | | | | | | | 1 | | 1 | 1 | | 2 | 2 | 15 | 4 | 16 | 16 | 15 | 61 | 10 | 120 | 39 | 3 | 10 | 2 | 1 | 10 | | | | 1 | | 1 | | | | | | 329 |
| 25 | | | | | | | | | | 1 | 3 | 6 | 1 | 5 | 7 | 2 | 23 | 14 | 112 | 66 | 51 | 27 | 17 | 27 | 174 | 282 | 22 | 3 | 9 | 4 | 1 | 9 | | | 1 | 4 | 2 | 4 | 1 | | | | | 878 |
| 26 | | | | | | 1 | | | | | 1 | 5 | 1 | 4 | 5 | 2 | 17 | 9 | 86 | 27 | 88 | 129 | 116 | 136 | 101 | 1436 | 140 | 9 | 22 | 8 | 2 | 26 | | | 2 | 5 | 2 | 4 | 2 | | | | | 2380 |
| 27 | | | | | | | | | | | | 1 | | 2 | 2 | 1 | 4 | 5 | 26 | 7 | 9 | 36 | 32 | 46 | 7 | 119 | 2363 | 65 | 311 | 56 | 15 | 69 | 1 | | 8 | 15 | 4 | 3 | 1 | | | | | 3159 |
| 28 | | | | | | | | | | | | | | | | | | 1 | 1 | | | 1 | 1 | 1 | | 2 | 17 | 96 | 23 | 13 | 7 | 3 | | | 3 | 3 | 1 | | | | | | | 174 |
| 29 | | | | | | | | | | | | 1 | | 1 | 1 | 1 | 3 | 8 | 21 | 4 | 5 | 9 | 8 | 16 | 4 | 25 | 418 | 118 | 484 | 90 | 21 | 69 | 1 | | 10 | 29 | 5 | 4 | 0 | | | | | 1336 |
| 30 | | | | | | | | | | | | 1 | | 2 | 2 | 1 | 2 | 13 | 15 | 4 | 3 | 5 | 4 | 7 | 3 | 18 | 145 | 126 | 175 | 280 | 23 | 39 | 3 | | 10 | 79 | 18 | 6 | 3 | | | | | 984 |
| 31 | | | | | | | | | | | | | | | | | | 1 | 2 | | | 1 | 1 | 1 | | 3 | 19 | 31 | 20 | 11 | 180 | 3 | 3 | 0 | 37 | 12 | 3 | 1 | 0 | | | | | 329 |
| 32 | | | | | | | | | | | | | | 1 | 1 | | 2 | 3 | 20 | 4 | 4 | 4 | 4 | 13 | 3 | 23 | 71 | 12 | 53 | 15 | 3 | 65 | | | | 4 | 2 | 2 | 1 | | | | | 307 |
| 33 | | | | | | | | | | | | | | | | | | 1 | 1 | | | | | | | 1 | 3 | 4 | 3 | 4 | 7 | 1 | 837 | 29 | 26 | 10 | 2 | 1 | 1 | | | | | 931 |
| 34 | | | | | | | | | | | | | | | | | | | | | | | | | | 1 | 6 | 8 | 4 | 2 | 12 | 1 | 229 | 124 | 58 | 5 | 1 | | | | | | | 439 |
| 35 | | | | | | | | | | | | | | | | | | | | | | | | | | | 2 | 4 | 2 | 1 | 8 | 1 | 3 | 1 | 55 | 2 | | | | | | | | 79 |
| 36 | | | | | | | | | | | | 1 | | 2 | 2 | 2 | 3 | 11 | 13 | 3 | 3 | 2 | 1 | 3 | 3 | 9 | 52 | 25 | 46 | 64 | 20 | 8 | 7 | | 13 | 563 | 110 | 21 | 22 | 0 | | | | 988 |
| 37 | | | | | | | | | | | | 1 | | 2 | 2 | 3 | 2 | 12 | 6 | 3 | 1 | 1 | 1 | 1 | 1 | 5 | 9 | 7 | 8 | 16 | 5 | 4 | 1 | | 4 | 117 | 201 | 56 | 34 | 3 | | | | 507 |
| 38 | | | | | | | | | | | | 1 | | 4 | 5 | 7 | 5 | 37 | 15 | 7 | 2 | 2 | 1 | 2 | 2 | 8 | 7 | 4 | 6 | 5 | 2 | 4 | 1 | | 1 | 23 | 56 | 139 | 29 | 4 | | | | 379 |
| 39 | | | | | | | | | | | | 2 | 1 | 8 | 10 | 11 | 10 | 26 | 14 | 7 | 3 | 2 | 2 | 3 | 4 | 11 | 9 | 6 | 9 | 10 | 5 | 5 | 2 | | 4 | 92 | 134 | 111 | 729 | 39 | 8 | 2 | 1 | 1289 |
| 40 | | | | | | | | | | | 1 | 4 | 1 | 15 | 19 | 26 | 20 | 21 | 6 | 4 | 1 | 1 | | 1 | 2 | 4 | 3 | 2 | 3 | 2 | 1 | 2 | | | 1 | 13 | 18 | 27 | 69 | 313 | 7 | 1 | 1 | 594 |
| 41 | | | | | | | | | | | | 2 | 1 | 9 | 11 | 11 | 11 | 11 | 6 | 2 | 1 | 1 | | 1 | 1 | 4 | 3 | 2 | 3 | 4 | 2 | 2 | | | 1 | 23 | 28 | 23 | 131 | 65 | 240 | 27 | 19 | 653 |
| 42 | | | | | | | | | | 1 | 1 | 10 | 2 | 40 | 62 | 64 | 67 | 94 | 45 | 22 | 8 | 3 | 2 | 0 | 8 | 26 | 23 | 16 | 20 | 44 | 13 | 11 | 3 | | 14 | 193 | 271 | 225 | 838 | 313 | 807 | 7742 | 2507 | 13702 |
| 43 | | | | | | | | | | | | | | 1 | 1 | 1 | 1 | 2 | 1 | | | | | | | | | | | | | | | | | 3 | 4 | 3 | 13 | 6 | 12 | 55 | 157 | 268 |
| $r_j$ | 510 | 9 | 120 | 248 | 20 | 654 | 251 | 1212 | 1614 | 331 | 591 | 717 | 1189 | 1453 | 638 | 264 | 1478 | 733 | 951 | 454 | 293 | 718 | 476 | 442 | 464 | 2422 | 3429 | 564 | 1268 | 656 | 333 | 387 | 1092 | 156 | 249 | 1227 | 888 | 699 | 1895 | 760 | 1077 | 7827 | 2685 | 43444 |

will affect the dual variables. Finally, it should be noted that the previous model can be applied to all types of allocation problems, for instance, migration problems, investment allocation problems, consumer allocation problems, and so forth. An extensive survey of all applications is contained in Wilson (1970).

Like in all programming problems, entropy models should have a dual interpretation. It is easily seen that the entropy model (6.4.5.8) bears a close resemblance to the dual geometric program represented in Appendix 5C. This relationship allows one to derive a dual interpretation of entropy models in terms of a primal geometric model (see Nijkamp and Paelinck [1974] and Nijkamp [1975]). In this way a more economic meaning of the entropy concept can be found, viz. a generalized cost minimizing behaviour. On the other hand, this economic-oriented interpretation implies that the entropy concept is only one class of organizing principles for spatial allocation, and certainly not the most general class. The advantage of the entropy concept is that it provides a more theoretical basis for the use of gravity-type models.

Finally, an application of entropy in interregional commodity flows will be presented. The data of this problem are derived from table 6.4.3.a. The results of the entropy approach are contained in table 6.4.5.a. (Computations by Specker and Kok.)

The results of table 6.4.5.a show that entropy maximizing models lead to less corner-solutions than the corresponding L.P. model: there is a higher degree of spatial dispersion of commodity flows when the entropy concept is used. As such, the entropy results are less rigid than the L.P. results, caused by the fact that the spatial attraction forces implicit in a gravity-type model lead to a more spatially dispersed pattern of flows.

## 6.5 Regional and interregional input-output programs

### 6.5.1. *A simple input-output program*

In section 6.4.4. attention was paid to a transportation model including input–output relationships. It appeared that the interregional distribution of products could be analysed and determined by means of L.P. techniques. In this section the input–output framework will be discussed in more detail (cf. Isard [1960] and Johansen [1967]). First, an example of the distribution of commodities within a single region will be given.

Suppose a firm wants to determine an optimal product 'mix', given the limited availability of (scarce) resources and given the assumption of linear activity analysis. Such a single-region ('spaceless') model can be represented in the following general way (using maximization of revenues as a criterion):

$$\left.\begin{array}{l} \max \omega = \mathbf{p}'\mathbf{x} \\ \text{s.t.} \\ \mathbf{A}\,\mathbf{x} \leqslant \mathbf{b} \\ \mathbf{x} \geqslant \mathbf{0} \end{array}\right\} \qquad (6.5.1.1)$$

where $\mathbf{p}$ denotes a $(J \times 1)$ vector of known prices, $\mathbf{x}$ the volume of corresponding goods $j$ $(j = 1, \ldots, J)$, $\mathbf{b}$ the maximum amount available of production factors or inputs $i (i = 1, \ldots, I)$ and $\mathbf{A}$ a $(I \times J)$ matrix of technical input–output coefficients (the typical element $a_{ij}$ represents the input of factor $i$ required per unit of commodity $j$).

The basic model (6.5.1.1) can be extended to an interregional commodity allocation model. For the sake of clarity such a model will be applied to two regions, viz. 1 and 2. Therefore, hereafter the variables will be provided with a subscript 1 or 2, related to the region concerned. Furthermore, the assumption is made that the regional production factors or resources can be classified into *mobile* factors (in particular, transportation services between regions), and *immobile* factors (for instance, natural resources *within* regions). Immobile factors in a certain region give rise to constraints of the type specified in (6.5.1.1), viz.

$$\left.\begin{array}{l} \mathbf{A}_1\,\mathbf{x}_1 \leqslant \mathbf{b}_1 \\ \mathbf{A}_2\,\mathbf{x}_2 \leqslant \mathbf{b}_2 \end{array}\right\} \qquad (6.5.1.2)$$

Mobile production factors are not distinguished according to regions of origin, so that constraints on mobile factors can be specified as aggregate constraints on the availability of these mobile production factors (distinguished by mode, for instance):

$$\mathbf{A}_1^*\,\mathbf{x}_1 + \mathbf{A}_2^*\,\mathbf{x}_2 \leqslant \mathbf{b}^* \qquad (6.5.1.3)$$

where $\mathbf{A}^*$ and $\mathbf{b}^*$ represent the matrix of technical input–output–coefficients and the vector of maximum amounts available of the aggregate mobile factors, respectively. Therefore, the resulting interregional I–O program can be formalized as the following L.P. model:

$$\left.\begin{array}{l}\max \omega = \mathbf{p}_1' \mathbf{x}_1 + \mathbf{p}_2' \mathbf{x}_2 \\ \text{s.t.} \\ \mathbf{A}_1 \mathbf{x}_1 \leqslant \mathbf{b}_1 \\ \mathbf{A}_2 \mathbf{x}_2 \leqslant \mathbf{b}_2 \\ \mathbf{A}_1^* \mathbf{x}_1 + \mathbf{A}_2^* \mathbf{x}_2 \leqslant \mathbf{b}^* \\ \mathbf{x}_1 \geqslant \mathbf{0} \\ \mathbf{x}_2 \geqslant \mathbf{0}\end{array}\right\} \qquad (6.5.1.4)$$

The shipments of mobile factors between regions are supposed to cause no additional costs. If, however, this assumption would be irrealistic, the costs of interregional shipments of mobile production factors could be included in the objective function by subtracting them from the revenues. In a similar way one may take into account the costs of interregional commodity shipments.

The model presented above gives a solution for the problem of the optimal interregional distribution of production, viz. in which region and to what amount production will take place.

The *dual* problem of (6.5.1.4) can be derived directly as:

$$\left.\begin{array}{l}\min \varphi = \mathbf{y}_1' \mathbf{b}_1 + \mathbf{y}_2' \mathbf{b}_2 + \mathbf{y}^{*\prime} \mathbf{b}^* \\ \text{s.t.} \\ \mathbf{A}_1' \mathbf{y}_1 + \mathbf{A}_1^{*\prime} \mathbf{y}^* \geqslant \mathbf{p}_1 \\ \mathbf{A}_2' \mathbf{y}_2 + \mathbf{A}_2^{*\prime} \mathbf{y}^* \geqslant \mathbf{p}_2 \\ \mathbf{y}_1 \geqslant \mathbf{0} \\ \mathbf{y}_2 \geqslant \mathbf{0} \\ \mathbf{y}^* \geqslant \mathbf{0}\end{array}\right\} \qquad (6.5.1.5)$$

The dual variables $\mathbf{y}_1$, $\mathbf{y}_2$ and $\mathbf{y}^*$ represent the shadow prices of the production factors. The dual objective function implies a minimization of the imputed costs of the production factors. The dual constraints can be interpreted as follows (cf. par. 6.3): at the optimum, a positive production will take place only if the total imputed costs of production in each region are equal to the product prices; if the accounting prices of the production factors embodied in a certain product exceed the product price, the result is a zero-production of this product in the region concerned. It should be noted, that mobile factors have the same shadow prices in either region whatever may be the regional distribution of production.

The basic L.P. model can be extended by allowing transfers of originally immobile production factors. These transfers bring about additional costs that can be imputed by means of the transportation sector. For instance, regional labour may become transferable to other regions by means of (mobile) transportation services. The (unknown) amount of a certain transferable production factor to be shipped from region 1 to 2 is denoted by $z_{12}$, while the known amount of a specific transportation factor required to ship one unit of a certain production factor from region 1 to region 2 is denoted by $c_{12}$. Therefore, our modified L.P. model becomes:

$$\left.\begin{aligned} & \max \omega = \mathbf{p}_1' \mathbf{x}_1 + \mathbf{p}_2' \mathbf{x}_2 \\ & \text{s.t.} \\ & \mathbf{A}_1 \mathbf{x}_1 + \mathbf{z}_{12} - \mathbf{z}_{21} \leqslant \mathbf{b}_1 \\ & \mathbf{A}_2 \mathbf{x}_2 + \mathbf{z}_{21} - \mathbf{z}_{12} \leqslant \mathbf{b}_2 \\ & \mathbf{A}_1^* \mathbf{x}_1 + \mathbf{A}_2^* \mathbf{x}_2 + \hat{\mathbf{c}}_{12} \mathbf{z}_{12} + \hat{\mathbf{c}}_{21} \mathbf{z}_{21} \leqslant \mathbf{b}^* \\ & \mathbf{x}_1 \geqslant \mathbf{0} \\ & \mathbf{x}_2 \geqslant \mathbf{0} \\ & \mathbf{z}_{12} \geqslant \mathbf{0} \\ & \mathbf{z}_{21} \geqslant \mathbf{0} \end{aligned}\right\} \qquad (6.5.1.6)$$

The matrices $\hat{\mathbf{c}}_{12}$ and $\hat{\mathbf{c}}_{21}$ are diagonal matrices. By multiplying these matrices by means of a vector $\mathbf{z}_{12}$ and a vector $\mathbf{z}_{21}$, respectively, one obtains the total transportation requirement in both directions for each specific transport mode. These additional transportation requirements are included in the transportation constraint. In a similar way one should take account of interregional shipments of production factors by including in the original constraints transfers of immobile production factors.

The dual program is equal to (6.5.1.5), apart from two additional constraints, viz.

$$\left.\begin{aligned} \mathbf{y}_1 - \mathbf{y}_2 + \hat{\mathbf{c}}_{12} \mathbf{y}^* \geqslant \mathbf{0} \\ \mathbf{y}_2 - \mathbf{y}_1 + \hat{\mathbf{c}}_{21} \mathbf{y}^* \geqslant \mathbf{0} \end{aligned}\right\} \qquad (6.5.1.7)$$

The interpretation of these constraints is facilitated by rewriting these constraints as:

$$\left.\begin{aligned} \mathbf{y}_2 - \mathbf{y}_1 \leqslant \hat{\mathbf{c}}_{12} \mathbf{y}^* \\ \mathbf{y}_1 - \mathbf{y}_2 \leqslant \hat{\mathbf{c}}_{21} \mathbf{y}^* \end{aligned}\right\} \qquad (6.5.1.8)$$

It appears that the difference in the regional shadow prices of transferable factors may not exceed the imputed costs of shipping one unit of these factors from one region to another. In case of non-zero interregional transfers of production factors this difference is exactly equal to the imputed shipping costs.

An extension of the basic model (6.1.5.6) towards another direction is obtained by allowing interregional trade of *products.* If one denotes the vector of commodities shipped from region 1 to region 2 by $\mathbf{q}_{12}$, the minimum product requirements, $\mathbf{r}$, in each region can be specified as:

$$\left.\begin{array}{l} x_1 + q_{21} - q_{12} \geqslant r_1 \\ x_2 + q_{12} - q_{21} \geqslant r_2 \end{array}\right\} \qquad (6.5.1.9)$$

A similar specification can be found *inter alia* in Mathur (1972). The specification of the dual problem can be modified in an analogous way.

Further extensions can be introduced by imposing minimum levels of production, of value of total production, or of minimum use of factors (for instance, a minimum level of regional employment).

A rather extensive treatment of interregional L.P. problems within the framework of activity analysis is contained in Isard (1960). This generalized I–0 analysis demonstrates again the significance of the $\alpha$–principle specified in the first chapter.

### 6.5.2. *A planning model for process industries*

In this section a planning model for investment decisions in the process industry will be discussed. It was developed by Kendrick (1967) in order to analyse sets of interdependent investment projects. These interdependencies arise from the fact that the production takes place in a series of successive processes, each of which uses a part of the output of the previous process as an input. Owing to these successive stages one often encounters bottlenecks in the sense of capacity limits in certain production processes. The purpose of this analysis was to devise a model for investment decisions in the Brazilian steel industry.

The model itself is a generalized input–output transportation model. The assumption is made that a planning committee seeks to minimize the aggregate investment, production and transportation costs of all branches of the industry concerned. Such an optimal scheduling of investment decisions over time should take account of capacity constraints and market requirements. In addition, the assumption is made that the production of the industry concerned can take place at multiple plants located at different places. The investment planner is then faced with the decision whether or not certain investment projects within the successive productive units of the plant concerned should be executed. Such a decision should be based on an analysis of the pattern of the corresponding commodity flows. The L.P. model associated with the previous problem includes, in addition to a cost minimizing objective function, product requirements for each of the industry's products in each market area, capacity limits for each productive unit of each plant, investment decision variables in each period, and imports and exports.

The basic version of this L.P. model is:

$$
\begin{aligned}
\min \omega = {} & \underbrace{\sum_{j=1}^{J}\sum_{i=1}^{I}\sum_{k=K^*+1}^{K} \gamma_{ji}^{k} x_{ji}^{k}}_{t_1} + \underbrace{\sum_{j=1}^{J}\sum_{\substack{j'=1 \\ j'\neq 1}}^{J}\sum_{k=1}^{K^*} \beta_{jj'}^{k} u_{jj'}^{k}}_{t_2} + \\
& \underbrace{\sum_{i=1}^{I}\sum_{k=K^*+1}^{K} \mu_i^k m_i^k}_{t_3} + \underbrace{\sum_{j=1}^{J}\sum_{k=1}^{K^*} \nu_j^k n_j^k}_{t_4} - \underbrace{\sum_{j=1}^{J}\sum_{k=1}^{K} \epsilon_j^k e_j^k}_{t_5} \\
\text{s.t.} \quad & \\
& \underbrace{\sum_{i=1}^{I}\sum_{k=K^*+1}^{K} a_j^{kp} x_{ji}^{k}}_{t_6} + \underbrace{\sum_{\substack{j'=1 \\ j'\neq j}}^{J}\sum_{k=1}^{K^*} a_j^{kp} u_{jj'}^{k}}_{t_7} - \underbrace{\sum_{\substack{j'=1 \\ j'\neq j}}^{J}\sum_{k=1}^{K^*} a_{j'}^{kp} u_{j'j}^{k}}_{t_8} \\
& \underbrace{-\sum_{k=1}^{K^*} a_j^{kp} n_j^k}_{t_9} + \underbrace{\sum_{k=1}^{K} a_j^{kp} e_j^k}_{t_{10}} \leqslant \underbrace{c_i^p}_{t_{11}} \qquad \forall j, p \\
& \underbrace{\sum_{j=1}^{J} x_{ji}^{k}}_{t_{12}} + \underbrace{m_i^k}_{t_{13}} \geqslant \underbrace{r_i^k}_{t_{14}} \qquad \forall\ i, k\ (k = K^* + 1, \ldots, K)
\end{aligned}
\qquad (6.5.2.1)
$$

taking also account of the non-negativity conditions of all variables.

The first term, $t_1$, of (6.5.2.1) represents the total production and transportation costs. The (unknown) variable $x_{ji}^{k}$ ($j = 1, \ldots, J$; $i = 1, \ldots, I$; $k = K^* + 1, \ldots, K$) represents the volume of commodity $k$ produced at plant $j$ and shipped to final market area $i$, whereas the coefficient $\gamma_{ji}^{k}$ represents the costs of producing one unit of commodity $k$ at plant $j$ and shipping it to market area $i$. It should be noted that the production of the industry concerned is divided among intermediate products $k$ ($k = 1, \ldots, K^*$) and final products $k$ ($k = K^* + 1, \ldots, K$). Intermediate products can be used either in the next stage (the next productive unit) of the *same plant* or in other plants within the *same industry*, while final products are supplied either to consumption markets or to plants belonging to another industry.

The next term, $t_2$, stands for the costs of shipping intermediate products between plants. The (unknown) variable $u_{jj'}^{k}$ denotes the amount of intermediate product $k$ ($k = 1, \ldots, K^*$) from plant $j$ ($j = 1, \ldots, J$) to plant $j'$ ($j' = 1, \ldots, J; j' \neq j$), while the (additional) unit costs of shipping product $k$ from plant $j$ to $j'$ are denoted by $\beta^k_{jj'}$.

The third term is related to imports of final products in order to meet the final product requirements in each market area. The (unknown) variable $m^k_i$ represents the volume of imports of final product $k$ ($k = K^*+1, \ldots, K$) to market area $i$; the coefficient $\mu^k_i$ represents the c.i.f. costs of importing a unit of final product $k$ to market area $i$.

The term $t_4$ is associated with imports of intermediate products. The (unknown) imports of intermediate products $k$ ($k = 1, \ldots, K^*$) to plant $j$ are denoted by $n^k_j$, while the additional costs to the system of importing a unit of intermediate product $k$ to plant $j$ (rather than using the intermediate product produced in plant $j$) are denoted by $\nu^k_j$.

The fifth term is associated with revenues obtained by exporting certain products (for instance, owing to the fact that indivisible production units may give rise to overcapacity). This term should be subtracted from the previous cost terms. The (unknown) variable $e^k_j$ represents the exports of product $k$ from plant $j$, while the coefficient $\epsilon^{k'}_j$ represents the expected profit from exporting a unit of product $k$ from plant $j$.

The first constraint of (6.5.2.1) is the aggregate capacity constraint of each productive unit $p$ ($p = 1, \ldots, P$) in each plant $j$ ($j = 1, \ldots, J$). The first term of this constraint, $t_6$, is related only to the pure capacity of a productive unit $p$ itself in plant $j$. The coefficient $a^{kp}_j$ represents the productive capacity required in productive unit $p$ in plant $j$ in order to produce one unit of a (final) product $k$.

The next term, $t_7$, represents the capacity required to produce intermediate goods shipped between plants of the same industry.

The term $t_8$ denotes savings in plant capacities owing to intermediate deliveries from other plants of the same industry. This term possesses a negative sign, since it serves to ease the capacity constraint.

In a similar way the next term, $t_9$, can be interpreted as the decline in capacity requirements owing to imports of intermediate products.

The last term of the capacity constraint, $t_{10}$, is related to the capacity required for the production of export goods.

Obviously, $t_{11}$ represents the actual maximum capacity available in productive unit $p$ at plant $j$.

The second constraint of (6.5.2.1) serves to fulfil the product requirements of each market area. The first term of this constraint, $t_{12}$, represents the total flows of final commodity $k$ from all plants $j$ to each market area $i$.

The next term, $t_{13}$, stands for the imports of final commodities to the market area concerned.

Finally, $t_{14}$ represents the various product requirements in each market area $i$.

The previous extensive model can be solved by means of standard solution methods of L.P. models. An application of this static model to the Brazilian steel industry is contained in Kendrick (1967). In this model the investment decisions of three important steel mills in Brazil are analyzed, viz. the Companhia Siderúrgica Paulista (Santos), the Companhia Siderúrgica Nacional (Volta Redonda) and the Usinas Siderúrgicas de Minas Gerais (Minas Gerais). Each of these three steel plants has six successive productive units, viz. steel furnaces, primary rolling mills, roughing mills, hot strip finishing mills, cold strip mills and tinning lines. Furthermore, three different market areas were distinguished, viz. São Paulo, Rio de Janeiro and Belo Horizonte. These market areas can be supplied with four different products, viz. steel plate, hot sheet and strip, cold sheet and strip and tin plate. Finally, only ingot steel is included as an intermediate product. The data for this allocation problem are derived from Kendrick (1967) and presented in table 6.5.2.a (all data are measured in millions of metric tons per year or in US dollars per metric ton).

Table 6.5.2.a

Data of the investment allocation model

| | | Unit production and transportation costs $\gamma_{ji}^k$ | | | |
|---|---|---|---|---|---|
| $j$ | $i \backslash k$ | 1 | 2 | 3 | 4 |
| | 1 | 64·82 | 62·87 | 66·27 | 70·64 |
| 1 | 2 | 68·54 | 66·59 | 69·99 | 74·36 |
| | 3 | 70·32 | 68·38 | 71·78 | 76·15 |
| | 1 | 63·71 | 63·76 | 65·03 | 68·96 |
| 2 | 2 | 62·27 | 60·52 | 63·58 | 67·52 |
| | 3 | 59·29 | 57·54 | 60·60 | 64·54 |
| | 1 | 69·56 | 67·52 | 71·09 | 75·68 |
| 3 | 2 | 68·22 | 66·18 | 69·75 | 74·35 |
| | 3 | 70·40 | 68·36 | 71·93 | 76·52 |

Market requirements $r_i^k$

| $i \backslash k$ | 1 | 2 | 3 | 4 |
|---|---|---|---|---|
| 1 | 0·20 | 0·20 | 0·30 | 0·15 |
| 2 | 0·16 | 0·12 | 0·16 | 0·06 |
| 3 | 0·02 | 0·08 | 0·14 | 0·04 |

Unit imports costs $\mu_i^k$

| $i \backslash k$ | 1 | 2 | 3 | 4 |
|---|---|---|---|---|
| 1 | 102 | 102 | 112 | 122 |
| 2 | 100 | 100 | 110 | 120 |
| 3 | 108 | 108 | 118 | 128 |

Unit export profits $\epsilon_j^k$

| $j \backslash k$ | 1 | 2 | 3 | 4 |
|---|---|---|---|---|
| 1 | 2 | 3 | 4 | 5 |
| 2 | 2 | 3 | 4 | 5 |
| 3 | 2 | 3 | 4 | 5 |

Unit intermediate costs $\beta_{jj'}^k$

| $j \backslash j'$ | 1 | 2 | 3 |
|---|---|---|---|
| 1 | – | 18·54 | 6·63 |
| 2 | 8·90 | – | 2·90 |
| 3 | 11·53 | 17·44 | – |

| | | Capacity data | | | | |
|---|---|---|---|---|---|---|
| | | Maximum capacity $c_j^p$ | Capacity coefficients $a_j^{kp}$ | | | |
| $j$ | $p$ | | 1 | 2 | 3 | 4 |
| 1 | 1 | 0·80 | 1·28 | 1·24 | 1·31 | 1·40 |
| | 2 | 1·80 | 1·28 | 1·24 | 1·31 | 1·40 |
| | 3 | 1·00 | 1·10 | 1·09 | 1·15 | 1·23 |
| | 4 | 1·50 | 0·00 | 1·05 | 1·12 | 1·20 |
| | 5 | 0·35 | 0·00 | 0·00 | 1·03 | 1·11 |
| | 6 | 0·00 | 0·00 | 0·00 | 0·00 | 1·05 |
| 2 | 1 | 0·60 | 1·28 | 1·24 | 1·31 | 1·40 |
| | 2 | 1·80 | 1·28 | 1·24 | 1·31 | 1·40 |
| | 3 | 1·00 | 1·10 | 1·09 | 1·15 | 1·23 |
| | 4 | 1·50 | 0·00 | 1·05 | 1·12 | 1·20 |
| | 5 | 0·15 | 0·00 | 0·00 | 1·03 | 1·11 |
| | 6 | 0·00 | 0·00 | 0·00 | 0·00 | 1·05 |
| 3 | 1 | 1·42 | 1·28 | 1·24 | 1·31 | 1·40 |
| | 2 | 1·22 | 1·28 | 1·24 | 1·31 | 1·40 |
| | 3 | 1·25 | 1·10 | 1·09 | 1·15 | 1·23 |
| | 4 | 1·50 | 0·00 | 1·05 | 1·12 | 1·20 |
| | 5 | 0·80 | 0·00 | 0·00 | 1·03 | 1·11 |
| | 6 | 0·17 | 0·00 | 0·00 | 0·00 | 1·05 |

The results of this L.P. model are included in table 6.5.2.b.

Table 6.5.2.b

Results of the L.P. model

| | Imports $m_i^k$ | | | |
|---|---|---|---|---|
| $i$ \ $k$ | 1 | 2 | 3 | 4 |
| 1 | – | – | – | – |
| 2 | – | – | – | 0·002 |
| 3 | – | – | – | – |

| | | Internal product flows $x_{ji}^k$ | | | |
|---|---|---|---|---|---|
| $j$ | $i \backslash k$ | 1 | 2 | 3 | 4 |
| | 1 | 0·020 | 0·160 | 0·300 | – |
| 1 | 2 | – | – | – | – |
| | 3 | – | – | – | – |
| | 1 | – | – | – | – |
| 2 | 2 | 0·160 | 0·064 | 0·006 | – |
| | 3 | 0·020 | 0·080 | 0·140 | – |
| | 1 | – | – | – | 0·150 |
| 3 | 2 | – | 0·096 | 0·154 | 0·058 |
| | 3 | – | – | – | 0·040 |

| | Exports $e_j^k$ | | | |
|---|---|---|---|---|
| $j \backslash k$ | 1 | 2 | 3 | 4 |
| 1 | – | 0·122 | 0·040 | – |
| 2 | – | – | – | – |
| 3 | – | 0·215 | 0·355 | – |

These results show once more the specific results of L.P. models, viz. the fact that many flows receive a zero value. Before these results can be used in the planning process, a set of sensitivity tests on the parameters (or groups of parameters) have to be carried out in order to inspect the stability of the solution with respect to changes or uncertainties in the data.

On the other hand, a significant shortcoming of this model is the fact that its static specification is less suitable for dynamic investment decisions. A dynamic version of the previous L.P. model has also been constructed by Kendrick (1967), so that the model can be used for multi-period planning purposes. In consequence, however, the number of unknown variables and parameters undergoes a formidable rise, since the number of variables and parameters is increased by a multiple of the number of time periods. The structure of the previous model does not undergo any change, but all variables and parameters are provided with a time index for each planning period. This implies that one should make projections about the future transportation, production and activity coefficients, as well as about future capacity constraints and market requirements. In addition, such a dynamic model requires the introduction of a discount rate, since one should minimize the present value of the total cost of the production system concerned.

Finally, the model can be extended by assuming that new investment projects can be implemented within the planning-horizon. The major part of new investment projects imply indivisibilities in the production process leading to overcapacities. Furthermore, another problem arises from the fact that a planner has to decide whether or not a certain investment project should be undertaken. This leads to a zero-one decision, which implies that the L.P. model is no longer of a continuous nature, but includes some integer elements. These integer elements are present both in the objective function, viz. the investment costs of a set of possible projects, and in the capacity constraints, viz. the capacity relaxations consequent upon the possible implementation of a set of investment projects in the productive units of certain plants. Such a mixed integer continuous version of a L.P. model is more difficult to solve. Apart from a complete enumeration of all possible combinations one may use standard solution methods for integer L.P. models (see, for instance, Gomory [1958]).

### 6.5.3 *An input–output transportation model for commodity shipments*

In this section a model will be presented which is again a combination of input–output models and transport models. This model is concerned with optimal patterns of interregional shipments and demonstrates some additional characteristics of transportation models. The model can also be used for programming interregional investments, since it determines patterns of trade for a number of commodities, making use of I – 0 analysis. For the moment only one single good and two different regions will be considered in order to simplify the structure of the model. A generalization to a multiple-commodity, multiple-region situation can be presented quite easily and directly (see, for instance, Hurter and Moses [1964]).

The objective function is specified as the minimization of the aggregate transportation and labour costs:

$$\begin{aligned} \min \omega = & (\tau_{11}^1 + w_1^1 \, l_1^1)\, x_{11}^1 + (\tau_{12}^1 + w_1^1 \, l_1^1)\, x_{12}^1 \\ & + (\tau_{21}^1 + w_2^1 \, l_2^1)\, x_{21}^1 + (\tau_{22}^1 + w_2^1 \, l_2^1)\, x_{22}^1 \end{aligned} \qquad (6.5.3.1)$$

where $\tau_{ji}^k$, $w_j^k$, $l_j^k$ and $x_{ji}^k$ are the unit costs of shipping commodity $k$ from region $j$ to region $i$, the unit price of labour input $l_j^k$, the labour input required to produce one unit of commodity $k$ in region $j$, and the amount of commodity $k$ shipped from region $j$ to region $i$, respectively. The region of production may coincide with the region of consumption. Since only one commodity category and 2 regions are assumed, it is obvious that $k = 1$ and $i, j = 1, 2$.

The following constraints are imposed:

$$\left.\begin{aligned} x_{11}^1 + x_{12}^1 &\leqslant c_1^1 \\ x_{21}^1 + x_{22}^1 &\leqslant c_2^1 \end{aligned}\right\} \tag{6.5.3.2}$$

These constraints state that there is a maximum production capacity for commodity $k$ in region $j$, viz. $c_j^k$.

In the second place, there are constraints on final and intermediate commodities:

$$\left.\begin{aligned} x_{11}^1 + x_{21}^1 &\geqslant r_1^1 + a_1^{11}\,(x_{11}^1 + x_{12}^1) \\ x_{12}^1 + x_{22}^1 &\geqslant r_2^1 + a_2^{11}\,(x_{21}^1 + x_{22}^1) \end{aligned}\right\} \tag{6.5.3.3}$$

These constraints are related to the minimum product requirements in each region; $r_i^k$ denotes the minimum requirements of final commodity $k$ in region $i$, while $a_i^{kk'}$ is an input–output coefficient, viz. the volume of input $k$ required per unit of total output $k'$ in region $i$; in other words, the last terms of constraint (6.5.3.3) are related to the intermediate requirements of regions 1 and 2. In our single-commodity situation these intermediate requirements are products of the same category.

The last set of constraints is:

$$\left.\begin{aligned} l_1^1\,(x_{11}^1 + x_{12}^1) &\leqslant e_1^1 \\ l_2^1\,(x_{21}^1 + x_{22}^1) &\leqslant e_2^1 \end{aligned}\right\} \tag{6.5.3.4}$$

These constraints specify the employment requirements; $e_j^k$ denotes the maximum amount of labour available for the production of commodity $k$ in region $j$. The stock of regional employment $e_j^k$ cannot be surpassed by the required labour inputs.

The dual problem can be constructed by transforming the constraints of the primal program into the standard L.P. form:

$$\begin{bmatrix} -1 & -1 & 0 & 0 \\ 0 & 0 & -1 & -1 \\ (1-a_1^{11}) & -a_1^{11} & 1 & 0 \\ 0 & 1 & -a_2^{11} & (1-a_2^{11}) \\ -l_1^1 & -l_1^1 & 0 & 0 \\ 0 & 0 & -l_2^1 & -l_2^1 \end{bmatrix} \begin{bmatrix} x_{11}^1 \\ x_{12}^1 \\ x_{21}^1 \\ x_{22}^1 \end{bmatrix} \geqslant \begin{bmatrix} -c_1^1 \\ -c_2^1 \\ r_1^1 \\ r_2^1 \\ -e_1^1 \\ -e_2^1 \end{bmatrix} \tag{6.5.3.5}$$

The dual problem associated with (6.5.3.5) is:

$$\left.\begin{array}{l}
\max \varphi = \rho_1^1\, r_1^1 + \rho_2^1\, r_2^1 - \gamma_1^1\, c_1^1 - \gamma_2^1\, c_2^1 - \lambda_1^1\, e_1^1 - \lambda_2^1\, e_2^1 \\
\text{s.t.} \\
\begin{bmatrix} -1 & 0 & (1-a_1^{11}) & 0 & -l_1^1 & 0 \\ -1 & 0 & -a_1^{11} & 1 & -l_1^1 & 0 \\ 0 & -1 & 1 & -a_2^{11} & 0 & -l_2^1 \\ 0 & -1 & 0 & (1-a_2^{11}) & 0 & -l_2^1 \end{bmatrix} \begin{bmatrix} \gamma_1^1 \\ \gamma_2^1 \\ \rho_1^1 \\ \rho_2^1 \\ \lambda_1^1 \\ \lambda_2^1 \end{bmatrix} \leqslant \begin{bmatrix} \tau_{11}^1 + w_1^1\, l_1^1 \\ \tau_{12}^1 + w_1^1\, l_1^1 \\ \tau_{21}^1 + w_2^1\, l_2^1 \\ \tau_{22}^1 + w_2^1\, l_2^1 \end{bmatrix} \\
\rho_i^1, \gamma_j^1, \lambda_j^1 \geqslant 0, \quad i, j = 1, 2
\end{array}\right\} \quad (6.5.3.6)$$

where $\rho_i^k$, $\gamma_j^k$ and $\lambda_j^k$ represent the shadow prices of the commodity requirements at point $i$, of the capacity requirements at point $j$ and of the labour requirements at point $j$, respectively. The dual objective function maximizes the fictitious returns of final commodities over the capital and labour costs. The meaning of the dual constraints can be clarified with respect to an arbitrary constraint (for instance, the second one) as follows:

$$-\gamma_1^1 - a_1^{11}\rho_1^1 + \rho_2^1 - l_1^1\lambda_1^1 \leqslant \tau_{12}^1 + w_1^1\, l_1^1 \qquad (6.5.3.7)$$

or:

$$\rho_2^1 \leqslant \gamma_1^1 + a_1^{11}\rho_1^1 + (l_1^1\, w_1^1 + l_1^1\lambda_1^1) + \tau_{12}^1 \qquad (6.5.3.8)$$

The latter constraint states that the shadow price of final commodity 1 in region 2 cannot exceed the production costs of commodity 1 in region 1 augmented with the transportation costs between region 1 and 2. These costs include respectively the price per unit of production capacity embodied in commodity 1 produced at location 1, the price of the required intermediate inputs for commodity 1, the price of the required labour input in region 1 (composed of a direct unit price $l_1^1 w_1^1$ and an opportunity price $l_1^1\lambda_1^1$ above the direct wage costs) and the unit transportation costs from region 1 to region 2. As far as the labour costs are concerned, it should be noted that the first term has to be paid as a direct cost element of labour. The second term is positive only if the supply of labour is completely exhausted. Then the use of labour requires an additional price, viz. the imputed unit value $\lambda_1^1$. If the dual constraint is an inequality at the optimum, one may conclude on the basis of the slack-duality conditions, that there is no interregional flow of commodities from region 1 to region 2, i.e. $x_{12}^1 = 0$.

The previous problem can be formulated in an alternative way, viz. by constructing an auto- or self-dual problem (see, for instance, Dorfman et al. [1958]). Such an auto-dual problem is specified as:

$$\max \chi = (\varphi - \omega) \qquad (6.5.3.9)$$

In an auto-dual problem the difference between the dual and primal objective function is maximized. It is evident that $\chi$ is always negative except at the optimum where the value of the dual objective function is equal to that of the primal one; in other words, where $\chi = 0$. This self-dual problem tries to maximize the surplus of the imputed revenues of production over direct transportation and labour costs. Since at the optimum $\chi = 0$, the rent (in the sense of the excess value produced by the entire system) is equal to zero. The latter result is an important point in interregional equilibrium studies (see Ch.7).

The foregoing model can be extended in various ways. An additional constraint specifying more explicitly interregional transportation services can be represented as:

$$\left.\begin{aligned} x_{12}^1 &\leqslant t_{12} \\ x_{21}^1 &\leqslant t_{21} \end{aligned}\right\} \qquad (6.5.3.10)$$

where $t_{ji}$ denotes the maximum total transportation capacity for shipping commodities from region $j$ to region $i$. It is evident that these constraints are more relevant in a multi-product case, where they are represented as:

$$\sum_{k=1}^{K} x_{ji}^k \leqslant t_{ji} \qquad (6.5.3.11)$$

The values of $t_{ji}$ can be derived from a matrix with maximum transportation flows between regions. The corresponding dual variable represents the imputed value of the interregional transportation structure concerned. Consideration of transportation services is necessary in case of multi-regional equilibrium situations.

Furthermore, one may assume an interregional mobility of labour. This results in interregional flows of labour, so that total labour available in region 1 is equal to:

$$l_1^1 + a_{21}^1 l_2^1 \qquad (6.5.3.12)$$

where $a_{21}^1$ denotes the proportion of labour in region 2 available for region 1. Instead of absolute values of labour flows in both directions one might include net migration flows in one direction. The introduction of interregional labour flows is another important point in studying interregional equilibria.

In a formal and more general way the basic model specified in (6.5.3.1) (6.5.3.2), (6.5.3.3) and (6.5.3.4) can be represented for a multi-product situation as:

$$\left.\begin{aligned}
&\min \omega = \sum_{i=1}^{I} \sum_{j=1}^{J} \sum_{k=1}^{K} (\tau_{ji}^k + w_j^k l_j^k)\, x_{ji}^k \\
&\text{s.t.} \\
&\sum_{i=1}^{I} x_{ji}^k \leqslant c_j^k && \forall j,\ k \\
&\sum_{j=1}^{J} x_{ji}^k \geqslant r_i^k + \sum_{k'=1}^{K} \sum_{i'=1}^{I} a_i^{kk'} x_{ii'}^{k'} && \forall i,\ k \\
&\sum_{k=1}^{K} \sum_{i=1}^{I} l_j^k x_{ji}^k \leqslant e_j && \forall j \\
&x_{ji}^k \geqslant 0 && \forall j,\ i,\ k
\end{aligned}\right\} \qquad (6.5.3.13)$$

The dual version of (6.5.3.13) is:

$$\left.\begin{aligned}
&\max \varphi = \sum_{k=1}^{K} \sum_{i=1}^{I} \rho_i^k r_i^k - \sum_{k=1}^{K} \sum_{j=1}^{J} \gamma_j^k c_j^k - \sum_{j=1}^{J} \lambda_j e_j \\
&\text{s.t.} \\
&\rho_i^k - \sum_{k'=1}^{K} a_j^{k'k} \rho_j^{k'} - l_j^k \lambda_j - \gamma_j^k \leqslant \tau_{ji}^k + w_j^k l_j^k, \quad \forall i, j, k \\
&\rho_i^k, \gamma_j^k, \lambda_j \geqslant 0 \qquad \forall i, j
\end{aligned}\right\} \qquad (6.5.3.14)$$

Expression (6.5.3.14) can be derived in a straightforward manner by means of (6.5.3.5) and (6.5.3.6); it can also be interpreted in a similar way.

## 6.6 L.P. models for plant locations

### 6.6.1 *Location decisions and zero-one programming*

The main difference between location models and transportation models is the fact that in transportation models fixed location patterns are assumed; only the transportation pattern of commodities can be manipulated in order to attain minimal transportation (or production) costs. Location models assume variable plant locations; the choice in favour of a specific location, made for instance on the basis of the criterion of minimal production costs, is essentially of a zero-one character. This can be illustrated by means of the following example (cf. Manne and Vietorisz [1963]).

Assume a plant can choose on a rectilinear market area among two locations $A$ and $B$; the final demand is uniformly dispersed along the straight line between $A$ and $B$ with a unit density of demand. If the length of the line segment between $A$ and $B$ is equal to $l$, total sales are equal to $l$. If the (unknown) production at $A$ is denoted by $x$, the production at $B$ will be equal to $l - x$. If the transportation costs per ton-mile are denoted by $\tau$, and the total transportation costs by $T$, it is evident that minimization of the aggregate transportation costs leads to an equal division of the market as the optimal solution.

$$\begin{aligned} T &= \tau \int_0^x z \, dz + \tau \int_0^{l-x} z \, dz \\ &= \tau (x^2 - lx + \tfrac{1}{2} l^2) \end{aligned} \tag{6.6.1.1}$$

Total transportation costs are at a minimum if

$$\frac{\partial T}{\partial x} = \tau \, (2x - l) = 0 \tag{6.6.1.2}$$

or:

$$x^{\mathrm{o}} = \tfrac{1}{2} l \tag{6.6.1.3}$$

If both plants do not have equal production costs, minimization of *total* production and transportation costs gives different results. For instance, assume that the plant located at $A$ has variable costs $c_1$ per unit of product and total fixed costs $k_1$, while the variable and constant costs of the plant at $B$ are equal to $c_2$ and $k_2$, respectively. Then total production costs $C$ are:

$$\begin{aligned} C &= T + c_1 x + c_2 \, (l - x) + k_1 + k_2 \\ &= \tau \, (x^2 - lx + \tfrac{1}{2} l^2) + c_1 \, x + c_2 \, (l - x) + k_1 + k_2 \end{aligned} \tag{6.6.1.4}$$

The first-order conditions for cost minimization are:

$$\frac{\partial C}{\partial x} = \tau \, (2x - l) + c_1 - c_2 = 0 \tag{6.6.1.5}$$

or:

$$x = \frac{c_2 - c_1 + \tau l}{2\tau} \tag{6.6.1.6}$$

The corresponding minimum costs can be calculated by substituting (6.6.1.6) into (6.6.1.4).

Until now, however, only a mixture of both production processes has been considered, while the implementation of one single production process (either at $A$ or at $B$) has been overlooked. Therefore, total costs $C$ determined in the way described previously must be compared with the successive costs of a concentrated production at $A$ and $B$, denoted by $C_A$ and $C_B$, respectively. These costs can be calculated as:

$$\begin{aligned} C_A &= T + c_1 l + k_1 \\ &= \int_0^l \tau z \, dz + c_1 l + k_1 \\ &= \tfrac{1}{2}\tau l^2 + c_1 l + k_1 \end{aligned} \tag{6.6.1.7}$$

and:

$$C_B = \tfrac{1}{2}\tau l^2 + c_2 l + k_2 \tag{6.6.1.8}$$

The latter problem is, in fact, a mixed integer-continuous problem which cannot be solved by means of classical optimizing techniques, because the classical solution techniques determine only *interior* solutions and no *corner* (or zero-one) solutions; the question as to whether a certain possible location will indeed be selected is a zero-one problem. This mixed integer-continuous problem might be solved, in principle, by inspecting all possible combinations and possibilities. This would in our case imply that a single location at $A$, a single location at $B$, and a combined location at *A and B* have to be inspected successively.

The following example may clarify the previous notions. Assume that $l = 1{,}000$; $\tau = 0{\cdot}01$; $c_1 = 4$; $c_2 = 6$; $k_1 = 6{,}000$ and $k_2 = 2{,}000$. One can easily calculate by means of (6.6.1.6), that in case of a combined location *A and B* $x^{\mathrm{o}} = 600$ and $C^{\mathrm{o}} = 15{,}400$. In a similar way one can calculate that in case of a single location at $A$ $C_A = 15{,}000$ and in case of a single location at $B$ $C_B = 13{,}000$. Therefore, the solution is provided by a single plant at $B$, since there total production costs are at a minimum.

It should be noted that in case of a large number of possible locations a complete enumeration of all possible combinations leads to a formidable rise in computing time. For instance, if in $n$ possible locations at least one plant must be built, the total number of possibilities to be inspected is equal to (cf. 5.19.3.1):

$$\sum_{k=1}^{n} \binom{n}{k} = 2^n - 1 \tag{6.6.1.9}$$

In this case an efficient heuristic mixed-integer solution algorithm could be used (cf. the cutting plane technique of Gomory [1958]). Sometimes, a *partial* enumeration based on non-parametric statistical sample theory might also give reliable results. The unknown size of a sample drawn from the entire population of possibilities of plant locations, i.e. (6.6.1.9), can be determined according to the following rule (see Manne and Vietorisz [1963]): if $s$ represents the *sample size* which is required in order to guarantee with a probability $a$ that at least a proportion $\beta$ of the entire *population* of all possible cost outcomes will have costs that exceed the minimal cost in the *sample* concerned, then:

$$s = \frac{\log (1 - a)}{\log \beta} \qquad (6.6.1.10)$$

However, this rather crude rule of thumb does not take into account the *level* of all possibilities: it only takes account of a proportion of the population with costs below the minimum cost level of a sample.

### 6.6.2 *A L.P. model for plant location*

The location theory discussed in Ch.3 was based on the assumption that each point in the location space could be a relevant location for a firm. The optimum location for such a continuous problem could be determined by solving the first-order conditions of a cost (or revenue) function with respect to the unknown co-ordinates $x$ and $y$. Frequently, however, a location problem is formulated as the choice of an optimal location among a number of pre-selected sites (for instance, the nodes of a network). This problem is obviously a mixed-integer (or zero-one) problem: which of a number of pre-selected sites should be chosen for the plants to optimize a cost or revenue function? A discussion of this problem can be found among others in Manne and Vietorisz (1963), Nicholson (1971) and Scott (1971).

The following location problem will be considered here in more detail. Suppose there are $K$ distinct points $k$ ($k = 1, \ldots, K$) to be considered for locating a plant (or a number of plants) as sources of supply of a certain intermediate product. This intermediate product has to be shipped to points of supply of a certain final product. It is assumed, that there are $J$ pre-selected relevant points $j$ ($j = 1, \ldots, J$), each of which can act as a supply point for final commodities. In addition, there are $I$ distinct market points $i$ ($i = 1, \ldots, I$) to be served. Finally, there is a known minimum rate of requirements $r_i$, to be satisfied at each market $i$.

The costs of satisfying the product requirement within the previous production transportation system are composed of fixed set-up costs on the one hand, and of manufacturing and transportation costs on the other hand. Deliveries of intermediate products from location $k$ to $j$ are denoted by $y_{kj}$ ($k = 1, \ldots, K; j = 1, \ldots, J$), while final commodities produced at location $j$ and shipped to market (or region) $i$ are denoted by $x_{ji}$ ($j = 1, \ldots, J; i = 1, \ldots, I$). The variable costs of producing one unit of intermediate product at location $k$ and shipping it to $j$ are denoted by $\beta_{kj}$, whereas the variable unit costs of final products plus unit transportation costs are denoted by $\gamma_{ji}$. The fixed costs of plants of intermediate products and of final products are represented by $a_k$ and $b_j$, respectively. Then the following L.P. model for zero-one plant locations decisions is constructed:

$$\left.\begin{aligned}
\min \omega = & \sum_{k=1}^{K} a_k \delta_k + \sum_{j=1}^{J} b_j \delta_j + \sum_{k=1}^{K} \sum_{j=1}^{J} \beta_{kj} y_{kj} \\
& + \sum_{j=1}^{J} \sum_{i=1}^{I} \gamma_{ji} x_{ji} \\
\text{s.t.} & \\
& \sum_{j=1}^{J} x_{ji} = r_i \qquad \forall i \\
& y_{kj}, x_{ji} \geqslant 0 \qquad \forall k, j, i \\
& \delta_k = \delta_k^2 \qquad \forall k \\
& \delta_j = \delta_j^2 \qquad \forall j
\end{aligned}\right\} \tag{6.6.2.1}$$

The last two zero-one constraints mean that $\delta_k$ and $\delta_j$ are either zero or one. They should be interpreted as follows:

$$\begin{cases}
\text{if } \delta_k \begin{cases} = 1 \\ = 0 \end{cases}, \text{then } \sum_{j=1}^{J} y_{kj} \begin{cases} \geqslant 0 \\ = 0 \end{cases} \quad \forall k \\
\text{if } \delta_j \begin{cases} = 1 \\ = 0 \end{cases}, \text{then } \sum_{i=1}^{I} x_{ji} \begin{cases} \geqslant 0 \\ = 0 \end{cases} \quad \forall j
\end{cases}$$

The latter representation demonstrates clearly the mixed integer-continuous character of this programming model. In addition to the market requirements $r_i$ one may introduce a capacity constraint for plants (cf. the transportation models). Furthermore, one may introduce a material balance condition, viz. that there is for each plant $j$ a balance between inputs and outputs, if outputs are measured in material input-equivalents. This would imply the following additional condition:

$$\sum_{k=1}^{K} y_{kj} = \sum_{i=1}^{I} x_{ji}, \ \forall j \tag{6.6.2.2}$$

The previous model has been tested for the Latin American ammonia fertilizer market by Manne and Vietorisz (1963). They considered 5 alternative production sites, which might be relevant both for ammonia production (i.e. an intermediate good) and for fertilizer production (i.e. a final good). In addition, they considered 12 distinct Latin American market points. In order to discuss the specific results of such a mixed integer-continuous L.P. model, the data of the Manne-Vietorisz problem are represented in table 6.6.2.a (imports are deleted). The costs are measured in thousands of US dollars and the volumes in millions of pounds per year in terms of ammonia-equivalents.

Table 6.6.2.a

Data of a zero-one location problem

| | $a_k$ | $b_j$ | $\beta_{kj}$ | | | | |
|---|---|---|---|---|---|---|---|
| | | | 1 | 2 | 3 | 4 | 5 |
| 1 | 1760 | 810 | 20·4 | 33·6 | 34·5 | 26·9 | 29·5 |
| 2 | 1656 | 951 | 33·4 | 20·2 | 26·7 | 31·3 | 28·1 |
| 3 | 1626 | 754 | 35·3 | 27·7 | 21·2 | 35·0 | 32·2 |
| 4 | 1784 | 856 | 41·8 | 46·4 | 49·1 | 35·3 | 42·1 |
| 5 | 1782 | 852 | 43·0 | 41·8 | 44·9 | 40·7 | 33·9 |

| | $\gamma_{ji}$ | | | | | | | | | | | |
|---|---|---|---|---|---|---|---|---|---|---|---|---|
| | 1 | 2 | 3 | 4 | 5 | 6 | 7 | 8 | 9 | 10 | 11 | 12 |
| 1 | 32·2 | 44·0 | 45·8 | 31·5 | 34·1 | 42·0 | 43·4 | 40·3 | 37·8 | 42·9 | 36·6 | 30·8 |
| 2 | 36·6 | 24·4 | 29·2 | 37·6 | 34·2 | 41·0 | 26·1 | 24·2 | 29·9 | 48·9 | 31·9 | 37·6 |
| 3 | 37·0 | 27·9 | 23·1 | 41·3 | 38·4 | 40·9 | 24·7 | 26·8 | 29·6 | 52·8 | 32·6 | 41·3 |
| 4 | 38·5 | 41·9 | 48·0 | 23·2 | 32·2 | 48·5 | 44·6 | 44·1 | 43·1 | 34·5 | 42·4 | 28·9 |
| 5 | 44·0 | 35·3 | 41·4 | 33·2 | 29·8 | 54·1 | 37·7 | 37·1 | 42·8 | 44·6 | 44·4 | 32·6 |

| | 1 | 2 | 3 | 4 | 5 | 6 | 7 | 8 | 9 | 10 | 11 | 12 |
|---|---|---|---|---|---|---|---|---|---|---|---|---|
| $r_i$ | 9·2 | 59·9 | 95·8 | 185·3 | 344·1 | 66·1 | 168·6 | 50·0 | 34·0 | 11·1 | 109·5 | 47·0 |

There are 10 variables of a zero-one character, viz. $\delta_k$ ($k = 1, \ldots, 5$) and $\delta_j$ ($j = 1, \ldots, 5$). This would imply that the total number of combinatorial possibilities is according to (6.6.1.9) equal to $2^{10} - 1$. By means of a complete enumeration it was found that the optimal solution of the previous zero-one problem is based upon utilizing a single joint plant (both for ammonia and for fertilizer production) at location 2. This implies that there are many zero-flows within the combined ammonia fertilizer system, a result which corresponds to our previous remarks about L.P. models. In the light of these results one may wonder whether non-linear programming models are not more satisfactory (in spite of the increase in mathematical complexity), for instance quadratic programming (see section 6.6.3) or geometric programming (see Ch.5 and 7).

A similar model applied to location decisions of steel plants serving the Canadian steel markets is contained in Casetti (1968). An extensive survey of general L.P. models for location problems is contained in Serck-Hanssen (1970). These models can be considered as generalizations of the model presented previously.

### 6.6.3 *Assignment models*

A specific type of general location models is formed by the so-called assignment models, which are in particular concerned with the spatial allocation of indivisible resources (see Koopmans and Beckmann [1957]). This type of problems is again of a zero-one nature, because an assignment model attempts to determine an optimal assignment of plants to locations.

An assignment model is in fact a certain type of the transportation models discussed previously. Suppose $J$ locations $j$ ($j = 1, \ldots, J$) and $I$ plants $i$ ($i = 1, \ldots, I$). The total number of plants is equal to the total number of locations. These $J$ plants have to be allocated among the $I$ locations, such that (a) each location receives precisely one plant, and (b) a certain decision criterion is optimized (for instance, minimization of costs, maximization of profits).

If one assumes the criterion of cost minimization, one has to construct a cost matrix for all plants at all locations. The typical element $c_{ji}$ of such a cost matrix represents the total costs expected from the operation of plant $j$ in location $i$. Then the assignment problem can be formulated as:

$$\left.\begin{array}{ll} \min \omega = \sum_{j=1}^{J} \sum_{i=1}^{I} c_{ji} x_{ji} & \\ \text{s.t.} & \\ \sum_{j=1}^{J} x_{ji} = 1 & \forall\, i \\ \sum_{i=1}^{I} x_{ji} = 1 & \forall\, j \\ x_{ji} \geqslant 0 & \forall\, j, i \end{array}\right\} \qquad (6.6.3.1)$$

Variable $x_{ji}$ is a zero-one variable: if there will be no plant $j$ located at point $i$, $x_{ji} = 0$; otherwise, $x_{ji} = 1$. The first constraint of (6.6.3.1) guarantees that exactly one location of each kind $i$ is available, whereas the second constraint guarantees that exactly one plant of each type $j$ is to be assigned.

If maximization of profits is assumed rather than a minimization of costs the objective function becomes:

$$\max \omega = \sum_{j=1}^{J} \sum_{i=1}^{I} \pi_{ji} x_{ji} \qquad (6.6.3.2)$$

where $\pi_{ji}$ represents the expected profits of plant $j$ at location $i$. An efficient solution algorithm for the previous types of L.P. transportation models can be found among others in Ford and Fulkerson (1956).

Next, one may assume that the profits of plant $j$ at location $i$ depend on the uses of other locations. Such interactions may result from flows of intermediate commodities between the successive plants. Then objective function (6.6.3.2) should be modified such that $\pi_{ji}$ represents gross revenue less costs of primary inputs except transportation costs of intermediate commodities between plants. These transportation costs have to be included separately.

Suppose a set of non-negative numbers $z_{jj'}^{ii'}$ $(j,j' = 1, \ldots, J;\ j \neq j';\ i,i' = 1, \ldots, I)$, each element of which represents the known intermediate commodity flows from plant $j$ at location $i$ to plant $j'$ at location $i'$. Next, suppose a set of non-negative numbers $\tau_{jj'}^{ii'}$, each element of which represents the costs of shipping one unit of $z_{jj'}^{ii'}$. Then the costs of shipping the required intermediate commodities between plant $j$ $(j = 1, \ldots, J)$ at location $i$ $(i = 1, \ldots, I)$, to a plant $j'$ $(j' = 1, \ldots, J;\ j' \neq j)$ at location $i'$ $(i' = 1, \ldots, I)$, denoted by $T_{jj'}^{ii'}$, are:

$$T_{jj'}^{ii'} = \tau_{jj'}^{ii'} z_{jj'}^{ii'} \qquad (6.6.3.3)$$

Now the total transportation costs of intermediate commodities within the system are:

$$\sum_{\substack{j=1 \\ j \neq j'}}^{J} \sum_{j'=1}^{J} \sum_{\substack{i=1 \\ i \neq i'}}^{I} \sum_{i'=1}^{I} T_{jj'}^{ii'} x_{ji} x_{j'i'} \qquad (6.6.3.4)$$

Ultimately, the new objective function of the assignment problem is:

$$\max \omega = \sum_{j=1}^{J} \sum_{i=1}^{I} \pi_{ji} x_{ji} - \sum_{\substack{j=1 \\ j \neq j'}}^{J} \sum_{j'=1}^{J} \sum_{\substack{i=1 \\ i \neq i'}}^{I} \sum_{i'=1}^{I} T_{jj'}^{ii'} x_{ji} x_{j'i'} \qquad (6.6.3.5)$$

Combined with the constraints of (6.6.3.1) this problem is called a quadratic assignment problem, because the maximand is a polynomial expression of the second degree in the unknown variables $x_{ji}$. The computational problems associated with this quadratic assignment problem are rather serious; a solution can be obtained by constructing an equivalent linear program (see Lawler [1963]).

## 6.7 Investment allocation models

### 6.7.1 *An interregional allocation model of investment*

In this section a programming model for an optimal distribution of a set of investment activities over a number of regions will be constructed (cf. Bernard [1963], and Blokland and Nijkamp [1974]).

This model contains the following elements:

$$I_r = \kappa_r q_r \tag{6.7.1.1}$$

where $I_r$ and $q_r$ represent respectively the total investments and the total production in region $r$ ($r = 1, \ldots, R$); $\kappa_r$ is a constant Leontief-coefficient for a linear relationship between investment and production.

$$L_r = l_r q_r \tag{6.7.1.2}$$

where $L_r$ represents the labour requirements in region $r$ and $l_r$ a constant labour-output ratio.

$$M_r = L_r^* - L_r \tag{6.7.1.3}$$

where $M_r$ represents net regional migration and $L_r^*$ the known regional labour supply.

$$\sum_{r=1}^{R} I_r \leqslant I \tag{6.7.1.4}$$

where $I$ is the total national investment budget.

$$\sum_{r=1}^{R} L_r \leqslant \sum_{r=1}^{R} L_r^* \tag{6.7.1.5}$$

which guarantees that the national labour requirement does not exceed total supply.

$$C_r = \gamma_r q_r + \beta_r M_r^2 \tag{6.7.1.6}$$

where $C_r$ represents regional costs, composed of production costs and migration costs; $\gamma_r$ represents the fixed marginal production costs, whereas the quadratic term indicates that the regional costs increase more than proportionally with a rise in migration.

$$Y_r = q_r - C_r \tag{6.7.1.7}$$

which defines regional income as the difference between regional production and regional costs.

The previous model describes the economic structure of the $R$ regions. An optimal interregional allocation of the investments is obtained by introducing a decision criterion, for instance the maximization of national income, i.e. the sum of regional incomes:

$$\begin{aligned}
\max \omega &= \sum_{r=1}^{R} Y_r \\
&= \sum_{r=1}^{R} (q_r - C_r) \\
&= \sum_{r=1}^{R} \left(\frac{L_r}{l_r} - \gamma_r q_r - \beta_r M_r^2\right) \\
&= \sum_{r=1}^{R} \left\{\frac{L_r}{l_r} - \gamma_r \frac{L_r}{l_r} - \beta_r (L_r^* - L_r)^2\right\} \\
&= \sum_{r=1}^{R} \left[\left\{\frac{(1-\gamma_r)}{l_r} + 2\,\beta_r L_r^*\right\} L_r - \beta_r L_r^2 - \beta_r L_r^{*2}\right]
\end{aligned} \tag{6.7.1.8}$$

Since the last term of the objective function is a constant, it can be deleted. By defining:

$$a_r = \frac{1-\gamma_r}{l_r} + 2\,\beta_r L_r^* \tag{6.7.1.9}$$

the objective function becomes the following quadratic expression:

$$\max \omega = \sum_{r=1}^{R} (a_r L_r - \beta_r L_r^2) \tag{6.7.1.10}$$

Until now constraints (6.7.1.1), (6.7.1.4) and (6.7.1.5) are left out of consideration. Constraint (6.7.1.4) can be written as:

$$\begin{aligned}
\sum_{r=1}^{R} I_r &= \sum_{r=1}^{R} \kappa_r q_r \\
&= \sum_{r=1}^{R} \frac{\kappa_r}{l_r} L_r \leqslant I
\end{aligned} \tag{6.7.1.11}$$

Therefore, the ultimate quadratic programming model is:

$$\left.\begin{aligned} &\max \omega = \sum_{r=1}^{R} (a_r L_r - \beta_r L_r^2) \\ &\text{s.t.} \\ &\sum_{r=1}^{R} \frac{\kappa_r}{l_r} L_r \leqslant I \\ &\sum_{r=1}^{R} L_r \leqslant \sum_{r=1}^{R} L_r^* \end{aligned}\right\} \qquad (6.7.1.12)$$

This problem can be solved by means of standard methods for quadratic programming, for instance constrained gradient methods.

### 6.7.2 *An interregional model for the allocation of investments under environmental constraints*

In this section attention will be paid to environmental deterioration resulting from production and consumption. It will be assumed that environmental degradation can be attacked (a) by a spatial reallocation of production; (b) by installing anti-pollution investments. The model presented here is based on a multi-sectoral approach contained in Mastenbroek and Nijkamp (1974).

This model is a L.P. model, in which the aggregated regional surplus is maximized subject to a set of side-conditions. The regional surplus is here defined as the aggregated sectoral values added minus the costs of environmental deterioration in each region $r (r = 1, \ldots, R)$. Therefore, the objective function is:

$$\max \omega = \sum_{r=1}^{R} \sum_{i=1}^{I} v_i^r q_i^r - \sum_{r=1}^{R} \sum_{k=1}^{K} c_k^r d_k^r \qquad (6.7.2.1)$$

where $q_i^r$ represents the production of sector $i$ $(i = 1, \ldots, I)$ in region $r$; $v_i^r$ the corresponding value added coefficients; $d_k^r$ the concentration of pollutant $k$ $(k = 1, \ldots, K)$ in region $r$; and $c_k^r$ the corresponding cost coefficients of pollution (for instance, agricultural damage, damage to materials and to health etc.). Since these cost coefficients can be estimated only very roughly, one should carry out a sensitivity analysis on the results of the model in order to inspect whether the results are invariant against errors in $c_k^r$.

The previous objective function has to be maximized subject to certain side-conditions. The first side-condition arises from the following I – O model.

$$q_i^r = \sum_{r'=1}^{R} \sum_{i'=1}^{I} a_{ii'}^{rr'} q_{i'}^{r'} + f_i^r + i_i^r + x_i^r \tag{6.7.2.2}$$

where $a_{ii'}^{rr'}$ is the well-known I – 0 coefficient between sector $i$ in region $r$ and sector $i'$ in region $r'$; $f_i^r$ the deliveries of the final products by sector $i$ in region $r$; and $x_i^r$ the known net exports from sector $i$ in region $r$ (cf. [5.10.1]).

The final commodities can be used both for internal consumption and consumption in other regions. Therefore, the final deliveries in region $r$ can be split up into:

$$f_i^r = \sum_{r'=1}^{R} f_i^{rr'} \tag{6.7.2.3}$$

where $f_i^{rr'}$ represents the quantity of final goods of sector $i$ produced in region $r$ and shipped to region $r'$. Next, one may assume that $f_i^{rr'}$ is a fixed proportion $\rho_i^{rr'}$ of the regional value added from the previous period (cf. also [5.10.3]):

$$f_i^{rr'} = \rho_i^{rr'} \sum_{i=1}^{I} v_i^{r'} q_{i,t-1}^{r'} \tag{6.7.2.4}$$

where $q_{i,t-1}^{r'}$ represents the known production value of sector $i$ in region $r'$ during a period before the planning period.

Next, one may consider in more detail the investments $i_i^r$. The assumption is made that investments can be used for two different purposes, viz. for productive purposes (machines, buildings, etc.) and for anti-pollution activities (water purifying installations, filters, etc.). In addition, one should be aware of the fact that $i_i^r$ represents *deliveries* of investments by sector $i$ (i.e., an output), and *not a capital increment* of sector $i$. The link between the input and output side is given by (5.10.10). In a way similar to (5.10.10) one may assume:

$$i_i^r = \sum_{r'=1}^{R} \sum_{i'=1}^{I} t_{ii'}^{rr'} I_{i'}^{Pr'} + \sum_{r'=1}^{R} \sum_{i'=1}^{I} \Theta_{ii'}^{rr'} I_{i'}^{Er'} \tag{6.7.2.5}$$

where $I_{i'}^{Pr'}$ *and* $I_{i'}^{Er'}$ represent the productive investments and the 'environmental' investments made by sector $i'$ in region $r'$, respectively. The coefficients $t_{ii'}^{rr'}$ and $\Theta_{ii'}^{rr'}$ denote which proportion of the corresponding investments are delivered by sector $i$ in region $r$. The total investments $\overline{I}$ within this multiregional system are:

$$\overline{I} = \sum_{r=1}^{R} \sum_{i=1}^{I} (I_i^{Pr} + I_i^{Er}) \qquad (6.7.2.6)$$

One may assume that the total investment budget is limited to a proportion $\beta$ of the national production value from the previous period, i.e.

$$\overline{I} \leqslant \beta \sum_{r=1}^{R} \sum_{i=1}^{I} q_{i,t-1}^{r} \qquad (6.7.2.7)$$

The productive investments serve both for replacement investments and for production extensions. In addition, the productive investments implemented in a certain period are only partially active in the period concerned. Therefore, the following condition is valid:

$$q_i^r \leqslant \kappa_i^r \left\{ (1-\delta_i^r)\, k_{i,t-1}^r + \eta_i^r\, I_i^{Pr} \right\} \qquad (6.7.2.8)$$

where $\kappa_i^r$ represents the (maximum) marginal productivity of capital in sector $i$ of region $r$; $\delta_i^r$ the average rate of depreciation; $k_{i,t-1}^r$ the capital stock of sector $i$ in region $r$ from a previous period; and $\eta_i^r$ the fraction of new productive investments which is already active in the period of installation.

Next, the environmental investments will be considered in more detail. They serve to reduce pollution; in other words, a unit of environmental investments $I_i^{Er}$ leads to a decline in the pollution, caused by sector $i$ in region $r$. The relationship between pollution, production, consumption and environmental investments can be represented in a simple way as follows:

$$t_k^r = \sum_{i=1}^{I} b_{ki}^r\, q_i^r + \sum_{i=1}^{I} \gamma_{ki}^r\, f_i^r - \sum_{i=1}^{I} \mu_{ki}^r\, I_i^{rE} \qquad (6.7.2.9)$$

where $t_k^r$ represents the emission of pollutant $k$ in region $r$. The coefficient $b_{ki}^r$ represents a pollution I – 0 coefficient denoting the volume of pollutant $k$ caused by a unit of production $i$ in region $r$ (see also [5.18.5]); $\gamma_{ki}^r$ is defined in a similar way for consumption activities; the coefficient $\mu_{ki}^r$ represents the decline in pollutant $k$, if a unit of anti-pollution investments $I_i^{rE}$ is implemented.

The relationship between *emission* of pollution at a certain point and *concentration* of pollution at another point is represented by (5.18.3), i.e.:

$$d_k^r = \sum_{r'=1}^{R} d_k^{r'r}$$
$$= \sum_{r'=1}^{R} h_k^{r'r} t_k^{r'} \qquad (6.7.2.10)$$

where $d_k^{r'r}$ represents the flow of pollutant $k$ from region $r'$ to $r$, and where $h_k^{r'r}$ represents which proportion of pollutant $k$ generated in region $r'$ ends up in region $r$.

In addition, the employment sector can be introduced. Assuming fixed labour coefficients one obtains:

$$L_i^r = l_i^r \, q_i^r \qquad (6.7.2.11)$$

where $L_i^r$ represents the demand for labour by sector $i$ in region $r$, and $l_i^r$ the average labour coefficient. By assuming an upper limit for the supply of labour in each region $r$ one finds:

$$\sum_{i=1}^{I} L_i^r = \sum_{i=1}^{I} l_i^r \, q_i^r \leqslant \bar{L}^r \qquad (6.7.2.12)$$

where $\bar{L}^r$ represents the maximum volume of labour available in region $r$ (apart from migration).

Finally, one may impose upper limits for the emission of pollution:

$$t_k^r \leqslant \bar{t}_k^r \qquad (6.7.2.13)$$

where $\bar{t}_k^r$ represents a pollution standard which may not be surpassed. If necessary one may impose also a pollution constraint on the concentration $d_k^r$ of pollution.

The previous model serves to determine an optimal spatial allocation of investments such that the total national surplus is maximized. The model is constructed such that simultaneously an optimal allocation of productive and environmental investments will take place, both over sectors and through space.

The previous model was applied to the Dutch industrialized area, the Rijnmond (around Rotterdam). For the sake of simplicity only two regions are considered here, viz. the Rijnmond-area itself and the remaining part of the Netherlands (denoted by region 1 and 2, respectively). Four sectors (denoted by 1,2,3 and 4) are distinguished in each region, viz. agriculture and fishery, industry, services, and transportation. Three pollutants are considered, viz. sulfur dioxide, nitrogen oxide, and particulates (denoted by 1,2 and 3, respectively). The data of this problem are contained in table 6.7.2.a.

Table 6.7.2.a

Data of the pollution control model

| | $i$ | $v_i^r$ | $x_i^r$ | $\rho_i^{r1}$ | $\rho_i^{r2}$ | $\kappa_i^r$ | $\delta_i^r$ | $\eta_i^r$ | $l_i^r$ | $q_{i,t-1}^r$ | $k_{i,t-1}^r$ |
|---|---|---|---|---|---|---|---|---|---|---|---|
| Region 1 | 1 | 0·63 | 3·0 | 0·005 | 0·002 | 0·40 | 0·037 | 0·3 | 0·078 | 12·0 | 42·0 |
| | 2 | 0·21 | 42·8 | 0·100 | 0·024 | 0·31 | 0·030 | 0·3 | 0·026 | 628·0 | 2832·0 |
| | 3 | 0·52 | 7·4 | 0·250 | 0·021 | 0·28 | 0·043 | 0·3 | 0·050 | 254·0 | 1188·0 |
| | 4 | 0·52 | 46·0 | 0·013 | 0·001 | 0·17 | 0·103 | 0·3 | 0·062 | 106·0 | 816·0 |
| Region 2 | 1 | 0·53 | 13·0 | 0·010 | 0·027 | 0·40 | 0·039 | 0·3 | 0·065 | 693·0 | 2112·0 |
| | 2 | 0·28 | 193·0 | 0·126 | 0·344 | 0·31 | 0·029 | 0·3 | 0·034 | 4625·0 | 18096·0 |
| | 3 | 0·53 | 220·0 | 0·115 | 0·315 | 0·28 | 0·056 | 0·3 | 0·074 | 1381·0 | 6072·0 |
| | 4 | 0·53 | 200·0 | 0·004 | 0·012 | 0·17 | 0·114 | 0·3 | 0·072 | 301·0 | 5796·0 |

| $a_{ii'}^{rr'}$ | | Region 1 | | | | Region 2 | | | |
|---|---|---|---|---|---|---|---|---|---|
| | | 1 | 2 | 3 | 4 | 1 | 2 | 3 | 4 |
| Region 1 | 1 | 0·072 | 0·006 | 0·000 | 0·000 | 0·001 | 0·000 | 0·000 | 0·000 |
| | 2 | 0·011 | 0·173 | 0·075 | 0·063 | 0·047 | 0·007 | 0·010 | 0·052 |
| | 3 | 0·040 | 0·036 | 0·088 | 0·037 | 0·003 | 0·001 | 0·002 | 0·009 |
| | 4 | 0·002 | 0·003 | 0·044 | 0·025 | 0·000 | 0·000 | 0·001 | 0·017 |
| Region 2 | 1 | 0·018 | 0·004 | 0·000 | 0·000 | 0·102 | 0·073 | 0·002 | 0·001 |
| | 2 | 0·053 | 0·003 | 0·010 | 0·015 | 0·290 | 0·283 | 0·125 | 0·138 |
| | 3 | 0·007 | 0·016 | 0·004 | 0·005 | 0·039 | 0·051 | 0·053 | 0·049 |
| | 4 | 0·000 | 0·000 | 0·007 | 0·004 | 0·003 | 0·007 | 0·085 | 0·037 |

| $t_{ii'}^{rr'} = \Theta_{ii'}^{rr'}$ | | Region 1 | | | | Region 2 | | | |
|---|---|---|---|---|---|---|---|---|---|
| | | 1 | 2 | 3 | 4 | 1 | 2 | 3 | 4 |
| Region 1 | 1 | 0·0 | 0·0 | 0·0 | 0·0 | 0·0 | 0·0 | 0·0 | 0·0 |
| | 2 | 0·68 | 0·68 | 0·68 | 0·68 | 0·17 | 0·17 | 0·17 | 0·17 |
| | 3 | 0·12 | 0·12 | 0·12 | 0·12 | 0·03 | 0·03 | 0·03 | 0·03 |
| | 4 | 0·0 | 0·0 | 0·0 | 0·0 | 0·0 | 0·0 | 0·0 | 0·0 |
| Region 2 | 1 | 0·0 | 0·0 | 0·0 | 0·0 | 0·0 | 0·0 | 0·0 | 0·0 |
| | 2 | 0·16 | 0·16 | 0·16 | 0·16 | 0·67 | 0·67 | 0·67 | 0·67 |
| | 3 | 0·04 | 0·04 | 0·04 | 0·04 | 0·13 | 0·13 | 0·13 | 0·13 |
| | 4 | 0·0 | 0·0 | 0·0 | 0·0 | 0·0 | 0·0 | 0·0 | 0·0 |

| $b_{ki}^r$ | Region 1 | | | | Region 2 | | | |
|---|---|---|---|---|---|---|---|---|
| | 1 | 2 | 3 | 4 | 1 | 2 | 3 | 4 |
| 1 | 30·4 | 55·3 | 4·4 | 12·1 | 0·0 | 0·0 | 0·0 | 0·0 |
| 2 | 0·0 | 4·6 | 0·0 | 15·4 | 0·0 | 0·0 | 0·0 | 0·0 |
| 3 | 0·0 | 30·0 | 0·0 | 55·3 | 0·0 | 0·0 | 0·0 | 0·0 |
| 1 | 0·0 | 0·0 | 0·0 | 0·0 | 17·5 | 24·0 | 4·2 | 13·9 |
| 2 | 0·0 | 0·0 | 0·0 | 0·0 | 0·0 | 4·5 | 0·0 | 15·3 |
| 3 | 0·0 | 0·0 | 0·0 | 0·0 | 0·0 | 50·4 | 0·0 | 47·3 |

| $\mu_{ki}^r$ | Region 1 | | | | Region 2 | | | |
|---|---|---|---|---|---|---|---|---|
| | 1 | 2 | 3 | 4 | 1 | 2 | 3 | 4 |
| 1 | 9·0 | 15·0 | 1·5 | 4·5 | 0 | 0 | 0 | 0 |
| 2 | 0·0 | 1·5 | 0 | 4·5 | 0 | 0 | 0 | 0 |
| 3 | 0·0 | 9·0 | 0 | 15·0 | 0 | 0 | 0 | 0 |
| 1 | 0·0 | 0 | 0 | 0 | 6·0 | 9·0 | 1·5 | 0 |
| 2 | 0·0 | 0 | 0 | 0 | 0 | 1·5 | 0 | 5·0 |
| 3 | 0·0 | 0 | 0 | 0 | 0 | 18·0 | 0 | 17·0 |

| | $k$ | $h_k^{1r}$ | $h_k^{2r}$ | $c_k^r$ | $\bar{t}_k^r$ |
|---|---|---|---|---|---|
| Region 2 | 1 | 0·80 | 0·05 | 0·005 | 54·000 |
| | 2 | 0·75 | 0·05 | 0·05 | 5·500 |
| | 3 | 0·90 | 0·05 | 0·07 | 32·000 |
| Region 1 | 1 | 0·20 | 0·95 | 0·0016 | 100·000 |
| | 2 | 0·25 | 0·95 | 0·012 | 21·000 |
| | 3 | 0·10 | 0·95 | 0·0008 | 190·000 |

$\beta = 0{\cdot}25$
$\bar{L}^1 = 100{\cdot}0$
$\bar{L}^2 = 360{\cdot}0$

$\gamma_{ki}^r = 0$

The results of the previous L.P. model showed again many zero-solutions. A set of sensitivity tests was carried out in order to inspect whether the results were rather stable with respect to parameter changes. Particular attention was paid to the cost coefficients of pollution. The coefficients $c_k^r$ were successively multiplied with a varying factor $r$. For instance, if $r = 0$, the following results are obtained for the investments:

| | Region 1 | | Region 2 | |
|---|---|---|---|---|
| $i$ | $I_i^{P1}$ | $I_i^{E1}$ | $I_i^{P2}$ | $I_i^{E2}$ |
| 1 | – | – | – | – |
| 2 | – | – | – | 1480·9 |
| 3 | 115·2 | – | – | – |
| 4 | – | – | 270·9 | 133·0 |

(6.7.2.14)

On the other hand, if $r = 1$, the results show a slightly different pattern:

| | Region 1 | | Region 2 | |
|---|---|---|---|---|
| $i$ | $I_i^{P1}$ | $I_i^{E1}$ | $I_i^{P2}$ | $I_i^{E2}$ |
| 1 | – | – | – | – |
| 2 | – | – | – | 1425·9 |
| 3 | – | – | – | – |
| 4 | – | 140·0 | 302·7 | 131·4 |

(6.7.2.15)

This difference is caused by the fact that in the latter problem the costs of environmental deterioration play a more significant role, reason why in this case in region 1 environmental investments are to be carried out. In addition, both results show many zero-values of investments. The only way to attack this problem is either to impose lower limits on the sectoral investments or to transform the pollution problem in a nonlinear programming model (see Nijkamp and Paelinck [1973] and Mastenbroek and Nijkamp [1974]).

## 6.8 A model for development planning

The previous models can also be used in the framework of development planning (see also Harris [1971]). In this last section an interregional-intersectoral planning model constructed by Mennes et al. (1969) will be treated. Products are classified into regional, national and international products dependent on the fact whether or not these products concerned remain within the boundaries of the original area of production. If necessary, one may also introduce local products.

The following hypotheses are made concerning this multi-level programming model:

H 1 Constant marginal production costs and marginal revenues.
H 2 A complete exhaustion of productive capacity.
H 3 Constant prices.
H 4 Constant marginal capital coefficients.
H 5 A static approach (for instance, no investment lags).
H 6 *Regional* commodities are only delivered within a relevant region, *national* commodities within a relevant country; the remaining commodities are *international* commodities.
H 7 The output of regional commodities is proportional to *regional* income (with fixed coefficients $a$).
H 8 The output of national commodities is proportional to *national* income.
H 9 Total output of all international commodities is given (for instance, on the basis of projections of international trade by means of comparative cost analysis).
H 10 The mobility of commodities is a function of the corresponding type of the commodities concerned.
H 11 Minimization of total investment costs.

The variables of the model are *income* variables (or increases in income). Some of these income variables are *a priori fixed* targets; others are unknown and have to be determined by a planning committee on the basis of the criterion of minimum investment costs. The typical element of all income variables is $y_s^r$, which denotes the increase of income in sectors $s$ of region $r$ ($r = 1, \ldots, R$). The sectors $s$ are distinguished according to regional, national and international sectors by means of the following successive indices: $s = 1, \ldots, S_1$; $s = S_1 + 1, \ldots, S_1 + S_2$; $s = S_1 + S_2 + 1, \ldots, S$. Thus, the total number of regional, national and international sectors is equal to $S_1$, $S_2$ and $S - S_1 - S_2$, respectively. Variables *a priori* fixed by a planning committee will be provided with an upper bar. When a certain index (either $r$ or $s$) has been deleted, the variable concerned is supposed to be aggregated over the index concerned; for instance, $y_s = \sum_{r=1}^{R} y_s^r$, and $y = \sum_{s=1}^{S} \sum_{r=1}^{R} y_s^r$.

The model is a combined fixed target-flexible target model. The *a priori* fixed targets are:

(a) $\bar{y}^r$ ($r = 1, \ldots, R$): regional income over all sectors;
(b) $\bar{y}_s$ ($s = 1, \ldots, S_1, S_1 + 1, \ldots, S_1 + S_2$): sectoral income over all

regions; only the regional and national sectors are assumed to have fixed income targets. Total income of regional and national sectors is respectively equal to $\bar{y}_1$ ($\triangleq \sum_{s=1}^{S_1} \bar{y}_s$) and $\bar{y}_2$ ($\triangleq \sum_{s=S_1+1}^{S_1+S_2} \bar{y}_s$);

(c) $\bar{y}_3 = \sum_{s=S_1+S_2+1}^{S} y_s$: total sectoral income of all international sectors; a division of fixed targets over international sectors is not assumed *a priori* (see H 9); and

(d) $\bar{y} = \bar{y}_1 + \bar{y}_2 + \bar{y}_3$: total national income generated by all sectors.

The model contains a set of balance equations, behavioral equations and technical equations for the three successive sectors.

a *Regional sectors*

$$\sum_{r=1}^{R} y_s^r \equiv \bar{y}_s, \quad s = 1, \ldots, S_1 \tag{6.8.1}$$

These $S_1$ equations are the balance equations of all regional sectors. On the basis of H 7 the following behavioral relationships can be assumed:

$$y_s^r = a_s^r \, \bar{y}^r \quad r = 1, \ldots, R; s = 1, \ldots, S_1 \tag{6.8.2}$$

The latter relationship describes the distribution of income over all regional sectors; in other words, given the value of $a_s^r$ the distribution of income over all regional sectors is fixed.

b *National sectors*

$$\sum_{r=1}^{R} y_s^r = \bar{y}_s = \beta_s \, \bar{y} \, , s = S_1 + 1, \ldots, S_1 + S_2 \tag{6.8.3}$$

These $S_2$ equations define sectoral output of national sectors as a constant proportion $\beta_s$ of national income (see H 8). The distribution within the sectors cannot be derived by means of (6.8.3); hereafter, some optimizing criterion will be introduced in order to solve these degrees of freedom.

c *International sectors*

$$\sum_{r=1}^{R} y_s^r \equiv y_s \, , s = S_1 + S_2 + 1, \ldots, S \tag{6.8.4}$$

The foregoing $S - S_1 - S_2$ equations are the sectoral balance equations of the international sectors. For these sectors even total income per sector is not fixed *a priori*. Therefore, this distribution of income for the international sectors must be determined simultaneously with the intersectoral distribution of income (see H 9). The income of the international sectors should satisfy the following condition:

$$\sum_{s=S_1+S_2+1}^{S} y_s = \bar{y}_3 \qquad (6.8.5)$$

In addition to balance and behavioral relationships per sector there are balance equations over all sectors:

$$\sum_{s=1}^{S} y_s^r = \bar{y}^r \quad r = 1, \ldots, R \qquad (6.8.6)$$

The program to be solved is a mixture of a fixed-target-approach, represented by the fixed income targets, and a flexible-target-approach, on which a number of unknown income variables should be determined on the basis of a certain criterion function. The objective function is assumed to be a minimization of investment costs:

$$\min \omega = \sum_{r=1}^{R} \sum_{s=1}^{S} c_s^r \, y_s^r \qquad (6.8.7)$$

where $c_s^r$ represents the marginal capital coefficients (see H 4), viz. the cost of investments required to generate the corresponding change in income. The marginal (incremental) capital coefficients (or capital output ratios) depend on the availability of natural resources, labour, capital and entrepreneurial behavior. They are estimated per sector and per region. Since $y_s^r$ $(s = 1, \ldots, S_1)$ can be determined directly by means of (6.8.2) without criterion (6.8.7), the income variables of the regional sectors can be left out of consideration in the optimization procedure. Therefore, the ultimate purpose of the program is: min $\omega$, subject to (6.8.3), (6.8.4), (6.8.5) and (6.8.6). Obviously, the non-negative conditions of the income variables should also be satisfied. Then, the total number of unknown variables is equal to $RS_2 + R(S - S_1 - S_2) + (S - S_1 - S_2)$, while the total number of relationships is equal to $S_2 + (S - S_1 - S_2) + 1 + R$. Since there is one dependent relationship owing to the balance conditions, the number of independent equations is reduced to $S - S_1 + R$. Therefore, the number of degrees of freedom of this system of equations is equal to $R(S - S_1 - 1) - S_2$. For instance, in the case of 10 regions (i.e., $R$ = 10), and 30 sectors equally divided among regional, national and international sectors (i.e., $S$ = 30, and $S_1 = S_2 = 10$), the number of degrees of freedom is equal to 180. These degrees of freedom can be solved by introducing objective function (6.8.7): minimization of $\omega$ permits the determination of the remaining number of unknown variables caused by the degrees of freedom.

The various fixed income variables as well as the unknown income variables are represented in a systematic way in table 6.8.a.

Table 6.8.a

A survey of the multi-regional multi-sectoral model

| Region / Sector | | 1 ......... $R$ | Total income per sector | |
|---|---|---|---|---|
| Regional | 1 ⋮ $S_1$ | $[y_s^r] = [a_s^r \bar{y}^r]$ | $[\bar{y}_s]$ | |
| | | | Total income of regional sectors | $\bar{y}_1 = \sum_{s=1}^{S_1} \bar{y}_s$ |
| National | $S_1+1$ ⋮ $S_1+S_2$ | $[y_s^r]$ | $[\bar{y}_s] = [\beta_s \bar{y}]$ | |
| | | | Total income of national sectors | $\bar{y}_2 = \sum_{s=S_1+1}^{S_1+S_2} \bar{y}_s$ |
| International | $S_1+S_2+1$ ⋮ $S$ | $[y_s^r]$ | $[y_s]$ | |
| | | | Total income of international sectors | $\bar{y}_3 = \sum_{s=S_1+S_2+1}^{S} \hat{y}_s$ |
| Total income per region | | $\bar{y}^1$ ......... $\bar{y}^R$ | Total national income | $\bar{y}$ |

All non-barred variables are unknown. It is easily seen that all income variables of the regional sector can be determined directly: they are independent of the minimization of $\omega$. Table 6.8.a contains the set of side-conditions subject to which objective function (6.8.7) must be minimized.

In fact the program is a particular type of a L.P. problem, since all linear constraints have an equality sign (i.e., all dual variables are analytically unequal to zero). The program bears a close resemblance to the transportation problems discussed previously. Therefore, the program specified above can be solved by means of certain standard techniques of transportation problems. Since, however, transportation problems may lead to many zero-values of the unknown variables, there is a high probability that in many sectors income will be zero. One can prevent such an undesirable situation by imposing *a priori* minimum levels for the sectoral incomes.

The previous analysis can be extended by considering transportation costs and input-output relationships between the sectors. An application of the previous model to development efforts in Mexico is contained in Mennes et al. (1969) and in Carillo Arronte (1968).

In correspondence with the dual interpretation of transportation models the dual program of the previous model implies a maximization of the aggregate imputed values of the fixed income (or production) variables, subject to the condition that the imputed prices of production are exactly equal to the production costs at the optimum.

## References


Allen, R.G.D., *Mathematical Economics*, Macmillan, London 1960.

Baumol, W.J., *Economic Theory and Operations Analysis,* Prentice-Hall, Englewood Cliffs, New Jersey 1961.

Beckmann, M. and Marschak, T., 'An Activity Analysis Approach to Location Theory', *Kyklos,* vol. VIII, 1955, pp. 125–143.

Bernard, Ph.J., 'Un Modèle de Croissance Régionale', *Cahiers de l'ISEA* (L, 13), 1963.

Berry, B.J.L., 'Cities as Systems within Systems of Cities', *Papers and Proceedings of the Regional Science Association,* vol. 13, 1964, pp. 147–163.

Blokland, J. and Nijkamp, P., 'Some Dynamic Models of Spatial Interactions', *Foundations of Empirical Economic Research,* Netherlands Economic Institute, Rotterdam, mimeo 1974.

Von Böventer, E., 'The Relationship between Transportation Costs and Location Rent in Transportation Problems', *Journal of Regional Science,* vol. 3, no. 2, 1961, pp. 27–40.
Carrillo-Arronte, R., *An Empirical Test on Interregional Planning; a Linear Programming Model for Mexico,* Grafisch Centrum 'Alfa', Den Haag 1968.
Casetti, E., 'Optimal Location of Steel Mills Serving the Quebec and Southern Ontario Steel Market', in: R.H.T. Smith, E.J. Taaffe and L.J. King, *Readings in Economic Geography,* Rand McNally & Company, Chicago, 1968, pp. 340–349.
Dantzig, G.B., 'Application of the Simplex Method to a Transportation Problem', in: T.C. Koopmans (ed.), *Activity Analysis of Production and Allocation,* Wiley, New York 1951.
Dorfman, R., Samuelson, P.A. and Solow, R.M., *Linear Programming and Economic Analysis*, McGraw-Hill, New York 1958.
Ford, L.R. and Fulkerson, D.R., 'Solving the Transportation Problem', *Management Science,* vol. 3, 1956, pp. 24–32.
Gale, D., *The Theory of Linear Economic Models,* McGraw-Hill, New York, 1960.
Ghosh, A., *Efficiency in Location and Interregional Flows,* North-Holland Publishing Co., Amsterdam 1965.
Gomory, R., 'Essentials of an Algorithm for Integer Solutions to Linear Programs', *Bulletin of the American Mathematical Society,* vol. 64, no. 5, 1958.
Gurevitch, B.L., 'Geographical Differentiation and its Measures in a Discrete System', *Soviet Geography,* vol. 10, nr. 7, 1969, pp. 387–412.
Hadley, G., *Nonlinear and Dynamic Programming,* Addison-Wesley Publishing Co., Reading, Massachusetts 1964.
Harris, J.R., 'Urban and Industrial Deconcentration in Developing Economies: an Analytical Framework', *Regional and Urban Economics,* vol. 1, no. 2, 1971, pp. 139–152.
Houthakker, H.S., 'On the Numerical Solution of the Transportation Problems', *Journal of the Operations Research Society of America,* 3, 1955, pp. 210–214.
Hurter Jr., A.P. and Moses, L.N., 'Regional Investment and Interregional Programming', *Papers and Proceedings of the Regional Science Association,* vol. 13, 1964, pp. 105–119.
Isard, W., *Methods of Regional Analysis: an Introduction to Regional Science,* MIT Press, Cambridge 1960.
Johansen, L., 'Regional Economic Problems Elucidated by Linear Programming', *International Economic Papers,* no. 12, 1967, pp. 63–81.

Kendrick, D.A., *Programming Investment in the Process Industries,* MIT Press, Cambridge 1967.

Koopmans, T.C. and Beckmann, M., 'Assignment Problems and the Location of Economic Activities', *Econometrica,* vol. 25, 1957, pp. 53–76.

Lancaster, K., *Mathematical Economics,* Macmillan, New York 1968.

Lawler, E.L., 'The Quadratic Assignment Model', *Management Science,* 1963, pp. 586–599.

Manne, A.S. and Vietorisz, T., 'Chemical Processes, Plant Location, and Economies of Scale', in: A.S. Manne and H.M. Markowitz (eds.), *Studies in Process Analysis,* Wiley, New York 1963.

Mastenbroek, A.P., and Nijkamp, P., 'Een Multi-regionaal Model voor een Ruimtelijke Allocatie van Investeringen' (A Multi-regional Model for a Spatial Allocation of Investments) in: P. Nijkamp (ed.), *Milieu en Economie* (Environment and Economics), Rotterdam University Press, Rotterdam, 1974.

Mathur, P.N., 'Multi-regional Analysis in a Dynamic Input-Output Framework', in: A. Bródy and A.P. Carter (eds.), *Input–Output Techniques*, North-Holland Publishing Co., Amsterdam 1972.

Medvedkov, Y.V., 'The Concept of Entropy in Settlement Patterns Analysis', *Papers and Proceedings of the Regional Science Association,* vol. 18, 1967, pp. 165–168.

Mennes, L.B.M., Tinbergen, J. and Waardenburg, J.G., *The Element of Space in Development Planning,* North-Holland Publishing Co., Amsterdam 1969.

Miller, R.E., *Modern Mathematical Methods for Economics and Business,* Holt, Rinehart and Winston, New York 1972.

Nicholson, T.A.J., *Optimization in Industry,* Longman, London 1971

Nijkamp, P., Reflections on Gravity and Entropy Models, *Regional Science and Urban Economics,* vol. 5, no. 2, 1975, pp. 203–226.

Nijkamp, P., *Planning of Industrial Complexes by Means of Geometric Programming,* Rotterdam University Press, Rotterdam 1972.

Nijkamp, P., and J.H.P. Paelinck, An Interregional Model of Environmental Choice, *Papers of the Regional Science Association,* vol. 31, 1973, pp. 51–71.

Nijkamp, P., and Paelinck, J.H.P., 'A Dual Interpretation and Generalization of Entropy Maximizing Models in Regional Science', *Papers of the Regional Science Association,* vol. 33, 1974, pp. 13–31.

Quandt, R.E., 'Models of Transportation and Optimal Network Construction', *Journal of Regional Science,* vol. 2, no. 1, 1960, pp. 27–45.

Rogers, A., *Matrix Methods in Urban and Regional Analysis,* Holden-Day, San Francisco 1971.

Saaty, T.L. and Bram, J., *Nonlinear Mathematics,* McGraw-Hill, New York 1964.

Scott, A.J., *Combinatorial Programming, Spatial Analysis and Planning,* Methuen & Co. Ltd., London 1971.

Serck-Hanssen, J., *Optimal Patterns of Location,* North-Holland Publishing Co., Amsterdam 1970.

Specker, H. and Kok, F., 'Het Entropiekonsept in de Ruimlelijke Ekonomie', Master's Thesis, Rotterdam (mimeo) 1974.

Stevens, B.H., 'Linear Programming and Location Rent', *Journal of Regional Science,* vol. 3, no. 2, 1961, pp. 15–26.

Theil, H., *Optimal Decision Rules for Government and Industry,* North-Holland Publishing Co., Amsterdam 1964.

Wilde, D.J. and Beightler, C.S., *Foundations of Optimization,* Prentice-Hall, Englewood Cliffs 1967.

Wilson, A.G., *Entropy in Urban and Regional Modelling,* Pion Limited, London 1970.

Zangwill, W.I., *Nonlinear Programming; a Unified Approach,* Prentice-Hall, Englewood Cliffs 1969.

PART III

# Synthesis

# 7 Multiregional Equilibrium and Growth

## 7.1 Introduction

In this chapter *multiregional equilibrium and growth* will be considered. The following pages provide a picture of interdependent spatial economic organization. The purpose is to give an introduction into multiregional equilibrium and growth analysis and into the existence conditions of spatial economic equilibrium, related to the neoclassical or Walrasian theory of general economic equilibrium. The neoclassical analysis, however, neglects almost completely the existence of space (even in the theory of international trade). Because of the latter omission it was impossible to analyze interregional trade patterns, choices of location, agglomeration and urbanization, migration, transportation networks, etc. More explicit attention to spatial phenomena was given by location theorists such as Von Thünen, Weber, Predöhl, and Palander (see Ch.2), albeit only in the context of a *partial* and not of a *general* spatial equilibrium.

The first general spatial equilibrium model was created by Lösch (see section 2.6.4). It contained a general formulation of interdependent spatial economic equilibrium, based on neoclassical equilibrium theory. As stated in section 2.6.4, the existence of spatial equilibrium was neither proved nor analyzed. Other criticisms on Lösch's model are also contained in section 2.6.4.

A highly enlightening contribution to the analysis of spatial equilibrium was presented by Isard (1956, 1969). His general equilibrium analysis takes explicitly account of the existing transportation structure. Since the distance factor is the heart of location theory, he introduces beside the classical production factors capital, labour and land a fourth one, viz. a *transport* or *distance input,* the price of which is the transport rate. In Isard's opinion, production is generated by the right choice of capital, labour, land and transport inputs.[1] The concept of transport inputs together with the substitution framework was interwoven by Isard into the concept of a *spatial transformation function,* which might be conceived of as a spatial implicit production function embracing the technical and spatial substitution between any pair of inputs and of outputs. This function encompasses the following variables: production inputs, transport inputs, and outputs. In order to define an interregional equilibrium, some criterion function (for instance a Weberian cost function) is optimized, subject to the condition of the spatial transformation function. By deriving the first-order marginal conditions and checking the second-order conditions, one may impose optimum conditions for a spatial equilibrium or investigate whether the equilibrium conditions are satisfied.

Isard's approach fails to differentiate between output produced at the production place and output delivered at the market, since production place and consumption market do not coincide generally (see the transportation models of the foregoing chapter). Furthermore, Isard does not indicate how the transport inputs are generated. Since one may assume that transport inputs absorb labour and capital, they may be conceived of as intermediate inputs in the production process. The way they are generated should be specified explicitly, as is done by Lefeber (1958) and Von Böventer (1962), whose ideas are viewed in section 7.3. The formal framework of equilibrium models will be presented first.

## 7.2 Formal presentation of equilibrium models

### 7.2.1 *Economic agents and states of the economy*

Equilibrium theory has received much attention in economic literature. In this text about regional economics, equilibrium theory will not be dealt with extensively. Only a set of relevant elements will be presented. For more details, the reader is referred to the existing literature.[2] Equilibrium theory studies the conditions under which an economy will attain an equilibrium, given a set of hypotheses concerning the economy. A brief exposition of such an equilibrium theory will be given here.

Let there be: $I$ goods and services $i$ ($i = 1, \ldots, I$), $J$ consumers $j$ ($j = 1, \ldots, J$), and $K$ producers $k$ ($k = 1, \ldots, K$).

Given the previous elements of a certain economy, we define,

$x_{ij}$ as the quantity of good $i$ consumed by (positive sign) or given up (negative sign) by consumer $j$. The consumption vector of $j$ is $\mathbf{x}_j$, and matrix $\mathbf{X}$ is the set of all actual consumer choices. Next, we define

$y_{ik}$ as the quantity of good $i$ absorbed (negative sign) or produced (positive sign) by producer $k$. In a similar way, we assume that

$\mathbf{y}_k$ is $k$'s production vector, and $\mathbf{Y}$ the matrix of all actual productions.

The *state* of the economy is represented by the following set of elements:

$$Z = [\mathbf{X},\mathbf{Y}] \tag{7.2.1.1}$$

obeying the evident feasibility conditions

$$(\mathbf{X}-\mathbf{Y})\mathbf{i} - \mathbf{r} \leqslant \mathbf{0} \tag{7.2.1.2}$$

where $\mathbf{r}$ is a vector of initial resources.

### 7.2.2 *Consumers' and producers' behaviour*

For the *consumer* the following hypotheses are postulated:

H 1 Convexity of preferences; this hypothesis simply excludes 'thick' equivalence (indifference) classes, which might be strictly or weakly convex (cf. Nikaido [1970]).
H 2 Individualistic behaviour; this means that if $Z_1$, $Z_2$, $Z_3$ and $Z_4$ are alternative states of the economy with $\mathbf{x}_{1j} = \mathbf{x}_{2j}$, $\mathbf{x}_{3j} = \mathbf{x}_{4j}$, then

$$Z_1 R_j Z_3 \longleftrightarrow Z_2 R_j Z_4 \tag{7.2.2.1}$$

where $R_j$ is a weak preference relation (preferred or indifferent).
H 3 Continuity of preferences.
H 4 'Maximizing behaviour', in the sense that the consumer will choose $Z^{\text{O}}$ such that

$$Z^{\text{O}} R Z, \forall\ Z \in S \tag{7.2.2.2}$$

if $Z^{\text{O}}$ exists, and where $S$ is the set of all possible states of the economy.

The *producers'* behaviour is hypothisized as follows:

H 1 Technological possibility of the production process (which, e.g., excludes $\mathbf{y}_k > \mathbf{0}$, since inputs should have a negative sign [cf. section 1.5.2]).
H 2 Independence of $\mathbf{y}_k$ and $\mathbf{y}_l, \forall\, k,l$ (no external effects).
H 3 $\mathbf{y} \leqslant \mathbf{0} \in Y$, the latter being convex (no increasing returns).
H 4 'Maximizing behaviour', in the sense that, if

$$\pi_k = \mathbf{p}'\mathbf{y}_k \tag{7.2.2.3}$$

where $\pi_k$ is profit and $\mathbf{p}$ a price vector, then the producer chooses $\mathbf{y}_k^{\text{O}}$ such that

$$\pi(\mathbf{y}_k^{\text{O}}) \gtrless \pi(\mathbf{y}_k) \quad \mathbf{y}_k \in Y \tag{7.2.2.4}$$

if $\mathbf{y}_k^{\text{O}}$ exists.

### 7.2.3 *Demand and supply*

Introduction of a price vector **p** allows us to define[3] micro-economic and macro-economic demand and supply functions or correspondences (multi-valued functions). Successive aggregations from individual consumers and producers onwards lead to the following aggregate demand and supply functions:

$$x_{ij}(\mathbf{p}) \longrightarrow x_i(\mathbf{p}) \longrightarrow \mathbf{x}(\mathbf{p}) \qquad (7.2.3.1)$$

$$y_{ik}(\mathbf{p}) \longrightarrow y_i(\mathbf{p}) \longrightarrow \mathbf{y}(\mathbf{p}) \qquad (7.2.3.2)$$

Define the excess-demand vector as:

$$\mathbf{e}(\mathbf{p}) = \mathbf{x}(\mathbf{p}) - \mathbf{y}(\mathbf{p}) - \mathbf{r} \qquad (7.2.3.3)$$

Then an *equilibrium* price-vector is generally defined by 3 conditions:

$$\mathbf{e}(\mathbf{p}^{\mathrm{o}}) \leqslant \mathbf{0} \qquad (7.2.3.4)$$

$$\mathbf{p}^{\mathrm{o}} \geqslant \mathbf{0} \qquad (7.2.3.5)$$

$$\mathbf{e}'\,\mathbf{p}^{\mathrm{o}} = 0 \qquad (7.2.3.6)$$

Excess demand should be either zero (Walrasian equilibrium) or negative (quasi-Walrasian equilibrium); at least one price should be strictly positive; either excess demand is zero, or the corresponding price is zero, or both ('efficient pricing'). These conditions bear some resemblance to duality conditions of programming models.

### 7.2.4 *Competitive equilibrium*

The problem is as follows: does a price vector as defined by (7.2.3.4) through (7.2.3.6) *exist,* when consumers and producers behave as described in section 7.2.2?

Formally, equilibrium should exist under the following conditions:

C 1 A privately owned economy in which the consumer possesses initial resources $\mathbf{r}_j$ forming an aggregate matrix **R** such that:

$$\mathbf{Ri} = \mathbf{r} \qquad (7.2.4.1)$$

being the total resources of the economy. Furthermore, the consumer possesses a set of shares in enterprises, representable by vectors $\mathbf{s}_j$ forming a matrix **S** such that the total shares add up to 1 for each production sector:

$$\mathbf{Si} = \mathbf{i} \;{}^{4} \qquad (7.2.4.2)$$

In an equilibrium situation, the expenditure pattern of the consumer is characterized by $\mathbf{x}_j^{\mathrm{O}} R_j x_j$, $\mathbf{x}_j^{\mathrm{O}} \in \mathbf{X}_j, \forall\, j$, such that

$$\mathbf{p}^{\mathrm{O}\prime}\, \mathbf{x}_j^{\mathrm{O}} \leqslant \mathbf{p}^{\mathrm{O}\prime}\, (\mathbf{r}_j + \mathbf{Y}^{\mathrm{O}} \mathbf{s}_j) \tag{7.2.4.3}$$

C 2 Firms select an activity vector $\mathbf{y}_k^{\mathrm{O}}$ such that

$$\mathbf{p}^{\mathrm{O}\prime}\, \mathbf{y}_k^{\mathrm{O}} \geqslant \mathbf{p}^{\mathrm{O}\prime}\, \mathbf{y}_k, \forall\, \mathbf{y}_k \in \mathbf{Y}_k \tag{7.2.4.4}$$

C 3 The following feasibility condition holds:

$$\mathbf{e}^{\mathrm{O}} \leqslant \mathbf{0} \tag{7.2.4.5}$$

which implies no excess demand.

C 4

$$\mathbf{p}^{\mathrm{O}\prime}\, \mathbf{e}^{\mathrm{O}} = 0, \ \mathbf{p}^{\mathrm{O}} \geqslant \mathbf{0} \tag{7.2.4.6}$$

which is the aforementioned condition of efficient pricing. Economic equilibrium can then be considered as a $J$+$K$+1–tuple of points in $R^I$ space.

It should be noted that the foregoing equilibrium theories are rather abstract. They do not prove the existence of an economic equilibrium in reality, but they show only under what conditions a possible equilibrium might exist. The equilibrium theories have been frequently criticized, among others owing to their lack of realism, the negligence of the existence of income inequalities and power structures in an economy, and the a-normative view of economic structures (cf. also Hunt and Schwarz [1972], Lindbeck [1971] and Sraffa [1960]).

### 7.2.5 *Multiregional extensions*

The foregoing discussion has been presented entirely in *spaceless* terms; e.g., no transport activities have been mentioned, necessary to move resources and produced goods from place to place, which would have implied the use of scarce resources (cf. Takayama and Judge [1971]).

Let us now suppose that the economy is composed of $R$ regions; an index $r$ ($r = 1, \ldots, R$) should be added systematically to all the symbols in the exercise. Moreover, a vector like $\mathbf{y}_{kr}$ now (potentially) comprises a sub-vector of transport-outputs, necessary to transport resources and goods from region $r$ to all other regions. The order of this sub-vector is equal to the number of possible routes.

Take any route $\rho$; $p_{r\rho}$ is now the price for the transport of a unit volume of any good from region $r$ via route $\rho$.

A symbol like $\epsilon_{irr'}$ stands for exports of good $i$ from region $r$ to region $r'$.

Conditions C 1 through C 4 from section 7.2.4 can now be generalized successively as follows:

$C_1^r$:

$$\forall j \begin{cases} \mathbf{x}_{jr}^{O} \in \mathbf{X}_{jr} & (7.2.5.1a) \\ \mathbf{x}_{jr}^{O}\, R_{jr}\, \mathbf{x}_{jr} & (7.2.5.1b) \\ \mathbf{p}_r^{O\prime}\, \mathbf{x}_{jr}^{O} \leqslant \mathbf{p}_r^{O\prime}\, (\mathbf{r}_{jr} + \mathbf{Y}^{O}\mathbf{s}_{jr}) & (7.2.5.1c) \end{cases}$$

$\mathbf{p}_r^{O}$ and $\mathbf{r}_{jr}$ are now of order $RI \times 1$; $\mathbf{p}_r^{O}$ is the vector of all prices in all regions, and $\mathbf{r}_{jr}$ the vector of all resources consumed in all regions; $\mathbf{s}_{jr}$ is of order $RK^* \times 1$, where $K^* = \Sigma_r K_r$; $\mathbf{Y}^{O}$ is a block-diagonal matrix (not necessarily square!) of all $\mathbf{Y}_r^{O}$'s.

$C_2^r: \forall k$

$$\mathbf{y}_{kr}^{O} \in \mathbf{Y}_{kr} \qquad (7.2.5.2a)$$

$$\mathbf{p}_r^{O\prime}\, \mathbf{y}_{kr}^{O} \geqslant \mathbf{p}_r^{O\prime}\, \mathbf{y}_{kr} \qquad (7.2.5.2b)$$

$C_3^r: \forall r$

$$\mathbf{e}_r^{O} + \boldsymbol{\epsilon}_r^{O} \leqslant \mathbf{0} \qquad (7.2.5.3a)$$

where $\boldsymbol{\epsilon}_r^{O}$ is an (equilibrium) vector of net exports out of region $r$. This condition applies to goods and services, and should be *complemented* with the analogous condition for transport services.

$$e_{rr'}^{O} = (\epsilon_{rr'}^{O\prime} + \mathbf{m}_{rr'}^{O\prime})\,\mathbf{i} - \mathbf{y}_{rr'}^{\rho\prime}\,\mathbf{i}_{\rho} \leqslant 0, \forall r' \qquad (7.2.5.3b)$$

where $\mathbf{m}_r^{O\prime}$ represents the (equilibrium) imports of region $r$, and $\boldsymbol{\epsilon}_{r'}^{O\prime}$ the *net* exports to region $r'$, so that the term between parentheses stands for gross exports; $\mathbf{y}_{rr'}^{\rho}$ represents transport services between $r$ and $r'$ along route $\rho$.

$C_4^r$: $\forall r$; the aforementioned price-efficiency applies to goods and services:

$$\mathbf{e}_r^{O\prime}\, \mathbf{p}_r^{O} = 0, \quad \mathbf{p}_r^{O} \geqslant \mathbf{0} \qquad (7.2.5.4a)$$

as well as to transport-services:

$$\tilde{\mathbf{e}}_r^{O\prime}\, \tilde{\mathbf{p}}_r^{O} = 0, \quad \tilde{\mathbf{p}}_r \geqslant \mathbf{0} \qquad (7.2.5.4b)$$

where $\tilde{\mathbf{e}}_r^{O}$ is the vector of $e_{rr'}^{O}$'s, and $\tilde{\mathbf{p}}_r$ the corresponding price vector.

Moreover we have spatial price-equilibrium in the sense that

$$\boldsymbol{\delta}_{rr'}^{O} \triangleq \mathbf{p}_{r'}^{O} - \mathbf{p}_r^{O} - \mathbf{p}_{rr'} \leqslant \mathbf{0} \qquad (7.2.5.4c)$$

$$\boldsymbol{\delta}_{rr'}^{O\prime}\, (\epsilon_{rr'}^{O} + \mathbf{m}_{rr'}^{O}) = 0 \qquad (7.2.5.4d)$$

$$(\boldsymbol{\epsilon}^{\mathrm{o}}_{rr\,'} + \mathbf{m}^{\mathrm{o}}_{rr\,'}) \geqslant \mathbf{0} \tag{7.2.5.4e}$$

$C^r_5$ is a new condition imposed on the model, viz. trade equilibrium:

$$\mathbf{p}^{\mathrm{o}\,'}_r \, \boldsymbol{\epsilon}^{\mathrm{o}}_r + \widetilde{\mathbf{p}}'_r \, \widetilde{\mathbf{y}}_r = 0 \tag{7.2.5.5}$$

where $\widetilde{\mathbf{y}}_r$ is the vector of all $\mathbf{y}^{\rho\,'}_{rr\,'}\, \mathbf{i}_\rho$ defined in (7.2.5.3b).

### 7.2.6 *Existence of multiregional equilibrium*

Spatial equilibrium models as such do not guarantee the *existence* of a spatial equilibrium. The existence conditions of a general economic equilibrium require the use of rather involved mathematical techniques (see, for instance, Arrow and Debreu [1954]); the same applies to proving the existence of *spatial* economic equilibria under the conditions described (see Isard [1957]; Isard and Ostroff [1958, 1960]). In analyzing equilibrium conditions frequent use is made of so-called 'fixed-point' theorems and advanced topological methods. This analysis, however, is beyond the scope of this text.

## 7.3 Some properties of general spatial equilibrium

### 7.3.1 *Introducing welfare functions*

In order to derive properties of the foregoing equilibrium system, a Paretian welfare function may be introduced.

A welfare function $W$ is said to satisfy Pareto-conditions, if a rise in individual welfare implies a rise in $W$:

$$\frac{\partial W(\mathbf{u}(\mathbf{x}))}{\partial u_i\,(\mathbf{x})} > 0 \tag{7.3.1.1}$$

where $\mathbf{u}$ is a set of individual welfare functions for a set of individuals living in the system of regions referred to above, and where $\mathbf{x}$ are the arguments of these functions. It can be proved that a Pareto optimum is an equilibrium point (see Debreu [1959]). In this 'selective' approach, which picks out one equilibrium point, it is important to separate the properties dependent on $W$ from those derived from the equilibrium state. In fact, every time a derivative of $W$ (or $\mathbf{u}$) pops up in a term of the final result, this term should be carefully inspected for its composition.

For further properties, particularly the derivation of equilibrium conditions from a mathematical programming framework, reference is made to Takayama and Judge (1971, 1973).

### 7.3.2 *Lefeber-type equilibrium models*

The first general spatial equilibrium analysis embracing the foregoing notions was specified by Lefeber; his static analysis allows to determine the spatial allocation of factors and the distribution of goods, and to investigate the pattern of industrial location. Therefore, Lefeber's analysis can be considered as a generalization of the neoclassical equilibrium theory by taking account of interactions of spatially dispersed economic activities. The following assumptions are made:

H 1 Existence of a fixed (finite) number of discrete location points, suitable for both production and consumption.
H 2 Each location point is endowed with a given assortment of productive factors; the latter may be transported to each other point by making use of transportation services.
H 3 Transportation services are generated by other production factors, so that the system is confronted with production functions for output as well as for transportation services. The production functions are additive, linear homogeneous, and for the same good equal in all locations.
H 4 Existence of a situation of pure competition: no individual supplier can influence the price of goods or factors.
H 5 Optimality conditions of consumer satisfaction and income distribution are ruled out. Prices of consumption goods are given (or determined by a welfare function provided by a central planning board).

On the basis of the foregoing assumptions a spatial equilibrium analysis is performed in three parts, viz. the allocation of productive factors, the distribution of final goods and the choice of production locations. The system as a whole needs an objective function defined as the maximization of the value of production. For a major part the analysis is carried out within the framework of L.P. techniques and shows close links to the generalized transportation problem (apart from the treatment of transportation services itself). The conditions for optimal spatial equilibrium can be derived both for linear and non-linear relationships, but the non-linear version of Lefeber's equilibrium model is not easily tractable, whence it is turned into a model with linear relationships, i.e. with (Leontief) fixed coefficient production functions[5] and linear demand functions for transportation services.

For the sake of clarity a general spatial equilibrium model is presented for a two-dimensional situation, i.e. two production locations, two production factors, two commodities and two consumption points. The production and consumption locations may not coincide. The following notation is used:

$q_{ji}^k$ : amount of good $k$ produced at $j$ and shipped to $i$;

$q_j^k$ : total amount of good $k$ produced at $j$;

$q^t$ : total amount of transportation services produced or demanded;

$f_{mj}^{lk}$ : productive factor $l$ from location $m$ for use in production process $k$ at location $j$;

$f_m^{lt}$ : factor $l$ from location $m$ for use in the production of transportation services;

$p_i^k$ : price of product $k$ at market $i$.[6]

Evidently: $i, j, k, l, m = 1,2$.

The maximand is expressed as:

$$\max \omega = p_1^1 (q_{11}^1 + q_{21}^1) + p_1^2 (q_{11}^2 + q_{21}^2) + p_2^1 (q_{12}^1 + q_{22}^1) + p_2^2 (q_{12}^2 + q_{22}^2) = \sum_{i=1}^{2} \sum_{k=1}^{2} p_i^k \sum_{j=1}^{2} q_{ji}^k \qquad (7.3.2.1)$$

The constraints imposed to the variables $q_{ji}^k$ are distinguished into three main groups, viz. restrictions upon transportation services, upon supply relations governing the distribution of goods, and on supply relations describing the distribution of factors among different occupations.

The constraints of the transportation services reflect the condition that the demand for transportation services should be smaller than its available supply:

$$\tau(f_{12}^{11} + f_{12}^{12}, f_{12}^{21} + f_{12}^{22}, f_{21}^{11} + f_{21}^{12}, f_{21}^{21} + f_{21}^{22}, q_{11}^1, q_{11}^2, q_{21}^1, q_{21}^2, q_{12}^1, q_{12}^2, q_{22}^1, q_{22}^2) \leqslant \varphi^t(\sum_{m=1}^{2} f_m^{1t}, \sum_{m=1}^{2} f_m^{2t}) \qquad (7.3.2.2)$$

The left-hand side of the transport inequality (7.3.2.2) represents the demand function for transportation services. The total amount of productive factors and commodities to be shipped determines the exact quantity of transportation services required. There are eight transportable factor variables[7] and eight final good variables. Homogeneous factors hauled from one location to another for employment in different occupations are additive. The right-hand side of (7.3.2.2) defines the production function for transportation services $q^t$. Since transportation services can be produced by factors of any origin, identical but spatially separated factors are homogeneous and may be added. Therefore:

$$q^t = \varphi^t \left( \sum_{m=1}^{2} f_m^{1t}, \sum_{m=1}^{2} f_m^{2t} \right) \quad (7.3.2.3)$$

The constraints for the distribution of goods are:

$$\sum_{i=1}^{2} q_{ji}^k \leqslant q_j^k \quad \forall\, j, k \quad (7.3.2.4)$$

or

$$\left.\begin{array}{l} q_{11}^1 + q_{12}^1 \leqslant q_1^1 \\ q_{21}^1 + q_{22}^1 \leqslant q_2^1 \\ q_{11}^2 + q_{12}^2 \leqslant q_1^2 \\ q_{21}^2 + q_{22}^2 \leqslant q_2^2 \end{array}\right\} \quad (7.3.2.5)$$

For each total amount of commodity $k$ produced at location $j$ the following relationship is valid:

$$q_j^k = \varphi^k \left( \sum_{m=1}^{2} f_{mj}^{1k}, \sum_{m=1}^{2} f_{mj}^{2k} \right) \quad \forall\, j, k \quad (7.3.2.6)$$

where the right-hand side of (7.3.2.6) denotes the production function of commodity $k$ produced at location $j$. Combination of (7.3.2.4) and (7.3.2.6) results in:

$$\sum_{i=1}^{2} q_{ji}^k \leqslant \varphi^k \left( \sum_{m=1}^{2} f_{mj}^{1k}; \sum_{m=1}^{2} f_{mj}^{2k} \right) \quad \forall\, j, k \quad (7.3.2.7)$$

The third kind of constraints relates to the distribution of factors among different occupations and is specified as:

$$\sum_{k=1}^{2} \sum_{j=1}^{2} f_{mj}^{lk} + f_m^{lt} \leqslant \bar{f}_m^l \quad \forall\, l, m \quad (7.3.2.8)$$

where $\bar{f}_m^l$ indicates the total level of productive factor $l$ available in location $m$. This maximum amount cannot be surpassed by the sum total of all production factors $l$ at $m$ required for the production of all commodities $k$ (at all locations $j$) and of transportation services. For the two-dimensional case condition (7.3.2.8) gives:

$$\left.\begin{array}{l} f_{11}^{11} + f_{11}^{12} + f_{12}^{11} + f_{12}^{12} + f_1^{1t} \leqslant \bar{f}_1^1 \\ f_{21}^{11} + f_{21}^{12} + f_{22}^{11} + f_{22}^{12} + f_2^{1t} \leqslant \bar{f}_2^1 \\ f_{11}^{21} + f_{11}^{22} + f_{12}^{21} + f_{12}^{22} + f_1^{2t} \leqslant \bar{f}_1^2 \\ f_{21}^{21} + f_{21}^{22} + f_{22}^{21} + f_{22}^{22} + f_2^{2t} \leqslant \bar{f}_2^2 \end{array}\right\} \quad (7.3.2.9)$$

Finally, non-negativity conditions for all variables should be imposed.

Thus the ultimate spatial equilibrium model consists of (7.3.2.1), (7.3.2.2), (7.3.2.7) and (7.3.2.8), i.e. of a maximand and 9 side-conditions. The total number of unknown variables is equal to 28, viz. 20 input variables $f_{mj}^{lk}$ and $f_m^{lt}$ and 8 output variables $q_{ji}^k$.

The equilibrium conditions of the whole system are satisfied by performing the maximization of the corresponding Lagrangean function:

$$L = \sum_{i=1}^{2} \sum_{k=1}^{2} p_i^k \sum_{j=1}^{2} q_{ji}^k - \lambda_1 (\tau - \varphi^t) - \sum_{j=1}^{2} \sum_{k=1}^{2} \lambda_j^k \left\{ \sum_{i=1}^{2} q_{ji}^k - \varphi^k \right\} - \sum_{l=1}^{2} \sum_{m=1}^{2} \lambda_m^l \left\{ \sum_{k=1}^{2} \sum_{j=1}^{2} f_{mj}^{lk} + f_m^{lt} - \bar{f}_m^l \right\} \tag{7.3.2.10}$$

where $\lambda_1$ is the shadow price of a unit of transportation service, $\lambda_j^k$ the shadow price of commodity $k$ at production place $j$ and $\lambda_m^l$ the shadow price of factor $l$ originating from location $m$.

According to chapter 6, the first-order conditions for the variables $q_{ji}^k, f_{mj}^{lk}$ and $f_m^{lt}$ are:

$$\left.\begin{aligned}
\frac{\partial L}{\partial q_{ji}^k} &= p_i^k - \lambda_1 \frac{\partial \tau}{\partial q_{ji}^k} - \lambda_j^k \leqslant 0 && \forall\, i, j, k \\
\frac{\partial L}{\partial f_{mj}^{lk}} &= -\lambda_1 \frac{\partial \tau}{\partial f_{mj}^{lk}} + \lambda_j^k \frac{\partial \varphi^k}{\partial f_{mj}^{lk}} - \lambda_m^l \leqslant 0^{8} && \forall\, j, k, l, m \\
\frac{\partial L}{\partial f_m^{lt}} &= \lambda_1 \frac{\partial \varphi^t}{\partial f_m^{lt}} - \lambda_m^l \leqslant 0 && \forall\, l, m
\end{aligned}\right\} \tag{7.3.2.11}$$

The first side-condition of (7.3.2.11) can be written as:

$$\lambda_j^k \geqslant p_i^k - \lambda_1 \frac{\partial \tau}{\partial q_{ji}^k} \tag{7.3.2.12}$$

which means that the imputed value of commodity $k$ produced at location $j$ should not be smaller than the price of the commodity at the market minus the imputed marginal transportation costs.

The second side-condition of (7.3.2.11), rewritten as:

$$\lambda_m^l \geqslant \lambda_j^k \frac{\partial \varphi^k}{\partial f_{mj}^{lk}} - \lambda_1 \frac{\partial \tau}{\partial f_{mj}^{lk}} \tag{7.3.2.13}$$

implies that the rent of factors in their local employment should exceed (or at least be equal to) the imputed value of its marginal product minus the imputed value of the demand for marginal transportation services.

The third restriction of (7.3.2.11) can be reformulated as:

$$\lambda_m^l \geqslant \lambda_1 \frac{\partial \varphi^t}{\partial f_m^{lt}} \tag{7.3.2.14}$$

and states that the shadow price of factors generating transportation services should not be smaller than the imputed value of its marginal product.

In order to facilitate some computational procedures the foregoing model is reformulated as a L.P. model. Evidently, only relationships (7.3.2.2) and (7.3.2.7) must be adapted.

The demand function for transportation services is reformulated as a linear relationship:

$$\begin{aligned}\tau = {} & \beta_{12}^1 (f_{12}^{11} + f_{12}^{12}) + \beta_{12}^2 (f_{12}^{21} + f_{12}^{22}) + \beta_{21}^1 (f_{21}^{11} + f_{21}^{12}) + \\ & + \beta_{21}^2 (f_{21}^{21} + f_{21}^{22}) + \gamma_{11}^1 q_{11}^1 + \gamma_{11}^2 q_{11}^2 + \gamma_{21}^1 q_{21}^1 + \gamma_{21}^2 q_{21}^2 \\ & + \gamma_{12}^1 q_{12}^1 + \gamma_{12}^2 q_{12}^2 + \gamma_{22}^1 q_{22}^1 + \gamma_{22}^2 q_{22}^2 \qquad (7.3.2.15) \\ = {} & \sum_{\substack{m=1 \\ m \neq j}}^{2} \sum_{j=1}^{2} \sum_{l=1}^{2} \beta_{mj}^l \left( \sum_{k=1}^{2} f_{mj}^{lk} \right) + \sum_{i=1}^{2} \sum_{j=1}^{2} \sum_{k=1}^{2} \gamma_{ji}^k q_{ji}^k\end{aligned}$$

where $\beta_{mj}^l$ and $\gamma_{ji}^k$ are transport coefficients denoting the amount of transportation services needed, if a unit of production factor $l$ must be shipped from point $m$ to $j$, and, if a unit of commodity $k$ must be shipped from location $j$ to market $i$, respectively.

Furthermore, the production functions of $q^t$ and $q_{ji}^k$ could be formulated as linear relationships by making use of Leontief relationships (as indicated above). Therefore, instead of (7.3.2.3) and (7.3.2.6) there is written:

$$a^{lt} q^t \leqslant \sum_{m=1}^{2} f_m^{lt} \qquad \forall\, l \tag{7.3.2.16}$$

and:

$$a^{lk} q_j^k \leqslant \sum_{m=1}^{2} f_{mj}^{lk} \qquad \forall\, j, k, l \tag{7.3.2.17}$$

The fixed production coefficients $a^{lt}$ and $a^{lk}$ denote the respective amounts of required input if one unit of transportation services and of commodity $k$ (at location $j$) is produced. Inequalities (7.3.2.16) and (7.3.2.17) mean that the amount of a factor used in a certain line of production should not exceed the total amount of the same factor available for that line of production.

The ultimate L.P. model is:

$$\left.\begin{array}{lr}
\max \omega = \sum_{i=1}^{2} \sum_{k=1}^{2} p_i^k \sum_{j=1}^{2} q_{ji}^k & \\
\text{s.t.} & \\
\sum_{m=1}^{2} \sum_{j=1}^{2} \sum_{l=1}^{2} \beta_{mj}^{l} \left(\sum_{k=1}^{2} f_{mj}^{lk}\right) + \sum_{i=1}^{2} \sum_{j=1}^{2} \sum_{k=1}^{2} \gamma_{ji}^k q_{ji}^k - q^t \leqslant 0 & \\
a^{lt} q^t - \sum_{m=1}^{2} f_m^{lt} \leqslant 0 & \forall\, l \\
\sum_{i=1}^{2} q_{ji}^k - q_j^k \leqslant 0 & \forall\, j, k \\
a^{lk} q_j^k - \sum_{m=1}^{2} f_{mj}^{lk} \leqslant 0 & \forall\, j, k, l \\
\sum_{k=1}^{2} \sum_{j=1}^{2} f_{mj}^{lk} + f_m^{lt} \leqslant \bar{f}_m^{l} & \forall\, l, m \\
q_j^k, q_{ji}^k, f_{mj}^{lk}, f_m^{lt} \geqslant 0 &
\end{array}\right\} \quad (7.3.2.18)$$

The foregoing basic spatial equilibrium model can be extended by including more dimensions and intermediate deliveries. Finally, the *a priori* given prices of final commodities can be determined endogenously within the model by including social and individual welfare functions as a representation of the whole system (see section 7.2).

### 7.3.3 *Alternative classes of spatial equilibrium models*

In addition to the Lefeber models of spatial economic equilibrium some other contributions in this field were presented among others by Von Böventer (1962) and Takayama and Judge (1971). These analyses bear a close resemblance to the Lefeber models and can be considered as extensions and generalizations of Lefeber's theory.

An important element in Von Böventer's approach is the fact that the linearity assumptions of Lefeber are abandoned, so that his analysis focuses on entirely non-linear spatial equilibrium models. His approach is based on a general utility approach,[9] so that the maximand for a set of 2 regions is equal to:

$$\omega = \omega\,(u_1, u_2) \qquad (7.3.3.1)$$

where $u_1$ and $u_2$ represent the utility levels of region 1 and 2, respectively. These utility levels are a function of the deliveries of products to the region in question,[10] i.e.,

$$u_i = u_i\,(\sum_{j=1}^{2} q_{ji}^1, \sum_{j=1}^{2} q_{ji}^2) \qquad i = 1,2 \qquad (7.3.3.2)$$

assuming again 2 commodity categories.

Criterion function (7.3.3.1) is maximized subject to a set of constraints. A first constraint may be an equilibrium condition for the regional balance-of-payment. For example, this constraint is for region 1:

$$\sum_{k=1}^{2} p_1^k q_{21}^k - \sum_{k=1}^{2} p_1^k q_{12}^k - p_1^t q_1^t + T \equiv 0 \qquad (7.3.3.3)$$

where the terms of (7.3.3.3) represent imports, exports, transport services and capital transfers, respectively.

In a manner similar to that in section 7.3.2 the demand for transportation services (cf. [7.3.2.2]), the production function of transportation services (cf. [7.3.2.3]), and the production function of commodities (cf. [7.3.2.6]) can be formalized. Furthermore, the condition that the total amount of regional production factors should not exceed the regional stock of production factors, can be represented in a way similar to (7.3.2.9).

The previous problem can be attacked in the same way as in section 7.3.2 by making use of Kuhn-Tucker-Lagrange conditions.

In addition to the previous analysis, Von Böventer introduces also situations of limited competition, price discrimination and demand elasticities, where prices are not given *a priori*. Furthermore, he pays attention to intermediate deliveries and capital goods, while problems of externalities and indivisibilities are also considered.

## 7.4 Approaches to regional growth

This section will give a short introduction to regional growth theories. Two main lines of thought extracted from literature[11] will be discussed briefly, viz. the neo-classical approach and the 'non-neo-classical' approach. Finally, a dynamic interregional simulation model will be presented.

### 7.4.1 *Neo-classical theory of regional growth*

The neo-classical growth theory assumes that entrepreneurial decisions about the use of labour and capital are guided by profit maximization. Given a certain stage of economic growth of a country (composed of various regions), the production factors (such as labour and capital) must be combined in various quantities in order to achieve a maximum profit for the activity in question.

Furthermore, the neo-classical theory of regional growth is primarily based on the openness of regions (cf. Ch.1), which implies free mobility of production factors and resources between regions (cf. also Borts and Stein [1968]). The relative availability of production factors in various regions, however, is in general not equal, involving different relative prices; mostly, a relative scarcity of one or of both factors does exist. If the economy is growing, this relative disequilibrium will induce forces tending to an equilibrium where the relative factor prices in all regions are equal. This equilibrium situation will be attained only if there is free interregional mobility of labour and capital.

The foregoing notions can be presented in a more systematic and formal way by stating the following hypotheses:

H 1 Complete equality of all regions:
- (a) equal regional production functions;
- (b) equal regional output.

H 2 Complete interregional mobility of commodities and production factors, i.e. negligible transportation costs.
H 3 Given total national amount of production factors.
H 4 Mobile capital, i.e. capital is decomposable and can be shifted to, and constructed in, all regions.

National growth is affected by a number of regional discrepancies; the size of these regional growth effects will be measured in terms of relative factor prices and of capital intensity, since the relative factor proportions are assumed to characterize the regional economic structure.[12]

For each region the production function is equal to (see H 1a and H 1b):

$$Y = f(K,L) \qquad (7.4.1.1)$$

where $Y$ is the regional output and where $K$ and $L$ are, respectively, equal to the amount of regional capital and labour. The following 'classical' assumptions are made:

$$\left.\begin{array}{l} f'_K > 0 \\ f'_L > 0 \end{array}\right\} \quad (7.4.1.2)$$

which implies positive marginal products of capital and of labour, and:

$$\begin{array}{l} f''_{KK} < 0 \\ f''_{LL} < 0 \\ f''_{LK} = f''_{KL} > 0 \end{array} \quad (7.4.1.3)$$

where the first two conditions indicate decreasing marginal revenues and where the last condition indicates that an addition of capital to labour brings on rising labour productivity and vice versa. The foregoing conditions may be checked for a Cobb-Douglas-type of production function:

$$f = \gamma K^{a} L^{\beta} \quad (7.4.1.4)$$

Then:

$$\left.\begin{array}{l} f'_K = a \frac{f}{K} > 0 \\ f'_L = \beta \frac{f}{L} > 0 \\ f''_{KK} = a\,(a-1)\frac{f}{K^2} < 0, \text{ if } a < 1 \\ f''_{LL} = \beta\,(\beta-1)\frac{f}{L^2} < 0, \text{ if } \beta < 1 \\ f''_{KL} = f''_{LK} = a\beta\,\frac{f}{KL} > 0 \end{array}\right\} \quad (7.4.1.5)$$

Neo-classical theory states that in the equilibrium point each productive factor is rewarded according to the value of its marginal product,[13] or:

$$f'_K\, p = r \quad (7.4.1.6)$$

and

$$f'_L\, p = w \quad (7.4.1.7)$$

where $p$ represents the price of output, and $r$ and $w$, respectively, the payments to capital and labour.

The influence of new investments, i.e. a rise in $K$, upon the wage rate (assuming a constant $L$) is measured by the total differential of (7.4.1.7):

$$\mathrm{d}w = f_L' \mathrm{d}p + p\, f_{LK}'' \mathrm{d}K \qquad (7.4.1.8)$$

or:

$$\frac{\mathrm{d}w}{w} = \frac{f_L'}{w} \mathrm{d}p + \frac{p}{w} f_{LK}'' \,\mathrm{d}K \qquad (7.4.1.9)$$

Making use of (7.4.1.7) and (7.4.1.9) results in:

$$\frac{\mathrm{d}w}{w} \doteq \frac{\mathrm{d}p}{p} + \frac{f_{LK}''}{f_L'} \mathrm{d}K \qquad (7.4.1.10)$$

In an analogous way one can prove:

$$\frac{dr}{r} = \frac{dp}{p} + \frac{f_{KK}''}{f_K'} \mathrm{d}K \qquad (7.4.1.11)$$

By subtracting (7.4.1.11) from (7.4.1.10) one obtains:

$$\frac{dw}{w} = \frac{dr}{r} + \left(\frac{f_{LK}''}{f_L'} - \frac{f_{KK}''}{f_K'}\right) \mathrm{d}K \qquad (7.4.1.12)$$

If one assumes that the amount of investments is a function of the rentability of capital, one may use the following simple investment function:

$$dK = \eta \frac{dr}{r} \qquad (7.4.1.13)$$

Substitution of (7.4.1.13) into (7.4.1.12) gives:

$$\frac{dw}{w} = \left\{ \eta \left(\frac{f_{LK}''}{f_L'} - \frac{f_{KK}''}{f_K'}\right) + 1 \right\} \frac{dr}{r} \qquad (7.4.1.14)$$

For each region of a country a relationship like (7.4.1.14) can be specified. Assuming different regional economic structures (i.e., a different availability of capital and labour) one may evaluate the various interregional effects. For instance, if a region possesses a surplus of labour accompanied with low wages and a rather small stock of capital, in general the profitability of capital (in terms of labour) will be positive, i.e. $dr/r > 0$. For this region the following effects may according to (7.4.1.13) and (7.4.1.14) be expected:

$$\left.\begin{array}{l} dK > 0\text{, i.e. a rise of capital} \\ d\frac{K}{L} > 0\text{, i.e. a rise in capital intensity} \\ \frac{dw}{w} > 0\text{, i.e. a rise in the wage rate.} \end{array}\right\} \qquad (7.4.1.15)$$

In the previous results use is made of the fact that according to the conditions (7.4.1.2) and (7.4.1.3) the term

$\left(\frac{f''_{LK}}{f'_L} - \frac{f''_{KK}}{f'_K}\right)$ is positive. The foregoing effects measured are, of course, strongly dependent on the hypotheses made *a priori*. A slight modification in one of the hypotheses may lead to quite different conclusions.

### 7.4.2 *Alternative growth theories*

The concept of alternative, i.e., 'non-neo-classical', growth theories is not a homogeneous one, but is composed of a number of various approaches to regional and interregional growth phenomena.

The first way of looking at regional growth originates from the concept of polarization, attraction and externalities. These elements were already mentioned in Ch.3 and 5.

Such an analysis of growth processes based on the relationship between specific activities at different geographical points was provided *inter alia* by the *centre-periphery theory* (cf. Friedmann [1966, 1972]). The general idea lying behind the centre-periphery notion was first introduced by Pottier (1963), and recently revisited by Hilhorst (1972). In the general notions about centre-periphery phenomena the concept of a *development axis* plays a crucial role. Such a development axis can be considered as the spatial representation of a set of geographical points, which constitute the dominating lines in a communications network such that they can act as transmittors of growth effects. These development axes constitute essentially a spatial diffusion mechanism for development processes. The centre-periphery notion is frequently used as an analytical tool for studying divergencies (or shifts in divergencies) in growth rates between central regions and peripheral regions.

Closely related to the centre-periphery notion is the *growth centre* concept (cf. Perroux [1955], Boudeville [1972] and Darwent [1969]). Growth centre theory assumes that selected geographical points can act as promotors of an accelerated growth, both for the city or region itself and for its surroundings. In a formal way the activities within a growth centre *c* can be characterized as:

$$\left.\begin{array}{l}\dfrac{\partial A_i^c}{\partial A_j^c} > 0 \\ \text{and:} \\ \dfrac{\partial A_i^s}{\partial A_j^c} > 0\end{array}\right\} \quad (7.4.2.1)$$

where $A_i^c$ and $A_i^s$ stand for activity level (employment, investment, or value added, e.g.) of industry $i$ ($i = 1, \ldots, j, \ldots I$) in the central region $c$ and in the set $s$ of adjacent regions, respectively (see also Higgins [1972]). Conditions (7.4.2.1) state that the mutual growth effects between activities reinforce each other, both within the centre and between the centre and its surroundings. A systematic way of integrating activities within such a growth centre taking account of their mutual interrelationships is contained in Nijkamp (1972).

In addition to a growth centre one may distinguish an *attraction* centre: an attraction centre attracts the activities from adjacent regions to the centre itself, so that the centre undergoes a positive effect of these attraction forces, but the surroundings a negative effect. Therefore, an attraction centre can be characterized as:

$$\left.\begin{array}{l}\dfrac{\partial A_i^c}{\partial A_j^c} > 0 \\ \text{and:} \\ \dfrac{\partial A_i^s}{\partial A_j^c} < 0\end{array}\right\} \quad (7.4.2.2)$$

In spite of the abundant quantity of literature in the field of growth centre theory, only a few attempts have been made to integrate the growth centre theory (and its related concept of development axes) in a formal dynamic model, which takes into account the interdependences within the evolution process of a spatio-temporal system. Some contributions in this field were made among others by Klaassen, Klein and Paelinck (1974), Paelinck (1971) and (1973), and Robinson and Salih (1971).

The second approach can be characterized as 'I – O access' (cf. Perloff et al. [1960], [1963]). It tries to provide insight into the complicated relationships between regional economic growth (or stagnation) and the availability of natural resources, by presenting a conceptual framework as a guide for research in resources and regions. 'I – O access' is a netting-out of the relative advantages and disadvantages of each region for its economic activities. When one considers 'access' as the sum of the relative advantages and disadvantages for the production of a particular commodity at some given place, one should examine the requirements of specific industries and for all economic activities together in terms of costs and markets. In this way the extent to which regions vary in their prospects for growth can become apparent. In this approach particular attention is paid to the question whether easy access to inputs or outputs (resulting in lower costs of transportation) affects regional growth significantly. The various regional-growth potentials can be measured as a weighted sum of a number of regional indicators. For some regions and some activities in the USA this approach has indeed led to positive results.

A third point of departure implies a division of public overhead capital into social overhead capital (SOC) and economic overhead capital (EOC) (cf. Hirschman [1958], Hansen [1968] and Gauthier [1973]), so that the following investment allocation may be distinguished:

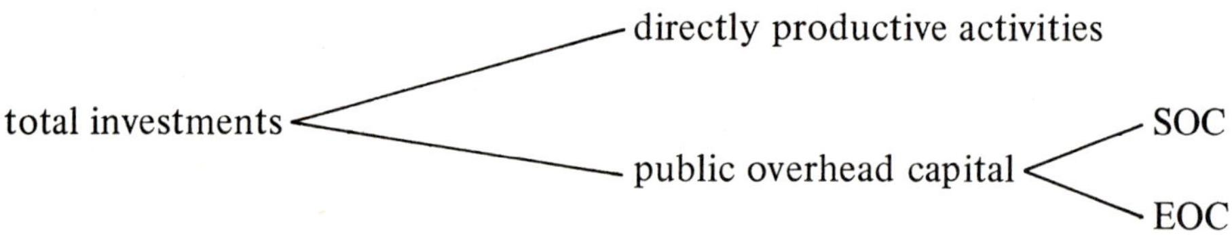


EOC projects are primarily oriented toward supporting directly productive activities or toward the movement of economic resources (e.g. roads, harbours, power installations etc.), while SOC projects are concerned with general social amenities like education, cultural and health programs, environment etc.

The division between SOC and EOC projects is not a completely fixed one like in the Leontief-type approach; see the system of isoquants in fig. 7.4.2.a.

Fig. 7.4.2.a A system of isoquants of SOC–EOC projects

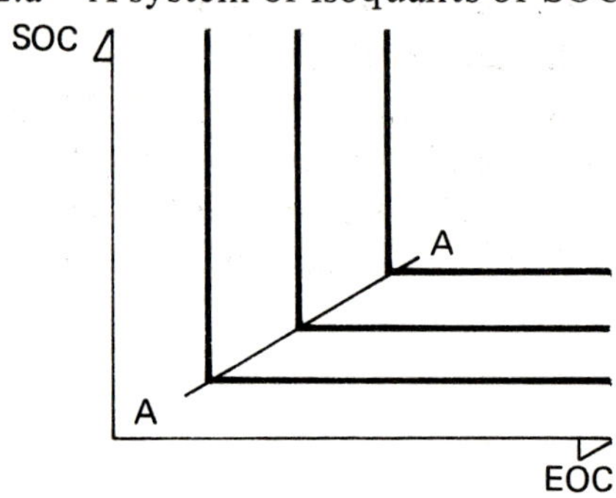

A fixed relation between SOC and EOC implies that the regional activity level resulting from a certain combination of SOC and EOC projects cannot be influenced by an addition to only *one* of the SOC or EOC projects: the regional growth path ($AA$) is fixed *a priori*.

A more flexible modification is obtained by allowing a limited substitution (between certain limits), as is denoted in figure 7.4.2.b.

Fig. 7.4.2.b  A system of isoquants of SOC–EOC projects with substitution

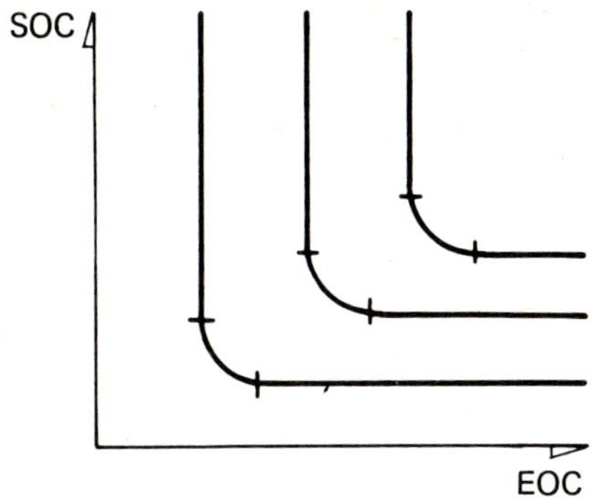


Figure 7.4.2.b denotes that there are (restricted) possibilities for choice between SOC and EOC, so that the regional growth path may have various shapes. The important value of this approach is, that it provides an explanation for regional stagnation: some regions may stagnate since their level of regional provisions may be situated at the limit of SOC or EOC, so that a rise of overhead capital in one direction will have no effect on regional growth.

### 7.4.3 *Conclusions*

The ideas laid down in section 7.4.1 and 7.4.2 give a number of possible explanations for regional growth and differences in regional growth. A more coherent approach seems to be desirable; before attempting to include in a more systematic way all relevant factors (section 7.6, where a simulation model is developed in order to explain spatial growth patterns in a dynamic context), it will be shown how the ideas set out above have led to further theoretical research.

## 7.5 Neoclassical theorems and extensions

On the basis of some foregoing neoclassical hypotheses a model can be set up to analyse the evolutionary properties of a system of regions (see Sakashita and Kamoike [1973]).

### 7.5.1 *The hypotheses*

The following hypotheses concerning the regional system are made:

H 1 Identical production functions.
H 2 Homogeneous output.
H 3 Adaptive mechanism through factor movements.
H 4 No transport cost on goods and services.
H 5 Complete product-capital substitutability.

### 7.5.2 *The model*

Each region $r$ ($r = 1, \ldots, R$) is supposed to possess a Cobb-Douglas production function which links regional output ($Y_r$) to labour ($L_r$) and to capital ($K_r$), i.e.

$$Y_r = L_r^{1-a} \; K_r^a = L_r k_r^a \tag{7.5.2.1}$$

where the capital intensity or capital-labour ratio ($k_r$) is defined as:

$$k_r = K_r L_r^{-1} \tag{7.5.2.2}$$

The regional growth rate of labour is assumed to be determined as follows:

$$\frac{1}{L_r} \frac{dL_r}{dt} \triangleq L_r^{-1} \; \dot{L}_r = \beta\lambda_r + l^* \tag{7.5.2.3}$$

where $\lambda_r$ represents the relative discrepancy between the regional and the average national marginal productivity of labour, i.e.,

$$\lambda_r = \frac{\left(\frac{\partial Y}{\partial L}\right)_r - \left(\frac{\partial Y}{\partial L}\right)}{\frac{\partial Y}{\partial L}} = \frac{k_r^a - k^a}{k^a} \tag{7.5.2.4}$$

which can directly be written in terms of differences in $k_r^a$ and $k^a$ by using (7.5.2.1). Furthermore, $l^*$ represents the average national growth rate of labour:

$$l^* = \frac{dL}{dt} \; L^{-1} \triangleq \dot{L} \; L^{-1} \tag{7.5.2.5}$$

where $L$ is defined in (7.5.2.12).
In a similar way, the growth rate of capital can be written as:

$$\frac{1}{K_r} \frac{dK_r}{dt} \triangleq K_r^{-1} \; \dot{K}_r = \gamma\pi_r + k^* \tag{7.5.2.6}$$

where $\pi_r$ and $k^*$ are defined in a way similar to $\lambda_r$ and $l^*$, respectively, i.e.,

$$\pi_r = \frac{\left(\frac{\partial Y}{\partial K}\right)_r - \frac{\partial Y}{\partial K}}{\frac{\partial Y}{\partial K}} = \frac{k_r^{a-1} - k^{a-1}}{k^{a-1}} \qquad (7.5.2.7)$$

$$k^* = \frac{dK}{dt} K^{-1} \triangleq \dot{K} K^{-1} \qquad (7.5.2.8)$$

where $K$ is defined in (7.5.2.11).

In a way similar to (7.5.2.1), the 'average' national production function is written as:

$$Y = L^{1-a} K^a = L k^a \qquad (7.5.2.9)$$

where the national capital intensity is defined as:

$$k = KL^{-1} \qquad (7.5.2.10)$$

and where the average national capital and labour stocks are defined as:

$$K = \sum_{r=1}^{R} K_r R^{-1} \qquad (7.5.2.11)$$

and:

$$L = \sum_{r=1}^{R} L_r R^{-1} \qquad (7.5.2.12)$$

The previous model describes the differential growth effects of a system of regions with factor mobility. Equations (7.5.2.1) and (7.5.2.9) are essentially definitional; the others are the adaptive equations. For instance, (7.5.2.3) indicates how demand (equals supply) of labour develops regionally as a function of relative marginal labour productivity (equals wages); (7.5.2.6) does the same for capital.

### 7.5.3 *The variance of per capita income and its evolution*

The previous regional system can be used to study the differential growth path of each region separately. The absolute variance of per capita output (income) among regions, denoted by $\sigma^2(Y/L)$, can be calculated as:

$$\sigma^2 \left(\frac{Y}{L}\right) = R^{-1} \sum_{r=1}^{R} \left(\frac{Y_r}{L_r} - R^{-1} \sum_{r'=1}^{R} \frac{Y_{r'}}{L_{r'}}\right)^2 \qquad (7.5.3.1)$$

$$= R^{-1} \sum_{r=1}^{R} (k_r^a - k^a)^2$$

$$= R^{-1} \sum_{r=1}^{R} (\lambda_r k^a)^2$$

$$= k^{2a} R^{-1} \sum_{r=1}^{R} \lambda_r^2$$

where use is made of (7.5.2.1) and (7.5.2.4). Next, by defining

$$\lambda_r \triangleq (1 + \theta_r)^a - 1 \tag{7.5.3.2}$$

one may rewrite (7.5.3.1) as:

$$\sigma \left(\frac{Y}{L}\right) = k^{2a} R^{-1} \sum_{r=1}^{R} \left\{(1 + \theta_r)^a - 1\right\}^2 \tag{7.5.3.3}$$

The new parameter $\theta_r$ is equal to the relative discrepancy between the regional and the average national capital-labour ratio, i.e.,

$$\theta_r = \frac{k_r - k}{k} \tag{7.5.3.4}$$

as is easily seen by substituting (7.5.2.4) into (7.5.3.2):

$$\frac{k_r^a}{k^a} - 1 = (1 + \theta_r)^a - 1 \tag{7.5.3.5}$$

or:

$$\frac{k_r}{k} = 1 + \theta_r \tag{7.5.3.6}$$

which is equal to (7.5.3.4). It should be noted that $\theta_r > -1$.

In a similar way one can show that the following relationship, which is complementary to (7.5.3.2), is also valid:

$$\pi_r = (1 + \theta_r)^{a-1} - 1 \tag{7.5.3.7}$$

The evolution of the income variance can be analyzed by differentiating (7.5.3.1) with respect to time:

$$\frac{d\sigma^2\left(\frac{Y}{L}\right)}{dt} \triangleq \dot{\sigma}^2 \left(\frac{Y}{L}\right) = \frac{d\left\{R^{-1} \sum_{r=1}^{R} (k_r^a - k^a)^2\right\}}{dt} \tag{7.5.3.8}$$

$$= 2R^{-1} \sum_{r=1}^{R} \left(\frac{dk_r^a}{dt} - \frac{dk^a}{dt}\right) (k_r^a - k^a)$$

$$= 2aR^{-1} \sum_{r=1}^{R} \left(k_r^{a-1} \frac{dk_r}{dt} - k^{a-1} \frac{dk}{dt}\right) (k_r^a - k^a)$$

$$= 2aR^{-1} \sum_{r=1}^{R} \left\{ k_r^{a-1} \frac{d(K_r/L_r)}{dt} - k^{a-1} \frac{d(K/L)}{dt} \right\} (k_r^a - k^a)$$

$$= 2aR^{-1} \sum_{r=1}^{R} \left\{ k_r^a (\gamma\pi_r - \beta\gamma_r + k^* - l^*) - k^a(k^* - l^*) \right\} (k_r^a - k^a)$$

$$= 2ak^{2a}R^{-1} \sum_{r=1}^{R} \left\{ (1+\theta_r)^a - 1 \right\} \Big[ (1+\theta_r)^a \left\{ \gamma\, (1+\theta_r)^{a-1} - \right.$$

$$\left. - \beta\, (1+\theta_r)^a + (\beta - \gamma + k^* - l^*) \right\} - (k^* - l^*) \Big]$$

where use is made of (7.5.2.1)–(7.5.2.8), and of (7.5.3.4)–(7.5.3.7).

It is easily seen that, in the case where $k^* = l^*$ (and thus $k$ is constant), $\dot{\sigma}^2\ (Y/L) < 0$: if $\theta_r = 0$, the $r^{th}$ term of the sum of (7.5.3.8) is zero, and if $\theta_r \neq 0$, the $r^{th}$ term is negative.

In the general case where $k^* \neq l^*$, a MacLaurin expansion on (7.5.3.8) gives, supposing $|\theta_r| < 1$ (cf. Sakashita and Kamoike [1973]):

$$\dot{\sigma}^2\ (Y/L) = 2\sigma^2 \left\{ -(1-a)\gamma - a\beta + a\,(k^* - l^*) \right\} \qquad (7.5.3.9)$$

which shows that $\dot{\sigma}^2\ (Y/L) > 0$ might be a possible case, viz. if $k^* > l^*$. This implies that in general no definite conclusion can be drawn concerning the evolution of the income variance over regions.

### 7.5.4 *The behaviour of $\theta_r$*

It seems to be worth while to examine the evolution of $\theta_r$. One can derive the following result:

$$\frac{d \ln (1+\theta_r)}{dt} = \frac{d \ln (k_r/k)}{dt} \qquad (7.5.4.1)$$

$$= \frac{k}{k_r} \; \frac{(dk_r/dt)k - (dk/dt)k_r}{k^2}$$

$$= \frac{k}{k_r} \; \frac{k_r\,(\gamma\pi_r - \beta\lambda_r + k^* - l^*)k - k(k^* - l^*)k_r}{k^2}$$

$$= \gamma\pi_r - \beta\lambda_r$$

$$= \gamma \left\{(1+\theta_r)^{a-1} - 1\right\} - \beta \left\{(1+\theta_r)^{a} - 1\right\}$$

where the results from (7.5.3.2), (7.5.3.6), (7.5.3.7) and (7.5.3.8) are employed. It is easily seen that $\theta_r = 0$ implies that (7.5.4.1) is equal to zero. Otherwise, after a series of mathematical exercises one can prove:

$$\frac{\mathrm{d}\,|\,\theta_r\,|}{\mathrm{d}t} < 0 \qquad (7.5.4.2)$$

A closer examination of the previous relationships shows that this process does, in fact, tend towards the equilibrium growth path $\theta_r = 0$, if $t \to \infty$ $\forall r$, which implies that $Y_r/L_r \to k^a, \forall r$. The latter balanced growth path can be proved by using the concept of a so-called Liapunov function (see among others La Salle and Lefschetz [1961] and Hahn [1963]). A possible Liapunov function is in fact the logarithmic or relative variance of per capita output among regions:

$$\rho^2 = R^{-1} \sum_{r=1}^{R} \left\{ \ln \left(\frac{Y}{L}\right)_r - \ln \left(\frac{Y}{L}\right)\right\}^2 \qquad (7.5.4.3)$$

$$= R^{-1} \sum_{r=1}^{R} \left\{ \ln k_r^a - \ln k^a \right\}^2$$

$$= a^2 R^{-1} \sum_{r=1}^{R} \left\{ \ln (1+\theta_r) \right\}^2$$

where use is made of (7.5.2.1), (7.5.2.9) and (7.5.3.6).

The time derivative of (7.5.4.3) is:

$$\dot{\rho}^2 = 2a^2 R^{-1} \sum_{r=1}^{R} (1+\theta_r)^{-1} \ln (1+\theta_r) - \frac{\mathrm{d}}{\mathrm{d}t} (1+\theta_r) \qquad (7.5.4.4)$$

where the terms are again equal to zero for $\theta_r = 0$, otherwise negative.

Now, a theorem of Liapunov tells us that a sufficient condition for stability of a dynamic system is that a scalar function $V(\mathbf{x})$ of the variables of the system can be found, such that:

(a) $V(\mathbf{x}) \in C^1$, the complex space
(b) $V(\mathbf{x}) \geqslant 0, \ \forall x_i$
(c) $V(\mathbf{x}) \equiv 0$, if $\mathbf{x} = \mathbf{0}$
(d) $\dot{V}(\mathbf{x}) \leqslant 0$

The search for a Liapunov function, i.e. a positive semi-definite function of $\mathbf{x}$, is an application of Liapunov's so-called 'direct' method.

It is easy to see that $\rho^2$ defined by (7.5.4.3) is a Liapunov function, and that the process defined by (7.5.2.1) – (7.5.2.12) tends to $\theta_r = 0, \forall\, r$. Such a system, defined by H 1 – H 5 of section 7.5.1, tends to equal $\theta$ and $Y/L$ characteristics in all regions.

This leads to the following growth proposition:

P.G.1 Under hypotheses H 1–H 5 relative income differences do not increase, and actually tend towards zero.

### 7.5.5 *Relaxing the hypotheses*

It suffices to relax hypothesis H 1, to show that a different dynamics may be the result.

Indeed suppose that for a certain region $r$, $a_r \gg a$, the latter being now an *average* value of the $a_r$ 's. In this case one can ultimately derive that

$$\frac{\mathrm{d} \ln (1+\theta_r)}{\mathrm{d}t} = \left\{(1+\theta_r)^{a_r} k^{a_r - a} - 1\right\} \times \left\{-\gamma \frac{1-(1+\theta_r)^{a_r-1} k^{a_r-a}}{(1+\theta_r)^{a_r} k^{a_r-a} - 1} - \beta\right\} \qquad (7.5.5.1)$$

For a sufficiently large value of $a_r$, (7.5.5.1) with $\theta_r > 0$ can be made to become positive, meaning relatively increasing regional capital intensity, and similar consequences for relative per capita income. In fact, even the difference $a_r - a$ may remain at a considerable level, as capital (and labour) is drawn to region $r$, when for instance capital productivity is higher owing to externalities. Economies of scale, meaning a production function of the following type:

$$Y_r = L_r^{\delta}\, k_r^{a} \qquad \delta > 1 \qquad (7.5.5.2)$$

would even increase the explosive effect.

Study along the lines previously sketched should proceed, showing for instance how capital and labour move in fact in and out of regions. The matter will not be pursued theoretically, but completed by means of a simulation model of the main economic activities through space.

## 7.6 Diffusion of growth processes in regional and urban systems

### 7.6.1 *Introduction*

The present section is an attempt to construct some formal models that describe the development processes of a system of mutually dependent spatial elements. Given a set of theoretical notions concerning such a system, some dynamic models will be presented which describe the variations of the state of the system – both through time and through space. Since these models suffer from a lack of adequate information, a simulation is carried out in order to inspect the possible evolution of the state of the system. Based on these outcomes, an attempt is made at formulating new 'second-order' hypotheses, which could underly relations to be tested empirically.

According to Perloff and Wingo (1961) the results of the successive stages of urban evolution were '. . . the great heartland nucleation of industry and the national market, the focus of large-scale national-serving industry, the seedbed of new industry responding to the dynamic structure of national final demand, and the centre of high levels of per capita income. Radiating out across the national landscape are the resource-dominant regional hinterlands specializing in the production of resource and intermediate outputs for which the heartland reaches out to satisfy the input requirements of its great manufacturing plants. Here in the hinterlands, resource-endowment is a critical determinant of the particular cumulative advantage of the region and hence its growth potential.'

It is evident that more insight in the backgrounds of these urban and regional development processes will be obtained, when the essential working of an economic system with spatial and temporal elements is analyzed more thoroughly. Therefore, it is necessary to develop a set of hypotheses concerning the structure and processes of regional and urban systems (see next section).

In addition to the *endogenous* functional working of such systems one should take account of *exogenous* factors that influence the endogenous development path. These exogenous factors may be so-called '*data*' (for instance, rise in population, technological changes, exhaustion of sources of new materials, and productivity changes) or *instrument variables* (for instance, institutional and political measures, locational subsidies, environmental protection measures, and infrastructural investments). It should be noted that in the long run a feed-back from the endogenous development of a system to the exogenous sector is possible, for instance an increased technological interest in alternative energy sources owing to the increased demand for traditional kinds of energy in relation to its possible supply, or a creation of favourable locational conditions in order to stimulate regional employment.

In a multiregional system one should also be aware of a functional interdependence between the various sub-regions. For instance, political measures earmarked for a specific region have side-effects in surrounding regions owing to the *openness* of the region concerned. This seems to be a crucial factor in interregional development processes, since the degree of openness of a region affects the entire working of a multiregional system. For that reason it is understandable that regions located on a development axis with many transport and communication lines to surrounding regions undergo a greater mutual influence than similar regions which are partially 'closed' with respect to each other, e.g. located far apart (one thinks of the problem in 'big jump policies' intended to develop peripheral regions).

The notion of the 'relative openness' of regions is essential in the so-called *filter* and *barrier* effects encountered in spatial diffusion problems (see, for instance, Yuill [1965]). For instance, a region may absorb activity streams or communication lines, so that the total interaction within the entire system is diminished. Or a region may act as a permeable barrier, so that it serves as a filter allowing the penetration of certain specific activity streams or communication lines. But this implies that a *functional analysis* of regional and urban systems should take into consideration the specific characteristics of each region separately, characteristics which explain its behaviour in the diffusion process.

Consequently, the dynamic evolution of a system of regions or of cities cannot be analyzed adequately, if one describes the interaction process between subsets of the system only by means of 'mechanical' allocation rules from the national level. In other words, an adequate analysis of space-time processes should be based mainly on the specific elements of spatial lay-outs. This implies that both sectoral and physical analysis should be carried out at a disaggregated level; it is obvious that a coherent analysis of these elements has to be based on detailed data concerning the structure and processes of the system. Therefore, in the future more and more attention should be paid to a systematic, objective-oriented data collection resulting in the emergence of functional data banks.

For the moment the major part of analyses concerning multiregional and multi-urban systems can not be based on reliable data, so that the construction of econometric models in this field is frequently an illusion (Paelinck [1972]). However, given a set of theoretical notions about entrepreneurial behaviour, about spatial and sectoral planning objectives and about the interwoven pattern of space and time, it is very well possible and also fruitful to construct a preliminary model in order to inspect the possible working and evolution of the underlying structure of the system. Such a model will be set out in next sections (see also Nijkamp and Paelinck [1974]).

### 7.6.2 *A dynamic model with spatial and temporal components*

Given the theoretical notions presented in the previous sections, a diffusion model with spatial and temporal elements should satisfy at least the following requirements:

(a) explicit introduction of time-elements as essential components;
(b) explicit introduction of a spatial interwovenness between specific regions, for instance, by means of spin-off and spill-over effects, of which the meaning should be made clear;
(c) functional relationships between all relevant phenomena which are responsible for a development or a diffusion process;
(d) presence of an institutional framework, for instance by means of political instrument variables (subsidies, infrastructural policy, etc.);
(e) presence of autonomous factors, for instance, demographic developments.

On the basis of the previous rules an attempt is made to construct a simplified model which shows some essential elements of a diffusion process with spatial and temporal aspects. This model is only of an illustrative nature; in a later section a more extensive and realistic model will be developed.

The model presented here possesses 4 equations describing the structure and evolution of the spatial system concerned. The assumption is made that this system is closed, and composed of $R$ regions $r$ ($r = 1, \ldots, R$), each of which has certain specific characteristics. These regions can be subdivided into:

(a) growth centres; these regions have according to (7.4.2.1) positive diffusion effects both within and outside the region;
(b) attraction centres; these regions have according to (7.4.2.2) negative diffusion effects with respect to surrounding regions; and
(c) intermediate regions; these regions stand between growth centres and attraction centres, because they undergo a positive stimulus from growth centres and a negative stimulus from attraction centres; they act as transmitters of growth effects, which leads to 'filter' and 'barrier' effects.

The model is composed of a set of four structural, dynamic equations. The first equation is the investment equation:

$$I^{r}_{t+1} = a^{r}_{t} A^{r}_{t} + \sum_{\substack{r' = 1 \\ r' \neq 1}}^{R} \beta^{rr'}_{t} K^{r'}_{t} + \gamma^{r}_{t} Y^{r}_{t} \qquad (7.6.2.1)$$

This equation states, that the investment decisions in region $r$ in period $t$+1 (denoted by $I^r_{t+1}$ ) are determined by some regional attractiveness in period $t$ (denoted by $A^r_t$, the relative 'locational vector' of region $r$, see (7.6.2.4)), by the aggregated spill-over effects from capital stocks in contiguous regions $r'$ ($r' = 1, \ldots, R$) in period $t$ (denoted by $K^{r'}_t$), and by regional production in period $t$ (denoted by $Y^r_t$ ). It is obvious that the second term on the right-hand side of (7.6.2.1) is responsible for an interwoven spatial development process, since capital stocks in surrounding regions induce investments in a central region.

The second equation is a definitional equation, which defines net investment as growth in capital sticks:

$$K^r_{t+1} \triangleq K^r_t + I^r_{t+1} \qquad (7.6.2.2)$$

The third equation is associated with the impulses for regional production:

$$Y^r_{t+1} = \sum_{r'=1}^{R} \delta^{rr'}_t P^{r'}_t + \sum_{r'=1}^{R} \epsilon^{rr'}_t Y^{r'}_t + c^r_t \qquad (7.6.2.3)$$

The first term of (7.6.2.3) indicates that the regional production is induced by total final demand in a previous period; this final demand (both *intraregional* and *interregional*) is assumed to be a linear function of the successive regional volume of population $P^{r'}_t$. The second term means that the regional production volume is stimulated by the volume of intermediate deliveries (again both *intraregional* and *interregional*) from a previous period; parameter $\epsilon^{rr'}_t$ is essentially an interregional input–output or 'attraction' coefficient (Klaassen [1974]). The last term of (7.6.2.3) is a trend term, which stands for general factors determining the volume of regional production (for instance, the efficiency of transportation systems, the availability of production factors, expected profits etc.); in view of the restrictiveness of the simplified model discussed here, this factor cannot be elaborated, but a discussion will be presented in a following section.

The last equation is concerned with the regional attractiveness:

$$A^r_{t+1} = A^r_t + \theta^r_t \; (\bar{K}^r_t - K^r_{t+1}) + e^r_t. \qquad (7.6.2.4)$$

Regional attractiveness can undergo a change owing to two factors: it will decrease if the regional capital stock exceeds a threshold value $\bar{K}^r_t$ (leading to problems of congestion and pollution); it will increase as a function of exogenous measures $e^r_t$ (for instance, infrastructural investments, creation of information and communication centres, recreation facilities, etc.).

The model includes four types of endogenous variables, viz. $I^r_t$, $K^r_t$, $Y^r_t$

and $A_t^r$. The endogenous dynamic mechanism between these variables can be controlled by means of instrument variables included in $c_t^r$ and $e_t^r$, while, in addition, the endogenous path is affected by exogenous data, for instance, population growth.

A first and provisional way of getting more insight in the structure of such dynamic models is to insert a set of reasonable coefficients into the model, as well as initial values for all variables, and next to simulate the spatio-temporal process. Inspection of the resulting growth path may lead to a revision of the model's structure, or to a set of new hypotheses as a basis for further experiments. It should be noted explicitly that without empirical calibration, the model is hardly suitable for spatio-temporal planning procedures (Naylor [1971]). We consider that, without adequate validation, the model can only be a demonstration or learning model; however, it may provide more analytical insight and could probably be used as the starting-point for operational, empirical approaches.

In the second place, it should be stressed that a necessary condition for using these models in economic policy and planning, is the determination of political and planning objectives. This evokes the problems of objective functions for dynamic spatial models (cf. Nijkamp [1974]). In spite of the importance of these problems no attention will be paid here to political preference functions; within the framework of the present paper, the major attention will be paid to the analysis of the properties of the development path of the spatio-temporal system itself. For that reason, in Appendix 7A some essential elements of dynamic models are discussed.

### 7.6.3 *A simulation of the simple model*

The model described in section 7.6.2 will now be used as the starting-point for analyzing the process of spatial interaction. The assumption is made that the regional (or urban) system is composed of 49 connex elementary spatial units (for instance grid cells, or operational taxonomic units).

According to the model there is both a *spin-off effect* (i.e. between the *same* endogenous variables $Y$ in equation (7.6.2.1) and a *spill-over effect* (i.e. between the *different* variables $K$ and $I$ in equation (7.6.2.3) as well as between $P$ and $Y$ in equation (7.6.2.3). Both the spin-off and the spill-over effects with respect to surrounding regions are assumed to be of first contiguity order. The positiveness or negativeness of these effects depends on the question as to whether a central region acts as an attraction centre or as a growth centre with respect to surrounding regions. For instance, if region $r'$ is an attraction centre with respect to region $r$, the spill-over coefficient $\beta_t^{rr'}$ in equation (7.6.2.1) will be negative. The same holds true for coefficients $\delta_t^{rr'}$ and $\epsilon_t^{rr'}$.

In addition to growth centres and attraction centres there are intermediate regions which transmit the spatial interaction effects from growth centres and attraction centres. The spatial system concerned is assumed to possess initially the following configuration:

Fig. 7.6.3.a The initial spatial system

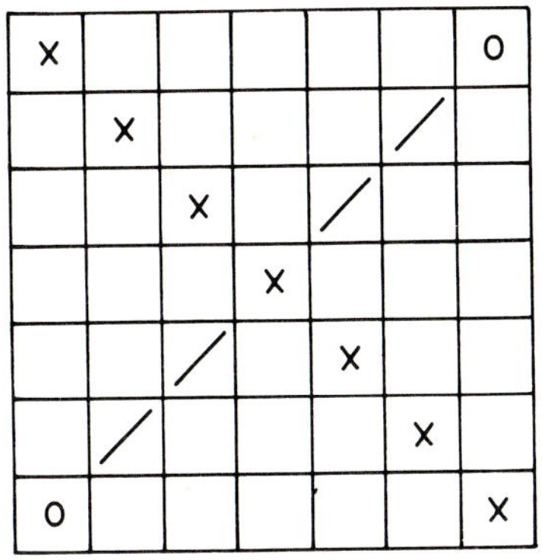

The grid cells containing the symbol 'x' represent a diagonal development axis (or a communication axis, for instance a railroad, a river or a highway), which acts as an attraction axis (or an attraction centre with 7 elements). The grid cells provided with the symbol 'O' represent growth centres. The cells with the symbol '/' constitute a counter-axis which transmits the growth impulses from the growth centres to the attraction axis. These interaction effects are assumed to be bilateral: the growth centres receive also a backward effect from positive impulses in surrounding regions. The remaining grid cells may undergo both positive and negative effects.

The attraction axis can be considered as an area with a favourable location vector. However, owing to the relatively small width of this area, it has a limited absorption potential for new activities. This implies that congestion phenomena will soon arise here, so that the capacity variable $\bar{K}$ has a relatively low value.

Next, a set of parameters will be introduced for each type of region. For the moment these parameters are assumed to be constant over time. The following data are used:

Table 7.6.3.a Data and starting-values of the simulation model

| | Growth pole | Intermediate region | Attraction centre |
|---|---|---|---|
| $K$ | 160.0 | 120.0 | 40.0 |
| $K$ | 40.0 | 0.0 | 0.0 |
| $A$ | 100.0 | 0.0 | 100.0 |
| $\alpha$ | 0.020 | 0.100 | 0.020 |
| $\beta$ | 0.002 | 0.002 | –0.003 |
| $\gamma$ | 0.05 | 0.04 | 0.03 |
| $Y$ | 50.0 | 40.0 | 20.0 |

| | Growth pole | Intermediate region | Attraction centre |
|---|---|---|---|
| $P$ | 100.0 | 30.0 | 50.0 |
| $c$ | 1.0 | 0.75 | 0.50 |
| $e$ | 2.0 | 1.5 | 1.0 |
| $\theta$ | 0.05 | 0.01 | 0.05 |
| $\delta^{rr}$ | 0.005 | 0.004 | 0.003 |
| $\epsilon^{rr}$ | 0.5 | 0.5 | 0.5 |
| $\delta^{rr'}$ | 0.0005 | 0.0004 | 0.0003 |
| $\epsilon^{rr'}$ | 0.10 | 0.01 | 0.04 |

Given the previous set of parameters, the model can be simulated in a recursive way in order to inspect the growth mechanism of such a dynamic system. Particularly important and interesting is here the dynamic evolution of the diffusion process between the growth centres and the attraction axis.

The foregoing dynamic model with the assumed parameters is recursively developed during 100 periods. For each 10 periods a figure is drawn representing the spatial configuration at that moment. These results are contained in Figures A 0 – A 10 of Appendix 7B; for the sake of simplicity only the capital variables are presented.

The results in Appendix 7B give rise to the following comments:

– The spin-off effects and spill-over effects are essential elements in the spatial diffusion process: they are responsible for transmitting growth impulses through a spatial system.

– It appears that in the simulation process a capital transmission from the growth pole to the surrounding regions is induced. In consequence, the major part of the intermediate regions receives already after 10 periods a certain rise in capital stocks.

– The aforementioned counter axis becomes clearly visible after 50 periods. In the next periods this counter axis is growing rather rapidly. From period 60 onwards certain cells on the counter axis have received such a growth in their capital stocks, that they exceed the capital stocks of the growth centres. This implies a relative decline of the development potential of the other regions, particularly of those at the attraction axis. In consequence, the attraction axis undergoes relatively a less rapid growth.

– The growth of capital implies that from period 60 onwards the capacity limits in certain regions become to be exceeded, so that a negative attractiveness begins to arise. This process arises first at the attraction axis.

– After 100 periods the attractiveness in all regions tends to be negative owing to the limits imposed by the capacity limits. In reality these limits are frequently less rapidly obtained owing to new technologies and innovations. This would imply a change in the parameters of the simulation model. The latter problem brings us again back to the aforementioned problems of estimating and projecting parameters in dynamic systems by means of statistical and econometric techniques.

### 7.6.4 *A general dynamic model of spatial interaction*

In this section a general dynamic model of spatial interactions will be developed. The initial simplified model in section 7.6.2 gave only a partial description of spatial interdependences, since it did not include explicitly entrepreneurial behaviour (for instance, profit maximization), labour markets, wage levels, and migration.

Therefore a more extended model will be presented now, which remedy the previous shortcomings, albeit that such a model is more complicated than the previous simple model. A first version of this model is contained in Paelinck (1973).

The first equation of the new model is again the investment equation. The assumption is made that investments in period $t + 1$ are determined by regional attractiveness in period $t$ (i.e., $A_t^r$), spill-over effects of capital stocks in surrounding regions (i.e., $K_t^{r'}$), realized profits in the previous period (i.e., $\Pi_t^r$), and an exogenous factor $b_t^r$ (for instance, investment subsidies). Therefore, the investment equation is:

$$I_{t+1}^r = a_t^r A_t^r + \sum_{\substack{r'=1 \\ r' \neq r}}^{R} \beta_t^{rr'} K_t^{r'} + \eta_t^r \Pi_t^r + b_t^r \qquad (7.6.4.1)$$

A comparison of (7.6.2.1) with (7.6.4.1) shows that in (7.6.4.1) production $Y_t^r$ is replaced by profits $\Pi_t^r$ (which are a more adequate impulse for entrepreneurial investments), while also an exogenous constant is added. Since in the theory of investment behaviour frequently *expected* profits instead of *realized* profits play an important role, one might also interpret $\Pi_t^r$ as expected profits.

It is evident, that $I_{t+1}^r$ can be defined as the growth in capital stock, so that:

$$K_{t+1}^r \triangleq K_t^r + I_{t+1}^r \qquad (7.6.4.2)$$

Furthermore, if total national investments are denoted by $I_t$, it is obvious that the following additivity condition is valid:

$$I_t = \sum_{r=1}^{R} I_t^r \qquad (7.6.4.3)$$

The system is said to be *neutral* at the national level, if in spite of the introduction of spin-off and spill-over effects the original level of investments would remain constant. A neutral effect, however, does not imply that the spatial dispersion of investments remains constant: growth and attraction effects can affect to a considerable degree the spatial configuration of investment patterns.

A spin-off effect is called *active*, if the net total spin-off and spill-over effects of the spatial system exert a positive influence on the total investment volume. An retro-active spin-off is defined the other way around.

The production level of region $r$ in period $t$+1 is induced by profits (or profit expectations) in a previous period, by the total volume of final demand and of intermediate deliveries, and by exogenous factors (for instance, transportation and communication systems, accessibility, etc.). Therefore one obtains (cf. [7.6.2.3]):

$$Y^{r}_{t+1} = \kappa^{r}_{t}\, \Pi^{r}_{t} + \sum_{r'=1}^{R} \delta^{rr'}_{t}\, p^{r'}_{t} + \sum_{r'=1}^{R} \epsilon^{rr'}_{t}\, Y^{r'}_{t} + c^{r}_{t} \qquad (7.6.4.4)$$

Regional profits (or profit expectations) are supposed to be a linear function of the regional production volume, of the difference between the national wage rate (i.e., $\bar{W}_t$) and the regional wage rate (i.e., $W^r_t$), of investment costs (in particular, depreciations), of the volume of regional labour supply (i.e., $L^r_t$), of infrastructural investments (i.e., $S^r_t$) and of exogenous factors (for instance, entrepreneurial subsidies). The result is:

$$\Pi^{r}_{t} = \lambda^{r}_{t}\, Y^{r}_{t} + \mu^{r}_{t}\, (\bar{W}_{t} - W^{r}_{t}) + \nu^{r}_{t}\, I^{r}_{t} + \epsilon^{r}_{t}\, L^{r}_{t} + \pi^{r}_{t}\, S^{r}_{t} + d^{r}_{t} \qquad (7.6.4.5)$$

The demand for labour (i.e., $E^r_t$) is a function of the regional production level, the regional wage difference and the regional technology $T^r_t$ (for instance, productivity changes in labour conditions) in previous periods:

$$E^{r}_{t+1} = \rho^{r}_{t}\, Y^{r}_{t} + \sigma^{r}_{t}\, (\bar{W}_{t} - W^{r}_{t}) + \tau^{r}_{t}\, T^{r}_{t} \qquad (7.6.4.6)$$

Regional labour supply is a function of the regional volume of population including net migration ($M^r_t$), of the regional wage difference with respect to the average national wage rate, of spill-over effects of wage differentials in contiguous regions and of exogenous factors (for instance, rigidity in mobility):

$$L^{r}_{t+1} = \varphi^{r}_{t}\, (P^{r}_{t} + M^{r}_{t}) + \chi^{r}_{t}(\bar{W}_{t} - W^{r}_{t}) + \sum_{\substack{r'=1 \\ r' \neq r}}^{R} \psi^{rr'}_{t}\, (\bar{W}_{t} - W^{r'}_{t}) + f^{r}_{t} \qquad (7.6.4.7)$$

The spill-over effect in (7.6.4.7) leads in fact to commuting.

Furthermore, net regional migration can be explained from wage differentials, spill-over effects of wage rates from contiguous regions, regional attractiveness factors, the degree of regional unemployment, and by exogenous factors (for instance, institutional decisions to move governmental services);

$$M^r_{t+1} = \omega^r_t (\overline{W}_t - W^r_t) + \sum_{\substack{r'=1 \\ r' \neq r}}^{R} k^{rr'}_t (\overline{W}_t - W^{r'}_t) + l^r_t A^r_t + m^r_t (L^r_t - E^r_t) + g^r_t \tag{7.6.4.8}$$

Regional attractiveness in period $t+1$ results from a shift of attractiveness in a previous period, caused by a threshold value of capital (owing to congestion and pollution), and by exogenous factors (such as degree of urbanization, public investments, recreation facilities, etc.). Therefore, the definitional equation of regional attractiveness is (cf. [7.6.2.4]):

$$A^r_{t+1} = A^r_t + \theta^r_t (\overline{K}^r_t - K^r_{t+1}) + e^r_t \tag{7.6.4.9}$$

Finally, the regional wage differential is supposed to be a result of regional unemployment levels, of spill-over effects of unemployment levels from contiguous regions, the level of regional technology, regional infrastructural investments and exogenous factors (for instance, the influence of trade union action). Therefore, the wage equation is:

$$\overline{W}_t - W^r_t = p^r_t (L^r_t - E^r_t) + \sum_{\substack{r'=1 \\ r' \neq r}}^{R} q^{rr'}_t (L^r_t - E^{r'}_t) + r^r_t T^r_t + s^r_t S^r_t + h^r_t \tag{7.6.4.10}$$

The previous system contains 9 equations for each region (leaving aside equation (7.6.4.3), so that the total number of equations is equal to 9 $R$. Each set of regional equations contains 9 unknown endogenous variables (viz., $I$, $K$, $Y$, $\Pi$, $E$, $L$, $M$, $A$, $W$), so that the system can in principle be solved in terms of the exogenous variables ($S$ and $T$) and in terms of the constant factors.

The previous system is still a rather simple representation of spatial interactions. Until now a sectoral breakdown of economic activities has not been introduced, although particularly in the field of input–output relationships strong spatial interactions may arise.

The previous system can again be written in the general structural form (7A.1) or (7A.4), and can be simulated in an analogous manner. The theory of dynamic systems presented in the previous section is also applicable here.

### 7.6.5 *Conclusion*

The models presented above can only be considered as illustrative ones: for the moment these models are simplified and non-validated representations of spatial diffusion and development processes. The various simulation runs show, however, that the assumption of development axes as the motor of regional and urban growth processes is quite reasonable. Such a situation can indeed be observed in reality, for instance, in the Ruhr-area in Germany, the Rhône-area in France and the Rhine-delta area in the Netherlands. This implies that agglomeration tendencies, spin-off and spill-over effects and diffusion effects are crucial elements in spatial interaction models.

It is evident, that the empirical calibration of the previous models will require a lot of work, but in certain respects meaningful results have already been obtained (for instance, for the employment equation and the migration equation). The conclusion is, that spatial econometrics is a discipline which is for the moment still underdeveloped, but which should receive more attention in the future.

## Appendix 7A The structure of dynamic models

The dynamic model presented in section 7.6.2 contains in each time period 4 $R$ equations with 4 $R$ unknown variables. This system can be represented in matrix notation as:

$$\mathbf{B}\,\mathbf{x}_{t+1} = \mathbf{C}\,\mathbf{x}_t + \mathbf{D}\,\mathbf{z}_t + \mathbf{v}_t \tag{7A.1}$$

where $\mathbf{x}_{t+1}$, $\mathbf{z}_t$ and $\mathbf{v}_t$ constitute a vector of endogenous variables in period $t$+1, of instrument variables in period $t$ and of exogenous data in period $t$, respectively. Matrices **B**, **C** and **D** contain all relevant coefficients of the previous dynamic spatial model. For the sake of simplicity the time-subscripts of these matrices are left out of consideration. In a more elaborate form the previous system can be represented as:

$$\begin{bmatrix} \mathbf{B}^{11} & \mathbf{B}^{12} & \\ \mathbf{B}^{21} & \ddots & \\ & & \mathbf{B}^{RR} \end{bmatrix} \begin{bmatrix} \mathbf{x}^1_{t+1} \\ \vdots \\ \mathbf{x}^R_{t+1} \end{bmatrix} = \begin{bmatrix} \mathbf{C}^{11} & \mathbf{C}^{12} & \\ \mathbf{C}^{21} & \ddots & \\ & & \mathbf{C}^{RR} \end{bmatrix} \begin{bmatrix} \mathbf{x}^1_{t} \\ \vdots \\ \mathbf{x}^R_{t} \end{bmatrix} + \begin{bmatrix} \mathbf{D}^{11} & \mathbf{D}^{12} & \\ \mathbf{D}^{21} & \ddots & \\ & & \mathbf{D}^{RR} \end{bmatrix} \begin{bmatrix} \mathbf{z}^1_{t} \\ \vdots \\ \mathbf{z}^R_{t} \end{bmatrix} + \begin{bmatrix} \mathbf{v}^1_{t} \\ \vdots \\ \mathbf{v}^R_{t} \end{bmatrix} \tag{7A.2}$$

Blocks $\mathbf{B}^{rr'}$, $\mathbf{C}^{rr'}$ and $\mathbf{D}^{rr'}$ are related to the coefficients which link region $r$ ($r = 1, \ldots, R$) to region $r'$ ($r' = 1, \ldots, R$). If there is no interregional interaction at all (i.e., $r = r'$), matrices **B**, **C** and **D** are block-diagonal. Then only blocks $\mathbf{B}^{rr}$, $\mathbf{C}^{rr}$ and $\mathbf{D}^{rr}$ are left, while all other blocks $\mathbf{B}^{rr'}$, $\mathbf{C}^{rr'}$ and $\mathbf{D}^{rr'}$ ($r, r' = 1, \ldots, R; r \neq r'$) drop out. It is evident that the spin-off and spill-over effects between regions are in fact represented by non-diagonal blocks. If there is no spatial interaction (i.e., if **B**, **C** and **D** are block-diagonal), the previous system can easily be solved for each region separately. Otherwise, the system has to be solved by multiplying (7A.1) by $\mathbf{B}^{-1}$ (supposing $\mathbf{B}^{-1}$ is non-singular):

$$\mathbf{x}_{t+1} = \mathbf{B}^{-1}\mathbf{C}\,\mathbf{x}_t + \mathbf{B}^{-1}\mathbf{D}\,\mathbf{z}_t + \mathbf{B}^{-1}\mathbf{v}_t \tag{7A.3}$$

or:

$$\mathbf{x}_{t+1} = \mathbf{X}\,\mathbf{x}_t + \mathbf{Z}\,\mathbf{z}_t + \mathbf{u}_t \tag{7A.4}$$

The latter set of equations is a system of non-homogeneous difference equations of the first order with constant coefficients (a more extensive description of systems of difference and differential equations is contained *inter alia* in Baumol (1952) and Goldberg (1958)). Such systems can in general be solved by determining first a *particular* solution for the homogeneous part of the system, and next a *general* solution with the aid of the particular solution. The general expression for the solution of the previous dynamic system can easily be obtained by developing (7A.4) in a recursive way: given the values of the exogenous variables $\mathbf{z}_t$ and $\mathbf{u}_t$ in each time period, and given the initial value of **x** in period $t = 0$, the successive values of $\mathbf{x}_t$ in later periods can be calculated as:

$$\left.\begin{aligned} \mathbf{x}_1 &= \mathbf{X}\,\mathbf{x}_0 + \mathbf{Z}\,\mathbf{z}_0 + \mathbf{u}_0 \\ \mathbf{x}_2 &= \mathbf{X}\,\mathbf{x}_1 + \mathbf{Z}\,\mathbf{z}_1 + \mathbf{u}_1 \\ &= \mathbf{X}^2\mathbf{x}_0 + \mathbf{X}\,\mathbf{Z}\,\mathbf{z}_0 + \mathbf{X}\,\mathbf{u}_0 + \mathbf{Z}\,\mathbf{z}_1 + \mathbf{u}_1 \\ &\;\vdots \\ \mathbf{x}_t &= \mathbf{X}^t\,\mathbf{x}_0 + \ldots\ldots\ldots\ldots\ldots\ldots \end{aligned}\right\} \tag{7A.5}$$

The question now arises as to whether $\mathbf{x}_t$ possesses a stable growth path. The growth path of $\mathbf{x}_t$ is determined by 2 factors, viz. by the endogenous growth mechanism of system (7A.4) and by the influence of the exogenous variables.

Leaving aside for the moment the exogenous part, it should be noted that the growth path of $\mathbf{x}_t$ depends on the eigenvalues of matrix **X**. These eigenvalues determine whether a stable, oscillating, explosive etc., growth path will occur. This can be inspected more accurately by means of the Cailey-Hamilton theorem. This theorem states that $\mathbf{X}^t$ can be written as:

$$\mathbf{X}^t = a_0 + a_1 \mathbf{X} + \ldots . a_{n-1} \mathbf{X}^{n-1} \tag{7A.6}$$

where $n$ is the total number of equations of the dynamic system. The as yet unknown parameters $a_0, \ldots ., a_{n-1}$ can be solved from the following system of linear equations:

$$\begin{bmatrix} 1 & \lambda_1 & \lambda_1^2 \ldots . \lambda_1^{n-1} \\ \vdots & & \\ 1 & \lambda_n & \lambda_n^2 \ldots . \lambda_n^{n-1} \end{bmatrix} \begin{bmatrix} a_0 \\ \vdots \\ a_{n-1} \end{bmatrix} = \begin{bmatrix} \lambda_1^t \\ \vdots \\ \lambda_n^t \end{bmatrix} \tag{7A.7}$$

where $\lambda_1, \ldots ., \lambda_n$ are the $n$ eigenvalues of the matrix $\mathbf{X}$, if there are no repetitive eigenvalues. Once the eigenvalues are known, the parameters $a_0, \ldots ., a_{n-1}$ can easily be calculated, and by means of (7A.6) a power series for $\mathbf{X}^t$. By means of the successive values of $\mathbf{X}^t$ the endogenous growth path of $\mathbf{x}_t$ can directly be inspected. Explosive developments of $\mathbf{x}_t$ result from eigenvalues which exceed 1 (in absolute value), whereas oscillating movements result from imaginary or complex eigenvalues.

It is easily seen that an unstable growth path in a certain region may lead to unstable movements in surrounding regions owing to the spin-off and spill-over effects. Therefore, by means of the previous model the endogenous growth mechanism of regional urban systems can be explained.[14]

Finally, some attention has to be paid to the non-homogeneous part of system (7A.4). This dynamic exogenous part can influence the endogenous growth mechanism. The exogenous part is partly composed of instrument variables, so that the endogenous growth mechanism of regional urban system can be influenced by regional and urban policy decisions. In this way a less desirable growth path of urban and regional systems can be corrected by governmental intervention (directly or indirectly). This evokes the problem of optimal decision taking in dynamic systems, which can be studied by means of optimal control theory (see, for instance, Nijkamp and Paelinck [1973] and Nijkamp [1974]). These problems will not be studied here.

## Appendix 7B Simulation results

In this Appendix the results of the simulation procedure described in section 7.6.3 are presented. For all successive 10 periods the results, measured in terms of the regional capital stocks, are in a figurative way included in the multiregional system of 49 areas. The volume of the stock of capital is defined by means of the following indices:

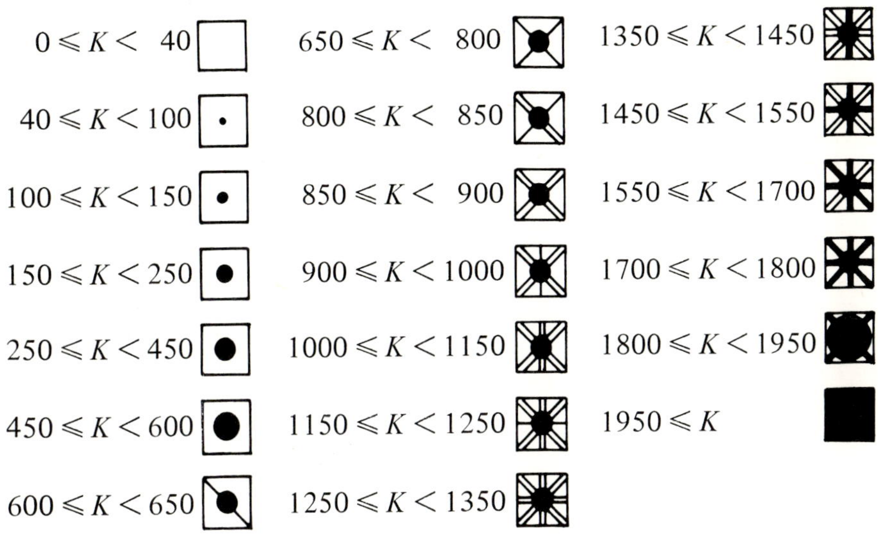


Diagram A0: period 0

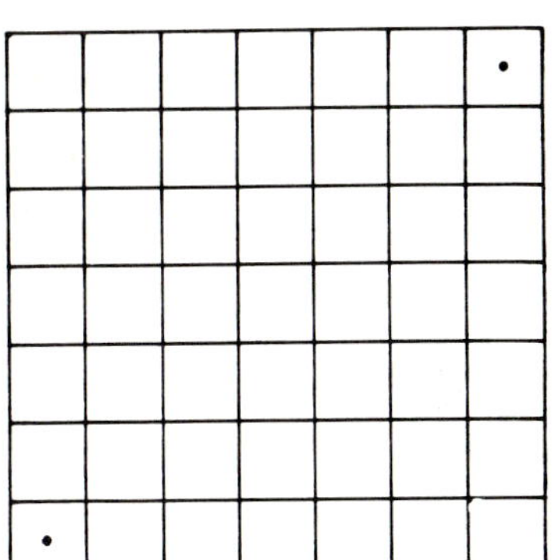

Diagram A1: period 10

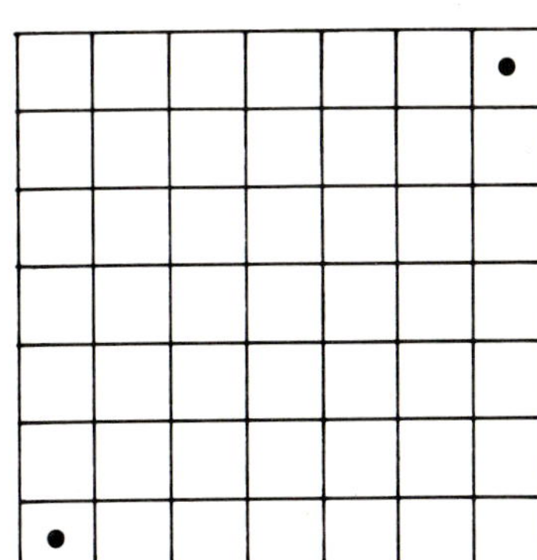

Diagram A2: period 20

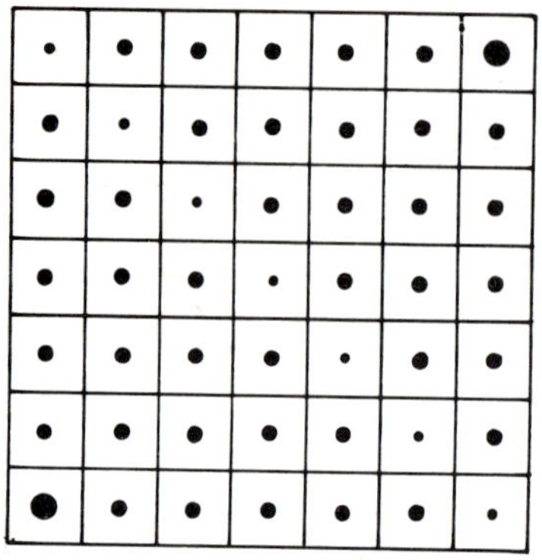

Diagram A3: period 30

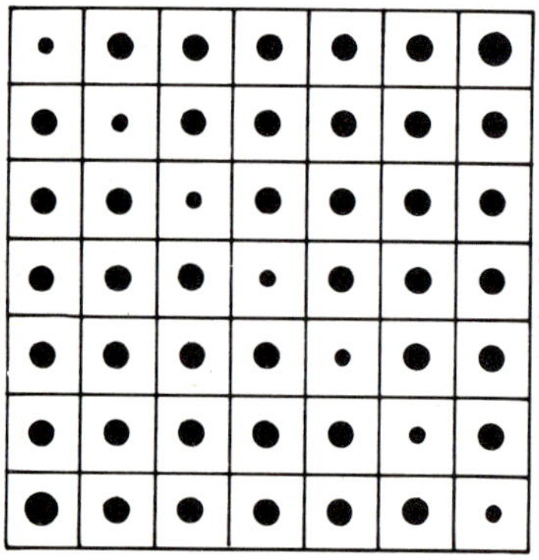

Diagram A4: period 40

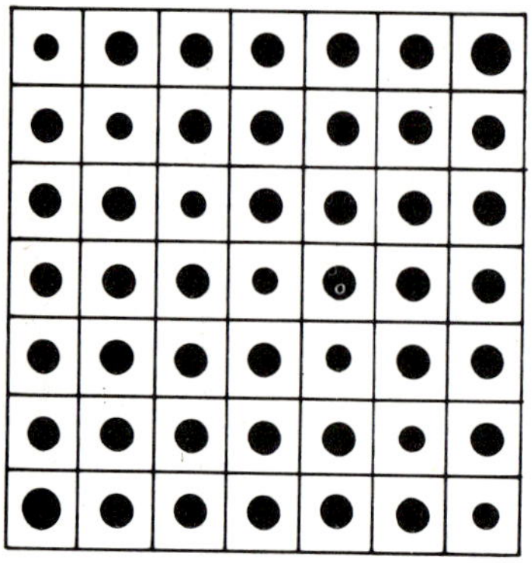

Diagram A5: period 50

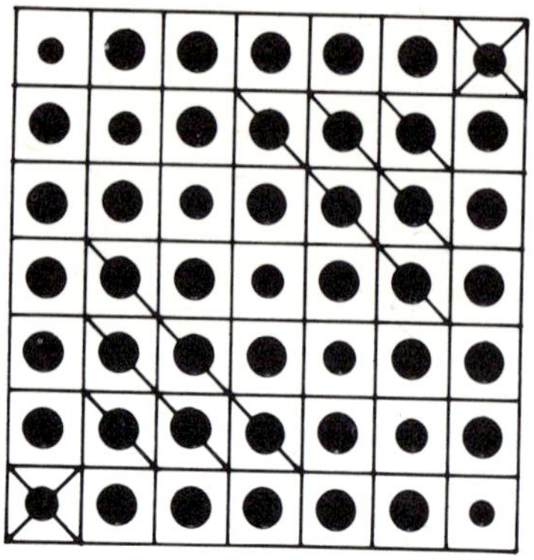

Diagram A6: period 60

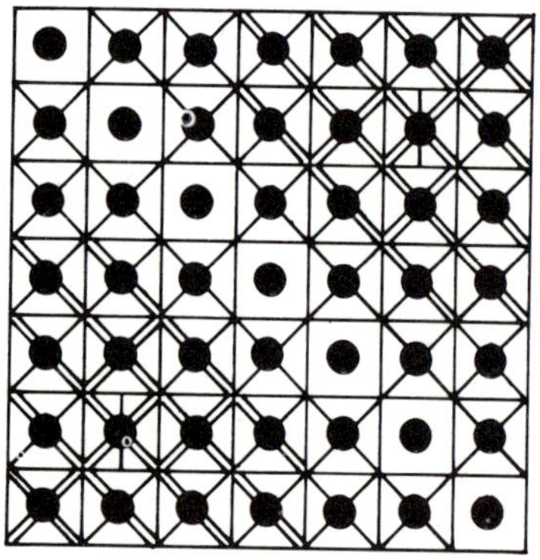

Diagram A7: period 70

Diagram A8: period 80

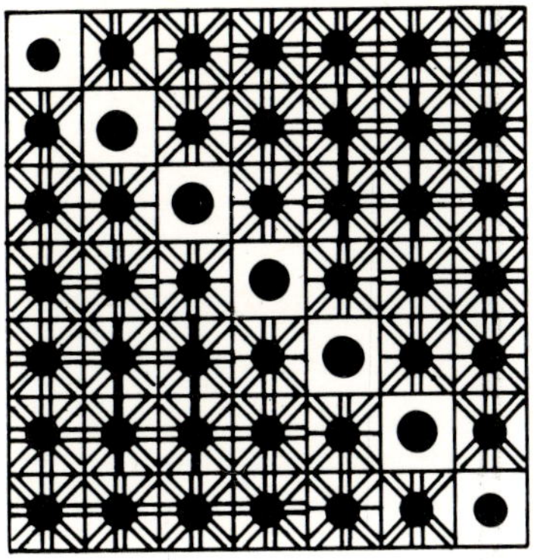

Diagram A10: period 100

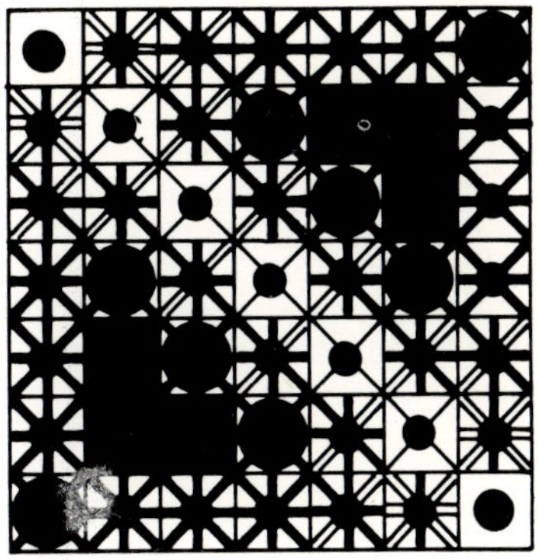

Diagram A9: period 90

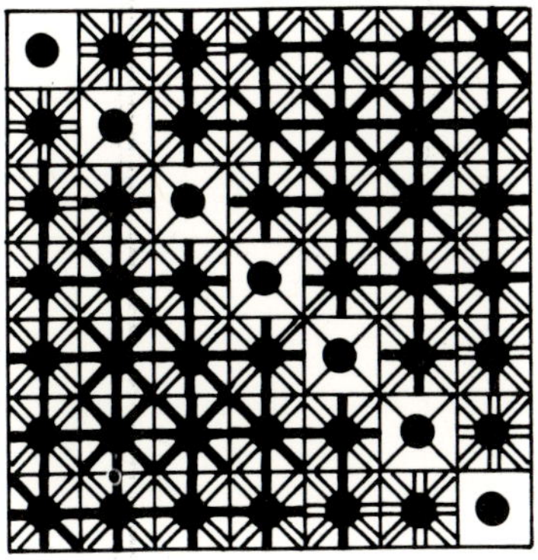

## Notes

[1] The problem of substitutable factors has been considered by, among others, Predöhl (see section 2.3).

[2] Elements can be found in Andersson and Marksjö (1972), Arrow and Debreu (1954), Arrow and Hahn (1971), Debreu (1959), Drèze (1973), Hansen (1970), Hildenbrand (1974), Isard (1969), Kraus and Johnson (1974), Kuenne (1963), Nikaido (1970), Quirk and Saposnik (1968), Sen (1970), Schwartz (1961), and Weintraub (1974).

[3] A discussion of their actual existence can be found in Nikaido (1970).

[4] It should be noted that the unit vectors have in general different (appropriate) order.

[5] A fixed coefficient production function is defined as:

$$x = \min \left\{ \frac{f_1}{a_1}, \frac{f_2}{a_2} \right\}$$

where $x$ = output,

$f_i$ = production factor $i$ (i = 1,2), and

$a_i$ = fixed technical coefficient: the amount of $f_i$ needed to produce one unit of output.

6 Identical goods shipped from different locations to the same market are assumed to have equal prices; thus, the price of $q_{ji}^k$ and $q_{j'i}^k$ is equal to $p_i^k$.

7 Productive factors originating from some location and needed for production within the same location are assumed not to absorb transportation services.

8 It should be noted that $\partial \tau / \partial f_{mj}^{lk} = 0$, if $m = j$; see (7.3.2.2).

9 This social criterion function is assumed to be known and may be any sort of social welfare (preference) function, monetary function, entropy maximizing criterion, or rent (e.g., consumer's surplus) maximizing function.

10 For normative issues, like in programming theory, $\omega$ may be assumed to be separable; for instance, $u_1$ and $u_2$ may represent the respective (weighted) regional income levels.

11 Elements of regional growth theory are contained, among others, in: Beckmann (1973), Borts and Stein (1968), Cameron (1972), Chisholm (1970), Hansen (1968), Mera (1968), Nijkamp and Paelinck (1974), Perloff et al. (1960, 1963), Richardson (1973), Sakashita and Kamoike (1973), Siebert (1969), Stilwell (1972), Takayama and Judge (1971, 1973), and Thoulen (1972a, 1972b).

12 If an interregional adaptation process leads finally to an equal relative availability of production factors, all regions will possess an equal regional structure.

13 This condition may be proved by assuming free competition and maximization of profits ($\Pi$). Then:

$$\Pi = pY - wL - rK$$

Maximization of $\Pi$ yields the first-order conditions:

$$\begin{cases} \Pi_L' = pf_L' + \dfrac{\partial p}{\partial L} Y - w - \dfrac{\partial w}{\partial L} L = 0 \\[2ex] \Pi_K' = pf_K' + \dfrac{\partial p}{\partial K} Y - r - \dfrac{\partial r}{\partial K} K = 0 \end{cases}$$

or:

$$\begin{cases} pf_L' \left(1 + \dfrac{\partial p}{\partial L} \dfrac{Y}{pf_L'}\right) = w \left(1 + \dfrac{\partial w}{\partial L} \dfrac{L}{w}\right. \\ pf_K' \left(1 + \dfrac{\partial p}{\partial K} \dfrac{Y}{pf_K'}\right) = r \left(1 + \dfrac{\partial r}{\partial K} \dfrac{K}{r}\right. \end{cases}$$

In the case of free competition there results:

$$\begin{cases} pf_L' = w \\ pf_K' = r \end{cases}$$

14 However, in the very long run, the movement of all variables will be dominated, at least for the endogenous part, by the dominating root, so that all variables would develop at the same rate. Non-linearities, and forcing terms, may prevent this from happening.

**References**


Andersson, A.E. and Marksjö, B., 'General Equilibrium Models for Allocation in Space under Interdependency and Increasing Returns to Scale', *Regional and Urban Economics*, vol. 2, no. 2, 1972, pp. 133–158.

Arrow, K.J. and Debreu, G., 'Existence of an Equilibrium for a Competitive Economy', *Econometrica*, vol. 22, 1954, pp. 265–290.

Arrow, K.J. and Hahn, F.H., *General Competitive Analysis*, Holden-Day, San Francisco 1971.

Baumol, W.J., *Economic Dynamics: An Introduction*, Macmillan, New York 1952.

Beckmann, M.J., 'The Isolated Region: A model of Regional Growth', *Regional and Urban Economics*, vol. 3, no. 3, 1973, pp. 223–231.

Von Böventer, E., *Theorie des Räumlichen Gleichgewichts*, Mohr, Tübingen 1962.

Borts, G.H. and Stein, J.L., 'Regional Growth and Maturity in the United States: A Study of Regional Structural Change', in: L. Needleman (ed.), *Regional Analysis*, Penguin Books, Baltimore 1968, pp. 159–197.

Boudeville, J.R., *Aménagement du Territoire et Polarisation*, Génin, Paris 1972.

Cameron, G.C., *Regional Economic Development, The Federal Role,* John Hopkins Press, Baltimore 1972.

Chisholm, M., (ed.), *Regional Forecasting*, Butterworth, London 1970.

Darwent, D.F., 'Growth Poles and Growth Centres in Regional Planning; A Review', *Environment and Planning*, vol. 1, 1969, pp. 5–31.

Debreu, G., *Theory of Value, An Axiomatic Analysis of Economic Equilibrium*, Wiley, New York 1959.

Drèze, J. (ed.), *Allocation under Uncertainty: Equilibrium and Optimality*, Macmillan, London 1973.

Friedmann, J.R., *Regional Development Policy; A case Study of Venezuela*, MIT Press, Cambridge 1966.

Friedmann, J.R., 'A General Theory of Polarized Development', in: N.M. Hansen (ed.), *Growth Centers in Regional Economic Development*, Free Press, New York 1972.

Gauthier, H.L., 'Geography, Transportation and Regional Development', in: B.S. Hoyle (ed.), *Transport and Development*, Macmillan, London, 1973, pp. 19–31.

Goldberg, S., *Introduction to Difference Equations*, Wiley, New York, 1958.

Hahn, W., *Theory and Applications of Liapunov's Direct Method*, Prentice-Hall, Englewood Cliffs, 1963.

Hansen, B., *A Survey of General Equilibrium Systems*, McGraw-Hill, New York 1970.

Hansen, N.M., *French Regional Planning*, Indiana University Press, Bloomington 1968.

Higgins, B., Growth Pole Theory in Canada, in: N.M. Hansen (ed.), *Growth Centers in Regional Economic Development*, The Free Press, New York 1972, pp. 204–228.

Hildenbrand, W., *Core and Equilibria of a Large Economy*, Princeton University Press, Princeton, 1974.

Hilhorst, J.G.M., *Development Axes and the Diffusion of Innovation*, Inaugural Address on Accepting the Chair of Economics and Regional Planning for Developing Countries, Institute of Social Studies, The Hague 1972.

Hirschman, A.O., *Strategy of Economic Development*, Yale University Press, New Haven 1958.

Hunt, E.K. and Schwarz, J.G. (eds.), *A Critique of Economic Theory*, Penguin, London 1972.

Isard, W., *Location and the Space-Economy*, MIT Press, Cambridge 1956.

Isard, W., 'General Interregional Equilibrium', *Papers and Proceedings of the Regional Science Association*, vol. 3, 1957, pp. 35–60.

Isard, W., *General Theory: Social, Political, Economic, and Regional*, MIT Press, Cambridge 1969.

Isard, W. and Ostroff, D.J., 'Existence of a Competitive Interregional Equilibrium', *Papers and Proceedings of the Regional Science Association*, vol. 4, 1958, pp. 49–76.

Isard, W. and Ostroff, D.J., 'General Interregional Equilibrium', *Journal of Regional Science*, vol. 2, no. 1, 1960, pp. 67–74.

Klaassen, L.H., 'Some Further Considerations on Attraction Analysis', *Foundations of Empirical Economic Research*, Netherlands Economic Institute, Rotterdam (mimeo) 1974.

Klaassen, L.H., Klein, P.W. and Paelinck, J.H.P., 'Very Long Term Evolution of a System of Regions', *Foundations of Empirical Economic Research,* Conference on Economic History, Copenhagen, 1974.

Kraus, M.B. and Johnson, H.G., *General Equilibrium Analysis,* Allen and Unwin, London 1974.

Kuenne, R.E., *The Theory of General Economic Equilibrium*, Princeton University Press, Princeton 1963.

La Salle, J. and Lefschetz, S., *Stability by Liapunov's Direct Method, with Applications,* Academic Press, New York 1961.

Lefeber, L., *Allocation in Space*, North-Holland Publishing Co., Amsterdam 1958.

Lindbeck, A., *The Political Economy of the New Left*, Harper & Row, New York 1971.

Mera, K., 'A Multiregion Multisector Model of Equilibrium Growth', *Papers of the Regional Science Association*, vol. 21, 1968, pp. 53–75.

Naylor, T.N., *Computer Simulation Experiments with Models of Economic Systems*, Wiley, New York 1971.

Nikaido, H., *Introduction to Sets and Mappings in Modern Economics*, North-Holland Publishing Co., Amsterdam 1970.

Nijkamp, P., *Planning of Industrial Complexes by Means of Geometric Programming*, Rotterdam University Press, Rotterdam 1972.

Nijkamp, P., 'Spatial Interdependencies and Environmental Effects', in: A. Karlquist, L. Lundquist and F. Snickars (eds.), *Dynamic Allocation of Urban Space*, Saxon House, Farnborough, 1974, pp. 175–209.

Nijkamp, P. and Paelinck, J.H.P., 'Some Models for the Economic Evaluation of the Environment', *Regional and Urban Economics*, vol. 3, no. 1, 1973, pp. 33–62.

Nijkamp, P. and Paelinck, J.H.P., 'Diffusion of Development Processes in Regional and Urban Systems', *Foundations of Empirical Economic Research*, Netherlands Economic Institute, Rotterdam, (mimeo) 1974.

Paelinck, J.H.P., 'Techniques of Regional Plan Formulation: Problems of Interregional Consistency' in: J.M. Dunham and J.G.M. Hilhorst (eds.), *Issues in Regional Planning*, Mouton, Paris 1971, pp. 184–194.

Paelinck, J.H.P., 'Economische Analyse van Ruimtelijke Diffusieprocessen', Mimeographed paper, Netherlands Economic Institute, Rotterdam 1973.

Paelinck, J.H.P., Alternative Methods for the Study of Urban Dynamics, in: R. Funck (ed.), *Recent Developments in Regional Science*, Pion Press, London 1972.

Perloff, H.S., Dunn Jr., E.S., Lampard, E.E. and Muth, R.F., *Regions, Resources, and Economic Growth*, The John Hopkins Press, Baltimore 1960.

Perloff, H.S. and Wingo, L., 'Natural Resource Endowment and Regional Economic Growth' in: J.J. Spengler (ed.), *Natural Resources and Economic Growth,* Resources for the Future, Washington 1961, pp. 191–212.

Perloff, H.S. and Dodds, V.W., *How a Region Grows*, Committee for Economic Development, New York 1963.

Perroux, F., 'Note sur la Notion de Pôle de Croissance', *Economie Appliquée,* vol. 1 and 2, 1955.

Pottier, P., 'Axes de Communication et Développement Economique', *Revue Economique*, nr. 1, 1963, pp. 58–132.

Quirk, J., and Saposnik, R. *Introduction to General Equilibrium Theory and Welfare Economics*, McGraw-Hill, New York 1968.

Richardson, H.W., *Regional Growth Theory*, Macmillan, London 1973.

Robinson, G. and Salih, K.B., 'The Spread of Development around Kuala Lumpur; A Methodology for an Exploratory Test of Some Assumptions of the Growth-Pole Model', *Regional Studies*, vol. 5, 1971, pp. 303–314.

Sakashita, N. and Kamoike, O., 'National Growth and Regional Income Inequality: A Consistent Model', *International Economic Review*, vol. 14, no. 2, 1973, pp. 372–382.

Schwartz, J.T., *Lectures on the Mathematical Method in Analytical Economics,* Gordon and Breach, New York 1961.

Sen, A.K., *Collective Choice and Social Welfare*, Holden-Day, San Francisco 1970.

Siebert, H., *Regional Economic Growth: Theory and Policy,* International Textbook Co., Scranton 1969.

Sraffa, P., *Production of Commodities by Means of Commodities,* Cambridge University Press, Cambridge 1960.

Stillwell, F.J.B., *Regional Economic Policy*, Macmillan, London 1972.

Takayama, T. and Judge, G.G., *Spatial and Temporal Price and Allocation Models,* North-Holland Publishing Co., Amsterdam 1971.

Takayama, T. and Judge, G.G., (eds.), *Studies in Economic Planning over Space and Time*, North-Holland Publishing Co., Amsterdam 1973.

Thoulen, M., 'Regional Growth and Factor Mobility', University of Louvain, Economics Institute, Working Paper 7218 (mimeo) 1972a.

Thoulen, M., *Les Modèles de Croissance Régionale, Une Synthèse*

*Théorique*, Université de Louvain, Master's Thesis (mimeo) 1972b.
Weintraub, E.R., *General Equilibrium Theory*, Macmillan, London 1974.
Yuill, R.S., 'A Simulation Study of Barrier Effects in Spatial Diffusion Problems', in: *Michigan Inter-University Community of Mathematical Geographers,* Discussion Paper no. 5, University of Michigan 1965.

# Index

# The Authors

Professor Paelinck has been Professor and Visiting Professor at the Universities of Bristol, Canterbury, Lille, Louvain, Namur, Paris and MIT, and is now Director of the Netherlands Economics Institute and Professor of Spatial Economics at the Erasmus University, Rotterdam.

Professor Nijkamp was educated in econometrics and regional economics at the Erasmus University, Rotterdam, and is now Professor of Regional Economics at the Free University, Amsterdam.